Community Care Law
and Local Authority Handbook

Community Care Law
and Local Authority Handbook

2nd Edition

Jonathan Butler
BA (Hons), MA, MEd, Barrister-at-Law

Contributor

Adam Fullwood
BA (Hons), MA (Law), Barrister-at-Law

JORDANS

Published by
Jordan Publishing Limited
21 St Thomas Street
Bristol BS1 6JS

British Library Cataloguing-in-Publication Data
A catalogue record for this book is available from the British Library.

ISBN 978 1 84661 293 0

Typeset by Letterpart Ltd, Reigate, Surrey

Printed and bound by CPI Group (UK) Ltd, Croydon, CR0 4YY

DEDICATIONS

Jonathan Butler

Dedicated to my parents
Philip Butler (5.12.18–19.3.99) and Margaret Butler (24.2.26–20.3.99)
and to my children
Katrina, Alexander and Lucy Butler

Adam Fullwood

To Mel, Joe and Maya who were very understanding
when I disappeared to complete my chapters.

FOREWORD TO 2ND EDITION

For one work to attempt to describe the detail of the law and practice relating to disabled and vulnerable adults and children, mental health, community care, health and social care, capacity, accommodation and finance is a very significant endeavour. To this list, can now be added two new chapters (by Adam Fullwood) on Social Housing, and Asylum Support. Both Jonathan Butler and Adam Fullwood are acknowledged specialists in the different courts and tribunals which administer and make these decisions. They have brought to this work both significant professional experience and an admirable dedication. The result is a work of scholarly detail, analytical erudition and practical application that is a real pleasure to use. Both lawyers and social and health care professionals will find this updated handbook an invaluable reference tool, a tutorial that sets out first principles but then develops the detail necessary for even the most complex problems and a step-by-step guide to the concepts that need to be considered.

With the extensive developments that have taken place since the commencement of the Mental Capacity Act 2005 and the Rules and Guidance that accompany it there could not have been a better time to review the law of capacity and in particular that which relates to the Deprivation of Liberty Safeguards. The handbook guides the reader through the up-to-date legislative concepts and principles that are the foundation of the statutory codes in each of the fields of study, giving detailed case-law examples and citations. The interrelationship between those codes and their occasional lacuna and dysfunctions are analysed and commented upon. Jonathan Butler's advice to the reader is both wise and helpful.

This timely and admirable contribution to what has previously been too disparate a field of study is both very welcome and necessary.

Ernest Ryder
Royal Courts of Justice
London
December 2011

PREFACE

There are currently approximately 20 statutes which govern the area of law considered in this textbook. The starting point for almost all of them has been described by Baroness Hale thus:

'The National Assistance Act 1948 was part of the package of measures which created the modern welfare state. It stood alongside the Children Act 1948, which is the origin of our modern child care services, the National Insurance Act 1946, which laid the foundations of the modern social security system, and the National Health Service Act 1946, which created the National Health Service. The Education Act 1944 had already led the way in the fight against what Sir William Beveridge had called the "five giants on the road of reconstruction" – Want, Disease, Ignorance, Squalor and Idleness (*Social Insurance and Allied Services*, Report by Sir William Beveridge (1942) (Cmd 6404)). The education and health services were universal, in the sense that they were available to all, and originally without any charge, irrespective of ability to pay. But people who could afford to do so remained, and still remain, free to make their own arrangements if they so wish. The social services were more limited, in that it was expected that families would continue to look after their children and their elderly or disabled relatives.'
(*YL (by her litigation friend the Official Solicitor) v Birmingham City Council* [2007] UKHL 27 [49]).

The purpose of this book is to attempt to provide a guide through the legislative maze that has been created over the past 60 years or so, and to assist those whose practice is what has come to be known as 'community care law', which in itself has 'been described at various times by judges as 'piecemeal ... numerous', 'exceptionally tortuous', 'labrynthine' and as including some of the 'worst drafted' subordinate legislation ever encountered' (The Law Commission (Law Com No 326) 'Adult Social Care' 10 May 2011). If the recommendations of the Law Commission are implemented, then the task facing judges, lawyers, and those whose lives are more directly affected by all of these legislative provisions will be made much easier. It is to be hoped that the suggested reforms are implemented as swiftly as possible. In the meantime, as another barrister reported Samuel Johnson as having said: 'Knowledge is of two kinds: we know a subject ourselves, or we know where we can find information upon it' (*Boswell's Life of Johnson* 17 April 1775). I can only hope that this book helps to fulfil the second function.

Jonathan Butler
Deans Court Chambers
24 St John Street
Manchester
December 2011

ACKNOWLEDGMENTS

The author would like to acknowledge and thank in particular Helen Wilson for her direct assistance and diligence in helping to prepare the first edition of this book but also in addition the following: Susan Alexander; Maureen Aspinall; Emma and Richard Atkinson; Victoria Cassidy; Christopher Curran; Anne Davies; Adam Fullwood; Tony Hawitt; Morris Hill; Janet Hughes; Kevin Lloyd; Linda Murphy; Damian Sanders; Eliza Sharron.

CONTENTS

Dedications	v
Foreword to 2nd Edition	vii
Preface	ix
Acknowledgments	xi
Table of Cases	xxiii
Table of Statutes	xxxv
Table of Statutory Instruments	xlv

Chapter 1
Mental Health Acts — **1**

General	1
Persons who are detained	2
After-care and care plans	6
Persons who cease to be detained	8
Health care needs v social care needs	9
Extent of duties of local authority	10
Relevant local authority	10
Recommendations of Report of the Inquiry into the Care and Treatment of Christopher Clunis (1994)	14
Continuation of after-care services	19
Ordinary residence	20
After-care services under s 117 of the Mental Health Act 1983	24
Establishing the responsible commissioner	25
Definition of services	26
Charges for services	26
Repayment of charges and restitution	27
Limitation periods	28
Independent Mental Capacity Advocates (Mental Capacity Act 2005) and Independent Mental Health Advocates (Mental Health Act 1983)	29
Independent Mental Health Advocates	30
Guardianship	33
Purpose and basis for guardianship	33
Implications of the Mental Capacity Act 2005	41
Practical aspects	43
Inappropriate/anomalous applications	45
New terms under the Mental Health Act 2007	46
Powers conferred as a result of guardianship order	46

Manner in which guardianship may be altered   48
The nearest relative and guardianship   50
Discharge of guardianship by nearest relative   55
Orders of Court in respect of guardianship   58
Responsibility for providing information   59
Guardianship and consent to treatment   60
The role and function of 'nearest relative'   61
Confidentiality of documentation   67
Determination of nature (and choice) of 'nearest relative'   68
Implementation of the Mental Health Act 2007   68
Alleged misuse of functions by nearest relative   70
Consultation and identification of nearest relative   70
The displacement of the nearest relative   89
The procedure for an application to displace the nearest relative   91
Applications in respect of displacing nearest relative   93
Interim and concurrent orders   94
Patients who lack capacity and displacement applications   95

Chapter 2
Capacity and the Court of Protection   **113**
Assessment of Capacity   113
Capacity – General Concepts   113
Subject Specific Capacity   118
   Capacity and medical treatment   118
   Capacity and adult contact/residence disputes   123
   Capacity and marriage   125
   Capacity and choice of residence   126
   Judicial review of decisions made by local authorities vs welfare
      decisions   127
   Capacity and sexual relationships/contraception   128
      Contraception   131
   Capacity to enter into tenancy agreements   132
   Capacity and transfer outside UK   136
   Capacity and abduction   136
   Capacity and deprivation of liberty   137
      The Bournewood Gap   137
      Deprivation of Liberty Safeguards – Code of Practice   140
      Role of local authority when DOLS regime cannot be applied   145
      What is deprivation of liberty?   150
Mental Capacity Act 2005 and the Court of Protection   165
   Principles of the Act   167
   Capacity   167
   Private/public hearings   168
   Interaction with Mental Health Act 1983   168
   After-care   169
   Definition of aims of Court of Protection   169
   Powers of Court   170
   Persons who lack capacity   170

Independent Mental Capacity Advocate (IMCA) 182
Procedure and the Court of Protection Rules 184
Applications and notification of P 184
Circumstances in which P must be notified 185
Permission and forms 186
How to start proceedings 187
Steps following issue of application form 189
The parties to the proceedings 190
Applications within proceedings (including emergency and ex parte
    applications) 191
Interim remedies 191
Private and public hearings 192
Expert evidence (rr 119–131) 194
Disclosure 194
Litigation friend 195
Costs (rr 156–160) 198
Practice Directions 199
Damages 202
Ordinary residence 204
Children and the Court of Protection 206

Chapter 3
Assessment of Community Care Needs for Adults **211**
General 211
  Putting People First 211
  Historical development 213
  Individual entitlement and the obligations of the local authority
    (*needs versus provision*) 213
  Determining eligibility 215
  Resources and assessment to pay 217
  The assessment process 218
  Mental capacity 219
  Assessing the needs of carers 219
  Ineligible for support 219
  Withdrawal of support 220
  Commissioning 220
  Contents of support plan 220
  Reviews of plans 222
  Personal budgets 222
  Use of resource allocation systems 223
Older People 225
  National Service Framework for Older People (NSF) 225
    Rationale behind NSF 225
    Different categories within older people 225
    Standards within NSF 226
    Mental health in older people 226
    Progress of the NSF 227

Parents with Learning Disabilities   227
  Ordinary residence   228
  Ordinary residence and children   229
  Needs   229
  Relevance of resources in considering needs   230
Chronically Sick and Disabled Persons Act 1970, s 1   234
  Assessments   234
Disabled Children   235
  Disabled Persons (Services, Consultation and Representation)
    Act 1986   236
  National Health Service and Community Care Act 1990   244
  Promotion and planning of services   245
  Mandatory provision for assessment   247
  Assessment of parents with learning disabilities   248
Vulnerable Adult Parents   249
  Eligibility thresholds   249
  Statistics   249
  Disability Discrimination Acts   249
  Ordinary residence and assessment   264
  No settled residence   265
  Inadequate care plans/assessments   266
  Refusal to assess/non-assessment   267
  Delay in assessments/maladministration   268
  Carers (Recognition and Services) Act 1995   268
Older and Vulnerable Adults   271
  Older adults   271
  Vulnerable adults   272
  Abuse   272
  Inter-agency framework and policy   273
  Protection of Vulnerable Adults Scheme   273
  Health Select Committee's Inquiry into Elder Abuse   273
  Duty of care by local authority towards vulnerable adults   273
  Role of the inherent jurisdiction and vulnerable adults   275

Chapter 4
Provision of Accommodation   **279**
Introduction   279
Background   279
  National Assistance Act 1948   281
Extent of Needs and Provision for Accommodation/Housing   282
  Psychological need   282
  Reasonableness of need   282
  Needs and resources   283
  Needs and housing   285
  Needs and lack of re-assessment   292
  Ordinary residence   293

Closure of Homes/Sales of Homes/Homes for life and Private Care
  Homes   297
  Private care/public body   297
  Sale of home/re-assessment   298
  Promise of home for life   298
  Closure of Homes: Art 2   300
  Procedure for closure; alternatives to litigation   301
  Home for life; re-assessment; resources   305
  Inadequate consultation; Art 8   305
  Movement of resident and flawed assessment   306
  Section 29 of the National Assistance Act 1948   306
  Sections 29 and 21 and eligible needs and resources   309
  Ordinary residence/mandatory and permissive functions   311
  Choice of accommodation   311
  Guidance   312
Disputes between Local Authorities and Care Home Owners (Choice
  of Contractors)   316
  Legislative background to dispute   316
  Community care in the next decade and beyond (LASSA Guidance
    1990)   317
  Choice of accommodation   317
  Outcome   317
  Disputes between care home owners and local authorities (levels of
    charges)   317
  Disputes regarding third party payments   318
Regulation of Accommodation   319
  General   319
  Care Standards Act 2000   319
  Definition of care homes   320
  What constitutes a care home   320
  Guidance to local authorities   323
  Personal care   324
  Care homes   324
  Domiciliary care   324
  Housing and care schemes   324
  Capacity and choice of accommodation   324
  Adult placements   325
  Safeguarding Vulnerable Groups Act 2006   325
  Regulated activity   325
  Regulated activity provider   325
  Controlled activity relating to vulnerable adults   326
  Local authority information and referrals   326
  Definition of a vulnerable adult   327

Chapter 5
Provisions for Older Children (Leaving Care) and Disabled Children   331
General   331
Children Leaving Care   331

Consultation Paper and Origins of the Act   332
Children (Leaving Care) Act 2000 – Guidance   334
  Summary of different categories   338
    Eligible children   338
    Relevant children   338
    Additional relevant children   338
    Former relevant children and former relevant children pursuing
      further education and training   338
    Persons qualifying for advice and assistance   339
    Unaffected children   339
    'Looked after, accommodated or fostered'   339
  Complaints by children   339
  Local authority planning and policy   340
  Needs assessments and pathway plans   340
  Personal advisers   340
  Accommodation   341
  Financial arrangements   341
Children Act 1989   352
  Ordinary residence and responsible local authority   359
Disputes Over Whether a Child Comes Within the Provisions of the
    Act   362
  Unaccompanied asylum-seeking children   362
  Detention   363
  Housing   363
  Assessment of needs and pathway plans   364
  Extent of obligation   365
  Disabled children, leaving care and education   366
Disabled Persons (Services, Consultation and Representation) Act 1986   367
  Implementation of ss 5 and 6 of the Disabled Persons (Services,
    Consultation and Representation) Act 1986   370
General Statutory Framework   374
Disabled children and the Chronically Sick and Disabled Persons
    Act 1970 and Children Act 1989   375
  Extent of general obligations of local authorities   382
Accommodation Needs   385
  Ordinary residence   390
  Disabled children and the Carers and Disabled Children Act 2000   390
  Summary   391
  The Community Care Assessment Directions 2004   395
  Delayed and deficient assessments   395
Children Act 2004   396
  Transitional services   399
Mental Capacity Act 2005   400
  Children   400
  Young people   401

Chapter 6
Finance and Charging **403**
General 403
Origins of the National Assistance Act 1948 403
Provision of Accommodation 404
Community Care (Delayed Discharges etc) Act 2003 406
Charges for residential accommodation 407
Charges for Residential Accommodation Guide 407
Capital 408
Capital to be disregarded indefinitely 409
Deprivation of capital 409
Income 410
Trust funds 410
Liability of relatives 413
Students 413
National Assistance (Assessment of Resources) Regulations 1992 413
Liability for charges and recovery of charges 413
Health and Social Services and Social Security Adjudications
  Act 1983 414
Section 29 of the National Assistance Act 1948 415
Section 2 of the Carers and Disabled Children Act 2000 417
Charging and reasonableness 417
Section 21 of the Health and Social Services and Social Security
  Adjudications Act 1983 419
Deprivation of assets 420
Subjective test for deprivation of assets 421
The use of charges and cautions on land 424
Deferred payments and charges 426
Choice of accommodation and third party top-ups 426
Direct payments 430
Recipients of direct payments 431
Lack of capacity 431
Use of direct payments 432
Amount of direct payments 433
Charging/contribution to cost of service 433
Employment of close relatives 434
Disabled parents with parental responsibility for a child 434
Seeking repayment of direct payments 435
Stopping direct payments 435
The recipient 445
Duty to make payments 445
Conditions 445
Termination of payments to those who lack capacity 445
Summary of changes to Direct Payment Regulations 446
Use of direct payments to support education/care of disabled child 449
Direct payments and s 17A of the Children Act 1989 450
Individual budgets, personal budgets, direct payments and resource
  allocation schemes 452

Prohibition on purchase of NHS services   456

Chapter 7
Health Care and Social Care   **459**
Distinction between Health Care and Social Services   459
Nursing Services   459
Section 117 of the Mental Health Act 1983 and Health Care   462
Health and Social Care Act 2001   463
  Community care (delayed discharges)   467
  Notice of needs   469
  Duties of local authority   471
  Duties of hospital   472
  Dispute resolution   474
  Adjustments   475
  Free provision of services   476
The Delayed Discharges (England) Regulations 2003, SI 2003/2277   478
  Acute care   478
  Dispute resolution   478
The National Health Service Act 2006   478
  The National Framework for Continuing Healthcare and NHS
      Funded Nursing Care   478
  Definitions   478
  Liaison between local authorities and NHS bodies   479
  Changes arising from the National Health Service Act 2006   479
  National Health Service Act 2006 and other community care
      legislation   480
  Local authority assessment   481
  Prohibition on provision   481
  The test for NHS versus local authority responsibility   481
  Specific criteria   482
  Core values   483
  Involvement of local authority in NHS assessment   485
  Direct payments   486
  Personal health budgets and personalisation   487
  Specific NHS provision   488
  Dispute resolution   489
  The statute   489
  Target duties   490
  Pooling of resources   492
  Community services   501
Ordinary Residence   503
  Ordinary/usual residence and the PCT   506
  Who Pays? Establishing the Responsible Commissioner   507
  No fixed abode   507
  Usually resident   507
  Patients who move   508
  Children and local authorities   508
  Adults and long-term care placements   509

Chapter 8
Social Housing **511**
Adam Fullwood
Introduction 511
Allocation 511
   The allocation scheme 511
   Exceptions 512
   Eligibility 514
   Advice and assistance 519
   Determining priorities 519
   The principal features of the allocation scheme 521
   Contracting out 524
Homelessness 525
   Duty to cooperate 525
   Applications 526
   Interim duty to accommodate pending decision 528
   Eligibility 529
   Priority need 530
   Intentionality 531
   Interim accommodation pending review 533
   Interim accommodation pending appeal 534
   Main duty 534
Equality and Diversity 534

Chapter 9
Asylum support **537**
Adam Fullwood
Introduction 537
Asylum Support 537
   Asylum seekers 537
   Failed asylum seekers 539
Community Care Services 540
   Introduction 540
   Immigration and Asylum Act 1999 541
   Age disputes 550

Index **553**

TABLE OF CASES

References are to paragraph numbers.

A and C (Equality and Human Rights Commission Intervening), Re [2010]
EWHC 978 (Fam), [2010] 2 FLR 1363   2.48, 2.51, 2.60, 3.93
A Local Authority v (1) MA (2) NA and (3) SA (by her children's guardian
LJ) [2005] EWHC 2942 (Fam), [2007] 10 CCLR 193, [2007] 10
CCLR 193, [2006] 1 FLR 867, [2007] 2 FCR 563, [2006] Fam Law
268   3.98
A v A Health Authority and linked applications: Re J and linked
applications [2001] EWHC Fam/Admin 18, [2002] 5 CCLR 165   2.23
AH v Hertfordshire Partnership NHS Foundation Trust [2011] EWHC 276
(COP)   2.19
Airedale NHS Trust v Bland [1993] AC 789, [1993] 1 FLR 1026, [1993] 1 All
ER 821, [1993] 2 WLR 316, [1993] Fam Law 473, HL   2.3, 2.13
AK v Central and North West London Mental Health NHS Trust and
Royal London Borough of Kensington and Chelsea [2008] EWHC
1217 (QB), [2008] 11 CCLR 543   1.4, 3.52
Anufrijeva v Southwark London Borough Council; R (on the application of
N) v Secretary of State for the Home Department; R (on the
application of M) v Same [2003] EWCA Civ 1406, [2004] QB 1124,
[2004] 1 All ER 833, [2004] 2 WLR 603, [2004] LGR 184, [2003] 3
FCR 673, [2004] 1 FLR 8, [2004] Fam Law 12, [2003] 44 LS Gaz R
30, (2003) *Times*, 17 October, 15 BHRC 526, [2003] All ER (D) 288
(Oct)   2.103
Associated Provincial Picture House v Wednesbury Corporation [1948] 1 KB
223, [1947] 2 All ER 680, 45 LGR 635, 112 JP 55   4.28
Austen and another v Commissioner of Police for the Metropolis [2009]
UKHL 5, [2009] 1 AC 564   2.60
Avon County Councilv Hooper (A Minor) and Bristol and District Health
Authority [1998] 1 CCLR 366, [1998] 1 CCLR 366, [1997] 1 WLR
1605, [1997] 1 All ER 532   6.25, 6.26
AVS (by his litigation friend, CS) v NHS Foundation Trust and B PCT
[2011] EWCA Civ 7, [2011] 2 FLR 1 967   2.13

B (A Local Authority) v RM, MM and AM [2010] EWHC 3802 (Fam),
[2011] 1 FLR 1635, [2011] Fam Law 459,   2.110
B Borough Council v Mr S [2006] EWHC 2584 (Fam), [2006] 9 CCLR 596,
[2007] 1 FLR 1600   2.18
Barnet London Borough Council v Robin [1999] 2 CCLR 455   1.46
Barnsley Metropolitan Borough Council v Norton [2011] EWCA Civ 834,
(2011) *Times*, 8 September, [2011] All ER (D) 191 (Jul)   8.84
BB; BB v Cygnet Healthcare [2008] EWHC 1259 (Admin), [2008] MHLR
106   1.47
Bell and Todd and Ryan v Liverpool Health Authority [2001] All ER (D)
348 (Jun)   6.14
Binomugisha v London Borough of Southwark [2006] EWHC 2254
(Admin), [2007] 1 FLR 916, [2007] 3 FCR 457, [2007] 1 FLR 916,
[2006] All ER (D) 83 (Sep)   5.37

BJ (Incapacitated Adult), Re [2009] EWHC 3310 (Fam), [2010] 1 FLR 1373   2.47
Botta v Italy (Application 21439/93) (1998) 26 EHRR 241, 4 BHRC 81,
    ECtHR   3.47
Buckinghamshire County Council v Royal Borough of Kingston upon
    Thames and (1) SL (by her litigation friend the Official Solicitor), (2)
    The National Society for Epilepsy and (3) Secretary of State for
    Health)(Interested Parties) [2011] EWCA Civ 457, [2011] 14 CCLR
    426   4.22

C (by his litigation friend the Official Solicitor) v (1) A Local Authority (2)
    LM (3) LPM (4) the PCT (4) An Organisation [2011] EWHC 1539
    (Admin), [2011] 14 CCLR 471   2.61, 2.111, 5.76
C (Mental Patient: Contact), Re [1993] 1 FLR 940, [1993] Fam Law 404   1.30
C (Refusal of Medical Treatment), Re [1994] 1 All ER 819, [1994] 1 WLR
    290, [1994] 2 FCR 151, [1994] 1 FLR 31, [1994] Fam Law 131, 15
    BMLR 77, [1993] NLJR 1642   2.3, 2.6, 2.7
C v Blackburn with Darwen Borough Council & A Care Home &
    Blackburn with Darwen Teaching Care Trust [2011] EWHC 3321
    (COP)   1.34
Cambridgeshire County Council v R, An Adult [1994] 2 FCR 973, [1995] 1
    FLR 50, [1995] Fam Law 12   1.30, 2.15
Casewell v Secretary of State for the Home Department [2008] EWCA Civ
    524, [2008] 11 CCLR 684   6.52
Cheshire West and Chester County Council v P and M [2011] EWHC 1330
    (Fam); [2001] EXCA Civ 1257, [2011] All ER (D) 150 (Nov)   2.60, 2.61, 2.96
City of Westminster v IC (by his friend the Official Solicitor) and KC and
    NN [2008] EWCA Civ 198, [2008] 2 FLR 267   2.22
Clunis (Christopher) (by his next friend Christopher Prince) v Camden and
    Islington Health Authority) [1998] QB 978, [1998] 1 CCLR 215   1.4, 1.18
Clunis and Richmond Borough Council v Watson [2000] EWCA Civ 239   1.3
Collins v United Kingdom (App No 11909/02) [2003] 6 CCLR 388   4.29
County Council v MB, JB and a Residential Home [2010] EWHC 2508
    (COP), [2011] 1 FLR 790   2.46
Crofton v National Health Service Litigation Authority [2007] EWCA Civ
    71, [2007] 10 CCLR 123   6.14
CX v A Local Authority & A NHS Foundation Trust [2011] EWHC 1918
    (Admin), [2011] All ER (D) 208 (Jul)   1.49

D (Mental Patient: Habeas Corpus), Re [2000] 2 FLR 848   1.47, 1.48
D Borough Council v AB [2011] EWHC 101 (COP), [2011] 2 FLR 72   2.29
Derbyshire County Council and another v Akrill and others [2005] EWCA
    Civ 308, [2005] 8 CCLR 173, [2005] All ER (D) 334 (Mar)   6.32, 6.36
DH NHS Foundation Trust v PS [2010] EWHC 1217 (Fam), [2010] 2 FLR
    1236   2.12

E (An Alleged Patient), Re; Sheffield City Council v E & S [2004] EWHC
    2808 (Fam), [2005] 1 FLR 965, [2005] 2 WLR 953   2.8
Enfield London Borough Council v SA (by her litigation friend, the Official
    Solicitor) FA & KA [2010] EWHC 196 (Admin), [2010] 1 FLR 1836   2.98
Engel and Others v The Netherlands (No 1) (1976) 1 EHRR 647   2.60

F (A Child), Re [1999] 2 CCLR 445, [2000] 1 FCR 11, [2000] 1 FLR 192,
    [2000] Fam Law 18, 51 BMLR 128, [1999] 39 LS Gaz R 38, [1999]
    All ER (D) 1043   1.30
F (Adult Patient), Re [2000] 3 CCLR 210   2.21, 2.22
F (Mental Capacity: Interim Jurisdiction), Re [2009] EWHC B30 (Fam),
    [2010] 2 FLR 28   2.66
Fox v Stirk [1970] 2 QB 463, [1970] 3 All ER 7, [1970] 3 WLR 147, 68 LGR
    644   1.15

G v E (by his litigation friend the Official Solicitor), a local authority, F
    [2010] EWCA Civ 822, [2011] 1 FLR 239; [2010] EWHC 621 (Fam),
    [2010] 2 FLR 294   2.9, 2.53–2.55, 2.60
GJ v (1) Foundation Trust; (2) PCT; (3) Secretary of State for Health [2009]
    EWHC 2972 (Fam), [2010] 1 FLR 1251   1.34, 2.45
Guzzardi v Italy (1981) 3 EHRR 333   2.60

HL v United Kingdom (Application No 45508/99) (2004) 40 EHRR 761,
    [2004] 7 CCLR 498, [2004] 1 FLR 1019   2.39, 2.40, 2.52, 2.103
HM (Vulnerable Adult:Abduction), Re [2010] EWHC 870 (Fam), [2010] 2
    FLR 1057   2.36
Husain v Asylum Support Adjudicator & Sec of State for the Home
    Department [2001] EWHC 832 (Admin)   9.4
Hussain v UK (1996) 2 EHRR 1   2.103

Independent News & Media v A [2010] EWCA Civ 343, [2010] 2 FLR 1290   2.96
Investigation into Complaint No 98/B/0341 against Wiltshire County
    Council [2000] 3 CCLR 60   1.22
Investigation into Complaint Nos 97/0177 and 97/0755 against the former
    Clwyd County Counciland Conwy County BC [1998] 1 CCLR 546   1.8
Islington London Borough Council v University College Hospital Trust
    [2005] EWCA Civ 596, [2005] 8 CCLR 337, [2006] LGR 50, 85
    BMLR 171, (2005) *Times*, 28 June, [2005] All ER (D) 165 (Jun)   6.13

JE v (1) DE (by his litigation friend the Official Solicitor) (2) Surrey County
    Council [2006] EWHC 3459 (Fam), [2007] 10 CCLR 149, [2007]
    MHLR 39   1.32
Jennifer Connor (application by for Judicial Review), Re [2005] 8 CCLR
    328, [2004] NICA 45   1.31
JT v UK [2000] MHLR 254, [2000] 1 FLR 909, [2000] Fam Law 533   1.43

KD & LD v Havering London Borough Council [2010] 1 FLR 1393, [2010]
    Fam Law 244   2.74
Khana (by her litigation friend the Official Solicitor) v The Mayor and
    Burgesses of Southwark London Borough Council [2001] EWCA Civ
    999, [2001] 4 CCLR 267, [2002] LGR 15, [2002] HLR 596, [2001] 31
    LS Gaz R 31, (2001) *Times*, 25 September, [2001] All ER (D) 316
    (Jun)   4.12
Kleinwort Benson v Lincoln City Council; Same v Birmingham City
    Council; Same v Southwark London Borough Council; Same v
    Kensington and Chelsea London Borough Council [1999] 2 AC 349,
    [1998] 3 WLR 1095, [1998] 4 All ER 513, HL   1.21

L (by his next friend GE), Re [1998] 1 CCLR 390, [1999] AC 458   2.40
LBH v GP & MP [2010] 13 CCLR 171   2.71
LBL v RYJ [2010] EWHC 2664 (Fam)   2.9
LBL v RYJ and VJ [2010] EWHC 2665 (COP), [2011] 1 FLR 1279   2.9
Levene v IRC [1928] AC 217, [1927] 2 KB 38, 13 TC 486   1.15
Lewis v Gibson and MH (by her litigation friend, the Official Solicitor)
    [2005] EWCA Civ 587, [2005] 8 CCLR 399, [2005] 2 FCR 241, 87
    BMLR 93, [2005] All ER (D) 292 (May)   1.54
LLBC v TG, JG and KR [2007] EWHC 2640; [2009] 1 FLR 414   2.60
Local Authority v (1) MA (2) NA and (3) SA (by her children's guardian
    LJ) [2005] EWHC 2942 (Fam), [2007] 10 CCLR 193, [2007] 10
    CCLR 193, [2006] 1 FLR 867, [2007] 2 FCR 563, [2006] Fam Law
    268   3.96
Local Authority v DL [2011] EWHC 1022 (Fam), [2011] 14 CCLR 443   3.99
Local Authority v DL, RL and ML [2010] EWHC 2675 (Fam), [2011] 1
    FLR 957   3.98

Local Authority v MRS A (Test for Capacity as to Contraception) [2010]
    EWHC 1549 (COP), [2011] 1 FLR 26   2.30
Local Authority v PB [2011] EWHC 502 (COP)   2.24
Local Authority X v MM (by her litigation friend the Official Solicitor) &
    KM [2007] EWHC 2003, [2009] 1 FLR 443   2.26–2.29
London Borough of Hillingdon v Steven Neary (by his litigation friend the
    Official Solicitor and Mark Neary [2011] EWHC 1377 (COP), [2011]
    Fam Law 944, [2011] NLJR 849   2.58, 2.60
London Borough of Hillingdon v Steven Neary (by his litigation friend the
    Official Solicitor) and Mark Neary [2011] EWHC 413 (COP), [2011]
    14 CCLR 239   2.96

M (by his litigation friend TM) v Hackney London Borough Council, East
    London NHS Foundation Trust, Secretary of State for Health) [2011]
    EWCA Civ 4, [2011] 14 CCLR 154 *reversing* R (on the application of
    TTM) by his litigation friend TM) v LB Hackney and East London
    NHS Foundation Trust [2010] EWHC 1349 (Admin), [2010] All ER
    (D) 88 (Jun)   1.47
M v B, A & S, by the Official Solicitor [2005] EWHC 1681 (Fam), [2006] 1
    FLR 117, [2005] Fam Law 860, (2005) *Times*, 10 August, [2005] All
    ER (D) 449 (Jul)   2.20, 3.97
M, Re [2011] EWHC 2443 (Fam), [2011] 39 LS Gaz R 18   2.13
Masterman-Lister v Brutton & Co (1) and Jewell and Home Counties
    Dairies (2) [2002] EWCA Civ 1889, [2004] 7 CCLR 5, [2003] 3 All
    ER 162, [2003] 1 WLR 1511, 73 BMLR 1, (2002) *Times*, 28
    December, 147 Sol Jo LB 60, [2002] All ER (D) 297 (Dec)   2.7, 2.8
MB (Medical Treatment), Re [1997] 2 FCR 541, [1997] 2 FLR 426, [1997]
    Fam Law 542, [1997] 8 Med LR 217, 38 BMLR 175, [1997] NLJR
    600   2.6, 2.11, 2.27
MIG & MEG, Re [2010] EWHC 785 (Fam)   2.60
MM (An Adult) [2007] EWHC 2689 (Fam), [2009] 1 FLR 487   2.28
MM, Re [2011] 1 FLR 712   2.67

Oldham Metropolitan Borough Council v GW and PW [2007] EWHC 136
    (Fam), [2007] 2 FLR 597   2.9
Osmani v Camden London Borough Council [2005] HLR 22   8.64

P (Forced Marriage), Re [2011] EWHC 3467 (Fam), [2011] 1 FLR 2060   2.20
P (otherwise known as MIG) and Q (otherwise known as MEG, by the
    Official Solicitor, their litigation friend v Surrey County Council, CA,
    LA and Equality and Human Rights Commission (Intervener) [2011]
    EWCA Civ 190, [2011] 14 CCLR 209; [2010] EWHC 785 (Fam)   2.48, 2.56, 2.59, 2.60
P (Vulnerable Adults: Deputies), Re [2010] EWHC 1592, [2010] 2 FLR 1712   2.83
PCT v P, AH and the Local Authority [2011] 1 FLR 287, [2010] Fam Law
    1275   2.55
Peters v (1) East Midlands Strategic Health Authority (2) Halstead and (3)
    Nottingham City Council [2009] EWCA Civ 145, [2009] 12 CCLR
    299   6.13
PH v A Local Authority & Z Ltd & R [2011] EWHC 1704 (Fam)   2.9
Pieretti v Enfield London Borough Council [2010] EWCA Civ 1104, [2011] 2
    All ER 642, [2010] LGR 944   3.49, 8.83

R (on the application of (1) Chavda (2) Fitzpatrick (by her daughter and
    litigation friend Pamela Fitzpatrick) (3) Maos) v Harrow London
    Borough Council [2007] EWHC 3064 (Admin), [2008] 11 CCLR 187   3.64
R (on the application of A) v LB or Croydon & ors [2009] UKSC 8, [2010]
    1 FLR 959, [2010] 1 All ER 469, [2009] 1 WLR 2557   9.34
R (on the application of A) v London Borough of Lambeth [2010] EWHC
    1652 (Admin), [2010] 2 FCR 539, [2010] NLJR 1013   5.36

R (on the application of AB and SB) v Nottingham County Council [2001]
EWHC Admin 235, [2001] 4 CCLR 295   5.55

R (on the application of Adrian Holloway) v Oxfordshire County
Counciland Oxford County Court [2007] EWHC 776 (Admin), [2007]
10 CCLR 264, [2007] LGR 891, [2007] All ER (D) 39 (Apr)   1.48

R (on the application of Ahmad) v Newham London Borough Council
[2009] UKHL 14, [2009] 3 All ER 755   8.27

R (on the application of Alloway) (by his father and litigation friend) v
Bromley London Borough Council [2004] EWHC 2108 (Admin),
[2005] 8 CCLR 61, [2004] All ER (D) 88 (Aug)   4.9

R (on the application of Alyson Booker) v NHS Oldham and Direct Line
Insurance PLC [2010] EWHC 2593 (Admin), [2011] 14 CCLR 315   6.13

R (on the application of Ariemuguvbe) v Islington London Borough
Council [2009] EWCA Civ 1308, [2010] HLR 254, [2010] All ER (D)
204 (Feb)   8.11

R (on the application of Aweys) v Birmingham County Council [2007]
EWHC 52 (Admin), [2007] 1 FLR 2066, [2007] Fam Law 493, [2007]
HLR 394   8.43

R (on the application of B) v Camden London Borough Council and
Camden and Islington Mental Health and Social Care Trust [2005]
EWHC 1366 (Admin), [2005] 8 CCLR 422, [2006] LGR 19, 85
BMLR 28, [2005] All ER (D) 43 (Jul)   1.4, 1.6

R (on the application of B) v Cornwall County Council and the Brandon
Trust [2009] EWHC 491 (Admin), [2009] 12 CCLR 381   3.9

R (on the application of B) v Merton London Borough Council [2003]
EWHC 1689 (Admin), [2003] 4 All ER 280   9.35

R (on the application of B) v Worcestershire County Council [2009] EWHC
2915 (Admin), [2010] 13 CCLR 13   4.42

R (on the application of Batantu) v Islington London Borough Council
[2001] 4 CCLR 445, [2000] All ER (D) 1744   4.10

R (on the application of Bauer-Czarnomski v Ealing London Borough
Council [2010] EWHC 130 (Admin)   8.30

R (on the application of Berhe, Kidane, Munir and Ncube) v Hillingdon
London Borough Council and Secretary of State for Education and
Skills (interested party) [2003] EWHC 2075 (Admin), [2003] 6 CCLR
471, [2004] 1 FLR 439, [2003] Fam Law 872, [2003] 39 LS Gaz R 38,
(2003) *Times*, 22 September, [2003] All ER (D) 01 (Sep)   5.30

R (on the application of Bernard) v Enfield London Borough Council
[2002] EWHC 2282 (Admin), [2002] 5 CCLR 577, [2003] LGR 423,
[2003] HLR 354, [2002] 48 LS Gaz R 27, (2002) *Times*, 8 November,
5 CCL Rep 577, [2002] All ER (D) 383 (Oct)   2.103, 3.77

R (on the application of Betteridge) v Parole Board [2009] EWHC 1638
(Admin)   2.103

R (on the application of BG) v Medway Council [2005] EWHC 1932
(Admin), [2005] 8 CCLR 448, [2005] 3 FCR 199, [2006] 1 FLR 663,
[2006] Fam Law 97, [2006] HLR 87, [2005] All ER (D) 40 (Sep)   5.60

R (on the application of Birmingham Care Consortium and others) v
Birmingham County Council [2002] EWHC 2118 (Admin), [2002] 5
CCLR 600, [2003] LGR 119, [2002] All ER (D) 232 (Oct)   4.51

R (on the application of Bodimeade and others) v Camden London
Borough Council [2001] EWHC Admin 271, [2001] 4 CCLR 246   4.27

R (on the application of Broster & Ors) v Wirral Metropolitan Borough
Council and Salisbury Independent Living [2010] EWHC 3086
(Admin)   3.25, 3.64

R (on the application of Burke) v General Medical Council [2005] EWCA
Civ 1003, [2005] 8 CCLR 463, [2006] QB 273, [2005] 3 WLR 1132,
[2005] 3 FCR 169, [2005] 2 FLR 1223, [2005] Fam Law 776, 85
BMLR 1, [2005] NLJR 1457, (2005) *Times*, 2 August, [2005] All ER
(D) 445 (Jul)   2.13

R (on the application of Carton and Larrad) v Coventry CC; R (on the
   application of Morgan and Pickering) v Coventry County Council
   [2001] 4 CCLR 41   6.28
R (on the application of CD) (a child by her litigation friend VD) v Isle of
   Anglesey County Council [2004] EWHC 1635 (Admin), [2004] 7
   CCLR 589, [2005] 1 FLR 59, [2004] 3 FCR 171   5.59
R (on the application of Cole) v Enfield London Borough Council [2003]
   EWHC 1454 (Admin)   8.74
R (on the application of Collins) v Lincolnshire Health Authority [2001]
   EWHC 685 (Admin), [2001] 4 CCLR 429   4.29
R (on the application of Cowl and others) v Plymouth County Council
   [2001] EWCA Civ 1935, [2002] 1 WLR 803; [2001] EWHC 734,
   [2001] 4 CCLR 475   4.31, 4.33
R (on the application of Daniel Falkner) v SoS for Justice (1) Parole Board
   (2) [2011] EWCA Civ 349   2.103
R (on the application of Dixon) v Wandsworth London Borough Council
   [2007] EWHC 3075 (Admin), [2007] All ER (D) 357 (Dec)   8.12, 8.29
R (on the application of E) v Bristol City Council [2005] EWHC 74
   (Admin), [2005] MHLR 83, [2005] All ER (D) 57 (Jan)   1.49, 1.59
R (on the application of F, J, S, R) v Wirral Borough Council [2009] EWHC
   1626 (Admin), [2009] 12 CCLR 452   3.19
R (on the application of FZ) v Croydon London Borough Council [2011]
   EWCA Civ 59, [2011] 1 FLR 2081, [2011] Fam Law 355, [2011] HLR
   343   9.36
R (on the application of G (FC)) v Southwark London Borough Council
   [2009] UKHL 26, [2009] 12 CCLR 437   5.32, 5.63
R (on the application of G) v Barnet London Borough Council; R (on the
   application of W) v Lambeth London Borough Council; R (on the
   application of A) v Lambeth London Borough Council [2003]
   UKHL 57, [2003] 6 CCLR 500   5.44, 5.56
R (on the application of G) v Nottingham City Council and Nottingham
   University Hospital [2008] EWHC 400 (Admin), [2008] 1 FLR 1668   5.35
R (on the application of Goldsmith) v Wandsworth London Borough
   Council [2004] EWCA Civ 1170, [2004] 7 CCLR 472, 148 Sol Jo LB
   1065, [2004] All ER (D) 154 (Aug)   4.37
R (on the application of Green (by her litigation friend Kempson)) v South
   West Strategic Health Authority and (1) North Somerset PCT (2)
   SoS Department of Health [2008] EWHC 2576 (Admin), [2009] 12
   CCLR 93   7.34
R (on the application of Greenwich London Borough Council) v Secretary
   of State for Health and Bexley London Borough Council [2006]
   EWHC 2576 (Admin), [2007] 10 CCLR 60, [2006] All ER (D) 178
   (Jul)   3.69, 4.18, 4.20, 7.53
R (on the application of Grogan) v Bexley NHS Care Trust and South East
   London Strategic Health Authority (First Interested Party) and
   Secretary of State for Health (Second Interested Party) [2006]
   EWHC 44 (Admin), [2006] 9 CCLR 188   7.12–7.14
R (on the application of Gunter) v South Western Staffordshire Primary
   Care Trust [2005] EWHC 1894 (Admin), [2006] 9 CCLR 121   6.71
R (on the application of H) v A City Council [2011] EWCA Civ 403, [2011]
   14 CCLR 381   6.46
R (on the application of H) v Wandsworth London Borough Council; R (on
   the application of Barhanu) v Hackney London Borough Council; R
   (on the application of B) v Islington London Borough Council [2007]
   EWHC 1082 (Admin), [2007] 10 CCLR 439, [2007] 2 FCR 378,
   [2007] 2 FLR 822   5.62
R (on the application of Haggerty and others) v St Helens Council [2003]
   EWHC 803 (Admin), [2003] 6 CCLR 352   4.36

R (on the application of Harrison) v SoS for Health, Wakefield District
  Primary Care Trust, Wakefield Metropolitan District Council
  (interested parties); R (on the application of Garnham) v SoS for
  Health and Islington PCT, Islington London Borough Council
  (interested party) [2009] EWHC 574 (Admin), [2009] 12 CCLR 355   6.71, 7.38

R (on the application of Heffernan) v Sheffield County Council [2004]
  EWHC 1377 (Admin), [2004] 7 CCLR 350   3.51

R (on the application of Hertfordshire County Council) v London Borough
  of Hammersmith and Fulham and JM (interested party) [2011]
  EWCA Civ 77, [2011] 14 CCLR 224   1.14, 1.15

R (on the application of Hide) v Staffordshire County Council [2007]
  EWCA Civ 860, [2008] 11 CCLR 28   4.30

R (on the application of Hughes) v Liverpool County Council [2005]
  EWHC 428 (Admin), [2005] 8 CCLR 243   4.40

R (on the application of Ireneschild) v Lambeth London Borough Council
  [2007] EWCA Civ 234, [2007] 10 CCLR 243   3.72

R (on the application of J) (by his litigation friend MW) v Caerphilly
  County Borough Council [2005] EWHC 586 (Admin), [2005] 8
  CCLR 255, [2005] 2 FLR 860   5.34, 5.36

R (on the application of J) v Enfield London Borough Council, Secretary of
  State for Health as Intervener [2002] EWHC 432 (Admin), [2002] 2
  FLR 1   5.58, 5.69

R (on the application of JL) v Islington London Borough Council [2009]
  EWHC 458 (Admin), [2009] 2 FLR 515   5.49

R (on the application of JM and NT) v Isle of Wight Council [2011]
  EWHC 2911 (Admin)   3.7

R (on the application of K) v Camden and Islington Health Authority
  [2001] EWCA Civ 240, [2001] 4 CCLR 170   1.4

R (on the application of KB) v MHRT [2003] EWHC 193 (Admin)   2.103

R (on the application of Kelly & Mehari) v Birmingham County Council
  [2009] EWHC 3240 (Admin)   8.52

R (on the application of Kelly) v Hammersmith and Fulham London
  Borough Council [2004] EWHC 435 (Admin), [2004] 7 CCLR 542   6.37

R (on the application of KM) v Cambridgeshire County Council [2010]
  EWHC 3065 (Admin), [2011] 14 CCLR 83; on appeal R (on the
  application of KM (by his mother and litigation friend JM)) v
  Cambridgeshire County Council [2011] EWCA Civ 682, [2011] 14
  CCLR 402   6.70

R (on the application of L) v Mayor and Burgesses of the London Borough
  of Barking and Dagenham [2001] EWCA Civ 533, [2001] 2 FLR 763,
  [2001] 4 CCLR 196   4.25

R (on the application of Lambeth London Borough Council) [2006] EWHC
  2362 (Admin), [2007] 10 CCLR 84   1.3, 1.4

R (on the application of Lawer) v Restormel BC [2007] EWHC 2299
  (Admin), [2008] HLR 327   8.53

R (on the application of LH and MH) v Lambeth London Borough
  Council [2006] EWHC 1190 (Admin), [2006] 9 CCLR 622   5.70

R (on the application of M (FC)) v Slough Borough Council [2008] UKHL
  52, [2008] 11 CCLR 733   3.5, 4.13–4.16, 4.41, 9.30

R (on the application of M) v Barking & Dagenham London Borough
  Council and Westminster County Council (Interested Party) [2002]
  EWHC 2663 (Admin), [2003] 6 CCLR 87   3.36, 5.28

R (on the application of M) v Hammersmith and Fulham London Borough
  Council [2008] UKHL 14, [2008] 1 FLR 1384   5.32, 5.63

R (on the application of M) v Homerton University Hospital [2008] EWCA
  Civ 197, [2008] MHLR 92   1.54

R (on the application of M) v Secretary of State for Health [2003] EWHC
  1094 (Admin), [2003] MHLR 348   1.43

R (on the application of M) v Suffolk County Council [2006] EWHC 2366
  (Admin), [2006] 9 CCLR 704   6.63

R (on the application of Madden) v Bury Metropolitan Borough Council
 [2002] EWHC 1882 (Admin), [2002] 5 CCLR 622   4.35
R (on the application of Manchester CC) v St Helens BC (PE interested
 party) [2009] EWCA Civ 1348, [2010] 13 CCLR 48   4.21
R (on the application of McDonald) (Appellant) v Royal Borough of
 Kensington and Chelsea (Respondent) [2011] UKSC 33, [2011] 14
 CCLR 341   3.4, 3.5, 3.7, 3.12, 3.46, 3.47, 3.77, 4.42, 8.84
R (on the application of MH) v Secretary of State for Health [2005] UKHL
 60, [2005] MHLR 302, [2006] 1 AC 441, [2005] 4 All ER 1311, [2005]
 3 WLR 867, 86 BMLR 71, (2005) *Times*, 25 October, [2005] All ER
 (D) 218 (Oct)   1.56, 1.58, 2.33
R (on the application of Michael Degainis) v SoS for Justice [2010] EWHC
 137 (Admin)   2.103
R (on the application of Michael Mwanza) v Greenwich London Borough
 Council and Bromley London Borough Council [2010] EWHC 1462
 (Admin), [2010] 13 CCLR 454   1.3
R (on the application of Mooney) v Southwark London Borough Council
 [2006] EWHC 1912 (Admin), [2006] 9 CCLR 670, [2006] All ER (D)
 73 (Jul)   5.61, 9.28
R (on the application of Moore and others) v Care Standards Tribunal
 Commission [2004] EWHC 2481 (Admin), [2005] 8 CCLR 91   4.58
R (on the application of Munjaz) v Merseycare NHS Trust [2005] UKHL
 58, [2005] MHLR 276   1.2
R (on the application of O) v Haringey London Borough Council [2004]
 EWCA Civ 535, [2004] LGR 672, [2004] 2 FCR 219, [2004] 2 FLR
 476, [2004] Fam Law 634, [2004] HLR 788, (2004) *Times*, 27 May,
 [2004] All ER (D) 22 (May)   5.61
R (on the application of O) v London Borough of Hammersmith & Fulham
 [2011] EWCA Civ 925   5.59
R (on the application of P) v Essex County Council and Basildon Council
 [2004] EWHC 2027 (Admin), [2004] All ER (D) 103 (Aug)   5.59
R (on the application of P) v Newham London Borough Council [2004]
 EWHC 2210 (Admin), [2004] 7 CCLR 553   5.33
R (on the application of Pennington) v Parole Board [2010] EWHC 78
 (Admin)   2.103
R (on the application of Phillips) (by her daughter and litigation friend) and
 Rowe (by her sister and litigation friend) v Walsall Metropolitan
 Borough Council [2001] EWHC Admin 789, [2002] 5 CCLR 383   4.34
R (on the application of PM) v Hertfordshire County Council [2010]
 EWHC 2056 (Admin), [2010] NLJR 1191, (2010) *Times*, 18
 November, [2010] All ER (D) 28 (Aug)   9.38
R (on the application of R) v Croydon London Borough Council [2011]
 EWHC 1473, [2011] LGR 691, [2011] All ER (D) 77 (Jun)   9.37
R (on the application of Rutter) v Stockton on Tees BC [2008] EWHC 2651
 (Admin), [2009] 12 CCLR 27   4.32
R (on the application of S) (by her mother and next friend Sandra Branch)
 v Leicester County Council [2004] EWHC 533 (Admin), [2004] 7
 CCLR 254   4.17
R (on the application of S) v SoS for the Home Department & Ors [2011]
 EWHC 2120 (Admin), 175 CL&J 551, [2011] All ER (D) 16 (Sep)   2.103
R (on the application of Savva) v Royal Borough of Kensington & Chelsea
 [2010] EWCA Civ 1209, [2011] 14 CCLR 75, (2010) *Times*, 15
 November   3.24, 6.69, 6.70
R (on the application of Spink) v Wandsworth London Borough Council
 [2005] EWCA Civ 302, [2005] 8 CCLR 272   5.44, 6.22
R (on the application of SSG) v Liverpool County Council (1) and
 Secretary of State for the Department of Health (2) and LS
 (Interested Party) [2002] 5 CCLR 639   1.43
R (on the application of St Helens Borough Council) v Manchester Primary
 Care Trust [2008] EWCA Civ 931, [2008] 11 CCLR 774   7.15

R (on the application of Stephenson) v Stockton-on-Tees BC [2005] EWCA
Civ 960, [2005] 8 CCLR 517, [2006] LGR 135, [2005] 3 FCR 248,
reversing [2004] EWHC 2228 (Admin), [2004] 7 CCLR 459, [2005] 1
FCR 165   6.26, 6.27

R (on the application of Stevens) v Plymouth City Council (C As Interested
Party) [2002] EWCA Civ 388, [2002] 1 WLR 2583, [2002] LGR 565,
[2002] 1 FLR 1177, [2002] All ER (D) 414 (Mar)   1.37, 1.42, 1.52

R (on the application of Stewart) v Wandsworth London Borough Council,
Hammersmith and Fulham London Borough Council and Lambeth
London Borough Council [2001] EWHC 709 (Admin), [2001] 4
CCLR 466, [2001] All ER (D) 08 (Oct)   3.36, 5.28

R (on the application of Sunderland City Council v South Tyneside Council
[2011] EWHC 2355 (Admin)   1.14

R (on the application of T and others) v Haringey London Borough
Council and another [2005] EWHC 2235 (Admin), [2006] 9 CCLR 58   7.16

R (on the application of TG) v London Borough of Lambeth and Shelter
(Intervener) [2011] EWCA Civ 526, [2011] 14 CCLR 366   5.63

R (on the application of V) v (1) South London & Maudsley NHS
Foundation Trust (2) Croydon London Borough Council [2010]
EWHC 742 (Admin), [2010] 13 CCLR 181   1.47

R (on the application of VC & ors) and R (on the application of K) v
Newcastle City Council [2011] EWHC 2673 (Admin), [2011] All ER
(D) 189 (Oct)   9.17

R (on the application of W) v Birmingham City Council [2011] EWHC
1147 (Admin), [2011] 14 CCLR 516   3.64

R (on the application of W) v Croydon London Borough Council [2011]
EWHC 696 (Admin), [2011] 14 CCLR 247   2.25, 3.12

R (on the application of W) v Doncaster Metropolitan Borough Council
[2003] EWHC 192 (Admin), [2003] 6 CCLR 301, (2003) *Times*, 12
March, [2003] All ER (D) 177 (Feb)   1.4

R (on the application of W) v North Lincolnshire Council [2008] EWHC
2299 (Admin), [2008] 2 FLR 2150   5.31

R (on the application of W, M and others) v Birmingham CC [2011] EWHC
1147 (Admin)   3.7

R (on the application of Wahid) v The Mayor and Burgesses of Tower
Hamlets London Borough Council [2002] EWCA Civ 287 [2002] 5
CCLR 239   4.11, 4.40, 9.30

R (on the application of Westminster CC) v National Asylum and Support
Service [2002] UKHL 38, [2002] 4 All ER 654, [2002] 1 WLR 2956,
[2003] LGR 23, [2002] HLR 1021, (2002) *Times*, 18 October, [2002]
All ER (D) 235 (Oct)   5.61, 9.28

R (on the application of Wilson) v Coventry City Council; R (on the
application of Thomas) v (1) Havering London Borough Council (2)
Secretary of State for Health [2008] EWHC 2300 (Admin), [2009] 12
CCLR 7   4.31

R (on the application of Zarzour) v Hillngdon London Borough Council &
Secretary of State for Home Department (Interested Party) [2009]
EWCA Civ 1529, [2010] 13 CCLR 157   4.16, 4.41

R (on the personal representatives of Beeson) v Dorset County Counciland
the Secretary of State for Health [2001] EWHC Admin 986, [2002] 5
CCLR 5   6.33

R v Avon County Council ex p M [1999] 2 CCLR 185, [1994] 2 FLR 1006   4.5

R v Bath Mental Healthcare NHS Trust, Wiltshire Health Authority and
Wiltshire County Council ex p Beck, Pearce, Doran and Burden
[2000] 3 CCLR 5   3.75

R v Berkshire County Council ex p P [1998] 1 CCLR 141   3.68

R v Bexley London Borough Council ex p B [2000] 3 CCLR 15   5.47

R v Bristol County Council ex p Penfold (Alice) [1998] 1 CCLR 315, [1998]
COD 210, (1998) 1 CCL Rep 315   3.73

R v Calderdale Metropolitan Borough Council ex p Houghton [2000] 3
  CCLR 228   3.71
R v Camden London Borough Council ex p Gillan (1988) 21 HLR 114   8.42
R v Camden London Borough Council ex p Mohammed (1998) 30 HLR
  315   8.73
R v Central London County Council ex p Ax London [1999] 2 CCLR 257,
  [1999] 2 FLR 161   1.55
R v Collins, Pathfinder Mental Health Services NHS Trust and St George's
  Healthcare NHS Trust ex p S [1998] 1 CCLR 410, [1998] 2 FLR 728   2.11
R v Cumbria County Council ex p Cumbria Professional Care Ltd [2000] 3
  CCLR 79   4.46
R v Ealing District Health Authority, ex p Fox [1993] 1 WLR 373, [1993] 3
  All ER 170, QBD   1.4
R v Ealing London Borough Council ex p C [2000] 3 CCLR 122   5.54
R v East Sussex County Council ex p Tandy [1998] AC 714, [1998] 2 All ER
  769, HL   3.39–3.42
R v East Sussex County Council ex p Ward [2000] 3 CCLR 132   4.52
R v Gloucestershire County Council ex p Barry [1997] 1 CCLR 40, [1997]
  AC 584, [1997] 2 All ER 1, [1997] 2 WLR 459, 95 LGR 638, 36
  BMLR 69, [1997] NLJR 453, 141 Sol Jo LB 91, 1 CCL Rep 40 HL   3.37, 3.38, 3.42, 3.44,
                                                                                 4.7, 4.8
R v Haringey London Borough Council ex p Norton [1998] 1 CCLR 168   3.50
R v Islington London Borough Council ex p Batantu; R (on the application
  of Wahid) v Tower Hamlets London Borough Council; R v Wigan
  Metropolitan Borough Council ex p Tammadge; R (on the
  application of G) v Barnet London Borough Council [2002] EWCA
  Civ 287, [2002] 5 CCLR 239   5.61
R v Islington London Borough Council ex p Rixon (Jonathan) [1998] 1
  CCLR 119, (1996) *Times* 17 April   3.3, 4.27
R v Jackson [1891] 1 QB 671   2.60
R v Kensington and Chelsea RLBC ex p Kujtim [1999] 2 CCLR 340, [1999]
  4 All ER 161, [1999] LGR 761, 32 HLR 579, 2 CCLR 340, (1999)
  Times, 5 August   4.6
R v Kent County Council ex p S [1999] 3 FCR 193, [2000] 1 FLR 155,
  [2000] Fam Law 15, [1999] All ER (D) 508   5.64
R v Kent County Council ex p Salisbury and Pierre [2000] 3 CCLR 38   3.35, 5.28
R v Kirklees Metropolitan Borough Council ex p Good [1998] 1 CCLR 506   3.83
R v Kirklees Metropolitan Borough Council, ex p Daykin (1996) 1 CCLR
  512   3.5
R v Lambeth London Borough Council ex p A1 and A2 [1998] 1 CCLR 336   3.51
R v Lambeth London Borough Council ex p K [2000] 3 CCLR 141   5.48
R v London Borough of Redbridge ex p East Sussex County Council (1992)
  Times, 31 December   3.67
R v Manchester County Council ex p Stennett and two other actions [2002]
  UKHL 34, [2002] 5 CCLR 500   1.7, 1.18, 1.19
R v Mental Health Review Tribunal ex p Hall (1999) 4 All ER 883   1.15
R v Mental Health Review Tribunal, Torfaen County BC and Gwent Health
  Authority ex p Hall [1999] 3 All ER 132, [1999] NLJR 638, [1999] 2
  CCLR 383   1.4, 1.9, 1.13
R v North and East Devon Health Authority, ex p Coughlan and Secretary
  of State for Health and Royal College of Nursing [1999] 2 CCLR
  285, [2000] 2 WLR 622   1.18, 4.26, 4.28, 4.29, 7.3, 7.6, 7.11, 7.33, 7.34
R v Oldham Metropolitan Borough Council ex p Garlick & another [1993]
  AC 509, HL   8.45
R v Paul-Coker v Southwark London Borough Council [2006] EWHC 497
  (Admin)   8.75
R v Powys County Council ex p Hambidge [1998] 1 CCLR 458, (1998)
  Times 20 July   6.21
R v Powys County Council ex p Hambidge (No 2) [2000] 3 CCLR 231   6.28

R v Richmond London Borough Council ex p Watson; R v Redcar and
  Cleveland BC ex p Armstrong; R v Manchester County Council ex p
  Stennett; R v Harrow London Borough Council ex p Cobham [1999]
  2 CCLR 402   1.7, 1.9, 1.14
R v Secretary of State for Health ex p M and K [1998] 1 CCLR 495   6.4
R v Sefton Metropolitan Borough Council ex p Help the Aged and
  Charlotte Blanchard [1997] 1 CCLR 57, [1997] 4 All ER 532   3.5, 4.7
R v Servite Houses and Wandsworth London Borough Council e p
  Goldsmith and Chatting [2000] 3 CCLR 325   4.23
R v Slough BC ex p Ealing London Borough Council [1981] QB 801, [1981]
  1 All ER 601, [1981] 2 WLR 399, CA   8.44
R v South Lanarkshire County Council ex p MacGregor [2001] 4 CCLR
  188   3.43
R v South Western Hospital Managers ex p M [1993] QB 683, [1994] 1 All
  ER 161   1.50
R v SSHD ex p Naughton [1997] 1 WLR 118, [1997] 1 Cr App Rep 151,
  [1997] Crim LR 146, [1996] NLJR 1507   2.103
R v Sutton London Borough Council ex p Tucker [1998] 1 CCLR 251   3.70
R v Tower Hamlets London Borough Council ex p Bradford (Anita,
  Raymond and Simon) [1998] 1 CCLR 294, (1997) 29 HLR 756   5.53
R v Waltham Forest London Borough Council, ex p Vale (1985) *Times*, 25
  February   1.15, 3.67
R v Wandsworth London Borough Council ex p O [2000] 1 WLR 2539,
  [2000] 4 All ER 590, [2000] 34 LS Gaz R 41   9.29
R v Westminster County Council ex p Ermakov [1996] 2 All ER 302, 95
  LGR 119   3.50
R v Westminster County Council ex p M, P, A & X (1997) 1 CCLR 85   4.11
R v Wigan Metropolitan Borough Council ex p Tammadge [1998] 1 CCLR
  581   3.74, 5.48
RK (Minor: Deprivation of Liberty), Re [2010] EWHC 3355 (COP)   2.60
RK v BCC (1); YB (2); AK(3) [2011] EWCA Civ 1305   2.61
Robertson v Fife [2002] UKHL 35, [2002] 5 CCLR 543, 68 BMLR 229,
  (2002) *Times*, 8 August, 2002 SLT 951, 2003 SCLR 39   6.34
RT v LT and a Local Authority [2010] EWHC 1910 (Fam), [2011] 1 FLR
  594   2.68

S (Adult Patient), Inherent Jurisdiction: Family Life, Re [2002] EWHC 2278
  (Fam), [2003] 1 FLR 292   2.16
S (Adult's Lack of Capacity: Carer and Residence), Re [2003] EWHC 1909
  (Fam), [2003] 2 FLR 1235   2.17
Salford City Council v GJ, NJ and BJ (by their respective litigation friends)
  [2008] EWHC 1097 (Fam), [2008] 2 FLR 1295   2.47
Sandford and Scherer v Waltham Forest London Borough Council [2008]
  EWHC 1106 (QB), [2008] 11 CCLR 480   3.52
SC (Mental Patient: Habeas Corpus), Re [1996] 1 FLR 548, [1996] 1 All ER
  532, [1996] 2 WLR 146   1.48
Secretary of State for the Home Department v JJ and others [2007] UKHL
  45, [2008] 1 AC 385   2.60
Sentges v The Netherlands (2003) 6 CCLR 400, 405   3.47
Shah v Barnet London Borough Council [1983] 2 AC 309, [1983] 1 All ER
  226, [1983] 2 WLR 16, 81 LGR 305, 127 Sol Jo 36   1.15
Sheffield City Council v E [2004] EWHC 2808 (Fam)   2.9
SK (Local Authority: Expert Evidence), Re [2007] EWHC 3289 (Fam),
  [2008] 2 FLR 707   2.97
SK, Re; A London Borough Council v KS and LU [2008] EWHC 636
  (Fam), [2008] 2 FLR 720   2.26
SL v Westminster City Council and The Medical Foundation/Mind
  (Intervening) [2011] EWCA Civ 954, [2011] All ER (D) 63 (Aug)   4.16, 9.31
SMBC v WMP,RG and CG (by their litigation friend the Official Solicitor),
  HSG, SK and SKG [2011] 14 CCLR 413   2.66

Sowden v Lodge; Crookdale v Drury [2004] EWCA Civ 1370, [2005] 1 All
    ER 581, [2005] 1 WLR 2129, 148 Sol Jo LB 1282, [2004] All ER (D)
    304 (Oct)   6.14
ST (Adult Patient), Re [2006] EWHC 3458 (Fam), [2008] 1 FLR 111   2.35
Stanley Johnson v The United Kingdom (1999) 27 EHRR 296   1.9
Storck v Germany (Application no 61603/00) (2005) 43 EHRR 96, [2005]
    ECHR 61603/00, ECtHR   2.51, 2.53, 2.56
Street v Mountford [1985] AC 809, [1985] 2 All ER 289, [1985] 2 WLR 877,
    129 Sol Jo 348   4.59

T (A Minor), Re [1998] 1 CCLR 352   3.40
T (An Adult), Consent to Medical Treatment, Re, *sub nom* T (Adult:
    Refusal of Treatment), Re [1993] Fam 95, [1992] 4 All ER 649, [1992]
    3 WLR 782, [1992] 2 FCR 861, [1992] 2 FLR 458, [1993] Fam Law
    27, 9 BMLR 46, [1992] NLJR 1125   2.3, 2.6

W (by her litigation friend, B) v M (by the Official Solicitor) *sub nom* W (by
    her litigation friend, B) v M (an adult patient by the Official
    Solicitor), S, NHS Primary Care Trus and *Times* Newspaper Ltd, Re
    [2011] EWHC 1197 (COP), [2011] 2 FLR 1143, [2011] Fam Law 811,
    [2011] NLJR 811   2.96
W Primary Care Trust v (1) TB (An Adult by her litigation friend the
    Official Solicitor); (2) V & S Metropolitan Borough Council (3) C &
    W Partnership NHS Foundation Trust (4) W Metropolitan Borough
    Council [2009] EWHC 1737 (Fam), [2010] 1 FLR 682 (COP)   2.45
Whitbread (Mental Patient: Habeas Corpus), Re (1998) 39 BMLR 94,
    (1997) *Times* 14 July   1.50
WM (Democratic Republic of Congo) v Sec of State for the Home
    Department [2006] EWCA Civ 1495   9.10
Woolwich Building Society v IRC [1993] AC 70, [1992] 3 WLR 366, [1992] 2
    All ER 737, (1992) 136 SJLB 230, [1992] STC 657, (1993) 5 Admin
    LR 265, (1992) NLJ 1196, (1992) *Times*, 22 July   1.21
Wychavon District Council v EM (HB) [2011] UKUT 144 (AAC)   2.34

X v Hounslow London Borough Council [2009] EWCA Civ 286, [2009] 2
    FLR 262   3.94

YA (F) v A Local Authority [2010] EWHC 2770 (COP), [2011] 1 FLR 2007   2.102
YL (by her litigation friend the Official Solicitor) v Birmingham City
    Council [2007] UKHL 27, [2007] 10 CCLR 505, [2007] 3 All ER 957,
    [2007] 3 WLR 112, 96 BMLR 1, [2007] NLJR 938, 151 Sol Jo LB
    860, [2007] All ER (D) 207 (Jun)   4.2, 4.24
Yule v South Lanarkshire Council (Court of Session (Inner House) Extra
    Division) [2001] 4 CCLR 383, 2001 SC 203, 2000 SLT 1249, 2001
    SCLR 26   6.33, 6.35

Z (An Adult: Capacity), Re [2005] 8 CCLR 146, [2004] All ER (D) 71 (Dec)   3.93
Z, Local Authority: Duty, Re [2004] EWHC 2817 (Fam), [2005] 3 All ER
    280, [2005] 1 WLR 959, [2005] LGR 709, [2005] 2 FCR 256, [2005] 1
    FLR 740, [2005] Fam Law 212, 84 BMLR 160, [2004] NLJR 1894,
    (2004) *Times*, 9 December, [2004] All ER (D) 71 (Dec)   2.48, 3.93, 3.94

TABLE OF STATUTES

References are to paragraph numbers.

Adoption and Children Act 2002	5.57
s 116	5.56
Asylum and Immigration Act 1996	8.46, 8.54
s 115	8.8
Births and Deaths Registration Act	
1953	1.37
Care Standards Act 2000	1.36, 3.54, 3.85,
	3.91, 4.45, 4.55, 4.56, 4.67, 7.22
Pt II	2.86, 2.90, 5.45, 7.29
Pt VII	4.54
s 3	4.57, 4.62
s 56	5.26
Carers (Recognition and Services) Act	
1995	3.3, 3.14, 3.73, 3.78, 5.65, 5.70,
s 1	3.82, 3.83, 5.66, 5.67
s 1(1)	5.67
s 1(2)	5.67
Carers and Disabled Children Act	
2000	3.3, 3.14, 3.78, 5.65, 5.67, 5.70,
	6.64, 7.35
s 1	3.82, 5.67, 7.18, 7.19, 7.22
s 2	5.67, 6.5, 6.20, 6.23, 6.55, 6.57, 7.18,
	7.19, 7.23
s 2(1)	6.61
s 4	5.67
s 6	3.82, 5.67, 5.69
s 6A	5.67
s 6A(3)(a)–(c)	5.66
Children Act 1989	2.97, 2.107, 2.110, 3.59,
	3.73, 3.78, 3.94, 5.32, 5.37, 5.41,
	5.71, 5.75, 6.53, 8.1, 8.37, 9.1, 9.29
Pt III	3.34, 3.36, 3.54, 3.58, 3.82, 5.43,
	5.44, 5.67, 5.70, 6.22
Pt IV	2.108, 3.36
s 1(1)	5.59
s 1(1)(a)	5.59
s 3	1.41
s 8	5.26
s 17	3.36, 3.54, 5.27, 5.30, 5.31, 5.44, 5.45,
	5.47–5.49, 5.53, 5.56, 5.57, 5.59,
	5.61, 5.62, 5.66, 5.67, 5.69, 6.22,
	6.55, 6.57, 6.63, 9.25, 9.26
s 17(1)	5.51, 5.59, 7.16, 9.34
s 17(2)	5.59
s 17(3)	5.66
s 17(4A)	6.64
s 17(6)	5.54, 5.56
s 17(7)–(9)	5.27

Children Act 1989—*continued*	
s 17(10(b)	5.72
s 17(10)	5.37, 5.45
s 17(11)	5.38, 5.45, 5.72, 6.65
s 17A	6.40, 6.55, 6.64, 6.65
s 17A(1)	6.55
s 17A(2)(c)	6.55
s 17A(6)	6.55
s 18	5.44, 6.22
s 20	2.61, 3.36, 5.30, 5.37, 5.42, 5.44, 5.45,
	5.59, 5.62, 9.34
s 20(1)	5.49, 5.51, 5.62, 5.63
s 20(2)	3.36
s 20(4)	5.49, 5.51
s 20(8)	2.61
s 21(3)	3.36
s 22	5.27, 5.45, 5.57, 5.59
s 22C(6)	5.26
s 23	5.19, 5.44, 5.45, 5.59
s 23(8)	5.59
s 23A	5.27
ss 23A–23D	5.62
ss 23A–24D	5.2
s 23A(2)	5.10, 5.26
s 23A(3)	5.26
s 23B	5.26, 5.27, 5.45
ss 23B–23D	5.19, 5.44
s 23B(1)	5.10
s 23B(2)	5.10, 5.26
s 23B(3)	5.26
s 23B(3)(a)	5.10
s 23B(3)(b)	5.10
s 23B(6)	5.27
s 23B(8)	5.10, 5.26
s 23B(8)(b)	5.11
s 23B(10)	5.26
s 23C	5.10, 5.18, 5.27, 5.37, 9.26
ss 23C–24D	5.72
s 23C(1)	5.10, 5.37
s 23C(2)	5.10
s 23C(3)	5.10, 5.37
s 23C(3)(a)	5.10
s 23C(3)(b)	5.10
s 23C(4)	5.10, 5.37
s 23C(4)(a)	5.10
s 23C(4)(b)	5.10
s 23C(5A)	5.10
s 23CA	5.26
s 23CA(1)	5.10
s 23CA(2)	5.10, 5.26
s 23CA(3)	5.26

Children Act 1989—*continued*
s 23CA(3)(a)   5.10
s 23CA(3)(b)   5.10
s 23D   5.27
s 23E   5.27
s 23E(1D)   5.10
s 24   5.4, 5.10, 5.15, 5.27, 5.37
s 24(1)   5.37
s 24(1A)   5.27
s 24(1B)   5.27, 5.37
s 24(2)   5.17
s 24(2)(a)   5.27
s 24A   5.10, 5.15, 5.19, 5.27, 5.37, 5.44,
                                                9.26
s 24A(2)   5.10
s 24A(3)   5.10
s 24B   5.10, 5.15, 5.19, 5.26, 5.27, 5.44,
                                          5.45, 9.26
s 24B(1)   5.10, 5.27
s 24B(2)   5.10, 5.18, 5.27
s 24B(3)   5.27
s 24B(5)   5.26, 5.27
s 24C   5.27
s 24D   5.18, 5.27
s 25   2.108, 2.111
s 25B(1)   5.26
s 26   5.27
s 26(3)   5.26
s 26A   5.26
s 29   6.22
s 29(7)   3.36
s 29(9)   3.36
s 30(2)   3.36
s 38   1.30
s 82(5)   5.45
s 105(6)   5.28
Sch 1, para 1   8.6, 8.7
Sch 1, Pt 1   5.44
Sch 2   5.44, 6.22
Sch 2, para 2   5.45
Sch 2, para 3(a)–(c)   5.27
Sch 2, para 6   5.45, 5.59
Sch 2, para 19(c)   5.34
Sch 2, para 19A   5.27
Sch 2, para 19B   5.10, 5.27
Sch 2, para 19B(2)   5.26
Sch 2, para 19B(2)(b)   5.26
Sch 2, para 19B(3)(b)   5.26
Sch 2, para 19B(4)   5.10, 5.26, 5.33
Sch 2, para 19B(5)   5.10
Sch 2, para 19C   5.26, 5.27
Children Act 2004   5.70
s 2(11)   5.71
s 2(12)   5.71
s 9   5.38, 5.71
s 10   5.72
s 17   5.72
s 49   5.45
Children (Leaving Care) Act 2000   2.108,
       2.111, 3.36, 5.2–5.5, 5.8, 5.9, 5.28,
                    5.30, 5.36, 5.64, 5.65, 9.33
Children (Scotland) Act 1995   5.71
Pt II   3.54
s 22   9.26

Children (Scotland) Act 1995—*continued*
s 29   9.26
s 30   9.26
Chronically Sick and Disabled Persons
      Act 1970   2.48, 3.46, 3.51, 3.55, 3.78,
                3.83, 3.84, 4.38, 5.43, 6.21, 7.15,
                                                7.16
s 1   3.45
s 1(2)   5.40
s 1(2)(b)   3.54
s 2   3.24, 3.34, 3.35, 3.45, 3.52, 3.54, 3.55,
                3.82, 4.40, 4.42, 5.44, 5.47, 5.51,
                5.59, 5.75, 6.21, 6.22, 6.69, 7.18
s 2(1)   3.5, 3.54, 4.8, 4.16, 5.38, 5.40
s 15   3.54
s 28A   2.111, 3.34, 3.36, 5.41, 5.43, 5.44,
                          5.51, 5.59, 5.64, 6.22
Civil Partnership Act 2004
Sch 5, Pt 2   8.6
Sch 7, para 9(2), (3)   8.6
Community Care (Delayed Discharges
      etc) Act 2003   4.45, 6.5, 7.25, 7.28,
                                                7.41
s 1   7.17, 7.22
s 2   7.17–7.21
s 2(1)   7.17
s 2(2)   7.17, 7.31
s 2(5)   7.22
s 2(6)   7.22
s 3   7.17
s 4   7.17, 7.18
s 4(2)   7.20
s 4(2)(b)   7.20, 7.21
s 4(3)   5.67
s 4(3)(b)   7.20, 7.21
s 4(7)   7.20
s 5   7.17, 7.19
s 5(3)   7.20
s 5(6)   7.22
s 6   7.17, 7.20
s 6(2)   7.17, 7.20
s 7   7.20
s 8   7.20
s 9   7.20
s 10   7.17, 7.21
s 12   7.22
s 14   7.22
s 15   6.4, 6.20, 7.23
s 15(1)   6.5
s 51(1)–(4)   6.5
Community Care (Direct Payments)
      Act 1996   6.40
County Courts Act 1984
s 38   1.55
Criminal Justice Act 1967
s 72   1.39
Criminal Justice Act 2003
Pt 12   1.37
ss 225–228   1.37
s 305(4)   1.37
Criminal Justice and Court Services
      Act 2000
Pt 1   4.75

Criminal Justice and Immigration Act
  2008
  Pt 1 — 5.28

Deregulation and Contracting Out Act
  1994 — 8.33
Disability Discrimination Act 1995 — 6.28
  s 4C(3) — 3.64
  s 4C(5) — 3.64
  s 4D — 3.64
  s 4E — 3.64
  s 4F(1) — 3.64
  s 15A(1) — 3.64
  s 21 — 3.48
  s 21B — 3.64
  s 21B(1) — 3.64
  s 21C(5) — 3.64
  s 21D — 3.64
  s 21D(2) — 3.64
  s 21D(5) — 3.48
  s 21E — 3.46, 3.64
  s 49A — 3.7, 3.49, 3.64, 5.51, 8.83, 8.84
  s 49A(1) — 8.83
  s 55 — 3.64
Disability Discrimination Act 2005
  s 2 — 3.46
Disabled Persons (Employment) Act
  1944 — 4.38
  s 15(1) — 7.52
Disabled Persons (Employment) Act
  1958
  s 3 — 7.52
Disabled Persons (Services,
  Consultation and
  Representation) Act 1986 — 3.3
  s 1 — 3.54
  s 1(3)(a)(i) — 3.54
  s 1(3)(a)(ii) — 3.54
  s 2 — 3.54, 5.39
  s 2(1) — 3.54
  s 3 — 3.54, 3.55, 3.57
  s 3(6) — 3.54
  s 3(7) — 3.54
  s 4 — 3.5, 3.54, 3.55, 3.57, 3.58, 5.40
  s 4(a) — 3.54
  s 4(c) — 3.54
  s 5 — 5.39, 5.40
  s 5(3) — 5.40
  s 5(4) — 5.40
  s 6 — 5.39, 5.40
  s 8 — 3.54, 3.55, 3.82
  s 8(1) — 3.54, 5.40
  s 9 — 3.54, 5.40
  s 10 — 3.54
  s 16 — 3.54, 3.58
  s 28A — 3.53

Education Act 1981
  s 7 — 5.39, 5.40
Education Act 1993
  s 168 — 5.39

Education Act 1996
  Pt IV — 5.39
  s 2(3) — 5.26
  s 2(5) — 5.26
  s 324 — 5.39
  s 337 — 4.75
  s 347 — 4.75
  s 347(5)(b) — 4.75
  s 434(5) — 5.26
  s 463 — 4.75
  s 579(1) — 7.52
  Sch 27, para 7 — 5.39
Employment and Training Act 1973 — 4.38
Equality Act 2010 — 3.49, 8.81
  Pt 3 — 3.64
  Pt 4 — 3.64
  Pt 5 — 3.64
  Pt 6 — 3.64
  Pt 7 — 3.64
  s 1 — 3.64
  s 4 — 3.64
  s 6 — 3.64
  s 13 — 3.64
  s 13(1) — 3.64
  s 14 — 3.64
  s 14(1) — 3.64
  s 15 — 3.64
  s 17 — 3.64
  s 18 — 3.64
  s 19 — 3.64
  s 20 — 3.64
  s 21 — 3.64
  s 24 — 3.64
  s 25 — 3.64
  s 149 — 3.7, 3.64, 8.83, 8.84
  Sch 2 — 3.64
  Sch 4 — 3.64
  Sch 8 — 3.64
  Sch 13 — 3.64
  Sch 15 — 3.64
  Sch 21 — 3.64

Firearms Act 1968
  s 51A(2) — 1.37
Further and Higher Education Act
  1992 — 5.39
  s 91 — 4.75

Health Act 1999 — 6.50, 7.42
  ss 29–31 — 7.46
  s 31 — 7.46
Health Act 2009
  s 11 — 6.71, 7.39
Health and Social Care Act 2001 — 6.37, 6.60,
  6.64, 7.42
  s 49 — 7.10, 7.12, 7.13, 7.16, 7.32
  s 54 — 4.3, 4.52, 6.37
  s 54(1) — 4.53
  s 55 — 6.37
  s 57 — 1.1, 4.73, 4.75, 6.55, 6.61
  s 57(1) — 6.55
  s 57(1A) — 6.55, 6.57
  s 57(1A)–(1C) — 6.61

Health and Social Care Act 2001—*continued*
s 57(2)(a)   6.55
s 57(3)   6.65
s 57(4)   6.55, 6.65
s 57(4)(a)   6.55, 6.65
s 57(4)(b)   6.55, 6.65
s 57(5)   6.55
s 57(5)(a)   6.65
s 57(5)(b)   6.65
s 57(5A)   6.55
s 57(5A)–(5C)   6.61
s 57(5B)   6.55
s 57(5C)   6.55
s 57(7)   6.65
s 57(7A)   6.61
Health and Social Care Act 2008   4.53, 4.61,
                                6.15, 6.42
  Pt 1   2.90
  s 8   4.62
Health and Social Care (Community
    Health and Standards) Act
    2003
  s 148   2.90
Health and Social Services and Social
    Security Adjudications Act
    1983   6.10, 7.51
  s 17   1.20, 6.20, 6.25
  s 17(1)   6.26
  s 17(2)(a)–(c)   6.5, 7.23
  s 17(2)(f)   6.5, 7.23
  s 17(3)   6.26
  s 21   6.29
  s 22   6.32, 6.33, 6.36, 6.37
  s 22(8)   6.37
  Sch 9, para 1   6.20
  Sch 9, Pt 2   7.52
Health Services and Public Health Act
    1968   3.3, 3.83
  s 45   3.56, 3.84, 7.18, 9.23, 9.26
  s 45(1)   6.20
  s 64   7.43
  s 65   7.43
Homelessness Act 2002
  s 1(2)   8.39
  s 1(6)   8.40
Housing Act 1985   3.56, 3.57, 8.16
  Pt 2   7.52
  s 5(4)   7.52
  s 5(5)   7.52
  s 65(2)   8.24
  s 68(2)   8.24
  s 84   8.8, 8.13
  s 89   8.6, 8.7
  s 90   8.6, 8.7
  s 92   8.6, 8.7
  Sch 2, Pt 1   8.8, 8.13
Housing Act 1996   4.40, 5.63, 8.1, 8.69, 9.30
  Pt VI   8.2, 8.5, 8.6, 8.24, 8.28, 8.31, 8.34,
                           8.37, 8.41, 8.58
  Pt VII   8.2, 8.36, 8.41, 8.59, 8.83
  s 72   8.35
  s 133   8.6
  s 133(2)   8.7

Housing Act 1996—*continued*
  s 159   8.5
  s 159(4)   8.24
  s 160   8.6
  s 160A   8.8
  s 160A(7)   8.13
  s 160A(8)   8.13
  s 160A(9)   8.24
  s 166(1)   8.14
  s 166(4)   8.16
  s 167   8.24
  s 167(4A)   8.16, 8.25
  s 167(8)   8.5
  s 167A(7)   8.26
  s 170   8.41
  s 184   8.46, 8.49
  s 184(1)   8.46
  s 184(3)   8.50
  s 188   5.32, 8.51, 8.77
  s 188(1)   8.51
  s 188(3)   9.26
  s 189(1)   8.61
  s 190   8.77
  s 190(2)   8.24, 8.66
  s 190(3)   8.59
  s 191   8.67
  s 191(1)   8.71
  s 192(3)   8.67
  s 193(2)   8.24, 8.46, 8.78
  s 193(3)   8.79
  s 193(7AD)   8.46
  s 193(7B)   8.79
  s 193(7C)   8.79
  s 195 (4A)   8.46
  s 195(2)   8.24, 8.46
  s 196   8.68
  s 198   8.46
  ss 198–200   8.51
  s 199   8.24
  s 200   8.77
  s 202   8.51
  s 202(1)   8.72
  s 204(1)   8.76
  s 204(4)   8.77, 9.26
  s 213(1)   8.41
  s 213A   8.41
Housing (Scotland) Act 1987
  s 29(1)(b)   9.26
Housing Associations Act 1985   3.54
Human Rights Act 1998   3.77, 3.99
  s 4   1.43
  s 6(1)   1.21
  s 6(3)(b)   4.24
  s 8   2.102

Immigration and Asylum Act 1999   3.84
  Pt VI   9.26
  Pt VIII   4.75
  s 4   9.12, 9.17, 9.18
  s 4(2)   9.14, 9.16
  s 4(3)   9.15, 9.16
  s 4(5)(a)   9.16
  s 4(5)(b)   9.16
  s 94(1)   9.7, 9.8, 9.10

Immigration and Asylum Act
 1999—*continued*
  s 94(3A) 9.26
  s 94(5) 9.13
  s 95 4.4, 9.3, 9.5, 9.13, 9.21, 9.23, 9.24
  s 95(1) 9.4
  s 95(2)–(7) 7.52
  s 95(3) 9.6
  s 98 9.3
  s 115 4.4, 7.52, 9.21–9.24
  s 115(9) 3.64, 9.22
  s 116 9.21
  s 117 9.21, 9.23, 9.24
  s 122(5) 9.25
  s 156 4.75
  Sch 4, para 17 9.22
  Sch 8 9.21, 9.23, 9.24
  Sch 8, para 2 4.4
Insolvency Act 1986
  s 423 6.32, 6.36
Interpretation Act 1978 3.65, 4.39

Land Charges Act 1972
  s 2 6.36
Land Registration Act 1925
  s 56 6.37
Law Reform (Personal Injuries) Act
 1948
  s 2(4) 6.13
Learning and Skills Act 2000
  s 114 5.72
Limitation Act 1980
  s 5 1.21
  s 9 6.25
  s 31(2)(c) 1.21
  s 32(1) 1.21
Local Authorities (Goods and
  Services) Act 1970
  s 1 4.74, 7.45
  s 1(5) 7.44
Local Authority Social Services Act
 1970 5.45, 6.18, 7.6, 7.22, 7.35, 7.48,
  7.52
  s 2(1) 3.43
  s 6 3.55
  s 7 3.2, 3.3, 3.9, 3.10, 3.22, 3.88, 4.27,
   4.40, 4.63, 5.2, 5.8, 5.31, 6.50, 6.68,
   7.47
  s 7(1) 3.2, 3.34, 6.6
  s 7A 3.2, 3.34, 4.44, 7.47
  s 7B(3) 6.33
Local Government (Wales) Measure
  2009
  s 39(4) 3.65
  s 41 3.65
  s 41(6) 3.65
Local Government Act 1970
  s 222 3.99
Local Government Act 1972
  s 111 6.37
  s 195(3) 4.2
  s 195(6) 4.2

Local Government Act 1972—*continued*
  s 222 3.93
  s 270(1) 3.54
  Sch 23, para 2(1) 4.2
Local Government Act 2000
  s 2 3.65, 9.26
  s 2(1) 3.65
  s 3 3.65
  s 4 3.64
  s 4A 3.65
Local Government Act 2003
  s 100 5.72
Local Government and Public
  Involvement in Health Act 2007
  s 103 3.64
  s 104 3.64
Local Government etc (Scotland) Act
  1994
  s 2 3.54
Local Government, Planning and
  Land Act 1980 7.52
Localism Act 2011 8.4, 8.32

Matrimonial and Family Proceedings
  Act 1984
  s 17(1) 8.6, 8.7
Matrimonial Causes Act 1973
  s 24 8.6, 8.7
Medical Act 1983
  s 2 7.35
Mental Capacity Act 2005 1.2, 1.27, 1.32,
  1.49, 1.53, 1.56, 2.2, 2.14, 2.20,
  2.28, 2.35, 2.36, 2.44, 2.46, 2.49,
  2.50, 2.58, 2.60, 2.63, 2.70, 2.72,
  3.95, 3.97–3.99, 4.62, 5.41, 6.38,
  6.61, 7.35
  s 1 2.73, 2.75
  s 1(2) 2.65
  s 1(3) 2.9, 2.65
  s 1(3)(a)–(c) 2.30
  s 1(4) 2.9, 2.65
  s 1(5) 2.65
  s 1(6) 2.65
  s 2 2.76, 2.77
  s 2(1) 2.9
  s 2(4) 2.9
  s 2(5) 2.107
  s 3 2.27, 2.77, 3.32
  s 3(1) 2.9, 2.68
  s 4 2.25, 2.78, 2.82
  s 4A 2.41
  s 4B 2.12, 2.41
  s 4B(1) 2.12
  s 4B(5) 2.12
  s 5 1.26, 2.79, 2.80
  s 6 2.79
  s 6(4) 2.43, 2.52
  s 7 2.33, 2.80
  s 9 4.75, 6.55
  s 15 2.81
  s 15(1)(c) 2.23
  s 16 2.41, 2.82–2.84, 4.75
  s 16(2)(a) 2.41

Mental Capacity Act 2005—*continued*

s 16(2)(b)	6.55
s 16A	2.41
s 17	2.83
s 17(1)(a)	2.22
s 18(3)	2.76
s 18(3))	5.77
s 19	2.84
s 20	2.83, 2.84
s 21A	2.85
ss 24–26	2.79
s 35	2.86, 4.75
s 36	2.86
s 37	2.86
s 39	1.24, 2.86
s 39A	1.24, 2.86
s 39C	1.24, 2.86
s 42	2.42
s 42(4)	2.42
s 43	2.42
s 44	2.37, 2.87, 3.88
s 45	2.73
s 46(2)(a)–(c)	2.101
s 47(1)	2.96
s 48	2.66, 2.89
s 49	2.67, 2.90
s 50(1)	2.93
s 64(5)	2.53
Sch A1	2.41–2.43, 2.45, 2.47, 2.85, 2.105
Sch A1, Pt 10	1.24, 2.86
Sch 1A	2.41, 2.43, 2.45
Sch 3, para 20	2.93
Sch 4	4.75

Mental Health (Care and Treatment)
    (Scotland) Act 2003

Pt 5	3.54
Pt 6	3.54
Pt 7	3.54
s 25	3.54, 6.29
s 193(7)	6.55

Mental Health Act 1959	1.30, 2.15
Mental Health Act 1983	1.6, 1.16, 2.3, 2.12,
	2.19, 2.39, 2.43–2.45, 2.70, 2.72,
	3.3, 3.83, 3.98
Pt II	3.54, 7.52
Pt III	7.52
s 1	5.72
s 1(2)	2.7
s 2	1.14, 1.16, 1.41, 1.49, 1.53–1.56, 2.11,
	2.108, 2.111
s 3	1.1–1.3, 1.14, 1.26, 1.29, 1.41, 1.47,
	1.49, 1.54–1.56, 2.108, 2.111
s 4	1.25, 1.41, 1.55
s 4(4)(a)	1.39
s 5	1.25, 1.47
s 5(2)	1.39, 1.47
s 5(4)	1.39
s 6(3)	1.48
s 7	1.1, 1.26, 1.27, 1.29, 1.30, 1.32, 1.34,
	1.40, 1.41, 1.56, 2.15, 3.32
s 8	1.26, 1.27, 1.34
s 8(1)(b))	1.30
s 9	1.34
s 10	1.34

Mental Health Act 1983—*continued*

s 10(1)(a)	1.35
s 10(1)(b)	1.35
s 10(3)	1.35
s 11	1.35
s 11(1)	1.26, 1.36, 1.41
s 11(3)	1.49
s 11(4)	1.36, 1.41, 1.49
s 12	1.36, 1.49
s 12(1)	1.36
s 12(2)	2.11
s 12A	1.35, 1.36
s 13	1.36, 1.49
s 13(4)	1.26, 1.36, 1.41
s 14	1.36
s 17	1.2, 1.5, 1.9
s 17A	1.58
s 17E	1.39, 1.57
s 17F	1.57
s 18	1.39
s 18(4)	1.34
s 18(7)	1.26
s 19	1.29, 1.56, 1.57
s 19(2)(c)	1.34
s 20	1.57
s 20A	1.57
s 21B	1.57
s 22	1.39
s 23	1.36, 1.37, 1.41, 1.57, 1.58
s 23(2)(a)	1.35–1.37
s 23(2)(b)	1.36, 1.37
s 23(3)	1.36, 1.41
s 23(4)	1.37
s 23(6)	1.37
s 24	1.36, 1.41
s 24(1)	1.14
s 24(5)	1.14
s 25	1.36, 1.37, 1.57, 1.58
s 25(1)	1.37
s 26	1.41, 1.44, 1.49, 2.94
s 26(1)	1.43
s 26(5)	1.44
s 26(6)	1.43, 1.44
s 26(7)	1.44
s 27	1.44
s 29	1.45, 1.49, 1.51–1.54, 1.56, 1.57
s 29(1)	1.46, 1.55, 1.56
s 29(3)	1.45, 1.56
s 29(3)(a)	1.53
s 29(3)(c)	1.52, 1.54, 1.55
s 29(3)(d)	1.52, 1.54
s 29(3)(e)	1.52
s 29(4)	1.53–1.56
s 29(5)	1.56, 1.57
s 29(6)	1.36
s 30	1.51, 1.53, 1.56
s 31	1.56
s 32	1.1, 1.37, 1.57
s 35	1.41, 1.56
s 36	1.41, 1.56
s 37	1.1, 1.2, 1.29, 1.37
s 37(2)(ii)	1.38
s 37(4)	1.39
s 38	1.39, 1.41, 1.56

Mental Health Act 1983—*continued*

s 38(4)	1.39
s 39A	1.38, 1.39
s 40	1.39
s 40(2)	1.38
s 42(2)	1.39, 6.55
s 44	2.71
s 45A	1.1, 1.2
s 45A(5)	1.39
s 47	1.1, 1.2
s 48	1.1, 1.2
s 56	1.39
ss 56–64	1.58
s 57	1.25, 1.39
s 58A	1.25, 1.39
s 59	1.39
s 60	1.39
s 61	1.39
s 62	1.39
s 66	1.29, 1.41, 1.51, 1.57, 1.58
s 66(1)(c)	1.29
s 66(1)(e)	1.29
s 66(1)(g)	1.58
s 66(1)(h)	1.36
s 66(1)(i)	1.36
s 66(2)(a)	1.56
s 66(2)(c)	1.29
s 66(2)(f)	1.29
s 66(2)(g)	1.36
s 67	1.29, 1.56
s 68(1)	1.29
s 68(6)	1.29
s 69	1.29, 1.51
s 69(1)(b)(ii)	1.36
s 69(b)(i)	1.29
s 69(b)(ii)	1.29
s 72	1.58
s 73	1.9, 1.39
s 73(4)	6.55
s 73(5)	6.55
s 74	1.39
s 75(3)	6.55
s 76(1)	1.41
s 94(2)	2.7
s 117	1.1–1.4, 1.7, 1.9, 1.11, 1.12, 1.14–1.16, 1.18–1.21, 1.24, 1.26, 1.36, 2.48, 2.86, 2.87, 2.108, 2.111, 3.52, 3.56, 4.11, 4.17, 6.55, 6.60, 6.61, 7.8, 7.18, 7.54, 9.20
s 117(2)	1.4
s 117(3)	1.9, 1.14
s 118	1.2, 1.58
s 118(2A)–(2D)	1.2
s 120	1.58
s 124	1.4
s 130A	1.25
s 131(1)	2.40
s 132	1.56, 1.58, 1.59
s 132(4)	1.41, 1.51
s 132A	1.58
s 133	1.51, 1.58, 1.59
s 133(2)	1.41
s 134	1.58
s 135	1.25, 1.39, 1.49

Mental Health Act 1983—*continued*

s 136	1.25, 1.39
s 137	1.26
s 139	1.47
s 145	1.43
s 145(1)	1.53
Sch 1, Pt I	1.39
Mental Health Act 2007	1.2, 1.24, 1.33, 1.44, 3.98
s 23	1.45, 1.52
s 24	1.45
s 25	1.58
s 26	1.44
s 50	2.41
s 50(2)	2.41
Sch 3, para 3(5)	1.27

National Assistance Act 1948	1.12, 1.49, 2.48, 3.3, 3.83, 4.45, 4.49, 5.28, 5.37, 5.64, 5.67, 6.2, 6.19, 7.15, 7.21, 7.56, 9.1
Pt III	3.54, 3.56, 3.57, 4.16, 4.18, 4.19, 4.44, 6.5, 7.23, 7.54
s 2(1)	3.38, 3.39
s 17	5.58
s 21	1.9, 1.14, 1.15, 1.24, 2.23, 2.86, 2.87, 2.105, 2.111, 3.73, 3.74, 4.3–4.5, 4.8, 4.11, 4.16–4.18, 4.21, 4.22, 4.24, 4.26, 4.27, 4.38, 4.40, 4.44, 4.45, 5.44, 5.58, 5.61, 5.75, 6.3, 6.13, 6.22, 7.6, 9.21, 9.26, 9.28
ss 21–26	4.38, 4.52, 6.29
s 21(1)	4.2, 4.7, 4.8, 4.11, 5.44, 5.61, 6.4
s 21(1)(a)	3.5, 4.2, 4.6, 4.11, 4.13, 4.14, 4.16, 9.28, 9.30, 9.31
s 21(1)(aa)	4.11, 4.75
s 21(1)(b)	9.30
s 21(1A)	4.13, 4.14, 4.16, 9.28, 9.29
s 21(2)	4.8
s 21(4)	4.2, 4.11
s 21(5)	4.26, 7.3
s 21(8)	4.26, 6.4, 7.3, 7.6
s 22	1.9, 4.2, 4.4, 4.8, 4.38, 6.4, 6.20, 6.29, 6.37
ss 22–26	4.7
s 22(2)	6.37
s 22(3)	6.35
s 22(4)	6.6
s 22(5)	4.8, 6.17
s 22(8A)	6.5
s 23	4.38
s 24	4.3, 4.17, 4.38
s 24(1)	3.66, 4.18
s 24(2)	4.18
s 24(3)	3.67
s 24(4)	4.11
s 24(5)	3.66, 3.69, 4.18–4.20, 7.53–7.55
s 24(6)	2.105, 3.66, 4.18, 4.19, 7.54
s 25	4.38
s 26	3.54, 3.69, 4.2–4.4, 4.18, 4.20, 4.23, 4.38, 4.54, 6.3, 6.4, 6.20
s 26(1)	4.11
s 26(1A)	4.45
s 26(2)	4.2, 6.37

National Assistance Act 1948—*continued*
s 26(3)   4.2, 4.52
s 26(3A)   4.45, 6.39
s 29   1.15, 1.24, 2.86, 2.87, 2.111, 3.5, 3.34,
       3.37, 3.44, 3.45, 3.51, 3.52, 3.58,
       3.66, 3.82, 4.3, 4.8, 4.16, 4.18, 4.21,
       4.38, 4.40, 4.42, 4.43, 5.43, 5.44,
       5.75, 6.20–6.22, 6.25, 7.18, 9.26
s 29(1)   3.46, 3.68, 4.18, 4.21, 4.39
s 29(4)   4.39
s 29(4)(g)   4.39
s 29(6)(b)   7.32
s 30(1)   4.39
s 32   4.38
s 32(1)   4.21
s 32(3)   2.105, 3.35, 3.36, 3.66, 3.68, 3.69,
                                            4.20, 7.58
s 32(3)–(5)   4.18
s 42   4.53, 6.15, 6.39
s 43   4.38, 6.15
s 45   6.18
s 47(11)   6.18
s 47(12)   6.18
s 56   6.18, 6.32
National Health Service Act 1977   7.3, 7.16,
                                               7.42
s 248   4.75
Sch 8   3.54, 4.11
Sch 8, para 1   4.75
Sch 8, para 2   4.11
National Health Service Act 2006   2.48, 3.3,
       3.57, 3.83, 3.84, 4.4, 4.38, 6.3, 6.71,
       7.1–7.3, 7.15, 7.17, 7.22, 7.26, 7.28,
       7.31, 7.32, 7.38, 7.39, 7.41
s 1   7.30, 7.42
s 2   7.35, 7.42
s 3   7.6, 7.7, 7.35, 7.42
s 3(1)(a)   3.54
s 12   7.43
s 12A(4)   1.1, 4.17
s 13   3.64
s 18   3.64, 7.47
s 25   7.47
s 74   7.44
s 75   7.46, 7.47, 7.49
s 75(2)(a)   7.47, 7.48
s 75(2)(b)   7.47, 7.48
s 75(2)(c)   7.48
s 75(8)   7.47, 7.48
s 76   7.46
s 77   7.47, 7.48
s 78   7.48, 7.49
s 78(1)   7.49
s 79   7.49
s 82   7.49
s 83(2)   7.42
s 99(2)   7.42
s 115(4)   7.42
s 191   7.50
s 254   3.56, 7.52, 9.26
s 256   7.46, 7.52
s 256(1)   7.52
s 256(3)   7.52
s 256(6)   7.52

National Health Service Act 2006—*continued*
s 257   7.46, 7.52
s 275(1)   5.26
Sch 3, para 15   7.44
Sch 20   3.56, 6.20, 9.24, 9.26
Sch 20, paras 1–4   7.52
National Health Service (Scotland)
   Act 1978
s 36(1)(a)   3.54
National Health Service (Wales) Act
   2006   3.54, 3.57, 4.4, 4.17, 4.38, 6.3,
                                          7.1, 7.22
s 3(1)(a)   3.54
s 187   4.75
s 192   3.56, 9.26
Sch 15   3.56, 6.20, 9.26
National Health Service and
   Community Care Act 1990   2.48, 3.37,
       3.46, 3.78, 4.27, 4.38, 4.47, 4.54,
       5.61, 5.67, 6.39, 7.15
Pt III   4.2
s 21   3.57, 7.5
s 22   3.57
s 23   3.57
s 24   3.57
s 26   3.57
s 29   3.57
s 32   3.57
s 46   3.5, 3.56, 3.57, 3.69, 4.2, 6.55, 6.57
s 46(2)   3.83
s 46(2)(d)   3.57
s 46(3)   3.5, 3.57, 3.82, 4.2, 4.73, 5.61,
                                            7.10, 7.22
s 47   1.6, 1.24, 2.86, 2.87, 2.111, 3.57–3.59,
       3.69, 3.74, 3.76, 3.79, 4.5, 4.9, 4.25,
       4.37, 4.42, 4.44, 5.61, 5.67, 6.66,
       7.18, 7.19, 7.31, 7.35, 7.36, 8.40,
                                             8.60
s 47(1)   3.5, 3.58, 3.68, 3.73, 4.6, 4.12,
                         4.43, 5.61, 7.18, 7.19
s 47(1)(a)   3.5, 3.82, 4.2, 4.10
s 47(1)(b)   3.5, 3.68, 3.70, 4.2
s 47(2)   3.5, 3.58
s 47(3)   3.58
s 47(3)(a)   7.31
Nationality, Immigration and Asylum
   Act 2002
Pt 2   9.26
Pt 5   9.26
s 18(2)   9.26
s 54   9.18, 9.26
s 113(1)   9.9
Sch 3   9.18, 9.26
Sch 3, para 1   5.37
Sch 3, para 1(1)(g)   5.37

Police Act 1997
s 113B   6.55
Powers of Criminal Courts
   (Sentencing) Act 2000
s 110(2)   1.37
s 111(2)   1.37
s 150   1.37

Prison Act 1952
  s 43 — 4.75
  s 53(1) — 4.75

Regional Development Agencies Act 1998 — 3.64
Registered Homes Act 1984
  Pt 1 — 4.11
Regulation of Care (Scotland) Act 2001 — 3.54
Residential Homes Act 1980
  s 8 — 6.20

Safeguarding Vulnerable Groups Act 2006 — 3.87, 4.3, 4.54, 4.70
  s 4 — 3.90
  s 5 — 3.90, 4.71
  s 6 — 3.90, 4.72
  s 16(5) — 4.75
  s 22 — 4.73
  s 39 — 4.74
  s 39(1)–(7) — 4.74
  s 40 — 4.74
  s 59 — 4.75
  Sch 3, para 1 — 4.74
  Sch 3, para 2 — 4.74
  Sch 3, para 4 — 4.74
  Sch 3, para 7 — 4.74
  Sch 3, para 8 — 4.74
  Sch 3, para 10 — 4.74
  Sch 4, para 7(1) — 4.71

Senior Courts Act 1981
  s 31A(3) — 9.36
Social Care Charges (Wales) Measure 2010
  s 12 — 6.61
Social Security Act 1980
  Sch 2 — 6.4
Social Security Administration Act 1992 — 4.75
Social Security Contributions and Benefits Act 1992
  Pt VII — 5.44
  Pt 7 — 6.65
Social Work (Scotland) Act 1968 — 6.29
  Pt IV — 3.54
  s 12 — 9.26
  s 13A — 9.26
  s 59(2)(c) — 3.54
Special Immigration Appeals Commission Act 1997 — 9.26
Supplementary Benefits Act 1976
  Sch 1 — 6.4

Teaching and Higher Education Act 1998
  s 22 — 5.26
  s 91(3) — 5.26

Violent Crime Reduction Act 2006
  s 29(4) — 1.37
  s 29(6) — 1.37

TABLE OF STATUTORY INSTRUMENTS

References are to paragraph numbers.

Allocation of Housing and
  Homelessness (Eligibility)
  (England) Regulations 2006,
  SI 2006/1294   8.54

Bodies and Local Authorities
  Partnership Arrangements
  Regulations 2000, SI 2000/617   7.47

Care Leavers (England) Regulations
  2010, SI 2010/2571   5.2
  Pt 2   5.20
  Pt 3   5.21
  regs 1–10   5.26
  reg 3   5.10
  reg 4   5.10
  reg 5   5.10
  reg 6   5.10
  reg 7   5.10
  reg 8   5.10
  reg 9   5.10, 5.22
  Schs 1, 2   5.26
Care Planning, Placement and Case
  Review (England) Regulations
  2010, SI 2010/959   5.2
  reg 40   5.10
  regs 40–46   5.26
  regs 41–43   5.20
  reg 42   5.10
  reg 43   5.10
  reg 44   5.10
  Sch 8   5.20, 5.26
Children Act 1989 (Higher Education
  Bursary) (England) Regulations
  2009, SI 2009/2274   5.10
Children (Leaving Care) (England)
  Regulations 2001, SI 2001/2874   5.33
  reg 3(1)   5.34
  reg 6(1)(a)   5.34
  reg 6(1)(b)   5.34
  reg 6(2)   5.34
  reg 7(2)(a)   5.34
Children (Northern Ireland) Order,
  SI 1995/755 (NI 2)   5.71
  Art 18   9.26
  Art 35   9.26
  Art 36   9.26

Civil Procedure Rules 1998,
  SI 1998/3132
  Pt 8   2.20
  Pt 12, r 12.4   1.53
  Pt 18, r 18.3(2)   1.54
  Pt 18, rr 18.1–18.7   1.53
  Pt 21   1.53, 1.56
  Pt 21, r 21.1   2.7
  Pt 29, r 29   1.56
  Pt 30, r 30.5(1)   2.23
  Pt 54   9.16
  Pt 54, r 54.20   2.23
Community Care (Delayed Discharges
  etc) Act (Qualifying Services)
  (England) Regulations 2003,
  SI 2003/1196   6.5
  reg 1   6.5
  reg 2   6.5
  reg 3   6.5
  reg 4   6.5
Community Care, Services for Carers
  and Children's Services (Direct
  Payments) (England)
  (Amendment) Regulations
  2010, SI 2010/2246   6.41
Community Care, Services for Carers
  and Children's Services (Direct
  Payments) (England)
  Regulations 2003, SI 2003/762
  reg 7(3)   6.63
Community Care, Services for Carers
  and Children's Services (Direct
  Payments) (England)
  Regulations 2009, SI 2009/1887   6.41
  regs 1–19   6.55
  reg 1(2)(a)(i)–(iii)   6.57
  reg 1(2)(b)   6.57
  regs 5–8   6.60
  reg 7(1)(c)   6.57
  reg 7(2)(a)   6.57
  reg 7(2)(b)   6.57
  reg 11   6.58
  reg 12   6.58
Community Care, Services for Carers
  and Children's Services (Direct
  Payments) (Wales) Regulations
  2011, SI 2011/831   6.41

Community Legal Service (Financial)
    Regulations 2000, SI 2000/516   6.55
County Court Rules 1981,
    SI 1981/1687
    Ord 49, r 12(3)(b)   1.54
Court of Protection Rules 2007,
    SI 2007/1744   2.91
    PD 9E   2.101
    Pt 9   2.95, 2.101
    Pt 10   2.95
    Pt 15   2.97
    Pt 16   2.98
    Pt 17   2.99
    r 32   2.99
    rr 40–49   2.92
    rr 42–45   2.92
    r 50   2.93
    r 54   2.93
    r 55   2.93
    r 55(c)   2.93
    r 56   2.93
    r 57   2.93
    r 61   2.94
    r 63   2.94
    r 64   2.94
    r 66   2.94
    r 69   2.94
    r 70   2.94
    r 71   2.101
    r 73   2.94
    r 74   2.94
    r 75   2.94
    r 76   2.94
    r 82   2.95
    r 85(2)   2.101
    r 90   2.95
    rr 90–93   2.69
    r 91   2.95
    r 91(1)–(3)   2.96
    r 91(2)(b), (3)   2.96
    r 92   2.95, 2.101
    r 93   2.95
    rr 119–131   2.97
    r 120   2.93, 2.94
    r 123   2.93, 2.94
    r 140   2.99
    r 140(1)   2.99
    r 141   2.99
    r 142   2.99
    r 143   2.99
    r 144   2.99
    r 145   2.99
    r 146   2.99
    r 147   2.99
    r 156   2.100
    r 157   2.100
    r 158   2.100
    r 159   2.100
Criminal Defence Service (Financial
    Eligibility) Regulations 2006,
    SI 2006/2492   6.55

Delayed Discharges (England)
    Regulations 2003, SI 2003/2277
    reg 3   7.24
    reg 14   7.25
    reg 17   7.25
    reg 18   7.25

Health and Personal Social Services
    (Northern Ireland) Order 1972,
    SI 1972/1265 (NI 14)
    Art 7   9.26
    Art 15   9.26
Health and Social Care Act 2008
    (Regulated Activities)
    Regulations 2010, SI 2010/781
    reg 2   4.61
    Sch 1   4.62
Homelessness (Priority Need for
    Accommodation) (England)
    Order 2002, SI 2002/2051   8.61

Immigration and Asylum (Provision of
    Accommodation to Failed
    Asylum-seekers) Regulations
    2005, SI 2005/930
    reg 2   9.13
    reg 3   9.16
    reg 4   9.16
    reg 6   9.16
Income Support (General) Regulations
    1987, SI 1987/1967   6.7

Local Authorities (Contracting Out of
    Allocation of Housing and
    Homelessness Functions) Order
    1996, SI 1996/3205   8.33
Local Health Board (Functions)
    (Wales) Regulations 2003,
    SI 2003/150   7.55

Mental Capacity Act 2005 (Transfer of
    Proceedings) Order 2007,
    SI 2007/1899
    r 1   2.109
    r 2   2.109
    r 3   2.109
    r 4   2.109
Mental Health (Hospital,
    Guardianship and Treatment)
    (England) Regulations 2008,
    SI 2008/1184   1.29, 1.41

National Assistance (Assessment of
    Resources) Regulations 1992,
    SI 1992/2977   6.7, 6.17, 6.35, 6.39, 6.47
    reg 9   6.50
    reg 10   6.50
    reg 25   6.33, 6.36

National Assistance (Residential
Accommodation) (Additional
Payments and Assessment of
Resources) (Amendment)
(England) Regulations 2001
SI 2001/3441   4.45
National Health Service Bodies and
Local Authorities Partnership
Arrangements (Wales)
Regulations 2000, SI 2000/2993   7.46
National Health Service (Functions of
Strategic Health Authorities
and Primary Care Trusts and
Administration Arrangements)
(England) (Amendment)
Regulations 2006, SI 2006/359   7.57

National Health Service (Functions of
Strategic Health Authorities
and Primary Care Trusts and
Administration Arrangements)
(England) Regulations 2002,
SI 2002/2375   1.16, 7.55
National Health Service (Payments by
Local Authorities to NHS
Bodies) (Prescribed Functions)
(Wales) Regulations 2001,
SI 2001/1543   7.52

Withholding and Withdrawal of
Support (Travel Assistance and
Temporary Accommodation)
Regulations 2002, SI 2002/3078   9.32

Chapter 1

MENTAL HEALTH ACTS

GENERAL

1.1   The purpose of this chapter is to consider certain specific and specialised aspects of mental health law which have a direct impact on the responsibilities of local authorities. In effect, this falls into three main areas. One is the obligations imposed by s 117 of the Mental Health Act 1983 (MHA 1983). These encompass the actual provision and extent of after-care to those who have been detained under the Act, and also the funding of such provision and, where appropriate, restitution for charges that have been made for those services. Another is the use by a local authority of applications for Guardianship Orders under s 7 of MHA 1983, and the limits of what such an order can and cannot do, together with the significance of the nearest relative in such situations. Finally, it considers the role and function of the nearest relative generally. This includes the extent to which a local authority should consult with a nearest relative, the choice that a patient may have in selecting his nearest relative, or if there may be an embargo on providing information to a nearest relative, or when it is imperative that information is provided to a nearest relative. It also considers the basis and process of an application to discharge a nearest relative.

Mental Health Act 1983

117 After Care

(1) This section applies to persons who are detained under section 3 above, or admitted to hospital in pursuance of a hospital order made under section 37 above, or transferred to a hospital in pursuance of a hospital direction made under section 45A above or a transfer direction made under section 47 or 48 above, and then cease to be detained and (whether or not immediately after so ceasing) leave hospital.

(2) It shall be the duty of the Primary Care Trust or Local Health Board and of the local social services authority to provide, in co-operation with relevant voluntary agencies, after-care services for any person to whom this section applies until such time as the Primary Care Trust or Local Health Board and the local social services authority are satisfied that the person concerned is no longer in need of such services; but they shall not be so satisfied in the case of a community patient while he remains such a patient.

(2B) Section 32 above shall apply for the purposes of this section as it applies for the purposes of Part II of this Act.

(2C) References in this Act to after-care services provided for a patient under this section include references to services provided to the patient –

> (a)   in respect of which direct payments are made under regulations under section 57 of the Health and Social Care Act 2001 or section 12A(4) of the National Health Service Act 2006, and
>
> (b)   which would be provided under this section apart from the regulations.

(3) In this section "the Primary Care Trust or Local Health Board" means the Primary Care Trust or Local Health Board, and "he local social services authority" means the local social services authority, for the area in which the person concerned is resident or to which he is sent on discharge by the hospital in which he was detained.

Persons who are detained

1.2   This section applies only to those who have been detained under the relevant sections of MHA 1983, and the provision of *after-care services* to them. The guidance issued by the Secretary of State is in the form of the Code of Practice (the Code). The references throughout this text are to the current Code of Practice. The Code is published pursuant to s 118 of the MHA 1983. Sections 18(2A)-(2D) have been inserted by the Mental Health Act 2007, which incorporate a slight alteration of its purpose in that there are additional matters to which the Code must address itself (s 118(2B)) all of which should 'inform decisions under the Act'. As the Code explains of itself:

> 'Whilst the Act does not impose a legal duty to comply with the Code ... The reasons for any departure should be recorded. Departures from the Code could give rise to legal challenge, and a court, in reviewing any departure from the Code, will scrutinise the reasons for the departure to ensure that there is sufficiently convincing justification in the circumstances.'
> (Introduction to Code of Practice (iv))

This observation in the introduction largely conforms to the decision in *R (Munjaz) v Merseycare NHS Trust* [2005] UKHL 58, [2005] MHLR 276 which is that the Code is for guidance, not instruction. However, it is guidance to which great weight should be given. The dissenting judgments of Lord Steyn and Lord Brown are of particular interest in this context. Lord Steyn held that:

> 'The Code of Practice is a special type of soft law which derives its status from the legislative context and the vulnerability of the patients that it serves to protect; it is designed to ensure that some minimum safeguards and a modicum of centralised protection are in place. Accordingly, it should be observed by all hospitals unless they have a very good reason for departing from it in relation to an individual patient; departure from the Code as a matter of policy is not permitted, since a dilution of the minimum centrally imposed safeguards, by pragmatic policy decisions from hospital to hospital is not appropriate.'

Lord Brown went further '... the Code must be given a status akin to law, which disentitles individual hospitals to depart from it on policy grounds'. However, despite the small amendments now in force as a result of the MHA 2007, it remains guidance only. The Code refers to *Refocusing the Care Programme Approach* (Department of Health, March 2008). This has the status of 'Best Practice Guidance'. The most significant part of this (from a practical perspective) is the creation of a care co-ordinator, who is 'pivotal to the success of the (new) CPA' (Section 6). It will be this individual who has the responsibility for devising what after-care services are required, and formalising those services in the format of a plan. The material contained in the *Care Programme Approach* is not a part of the Code.

This Code came into force on 3 November 2008, and replaces the previous Code. There is a separate Code for Wales and England. The differences between the two are very slight indeed. There is more detail on after care planning in the English Code. There is no mention of the distinction between guardianship, leave and SCT in the Welsh Code (Chapter 28).

Chapter 27 After-care

27.1 This chapter gives guidance on the duty to provide after-care for patients under section 117 of the Act.

Section 117 after-care

27.2 Section 117 of the Act requires primary care trusts (PCTs) and local social services authorities (LSSAs), in co-operation with voluntary agencies, to provide aftercare to patients detained in hospital for treatment under section 3, 37, 45A, 47 or 48 of the Act who then cease to be detained. This includes patients granted leave of absence under section 17 and patients going onto supervised community treatment (SCT).

27.3 The duty to provide after-care services continues as long as the patient is in need of such services. In the case of a patient on SCT, after-care must be provided for the entire period they are on SCT, but this does not mean that the patient's need for after-care will necessarily cease as soon as they are no longer on SCT.

27.4 Services provided under section 117 can include services provided directly by PCTs or LSSAs as well as services they commission from other providers.

27.5 After-care is a vital component in patients' overall treatment and care. As well as meeting their immediate needs for health and social care, after-care should aim to support them in regaining or enhancing their skills, or learning new skills, in order to cope with life outside hospital.

27.6 Where eligible patients have remained in hospital informally after ceasing to be detained under the Act, they are still entitled to after-care under section 117 once they leave hospital. This also applies when patients are released from prison, having spent part of their sentence detained in hospital under a relevant section of the Act.

After-care planning

27.7 When considering relevant patients' cases, the Tribunal and hospital managers will expect to be provided with information from the professionals concerned on what after-care arrangements might be made for them under section 117 if they were to be discharged. Some discussion of after-care needs, involving LSSAs and other relevant agencies, should take place in advance of the hearing.

27.8 Although the duty to provide after-care begins when the patient leaves hospital, the planning of after-care needs to start as soon as the patient is admitted to hospital. PCTs and LSSAs should take reasonable steps to identify appropriate after-care services for patients before their actual discharge from hospital.

27.9 Where a Tribunal or hospital managers' hearing has been arranged for a patient who might be entitled to after-care under section 117 of the Act, the hospital managers should ensure that the relevant PCT and LSSA have been informed. The PCT and LSSA should consider putting practical preparations in hand for after-care in every case, but should in particular consider doing so where there is a strong possibility that the patient will be discharged if appropriate after-care can be arranged. Where the Tribunal has provisionally decided to give a restricted patient a conditional discharge, the PCT and LSSA must do their best to put after-care in place which would allow that discharge to take place.

27.10 Before deciding to discharge, or grant more than very short-term leave of absence to, a patient, or to place a patient onto SCT, the responsible clinician should ensure that the patient's needs for after-care have been fully assessed, discussed with the patient and addressed in their care plan. If the patient is being given leave for only a short period, a less comprehensive review may be sufficient, but the arrangements for the patient's care should still be properly recorded.

27.11 After-care for all patients admitted to hospital for treatment for mental disorder should be planned within the framework of the Care Programme Approach (or its equivalent), whether or not they are detained or will be entitled to receive after-care under section 117 of the Act. But because of the specific statutory obligation it is important that all patients who are entitled to after-care under section 117 are identified and that records are kept of what after-care is provided to them under that section.

27.12 In order to ensure that the after-care plan reflects the needs of each patient, it is important to consider who needs to be involved, in addition to patients themselves. This may include:

- the patient's responsible clinician;
- nurses and other professionals involved in caring for the patient in hospital;
- a clinical psychologist, community mental health nurse and other members of the community team;
- the patient's GP and primary care team;
- subject to the patient's views, any carer who will be involved in looking after them outside hospital, the patient's nearest relative or other family members;
- a representative of any relevant voluntary organisations;

- in the case of a restricted patient, the probation service;
- a representative of housing authorities, if accommodation is an issue;
- an employment expert, if employment is an issue;
- an independent mental health advocate, if the patient has one;
- an independent mental capacity advocate, if the patient has one;
- the patient's attorney or deputy, if the patient has one; and
- any other representative nominated by the patient.

27.13 A thorough assessment is likely to involve consideration of:

- continuing mental healthcare, whether in the community or on an out-patient basis;
- the psychological needs of the patient and, where appropriate, of their family and carers;
- physical healthcare;
- daytime activities or employment;
- appropriate accommodation;
- identified risks and safety issues;
- any specific needs arising from, for example, co-existing physical disability, sensory impairment, learning disability or autistic spectrum disorder;
- any specific needs arising from drug, alcohol or substance misuse (if relevant);
- any parenting or caring needs;
- social, cultural or spiritual needs;
- counselling and personal support;
- assistance in welfare rights and managing finances;
- the involvement of authorities and agencies in a different area, if the patient is not going to live locally;
- the involvement of other agencies, for example the probation service or voluntary organisations;
- for a restricted patient, the conditions which the Secretary of State for Justice or the Tribunal has imposed or is likely to impose on their conditional discharge; and
- contingency plans (should the patient's mental health deteriorate) and crisis contact details.

27.14 The professionals concerned should, in discussion with the patient, establish an agreed outline of the patient's needs and agree a timescale for the implementation of the various aspects of the after-care plan. All key people with specific responsibilities with regard to the patient should be properly identified.

27.15 It is important that those who are involved are able to take decisions regarding their own involvement and, as far as possible, that of their agency. If approval for plans needs to be obtained from more senior levels, it is important that this causes no delay to the implementation of the after-care plan.

27.16 If accommodation is to be offered as part of the after-care plan to patients who are offenders, the circumstances of any victims of the patient's offence(s) and their families should be taken into account when deciding where the accommodation should be offered. Where the patient is to live may be one of the conditions imposed by the Secretary of State for Justice or the Tribunal when conditionally discharging a restricted patient.

27.17 The after-care plan should be recorded in writing. Once the plan is agreed, it is essential that any changes are discussed with the patient as well as others involved with the patient before being implemented.

27.18 The after-care plan should be regularly reviewed. It will be the responsibility of the care co-ordinator (or other officer responsible for its review) to arrange reviews of the plan until it is agreed that it is no longer necessary.

Ending section 117 after-care services

27.19 The duty to provide after-care services exists until both the PCT and the LSSA are satisfied that the patient no longer requires them. The circumstances in which it is appropriate to end section 117 after-care will vary from person to person and according to the nature of the services being provided. The most clear-cut circumstance in which after-care will end is where the person's mental health has improved to a point where they no longer need services because of their mental disorder. But if these services include, for example, care in a specialist residential setting, the arrangements for their move to more appropriate under section 117 is finally withdrawn. Fully involving the patient in the decision-making process will play an important part in the successful ending of after-care.

27.20 After-care services under section 117 should not be withdrawn solely on the grounds that:

- the patient has been discharged from the care of specialist mental health services;
- an arbitrary period has passed since the care was first provided;
- the patient is deprived of their liberty under the Mental Capacity Act 2005;
- the patient may return to hospital informally or under section 2; or
- the patient is no longer on SCT or section 17 leave.

27.21 Even when the provision of after-care has been successful in that the patient is now well settled in the community, the patient may still continue to need after-care services, for example to prevent a relapse or further deterioration in their condition.

27.22 Patients are under no obligation to accept the after-care services they are offered, but any decisions they may make to decline them should be fully informed. An unwillingness to accept services does not mean that patients have no need to receive services, nor should it preclude them from receiving them under section 117 should they change their minds.

After-care and care plans

1.3 There is no definition of what constitutes after-care services, but the key elements of any plan should include an assessment of the health and social care needs of the patient, and a plan which reflects those needs, the appointment of a key worker to keep in touch with the patient, and regular reviews and/or changes to the plan. It is clear that there is an obligation to provide appropriate accommodation (including ordinary housing, if appropriate, cf *R (on the application of Lambeth LBC)*, see **1.4** below). What the nature of that accommodation might be will plainly depend upon each case, and all aspects of the care plan need to be clearly set out. However, in *R(on the application of Michael Mwanza) v Greenwich LBC and Bromley LBC* [2010] EWHC 1462 (Admin), [2010] 13 CCLR 454 the matters which might come within s 117 were revisited. On the facts of the case, Mr Mwanza (whose immigration status was dependent upon his wife's student visa) had been admitted pursuant to s 3 of the MHA 1983, and duly discharged with various support services. His claim for judicial review was based upon refusals by the Local Authorties to provide him with financial and housing support. In so doing, he relied upon (in part) s 117. It was held that by Hickinbottom J that:

> '[68] I consider my construction of section 117 – restricting its scope to services necessary to meet a need arising from a mental disorder – is generally supported by those authorities.'

He then referred to *Clunis* and *Richmond Borough Council v Watson* [2000] EWCA Civ 239 as authorities for that judgment. In short, and on the facts in this case, the need for accommodation arose not as a result of the mental disorder of Mr Mwanza, but because he was unable to work. The requirement for accommodation was common to all individuals, and did not in this instance have any causal connection with the mental disorder from which Mr Mwanza suffered.

1.4   Whilst the duty to provide such services generally does not apply until a patient has actually been discharged (*R (on the Application of B) v Camden LBC and Camden and Islington Mental Health and Social Care Trust* [2005] EWHC 1366 (Admin), [2005] 8 CCLR 422), it is important to note a plan should be considered prior to discharge. This is more than a mere technicality when the necessity for detention is being considered not by the detaining authority, but (for example) by the First Tier Tribunal (Health, Education and Social Care (the Tribunal) or a Hospital Managers Meeting. It is the responsibility of the Responsible Clinician (RC) to ensure that the needs of the patient for health and social care are fully assessed, and that the care plan addresses those needs. This plan should be devised in consultation with all the professionals concerned with the patient. This includes the patient himself, named nurse, social worker, GP, CPN and possibly probation services, informal carers, nearest relative (if the patient has given permission for consultation), and the relevant housing authorities should accommodation be an issue. In order for Health Authorities and Local Authority Social Services to fulfil their obligations, they must take 'reasonable steps to identify appropriate after care facilities for a patient before his or her actual discharge from hospital' (para 27.7 of the Code and *R v Ealing District Health Authority ex parte Fox* [1993] 3 All ER 170). The extent of such preparation does not need to be any greater than discussion, and a failure to do no more than this within the context of a contested hearing before a Tribunal does not mean that there is a breach of any duty arising from s 117 (*R (on the Application of W) v Doncaster MBC* [2003] EWHC 192 (Admin), [2003] 6 CCLR 301). Within the context of the Tribunal, it is appropriate for there to be an adjournment if the care plan is undeveloped or lacking in specificity, so that the burden is passed to the health authority and local authority to prepare and implement the plan within a reasonable period of time (*R v Mental Health Review Tribunal, Torfaen County BC and Gwent Health Authority ex p Hall* [1999] 2 CCLR 383). It is not a breach of the duty imposed by s 117 where a health authority is unable to provide psychiatric supervision of a patient simply because no doctor could be found to provide such supervision (*R (on the application of K) v Camden and Islington Health Authority* [2001] EWCA Civ 240, [2001] 4 CCLR 170). However, a local authority was found to be in breach of its duty when it failed to provide alternative accommodation to a patient who was subject to possession proceedings based upon her behaviour, which was in turn caused by her mental illness (*R (on the application of Lambeth LBC)* [2006] EWHC 2362 (Admin), [2007] 10 CCLR 84). It had been though that should a health authority fail to comply with its obligations pursuant to s 117(2), it would not found an action for breach of statutory care, nor an action for breach of a common law duty of care. The appropriate remedy would be via the default powers of the Secretary of State (s 124 of MHA 1983), or by way of judicial review (*Clunis (Christopher) (by his next friend Christopher Prince) v Camden and Islington Health Authority)* [1998] 1 CCLR 215). However, this is no longer the law. In *AK v Central and North West London Mental Health NHS Trust and Royal Borough of Kensington and Chelsea* [2008] EWHC 1217 (QB), [2008] 11 CCLR 543 Mr Justice King reviewed all the authorities that lead to the judgment in *Clunis*. He held that liability derived from s 117 (and not the CPA, which did not create powers or responsibilities), and that since *Clunis* had been decided, the law in this area of negligence had developed considerably. The allegation of negligence arose from the failure to appoint a competent social worker, and that the former patient was in appropriate accommodation (on the facts, he was in a flat where he was able to jump from a window, which he did and sustained injuries as a result). A full commentary on the law is contained in *Section 117 1983 re-visited: the liability of the State and the existence of a duty of care* (Butler, J *Journal of Mental Health Law* 2011; 21, pp 84–92).

Persons who cease to be detained

1.5   This includes not only patients who have been fully discharged from detention (through whichever route) but also those who: (a) stay in hospital as a voluntary patient after discharge; or (b) when a patient is released from prison if a part of their sentence has been spent in hospital under detention; or (c) if a patient is given leave pursuant to s 17 of MHA 1983.

1.6   Where a patient is the subject of a provisional decision of the MHRT to conditionally discharge him, then he is still detained under MHA 1983, and the actual duty to provide him with after-care services does not arise (*R (B) v (1) Camden LBC (2) Camden & Islington Health and Social Care Trust* [2005] EWHC 1366 (Admin)). The same case held that a local authority was not under a parallel obligation (in such circumstances) under s 47 of the National Health Service and Community Care Act 1990.

Health care needs v social care needs

1.7   Once a patient ceases to be detained, then the duty of service provision arises. Chapter 27 of the Code provides a list of those areas that an *assessment* should cover (para 27.13), but there is no list of what might actually be contained in an after-care plan by way of services. Clearly, this will depend on each individual case. There may be an argument as between the providers of health services, and social services, as to who should provide which, and what constitutes a health need, and what constitutes a social care need. The full extent of this area of law is explored in Chapter 7. In *Special Report NHS Funding for Long-Term Care – investigation into Complaints Nos E208/99–00* an attempt was made to identify criteria which might differentiate the two areas of responsibility. Within the report the guidance of the Department of Health (in 1995) was cited as suggesting that the NHS should be responsible:

> 'Where the complexity or intensity of their medical, nursing or other care or the need for frequent not easily predictable interventions requires the regular ... supervision of a consultant, specialist nurse or other NHS member of the multidisciplinary team ... who routinely use specialist health care equipment or treatments which require the supervision of specialist NHS staff ... who have a rapidly degenerating or unstable condition which means that they will require specialist medical or nursing supervision [and] the in patient care might be provided in a hospital or nursing home.'

This dispute is likely to be particularly acute where the condition from which the patient suffers is chronic and deteriorating, such as with forms of dementia. As Sullivan J observed in the first tier of decisions that culminated in *R v Manchester CC ex p Stennett and two other actions* [2002] UKHL 34, [2002] 5 CCLR 500 (*R v Richmond LBC ex p Watson; R v Redcar and Cleveland BC ex p Armstrong; R v Manchester CC ex p Stennett; R v Harrow LBC ex p Cobham* [1999] 2 CCLR 402):

> '[416J–416K] There may be cases where in due course there will be no need for after care services for the persons mental condition, but he or she will still need social services provision for other needs e g physical disability. Such cases will have to be examined individually on their facts ... in such a case as Mrs W, where the illness is dementia, it is difficult to see how such a situation could arise in practice.'

The Law Commission (Law Com No 326) *Adult Social Care* (May 2011) has also made observations on this area of law, together with recommendations. These are are follows:

> '11.93 Section 117 is a joint duty placed on health and social service authorities but it is not clear from the statute whether the duty falls jointly and severally on health and social services authorities, in that both are responsible for the entire duty, or whether the duty falls primarily on health authorities to provide **healthcare after-care** and social services to provide **social care after-care**. In the consultation paper we argued that it is unlikely that a court would regard a health body as being accountable for the provision of **social care after-care**, or a social services authority as being accountable for **healthcare after-care.** However, the

position is not clear in law and this could cause difficulties. We therefore proposed that section 117 should be amended to state expressly that the duty falls on health authorities to provide **healthcare after-care** and on social services authorities to provide **social care after-care** ...

11.94 Since consultation, the Health and Social Care Bill 2011 has been introduced to Parliament and, amongst other matters, proposes to amend section 117 to make clear that in England the commissioning consortia are responsible only for the health (rather than social) services provided under section 117. It also proposes to split the termination of the section 117 duty. The section 117 duty on the consortia in question continues until it (rather than it and the local social services authority together) is satisfied that the after-care is no longer required. Likewise, the duty on the local social services authority continues until it (rather than it and the consortia) is satisfied that after-care is no longer required. These amendments would apply in England, but not in Wales.'

Extent of duties of local authority

1.8   The extent of the duties of a local authority were also considered at length in *Investigation into Complaint Nos 97/0177 and 97/0755 against the former Clwyd CC and Conwy County BC* [1998] 1 CCLR 546. The complaint arose out of circumstances where the services to be provided ceased. There was no consultation, and the complainant was required to pay for her own residential accommodation. The complaint was upheld, and the Local Government Ombudsman concluded that the local authority had a duty to provide after-care until it was satisfied (as a social services authority and irrespective of the views of the district health authority) that the complainant was no longer in need of such services. It was also concluded that the local authority had taken into account irrelevant matters in deciding not to provide after-care services, and had failed to consult at all with the complainant herself. It was also concluded that she had been wrongly charged for the services and that there had been further maladministration by virtue of a decision to register a caution upon her property. It stressed the need to conform to the Code.

Relevant local authority

1.9   The relevant after-care bodies responsible for arranging the after-care, and providing it, are those in which the patient was resident at the time that he was detained (*R v MHRT ex parte Hall* [1999] 3 All ER 131). Those bodies will continue to be responsible until the patient is no longer in need of such services. A decision that such after-care services are not required should be formally recorded together with the reasons for discontinuance and include the same generic professionals as those who were involved in formulating the original plan. The decision in *Hall* was subject to Department of Health Guidance (Circular No LAC (2000) 3: HSC 2000/3, 10 February 2000) which alerted local authorities to their obligations including that if the patient had no ordinary residence when admitted, the authorities where the patient must reside as a part of his conditional discharge have responsibility for providing after-care.

Circular No LAC (2000) 3 – After-Care Under the Mental Health Act 1983

Section 117 After-Care Services

Summary

This circular covers three recent judgments affecting the provision of after-care under the Mental Health Act 1983 (MHA). Section 117 of the MHA places a duty on health and social services authorities to provide after-care services for certain patients discharged from detention under the Act.

It does not specify services to be provided or confer powers to charge.

(1) The High Court judgment of 28 July 1999 made clear that local authorities may not charge for residential care provided under section 117. This is a free-standing duty and should not be seen as a gateway for services provided under other legislation.

(2) The Court of Appeal on 30 July 1999 clarified which health and social services authorities are responsible for providing section 117 after-care services.

(3) The European Court of Human Rights (ECHR) issued a judgment in 1997 that the UK was in breach of the European Convention on Human Rights in a case where the Mental Health Review Tribunal (MHRT) had given a restricted patient a deferred conditional discharge which was not implemented within a reasonable time.

Action

The Court gave the four authorities involved in the first case leave to appeal. But social services authorities still charging for after-care services provided under section 117 should immediately cease charging since there is no power to do so. In relation to the ECHR judgment, social services and health authorities should ensure that the conditions of deferred conditional discharges are implemented timeously.

Judgment 1

R v London Borough of Richmond ex parte Watson

R v Redcar and Cleveland Borough Council ex parte Armstrong

R v Manchester City Council ex parte Stennett

R v London Borough of Harrow ex parte Cobham

1. The Court considered four cases relating to the provision of after-care services under section 117 and whether it is lawful to make a charge for these services. The judgment confirmed that:

- where the responsible social services authority assesses the patient as needing to be provided as part of their after-care following detention with residential accommodation of the kind covered by section 117, there is a duty to provide this accommodation under section 117. The authority may not provide it under section 21 of the National Assistance Act 1948 nor charge for it under section 22;

- patients may not be charged for residential accommodation provided as part of a package of after-care services under section 117; *Health Service Circular / Local Authority Circular HSC 2000l003: LAC (2000) 10 February 2000 Page 4*

- patients who are required to live in residential accommodation as a condition of leave under section 17 are entitled to this accommodation as an after-care service under section 117 if they would be entitled to receive after-care services under section 117 when discharged from detention under the Act.

Implications of the Judgment

2. The Court did not address the question of charging for non-residential services provided under section 117 but there is a strong implication that the responsible authorities may not charge for such services. Occasionally, there may be other non-residential community care services provided by the authority which are not part of the section 117 after-care plan. These may relate to physical disabilities or illnesses which have no direct bearing on the person's mental health.

Such services will generally fall outside section 117 after-care.

Points for Action

3. Social services and health authorities should establish jointly agreed local policies on providing section 117 after-care. Policies should set out clearly the criteria for deciding which services fall under section 117 and which authorities should finance them. The section 117 after-care plan should indicate which services are provided as part of the plan.

4. After-care provision under section 117 does not have to continue indefinitely. It is for the responsible health and social services authorities to decide in each case when after-care provided under section 117 should end, taking account of the patient's needs at the time. It is for the authority responsible for providing particular services to take the lead in deciding when those services are no longer required. The patient, his/her carers, and other agencies should always be consulted.

Judgment 2

R v Mental Health Review Tribunal ex parte Hall [1999] 3 All ER 131

5. This judgment concerns a restricted patient who was granted a deferred conditional discharge by the MHRT. One of the conditions set by the Tribunal was that the patient should not return to where he lived before admission to hospital. The judgment confirmed that:

- the health and social services authorities where the patient was resident at the time of admission to hospital have legal responsibility for providing after-care under section 117.

6. If the patient has no current residence when admitted to hospital, the authorities for the area where the patient must reside as part of his/her conditional discharge have responsibility for providing after-care under section 117(3).

Implications of Judgment

7. A patient who was resident in an area before admission to hospital does not cease to be resident there because of his/her detention under the Act. If a patient with ordinary residence in one area is sent to another area on discharge, it is the responsibility of the health and social services authorities in the area where the patient was resident before admission to make the necessary arrangements under section 117. However, where a patient does not have a current residence, the responsibility for providing after-care under section 117 falls to the health and social services authorities covering the area to which the person is sent on discharge. When a patient is conditionally discharged, the Tribunal may send the patient to an area by imposing a residence condition.

Points for Action

8. Guidance in the revised *Mental Health Code of Practice* makes clear that where section 117 applies and there is to be a hearing of the MHRT, the 'responsible authorities' should prepare an after-care plan under section 117 and submit this to the Tribunal to assist it in reaching its decisions. The hospital where the patient is detained will always be expected to assist.

9. Where a patient is discharged to an area different from that where he/she was resident at the time of admission, the 'responsible authorities' may need to purchase services in that area. They should inform the health and social services authorities in the receiving area of the arrangements made for the patient's after-care.

10. LAC(93)7 on 'Ordinary Residence' provides guidance to local authorities on ordinary residence.

Guidance for health authorities is in a booklet 'Establishing District of Residence' (1993).

Stanley Johnson v The United Kingdom [1997] series A 1991 VII 2391

11. In the 1997 judgment of the ECHR in this case ((1999) 27 EHRR 296) (http://www.dhcour.coe.fr/hudoc), the Court found the UK in breach of article 5 of the European Convention on Human Rights because for a considerable period the patient concerned was not lawfully detained.

12. Successive MHRTs had given the patient a deferred conditional discharge under section 73 of the MHA. Discharge from hospital was delayed for several years because the responsible social services authority had been unable to

implement the conditions set by the MHRT by finding suitable supervised hostel accommodation and the Tribunal lacked the power to ensure that the discharge conditions were implemented within a reasonable time.

13. Where social services and health authorities are unable to implement conditions set by a MHRT they should follow guidance in Dr Graham Winyard's and Sir Herbert Laming's June 1997 letter 'Implementation of Mental Health Review Tribunals' Decisions'.

This Circular has been issued by:

Dr Sheila Adam Denise Platt

Director of Health Services Chief Social Services Inspector

Recommendations of Report of the Inquiry into the Care and Treatment of Christopher Clunis (1994)

1.10   This Report arose out of the now notorious facts and consequences of the care and treatment of Christopher Clunis. In part, the terms of reference for the Inquiry was: 'To make recommendations for the future delivery of care including admission, treatment, discharge and continuing care to people in similar circumstances so that, as far as possible, harm to patients and the public is avoided' (Section 1, para 1.1.1).

1.11   The specific recommendations in respect of s 117 are contained in Section V of the Report (paras 44–45). These are set out below. It is noteworthy that many of the recommendations are still routinely ignored, although the concept of a 'befriender' (para 45.4.3) is perhaps now partially in existence in the form of an Independent Mental Capacity Advocate (although only if the patient lacked capacity). The potential for this form of 'befriender' is also augmented by the Independent Mental Health Advocate. However, in particular, where a patient moves from one area to another, the Report recommended that:

'44.03 (xi) When the patient moves from the district where he has previously been receiving care, responsibility for his after-care should be formally transferred to the services responsible for his care in the district to which he moves ...

45.5.2 Before a patient who is subject to Section 117 aftercare moves from the area he is being cared for, a joint case conference should be held between those who are currently providing his after care, and those who will be providing his aftercare in the future. Responsibility will remain with the original multidisciplinary team unless and until Section 117 aftercare is effectively transferred and a new Section 117 from is completed by the new multidisciplinary team.'

44.0 THE PRINCIPLES UNDERLYING SECTION 117 MENTAL HEALTH ACT 1983 AFTERCARE AND THE CARE PROGRAMME APPROACH

44.0.1 Section 117 Mental Health Act 1983 and the Care Programme Approach under Health Circular (90)23/LASS letter 90/11 require Health Services and Social Services to provide, in co-operation with voluntary agencies, aftercare services for patients on their discharge from hospital. Section 117 comes into play when the patient has been detained under the Act in hospital. The Care Programme Approach comes into play for other mentally ill patient[s] on discharge from hospital.

44.0.2 We are concerned that doctors, nurses and social workers who are primarily responsible for providing this aftercare may not fully understand that the principles underlying Section 117 and Care Programme Approach aftercare are the same. We therefore set out common principles as we understand them. Although a great deal of very helpful guidance has been published by the Department of Health and others as to the way the Care Programme Approach should work, we are driven to say that we found that the terms in which such advice has been given, was often difficult to understand and couched in unhelpful jargon. We are sure that it is in everyone's interests; that is in the interests of the patient, those who care for the patient, the patient's relatives and the general public, that official guidance should try to be clear and simple. We suggest the following recommendations as a guide to aftercare.

44.0.3

(i) The aftercare needs of each individual patient must be assessed by health and social services before the patient is discharged into the community. Such assessment must take into account the patient's own wishes and choices.

(ii) A plan of care must be formulated for each individual patient, under the direction of the Consultant Psychiatrist under whose care the patient has been admitted.

(iii) The plan must be formulated by all those who will afterwards be responsible for providing any part of the aftercare, so that the plan is made by a team of people who work in a variety of different fields. Such a team for convenience is called a multi-disciplinary team. The aftercare plan must be recorded in detail and a copy of the plan must be given to the patient and to all those who are to provide the care.

(iv) The plan of care must fully consider and provide for both the immediate and long term needs of the patient.

(v) The Consultant Psychiatrist with responsibility for the patient must assess, together with the multi-disciplinary team, the risk of the patient harming himself or others.

(vi) Members of the multi-disciplinary team should be aware that aftercare is not provided by medication alone, although it is obviously a useful part of the armoury. There is always a need to help the patient come to terms with his illness and for the patient to have proper contact with those people who will be providing him with aftercare.

(vii) A keyworker must be agreed who will act to coordinate the care that has been planned by the multi-disciplinary team.

(viii) All members of the team should be alerted to signs and symptoms in the patient which may indicate that the patient is likely to relapse. Such signs and symptoms may be identified by the doctors but may also be identified by the patient himself or his relatives or friends. Non compliance with medication should be recognised as a significant pointer to a relapse.

(xi) The aftercare which is provided must be properly coordinated and supervised; it is severely to the patient's detriment if each member of the team acts in isolation. The Consultant Psychiatrist and Care Manager from social services must together be responsible for supervising aftercare.

(x)   It is essential that each member of the team who is providing care for the patient responds effectively to signs and symptoms which suggest that the patient is likely to relapse. Help which can be given before a crisis develops is more beneficial to the patient than the care that can be provided once the patient is in crisis.

(xi) When the patient moves from the district where he has previously been receiving care, responsibility for his aftercare should be formally transferred to the services responsible for his care in the district to which he moves.

(xii) Although Health and Social Services often have boundaries and catchment areas which do not overlap, proper co-operation between those who are providing care is likely to resolve any potential problems. Catchment areas should never be allowed to interfere with proper care in the community.

(xiii) It is essential that the aftercare for patients is properly monitored by Health and Social Services.

(xiv) Any area of unmet need which is identified by the multi-disciplinary team must be brought to the attention of the managers of the Health and Social Services.

45.0 PARTICULAR CONSIDERATIONS IN ADDITION TO THE CARE PROGRAMME APPROACH FOR SECTION 117 MENTAL HEALTH ACT 1983 AFTERCARE

45.0.1 Section 117 Mental Health Act 1983 imposes a statutory obligation on Health Authorities and Social Service Authorities to provide aftercare for patients who have been detained under the Act. We consider that this is a vital provision to ensure effective care in the community. Its impact should not be diminished by any other provisions for care in the community.

45.1 SECTION 117 FORM

45.1.1 We have seen a variety of Section 117 forms which have been prepared by individual hospitals or Health Authorities. Some are good, but some are not so good. We consider that Section 117 form should be standardised to ensure uniformity of approach throughout England and Wales. Plans made at Section 117 meetings and subsequent reviews should be recorded on a newly designed form, similar to other Mental Health Act 1983 documentation, the 'pink form'. Information about the plan should be recorded on the form, as also should any modification of the plan, and the form should identify who in Health and Social Services is responsible for supervising the plan.

45.1.2 RECOMMENDATIONS

(i) A new form should be designed for use in all Section 117 aftercare cases, similar to other forms which are presently standardised under the Mental Health Act 1983.

(ii) The form should record details of the plan that have been agreed, and should name the Consultant Psychiatrist, the Care Manager and the keyworker who together are responsible for the supervision and co-ordination of the plan.

(iii) Details of the signs and symptoms which suggest a likely relapse should be recorded as should details of the steps that the patient would like to be followed in the event of a relapse occurring. An assessment should be made as to whether the patient's propensity for violence presents any risk to his own health or safety or to the protection of the public.

(iv) Decisions and further plans that are made subsequently at S 117 review meetings, should be recorded on the form as should the decision to discharge the patient from Section 117 aftercare.

45.2 SECTION 117 REGISTER

45.2.1 We consider that the Section 117 plan should be lodged with the Mental Health Act Commission, just as other lists are maintained pursuant to the Mental Health Act 1983 and Regulations made thereunder, but always subject to strict confidentiality. When the patient presents in a new district a doctor or social worker will have immediate access to the Section 117 Register to find out if the patient is already subject to a Section 117 aftercare plan.

45.2.2 The Register should contain the following information only: the patient's name (and any know aliases), the patient's date of birth, a description of the patient, the name of patient's General Practitioner, the name of the patient's Responsible Medical Officer and the name of the last hospital at which the patient was detained, together with telephone and Facsimile numbers of the relevant hospital. Such information would enable ready identification of the patient who is subject to a Section 117 aftercare and would indicate whence information about the patient could be obtained.

45.2.3 RECOMMENDATION

(v) A nationally based Register for patients subject to Section 117 Mental Health Act 1983 aftercare should be set up, where information which leads to ready identification of the patient would be stored, and which would indicate whence confidential information about the patient could be obtained.

45.3 KEYWORKERS

45.3.1 We consider that the role of a keyworker in the provision of Section 117 aftercare should be undertaken by qualified and experienced Social Workers or Community Psychiatric Nurses. The keyworker should have direct access to the patient's Responsible Medical Officer. The patient and his family, and members of the multi-disciplinary team must have ready access to the keyworker. In our view the role of the keyworker is crucial to the co-ordination and supervision of aftercare, although ultimate responsibility must remain with the Responsible Medical Officer and Care Manager.

45.3.2 RECOMMENDATION

(vi) The nominated keyworker in Section 117 aftercare should always be a qualified and experienced Social Worker or Community Psychiatric Nurse.

45.4 BEFRIENDER/ADVOCATE

45.4.1 We are concerned that the patient very often considers that the Section 117 Mental Health Act 1983 aftercare plan is made at his expense rather than for his benefit. Although it is vital that the patient should, himself, participate in his formation of the plan, we consider that the patient needs someone to be his ally/befriender/advocate in relation to Section 117 aftercare. That befriender should attend all Section 117 meetings with the patient, should champion his cause, and should ensure that action which is supposed to happen under the plan, does in fact happen. If there is a failure to provide a service that has been agreed or if the befriender becomes aware of an area of need which has not been catered for, he should have access to the keyworker to prompt action. The befriender would be assertive in keeping in touch with the patient and in picking up any signs or symptoms of relapse, just as a caring relative would do. The befriender would only be able to relinquish responsibility when another befriender has agreed to take on the role.

45.4.2 We envisage the befriender as being a relative or friend of the patient or a volunteer. Volunteers would be able to join a local panel of befrienders after they have received training in basic mental health skills. The patient would have to agree a particular volunteer being his befriender.

45.4.3 RECOMMENDATIONS

(vi)   Every patient, subject to Section 117 Mental Health Act 1983 aftercare, should have a nominated relative, friend or volunteer to act as his befriender/advocate, unless the patient expressly states to the contrary.
(vii) Statutory Authorities and Voluntary Agencies working in the field of mental health should recruit, train and support members of the public who wish to be Section 117 befrienders.
(viii) A copy of the current aftercare plan should be given to the befriender.

45.5 SECTION 117 PLANNING ACROSS BOUNDARIES

45.5.1 We have seen during our investigations that many problems occur in respect of the aftercare of a patient who intends to move away from the locality where he has previously been receiving aftercare. We consider that for patients subject to Section 117, special provision is required to ensure proper continuation of aftercare.

45.2.2 RECOMMENDATION

(x)   Before a patient , who is subject to Section 117 aftercare, moves from the area where he is being cared for, a joint case conference should be held between those who are currently providing his aftercare and those who will be providing his aftercare in the future. Responsibility will remain with the original multi-disciplinary team unless and until Section 117 aftercare is effectively transferred and a new Section 117 form is completed by the new multi-disciplinary team.

45.6 MONITORING

45.6.1 In our view it is vital that Health Authorities and Social Services Departments should review Section 117 forms regularly. Section 117 forms and the records of scrutiny and review should be presented to the Mental Health Act Commissioners on each statutory visit so that external monitoring can also be provided.

45.6.2 RECOMMENDATIONS

(xi)   Section 117 forms should be reviewed regularly by Hospital Managers as defined under the Mental Health Act 1983.

(xii)   The Mental Health Act Commission should carry out external monitoring of Section 117 forms on each statutory visit.

Continuation of after-care services

1.12 Whilst it is clear that after-care services do not have to continue indefinitely, a retrospective decision by a responsible body that s 117 no longer applied to the services provided (which might result in charging for the services under the National Assistance Act 1948) is likely to be susceptible to remedy by way of judicial review. The caution that should be used in considering the use of retrospective assessments was the basis of complaints made to the Local Government Ombudsman, which resulted in the *Special Report (The Local Government Ombudsmen) Advice and Guidance on the funding of AfterCare under Section 117 of the Mental Health Act 1983*. This was published in July 2003. It stated (Section D, para 4):

'We see very little scope under the Code for a retrospective decision to be made – in default of consultation, review and a formal decision communicated to all relevant parties – that a patient's status as a recipient of Section 117 after-care can have changed. It is difficult to see how such a retrospective assessment could operate fairly. If a decision had been taken at the right time and upon the right assumptions, that is that aftercare had to be provided free until the authorities no longer considered it to be required, a patient or relative could, in the event of a decision to discontinue Section 117 after-care, then decide whether or not to have the aftercare at his own expense. If the effect of a retrospective decision is to disentitle a patient or relative to reimbursement of charges until after the date of the notional decision to discontinue (on the grounds of the absence of need) this would deprive those persons of the opportunity, which they otherwise would have had, not to continue with the aftercare and not to incur the cost of its provision. For all those reasons a retrospective assessment may be found to be maladministration, subject always to the facts of each case.'

Ordinary residence

1.13   The issue of residence is touched upon in *Hall* (above) and is a much traversed route in respect of virtually all areas of litigation where a subsidiary branch of the state (that is to say local authority or health care provider) may be obliged to pay for services to a citizen who comes within its geographic jurisdiction. It tends to involve somewhat sterile and technical arguments designed to ensure that someone else pays, or so that an authority is able to manage its budget effectively in a predictable fashion. Almost all such arguments are likely to be determined upon the facts peculiar to the case, but a number of principles have emerged within the context of community care law generally which it is worth considering at this point.

1.14   With specific reference to s 117(3) it is enough that the service user is 'resident' in the area of the local authority. However, the issue has been re-visited both in terms of case law, and guidance provided by the Department of Health. In *R (on the application of Hertfordshire County Council) v London Borough of Hammersmith and Fulham and JM (interested party)* [2011] EWCA Civ 77, [2011] 14 CCLR 224 the provisions of s 21 of the National Assistance Act 1948 and s 117 of the MHA 1983 were considered. In effect, the problem that both Local Authorities wished to have considered arose out of what happened when (as a matter of fact) it could be argued that the provisions of s 117 were incompatible with the provisions of s 21. JM himself had lived within the jurisdiction of the London Borough of Hammersmith and Fulham for a considerable number of years. His accommodation had been provided by way of s 21 of the NAA 1948. However, he was then placed in another local authority area, following an assessment of his mental health. Ultimately, he was detained under s 3 of the MHA 1983 (after having been detained under s 2), and reached a stage where he was able to be discharged. By this time, the original local authority had decided that it would not be responsible for his after care. Section 24(1) provides that responsibility lies with the local authority in whose area the person was ordinarily resident and s 24(5) deems that the ordinary residence of that person remains where the person had been provided with accommodation under Part 3 of the NAA 1948. Thus, it was argued that the London Borough of Hammersmith and Fulham should have responsibility for him, as he was (on that construction) ordinarily resident in their area. However, s 117 has no such 'deeming' provision, and simply places the responsibility for after-care services on the local authority for the area in which the person was resident, or to which the hospital sent him on discharge. The court held that (following *Stennett*) s 117 was a free-standing provision which was not dependent on the NAA 1948. It also held that the period of detention could not be considered as pointing towards residence. The provisions of s 117(3) in respect of residence could not be taken to mean that period when the person was compulsorily detained by virtue of s 2 or 3 of the MHA 1983.

The consequence of the decision, therefore, tends to re-affirm the existing law as to the separate status of s 117 in terms of the issue of residence. The Law Commission (Law Com No 326) Adult Social Care (May 2011) also commented on this case, and this same issue. It was concerned about the distinction between the NAA and the MHA on this point and commented (at Chapter 11, paras 11.89, 11.90, 11.92):

'11.89 In our view, extending the concept of ordinary residence to apply to section 117 after-care services would bring greater clarity and consistency. As pointed out in the consultation paper, it would also ensure that section 117 service users would benefit from having access to the dispute resolution procedures that apply to ordinary residence ...

11.90 ... the decision in *R (M) v London Borough of Hammersmith and Fulham* raises serious questions about the efficacy of current policy ...

11.92 ... **Recommendation 63: The concept of ordinary residence should be extended to apply to after-care services provided under section 117 of the Mental Health Act 1983. The issue of how ordinary residence rules should be applied to section 117 should be taken forward as a general review of the policy of the Government and Welsh Assembly Government.**'

Consequently, it would appear that the tide is changing, and that in the reasonably near future, the law on ordinary residence will be harmonious as between different areas of law. The Law Commission have also recommended that s 117 should no longer be a free-standing duty (Recommendation 66, Chapter 11, para 11.111). Nevertheless, for the present, disputes between local authorities, based upon the interpretation of what is meant by the term 'ordinary residence' continue. In *R (on the application of Sunderland City Council v South Tyneside Council* [2011] EWHC 2355 (Admin) two councils were in dispute over the residence of a patient, and as to which one of them was responsible for the provision of s 117 after-care services. As ever, the facts on each case will be of particular relevance, but in this instance the patient had been informally admitted to hospital in one area, prior to moving to the other area, where she was subsequently detained under s 3 of the MHA. The judgment sets out a clear and helpful summary of the law in this area (concluding, inter alia, that an unavoidable voluntary stay in a hospital did not make the patient case to be a resident in the area where she had been previously resident). The attention of the Court did not seem to have been drawn to the new Guidance (referred to below).

1.15 Guidance to local authorities on the issue of ordinary residence had existed for many years in the form of Circular No LAC (93) 7 (issued in March 1993 by the Department of Health). This was long overdue for a replacement, which was duly provided in April 2010, and then in an amended form on 15 April 2011. It is called *Ordinary Residence: Guidance on the identification of the ordinary residence of people in need of community care services, England*. The basic principles remain those as set out in *Shah v Barnet LBC* [1983] 2 AC 309. It means:

'[343G-343H] a man's abode in a particular place or country which he has adopted **voluntarily** [emphasis added] **and for settled purposes as part of the regular order of his life for the time being, whether of long or short duration.**'

It is an essential component of this test that the move must be voluntary, thus excluding prisoners, those detained under the MHA 1983, and (surely) those who lack capacity to make a decision as to where they reside or wish to reside. Similarly, ordinary residence can be lost in a day, if there is a move with an intention not to return. Where new ordinary residence is concerned, this may also be acquired with some rapidity, but as with all these cases, the determination is likely to be fact specific. The substance of the authorities is that it takes longer to acquire a new ordinary residence than it does to lose it, but there is no time limit which exists. Other complexities which may arise is where a service user has dual residence (or a primary and secondary residence). The relevant parts of the Guidance are set out at appropriate parts of this book where they relate to the law to which it refers, apart from the general test, which is produced below. The Guidance itself is a much more substantial document than its predecessor, and it is to be hoped that it may be amended with greater regularity (ie on an annual basis).

ORDINARY RESIDENCE

Meaning of ordinary residence

18. Responsibility for the provision of accommodation and community care services under sections 21 and 29 of the 1948 Act is largely based on the concept of "ordinary residence". However, there is no definition of "ordinary residence" in the 1948 Act. Therefore, the term should be given its ordinary and natural meaning subject to any interpretation by the courts.

19. In many cases, establishing a person's ordinary residence is a straightforward matter. However, this is not always the case and where uncertainties arise, local authorities should consider each case on its own merits, taking relevant court judgments and Secretary of State determinations (see paragraphs 67–71) into account. The concept of ordinary residence involves questions of fact and degree. Factors such as time, intention and continuity (each of which may be given different weight according to the context) have to be taken into account.

20. The courts have considered the meaning of "ordinary residence" and the leading case is that of *Shah v London Borough of Barnet* (1983) 1 All ER 226. In this case, Lord Scarman stated that:

'unless ... it can be shown that the statutory framework or the legal context in which the words are used requires a different meaning I unhesitatingly subscribe to the view that "ordinarily resident" refers to a man's abode in a particular place or country which he has adopted voluntarily and for settled purposes as part of the regular order of his life for the time being, whether of short or long duration.'

21. Local authorities should always have regard to this case when determining the ordinary residence of people who have capacity to make their own decisions about where they wish to live (for people who lack capacity to make decisions about their accommodation, one of the alternative tests set out in *R v Waltham Forest London Borough Council, ex Parte Vale* (1985) *Times* 25 February (the "Vale case", see paragraphs 27–34 below) should be used). The starting presumption is that a person does have such capacity unless it is shown otherwise.

22. Particular attention should be paid to Lord Scarman's statement that ordinary residence is the place a person has voluntarily adopted for a settled purpose for **short or long duration**. Ordinary residence can be acquired as soon as a person moves to an area if their move is voluntary and for settled purposes, irrespective of whether they own, or have an interest in, a property in another local authority area. **There is no minimum period in which a person has to be living in a particular place for them to be considered ordinarily resident there**, because it depends on the nature and quality of the connection with the new place.

Temporary absences

23. Local authorities should have regard to the case of *Levene v Inland Revenue Commissioners* (1928) AC 217. This case is particularly useful for considering the effect of temporary absences on a person's ordinary residence or when assessing whether someone has lost their ordinary residence in a particular place. In this case, Viscount Cave stated:

'It [ordinary residence] connotes residence in a place with some degree of continuity and apart from accidental or temporary absences.'

24. Viscount Cave went on to give examples of temporary absence as being absences for the purpose of business or pleasure, such as a fisherman going away to sea. This issue of absence and its effect on ordinary residence was further considered in the case of *Fox v Stirk* [1970] 2 QB 463. In this case, Lord Denning MR set out the principle that temporary absence does not deprive a person of their ordinary residence:

'If he happens to be away for a holiday or away for the weekend or in hospital, he does not lose his residence on that account.'

Urgent need during temporary absences

25. The fact that a person may be temporarily away from the local authority in which they are ordinarily resident does not preclude them from receiving accommodation and/or services from another local authority if they become in urgent need (see paragraphs 47–50).

More than one place of residence

26. Although in general terms it would be possible for a person to have more than one ordinary residence (for example, a person who divides their time equally between two homes), this is not possible for the purposes of the 1948 Act. The purpose of the ordinary residence test in the 1948 Act is to determine which single

local authority has responsibility for meeting a person's eligible social care needs, and this purpose would be defeated if a person could have more than one ordinary residence. If a person appears genuinely to divide their time equally between two homes, it would be necessary to establish (from all of the circumstances) to which of the two homes the person has the stronger link. Where this is the case, it would be the responsibility of the local authority in which the person is ordinarily resident to provide or arrange services during the time the person is temporarily away at their second home. Scenario 4 on page 53 provides further guidance on how the ordinary residence provisions operate where a person lives in two different local authority areas.

After-care services under s 117 of the Mental Health Act 1983

After-care services under section 117 of the Mental Health Act 1983

182. Under section 117 of the Mental Health Act 1983 ("the 1983 Act"), local authorities, together with Primary Care Trusts (PCTs), have a duty to provide after-care services to people who have been detained in hospital under certain provisions of the 1983 Act. This duty stands by itself and is not a "gateway" to the provision of services under other legislation, such as the 1948 Act.

183. Section 117 of the 1983 Act sets out that the duty falls on the authorities "for the area in which the person concerned is resident or to which the person is sent on discharge by the hospital in which the person was detained."

184. The term "resident" in the 1983 Act is not the same as "ordinarily resident" in the 1948 Act and therefore the deeming provisions (and other rules about ordinary residence explained in this guidance) do not apply.

185. Guidance on section 117 of the 1983 Act was given in the case of *R v Mental Health Review Tribunal Ex p. Hall* (1999) 4 All ER 883. This case made clear that responsibility for the provision of such services falls to the local authority and PCT for the area in which the person was resident before being detained in hospital, even if the person does not return to that area on discharge. If no such residence can be established, the duty falls on the authority where the person is to go on discharge from hospital.

186. For example, the Local Government Ombudsman's investigation into the provision of after-care services by Medway Council (06/B/12248) and Wigan Metropolitan Borough Council (06/B12247) considered the case of a man who was detained under section 3 of the 1983 Act and required section 117 after-care following his discharge. He was discharged to a specialist care facility in Wigan Metropolitan Borough Council but had been living in Medway Council prior to his detention. Both local authorities refused to meet the cost of providing after-care services. The Ombudsman considered the man to have been 'resident' in Medway prior to his compulsory admission and therefore found Medway Council to be responsible for the provision of the after-care services.

187. The term "resident" is not defined in the 1983 Act, and so, like "ordinarily resident" the term should be given its ordinary and natural meaning subject to any interpretation by the courts.

188. The duty to provide after-care services remains with the same local authority even if the person subsequently becomes resident in another area, unless they are then re-detained under a provision of the 1983 Act which again entitles them to section 117 after-care. In this situation, the rules would need to be applied again from scratch, to decide which authority has responsibility for any after-care once the person leaves hospital again.

189. Disputes arising in connection with section 117 of the 1983 Act cannot be referred to the Secretary of State or Welsh Ministers for determination under section 32(3) of the 1948 Act. If such a dispute could not be resolved locally, it would be necessary to involve the courts.

It is to be noted that despite the anomalies identified by the Law Commission, the current state of the law in respect of s 117 and ordinary residence is summarised at para 188. In particular, where the patient is discharged and then re-detained, the law is re-applied 'from scratch'. There is no formal method of resolving a dispute between local authorities apart from recourse to the Courts (which would be by way of judicial review). The scenario set out at para 189 is clearly based upon *R (on the application of Hertfordshire County Council) v London Borough of Hammersmith and Fulham and JM (interested party)*.

Establishing the responsible commissioner

1.16 The Department of Health has published some guidance for Primary Care Trusts and Strategic Health Authorities (*Who Pays? Establishing the Responsible Commissioner September 2007*). This is considered at greater length in Chapter 7. However, it contains a helpful summary of the responsible PCT for those who have been detained under the Mental Health Act 1983 (paras 84–87). This includes those detained under s 2 (for example) and who would not therefore come within the ambit of s 117. The Guidance also refers to this framework and for the sake of convenience, it is set out below.

ESTABLISHING THE RESPONSIBLE COMMISSIONER

179. The concept of "ordinary residence" does not apply to the NHS and the NHS has its own rules for determining who pays for the provision of care at a local level. Primary Care Trusts (PCTs) have responsibility for commissioning secondary care for people in need of treatment and care. The legal framework relating to secondary care commissioning responsibilities for PCTs is set out in the National Health Service (Functions of Strategic Health Authorities and Primary Care Trusts and Administration Arrangements) (England) Regulations 2002. Guidance on the application of this legal framework is contained in *Who Pays?*

180. In general, where a person is registered with a GP in England, the responsible commissioner is the PCT that holds the contract with that GP practice. Where a person is not registered with a GP practice, the responsible commissioner is the PCT in whose geographic area the person is 'usually resident'. 'Usually resident' is largely determined by the person's own perception of where they are resident (either currently, or failing that, most recently) as evidenced by the address they give. If a person is unable to give an address, and their place of residence cannot

be established by any other means, the responsible commissioner is the PCT in whose area the unit providing treatment is located.

181. An exception to the general approach for establishing the responsible commissioner exists in relation to NHS CHC. Where a PCT places a person in a care home or independent hospital in the area of another PCT for the purpose of receiving NHS CHC, the "placing PCT" remains responsible for the provision of continuing care, even where the person changes their GP practice. See paragraphs 112–115 for more information on NHS CHC.

Definition of services

1.17 As observed above, the Code contains no guidance as to what actually constitutes an after-care service, and neither did its predecessors. However, the old Codes did include a statement that purpose of after-care is 'to enable a patient to return to his home or accommodation other than a hospital or nursing home, and to minimise the chances of him needing any future in-patient hospital care'. The revised version (effective from April 1999) states 'a central purpose of all treatment and care is to equip patients to cope with life outside hospital and function there without danger to themselves or other people'.

1.18 In *Clunis v Camden & Islington Health Authority* [1998] QB 978, after-care services were held to include residential facilities. If there was any doubt as to this, it has been confirmed in *R v Manchester CC ex parte Stennett* [2002] UKHL 34. Also, in *Clunis* it was held that after-care services would include social work support, support in helping the discharged patient with problems of employment, accommodation or family relationships, provision of domiciliary services and the use of day centres and residential facilities. In *R v North East Devon Health Authority ex parte Coughlan* [1999] 2 CCLR 285, [2000] 2 WLR 622 it was held that nursing care could in appropriate cases be provided by a local authority as a social service. Finally, see **1.3** and **1.4** above for the proposition that ordinary private accommodation may be a part of the type of accommodation to be provided pursuant to s 117.

Charges for services

1.19 None of those responsible for providing services are able to charge for them (*R v Manchester CC ex parte Stennett* [2002] UKHL 34, [2002] 5 CCLR 500). The series of decisions that ended in this judgment started on 28 July 1999. It also gave rise to Circular No LAC (2000) 3: HSC 2000/3 in which local authorities were alerted to the consequences of the developments and instructed them to cease charging for s 117 after-care services immediately (even prior to the decision in the House of Lords). The complete text of this circular is set out at **1.9** above. Thus, no local authority can have any justification for having levied charges since (at least) 10 February 2000. It also states that:

'The Court did not address the question of charging for non-residential services provided under section 117 but there is a strong implication that the responsible authorities may not charge for such services.'

It also advised that:

'Social Services and Health Authorities should jointly agree local policies on providing section 117 after-care. Policies should set out clearly the criteria for deciding which services fall under section 117 and which authorities should finance them. The section 117 after-care plan should indicate which services are provided as a part of the plan.'

In Circular LAC (2002) 15 (14 October 2002) this advice was confirmed in the light of the judgment in the House of Lords, and added that 'those authorities that have made such a charge will no doubt wish to address that issue and will each wish to seek their own advice as to the extent of their liability'.

CIRCULAR LAC (2002) 15

VI SECTION 117 AFTERCARE SERVICES

22. The House of Lord's judgment in the case of *R v Manchester City Council ex parte Stennett* and two other actions has confirmed Department of Health guidance that Mental Health Act 1983 section 117 aftercare should not be charged for. Those authorities that have made such a charge will no doubt wish to address that issue and will each wish to seek their own advice as to the extent of their liability. Paragraph 1.005A of CRAG refers.

Paragraph 1.005A of CRAG no longer exists in its current form (April 2011) although the reference to LAC (2002) 15 is preserved in Annex K (Summary of LAC Circulars) which simply confirms the above.

Repayment of charges and restitution

1.20 The remedy for those who have been charged is almost certainly for a restitutionary claim for monies paid under a mistake of law, or a restitutionary claim for monies paid pursuant to an *ultra vires* demand. The *Special Report (The Local Government Ombudsmen) Advice and guidance on the funding of AfterCare under Section 117 of the Mental Health Act 1983* noted that as long ago as January 1994 the Department of Health had issued advice stating that 'Services provided under Section 117 ... are not subject to charging under Section 17 of the 1983 [Health and Social Services and Social Security Adjudication Act]' (Section B, para 3 of the Report). It also suggested that Social Services Authorities should be proactive in identifying those who had paid for aftercare services and should be reimbursed. That is to say, local authorities should seek out those service users who may have paid for services to which they were entitled free of charge, and reimburse them accordingly. If necessary, it suggested advertising in the press. It also notes that some complexities may arise where the major source of the income of a service user might be another arm of the Government (that is to say from state benefits). The view of the Ombudsman was that in these instances it would be a matter for the relevant Government Department (rather than the Social Service Authority) to consider clawing back any windfall. It also suggests that one local authority had received advice that it should search its files only back to 28 July 1993 (6 years back from the decision of Mr Justice Sullivan). It also suggested that caution was exercised in providing reimbursement to vulnerable recipients, and consider the most appropriate method in which this might take place.

Limitation periods

1.21   The limitation period for such claims is not entirely clear. In *Kleinwort Benson v Lincoln City Council* [1999] 2 AC 349 it was held that there is a cause of action in such a claim, and that it is not a defence to such a claim that at the time the money was paid the law was settled to the extent that the mistake was unknown to either or both parties. If it subsequently appeared that on the law held to be applicable at the date that the payment was made that the Claimant was not bound so to do, then he or she was entitled to recover the money paid. The House of Lords also considered s 31(2)(c) of the Limitation Act 1980, which provides for an extension of the normal limitation period (of 6 years) from the date upon which the mistake might have been discovered with due diligence, or did discover the mistake. If the claim is for unjust enrichment, this is a cause of action that was unrecognised in law until 1991, and therefore falls outside the Limitation Act 1980 altogether. The consensus appears to be that a 6-year period is appropriate, from the date upon which the defendant was unjustly enriched (cf Law Commission (Law Com No 270) *Limitation of Actions, Claims for Restitution* at **2.48** et seq). A further glossary upon this was provided in the report by the Local Government Ombudsman referred to above. This states that there were three possible heads of claim (the two referred to above) and in addition a claim dependent upon s 6(1) of the Human Rights Act 1998 (but only in respect of those actions post 2 October 2000). The report continues (Section B, para 14) as follows:

> '14 If charges for section 117 accommodation were demanded under a mistaken view of section 117, then local authorities would prima facie be liable to restitution. The advice [given to Nottinghamshire County Council] added that section 32(1) of the Limitation Act 1980 applies to such actions and a six year time limit begins to run from the time when the mistake in law is established. This would mean that there would be no statutory limit on the period for which reimbursement of charges could be claimed – only a six year period forwards, from the time when the law was clarified, in which to claim.

> 15 Finally [with regard to a claim for monies paid pursuant to an ultra vires demand] the advice said that the case of *Woolwich Building Society v IRC* [1993] established that claims could be made in respect of paid pursuant to an ultra vires demand. It suggested that section 5 of the Limitation Act may apply to such claims and that the limitation period of six years would run from the date of cause

of action – in these cases the date of payment of the charges. So the claim could extend only to charges paid within the last six years of the date when the proceedings are commenced.'

1.22 It was held to be maladministration to continue to charge service users for 2 years after receipt of legal advice that charges were unlawful (*Investigation into Complaint No 98/B/0341 against Wiltshire CC* [2000] 3 CCLR 60).

1.23 Whatever sums are paid, they should have added to them the relevant rate of interest for the material period. However, given the length of time that has expired since this area of law was last considered by the Court, it is unlikely that this is anything more than of academic interest.

Independent Mental Capacity Advocates (Mental Capacity Act 2005) and Independent Mental Health Advocates (Mental Health Act 1983)

1.24 If a local authority provides accommodation or wishes to change accommodation (pursuant to s 117, amongst other statutes set out below) and the patient lacks capacity and the accommodation is not provided as a result of an obligation imposed upon him by the Mental Health Act itself, then an Independent Mental Capacity Advocate must be instructed by a local authority. In addition to the MCA 2005, the Code of Practice (*Mental Capacity Act 2005 Code of Practice April 2007*) contains further information on the role of IMCA's (Chapter 10). The Code of Practice has a different legal status to that of the Code of Practice for the MHA 1983, in that it has statutory force. It is also remarkable for its lucidity, clarity and excellent style. The role of the IMCA service is described thus (at Chapter 10):

'to provide independent safeguards for people who lack capacity to make certain important decisions and, at the time of such decisions need to be made, have no-one else (other than paid staff) to support or represent them or be consulted. IMCA's must be independent.'

Mental Capacity Act 2005

39 Provision of accommodation by local authority

(1) This section applies if a local authority propose to make arrangements –

    (a)   for the provision of residential accommodation for a person ("P") who lacks capacity to agree to the arrangements, or

    (b)   for a change in P's residential accommodation,

and are satisfied that there is no person, other than one engaged in providing care or treatment for P in a professional capacity or for remuneration, whom it would be appropriate for them to consult in determining what would be in P's best interests.

(2) But this section applies only if the accommodation is to be provided in accordance with –

(a)   section 21 or 29 of the National Assistance Act 1948 (c 29), or

(b)   section 117 of the Mental Health Act,

as the result of a decision taken by the local authority under section 47 of the National Health Service and Community Care Act 1990 (c 19).

(3) This section does not apply if P is accommodated as a result of an obligation imposed on him under the Mental Health Act.

(3A) And this section does not apply if –

(a)   an independent mental capacity advocate must be appointed under section 39A or 39C (whether or not by the local authority) to represent P, and

(b)   the place in which P is to be accommodated under the arrangements referred to in this section is the relevant hospital or care home under the authorisation referred to in that section.

(4) Before making the arrangements, the local authority must instruct an independent mental capacity advocate to represent P unless they are satisfied that –

(a)   the accommodation is likely to be provided for a continuous period of less than 8 weeks, or

(b)   the arrangements need to be made as a matter of urgency.

(5) If the local authority –

(a)   did not instruct an independent mental capacity advocate to represent P before making the arrangements because they were satisfied that subsection (4)(a) or (b) applied, but

(b)   subsequently have reason to believe that the accommodation is likely to be provided for a continuous period that will end 8 weeks or more after the day on which accommodation was first provided in accordance with the arrangements,

they must instruct an independent mental capacity advocate to represent P.

(6) The local authority must, in deciding what arrangements to make for P, take into account any information given, or submissions made, by the independent mental capacity advocate.

(7) For the purposes of subsection (1), a person appointed under Part 10 of Schedule A1 to be P's representative is not, by virtue of that appointment, engaged in providing care or treatment for P in a professional capacity or for remuneration.

Independent Mental Health Advocates

1.25 This role was created by s 130A of the Mental Health Act 1983. The Code (Chapter 20) sets out the purpose of the Independent Mental Health Advocate (IMHA). This is self-explanatory and is set out below (para 20.8). In addition, the National Institute for Mental Health in England have published *Independent Mental Health Advocacy – Guidance for Commissioners' (December 2008)* which provides additional information. PCT commissioners have been responsible for ensuring that IMHA services have been available since 1 April 2009.

CHAPTER 20 OF MHA CODE

20.1 This chapter explains the role of independent mental health advocates (IMHAs) under the Act.

Purpose of independent mental health advocacy services

20.2 Independent mental health advocacy services provide an additional safeguard for patients who are subject to the Act. IMHAs are specialist advocates who are trained specifically to work within the framework of the Act to meet the needs of patients.

20.3 Independent mental health advocacy services do not replace any other advocacy and support services that are available to patients, but are intended to operate in conjunction with those services.

Patients who are eligible for independent mental health advocacy services (qualifying patients)

20.4 Patients are eligible for support from an IMHA if they are:

- detained under the Act (even if they are currently onleave of absence from hospital);
- conditionally discharged restricted patients;
- subject to guardianship; or
- supervised community treatment (SCT) patients.

20.5 For these purposes, detention does not include being detained:

- on the basis of an emergency application (section 4) until the second medical recommendation is received (see chapter 5);
- under the holding powers in section 5; or
- in a place of safety under section 135 or 136.

20.6 Other patients ("informal patients") are eligible if they are:

- being considered for a treatment to which section 57 applies ("a section 57 treatment"); or
- under 18 and being considered for electro-convulsive therapy or any other treatment to which section 58A applies ("a section 58A treatment").

20.7 The Act calls patients who are eligible for the support of an IMHA "qualifying patients".

The role of independent mental health advocates

20.8 The Act says that the support which IMHAs provide must include helping patients to obtain information about and understand the following:

- their rights under the Act;

- the rights which other people (eg nearest relatives) have in relation to them under the Act;
- the particular parts of the Act which apply to them (eg the basis on which they are detained) and which therefore make them eligible for advocacy;
- any conditions or restrictions to which they are subject (eg as a condition of leave of absence from hospital, as a condition of a community treatment order, or as a condition of conditional discharge);
- any medical treatment that they are receiving or might be given;
- the reasons for that treatment (or proposed treatment); and
- the legal authority for providing that treatment, and the safeguards and other requirements of the Act which would apply to that treatment.

20.9 It also includes helping patients to exercise their rights, which can include representing them and speaking on their behalf.

20.10 IMHAs may also support patients in a range of other ways to ensure they can participate in the decisions that are made about their care and treatment.

20.11 The involvement of an IMHA does not affect a patient's right (nor the right of their nearest relative) to seek advice from a lawyer. Nor does it affect any entitlement to legal aid.

Duty to inform patients about the availability of independent mental health advocacy services

20.12 Certain people have a duty to take whatever steps are practicable to ensure that patients understand that help is available to them from IMHA services and how they can obtain that help, as set out in the following table. This must include giving the relevant information both orally and in writing.

Mental Health Act 1983

130A Independent mental health advocates

(1) The appropriate national authority Secretary of State shall make such arrangements as it considers reasonable to enable persons ("independent mental health advocates") to be available to help qualifying patients.

(2) The appropriate national authority Secretary of State may by regulations make provision as to the appointment of persons as independent mental health advocates.

(3) The regulations may, in particular, provide –

    (a)   that a person may act as an independent mental health advocate only in such circumstances, or only subject to such conditions, as may be specified in the regulations;
    (b)   for the appointment of a person as an independent mental health advocate to be subject to approval in accordance with the regulations.

(4) In making arrangements under this section, the appropriate national authority Secretary of State shall have regard to the principle that any help available to a

patient under the arrangements should, so far as practicable, be provided by a person who is independent of any person who is professionally concerned with the patient's medical treatment.

(5) For the purposes of subsection (4) above, a person is not to be regarded as professionally concerned with a patient's medical treatment merely because he is representing him in accordance with arrangements –

(a) under section 35 of the Mental Capacity Act 2005; or
(b) of a description specified in regulations under this section.

(6) Arrangements under this section may include provision for payments to be made to, or in relation to, persons carrying out functions in accordance with the arrangements.

(7) Regulations under this section –

(a) may make different provision for different cases;
(b) may make provision which applies subject to specified exceptions;
(c) may include transitional, consequential, incidental or supplemental provision.

GUARDIANSHIP

Purpose and basis for guardianship

1.26 In practice it is the local authority who will most commonly be responsible for making an application for guardianship (via an approved mental health professional (AMHP)), although the nearest relative may also make an application (s 11(1) of MHA 1983). Also, a nearest relative may require an AMHP to take the patient's case into consideration with a view to making an application for guardianship (s 13(4)). The typical scenario in which circumstances arise where a local authority may intervene are likely to be where an elderly patient has a mental impairment caused by some form of dementia, which in turn may have compromised his ability to care for himself. This is sometimes coupled with concerns regarding vulnerability to financial and/or emotional abuse. It may be the case that the nearest relative is suspected of being involved in such activities, in which case consideration would have to be given to an application to displace. Very frequently, the aim of the Local Authority will be to remove the patient from his own home, and to place him in a setting such as a care home (of some description). However, it is worth noting that this is not the intention of the statute, and a patient may be maintained in his own home if sufficient and appropriate support can be provided by the local authority, and other agencies (such as health authorities). Also, this section does not trigger s 117 of MHA 1983. However, by way of example, a patient may be subject to s 3 of MHA 1983, who could equally as easily have been made subject to s 7 of MHA 1983. If made subject to s 3, then the consequences for funding and service provision pursuant to s 117 will follow. If made subject to s 7, then there are no such consequences (or benefits for the patient). Clearly, the use of s 7 may be of considerable importance in terms of the financial impact upon a patient (and a local authority). Financial considerations should not, of course, form any part of the basis for such an application. The Code of Practice (MHA 1983) deals with Guardianship in Chapter 26.

Mental Health Act 1983

7 Application for guardianship

(1) A patient who has attained the age of 16 years may be received into guardianship, for the period allowed by the following provisions of this Act, in pursuance of an application (in this Act referred to as "a guardianship application") made in accordance with this section.

(2) A guardianship application may be made in respect of a patient on the grounds that –

    (a)   he is suffering from mental disorder of a nature or degree which warrants his reception into guardianship under this section; and

    (b)   it is necessary in the interests of the welfare of the patient or for the protection of other persons that the patient should be so received.

(3) A guardianship application shall be founded on the written recommendations in the prescribed form of two registered medical practitioners, including in each case a statement that in the opinion of the practitioner the conditions set out in subsection (2) above are complied with; and each such recommendation shall include –

    (a)   such particulars as may be prescribed of the grounds for that opinion so far as it relates to the conditions set out in paragraph (a) of that subsection; and

    (b)   a statement of the reasons for that opinion so far as it relates to the conditions set out in paragraph (b) of that subsection.

(4) A guardianship application shall state the age of the patient or, if his exact age is not known to the applicant, shall state (if it be the fact) that the patient is believed to have attained the age of 16 years.

(5) The person named as guardian in a guardianship application may be either a local social services authority or any other person (including the applicant himself); but a guardianship application in which a person other than a local social services authority is named as guardian shall be of no effect unless it is accepted on behalf of that person by the local social services authority for the area in which he resides, and shall be accompanied by a statement in writing by that person that he is willing to act as guardian.

8 Effect of guardianship application, etc

(1) Where a guardianship application, duly made under the provisions of this Part of this Act and forwarded to the local social services authority within the period allowed by subsection (2) below is accepted by that authority, the application shall, subject to regulations made by the Secretary of State, confer on the authority or person named in the application as guardian, to the exclusion of any other person –

    (a)   the power to require the patient to reside at a place specified by the authority or person named as guardian;

(b)   the power to require the patient to attend at places and times so specified for the purpose of medical treatment, occupation, education or training;

(c)   the power to require access to the patient to be given, at any place where the patient is residing, to any registered medical practitioner, approved mental health professional or other person so specified.

(2) The period within which a guardianship application is required for the purposes of this section to be forwarded to the local social services authority is the period of 14 days beginning with the date on which the patient was last examined by a registered medical practitioner before giving a medical recommendation for the purposes of the application.

(3) A guardianship application which appears to be duly made and to be founded on the necessary medical recommendations may be acted upon without further proof of the signature or qualification of the person by whom the application or any such medical recommendation is made or given, or of any matter of fact or opinion stated in the application.

(4) If within the period of 14 days beginning with the day on which a guardianship application has been accepted by the local social services authority the application, or any medical recommendation given for the purposes of the application, is found to be in any respect incorrect or defective, the application or recommendation may, within that period and with the consent of that authority, be amended by the person by whom it was signed; and upon such amendment being made the application or recommendation shall have effect and shall be deemed to have had effect as if it had been originally made as so amended.

(5) Where a patient is received into guardianship in pursuance of a guardianship application, any previous application under this Part of this Act by virtue of which he was subject to guardianship or liable to be detained in a hospital shall cease to have effect.

18 Return and readmission of patients absent without leave

. . .

(7) In relation to a patient who has yet to comply with a requirement imposed by virtue of this Act to be in a hospital or place, references in this Act to his liability to be returned to the hospital or place shall include his liability to be taken to that hospital or place; and related expressions shall be construed accordingly.

137 Provisions as to custody, conveyance and detention

(1) Any person required or authorised by or by virtue of this Act to be conveyed to any place or to be kept in custody or detained in a place of safety or at any place to which he is taken under section 42(6) above shall, while being so conveyed, detained or kept, as the case may be, be deemed to be in legal custody.

(2) A constable or any other person required or authorised by or by virtue of this Act to take any person into custody, or to convey or detain any person shall, for the purposes of taking him into custody or conveying or detaining him, have all the powers, authorities, protection and privileges which a constable has within the area for which he acts as constable.

(3) In this section "convey" includes any other expression denoting removal from one place to another.

Mental Health Act 1983 Code of Practice

GUARDIANSHIP

26.1 This chapter gives guidance on guardianship under the Act.

Purpose of guardianship

26.2 The purpose of guardianship is to enable patients to receive care outside hospital when it cannot be provided without the use of compulsory powers. Such care may or may not include specialist medical treatment for mental disorder.

26.3 A guardian may be a local social services authority (LSSA) or someone else approved by an LSSA (a "private guardian"). Guardians have three specific powers as follows:

- they have the exclusive right to decide where a patientshould live, taking precedence even over an attorney or deputy appointed under the Mental Capacity Act 2005 (MCA);
- they can require the patient to attend for treatment,work, training or education at specific times and places(but they cannot use force to take the patient there);
- they can demand that a doctor, approved mental health professional (AMHP) or another relevant person hasaccess to the patient at the place where the patient lives.

26.4 Guardianship therefore provides an authoritative framework for working with a patient, with a minimum of constraint, to achieve as independent a life as possible within the community. Where it is used, it should be part of the patient's overall care plan.

26.5 Guardianship does not give anyone the right to treat the patient without their permission or to consent to treatment on their behalf.

26.6 While the reception of a patient into guardianship does not affect the continued authority of an attorney or deputy appointed under the MCA, such attorneys and deputies will not be able to take decisions about where a guardianship patient is to reside, or take any other decisions which conflict with those of the guardian.

Assessment for guardianship

26.7 An application for guardianship may be made on the grounds that:

- the patient is suffering from mental disorder of a nature or degree which warrants their reception into guardianship; and
- it is necessary, in the interests of the welfare of the patient or for the protection of other persons, that the patient should be so received.

26.8 Guardianship is most likely to be appropriate where:

- the patient is thought to be likely to respond well to the authority and attention of a guardian and so be more willing to comply with necessary treatment and care for their mental disorder; or
- there is a particular need for someone to have the authority to decide where the patient should live or to insist that doctors, AMHPs or other people be given access to the patient.

26.9 As with applications for detention in hospital, AMHPs and doctors making recommendations should consider whether the objectives of the proposed application could be achieved in another, less restrictive, way, without the use of guardianship.

26.10 Where patients lack capacity to make some or all important decisions concerning their own welfare, one potential alternative to guardianship will be to rely solely on the MCA – especially the protection from liability for actions taken in connection with care or treatment provided by section 5 of the MCA. While this is a factor to be taken into account, it will not by itself determine whether guardianship is necessary or unnecessary. AMHPs and doctors need to consider all the circumstances of the particular case.

26.11 Where an adult is assessed as requiring residential care but lacks the capacity to make a decision about whether they wish to be placed there, guardianship is unlikely to be necessary where the move can properly, quickly and efficiently be carried out on the basis of:

- section 5 of the MCA or the decision of an attorney or deputy; or
- (where relevant) the MCA's deprivation of liberty safeguards.

26.12 But guardianship may still be appropriate in such cases if:

- there are other reasons – unconnected to the move to residential care – to think that the patient might benefit from the attention and authority of a guardian;
- there is a particular need to have explicit statutory authority for the patient to be returned to the place where the patient is to live should they go absent; or
- it is thought to be important that decisions about where the patient is to live are placed in the hands of a single person or authority – for example, where there have been long-running or particularly difficult disputes about where the person should live.

26.13 However, it will not always be best to use guardianship as the way of deciding where patients who lack capacity to decide for themselves must live. In cases which raise unusual issues, or where guardianship is being considered in the interests of the patient's welfare and there are finely balanced arguments about where the patient should live, it may be preferable instead to seek a best interests decision from the Court of Protection under the MCA.

26.14 Where the relevant criteria are met, guardianship may be considered in respect of a patient who is to be discharged from detention under the Mental Health Act. However, if it is thought that the patient needs to remain liable to be recalled to hospital (and the patient is eligible), supervised community treatment is likely to be more appropriate (see chapter 28).

Responsibilities of local social services authorities

26.15 Each LSSA should have a policy setting out the arrangements for:

- receiving, scrutinising and accepting or refusing applications for guardianship. Such arrangements should ensure that applications are properly but quickly dealt with;
- monitoring the progress of each patient's guardianship, including steps to be taken to fulfil the authority's statutory obligations in relation to private guardians and to arrange visits to the patient;
- ensuring the suitability of any proposed private guardian, and that they are able to understand and carry out their duties under the Act;
- ensuring that patients under guardianship receive, both orally and in writing, information in accordance with regulations under the Act;
- ensuring that patients are aware of their right to apply to the Tribunal and that they are given the name of someone who will give them the necessary assistance, on behalf of the LSSA, in making such an application;
- authorising an approved clinician to be the patient's responsible clinician;
- maintaining detailed records relating to guardianship patients;
- ensuring that the need to continue guardianship isreviewed in the last two months of each period ofguardianship in accordance with the Act; and
- discharging patients from guardianship as soon as itis no longer required.

26.16 Patients may be discharged from guardianship at any time by the LSSA, the responsible clinician authorised by the LSSA, or (in most cases) the patient's nearest relative.

26.17 Discharge decisions by LSSAs may be taken only by the LSSA itself, or by three or more members of the LSSA or of a committee or sub-committee of the LSSA authorised for that purpose. Where decisions are taken by three or more members of the LSSA (or a committee or subcommittee), all three people (or at least three of them, if there are more) must agree.

26.18 LSSAs may consider discharging patients from guardianship at any time, but must consider doing so when they receive a report from the patient's nominated medical attendant or responsible clinician renewing their guardianship under section 20 of the Act.

Components of effective guardianship

Care planning

26.19 An application for guardianship should be accompanied by a comprehensive care plan established on the basis of multi-disciplinary discussions in accordance with the Care Programme Approach (or its equivalent).

26.20 The plan should identify the services needed by the patient and who will provide them. It should also indicate which of the powers that guardians have under the Act are necessary to achieve the plan. If none of the powers are required, guardianship should not be used.

26.21 Key elements of the plan are likely to be:

- suitable accommodation to help meet the patient's needs;
- access to day care, education and training facilities, as appropriate;
- effective co-operation and communication between all those concerned in implementing the plan; and
- (if there is to be a private guardian) support from the LSSA for the guardian.

26.22 A private guardian should be prepared to advocate on behalf of the patient in relation to those agencies whose services are needed to carry out the care plan. So should an LSSA which is itself the guardian.

26.23 A private guardian should be a person who can appreciate any special disabilities and needs of a mentally disordered person and who will look after the patient in an appropriate and sympathetic way. The guardian should display an interest in promoting the patient's physical and mental health and in providing for their occupation, training, employment, recreation and general welfare in a suitable way. The LSSA must satisfy itself that a proposed private guardian is capable of carrying out their functions and it should assist them with advice and other forms of support.

26.24 Regulations require private guardians to appoint a doctor as the patient's nominated medical attendant. It is the nominated medical attendant who must examine the patient during the last two months of each period of guardianship and decide whether to make a report extending the patient's guardianship. (Where the patient's guardian is the LSSA itself, this is done by the responsible clinician authorised by the LSSA.)

26.25 It is for private guardians themselves to decide whom to appoint as the nominated medical attendant, but they should first consult the LSSA. The nominated medical attendant may be the patient's GP, if the GP agrees.

Power to require a patient to live in a particular place

26.26 Guardians have the power to decide where patients should live. If patients leave the place where they are required to live without the guardian's permission, they can be taken into legal custody and brought back there (see chapter 22).

26.27 This power can also be used to take patients for the first time to the place they are required to live, if patients do not (or, in practice, cannot) go there by themselves.

26.28 Patients should always be consulted first about where they are to be required to live, unless their mental state makes that impossible. Guardians should not use this power to make a patient move without warning.

26.29 The power to take or return patients to the place they are required to live may be used, for example, to discourage them from:

- living somewhere the guardian considers unsuitable;
- breaking off contact with services;
- leaving the area before proper arrangements can be made; or
- sleeping rough.

But it may not be used to restrict their freedom to come and go so much that they are effectively being detained.

26.30 The power to require patients to reside in a particular place may not be used to require them to live in a situation in which they are deprived of liberty, unless that is authorised separately under the MCA. That authorisation will only be possible if the patient lacks capacity to decide where to live. If deprivation of liberty is authorised under the MCA, the LSSA should consider whether guardianship remains necessary, bearing in mind the guidance earlier in this chapter.

Guardianship and hospital care

26.31 Guardianship does not restrict patients' access to hospital services on an informal basis. Patients who require treatment but do not need to be detained may be admitted informally in the same way as any other patient. This applies to both physical and mental healthcare.

26.32 Nor does guardianship prevent an authorisation being granted under the deprivation of liberty safeguards2 in the MCA, if the person needs to be detained in a hospital in their best interests in order to receive care and treatment, so long as it would not be inconsistent with the guardian's decision about where the patient should live.

26.33 Otherwise, guardianship should not be used to require a patient to reside in a hospital except where it is necessary for a very short time in order to provide shelter while accommodation in the community is being arranged.

26.34 Guardianship can remain in force if the patient is detained in hospital under section 2 or 4 of the Mental Health Act for assessment, but it ends automatically if a patient is detained for treatment as a result of an application under section 3. Regulations also allow a patient to be transferred from guardianship to detention in hospital under section 3. The normal requirements for an application and medical recommendations must be met, and the transfer must be agreed by the LSSA.

Patients who resist the authority of the guardian

26.35 If a patient consistently resists exercise by the guardian of any of their powers, it can normally be concluded that guardianship is not the most appropriate form of care for that person, and the guardianship should be discharged. However, the LSSA should first consider whether a change of guardian – or change in the person who, in practice, exercises the LSSA's powers as guardian – might be appropriate instead.

Guardianship orders under section 37

26.36 Guardianship may be used by courts as an alternative to hospital orders for offenders with mental disorders where the criteria set out in the Act are met. The court must first be satisfied that the LSSA or named person is willing to act as guardian. In considering the appropriateness of the patient being received into their guardianship, LSSAs should be guided by the same considerations as apply to applications for guardianship under Part 2 of the Act.

26.37 The guidance in this chapter on components of effective guardianship applies to guardianship order patients in the same way as it applies to other guardianship patients. The main difference between applications for guardianship under Part 2 of the Act and guardianship orders is that nearest relatives may not discharge patients from guardianship orders. Nearest relatives have rights to apply to the Tribunal instead.

Implications of the Mental Capacity Act 2005

1.27   It is worth briefly considering the interaction between the Mental Capacity Act 2005 and the provisions of MHA 1983. When an application is considered under MHA 1983 it is always appropriate to consider the least restrictive regime for the patient. If a patient lacked capacity, it may be that the Mental Capacity Act 2005 is the more appropriate route. However, much will turn on whether or not it is felt by the professionals involved that it would be preferable that the compulsory aspects of s 7 are appropriate. Those powers of compulsion are contained at s 8 of the MHA 1983 (above) and commented upon in the Code of Practice (MHA 1983). The Mental Capacity Act 2005 may not be used as a way of challenging decisions made by a guardian appointed under MHA 1983. Useful guidance on the distinction between the two jurisdictions are given at paras 13.16–13.21 of the Code of Practice (Mental Capacity Act 2005). However, the Mental Health Act 2007 has extended the ambit of guardianship to anyone who suffers from 'any disorder or disability of mind' and also (via Sch 3, para 3(5)) which 'broadens the power of the guardian by introducing a new power to take and convey a person to their required place of residence under guardianship alongside the power which already exists to return a guardianship patient who has absconded to their place of residence' (see Professor Philip Fennell *Mental Health – The New Law* (Jordan Publishing, 2007) at para 8.19). Together with the developing jurisprudence of the Mental Capacity Act 2005, and in particular the effect of the Deprivation of Liberty Safeguards (which are discussed at greater length in Chapter 2) there is an ongoing debate about certain aspects of the extent to which guardianship can be used. The Code of Practice (MCA 2005) (para 13.16),which has the force of statute, asserts that guardianship cannot be used to deprive someone of their liberty. However, it is at least very arguable that the regime created by an admission to guardianship (as a matter of law and fact) actually *does* deprive an individual of their liberty (power to remove and place elsewhere; power to force residence at a specific place; power to return if the person *'absents'* themselves; power to take the person to a place for purposes of receiving medical treatment. If this interpretation is correct, then the Code of Practice (MCA 2005) does not state accurately the legal position.

Mental Capacity Act 2005 Code of Practice

How does the MCA apply to a patient subject to guardianship under the MHA?

13.16 Guardianship gives someone (usually a local authority social services department) the exclusive right to decide where a person should live – but in doing this they cannot deprive the person of their liberty. The guardian can also require the person to attend for treatment, work, training or education at specific times and places, and they can demand that a doctor, approved social worker or another relevant person have access to the person wherever they live. Guardianship can apply whether or not the person has the capacity to make decisions about care and treatment. It does not give anyone the right to treat the person without their permission or to consent to treatment on their behalf.

13.17 An application can be made for a person who has a mental disorder to be received into guardianship under section 7 of the MHA when:

- the situation meets the conditions summarised in paragraph 13.18,
- the relevant people agree an application for guardianship should be made (normally two doctors and an approved social worker), and
- the person's nearest relative does not object.

13.18 An application can be made in relation to any person who is 16 years or over if:

- they have a mental illness, severe mental impairment, psychopathic disorder or mental impairment that is serious enough to justify guardianship (see paragraph 13.20 below), and
- guardianship is necessary in the interests of the welfare of the patient or to protect other people.

13.19 Applicants (usually approved social workers) and doctors supporting the application will need to determine whether they could achieve their aims without guardianship. For patients who lack capacity, the obvious alternative will be action under the MCA.

13.20 But the fact that the person lacks capacity to make relevant decision is not the only factor that applicants need to consider. They need to consider all the circumstances of the case. They may conclude that guardianship is the best option for a person with a mental disorder who lacks capacity to make those decisions if, for example:

–   they think it is important that one person or authority should be in charge of making decisions about where the person should live (for example, where there have been long-running or difficult disagreements about where the person should live)
–   they think the person will probably respond well to the authority and attention of a guardian, and so be more prepared to accept treatment for the mental disorder (whether they are able to consent to it or it is being provided for them under the MCA), or
–   they need authority to return the person to the place they are to live (for example, a care home) if they were to go absent.

Decision-makers must never consider guardianship as a way to avoid applying the MCA.

13.21 A guardian has the exclusive right to decide where a person lives, so nobody else can use the MCA to arrange for the person to live elsewhere. Somebody who knowingly helps a person leave the place a guardian requires them to stay may be committing a criminal offence under the MHA. A guardian also has the exclusive power to require the person to attend set times and places for treatment, occupation, education or training. This does not stop other people using the MCA to make similar arrangements or to treat the person in their best interests. But people cannot use the MCA in any way that conflicts with decisions which a guardian has a legal right to make under the MHA. See paragraph 13.16 above for general information about a guardian's powers.

Practical aspects

1.28   The format in which an application should be made is self-explanatory. However, the requirement that such an order is required as being necessary for the welfare of the patient is often given less attention by the AMHP and the recommendations of the medical practitioners than it should be, and there may be an inadequate analysis of the needs of the patient in any subsequent care plan provided for the patient.

1.29   Guardianship lasts for 6 months in the first instance, and can be renewed for a further 6 months and then for periods of one year at a time. The Responsible Clinician (RC) must examine the patient within 2 months of the date of expiry of the order. If he is satisfied that the order should continue, then he must report in writing to the local authority (if it is the local authority that has responsibility). Once this is done, there is an automatic renewal of the order (subject to the appropriate forms having been completed (Parts I and II of Form 31)), and unless the local authority decide to discharge the patient. The order itself can be brought to an end in various ways. The most obvious is that the responsible local social services authority can discharge the order. However, the RC also has this power as does the nearest relative. The consequences for a nearest relative in taking such a course of action is likely to be an application to displace them (see **1.54** et seq). All such discharges have to be in writing. Finally, an application for discharge can be made to the First-Tier Tribunal (Health, Education and Social Care Chamber) Mental Health (referred to throughout this book by the shorthand 'Mental Health

Tribunal' or 'Tribunal'). However, there is a type of individual who may have been admitted to guardianship which may in turn have created a situation analogous to that of the 'Bournewood' patient (ie where that individual lacks capacity and never makes an application to the Mental Health Tribunal). In practice, many local authorities have adopted a pragmatic and responsible approach to the problem that exists where a person who lacks capacity and who is subject to a guardianship order. Section 66 of the Act covers Part II patients (in this case, s 7 patients). Section 66(1)(c) deals with those received into guardianship. Section 66(2)(c) states that an application can be made to the Tribunal within 6 months of reception into guardianship or (s 66(2)(f)) within the period beginning with the date upon which authority for guardianship was renewed (by virtue of reports). These applications may be made by the patient. The hospital managers (if relevant) must refer certain types of cases to the Tribunal. This includes those in respect of whom a guardianship order exists, and are transferred to a hospital (s 68(1)(e)) pursuant to regulations made under s 19. The relevant circumstances under which a referral would take place (which are subject to a number of exceptions) all commence once a period of 6 months has expired. Section 68(6) states that a patient shall be referred if a period of more than 3 years has elapsed since a Tribunal considered the matter. If a patient who is subject to a guardianship order is transferred to hospital, they are (of course) still subject to that order unless either admitted pursuant to s 3 of the MHA, or transferred via reg 8 of the Mental Health (Hospital, Guardianship and Treatment) (England) Regulations, SI 2008/1184 (the Regulations). The purpose of the admission would clearly be treatment for a mental disorder. Once such a transfer has taken place, then a right to apply to a Tribunal within six months of the transfer exists (s 66(1)(e), (2)(e)) and if he does not exercise that right, then he must be referred by the hospital managers automatically (s 68(1)). The Secretary of State may refer any patient to a Tribunal, and this includes someone subject to a guardianship order. This is included in the MHA (s 67) and is also set out in the *Reference Guide to the Mental Health Act 1983* (DoH 2008) at para 23.16. There is no other statutory route by which a referral can be made. If a Court has ordered that someone be subject to a guardianship order, then they are subject to Part III of the Act, and s 69 of the Act (in terms of *referrals* and *applications* to the Tribunal). Section 69(b)(i) and (ii) deals with applications that can be made by either the patient or the nearest relative. However, it is most unlikely that this can apply to many (if any patients) and it is therefore probably almost irrelevant. Two months before the date upon which a guardianship order expires, the RC must report to the local authority (if it is the local authority that has responsibility) that an extension of the order is required. An extension of the order is then automatic. Chapter 25 of the Code of Practice (para 26.15) states that it is the responsibility of the LSSA to ensure that patients are aware of their right to apply to a Tribunal, and that they are given the name of someone who will assist them in making such an application.In respect of **references** the *Reference Guide* (paras 23.16–23.19) is of assistance and makes similar observations in particular that LSSA's 'should consider doing so where a patient's rights under the European Convention on Human Rights might be jeopardised'. This is by way of specific reference to s 67 (and the power of the SoS to make a referral).

It is also clearly a reference to Arts 5 and 6 of the ECHR. Thus, where there is an order pursuant to s 7 of the MHA in force, and the subject of the order **is in a hospital**, then the regime as summarised above applies but the responsibility lies with the hospital managers. It is unlikely that there is any difference if the patient has been the subject of an order of the Court via s 37 of the MHA (ie if they are in a hospital). If, however, someone is **not** in a hospital (which will be most, if not all individuals), then the relevant regime for *referrals* is s 67. If a patient is not exercising his right to *apply* to a Tribunal (and neither is his nearest relative) then there is an obligation upon the LSSA to request the SoS to make such a reference. Although there is no specific legislation or regulation which covers **when** this should be done, it would be wise for the LSSA should adopt the regime which exists within the context of a hospital (ie the manner in which Hospital Managers are obliged to make referrals). The reason for this is that if there is no access to a Tribunal then it is certain that Arts 5 and 6 have been breached, and that a quasi *Bournewood* situation then would exist. In all other contexts other than a placement in a hospital, it likely that the LSSA does have a positive responsibility to enable references to be made (via the SoS) and indeed that this is the **only** formal route available.

Inappropriate/anomalous applications

1.30   There have been a number of cases where an application has foundered (due to the avowed intention being at odds with the statutory basis upon which it should have been made, or other incongruities between what is possible pursuant to s 7, and that which a local authority wished to achieve). In *Re F (A Child)* [1999] 2 CCLR 445, [2000] 1 FLR 192 an application was made in respect of a child who had reached her 16th birthday. Had she been below this age, the local authority would have applied for an interim care order (s 38 of the Children Act 1989). The child had expressed a strong wish to return home and the local authority wished to use the power of an order pursuant to s 7 to require her to live elsewhere (s 8(1)(b)). It was held on the facts that the risk posed to the child had been inadequately assessed, and that it had been inapt to try to construe the wishes of the child to return home as being such to amount to seriously irresponsible conduct. It was further held that the effect of the application had been to divert the child into a statutory field where the power lay within the MHRT, and moreover imposed restrictions upon her liberty in an area of jurisdiction that was not child-centred. The better course of action would have been to consider wardship, in which case the Official Solicitor would have been able to represent the interests of the child. There were also seven siblings who were subject to proceedings under the Children Act 1989, and it was more appropriate for one judge to consider the entire family at once. The Court of Appeal cited *Cambridgeshire County Council v R (An Adult)* [1995] 1 FLR 50 with approval thus:

'It is clear, however, from the troubling circumstances of this case that there exists no wholly appropriate legal mechanism for examining whether or not W should be free to make her own decisions in the vital matter of her relationship with her family and if she should not what decisions should be made on her behalf. I share the view expressed by Eastham J in *Re C Mental Patient: Contact* [1993] 1 FLR 940 at 946 that it is a sad state of affairs that the law is unable to provide suitable protection in such a situation. The 1959 Act was thought to have placed all the necessary features of an ancient prerogative jurisdiction on a statutory footing. Cases such as this have proved that judgment wrong and it is to be hoped that parliament will before too long turn its attention to the matter once more.'

The ancient prerogative jurisdiction to which Hale J (as she then was) was referring is of course that of *parens patriae*.

1.31 In *Re an Application by Jennifer Connor for Judicial Review* [2005] 8 CCLR 328, [2004] NICA 45 the disproportionate effect upon a patient subject to a guardianship order was considered. The relevant public authority refused to permit Mrs Connor to live with her husband, or to consider her request. It was held that such a refusal was an interference with her rights under Art 8 of the European Convention on Human Rights, in that such an interference required justification and should be confined to the minimum necessary to secure the objective of protection of Mrs Connor. The outcome was that the decision of the public authority to refuse to accede to the request to live with her husband was quashed.

1.32 In *JE v (1) DE (by his litigation friend the Official Solicitor) (2) Surrey County Council* [2006] EWHC 3459 (Fam), [2007] 10 CCLR 149, [2007] MHLR 39 an adult disabled man (who was declared to lack capacity on an interim basis) was held to have been deprived of his liberty, having been accommodated in residential care as a matter of necessity. It is unclear why s 7 was not used, although presumably if the criteria were not felt to be met, then the apparent difficulty in the case could now be resolved by the use of the Mental Capacity Act 2005.

New terms under the Mental Health Act 2007

1.33 Some new terminology is introduced to replace the older forms with which practitioners have become familiar and these have been referred to already. An approved social worker has become 'an approved mental health professional'. These are defined as 'A Social worker or other professional approved by a local social services authority (LSSA) to act upon behalf of an LSSA in carrying out a variety of functions under the Act' (Annex A – Code of Practice for MHA 1983). A Responsible Medical Officer (RMO) is now called a *'responsible clinician'* which is defined in Annex A as:

> 'the approved clinician with overall responsibility for a patient's case. Certain decisions (such as renewing a patient's detention or placing a patient on supervised community treatment) can only be taken by the responsible clinician).'

Powers conferred as a result of guardianship order

1.34 There is an explicit power to enable a local authority to remove a patient from his home (if it is necessary for this to happen) in order to impose upon him the requirement of residence. Once so placed, if the subject of the guardianship order leaves without the consent of the guardian, he may be taken into custody and returned (s 18(4)). At **1.26**, reference was made to the effect of s 8 of the MHA 1983, to the effect that once an order is in place it confers upon the guardian 'to the exclusion of any other person' decisions on a number of matters (the most significant of which is the issue of where the individual shall live). This section, and the interrelationship that guardianship has with the jurisdiction of the Court of Protection, has been considered in *C v Blackburn with Darwen Borough Council & A Care Home & Blackburn with Darwen Teaching Care Trust* [2011] EWHC 3321 (COP). It was argued on behalf of C that the word 'person' could not extend to preventing a judge of the Court of Protection deciding where an individual should live, where that issue was before the Court, and P was also subject to an order pursuant to s 7 of the MHA 1983. The Local Authority and the Trust argued that: (a) in the particular circumstances of the case C was not deprived of his liberty (there being a secondary issue as to whether he either could be, or needed to be, subject to a standard authorisation via 'DOLS') and was also ineligible for this scheme; and (b) that s 8 prevents any Court from exercising a juridiction that would have the effect of emasculating the MHA 1983. In respect of the matter of s 8, and its legal effect, Mr Justice Peter Jackson relied upon *GJ v The Foundation Trust & Ors* to the effect that in general the MHA 1983, where it applies, has primacy over the MCA. He also held, at [34] and [35] that:

'there are good reasons why the provisions of the MHA should prevail where they apply. It is a self-contained system with inbuilt checks and balances and it is well understood by professionals working in that field. It is cheaper than the Court of Protection.'

However, it is important to note the following caveat:

'[37] On the other hand, it is not in my view appropriate for genuinely contested issues about the place of residence of a resisting incapacitated person to be determined either under the guardianship regime or by means of a standard authorisation under the DOLS regime. Substantial decisions of that kind ought properly to be made by the Court of Protection, using its power to make welfare decisions under section 16 MCA.'

In other words, local authorities may well conclude that in cases where there is a dispute about residence, and as to whether that is in the best interests of P or not, the correct court within which to determine that point (assuming a lack of capacity) is not by using ss 7 and 8 at all, but by way of an application to the Court of Protection instead.

9 Regulations as to guardianship

(1) Subject to the provisions of this Part of this Act, the Secretary of State may make regulations –

    (a)   for regulating the exercise by the guardians of patients received into guardianship under this Part of this Act of their powers as such; and

(b)   for imposing on such guardians, and upon local social services authorities in the case of patients under the guardianship of persons other than local social services authorities, such duties as he considers necessary or expedient in the interests of the patients.

(2) Regulations under this section may in particular make provision for requiring the patients to be visited, on such occasions or at such intervals as may be prescribed by the regulations, on behalf of such local social services authorities as may be so prescribed, and shall provide for the appointment, in the case of every patient subject to the guardianship of a person other than a local social services authority, of a registered medical practitioner to act as the nominated medical attendant of the patient.

10 Transfer of guardianship in case of death, incapacity, etc of guardian

(1) If any person (other than a local social services authority) who is the guardian of a patient received into guardianship under this Part of this Act –

(a)   dies; or
(b)   gives notice in writing to the local social services authority that he desires to relinquish the functions of guardian,

the guardianship of the patient shall thereupon vest in the local social services authority, but without prejudice to any power to transfer the patient into the guardianship of another person in pursuance of regulations under section 19 below.

(2) If any such person, not having given notice under subsection (1)(b) above, is incapacitated by illness or any other cause from performing the functions of guardian of the patient, those functions may, during his incapacity, be performed on his behalf by the local social services authority or by any other person approved for the purposes by that authority.

(3) If it appears to the county court, upon application made by an approved mental health professional acting on behalf of the local social services authority, that any person other than a local social services authority having the guardianship of a patient received into guardianship under this Part of this Act has performed his functions negligently or in a manner contrary to the interests of the welfare of the patient, the court may order that the guardianship of the patient be transferred to the local social services authority or to any other person approved for the purpose by that authority.

(4) Where the guardianship of a patient is transferred to a local social services authority or other person by or under this section, subsection (2)(c) of section 19 below shall apply as if the patient had been transferred into the guardianship of that authority or person in pursuance of regulations under that section.

(5) In this section "the local social services authority", in relation to a person (other than a local social services authority) who is the guardian of a patient, means the local social services authority for the area in which that person resides (or resided immediately before his death).

Manner in which guardianship may be altered

1.35   Although in the majority of cases it will be the local authority who are responsible for the guardianship order, in some circumstances this is not the case. If so, and if it is no longer possible or appropriate for the existing guardian to continue, the above provisions apply. As soon as the pre-conditions at s 10(1)(a) and (b) apply, then the guardianship vests in the local social services authority. There is no mention of residence in this part of the statute, but the concepts of ordinary residence as set out elsewhere are likely to apply if there is a dispute over which local authority will be responsible. Once the application has been accepted by a local authority, then it will become the responsible social services authority. Even if no notice pursuant to s 10(1)(b) has been given, then either the local authority or any other person approved by the authority may be (temporarily) taken over by that local authority or person. Section 10(3) is an interesting alternative to an application to displace a nearest relative (if the nearest relative happens to be the person in whom the guardianship order is vested). It permits the Court to order that the guardianship order itself is transferred to the local social services authority (or any other person approved for that purpose by the authority) where the functions of the guardian have been performed negligently or contrary to the interests of the patient. It seems likely that whatever the mechanism used, the criteria for displacing the nearest relative and the case-law on those applications would be relevant, if not determinative.

11 General provisions as to applications

(1) Subject to the provisions of this section, an application for admission for assessment, an application for admission for treatment and a guardianship application may be made either by the nearest relative of the patient or by an approved mental health professional; and every such application shall specify the qualification of the applicant to make the application.

(1A) No application mentioned in subsection (1) above shall be made by an approved mental health professional if the circumstances are such that there would be a potential conflict of interest for the purposes of regulations under section 12A below.

(2) Every application for admission shall be addressed to the managers of the hospital to which admission is sought and every guardianship application shall be forwarded to the local social services authority named in the application as guardian, or, as the case may be, to the local social services authority for the area in which the person so named resides.

(3) Before or within a reasonable time after an application for the admission of a patient for assessment is made by an approved mental health professional, that professional shall take such steps as are practicable to inform the person (if any) appearing to be the nearest relative of the patient that the application is to be or has been made and of the power of the nearest relative under section 23(2)(a) below.

(4) An approved mental health professional may not make an application for admission for treatment or a guardianship application in respect of a patient in either of the following cases –

    (a)   the nearest relative of the patient has notified that professional, or the local social services authority on whose behalf the professional is acting, that he objects to the application being made; or

    (b)   that professional has not consulted the person (if any) appearing to be
the nearest relative of the patient, but the requirement to consult that
person does not apply if it appears to the professional that in the
circumstances such consultation is not reasonably practicable or would
involve unreasonable delay.

(5) None of the applications mentioned in subsection (1) above shall be made by
any person in respect of a patient unless that person has personally seen the
patient within the period of 14 days ending with the date of the application.

(6) ...

(7) Each of the applications mentioned in subsection (1) above shall be sufficient
if the recommendations on which it is founded are given either as separate
recommendations, each signed by a registered medical practitioner, or as a joint
recommendation signed by two such practitioners.

The nearest relative and guardianship

1.36 Section 11(1) means that a nearest relative can make an application for
guardianship. There may be circumstances where this method is to be preferred
by the family of the patient, or where a local authority is proving dilatory.
Similarly, there may be circumstances in which those who are not the nearest
relative (but who are members of the family, or others) may have concerns
about the probity of the *de jure* nearest relative achieving the degree of control
over the patient which a guardianship order confers. The nearest relative can
also make a request that the authority consider whether a guardianship order is
appropriate, and if a decision is made not to make such an application, it shall
notify the nearest relative of the reasons for not making such an application in
writing (s 13(4)). If the nearest relative does make an application, and the
patient is admitted as a result, then the managers of the hospital are in any
event obliged to give notice of that fact to the local social services authority for
the area in which the patient resided immediately before his admission (s 14).
The significance of this section is twofold. First, a local authority will be
notified of (and involved in) all guardianship orders to a greater or lesser
degree. Secondly, the provision as to the relevant responsible local authority
mirrors the provision as to residence (and therefore the case-law upon the
point) should there be any argument on this aspect. If it is the local authority
that makes the application, then the nearest relative still retains considerable
power (s 23(2)(a) and (b)). In any event, there is a prohibition upon such
application being made if the nearest relative has notified the social worker
who has recommended that such an order should be made that he objects to
such an application. There is also a requirement that whomsoever makes the
application must have seen the patient personally within 14 days ending with
the date of the application. The provision for personal examination also applies
to the medical recommendations (albeit with different timescales) (s 12(1)). A
nearest relative does have a statutory right to apply to a Tribunal for the
discharge of the patient (s 69(1)(b)(ii)), and if displaced can also apply on his
own behalf once within every 12-month period after a court order replacing
him (ss 29(6), 66(1)(h) and (i) and (2)(g)).

12 General provisions as to medical recommendations

(1) The recommendations required for the purposes of an application for the admission of a patient under this Part of this Act or a guardianship application (in this Act referred to as "medical recommendations") shall be signed on or before the date of the application, and shall be given by practitioners who have personally examined the patient either together or separately, but where they have examined the patient separately not more than five days must have elapsed between the days on which the separate examinations took place.

(2) Of the medical recommendations given for the purposes of any such application, one shall be given by a practitioner approved for the purposes of this section by the Secretary of State as having special experience in the diagnosis or treatment of mental disorder; and unless that practitioner has previous acquaintance with the patient, the other such recommendation shall, if practicable, be given by a registered medical practitioner who has such previous acquaintance.

(2A) A registered medical practitioner who is an approved clinician shall be treated as also approved for the purposes of this section under subsection (2) above as having special experience as mentioned there.

(3) No medical recommendation shall be given for the purposes of an application mentioned in subsection (1) above if the circumstances are such that there would be a potential conflict of interest for the purposes of regulations under section 12A below.

12A Conflicts of interest

(1) The appropriate national authority may make regulations as to the circumstances in which there would be a potential conflict of interest such that –

    (a)   an approved mental health professional shall not make an application mentioned in section 11(1) above;

    (b)   a registered medical practitioner shall not give a recommendation for the purposes of an application mentioned in section 12(1) above.

(2) Regulations under subsection (1) above may make –

    (a)   provision for the prohibitions in paragraphs (a) and (b) of that subsection to be subject to specified exceptions;

    (b)   different provision for different cases; and

    (c)   transitional, consequential, incidental or supplemental provision.

(3) In subsection (1) above, "the appropriate national authority" means –

    (a)   in relation to applications in which admission is sought to a hospital in England or to guardianship applications in respect of which the area of the relevant local social services authority is in England, the Secretary of State;

    (b)   in relation to applications in which admission is sought to a hospital in Wales or to guardianship applications in respect of which the area of the relevant local social services authority is in Wales, the Welsh Ministers.

(4) References in this section to the relevant local social services authority, in relation to a guardianship application, are references to the local social services

authority named in the application as guardian or (as the case may be) the local social services authority for the area in which the person so named resides.

13 Duty of approved mental health professionals to make applications for admission or guardianship

(1) If a local social services authority have reason to think that an application for admission to hospital or a guardianship application may need to be made in respect of a patient within their area, they shall make arrangements for an approved mental health professional to consider the patient's case on their behalf.

(1A) If that professional is –

(a)   satisfied that such an application ought to be made in respect of the patient; and

(b)   of the opinion, having regard to any wishes expressed by relatives of the patient or any other relevant circumstances, that it is necessary or proper for the application to be made by him,

he shall make the application.

(1B) Subsection (1C) below applies where –

(a)   a local social services authority makes arrangements under subsection (1) above in respect of a patient;

(b)   an application for admission for assessment is made under subsection (1A) above in respect of the patient;

(c)   while the patient is liable to be detained in pursuance of that application, the authority have reason to think that an application for admission for treatment may need to be made in respect of the patient; and

(d)   the patient is not within the area of the authority.

(1C) Where this subsection applies, subsection (1) above shall be construed as requiring the authority to make arrangements under that subsection in place of the authority mentioned there.

(2) Before making an application for the admission of a patient to hospital an approved mental health professional shall interview the patient in a suitable manner and satisfy himself that detention in a hospital is in all the circumstances of the case the most appropriate way of providing the care and medical treatment of which the patient stands in need.

(3) An application under subsection (1A) above may be made outside the area of the local social services authority on whose behalf the approved mental health professional is considering the patient's case.

(4) It shall be the duty of a local social services authority, if so required by the nearest relative of a patient residing in their area, to make arrangements under subsection (1) above for an approved mental health professional to consider the patient's case with a view to making an application for his admission to hospital; and if in any such case that professional decides not to make an application he shall inform the nearest relative of his reasons in writing.

(5) Nothing in this section shall be construed as authorising or requiring an application to be made by an approved mental health professional in contravention of the provisions of section 11(4) above or of regulations under

section 12A above, or as restricting the power of a local social services authority to make arrangements with an approved mental health professional to consider a patient's case or of an approved mental health professional to make any application under this Act.

14 Social reports

Where a patient is admitted to a hospital in pursuance of an application (other than an emergency application) made under this Part of this Act by his nearest relative, the managers of the hospital shall as soon as practicable give notice of that fact to the local social services authority for the area in which the patient resided immediately before his admission; and that authority shall as soon as practicable arrange for an approved mental health professional ... to interview the patient and provide the managers with a report on his social circumstances.

23 Discharge of Patients

(1) Subject to the provision of this section and Section 25 below, a patient who is for the time being liable to be detained or subject to guardianship under this Part of this Act shall cease to be so liable or subject if an order in writing discharging him absolutely from detention or guardianship is made in accordance with this section.

(1A) Subject to the provisions of this section and section 25 below, a community patient shall cease to be liable to recall under this Part of this Act, and the application for admission for treatment cease to have effect, if an order in writing discharging him from such liability is made in accordance with this section.

(1B) An order under subsection (1) or (1A) above shall be referred to in this Act as "an order for discharge".

(2) An order for discharge may be made in respect of a patient –

    (a)   where the patient is liable to be detained in a hospital in pursuance of an application for admission for assessment or for treatment by the responsible clinician, by the managers or by the nearest relative of the patient;

    (b)   where the patient is subject to guardianship, by the responsible clinician, by the responsible local social services authority or by the nearest relative of the patient;

    (c)   where the patient is a community patient, by the responsible clinician, by the managers of the responsible hospital or by the nearest relative of the patient.

(3) Where the patient falls within subsection (3A) below, an order for his discharge may, without prejudice to subsection (2) above, be made by the Secretary of State and, if arrangements have been made in respect of the patient under a contract with a National Health Service trust, NHS foundation trust, Local Health Board, Special Health Authority or Primary Care Trust, by that National Health Service trust, NHS foundation trust, Local Health Board, Special Health Authority or Primary Care Trust.

(3A) A patient falls within this subsection if –

    (a)   he is liable to be detained in a registered establishment in pursuance of an application for admission for assessment or for treatment; or

(b)   he is a community patient and the responsible hospital is a registered establishment.

(4) The powers conferred by this section on any authority trust, board (other than an NHS foundation trust), board or body of persons may be exercised subject to subsection (3) below by any three or more members of that authority trust, board or body authorised by them in that behalf or by three or more members of a committee or sub-committee of that authority trust, board or body which has been authorised by them in that behalf.

(5) The reference in subsection (4) above to the members of an authority, trust, board or body or the members of a committee or sub-committee of an authority, trust, board or body –

(a)   in the case of a Local Health Board, Special Health Authority or Primary Care Trust or a committee or sub-committee of a Local Health Board, Special Health Authority or Primary Care Trust, is a reference only to the chairman of the authority, trust or board and such members (of the authority, trust, board, committee or sub-committee, as the case may be) as are not also officers of the authority, trust or board within the meaning of the National Health Service Act 2006 or the National Health Service (Wales) Act 2006; and

(b)   in the case of a National Health Service trust or a committee or sub-committee of such a trust, is a reference only to the chairman of the trust and such directors or (in the case of a committee or sub-committee) members as are not also employees of the trust.

(6) The powers conferred by this section on any NHS foundation trust may be exercised by any three or more persons authorised by the board of the trust in that behalf each of whom is neither an executive director of the board nor an employee of the trust.

24 Visiting and examination of patients

(1) For the purpose of advising as to the exercise by the nearest relative of a patient who is liable to be detained or subject to guardianship under this Part of this Act , or who is a community patient, of any power to order his discharge, any registered medical practitioner or approved clinician authorised by or on behalf of the nearest relative of the patient may, at any reasonable time, visit the patient and examine him in private.

(2) Any registered medical practitioneror approved clinician authorised for the purposes of subsection (1) above to visit and examine a patient may require the production of and inspect any records relating to the detention or treatment of the patient in any hospital or to any after-care services provided for the patient under section 117 below.

(3) Where application is made by the Secretary of State or a Local Health Board, Special Health Authority, Primary Care Trust, National Health Service trust or NHS foundation trust to exercise any power under section 23(3) above to make an order for a patient's discharge, the following persons, that is to say –

(a)   any registered medical practitioner or approved clinician authorised by the Secretary of State or, as the case may be, that Local Health Board, Special Health Authority, Primary Care Trust, National Health Service trust or NHS foundation trust; and

(b)   any other person (whether a registered medical practitioner or approved clinician or not) authorised under Part II of the Care Standards Act 2000 to inspect the establishment in question;

may at any reasonable time visit the patient and interview him in private.

(4) Any person authorised for the purposes of subsection (3) above to visit a patient may require the production of and inspect any documents constituting or alleged to constitute the authority for the detention of the patient, or (as the case may be) for his liability to recall, under this Part of this Act; and any person so authorised, who is a registered medical practitioner or approved clinician, may examine the patient in private, and may require the production of and inspect any other records relating to the treatment of the patient in the establishment or to any after-care services provided for the patient under section 117 below.

Discharge of guardianship by nearest relative

1.37   The nearest relative may discharge the patient from the order for guardianship (and s 25(1) below has *no* effect upon this right). There is no equivalent 'barring order' in respect of the discharge of a patient subject to guardianship. In other words, there exists no statutory power to block the use of s 23(2)(a) or (b) in respect of guardianship. Once discharged, the patient will remain so until another order is made. However, before that happened, the normal course that would be taken by a local authority would be to make an application to displace him as nearest relative. As Hale LJJ (as she then was) observed in *R (on the Application of Stevens) v Plymouth City Council (C as Interested Party)* [2002] EWCA Civ 388, [2002] 1 FLR 1177:

'Any sensible nearest relative who was unhappy about the decisions made by the professionals would wish to seek such advice rather than rush to discharge the patient, thus placing at possible risk not only the patient's welfare but also her own status as nearest relative.'

25 Restrictions on discharge by nearest relative

(1) An order for the discharge of a patient who is liable to be detained in a hospital shall not be made under section 23 above by his nearest relative except after giving not less that 72 hours notice in writing to the managers of the hospital; and if, within 72 hours after such notice has been given, the responsible clinician furnishes to the managers a report certifying that in the opinion of that clinician the patient, if discharged, would be likely to act in a manner dangerous to other persons or to himself –

(a)   any order for the discharge of the patient made by that relative in pursuance of the notice shall be of no effect; and

(b)   no further order for the discharge of the patient shall be made by that relative during the period of six months beginning with the date of the report.

(1A) Subsection (1) above shall apply to an order for the discharge of a community patient as it applies to an order for the discharge of a patient who is liable to be detained in a hospital, but with the reference to the managers of the hospital being read as a reference to the managers of the responsible hospital.

(2) In any case where a report under sub-section (1) above is furnished in respect of a patient who is liable to be detained in pursuance of an application for admission for treatment , or in respect of a community patient, the managers shall cause the nearest relative of the patient to be informed.

32 Regulations for purposes of Part II

(1) The Secretary of State may make regulations for prescribing anything which, under this Part of this Act, is required or authorised to be prescribed, and otherwise for carrying this Part of this Act into full effect.

(2) Regulations under this section may in particular make provision –

   (a)   for prescribing the form of any application, recommendation, report, order, notice or other document to be made or given under this Part of this Act;
   (b)   for prescribing the manner in which any such application, recommendation, report, order, notice or other document may be proved, and for regulating the service of any such application, report, order or notice;
   (c)   for requiring such bodies as may be prescribed by the regulations to keep such registers or other records as may be so prescribed in respect of patients liable to be detained or subject to guardianship under this Part of this Act or community patients, and to furnish or make available to those patients, and their relatives, such written statements of their rights and powers under this Act as may be so prescribed;
   (d)   for the determination in accordance with the regulations of the age of any person whose exact age cannot be ascertained by reference to the registers kept under the Births and Deaths Registration Act 1953; and
   (e)   for enabling the functions under this Part of this Act of the nearest relative of a patient to be performed, in such circumstances and subject to such conditions (if any) as may be prescribed by the regulations, by any person authorised in that behalf by that relative;

and for the purposes of this Part of this Act any application, report or notice the service of which is regulated under paragraph (b) above shall be deemed to have been received by or furnished to the authority or person to whom it is authorised or required to be furnished, addressed or given if it is duly served in accordance with the regulations.

(3) Without prejudice to subsections (1) and (2) above, but subject to section 23(4) and (6) above, regulations under this section may determine the manner in which functions under this Part of this Act of the managers of hospitals, local social services authorities, Local Health Board, Special Health Authorities, Primary Care Trusts, National Health Service trusts or NHS foundation trusts are to be exercised, and such regulations may in particular specify the circumstances in which, and the conditions subject to which, any such functions may be performed by officers of or other persons acting on behalf of those managers, boards, authorities and trusts.

37 Powers of courts to order hospital admission or guardianship

(1) Where a person is convicted before the Crown Court of an offence punishable with imprisonment other than an offence the sentence for which is fixed by law or is convicted by a magistrates' court of an offence punishable on summary conviction with imprisonment, and the conditions mentioned in subsection (2)

below are satisfied, the court may by order authorise his admission to and detention in such hospital as may be specified in the order or, as the case may be, place him under the guardianship of a local social services authority or of such other person approved by a local social services authority as may be so specified.

(1A) In the case of an offence the sentence for which would otherwise fall to be imposed –

(a)   under section 51A(2) of the Firearms Act 1968,

(b)   under section 110(2) or 111(2) of the Powers of Criminal Courts (Sentencing) Act 2000,

(c)   under any of sections 225 to 228 of the Criminal Justice Act 2003, or

(d)   under section 29(4) or (6) of the Violent Crime Reduction Act 2006 (minimum sentences in certain cases of using someone to mind a weapon),

nothing in those provisions shall prevent a court from making an order under subsection (1) above for the admission of the offender to a hospital.

(1B) References in subsection (1A) above to a sentence falling to be imposed under any of the provisions mentioned in that subsection are to be read in accordance with section 305(4) of the Criminal Justice Act 2003.

(2) The conditions referred to in subsection (1) above are that –

(a)   the court is satisfied, on the written or oral evidence of two registered medical practitioners, that the offender is suffering from mental disorder and that either –

(i)   the mental disorder from which the offender is suffering is of a nature or degree which makes it appropriate for him to be detained in a hospital for medical treatment and, appropriate medical treatment is available for him; or

(ii)   in the case of an offender who has attained the age of 16 years, the mental disorder is of a nature or degree which warrants his reception into guardianship under this Act; and

(b)   the court is of the opinion, having regard to all the circumstances including the nature of the offence and the character and antecedents of the offender, and to the other available methods of dealing with him, that the most suitable method of disposing of the case is by means of an order under this section.

(3) Where a person is charged before a magistrates' court with any act or omission as an offence and the court would have power, on convicting him of that offence, to make an order under subsection (1) above in his case then, if the court is satisfied that the accused did the act or made the omission charged, the court may, if it thinks fit, make such an order without convicting him.

(4) An order for the admission of an offender to a hospital (in this Act referred to as "a hospital order") shall not be made under this section unless the court is satisfied on the written or oral evidence of the approved clinician who would have overall responsibility for his case or of some other person representing the managers of the hospital that arrangements have been made for his admission to that hospital ... and for his admission to it within the period of 28 days beginning with the date of the making of such an order; and the court may, pending his admission within that period, give such directions as it thinks fit for his conveyance to and detention in a place of safety.

(5) If within the said period of 28 days it appears to the Secretary of State that by reason of an emergency or other special circumstances it is not practicable for the patient to be received into the hospital specified in the order, he may give directions for the admission of the patient to such other hospital as appears to be appropriate instead of the hospital so specified; and where such directions are given –

    (a)   the Secretary of State shall cause the person having the custody of the patient to be informed, and

    (b)   the hospital order shall have effect as if the hospital specified in the directions were substituted for the hospital specified in the order.

(6) An order placing an offender under the guardianship of a local social services authority or of any other person (in this Act referred to as "a guardianship order") shall not be made under this section unless the court is satisfied that that authority or person is willing to receive the offender into guardianship.

(7) ...

(8) Where an order is made under this section, the court shall not –

    (a)   pass sentence of imprisonment or impose a fine or make a community order (within the meaning of Part 12 of the Criminal Justice Act 2003) in respect of the offence,

    (b)   if the order under this section is a hospital order, make a referral order (within the meaning of the Powers of Criminal Courts (Sentencing) Act 2000) in respect of the offence, or

    (c)   make in respect of the offender a supervision order (within the meaning of that Act) or an order under section 150 of that Act (binding over of parent or guardian),

but the court may make any other order which it has power to make apart from this section; and for the purposes of this subsection "sentence of imprisonment" includes any sentence or order for detention.

Orders of Court in respect of guardianship

1.38 An order of the Court (a 'hospital order') can also be made, without an application having been made by anybody. This may be to a local authority, or such other person approved by a local authority. The evidential pre-conditions are identical to other hospital orders save for s 37(2)(ii) which specifically refers to guardianship orders as being appropriate where the mental disorder is of a nature or degree which warrants reception into guardianship. An order cannot be made unless the local authority or approved person is willing to receive the patient into guardianship, and the Court must be satisfied that such is the case before the order can be made.

39A Information to facilitate guardianship orders

Where a court is minded to make a guardianship order in respect of any offender, it may request the local social services authority for the area in which the offender resides or last resided, or any other local social services authority that appears to the court to be appropriate –

(a)   to inform the court whether it or any other person approved by it is willing to receive the offender into guardianship; and

(b)   if so, to give such information as it reasonably can about how it or the other person could be expected to exercise in relation to the offender the powers conferred by section 40(2) below;

and that authority shall comply with any such request.

Responsibility for providing information

1.39   If the Court is considering making an order for guardianship, then it may request the local social services authority for the area in which the offender either resides, or last resided *or any other local social services that appears to the court to be appropriate* to inform the Court of those matters set out at s 39A below. In respect of the italicised words above, this provides the Court with apparent discretion to override any considerations of ordinary residence in considering which local authority should be responsible for providing information (but not which local authority would be responsible for the order itself).

40 Effect of hospital orders, guardianship orders and interim hospital orders

(1) A hospital order shall be sufficient authority –

(a)   for a constable, an approved mental health professional or any other person directed to do so by the court to convey the patient to the hospital specified in the order within a period of 28 days; and

(b)   for the managers of the hospital to admit him at any time within that period and thereafter detain him in accordance with the provisions of this Act.

(2) A guardianship order shall confer on the authority or person named in the order as guardian the same powers as a guardianship application made and accepted under Part II of this Act.

(3) Where an interim hospital order is made in respect of an offender –

(a)   a constable or any other person directed to do so by the court shall convey the offender to the hospital specified in the order within the period mentioned in section 38(4) above; and

(b)   the managers of the hospital shall admit him within that period and thereafter detain him in accordance with the provisions of section 38 above.

(4) A patient who is admitted to a hospital in pursuance of a hospital order, or placed under guardianship by a guardianship order, shall, subject to the provisions of this subsection, be treated for the purposes of the provisions of this Act mentioned in Part I of Schedule 1 to this Act as if he had been so admitted or placed on the date of the order in pursuance of an application for admission for treatment or a guardianship application, as the case may be, duly made under Part II of this Act, but subject to any modifications of those provisions specified in that Part of that Schedule.

(5) Where a patient is admitted to a hospital in pursuance of a hospital order, or placed under guardianship by a guardianship order, any previous application,

hospital order or guardianship order by virtue of which he was liable to be detained in a hospital or subject to guardianship shall cease to have effect; but if the first-mentioned order, or the conviction on which it was made, is quashed on appeal, this subsection shall not apply and section 22 above shall have effect as if during any period for which the patient was liable to be detained or subject to guardianship under the order, he had been detained in custody as mentioned in that section.

(6) Where –

- (a) a patient admitted to a hospital in pursuance of a hospital order is absent without leave;
- (b) a warrant to arrest him has been issued under section 72 of the Criminal Justice Act 1967; and
- (c) he is held pursuant to the warrant in any country or territory other than the United Kingdom, any of the Channel Islands and the Isle of Man,

he shall be treated as having been taken into custody under section 18 above on first being so held.

56 Patients to whom Part 4 applies

(1) Section 57 and, so far as relevant to that section, sections 59 to 62 below apply to any patient.

(2) Subject to that and to subsection (5) below, this Part of this Act applies to a patient only if he falls within subsection (3) or (4) below.

(3) A patient falls within this subsection if he is liable to be detained under this Act but not if –

- (a) he is so liable by virtue of an emergency application and the second medical recommendation referred to in section 4(4)(a) above has not been given and received;
- (b) he is so liable by virtue of section 5(2) or (4) or 35 above or section 135 or 136 below or by virtue of a direction for his detention in a place of safety under section 37(4) or 45A(5) above; or
- (c) he has been conditionally discharged under section 42(2) above or section 73 or 74 below and he is not recalled to hospital.

(4) A patient falls within this subsection if –

- (a) he is a community patient; and
- (b) he is recalled to hospital under section 17E above.

(5) Section 58A and, so far as relevant to that section, sections 59 to 62 below also apply to any patient who –

- (a) does not fall within subsection (3) above;
- (b) is not a community patient; and
- (c) has not attained the age of 18 years.

Guardianship and consent to treatment

1.40 A patient who is subject to an order pursuant to s 7 is not liable to be detained, and therefore he will not come within the scope of this part of MHA 1983.

The role and function of 'nearest relative'

1.41 The role of the nearest relative is extensive and significant. That role has been the subject of some modification where there has been a conflict between the powers of the nearest relative, and the rights of the patient. The Code of Practice (MHA 1983) referred to above includes (for the first time) extensive guidance as to the role of the nearest relative (in Chapter 8) and it stresses the need for practitioners to be aware of the significance of the nearest relative. However, the involvement of the nearest relative remains great, and its main implications are as follows:

(a)   the nearest relative may make an application for admission for assessment (s 2);

(b)   he may make an application for an emergency admission for assessment (s 4);

(c)   he may make an application for admission for treatment (s 3) or for guardianship (ss 7 and 11(1));

(d)   an AMHP is required to consult with the nearest relative prior to making an application either for admission pursuant to s 3 or s 7 unless the social worker considers that such consultation is not reasonably practicable or would involve unreasonable delay (s 11(4));

(e)   the managers of a hospital in which the patient is detained are obliged to inform the nearest relative on the right to apply to a Mental Health Tribunal, the right to be discharged, the right to receive and send correspondence and the right to consent to or refuse treatment (s 132(4));

(f)   the nearest relative can order the discharge of a patient who is detained under either s 3 or s 7 (s 23(3));

(g)   the nearest relative can arrange an assessment of the patient by a doctor, who can in turn require the production of the medical records of the patient (s 24);

(h)   where a patient is to be discharged (other than by the nearest relative), the detaining authority is required to notify the nearest relative of this. The only way in which the patient can prevent this is by making a request that no such information is supplied (s 133(2));

(i)   the nearest relative can make an application for a local authority to consider making an application into hospital or guardianship (s 13(4));

(j)   he may make an application to a Mental Health Tribunal for the discharge of the patient (s 66(g) and (h));

(k)   he is entitled to be informed of the progress of the Tribunal, be represented at the hearing, and take such part in proceedings as the Tribunal thinks proper;

(l)   he is entitled to receive a copy of the decision and the reasons for the decision;

(m) if he has made an application for discharge he can appoint a doctor to examine the patient, and the records in respect of detention (s 76(1));

(n)   if he is the applicant, he can attend the hearing, call witnesses and cross-examine witnesses;

(o)   if he is an applicant, he should receive all the documentation that the Tribunal receives.

(p)   the nearest relative can seek to discharge a CTO (s 23).

For a full consideration of the law in respect of the nearest relative, the reader is directed to *The Nearest Relative Handbook* (D Hewitt, 2009, 2nd Edition, Jessica Kinsgley).

If a patient has been remanded to hospital under MHA 1983 s 35, 36 or 38 there is no nearest relative for the purposes of the MHA 1983. If a patient is a restricted patient, or conditionally discharged, then there is no nearest relative. However, if a patient is the subject of an unrestricted hospital order, or hospital directions to which limitation directions do not apply, or unrestricted transfer directions, then the patient will have a nearest relative.

Mental Health Act 1983 Code of Practice

CHAPTER 8

The nearest relative

8.1 This chapter gives guidance on the identification, appointment and displacement of nearest relatives under the Act.

Identification of the nearest relative

8.2 Section 26 of the Act defines "relative" and "nearest relative" for the purposes of the Act. It is important to remember that the nearest relative for the purposes of the Act may not be the same person as the patient's next of kin. The identity of the nearest relative may also change with the passage of time (eg if the patient enters into a marriage or civil partnership). (See paragraphs 4.56–4.65.)

8.3 Patients remanded to hospital under sections 35 and 36 of the Act and people subject to interim hospital orders under section 38 do not have nearest relatives (as defined by the Act). Nor do patients subject to special restrictions under Part 3 of the Act (restricted patients).

Delegation of nearest relative functions

8.4 A nearest relative is not obliged to act as such. They can authorise, in writing, another person to perform the functions of the nearest relative on their behalf. The procedure for doing this is set out in the Mental Health (Hospital, Guardianship and Treatment) (England) Regulations 2008.

Where there is no nearest relative

8.5 Where an approved mental health professional (AMHP) discovers, when assessing a patient for possible detention or guardianship under the Act (or at any other time), that the patient appears to have no nearest relative, the AMHP should advise the patient of their right to apply to the county court for the appointment of a person to act as their nearest relative.

Displacement of nearest relatives and appointment ofacting nearest relatives by the county court

Grounds for displacement and appointment

8.6 An acting nearest relative can be appointed by the county court on the grounds that:

- the nearest relative is incapable of acting as such because of illness or mental disorder;
- the nearest relative has objected unreasonably to an application for admission for treatment or a guardianship application;
- the nearest relative has exercised the power to discharge a patient without due regard to the patient's health or wellbeing or the safety of the public;
- the nearest relative is otherwise not a suitable person to act as such; or
- the patient has no nearest relative within the meaning of the Act, or it is not reasonably practicable to ascertain whether the patient has a nearest relative or who that nearest relative is.

8.7 The effect of a court order appointing an acting nearest relative is to displace the person who would otherwise be the patient's nearest relative.

8.8 However, as an alternative to an order by the court, it may sometimes be enough for the actual nearest relative to delegate their role to someone else (see paragraph 8.4).

Who can make an application to the court?

8.9 An application to displace the nearest relative may be made by any of the following people:

- the patient;
- any relative of the patient;
- anyone with whom the patient is residing (or was residing prior to admission); or
- an AMHP.

Applications to the court by AMHPs

8.10 AMHPs will need to consider making an application for displacement or appointment if:

- they believe that a patient should be detained in hospital under section 3 of the Act, or should become a guardianship patient, but the nearest relative objects; or
- they believe that the nearest relative is likely to discharge a patient from detention or guardianship unwisely.

8.11 They should also consider doing so if they think that:

- a patient has no identifiable nearest relative or their nearest relative is incapable of acting as such; or
- they have good reasons to think that a patient considers their nearest relative unsuitable and would like them to be replaced;

and it would not be reasonable in the circumstances to expect the patient, or anyone else, to make an application.

8.12 AMHPs should bear in mind that some patients may wish to apply to displace their nearest relative but may be deterred from doing so by the need to apply to the county court.

8.13 It is entirely a matter for the court to decide what constitutes "suitability" of a person to be a nearest relative. But factors which an AMHP might wish to consider when deciding whether to make an application to displace a nearest relative on grounds of unsuitability, and when providing evidence in connection with an application, could include:

- any reason to think that the patient has suffered, or is suspected to have suffered, abuse at the hands of the nearest relative (or someone with whom the nearest relative is in a relationship), or is at risk of suffering such abuse;
- any evidence that the patient is afraid of the nearest relative or seriously distressed by the possibility of the nearest relative being involved in their life or their care; and
- a situation where the patient and nearest relative are unknown to each other, there is only a distant relationship between them, or their relationship has broken down irretrievably.

This is not an exhaustive list.

8.14 In all cases, the decision to make an application lies with the AMHP personally.

8.15 Before making an application for displacement, AMHPs should consider other ways of achieving the same end, including:

- whether the nearest relative will agree to delegate their role as the patient's nearest relative to someone else; or
- providing or arranging support for the patient (or someone else) to make an application themselves. This could include support from an independent mental health advocate.

8.16 Local social services authorities (LSSAs) should provide clear practical guidance to help AMHPs decide whether to make an application and how to proceed. Before producing such guidance, LSSAs should consult with the county court. LSSAs should ensure that they have access to the necessary legal advice and support.

Making an application

8.17 People making an application to the county court will need to provide the court with the facts that will help it make a decision on the application. Exactly what will be required will depend on the type of application and the specific circumstances of the case.

8.18 When applying to displace a nearest relative, AMHPs should nominate someone to become the acting nearest relative in the event that the application is successful. Wherever practicable, they should first consult the patient about the patient's own preferences and any concerns they have about the person the AMHP proposes to nominate. AMHPs should also seek the agreement of the proposed nominee prior to an application being made, although this is not a legal requirement.

8.19 LSSAs should provide clear practical guidance to help the AMHP decide who it is appropriate to nominate when making an application to displace a nearest relative.

8.20 If the patient has any concerns that any information given to the court on their views on the suitability of the nearest relative may have implications for their own safety, an application can be made to the court seeking its permission not to make the current nearest relative a party to the proceedings. The reasons for the patient's concerns should be set out clearly in the application.

8.21 Hospital managers should provide support to detained patients to enable them to attend the court, if they wish, subject to the patient being granted leave under section 17 for this purpose.

8.22 If, exceptionally, the court decides to interview the patient (as the applicant), the court has the discretion to decide where and how this interview may take place and whether it should take place in the presence of, or separate from, other parties.

8.23 If the court decides that the nearest relative should be displaced and finds the proposed replacement to be suitable, and that person is willing to act as nearest relative, then the court will appoint them.

Mental Health Act 1983

26 Definition of 'relative' and 'nearest relative'

(1) In this Part of this Act "relative" means any of the following persons –

   (a)   husband or wife or civil partner;
   (b)   son or daughter;
   (c)   father or mother;
   (d)   brother or sister;
   (e)   grandparent;
   (f)   grandchild;
   (g)   uncle or aunt;
   (h)   nephew or niece.

(2) In deducing relationships for the purposes of this section, any relationship of the half-blood shall be treated as a relationship of the whole blood, and an illegitimate person shall be treated as the legitimate child of –

   (a)   his mother, and
   (b)   if his father has parental responsibility for him within the meaning of section 3 of the Children Act 1989, his father.

(3) In this Part of this Act, subject to the provisions of this section and to the following provisions of this Part of this Act, the "nearest relative" means the person first described in subsection (1) above who is for the time being surviving, relatives of the whole blood being preferred to relatives of the same description of the half-blood and the elder or eldest of two or more relatives described in any paragraph of that subsection being preferred to the other or others of those relatives, regardless of sex.

(4) Subject to the provisions of this section and to the following provisions of this Part of this Act, where the patient ordinarily resides with or is cared for by one or more of his relatives (or, if he is for the time being an in-patient in a hospital, he last ordinarily resided with or was cared for by one or more of his relatives) his nearest relative shall be determined –

   (a)   by giving preference to that relative or those relatives over the other or others; and
   (b)   as between two or more such relatives, in accordance with subsection (3) above.

(5) Where the person who, under subsection (3) or (4) above, would be the nearest relative of a patient –

   (a)   in the case of a patient ordinarily resident in the United Kingdom, the Channel Islands or the Isle of Man, is not so resident; or
   (b)   is the husband or wife or civil partner of the patient, but is permanently separated from the patient, either by agreement or under an order of a court, or has deserted or has been deserted by the patient for a period which has come to an end; or
   (c)   is a person other than the husband, wife, civil partner, father or mother of the patient, and is for the time being under 18 years of age; ...
   (d)   ...

the nearest relative of the patient shall be ascertained as if that person were dead.

(6) In this section "husband", "wife" and "civil partner" include a person who is living with the patient as the patient's husband or wife or as if they were civil partners, as the case may be (or, if the patient is for the time being an in-patient in a hospital, was so living until the patient was admitted), and has been or had been so living for a period of not less than six months; but a person shall not be treated by virtue of this subsection as the nearest relative of a married patient or a patient in a civil partnership unless the husband, wife or civil partner of the patient is disregarded by virtue of paragraph (b) of subsection (5) above.

(7) A person, other than a relative, with whom the patient ordinarily resides (or, if the patient is for the time being an in-patient in a hospital, last ordinarily resided before he was admitted), and with whom he has or had been ordinarily residing for a period of not less than five years, shall be treated for the purposes of this Part of this Act as if he were a relative but –

(a)   shall be treated for the purposes of subsection (3) above as if mentioned last in subsection (1) above; and

(b)   shall not be treated by virtue of this subsection as the nearest relative of a married patient or a patient in a civil partnership unless the husband, wife or civil partner of the patient is disregarded by virtue of paragraph (b) of subsection (5) above.

Confidentiality of documentation

1.42   In *R (on the Application of Stevens) v Plymouth City Council (C As Interested Party)* [2002] EWCA Civ 388, [2002] 1 FLR 1177 the nearest relative was the mother of a patient who lacked capacity. He had been the subject of a guardianship order with the reluctant agreement of his mother. She had asked the local authority for access to his files, including the reports upon which it had relied to make its recommendations for the necessity for an order. It was held that a balance had to be struck between public and private interests in maintaining confidentiality of information, and public and private interests in disclosing information. In this instance, the mother required the information (which had been produced for a particular purpose, ie an application for guardianship) in order to make a decision as to her position. Further, the proper administration of justice (within the context of litigation) normally required that both sides had access to anything relevant to the decision of the Court. The decision to permit access was founded both on common law principles, and Arts 6 and 8 of the European Convention on Human Rights. Furthermore, the mother (by virtue of her ultimate objection to renewal of the order) had been faced with an application to displace her as the nearest relative. Although she had the power to discharge the order (see **1.41**) she would have been obliged to justify this position at the hearing for her displacement by the local authority. Without access to the relevant documents, this would have been impossible. In the circumstances of this particular case, the mother and her lawyers properly required access to the information requested. The Court also relied upon the statutory basis of the nearest relative as having 'an important role, not only in securing a patient's reception into guardianship but also in bringing that guardianship to an end' (1184/5 [21]).

Determination of nature (and choice) of 'nearest relative'

1.43 In *R (on the Application of SSG) v Liverpool CC (1) and Secretary of State for the Department of Health (2) and LS (Interested Party)* [2002] 5 CCLR 639 the local authority had (correctly) identified the patient's mother as being the nearest relative. However, the patient herself had been living with her female partner and wished for her partner to be her nearest relative. The application (unopposed by the local authority) was that either it treated her partner as her nearest relative, or that the Court make an order that the legislation was incompatible with her rights pursuant to the European Convention on Human Rights. The orders made were that a difference in treatment between a homosexual unmarried couple and a heterosexual unmarried couple could not be justified, and that a homosexual partner of a patient can be treated as a nearest relative within s 26(1), and that where there has been cohabitation in a sexual relationship for a period of 6 months or more, that partner will be the patient's nearest relative. There was a declaration that the partner of the patient could be treated as a relative within the meaning of s 145 of MHA 1983 and consequently, s 26(1) and (6). However, in *R (on the Application of M) v Secretary of State for Health* [2003] EWHC 1094 (Admin), [2003] MHLR 348, the patient objected to her nearest relative (her father) having access to confidential documentation. She had also made allegations that she had been sexually abused by her father. She wanted to change her nearest relative. The Court granted a declaration of incompatibility (pursuant to s 4 of the Human Rights Act 1998). Mr Justice Kay held:

> 'It is not necessary for me to dwell on the issue of incompatibility in this case for the simple reason that it is admitted by the Secretary of State. This is hardly surprising. In *JT v UK* (appn. 26494, 26th February 1997) the European Commission of Human Rights declared the admissibility of a complaint concerning the incompatibility of the nearest relative provisions with Article 8. In its subsequent report adopted on 20th May 1998 the Commission considered that "even taking account of the Government's margin of appreciation, the absence of any possibility to apply to the County Court to change the applicant's nearest relative on the grounds of her concerns about the identity of that person renders the interference in her rights under Article 8 para 1 of the Convention disproportionate to the aims pursued". The judgment of the European Court of Human Rights [2000] MHLR 254 records a friendly settlement between JT and the Government ... in fact following the friendly settlement in *JT* no amending legislation has been enacted.'

Implementation of the Mental Health Act 2007

1.44 The Department of Health has given guidance on the early implementation of some parts of the Mental Health Act 2007 (as it amends MHA 1983). The amendments to s 26 came into force on 1 December 2007. The amendment is that the list at s 26 now provides that a civil partner has equal status to that of a husband or wife (and all references to such have been amended at ss 26(5), (6), (7) and 27). The Guidance adds:

'The effect of these amendments will be that a patient's civil partner will become their nearest relative if they are not already. Any person (not a civil partner) who is the patient's nearest relative prior to the enactment of these provisions will cease to be the patient's nearest relative. Any action taken by the former nearest relative when they were the nearest relative is unaffected by the change. It is not unusual for a person who is the nearest relative to be replaced by another person, for example, where a person on the list assumes caring responsibilities for the patient, or a person higher on the list of relatives comes of age, or returns to reside in the UK or where a spouse and patient separate. However it may be useful to remind those with duties to the nearest relative on what action they should take in the event that the nearest relative of a patient changes. It is not known how many patients and existing nearest relatives will be affect [sic] by this change. It is likely that only a very few of the people who have entered into civil partnerships in England and Wales will have subsequently been detained in hospital or subject to guardianship under the Mental Health Act 1983. Also, any person who has resided with the patient for 5 years or more is counted as a relative (s 26 of MHA 1983 as amended by s 26 of the Mental Health Act 2007).'

1.45   The new Mental Health Act 2007 also introduces the possibility of a patient applying to seek displacement of an unsuitable nearest relative. The alterations in the law are in response to the authorities discussed above and below. This possibility is available via s 23 of the Mental Health Act 2007, which amends s 29 of MHA 1983. Fennell comments as follows:

'**5.15** Section 29 of the 1983 Act empowers a county court to make an order directing that the functions of nearest relative be exercised by another person or by the local social services authority. Section 23 of the MHA 2007 amends s 29 and introduces the possibility for the patient him or herself to seek displacement of an unsuitable nearest relative. An application for such an order may be made by the patient, any relative of the patient, any other person with whom the patient is residing (or was last residing before admitted to hospital), or by an AMHP A relative or person residing with the patient may apply for the functions of nearest relative to be conferred on him or her personally or on any other willing person whom the court considers suitable. If the applicant is an AMHP, the effect of a successful application will be that the local social services authority will be appointed as acting nearest relative. An application may be made on any of the following grounds in s 29(3):

(a)   that the patient has no nearest relative within the meaning of the Act, or that it is not reasonably practicable to ascertain whether he or she has such a relative, or who that relative is;

(b)   that the nearest relative is incapable of acting as such by reason of mental disorder or other illness;

(c)   that the nearest relative of the patient unreasonably objects to the making of an application for admission for treatment or guardianship;

(d)   that the nearest relative has exercised, without due regard to the welfare of the patient or the interests of the public, his or her power to discharge the patient from hospital or guardianship, or is likely to do so.

...

5.18 Section 25 of the MHA 2007 has amended s 66 of the MHA 1983 and limits applications to the Mental Health Tribunal (MHT) from displaced NRs. Such an application may be made only by a NR displaced on grounds of unreasonable objection to admission or exercising the power of discharge without due regard to the welfare of the patient or the protection of the public. A person displaced as the NR because he or she is too ill to act, or unsuitable to act, will not have the right to apply to the MHT.'

Alleged misuse of functions by nearest relative

1.46 It is also possible to transfer the functions of the nearest relative. In *Barnet LBC v Robin* [1999] 2 CCLR 455 it was held that even where there had been *no* past misuse of the powers of the nearest relative, but where there was a likelihood that this might happen in the future (on the facts in the case this seems to have been based upon an application by the nearest relative for discharge from the order at a Tribunal), such an order can be made. The instant application was considered under s 29(1).

Consultation and identification of nearest relative

1.47 The obligation upon the local authority is to consult the person appearing to be the nearest relative (s 11(4)). The text of the statute is set out above at **1.35**. In *Re D (Mental Patient: Habeas Corpus)* [2000] 2 FLR 848, the nearest relative was the elder of his two children. Section 26(4) provides that if the patient ordinarily resides with or is cared for by one or more of his relatives the nearest relative would be that carer. The dispute arose as to which of his relatives provided the majority of the care, and whether (as a matter of fact) the local authority had consulted the correct one, and if not then whether the consequences of such a failure vitiated the original admission. It was held that the word 'ordinarily' does not qualify both 'resides with' and 'is cared for'. The words 'care for' fall to be interpreted in their common and everyday meaning and effect. The issue in the case was not whether the local authority had consulted with the legally correct nearest relative, but whether it had consulted with the person 'appearing to be' that relative. All that was required of the social worker was that he had carried out his duties honestly. Where a decision was made by an AMHP **not** to consult the nearest relative at all (on an erroneous basis) the result will be very different. In *R (on the application of V) v (1) South London & Maudsley NHS Foundation Trust (2) Croydon LBC* [2010] EWHC 742 (Admin), [2010] 13 CCLR 181 there had been a fundamental error in respect of the relevant powers as to detention created by the MHA 1983. The patient had been detained under s 3, but concerns existed as to the procedural propriety of that detention. The hospital in which he was detained elected to use s 5(2) of the MHA 1983 (which permits detention for 72 hours if where the patient is already an in-patient). The time period elapsed without any application for detention via s 3 having been made. The AMHP attempted to assess the patient for this purpose, but he refused to be assessed. The AMHP was aware that his nearest relative was his mother, and proceeded with the application, having tried to contact his mother, by way of leaving a message with the father of the patient. The actual application form stated that the identity of the nearest relative was unknown. The application to challenge the admission was by way of issuing a writ of *habeas corpus,* rather than judicial review. The order was granted. The basis of the order was that the decision (and procedure) in respect of admission was: (a) unreasonable; and (b) factually incorrect. A virtually identical scenario existed in *In re BB; BB v Cygnet Healthcare* [2008] EWHC 1259 (Admin), [2008] MHLR 106. The holding power (s 5) was used in respect of a patient whilst inquiries were made of his nearest relative. There was a conflict of fact as to whether the AMHP had ever consulted at all with the nearest relative, albeit this process was confused and poorly documented (and compounded by language barriers). The Court heard evidence on the point, and decided that on balance it had not been established that there had been consultation (although it was acceptable to make inquiries of a nearest relative via an intermediary). Consequently, the admission was unlawful, and a writ of habeas corpus was granted. A similar issue arose at first instance in *R (TTM) by his litigation friend TM) v LB Hackney and East London NHS Foundation Trust* [2010] EWHC 1349 (Admin), albeit from a slightly different perspective. On the facts in this case, the nearest relative had not objected to detention. However, he then gave notice that he was intending to discharge the patient. The procedure for 'barring' the discharge was not completed. The nearest relative again made it clear that he objected to his brother being detained under the MHA (albeit he did not object to him being admitted as an 'informal' patient. This was treated as an application to discharge, and was then barred by the RC. The AMHP believed that a further conversation that she had had with the nearest relative led her to believe that any objection had been lifted, and that the nearest relative did not object to detention. It appeared that she had made an honest mistake (ie that the nearest relative had never resiled from his position). In the interim, a writ of habeas corpus had been made. The court had to consider whether: (a) the managers of the hospital could rely upon the defective application; (b) whether there was a duty of care as between the AMHP and the patient; (c) whether the requirement to seek leave to issue proceedings for negligence (pursuant to s 139 of the MHA 1983) would be granted; (d) what damages might flow from the period that the patient was detained under an application that was flawed. It was held that: (a) the hospital managers were entitled to rely upon the application (as it had been 'duly made' in accordance with the MHA 1983); (b) there might be a duty of care as between the AMHP and the patient, but the case itself was without merit, and therefore (c) leave would be refused – the AMHP had acted properly but had made an honest mistake; (d) that the admission was lawful until set aside, and that therefore no damages could be awarded. It was held that the only remedy to which the patient might be entitled was that his detention was unlawful as at the date that the remedy of habeas corpus was granted. *Per curiam* the Court held that the AMHP was acting for the local authority, which was therefore vicariously liable for her actions. If bad faith had been asserted and proved, then there would be an action in misfeasance in public office available to the patient. The original application for the writ of habeas corpus is reported at [2009] MHLR 154. The first instance decision referred to above was the subject of a successful appeal to the Court of Appeal. It was held that the detention had been unlawful throughout (and not just from the date of detention) and that merely because the hospital had a lawful basis for detaining the patient did not remedy the unlawful act of the AMHP. It also followed, therefore, that the patient had a right both at common law, and pursuant to Art 5(5) of the ECHR to a claim for damages (*M (by his litigation friend TM) v Hackney LBC, East London NHS Foundation Trust, Secretary of State for Health*) [2011] EWCA Civ 4, [2011] 14 CCLR 154).

1.48 In *Re SC (Mental Patient: Habeas Corpus)* [1996] 1 FLR 548, it was known that the nearest relative of the patient (the father) objected to detention. However, the social worker completed the forms stating that the mother was the nearest relative (who did not object to detention). The social worker had therefore opted to deliberately ignore the status and wishes of the legal nearest relative. The consequence was that the admission itself was unlawful (and it was not permissible for a hospital to rely upon an apparently valid application for admission by virtue of s 6(3)). In terms of the remedy available, the correct avenue was by way of an application for a writ of habeas corpus. Plainly, this is a case where the ASW seems to have acted in bad faith, and dishonestly, and therefore is easily distinguished from *Re D (Mental Patient: Habeas Corpus)* [2000] 2 FLR 848. A different approach, however, was taken in *R (on the application of Adrian Holloway) v Oxfordshire CC and Oxford County Court* [2007] EWHC 776 (Admin), [2007] 10 CCLR 264. The local authority did identify the correct nearest relative, and discovered that she objected to the detention of her son. It therefore applied to the County Court to displace her as nearest relative. It would appear that there was no attempt to serve the mother with notice of the hearing, despite being aware of her views, and that she was legally represented. An interim order was made, displacing her as nearest relative (subsequently ratified at a final hearing). An application was made to judicially review the local authority in respect of its original behaviour. The local authority was heavily criticised for its behaviour, as was the social worker involved. Nevertheless, the County Court had been entitled to make an interim order. This was because: (a) it was just that – an interim order; (b) there could have been an application to set the order aside; (c) if the interim order had not been made final, then the mother could at that stage have applied to discharge the patient herself. It was also held that it would have been good practice (if there was any doubt) to have adjourned the application in order to be certain that the mother had been served with notice of the application.

1.49 In *R (E) v Bristol City Council* [2005] EWHC 74 (Admin), [2005] MHLR 83, the nearest relative was the sister of the patient. The patient did not wish her sister to be consulted at all in respect of the Act. The local authority believed that it was obliged (pursuant to s 11(3)) to inform the sister of any intentions it might have under the Act in respect of admission for assessment, treatment or guardianship. In this instance, the Court focused on an interpretation of the word 'practicable' in s 11(3) and (4), and reached the conclusion that in order for the statute to be compatible with the rights of the patient pursuant to Art 8, that it could be interpreted so as to remove the obligation to consult the sister in this instance. The construction suggested at para 2.16 of the old MHA 1983 Code (which does not have the force of a primary statute) was wrong, and that practicability was not just a question of availability, but also went to the question of whether it was appropriate to notify the sister. The declaration was to the effect that the social worker was not bound to notify or consult where the nearest relative may not act in the best interest of the patient, or dislikes of the patient, and where the patient herself was competent and had expressed a strong wish that the nearest relative should not be contacted. The relevant parts of the current Code are set out below. However, it is fairly clear that in recent years the Courts have been readily amenable to argument that where even honest mistakes have been made about the procedure for admission via s 3, if there has (as a matter of fact) been a mistake, then the admission will be vitiated by that error, and an application for habeas corpus will meet with success. This principle was affirmed in *CX v A Local Authority & A NHS Foundation Trust* [2011] EWHC 1918 (Admin), albeit that Spencer J was clear that: 'This case turns entirely upon its unusual facts' [68] albeit these were that the AMHP had misrepresented the law to the nearest relative (not in bad faith), leading her to reluctantly withdraw her objection to the detention of her son. The misrepresentation vitiated the process of consultation, and a writ of habeas corpus was granted, and thus detention under s 3 ceased.

Mental Health Act 1983 Code of Practice

CHAPTER 4

Applications for detention in hospital

4.1 This chapter gives guidance on the making of applications for detention in hospital under Part 2 of the Act.

Grounds for making an application for detention

4.2 An application for detention may only be made where the grounds in either section 2 or section 3 of the Act are met (see box below).

Criteria for applications

A person can be detained for assessment under section 2 only if both the following criteria apply:

- the person is suffering from a mental disorder of a nature or degree which warrants their detention in hospital for assessment (or for assessment followed by treatment) for at least a limited period; and
- the person ought to be so detained in the interests of their own health or safety or with a view to the protection of others.

A person can be detained for treatment under section 3 only if all the following criteria apply:

- the person is suffering from a mental disorder of a nature or degree which makes it appropriate for them to receive medical treatment in hospital;
- it is necessary for the health or safety of the person or for the protection of other persons that they should receive such treatment and it cannot be provided unless the patient is detained under this section; and
- appropriate medical treatment is available.

4.3 The criteria require consideration of both the nature and degree of a patient's mental disorder. Nature refers to the particular mental disorder from which the patient is suffering, its chronicity, its prognosis, and the patient's previous response to receiving treatment for the disorder. Degree refers to the current manifestation of the patient's disorder.

4.4 Before it is decided that admission to hospital is necessary, consideration must be given to whether there are alternative means of providing the care and treatment which the patient requires. This includes consideration of whether there might be other effective forms of care or treatment which the patient would be willing to accept, and of whether guardianship would be appropriate instead.

4.5 In all cases, consideration must be given to:

- the patient's wishes and view of their own needs;
- the patient's age and physical health;
- any past wishes or feelings expressed by the patient;
- the patient's cultural background;
- the patient's social and family circumstances;
- the impact that any future deterioration or lack of improvement in the patient's condition would have on their children, other relatives or carers, especially those living with the patient, including an assessment of these people's ability and willingness to cope; and
- the effect on the patient, and those close to the patient, of a decision to admit or not to admit under the Act.

Factors to consider – the health or safety of the patient

4.6 Factors to be considered in deciding whether patients should be detained for their own health or safety include:

- the evidence suggesting that patients are at risk of: – suicide; – self-harm; – self-neglect or being unable to look after their own health or safety; or – jeopardising their own health or safety accidentally, recklessly or unintentionally; or that their mental disorder is otherwise putting their health or safety at risk;
- any evidence suggesting that the patient's mental health will deteriorate if they do not receive treatment;
- the reliability of such evidence, including what is known of the history of the patient's mental disorder;
- the views of the patient and of any carers, relatives or close friends, especially those living with the patient, about the likely course of the disorder and the possibility of it improving;
- the patient's own skills and experience in managing their condition;

- the potential benefits of treatment, which should be weighed against any adverse effects that being detained might have on the patient's wellbeing; and
- whether other methods of managing the risk are available.

Factors to consider – protection of others

4.7 In considering whether detention is necessary for the protection of other people, the factors to consider are the nature of the risk to other people arising from the patient's mental disorder, the likelihood that harm will result and the severity of any potential harm, taking into account:

- that it is not always possible to differentiate risk of harm to the patient from the risk of harm to others;
- the reliability of the available evidence, including any relevant details of the patient's clinical history and past behaviour, such as contact with other agencies and (where relevant) criminal convictions and cautions;
- the willingness and ability of those who live with the patient and those who provide care and support to the patient to cope with and manage the risk; and
- whether other methods of managing the risk are available.

4.8 Harm to other people includes psychological as well as physical harm.

Alternatives to detention – patients with capacity to consent to admission

4.9 When a patient needs to be in hospital, informal admission is usually appropriate when a patient who has the capacity to do so consents to admission. (See chapter 36 for guidance on when parents might consent to admission on behalf of children and young people.)

4.10 However, this should not be regarded as an absolute rule, especially if the reason for considering admission is that the patient presents a clear danger to themselves or others because of their mental disorder.

4.11 Compulsory admission should, in particular, be considered where a patient's current mental state, together with reliable evidence of past experience, indicates a strong likelihood that they will have a change of mind about informal admission, either before or after they are admitted, with a resulting risk to their health or safety or to the safety of other people.

4.12 The threat of detention must not be used to induce a patient to consent to admission to hospital or to treatment (and is likely to invalidate any apparent consent).

Alternatives to detention – patients who lack capacity to consent to admission or treatment

4.13 In deciding whether it is necessary to detain-patients, doctors and approved mental health professionals (AMHPs) must always consider the alternative ways of providing the treatment or care they need.

4.14 The fact that patients cannot consent to the treatment they need, or to being admitted to hospital, does not automatically mean that the Act must be used. It may be possible to rely instead on the provisions of the Mental Capacity Act 2005 (MCA) to provide treatment in the best interests of patients who are aged 16 or over and who lack capacity to consent to treatment.

4.15 This may be possible even if the provision of treatment unavoidably involves depriving patients of their liberty. Deprivation of liberty for the purposes of care or treatment in a hospital or care home can be authorised in a person's best interests under the deprivation of liberty safeguards in the MCA if the person is aged 18 or over.

4.16 If admission to hospital for assessment or treatment for mental disorder is necessary for a patient who lacks capacity to consent to it, an application under the Mental Health Act should be made if:

- providing appropriate care or treatment for the patient will unavoidably involve depriving them of their liberty and the MCA deprivation of liberty safeguards cannot be used; or
- for any other reason, the assessment or treatment the patient needs cannot be safely or effectively delivered by relying on the MCA alone.

4.17 The MCA deprivation of liberty safeguards can be used only if the six qualifying requirements summarised in the table below are met.

Summary of qualifying requirements in the MCA's deprivation of liberty safeguards

Age requirement	The person is at least 18 years old.
Mental health requirement	The person has a mental disorder.
Mental capacity requirement	The person lacks capacity to decide whether to be in a hospital or care home for the proposed treatment or care.
Best interests requirement	The proposed deprivation of liberty is in the person's best interests and it is a necessary and proportionate response to the risk of them suffering harm.
Eligibility requirement	The person is not subject, or potentially subject, to specified provisions of the Mental Health Act in a way that makes them ineligible.
No refusals requirement	There is no advance decision, or decision of an attorney or deputy which makes the proposed deprivation of liberty impossible.

4.18 The key points when considering whether an application for detention should be made under the Mental Health Act instead of relying on the MCA's deprivation of liberty safeguards are that those safeguards cannot be used if:

- the patient is aged under 18;

- the patient has made a valid and applicable advancedecision refusing a necessary element of the treatmentfor which they are to be admitted to hospital (see chapter 17);
- the use of the safeguards would conflict with a decision of the person's attorney or deputy or of the Court of Protection; or
- the patient meets the criteria in section 2 or section 3 of the Mental Health Act and is objecting to being admitted to (or remaining in) hospital for mental health treatment (unless an attorney or deputy consents on their behalf).

4.19 In that last case, whether a patient is objecting has to be considered in the round, taking into account all the circumstances, so far as they are reasonably ascertainable. The decision to be made is whether the patient objects to treatment – the reasonableness of that objection is not the issue. In many cases the patient will be perfectly able to state their objection. But in other cases doctors and AMHPs will need to consider the patient's behaviour, wishes, feelings, views, beliefs and values, both present and past, so far as they can be ascertained. If there is reason to think that a patient would object, if able to do so, then the patient should be taken to be objecting.

4.20 Even if providing appropriate care or treatment will not unavoidably involve a deprivation of liberty, it may be necessary to detain a patient under the Mental Health Act rather than relying on the MCA because:

- the patient has, by means of a valid and applicable advance decision, refused a necessary element of the treatment required; or
- the patient lacks capacity to make decisions on some elements of the care and treatment they need, but has capacity to decide about a vital element – e g admission to hospital – and either has already refused it or is likely to do so.

4.21 Whether or not the deprivation of liberty safeguards could be used, other reasons why it may not be possible to rely on the MCA alone include the following:

- the patient's lack of capacity to consent is fluctuating or temporary and the patient is not expected to consent when they regain capacity. This may be particularly relevant to patients having acute psychotic, manic or depressive episodes;
- a degree of restraint needs to be used which is justified by the risk to other people but which is not permissible under the MCA because, exceptionally, it cannot be said to be proportionate to the risk to the patient personally; and
- there is some other specific identifiable risk that the person might not receive the treatment they need if the MCA is relied on and that either the person or others might potentially suffer harm as a result.

4.22 Otherwise, if the MCA can be used safely and effectively to assess or treat a patient, it is likely to be difficult to demonstrate that the criteria for detaining the patient under the Mental Health Act are met.

4.23 For further information on the MCA deprivation of liberty safeguards, see the addendum to the MCA Code of Practice.

4.24 For the different considerations which apply to children and young people, see chapter 36.

4.25 An application for detention can be made under either section 2 or section 3 of the Mental Health Act.

4.26 Section 2 should be used if:

- the full extent of the nature and degree of a patient'scondition is unclear;
- there is a need to carry out an initial in-patientassessment in order to formulate a treatment plan, orto reach a judgement about whether the patient willaccept treatment on a voluntary basis following admission; or
- there is a need to carry out a new in-patient assessment in order to re-formulate a treatment plan, or to reach a judgement about whether the patient will accept treatment on a voluntary basis.

4.27 Section 3 should be used if:

- the patient is already detained under section 2 (detention under section 2 cannot be renewed by a new section 2 application); or
- the nature and current degree of the patient's mental disorder, the essential elements of the treatment plan to be followed and the likelihood of the patient accepting treatment on a voluntary basis are already established.

The assessment process

4.28 An application for detention may be made by an AMHP or the patient's nearest relative. An AMHP is usually a more appropriate applicant than a patient's nearest relative, given an AMHP's professional training and knowledge of the legislation and local resources, together with the potential adverse effect that an application by the nearest relative might have on their relationship with the patient.

4.29 An application must be supported by two medical recommendations given in accordance with the Act.

4.30 Doctors who are approached directly by a nearest relative about making an application should advise the nearest relative that it is preferable for an AMHP to consider the need for a patient to be admitted under the Act and for the AMHP to make any consequent application. Doctors should also advise the nearest relative of their right to require a local social services authority (LSSA) to arrange for an AMHP to consider the patient's case. Doctors should never advise a nearest relative to make an application themselves in order to avoid involving an AMHP in an assessment.

Objective of the assessment

4.31 The objective of the assessment is to determine whether the criteria for detention are met and, if so, whether an application for detention should be made.

4.32 Because a proper assessment cannot be carried out without considering alternative means of providing care and treatment, AMHPs and doctors should, as far as possible in the circumstances, identify and liaise with services which may potentially be able to provide alternatives to admission to hospital. That could include crisis and home treatment teams.

Responsibilities of local social services authorities

4.33 LSSAs are responsible for ensuring that sufficient AMHPs are available to carry out their roles under the Act, including assessing patients to decide whether an application for detention should be made. To fulfil their statutory duty, LSSAs must have arrangements in place in their area to provide a 24-hour service that can respond to patients' needs.

4.34 Section 13 of the Act places a specific duty on LSSAs to arrange for an AMHP to consider the case of any patient who is within their area if they have reason to believe that an application for detention in hospital may need to be made in respect of the patient. LSSAs must make such arrangements if asked to do so by (or on behalf of) the nearest relative.

4.35 If a patient is already detained under section 2 as the result of an application made by an AMHP, the LSSA on whose behalf that AMHP was acting is responsible for arranging for an AMHP to consider the patient's case again if the LSSA has reason to believe that an application under section 3 may be necessary. This applies even if the patient has been detained outside that LSSA's area.

4.36 These duties do not prevent any other LSSA from arranging for an AMHP to consider a patient's case if that is more appropriate.

Setting up the assessment

4.37 Local arrangements should, as far as possible, ensure that assessments are carried out by the most appropriate AMHP and doctors in the particular circumstances.

4.38 Where a patient is known to belong to a group for which particular expertise is desirable (e g they are aged under 18 or have a learning disability), at least one of the professionals involved in their assessment should have expertise in working with people from that group, wherever possible.

4.39 If this is not possible, at least one of the professionals involved in the person's assessment should, if at all possible, consult with one or more professionals who do have relevant expertise and involve them as closely as the circumstances of the case allow.

4.40 Unless different arrangements have been agreed locally between the relevant authorities, AMHPs who assess patients for possible detention under the Act have overall responsibility for co-ordinating the process of assessment. In doing so, they should be sensitive to the patient's age, gender (and gender identity), social, cultural, racial and religious background and sexual orientation. They should also consider how any disability the patient has may affect the way the assessment needs to be carried out.

4.41 Given the importance of good communication, it is essential that those professionals who assess patients are able to communicate with the patient effectively and reliably to prevent potential misunderstandings. AMHPs should establish, as far as possible, whether patients have particular communication needs or difficulties and take steps to meet them, for example by arranging a signer or a professional interpreter. AMHPs should also be in a position, where appropriate, to supply suitable equipment to make communication easier with patients who have impaired hearing, but who do not have their own hearing aid.

4.42 See paragraphs 4.106–4.110 for specific guidance in relation to the assessment of people who are deaf. For further guidance on specific issues that may arise when assessing people who have a learning disability or an autistic spectrum disorder, or who have a personality disorder, see chapter 34 and chapter 35 respectively.

4.43 Doctors and AMHPs undertaking assessments need to apply professional judgement and reach decisions independently of each other, but in a framework of co-operation and mutual support.

4.44 Unless there is good reason for undertaking separate assessments, patients should, where possible, be seen jointly by the AMHP and at least one of the two doctors involved in the assessment.

4.45 While it may not always be feasible for the patient to be examined by both doctors at the same time, they should both discuss the patient's case with the person considering making an application for the patient's detention.

4.46 Everyone involved in an assessment should be alert to the need to provide support for colleagues, especially where there is a risk of the patient causing physical harm. People carrying out assessments should be aware of circumstances in which the police should be asked to provide assistance, in accordance with arrangements agreed locally with the police, and of how to use that assistance to maximise the safety of everyone involved in the assessment.

4.47 Locally agreed arrangements on the involvement of the police should include a joint risk assessment tool to help determine the level of risk, what (if any) police assistance may be required and how quickly it is needed. In cases where no warrant for the police to enter premises under section 135 of the Act is being applied for (see chapter 10), the risk assessment should indicate the reasons for this and explain why police assistance is nonetheless necessary.

The role of approved mental health professionals

4.48 AMHPs may make an application for detention only if they:

- have interviewed the patient in a suitable manner;
- are satisfied that the statutory criteria for detention are met; and

- are satisfied that, in all the circumstances of the case, detention in hospital is the most appropriate way of providing the care and medical treatment the patient needs.

4.49 Once AMHPs have decided that an application should be made, they must then decide whether it is necessary or proper for them to make the application themselves. If they decide it is, having considered any views expressed by the patient's relatives and all the other relevant circumstances, AMHPs must make the application.

4.50 At the start of an assessment, AMHPs should identify themselves to the person being assessed, members of the person's family, carers or friends and the other professionals present. AMHPs should ensure that the purpose of the visit, their role and that of the other professionals are explained. They should carry documents with them at all times which identify them as AMHPs and which specify both the LSSA which approved them and the LSSA on whose behalf they are acting.

4.51 Although AMHPs act on behalf of a LSSA, they cannot be told by the LSSA or anyone else whether or not to make an application. They must exercise their own judgement, based on social and medical evidence, when deciding whether to apply for a patient to be detained under the Act. The role of AMHPs is to provide an independent decision about whether or not there are alternatives to detention under the Act, bringing a social perspective to bear on their decision.

4.52 If patients want someone else (eg a familiar person or an advocate) to be present during the assessment and any subsequent action that may be taken, then ordinarily AMHPs should assist in securing that person's attendance, unless the urgency of the case makes it inappropriate to do so. Patients may feel safer or more confident with a friend or other person they know well in attendance. Equally, an advocate can help to reassure patients. Some patients may already be receiving help from an advocate.

4.53 Patients should usually be given the opportunity of speaking to the AMHP alone. However, if AMHPs have reason to fear physical harm, they should insist that another professional is present.

4.54 It is not desirable for patients to be interviewed through a closed door or window, and this should be considered only where other people are at serious risk. Where direct access to the patient is not possible, but there is no immediate risk of physical danger to the patient or to anyone else, AMHPs should consider applying for a warrant under section 135 of the Act, allowing the police to enter the premises (see chapter 10).

4.55 Where patients are subject to the short-term effects of alcohol or drugs (whether prescribed or self-administered) which make interviewing them difficult, the AMHP should either wait until the effects have abated before interviewing the patient or arrange to return later. If it is not realistic to wait, because of the patient's disturbed behaviour and the urgency of the case, the assessment will have to be based on whatever information the AMHP can obtain from reliable sources. This should be made clear in the AMHP's record of the assessment.

The AMHP and the nearest relative

4.56 AMHPs are required by the Act to attempt to identify the patient's nearest relative as defined in section 26 of the Act.

4.57 When AMHPs make an application for detention under section 2, they must take such steps as are practicable to inform the nearest relative that the application is to be (or has been) made and of the nearest relative's power to discharge the patient.

4.58 Before making an application for detention under section 3, AMHPs must consult the nearest relative, unless it is not reasonably practicable or would involve unreasonable delay.

4.59 Circumstances in which the nearest relative need not be informed or consulted include those where:

• it is not practicable for the AMHP to obtain sufficient information to establish the identity or location of the nearest relative, or where to do so would require an excessive amount of investigation involving unreasonable delay; and

• consultation is not possible because of the nearest relative's own health or mental incapacity.

4.60 There may also be cases where, although physically possible, it would not be reasonably practicable to inform or consult the nearest relative because there would be a detrimental impact on the patient which would result in infringement of the patient's right to respect for their privacy and family life under article 8 of the European Convention on Human Rights and which could not be justified by the benefit of the involvement of the nearest relative.4 Detrimental impact may include cases where patients are likely to suffer emotional distress, deterioration in their mental health, physical harm, or financial or other exploitation as a result of the consultation.

4.61 Consulting and notifying the nearest relative is a significant safeguard for patients. Therefore decisions not to do so on these grounds should not be taken lightly. AMHPs should consider all the circumstances of the case, including:

• the benefit to the patient of the involvement of their nearest relative;

• the patient's wishes (taking into account whether they have the capacity to decide whether they would want their nearest relative involved and any statement of their wishes they have made in advance);

• any detrimental effect that involving the nearest relative would have on the patient's health and wellbeing; and

• whether there is any good reason to think that the patient's objection may be intended to prevent information relevant to the assessment being discovered.

4.62 AMHPs may also consider the degree to which the nearest relative has been willing to be involved on previous occasions, but unwillingness to act previously should not automatically be taken to imply current unwillingness.

4.63 If they do not consult or inform the nearest relative, AMHPs should record their reasons. Consultation must not be avoided purely because it is thought that the nearest relative might object to the application.

4.64 When consulting nearest relatives AMHPs should, where possible:

- ascertain the nearest relative's views about both the patient's needs and the nearest relative's own needs in relation to the patient;
- inform the nearest relative of the reasons for considering an application for detention and what the effects of such an application would be; and
- inform the nearest relative of their role and rights under the Act.

4.65 If the nearest relative objects to an application being made for admission for treatment under section 3, the application cannot be made. If it is thought necessary to proceed with the application to ensure the patient's safety and the nearest relative cannot be persuaded to agree, the AMHP will need to consider applying to the county court for the nearest relative's displacement under section 29 of the Act (see chapter 8).

Consultation with other people

4.66 Although there are specific requirements to consult the nearest relative, it is important to recognise the value of involving other people, particularly the patient's carers and family, in the decision-making process as well. Carers and family members are often able to provide a particular perspective on the patient's circumstances. Insofar as the urgency of the case allows, AMHPs should consider consulting with other relevant relatives, carers or friends and should take their views into account.

4.67 Where patients are under 18, AMHPs should in particular consider consulting with the patient's parents (or other people who have parental responsibility for the patient), assuming they are not the patient's nearest relative anyway.

4.68 In deciding whether it is appropriate to consult carers and other family members, AMHPs should consider:

- the patient's wishes;
- the nature of the relationship between the patient and the person in question, including how long the relationship has existed; and
- whether the patient has referred to any hostility between them and the person in question, or there is other evidence of hostility, abuse or exploitation.

4.69 AMHPs should also consult wherever possible with other people who have been involved with the patient's care. These could include people working for statutory, voluntary or independent mental health services and other service providers who do not specialise in mental health services but have contact with the patient. For example, the patient may be known to services for older people or substance misuse services.

4.70 Some patients may have an attorney or deputy appointed under the MCA who has authority to make decisions about their personal welfare. Where such a person is known to exist, AMHPs should take reasonable steps to contact them and seek their opinion. Where attorneys or deputies have the power to consent or refuse treatment for mental disorder on the patient's behalf, they should also be given the opportunity to talk directly to the doctors assessing the patient, where practicable.

Medical examination by doctors as part of the assessment

4.71 A medical examination must involve:

- direct personal examination of the patient and their mental state; and
- consideration of all available relevant clinical information, including that in the possession of others, professional or non-professional.

4.72 If direct physical access to the patient is not immediately possible and it is not desirable to postpone the examination in order to negotiate access, consideration should be given to requesting that an AMHP apply for a warrant under section 135 of the Act (see paragraph 4.54).

4.73 Where practicable, at least one of the medical recommendations must be provided by a doctor with previous acquaintance with the patient. Preferably, this should be a doctor who has personally treated the patient. But it is sufficient for the doctor to have had some previous knowledge of the patient's case.

4.74 It is preferable that a doctor who does not have previous acquaintance with the patient be approved under section 12 of the Act. The Act requires that at least one of the doctors must be so approved.

4.75 If the doctors reach the opinion that the patient needs to be admitted to hospital, it is their responsibility to take the necessary steps to secure a suitable hospital bed. It is not the responsibility of the applicant, unless it has been agreed locally between the LSSA and the relevant NHS bodies that this will be done by any AMHP involved in the assessment. Primary care trusts are responsible for commissioning mental health services to meet the needs of their areas. They should ensure that procedures are in place through which beds can be identified where required.

4.76 Doctors must give reasons for the opinions stated in their recommendations. When giving a clinical description of the patient's mental disorder as part of these reasons, doctors should include a description of the patient's symptoms and behaviour, not merely a diagnostic classification.

4.77 When making recommendations for detention under section 3, doctors are required to state that appropriate medical treatment is available for the patient (see chapter 6). Preferably, they should know in advance of making the recommendation the name of the hospital to which the patient is to be admitted. But, if that is not possible, their recommendation may state that appropriate medical treatment will be available if the patient is admitted to one or more specific hospitals (or units within a hospital).

Communicating the outcome of the assessment

4.78 Having decided whether or not to make an application for detention, AMHPs should inform the patient, giving their reasons. Subject to the normal considerations of patient confidentiality, AMHPs should also give their decision and the reasons for it to:

- the patient's nearest relative;
- the doctors involved in the assessment;
- the patient's care co-ordinator (if they have one); and
- the patient's GP, if they were not one of the doctorsinvolved in the assessment.

4.79 An AMHP should, when informing the nearest relative that they not do intend to make an application, advise the nearest relative of their right to do so instead. If the nearest relative wishes to pursue this, the AMHP should suggest that they consult with the doctors involved in the assessment to see if they would be prepared to provide recommendations anyway.

4.80 Where the AMHP has considered a patient's case at the request of the nearest relative, the reasons for not applying for the patient's detention must be given to the nearest relative in writing. Such a letter should contain, as far as possible, sufficient details to enable the nearest relative to understand the decision while at the same time preserving the patient's right to confidentiality.

Action when it is decided not to apply for detention

4.81 There is no obligation on an AMHP or nearest relative to make an application for detention just because the statutory criteria are met.

4.82 Where AMHPs decide not to apply for a patient's detention they should record the reasons for their decision. The decision should be supported, where necessary, by an alternative framework of care and treatment. AMHPs must decide how to pursue any actions which their assessment indicates are necessary to meet the needs of the patient. That might include, for example, referring the patient to social, health or other services.

4.83 The steps to be taken to put in place any new arrangements for the patient's care and treatment, and any plans for reviewing them, should be recorded in writing and copies made available to all those who need them (subject to the normal considerations of patient confidentiality).

4.84 It is particularly important that the patient's care coordinator (if they have one) is fully involved in decisions about meeting the patient's needs.

4.85 Arrangements should be made to ensure that information about assessments and their outcome is passed to professional colleagues where appropriate, for example where an application for detention is not immediately necessary but might be in the future. This information will need to be available at short notice at any time of day or night.

4.86 More generally, making out-of-hours services aware of situations that are ongoing – such as when there is concern over an individual but no assessment has begun, or when a person has absconded before an assessment could start or be completed – assists out-of-hours services in responding accordingly.

Action when it is decided to make an application

4.87 Most compulsory admissions require prompt action. However, applicants have up to 14 days (depending on when the patient was last examined by a doctor as part of the assessment) in which to decide whether to make the application, starting with the day they personally last saw the patient. There may be cases where AMHPs conclude that they should delay taking a final decision, in order to see whether the patient's condition changes, or whether successful alternatives to detention can be put in place in the interim.

4.88 Before making an application, AMHPs should ensure that appropriate arrangements are in place for the immediate care of any dependent children the patient may have and any adults who rely on the patient for care. Their needs should already have been considered as part of the assessment.

4.89 Where relevant, AMHPs should also ensure that practical arrangements are made for the care of any pets and for the LSSA to carry out its other duties under the National Assistance Act 1948 to secure the patient's home and protect their property.

4.90 Applications for detention must be addressed to the managers of the hospital where the patient is to be detained. An application must state a specific hospital. An application cannot, for example, be made to an NHS trust without specifying which of the trust's hospitals the patient is to be admitted to.

4.91 Where units under the management of different bodies exist on the same site (or even in the same building), they will be separate hospitals for the purposes of the Act, because one hospital cannot be under the control of two sets of managers. Where there is potential for confusion, the respective hospital managers should ensure that there are distinct names for the units. In collaboration with LSSAs, they should take steps to ensure that information is available to AMHPs who are likely to be making relevant applications to enable them effectively to distinguish the different hospitals on the site and to describe them correctly in applications.

4.92 Once an application has been completed, the patient should be conveyed to the hospital as soon as possible, if they are not already in the hospital. But patients should not be moved until it is known that the hospital is willing to accept them.

4.93 A properly completed application supported by the necessary medical recommendations provides the applicant with the authority to convey the patient to hospital even if the patient does not wish to go. That authority lasts for 14 days from the date when the patient was last examined by one of the doctors with a view to making a recommendation to support the application. See chapter 11 for further guidance on conveyance.

4.94 The AMHP should provide an outline report for the hospital at the time the patient is first admitted or detained, giving reasons for the application and details of any practical matters about the patient's circumstances which the hospital should know. Where possible, the report should include the name and telephone number of the AMHP or a care co-ordinator who can give further information. LSSAs should consider the use of a standard form on which AMHPs can make this outline report.

4.95 Where it is not realistic for the AMHP to accompany the patient to the hospital – for example, where the admitting hospital is some distance from the area in which the AMHP operates – it is acceptable for them to provide the information outlined above by telephone or fax or other means compatible with transferring confidential information. If providing the information by telephone, the AMHP should ensure that a written report is sent to the admitting hospital as soon as possible.

4.96 An outline report does not take the place of the full report which AMHPs are expected to complete for their employer or the LSSA on whose behalf they are acting (if different).

4.97 If the patient is a restricted patient, the AMHP should ensure that the Mental Health Unit of the Ministry of Justice is notified of the detention as soon as possible. A duty officer is available at all times to receive this information, which should not be left until office hours.

4.98 An application cannot be used to admit a patient to any hospital other than the one stated in the application (although once admitted a patient may be transferred to another hospital – see chapter 30).

4.99 In exceptional circumstances, if patients are conveyed to a hospital which has agreed to accept them, but there is no longer a bed available, the managers and staff of that hospital should assist in finding a suitable alternative for the patient. This may involve making a new application to a different hospital. If the application is under section 3, new medical recommendations will be required, unless the original recommendations already state that appropriate medical treatment is available in the proposed new hospital. The hospital to which the original application was made should assist in securing new medical recommendations if they are needed. A situation of this sort should be considered a serious failure and should be recorded and investigated accordingly.

Resolving disagreements

4.100 Sometimes there will be differences of opinion between professionals involved in the assessment. There is nothing wrong with disagreements: handled properly they offer an opportunity to safeguard the interests of the patient by widening the discussion on the best way of meeting their needs. Doctors and AMHPs should be ready to consult other professionals (especially care co-ordinators and others involved with the patient's current care), while themselves retaining the final responsibility for their decision. Where disagreements do occur, professionals should ensure that they discuss these with each other.

4.101 Where there is an unresolved dispute about an application for detention, it is essential that the professionals do not abandon the patient. Instead, they should explore and agree an alternative plan – if necessary on a temporary basis. Such a plan should include a risk assessment and identification of the arrangements for managing the risks. The alternative plan should be recorded in writing, as should the arrangements for reviewing it. Copies should be made available to all those who need them (subject to the normal considerations of patient confidentiality).

4.102 The Secretary of State has delegated to strategic health authorities (SHAs) the task of approving medical practitioners under section 12(2) of the Act. Medical practitioners who are approved clinicians under the Act are automatically treated as being approved under section 12 as well.

4.103 SHAs should:

- take active steps to encourage sufficient doctors, including GPs and those working in prison health services and the police service, to apply for approval;
- ensure that arrangements are in place for 24-hour on-call rotas of approved doctors (or an equivalent arrangement) sufficient to cover each area for which they are responsible;
- ensure that regularly updated lists of approved doctors are maintained which indicate how they can be contacted and the hours that each is available; and
- ensure that the up-to-date list of approved doctors and details of 24-hour on-call rotas (or the equivalent arrangement) are available to all those who may need them, including GPs, providers of hospital and community mental health services and social services.

Co-operation between local agencies

4.104 NHS bodies and LSSAs should co-operate in ensuring that there are opportunities for regular communication between professionals involved in mental health assessments, in order to promote understanding and to provide a forum for clarification of their respective roles and responsibilities. NHS bodies and LSSAs should also keep in mind the interface with the criminal justice agencies, including the probation service and the police.

4.105 Opportunities should also be sought to involve and learn directly from people with experience of being assessed.

Patients who are deaf

4.106 AMHPs and doctors assessing a deaf person should, wherever possible, have had deaf awareness training, including basic training in issues relating to mental health and deafness. Where required, they should also seek assistance from specialists with appropriate expertise in mental health and deafness. This may be available from one of the specialist hospital units for deafness and mental health. Contact with such units may, in particular, help to prevent deaf people being wrongly assessed as having a learning disability or another mental disorder.

4.107 Unless different arrangements have been agreed locally, the AMHP involved in the assessment should be responsible for booking and using registered qualified interpreters with expertise in mental health interpreting, bearing in mind that the interpretation of thought-disordered language requires particular expertise. Relay interpreters (interpreters who relay British Sign Language (BSL) to hands-on BSL or visual frame signing or close signing) may be necessary, such as when the deaf person has a visual impairment, does not use BSL to sign or has minimal language skills or a learning disability.

4.108 Reliance on unqualified interpreters or health professionals with only limited signing skills should be avoided. Family members may (subject to the normal considerations about patient confidentiality) occasionally be able to assist a professional interpreter in understanding a patient's idiosyncratic use of language. However, family members should not be relied upon in place of a professional interpreter, even if the patient is willing for them to be involved.

4.109 Pre-lingual deafness may cause delayed language acquisition, which may in turn influence social behaviour. People carrying out assessments of deaf people under the Act should have an awareness and knowledge of how mental health problems present in pre-lingually deaf people.

4.110 Cultural issues need to be taken into account, for instance in people who are pre-lingually deaf, as they have a visual perspective of the world and may consider themselves to be part of a cultural and linguistic minority. This means that they may behave in ways which are misperceived as evidence of mental disorder. For example, animated signing may be misunderstood as aggression, while touching a hearing person to talk to them may be misunderstood as an assault. Deaf people's spoken or written English may be poor, giving rise to a false assumption of thought disorder.

1.50 The issue of what is meant by 'consultation' has also been considered by the Courts. The following principles have emerged. First, there is no embargo on when the consultation should take place, and the purpose of the consultation is to provide the social worker with information as to whether to apply for an admission, and secondly to put the nearest relative into a position where he may object to the application (*Re Whitbread (Mental Patient: Habeas Corpus)* (1998) 39 BMLR 94, (1997) *Times* 14 July. Thirdly, it is not necessary for the social worker to carry out the assessment himself, but it is preferable for this to happen (*R v South Western Hospital Managers ex p M* [1994] 1 All ER 161).

The displacement of the nearest relative

1.51 Circumstances in which an nearest relative need not be informed or consulted include where the AMHP cannot obtain sufficient information to establish either identity or location, or where to do so would require an excessive amount of investigation involving unreasonable delay. Also, there is a proviso to the effect that there may be situations where although possible to identify and consult the nearest relative it would be an infringement of the right to privacy and family life (Art 8) of the patient.

Mental Health Act 1983

29 Appointment by court of acting nearest relative

(1) The county court may, upon application made in accordance with the provisions of this section in respect of a patient, by order direct that the functions of the nearest relative of the patient under this Part of this Act and sections 66 and 69 below shall, during the continuance in force of the order, be exercisable by the person specified in the order.

(1A) If the court decides to make an order on an application under subsection (1) above, the following rules have effect for the purposes of specifying a person in the order –

   (a)   if a person is nominated in the application to act as the patient's nearest relative and that person is, in the opinion of the court, a suitable person to act as such and is willing to do so, the court shall specify that person (or, if there are two or more such persons, such one of them as the court thinks fit);

   (b)   otherwise, the court shall specify such person as is, in its opinion, a suitable person to act as the patient's nearest relative and is willing to do so.

(2) An order under this section may be made on the application of –

   (za)   the patient;
   (a)   any relative of the patient;
   (b)   any other person with whom the patient is residing (or, if the patient is then an in-patient in a hospital, was last residing before he was admitted); or
   (c)   an approved mental health professional;

(3) An application for an order under this section may be made upon any of the following grounds, that is to say –

   (a)   that the patient has no nearest relative within the meaning of this Act, or that it is not reasonably practicable to ascertain whether he has such a relative, or who that relative is;

   (b)   that the nearest relative of the patient is incapable of acting as such by reason of mental disorder or other illness;

   (c)   that the nearest relative of the patient unreasonably objects to the making of an application for admission for treatment or a guardianship application in respect of the patient;

   (d)   that the nearest relative of the patient has exercised without due regard to the welfare of the patient or the interests of the public his power to discharge the patient under this Part of this Act, or is likely to do so; or

   (e)   that the nearest relative of the patient is otherwise not a suitable person to act as such.

(4) If, immediately before the expiration of the period for which a patient is liable to be detained by virtue of an application for admission for assessment, an application under this section, which is an application made on the ground specified in subsection (3)(c) or (d) above, is pending in respect of the patient, that period shall be extended –

   (a)   in any case, until the application under this section has been finally disposed of; and

(b) if an order is made in pursuance of the application under this section, for a further period of seven days;

and for the purposes of this subsection an application under this section shall be deemed to have been finally disposed of at the expiration of the time allowed for appealing from the decision of the court or, if notice of appeal has been given within that time, when the appeal has been heard or withdrawn, and "pending" shall be construed accordingly.

(5) An order made on the ground specified in subsection (3)(a), (b) or (e) above may specify a period for which it is to continue in force unless previously discharged under section 30 below.

(6) While an order made under this section is in force, the provisions of this Part of this Act (other than this section and section 30 below) and sections 66, 69, 132(4) and 133 below shall apply in relation to the patient as if for any reference to the nearest relative of the patient there were substituted a reference to the person having the functions of that relative and (without prejudice to section 30 below) shall so apply notwithstanding that the person who was the patient's nearest relative when the order was made is no longer his nearest relative; but this subsection shall not apply to section 66 below in the case mentioned in paragraph (h) of subsection (1) of that section.

The procedure for an application to displace the nearest relative

1.52 The grounds upon which an order may be made are relatively self-explanatory. The commonest grounds are those set out in s 29(3)(c) or (d). If a local authority is to succeed in its application, then it will require not just evidence from a social worker, but preferably also from an appropriately qualified and experienced medical practitioner in support of the order. Similarly, the nearest relative is entitled to all the documentation if he is to attempt to resist the application (see *R (on the Application of Stevens) v Plymouth City Council (C as Interested Party)*). The hearing itself must be before a County Court judge (and *not* a District Judge, who has no jurisdiction). All practitioners in such proceedings must be aware that this jurisdiction exercised in the County Court is specialised, fairly technical, and in comparison with normal Court business, rare. There are numerous traps for the unwary. Representatives should take particular additional care to be prepared to explain the law and procedure in more detail to the Court than might ordinarily be expected. The hearings are in private. Further Fennell comments:

'**5.14** The MHA 2007 introduces an additional ground in new s 29(3)(e) "that the nearest relative is otherwise unsuitable to act". The patient may apply for displacement on any of the above grounds. Section 23 also amends s 29 of the MHA 1983 to provide that where the person nominated by the applicant is, in the court's opinion, not "suitable" or there is no nomination, the court can appoint any other person it thinks is "suitable".'

1.53 The former procedure for making an application to displace the nearest relative was changed in April 2007 (and now exists in a similar form). The relevant part of the CPR (as amended) is set out below. The only actual

alteration between the old format and the new (apart from some
re-arrangements in the way in which it is set out) is that the repealed CPR 12(4)
read:

> '... the respondent shall be told the substance of any part of the report bearing on
> his fitness or conduct which the judge considers to be material for the **fair**
> determination of the application.'

The equivalent in the amended CPR 1998 (Practice Direction 8A; 8APD.18
'Application made under Mental Health Act 1983') omits the word 'fair'. This
would seem to be a rather capricious omission, but unlikely to be of much
consequence given the authorities referred to elsewhere, and the implications of
Art 6 of the European Convention for the Protection of Human Rights and
Fundamental Freedoms. In summary, the following steps need to be taken. A
claim form has to be filed in the Court where either the patient's place of
residence is situated, or if it is for the variation of an earlier order, in the
County Court where such an order was made. The nearest relative should be a
respondent (unless the grounds are s 29(3)(a)) and the Court can make any
other person a Respondent. It is noteworthy that the patient is not
automatically a party to the proceedings. Since the patient is intrinsically
involved in the litigation, this is a matter which may require careful thought at
a hearing. It is not unusual for the patient himself to have a view on the issue of
what should or should not happen to the nearest relative. In addition, the
consequences of a displacement will have a direct impact on the patient himself.
If the patient has capacity in respect of the litigation, then it follows that there
is unlikely to be a compelling reason why he should not be a party to
proceedings, and have legal representation in this very specialised area of law. If
the patient does not have capacity on this specific issue, then he will have the
status of a protected party (CPR 21) and in the absence of any suitable
alternative, the Official Solicitor would be appointed as his litigation friend. In
order to establish a lack of capacity, evidence will be required. The test for
capacity is set out in the Mental Capacity Act 2005 (see Chapter 2). Thus, if the
patient is excluded from proceedings, it is almost certain that he is being
prevented from having access to a hearing in which his civil rights are being
determined, which in turn might lead to a breach of Art 6 of the ECHR. For
example, if he had been detained under s 2 of the MHA 1983, and an
application to displace had been made in circumstances that caused an
extension of that detention (via s 29(4)) then his access to a Mental Health
Tribunal may be limited or compromised. Whilst it is the case that the Practice
Direction provides that the Circuit Judge can interview the patient or direct a
District Judge to do so, and report to the Judge in writing, this is not a practice
which can be common, and in any event if deployed would trigger yet further
evidential problems, and still not render the hearing compliant with the ECHR.

Application under Mental Health Act 1983

18.1 In this paragraph –

(1)   a section referred to by a number refers to the section so numbered in
      the Mental Health Act 1983 and "Part II" means Part II of that Act;

(2)   "hospital manager" means the manager of a hospital as defined in section 145(1) of the Act; and

(3)   "place of residence" means, in relation to a patient who is receiving treatment as an in-patient in a hospital or other institution, that hospital or institution.

18.2 The claim form must be filed –

(1)   in the court for the district in which the patient's place of residence is situated; or

(2)   in the case of an application under section 30, in the court that made the order under section 29 which the application seeks to discharge or vary.

18.3 Where an application is made under section 29 for an order that the functions of the nearest relative of the patient are to be exercisable by some other person –

(1)   the nearest relative must be made a respondent, unless –
     (a)   the application is made on the grounds that the patient has no nearest relative or that it is not reasonably practicable to ascertain whether he has a nearest relative; or
     (b)   the court orders otherwise; and

(2)   the court may order that any other person shall be made a respondent.

18.4 Subject to paragraph 18.5, the court may accept as evidence of the facts relied upon in support of the application, any report made –

(1)   by a medical practitioner; or

(2)   by any of the following acting in the course of their official duties –
     (a)   a probation officer;
     (b)   an officer of a local authority;
     (c)   an officer of a voluntary body exercising statutory functions on behalf of a local authority; or
     (d)   an officer of a hospital manager.

18.5 The respondent must be informed of the substance of any part of the report dealing with his fitness or conduct that the court considers to be material to the determination of the claim.

18.6 An application under Part II shall be heard in private unless the court orders otherwise.

18.7 The judge may, for the purpose of determining the application, interview the patient. The interview may take place in the presence of, or separately from, the parties. The interview may be conducted elsewhere than at the court. Alternatively, the judge may direct the district judge to interview the patient and report to the judge in writing.

Applications in respect of displacing nearest relative

1.54   In *Lewis v Gibson and MH (by her litigation friend, the Official Solicitor)* [2005] 8 CCLR 399, [2005] EWCA Civ 587, an order had been made in the conventional manner pursuant to s 29. It had been suggested that an appropriate alternative method of determining the issue would have been to have made an application for a declaration of the best interests of the patient. This argument was rejected, but there was endorsement for the proposition that

CCR Ord 49, r 12(3)(b) should be amended in such a way as to ensure that the Convention rights of the patient were upheld. This has now been amended (CPR 18.3(2)) so that a patient may be made a party to proceedings. The authority is also important in another aspect, which relates to applications to displace generally. In order for an application under this part of the MHA to succeed, the criteria must be made out both as at the date of the application and at the hearing (whether interim or final). Thus, for example, if a nearest relative objected (unreasonably) as at the date of the issuing of proceedings, but by the time of the first hearing withdrew his objections, then that would end the case. It may well be that there are other grounds upon which a local authority might be able to rely upon (eg that he is not a suitable person to act as such under (e)). If this is the case, then it would be better to rely on both grounds. In *R (M) v Homerton University Hospital* [2008] EWCA Civ 197, [2008] MHLR 92 the following legal context was analysed when an application to displace (upon the basis of an unreasonable objection) and an interim order was made displacing the nearest relative. At the time that this order was made, the patient was detained under s 2 of the MHA 1983. The effect of this is to extend the life of a s 2 order until final determination of the application (see below, and s 29(4)). This only applies to applications made using s 29(3)(c) or (d). Once the nearest relative was so displaced on an interim basis (and therefore could no longer object in a manner that could prevent an application being made for admission under s 3 of the MHA1983) the Local Authority duly made such an application, and the patient was admitted via s 3. This created a situation where she was detained both under s 2 and s 3 (until the substantive application could be determined). A Mental Health Tribunal convened, and upheld the detention under s 3, after which the main application for displacement became delayed. The patient applied for judicial review of the decision to admit her under s 3 of the MHA 1983. The basis for this argument was that it was unlawful for there to be in existence detention under both ss 2 and 3, and that by virtue of the latter admission, the jurisdiction of the County Court to decide the issue had been pre-empted. The Court of Appeal held that: (a) there was no legal basis upon which it could be said that a concurrent use of s 2 and s 3 was unlawful; (b) had Parliament wished to prohibit the use of detention under s 3 whilst proceedings for displacement were being conducted in the County Court, it would have expressly incorporated that proposition into s 29 of the MHA 1983. Thus, it is possible to obtain an interim displacement using s 29(3)(c) or (d), and once so obtained, proceed to make an application for detention via s 3, (but whilst the lifespan of s 2 is extended beyond its 28 day period by virtue of s 29(4)).

Interim and concurrent orders

1.55   Other difficulties have arisen over applications made under different sections of the Mental Health Act. This may be a problem for those involved in applications to displace a nearest relative. In *R v Central London CC ex parte Ax London* [1999] 2 CCLR 257, [1999] 2 FLR 161 the issue of interim orders (s 29(1)) and concurrent detention (under s 2) were considered. The interplay between various parts of the Mental Health Act is quite tortuous. The nearest relative of the patient was his mother. The patient was first admitted pursuant to s 4, and then pursuant to s 2 (admission for assessment). At all times the nearest relative had the power to object to the making of an application for admission for treatment. Two days after the admission under s 2, the local authority made an application to displace the mother as nearest relative. The ground relied upon was s 29(3)(c) (unreasonable objection to the making of an application for admission for treatment). The County Court made an order *ex parte* with a return date for a contested hearing 7 days later. The order was extended (after an *inter partes* hearing) for a further period of time, during which (and before the final hearing pursuant to s 29(1) was heard) the patient was detained under s 3 (admission for treatment). This was, of course, the very issue that had been before the Court in respect of the function of the nearest relative. The issues before the Court were: (a) whether the there was jurisdiction to make interim orders; and (b) if there was no such jurisdiction, then whether his detention had been lawful. It was held that the Court did have jurisdiction to make interim orders (s 38 of the County Courts Act 1984). It was also held that unless there were cogent reasons to the contrary, the issue as to displacement should be finally determined *before* any detention is made under s 3. It also held that whilst the s 29(1) application is undetermined, then the power of s 29(4) should be used. The effect of s 29(4) is to enable detention under s 2 to be extended until: (a) the application under s 29(1) is finally disposed of; or (b) for a further period of 7 days (if an order is made). In respect of the wording 'finally disposed of' this includes the period of time permissible for appealing, and/or the determination of the appeal itself. During this period, it follows that the nearest relative will have been displaced, with the consequence that all the powers adumbrated at **1.41** no longer vest in the nearest relative. Furthermore, the period of detention pursuant to s 2 (which is not supposed to last for more than 28 days) will continue for an indefinite period of time. If there is any message to be discerned from the authorities on interim orders in the County Court, and detention under the MHA 1983, it is to ensure that the correct procedural steps are taken prior to and upon issue, and that there is robust case management at an early CMC in the County Court. It is unfortunate that many AMHP's have insufficient training and/or legal support in such circumstances, and the County Court administration itself may not have regular experience of processing what amounts to hybrid claim from a different jurisdiction. In addition, a degree of co-ordination will be required between a local authority applicant, and the RC of the patient (who is, of course a witness, but employed by a separate legal entity eg a Hospital Trust). This can lead to confusion, and delay, and the type of problems which are illustrated above.

Patients who lack capacity and displacement applications

1.56 The problem of extended detention and the interplay of the different sections was again considered in *R (MH) v Secretary of State for Health* [2005] UKHL 60, [2005] MHLR 302. The factual background to the case was that the patient herself lacked capacity. She was detained pursuant to s 2 (for assessment). Her mother (who was her nearest relative) tried to discharge her

from this section. The result was a 'barring order'. The local authority wished
to make the patient subject to a guardianship order (s 7). The mother objected,
and consequently an application was made pursuant to s 29(1). The
consequence of such an application was to automatically extend the duration
of detention under s 2 (s 29(4)). Since the patient herself lacked capacity, she
had not applied to a MHRT within the 14-day period required by s 66(2)(a).
The solicitors acting for the patient subsequently requested the Secretary of
State to make a referral to the Tribunal using powers under s 67. This was done,
and the matter came before a Tribunal. The County Court made an interim
order in due course, and the patient was duly admitted into guardianship.
Baroness Hale gave the leading judgment, and it rewards close reading. In
general, the judgment held that:

> '[305] It must have been originally contemplated that county courts would deal
> with these cases very quickly. In practice, however, they may drag on for a
> considerable time: the county court order in this case was made after a 3 day trial
> in July 2004 and the application not 'finally disposed of' until the Court of Appeal
> dismissed the mother's appeal in May 2005, more than two years after the
> proceedings had begun.'

It comments on upon the effect of s 29(4) thus:

> '[305] Section 29(4) of the 1983 Act places the patient in a most unsatisfactory
> legal position. She has been compulsorily admitted to hospital under a power
> which is meant to last for 28 days at most before either lapsing or being replaced
> with a longer term power for which the procedure and criteria are more stringent.'

The judgment then lists the protection conferred upon the patient in terms of
access to a Tribunal where there s 29(4) does not operate. However:

> 'None of these rights to a review arises if the patient is kept waiting under
> Section 29(4). Yet the timetable for proceedings under Section 29 has nothing to
> do with the patient's needs and is not under her control ... nor does the nearest
> relative have any right to apply to a Tribunal instead.'

What remains in this interregnum is 'a discretionary power in the Secretary of
State for Health at any time to refer the case of any patient who is liable to be
detained (whether or not she is actually in hospital) or is subject to
guardianship' [306]. The issue before the Court was whether or not the
situation created by virtue of the effect of s 29(4) was compatible with the
rights of the patient under Art 5(4) of the European Convention on Human
Rights. The House of Lords held that it was compatible. The Court relied upon
the existing safeguards that exist (even with patients who lack capacity) in the
following terms. First, the managers of the hospital have an obligation to take
such steps as are practical to ensure that the patient understands the effect of
the provisions of detention, and the right to apply to a MHRT (s 132).
Secondly, a referral is treated in the same manner as if the patient herself had

made an application (r 29). An application can be signed by any person authorised by the patient so to do and even where a patient's capacity is compromised:

> '[308] The common law presumes that every person has capacity until the contrary is shown and the threshold for capacity is not a demanding one. These principles have recently been confirmed by Parliament in the Mental Capacity Act 2005.'

As set out at **1.52** above, should the patient lack capacity, the CPR 21 provides that the Official Solicitor may be appointed as the litigation friend.

Thirdly, as in this case, the nearest relative stimulated the reference by the Secretary of State. Fourthly, in respect of s 29(4) itself:

> '[308] The system is obviously **capable** of being operated compatibly ... the county court proceedings may produce a swift displacement order, whether interim or final, after which the patient is admitted under section 3 ... alternatively, a displacement order may be refused ... the problem arises when the county court proceedings drag on and the patient is detained indefinitely without recourse to a Tribunal ... Hence there may well come a time when her Article 5(4) rights will be violated unless some means of taking proceedings is available to her.'

The judgment then returns to the facts of the case, in which the Secretary of State did act to refer the case to a Tribunal. Had this not been the case, then 'judicial review would be swiftly available to oblige her to do so'.

Finally the remedy of judicial review/habeas corpus remains available to challenge the lawfulness of the detention of the patient, although this remedy was not felt to be the most appropriate.

Mental Health Act 1983

30 Discharge and variation of orders under s 29

(1) An order made under section 29 above in respect of a patient may be discharged by the county court upon application made –

    (a)   in any case, by the patient or the person having the functions of the nearest relative of the patient by virtue of the order;

    (b)   where the order was made on the ground specified in paragraph (a), (b) or (e) of section 29(3) above, or where the person who was the nearest relative of the patient when the order was made has ceased to be his nearest relative, on the application of the nearest relative of the patient.

(1A) But, in the case of an order made on the ground specified in paragraph (e) of section 29(3) above, an application may not be made under subsection (1)(b) above by the person who was the nearest relative of the patient when the order was made except with leave of the county court.

(2) An order made under section 29 above in respect of a patient may be varied by the county court, on the application of the patient or of the person having the

functions of the nearest relative by virtue of the order or on the application of an approved mental health professional, by substituting another person for the person having those functions.

(2A) If the court decides to vary an order on an application under subsection (2) above, the following rules have effect for the purposes of substituting another person –

    (a)   if a person is nominated in the application to act as the patient's nearest relative and that person is, in the opinion of the court, a suitable person to act as such and is willing to do so, the court shall specify that person (or, if there are two or more such persons, such one of them as the court thinks fit);

    (b)   otherwise, the court shall specify such person as is, in its opinion, a suitable person to act as the patient's nearest relative and is willing to do so.

(3) If the person having the functions of the nearest relative of a patient by virtue of an order under section 29 above dies –

    (a)   subsections (1) and (2) above shall apply as if for any reference to that person there were substituted a reference to any relative of the patient, and

    (b)   until the order is discharged or varied under those provisions the functions of the nearest relative under this Part of this Act and sections 66 and 69 below shall not be exercisable by any person.

(4) An order made on the ground specified in paragraph (c) or (d) of section 29(3) above shall, unless previously discharged under subsection (1) above, cease to have effect as follows –

    (a)   if –

        (i)   on the date of the order the patient was liable to be detained or subject to guardianship by virtue of a relevant application, order or direction; or

        (ii)   he becomes so liable or subject within the period of three months beginning with that date; or

        (iii)   he was a community patient on the date of the order,

it shall cease to have effect when he is discharged under section 23 above or 72 below or the relevant application, order or direction otherwise ceases to have effect (except as a result of his being transferred in pursuance of regulations under section 19 above);

    (b)   otherwise, it shall cease to have effect at the end of the period of three months beginning with the date of the order.

(4A) In subsection (4) above, reference to a relevant application, order or direction is to any of the following –

    (a)   an application for admission for treatment;

    (b)   a guardianship application;

    (c)   an order or direction under Part 3 of this Act (other than under section 35, 36 or 38).

(4B) An order made on the ground specified in paragraph (a), (b) or (e) of section 29(3) above shall –

(a) if a period was specified under section 29(5) above, cease to have effect on expiry of that period, unless previously discharged under subsection (1) above;

(b) if no such period was specified, remain in force until it is discharged under subsection (1) above.

(5) The discharge or variation under this section of an order made under section 29 above shall not affect the validity of anything previously done in pursuance of the order.

31 Procedure on applications to county court

County court rules which relate to applications authorised by this Part of this Act to be made to a county court may make provision –

(a) for the hearing and determination of such applications otherwise than in open court;

(b) for the admission on the hearing of such applications of evidence of such descriptions as may be specified in the rules notwithstanding anything to the contrary in any enactment or rule of law relating to the admissibility of evidence;

(c) for the visiting and interviewing of patients in private by or under the directions of the court.

1.57 In terms of applications by a nearest relative for discharge of the original order, it is important that practitioners are aware of the implications for s 29(5) of the MHA 1983. In respect of judgments made upon the basis of grounds (a); (b) and (e) the Court may specify the period that such an order can last. In other words, it may be argued that it is not proportionate to remove the nearest relative for more than a finite period. The length of any period of displacement will (of course) be decided upon the individual facts in each case (eg if on ground (a), then how likely it is that a nearest relative will be found, or if on ground (b) the prognosis for the illness, whether physical or mental, and if on ground (c) the nature of the lack of suitability). These are further matters to which the Local Authority should direct its mind prior to making an application for displacement.

66 Applications to tribunals

(1) Where –

(a) a patient is admitted to a hospital in pursuance of an application for admission for assessment; or

(b) a patient is admitted to a hospital in pursuance of an application for admission for treatment; or

(c) a patient is received into guardianship in pursuance of a guardianship application; or

(ca) a community treatment order is made in respect of a patient; or

(cb) a community treatment order is revoked under section 17F above in respect of a patient; or

(d) ...

(e) a patient is transferred from guardianship to a hospital in pursuance of regulations made under section 19 above; or

(f)   a report is furnished under section 20 above in respect of a patient and the patient is not discharged under section 23 above; or

(fza) a report is furnished under section 20A above in respect of a patient and the patient is not discharged under section 23 above; or

(fa)   a report is furnished under subsection (2) of section 21B above in respect of a patient and subsection (5) of that section applies (or subsections (5) and (6)(b) of that section apply) in the case of the report; or

(faa) a report is furnished under subsection (2) of section 21B above in respect of a community patient and subsection (6A) of that section applies (or subsections (6A) and (6B)(b) of that section apply) in the case of the report; or

(fb)   ...

(g)   a report is furnished under section 25 above in respect of a patient who is detained in pursuance of an application for admission for treatment or a community patient; or

(ga)   ...

(gb)   ...

(gc)   ...

(h)   an order is made under section 29 above on the ground specified in paragraph (c) or (d) of subsection (3) of that section in respect of a patient who is or subsequently becomes liable to be detained or subject to guardianship under Part II of this Act or who is a community patient,

an application may be made to a Mental Health Review Tribunal within the relevant period –

(i)   by the patient (except in the cases mentioned in paragraphs (g) and (h) above), and

(ii)   in the cases mentioned in paragraphs (g) and (h) above, by his nearest relative.

(2) In subsection (1) above "the relevant period" means –

(a)   in the case mentioned in paragraph (a) of that subsection, 14 days beginning with the day on which the patient is admitted as so mentioned;

(b)   in the case mentioned in paragraph (b) of that subsection, six months beginning with the day on which the patient is admitted as so mentioned;

(c)   in the case mentioned in paragraph (c) of that subsection, six months beginning with the day on which the application is accepted;

(ca)   in the case mentioned in paragraph (ca) of that subsection, six months beginning with the day on which the community treatment order is made;

(cb)   in the case mentioned in paragraph (cb) of that subsection, six months beginning with the day on which the community treatment order is revoked;

(d)   in the case mentioned in paragraph (g) of that subsection, 28 days beginning with the day on which the applicant is informed that the report has been furnished;

(e)   in the case mentioned in paragraph (e) of that subsection, six months beginning with the day on which the patient is transferred;

(f)   in the case mentioned in paragraph (f) or (fa) of that subsection, the period or periods for which authority for the patient's detention or guardianship is renewed by virtue of the report;

(fza)   in the cases mentioned in paragraphs (fza) and (faa) of that subsection, the period or periods for which the community treatment period is extended by virtue of the report;

(fa)   ...

(g)   in the case mentioned in paragraph (h) of that subsection, 12 months beginning with the date of the order, and in any subsequent period of 12 months during which the order continues in force.

(2A) Nothing in subsection (1)(b) above entitles a community patient to make an application by virtue of that provision even if he is admitted to a hospital on being recalled there under section 17E above.

(3) Section 32 above shall apply for the purposes of this section as it applies for the purposes of Part II of this Act.

1.58 The above are (in part) the statutory regime which provided the safeguards referred to in *R (MH) v Secretary of State for Health*. The Mental Health Act 2007 has made further changes, upon which Fennel comments as follows:

'**5.16** Section 25 of the MHA 2007 amends s 66 of the MHA 1983 and limits applications to the MHRT from displaced NRs. Such an application may be made only by a NR displaced on grounds of unreasonable objection to admission or exercising the power of discharge without due regard to the welfare of the patient or the protection of the public. A person displaced as the NR because he or she is too ill to act, or unsuitable to act, will not have the right to apply to the MHRT.'

132 Duty of managers of hospitals to give information to detained patients

(1) The managers of a hospital or registered establishment in which a patient is detained under this Act shall take such steps as are practicable to ensure that the patient understands –

(a)   under which of the provisions of this Act he is for the time being detained and the effect of that provision; and

(b)   what rights of applying to a Mental Health Review Tribunal are available to him in respect of his detention under that provision;

and those steps shall be taken as soon as practicable after the commencement of the patient's detention under the provision in question.

(2) The managers of a hospital or registered establishment in which a patient is detained as aforesaid shall also take such steps as are practicable to ensure that the patient understands the effect, so far as relevant in his case, of sections 23, 25, 56 to 64, 66(1)(g), 118 and 120 above and section 134 below; and those steps shall be taken as soon as practicable after the commencement of the patient's detention in the hospital or establishment.

(3) The steps to be taken under subsections (1) and (2) above shall include giving the requisite information both orally and in writing.

(4) The managers of a hospital or registered establishment in which a patient is detained as aforesaid shall, except where the patient otherwise requests, take such

steps as are practicable to furnish the person (if any) appearing to them to be his nearest relative with a copy of any information given to him in writing under subsections (1) and (2) above; and those steps shall be taken when the information is given to the patient or within a reasonable time thereafter.

132A Duty of managers of hospitals to give information to community patients

(1) The managers of the responsible hospital shall take such steps as are practicable to ensure that a community patient understands –

    (a)   the effect of the provisions of this Act applying to community patients; and

    (b)   what rights of applying to a Mental Health Review Tribunal are available to him in that capacity;

and those steps shall be taken as soon as practicable after the patient becomes a community patient.

(2) The steps to be taken under subsection (1) above shall include giving the requisite information both orally and in writing.

(3) The managers of the responsible hospital shall, except where the community patient otherwise requests, take such steps as are practicable to furnish the person (if any) appearing to them to be his nearest relative with a copy of any information given to him in writing under subsection (1) above; and those steps shall be taken when the information is given to the patient or within a reasonable time thereafter.

133 Duty of managers of hospitals to inform nearest relatives of discharge

(1) Where a patient liable to be detained under this Act in a hospital or registered establishment is to be discharged otherwise than by virtue of an order for discharge made by his nearest relative, the managers of the hospital or registered establishment shall, subject to subsection (2) below, take such steps as are practicable to inform the person (if any) appearing to them to be the nearest relative of the patient; and that information shall, if practicable, be given at least seven days before the date of discharge.

(1A) The reference in subsection (1) above to a patient who is to be discharged includes a patient who is to be discharged from hospital under section 17A above.

(1B) Subsection (1) above shall also apply in a case where a community patient is discharged under section 23 or 72 above (otherwise than by virtue of an order for discharge made by his nearest relative), but with the reference in that subsection to the managers of the hospital or registered establishment being read as a reference to the managers of the responsible hospital.

(2) Subsection (1) above shall not apply if the patient or his nearest relative has requested that information about the patient's discharge should not be given under this section.

1.59   Section 132 obliges the relevant personnel to provide the nearest relative with certain (albeit limited) information, unless the patient objects to such information being given. The relevance of *R (E) v Bristol City Council* is clear in respect of this part of the statute, as it is in respect of s 133 (where a patient has been discharged from hospital). These obligations are also considered in the Code of Practice in Chapter 2. For the sake of completeness, this Chapter is set out below in its entirety.

Mental Health Act 1983 Code of Practice

CHAPTER 2

Information for patients, nearest relatives and others

2.1 This chapter gives guidance on the information that must be given to patients and their nearest relatives. It also gives guidance on communication with patients and others generally.

Communication with patients

2.2 Effective communication is essential in ensuring appropriate care and respect for patients' rights. It is important that the language used is clear and unambiguous and that people giving information check that the information that has been communicated has been understood.

2.3 Everything possible should be done to overcome barriers to effective communication, which may be caused by any of a number of reasons – for example, if the patient's first language is not English. Patients may have difficulty in understanding technical terms and jargon or in maintaining attention for extended periods. They may have a hearing or visual impairment or have difficulty in reading or writing. A patient's cultural background may also be very different from that of the person speaking to them.

2.4 Those with responsibility for the care of patients need to identify how communication difficulties affect each patient individually, so that they can assess the needs of each patient and address them in the most appropriate way. Hospitals and other organisations should make people with specialist expertise (eg in sign language or Makaton) available as required.

2.5 Where an interpreter is needed, every effort should be made to identify who is appropriate to the patient, given the patient's gender, religion, language, dialect, cultural background and age. The patient's relatives and friends should only exceptionally be used as intermediaries or interpreters. Interpreters (both professional and nonprofessional) must respect the confidentiality of any personal information they learn about the patient through their involvement.

2.6 Independent advocates1 engaged by patients can be invaluable in helping patients to understand the questions and information being presented to them and in helping them to communicate their views to staff. (See chapter 20.)

2.7 Wherever possible, patients should be engaged in the process of reaching decisions which affect their care and treatment under the Act. Consultation with patients involves assisting them in understanding the issue, their role and the roles of others who are involved in taking the decision. Ideally decisions should be agreed with the patient. Where a decision is made that is contrary to the patient's wishes, that decision and the authority for it should be explained to the patient using a form of communication that the patient understands.

Information for detained patients and patients onsupervised community treatment

2.8 The Act requires hospital managers to take steps to ensure that patients who are detained in hospital under the Act, or who are on supervised community treatment (SCT), understand important information about how the Act applies to them. This must be done as soon as practicable after the start of the patient's detention or SCT. This information must also be given to SCT patients who are recalled to hospital.

2.9 Information must be given to the patient both orally and in writing. These are not alternatives. Those providing information to patients should ensure that all relevant information is conveyed in a way that the patient understands.

2.10 It would not be sufficient to repeat what is already written on an information leaflet as a way of providing information orally.

Information about detention and SCT

2.11 Patients must be informed:

- of the provisions of the Act under which they are detained or on SCT, and the effect of those provisions;
- of the rights (if any) of their nearest relative to discharge them (and what can happen if their responsible clinician does not agree with that decision); and
- for SCT patients, of the effect of the community treatment order, including the conditions which they are required to keep to and the circumstances in which their responsible clinician may recall them to hospital.

2.12 As part of this, they should be told:

- the reasons for their detention or SCT;
- the maximum length of the current period of detention or SCT;
- that their detention or SCT may be ended at any time if it is no longer required or the criteria for it are no longer met;
- that they will not automatically be discharged when the current period of detention or SCT ends; and
- that their detention or SCT will not automatically be renewed or extended when the current period of detention or SCT ends.

2.13 Patients should also be told the essential legal and factual grounds for their detention or SCT. For the patient to be able to effectively challenge the grounds for their detention or SCT, should they wish, they should be given the full facts rather than simply the broad reasons. This should be done promptly and clearly.

2.14 In addition, a copy of the detention or SCT documentation should be made available to the patient, unless the hospital managers are of the opinion (based on the advice of the authors of the documents) that the information disclosed would adversely affect the health or wellbeing of the patient or others. It may be necessary to remove any personal information about third parties.

2.15 Where the section of the Act under which the patient is being detained changes, they must be provided with the above information to reflect the new situation. This also applies where a detained patient becomes an SCT patient, where an SCT patient's community treatment order is revoked, or where a conditionally discharged patient is recalled to hospital.

Information about consent to treatment

2.16 Patients must be told what the Act says about treatment for their mental disorder. In particular they must be told:

- the circumstances (if any) in which they can be treated without their consent – and the circumstances in which they have the right to refuse treatment;
- the role of second opinion appointed doctors (SOADs) and the circumstances in which they may be involved; and
- (where relevant) the rules on electro-convulsive therapy (ECT).

Information about seeking a review of detention or SCT

2.17 Patients must be informed:

- of the right of the responsible clinician and the hospital managers to discharge them (and, for restricted patients, that this is subject to the agreement of the Secretary of State for Justice);
- of their right to ask the hospital managers to discharge them;
- that the hospital managers must consider discharging them when their detention is renewed or their SCT extended;
- (for NHS patients in independent hospitals) of the power of the relevant NHS body to discharge them;
- of their rights to apply to the Tribunal;
- of the rights (if any) of their nearest relative to apply to the Tribunal on their behalf;
- about the role of the Tribunal; and
- how to apply to the Tribunal.

2.18 Hospital managers should ensure that patients are offered assistance to request a hospital managers' hearing or make an application to the Tribunal. They should also be told:

- how to contact a suitably qualified legal representative (and should be given assistance to do so if required);
- that free legal aid may be available; and
- how to contact any other organisation which may be able to help them make an application to the Tribunal.

2.19 It is particularly important that patients on SCT who may not have daily contact with people who could help them make an application to the Tribunal are informed and supported in this process.

2.20 SCT patients whose community treatment orders are revoked, and conditionally discharged patients recalled to hospital, should be told that their cases will be referred automatically to the Tribunal.

Information about the Commission

2.21 Patients must be informed about the role of the Commission and of their right to meet visitors appointed by the Commission in private. Patients should be told when the Commission is to visit their hospital and be reminded of the Commission's role.

2.22 Patients may also make a complaint to the Commission, and they should be informed of the process for this. Support should be made available to patients to do this, if required. Patients should also be given information about the hospital's own complaints system and how to use it.

Information about withholding of correspondence

2.23 Detained patients must be told that post sent by them may be withheld if the person to whom it is addressed asks the hospital managers to do so. Patients in high security psychiatric hospitals must be told about the other circumstances in which their correspondence may be withheld, the procedures that will be followed and their right to ask the Commission to review the decisions taken.

Keeping patients informed of their rights

2.24 Those with responsibility for patient care should ensure that patients are reminded from time to time of their rights and the effects of the Act. It may be necessary to convey the same information on a number of different occasions or in different formats and to check regularly that the patient has fully understood it. Information given to a patient who is unwell may need to be repeated when their condition has improved.

2.25 A fresh explanation of the patient's rights should be considered in particular where:

- the patient is considering applying to the Tribunal, or when the patient becomes eligible again to apply to the Tribunal;
- the patient requests the hospital managers to consider discharging them;
- the rules in the Act about their treatment change (for example, because three months have passed since they were first given medication, or because they have regained capacity to consent to treatment – see chapters 23 and 24);
- any significant change in their treatment is beingconsidered;
- there is to be a Care Programme Approach review (or its equivalent);
- renewal of their detention or extension of their SCT is being considered; or
- a decision is taken to renew their detention or toextend their SCT.

2.26 When a patient is discharged from detention or SCT, or the authority for their detention or SCT expires, this fact should be made clear to them. The patient should also be given an explanation of what happens next, including any section 117 after-care or other services which are to be provided.

Information for nearest relatives

2.27 The Act also requires hospital managers to take such steps as are practicable to give the patient's nearest relative a copy of any information given to the patient in writing, unless the patient requests otherwise. The information should be given to the nearest relative when the information is given to the patient, or within a reasonable time afterwards.

2.28 When a patient detained under the Act or on SCT is given information, they should be told that the written information will also be supplied to their nearest relative, so that they have a chance to object.

2.29 The nearest relative should also be told of the patient's discharge from detention or SCT (where practicable), unless either the patient or the nearest relative has requested that information about discharge should not be given. This includes discharge from detention onto SCT. If practicable, the information should be given at least seven days in advance of the discharge.

2.30 In addition, regulations require nearest relatives to be informed of various other events, including the renewal of a patient's detention, extension of SCT and transfer from one hospital to another.

2.31 These duties to inform nearest relatives are not absolute. In almost all cases, information is not to be shared if the patient objects.

2.32 In addition, there will occasionally be cases where these duties do not apply because disclosing information about the patient to the nearest relative cannot be considered practicable, on the grounds that it would have a detrimental impact on the patient that is disproportionate to any advantage to be gained from informing the nearest relative. This would therefore be a breach of the patient's right to privacy under the European Convention on Human Rights. The risk of this is greatest where the nearest relative is someone whom the patient would not have chosen themselves.

2.33 Before disclosing information to nearest relatives without a patient's consent, the person concerned must consider whether the disclosure would be likely to:

- put the patient at risk of physical harm or financial or other exploitation;
- cause the patient emotional distress or lead to a deterioration in their mental health; or
- have any other detrimental effect on their health or wellbeing, and if so whether the advantages to the patient and the public interest of the disclosure outweigh the disadvantages to the patient, in the light of all the circumstances of the case.

Communication with other people nominated by the patient

2.34 Patients may want to nominate one or more people who they would wish to be involved in, or notified of, decisions related to their care and treatment.

2.35 Patients may nominate an independent mental health advocate, another independent advocate or a legal professional. But they may also nominate a relative, friend or other informal supporter.

2.36 The involvement of such friends, relatives or other supporters can have significant benefits for the care and treatment of the patient. It can provide reassurance to the patient, who may feel distrustful of professionals who are able to impose compulsory measures on them, or are relatively unfamiliar and unknown to the patient. People who know the patient well can provide knowledge of the patient and perspectives that come from long-standing and intimate involvement with the patient prior to (and during) their involvement with mental health services. They can provide practical assistance in helping the patient to convey information and views and may have knowledge of advance decisions or statements made by the patient (see chapter 17).

2.37 Professionals should normally agree to a patient's request to involve relatives, friends or other informal supporters. They should tell the patient whenever such a request will not be, or has not been, granted. Where a patient's request is refused, it is good practice to record this in the patient's notes, giving reasons for the refusal. It may not always be appropriate to involve another person as requested by the patient, for example where:

• contacting and involving the person would result in a delay to the decision in question that would not be in the patient's best interests;
• the involvement of the person is contrary to the best interests of the patient; or
• that person has requested that they should not be involved.

2.38 Professionals should also take steps to find out whether patients who lack capacity to take particular decisions for themselves have an attorney or deputy with authority to take the decision on their behalf. Where there is such a person, they act as the agent of the patient, and should be informed in the same way as the patient themselves about matters within the scope of their authority.

Involvement of carers

2.39 Carers frequently play a vital role in helping to look after relatives and friends who have mental disorders. It is important to identify all individuals who provide regular and substantial care for patients, to ensure that health and social services assess those carers' needs and, where relevant, provide services to meet them.

2.40 Unless there are reasons to the contrary, patients should be encouraged to agree to their carers being involved in decisions under the Act and to them being kept informed. If patients lack capacity to consent to this, it may be appropriate to involve and inform carers if it is in the patient's best interests – although that decision must always be made in the light of the specific circumstances of the case.

2.41 In order to ensure that carers can, where appropriate, participate fully in decision-making, it is important that they have access to:

- practical and emotional help and support to help them to participate; and
- timely access to comprehensive, up-to-date and accurate information.

2.42 Even if carers cannot be given detailed information about the patient's case, where appropriate they should be offered general information which may help them understand the nature of mental disorder, the way it is treated, and the operation of the Act.

Information for patients' children

2.43 In considering the kind and amount of information which children and young people (especially young carers) should receive about a parent's condition or treatment, the people giving the information will need to balance the interests of the child or young person against the patient's right to privacy and their wishes and feelings. Any such information should be appropriate to the age and understanding of the child or young person.

Hospital managers' information policy

2.44 The formal duty to ensure that detained and SCT patients and their nearest relatives have been informed about their legal situation and rights falls to the hospital managers. In practice, it would usually be more appropriate for professionals working with the patient to provide them with the information. In order to fulfil their statutory duties hospital managers should have policies in place to ensure that:

- the correct information is given to patients and their nearest relatives;
- information is given in accordance with the requirements of the legislation, at a suitable time and in an accessible format, where appropriate with the aid of assistive technologies and interpretative and advocacy services;
- people who give the information have received sufficient training and guidance;
- a record is kept of the information given, including how, when, where and by whom it was given, and an assessment made of how well the information was understood by the recipient; and
- a regular check is made that information has been properly given to each patient and understood by them.

Information for informal hospital in-patients

2.45 Although the Act does not impose any duties to give information to informal patients, these patients should be made aware of their legal position and rights. Local policies and arrangements about movement around the hospital and its grounds must be clearly explained to the patients concerned. Failure to do so could lead to a patient mistakenly believing that they are not allowed freedom of movement, which could result in an unlawful deprivation of their liberty.

Information for those subject to guardianship

2.46 Responsible local social service authorities (LSSAs) are required to take steps to ensure that guardianship patients understand their rights to apply to the Tribunal and the rights of their nearest relatives. The same information must also normally be given to nearest relatives. More generally, LSSAs (and private guardians) should do what they can to ensure that patients understand why they have been made subject to guardianship and what it means for them.

1.60   Chapter 18 of the Code of Conduct addressed matters of confidentiality generally, and information sharing. For the sake of brevity, only para 18.2 (General Points and Summary) is set out below.

General points

18.2 Except where the Act itself says otherwise, the law on confidentiality is the same for patients subject to the Act as it is for any other patients. The box below gives a brief summary of the most fundamental points of the general law. There are some additional considerations in relation to children and young people (see chapter 36).

Confidentiality – a brief summary

In common law, a duty of confidence arises when one person discloses information to another in circumstances where it is reasonable to expect that the information will be held in confidence. Certain situations, such as discussions with a health professional or social worker, are generally presumed to be confidential.

However, there are circumstances in which it is both justifiable and important to share otherwise confidential patient information with people outside the immediate team treating a patient.

Before considering such disclosure of confidential patient information, the individual's consent should normally be sought.

If a person lacks the capacity to consent to the disclosure, it may nonetheless be acceptable and appropriate to disclose the information in the person's best interests.

Otherwise, confidential patient information should be disclosed outside the team only:

- with the person's consent (where the person has capacity to consent);
- if there is a specific legal obligation or authority to do so; or
- where there is an overriding public interest in disclosing the information.

The "public interest" is not the same as what might be of interest to the public. Where confidential patient information is involved, public interest justifications for overriding confidentiality could include (but are not limited to) protecting other people from serious harm and preventing serious crime.

The common law does not normally permit disclosure of confidential patient information solely in the person's own interests, where they have capacity to consent to the disclosure but refuse to do so.

A person's right to have their privacy respected is also protected by Article 8 of the European Convention on Human Rights. The disclosure of confidential information may be a breach of that right unless it is a necessary and proportionate response to the situation.

Chapter 2

CAPACITY AND THE COURT OF PROTECTION

ASSESSMENT OF CAPACITY

2.1 The issue of capacity may become inextricably linked with matters of assessment and protection. These have an impact upon the role of the local authority in ensuring that the implications which flow from a lack of capacity are fully understood and considered. The law in respect of the role of a local authority in protecting those adults who may not lack capacity, but are nevertheless classed as 'vulnerable adults' is partially considered in this Chapter, but mainly in Chapter 3.

2.2 The Mental Capacity Act 2005 is considered insofar as it is relevant to local authorities. However, the majority of the law in this area is still based on common law principles. The main developments have been within the past decade or so, but as a result of vast numbers of cases that have been heard in the Court of Protection (since October 2007) there has been an acceleration of those developments during the period of its existence. The majority of authorities referred to in this Chapter derive from the jurisdiction of the Court of Protection, but the principles upon which the Court of Protection operates were more often than not in existence prior to that date. For those who require a detailed and specialist guide to the Court of Protection, the only textbook in this area is *Court of Protection Practice* (Jordan Publishing). This is published on an annual basis.

CAPACITY – GENERAL CONCEPTS

2.3 A useful starting point for considering capacity is *Re C (Refusal of Medical Treatment)* [1994] 1 FLR 31. The application concerned itself in part with the jurisdiction of the court to grant injunctive or declaratory relief. The subject matter was whether or not a patient (within the meaning of the Mental Health Act 1983 (MHA 1983)) was capable of making a decision about the amputation of his leg. In a short but significant judgment the following principles emerged. First, (by reference to *Re T (An Adult) (Consent to Medical Treatment)* [1992] 2 FLR 458 and *Airedale NHS Trust v Bland* [1993] 1 FLR 1026) there are four propositions adopted from *Re T*. These are:

> '(1) Prima facie every adult has the right and capacity to decide whether or not he will accept medical treatment ... it matters not whether the reasons for the refusal

were rational or irrational, unknown or even non-existent ... however, the presumption of capacity to decide, which stems from the fact that the patient is an adult, is rebuttable. (2) An adult patient may be deprived of his capacity to decide ... by long term mental incapacity ... (3) If an adult patient did not have the capacity to decide at the time of the purported refusal and still does not have that capacity, it is the duty of the doctors to treat him in whatever way they consider, in the exercise of their clinical judgment, to be in his best interests. (4) Doctors faced with a refusal of consent have to give very careful and detailed consideration to what was the patient's capacity to decide at the time when the decision was made. **It may not be a case of capacity or no capacity: it may be a case of reduced capacity** [emphasis added]. What matters is whether at the time the patient's capacity was reduced below the level needed in the case of a refusal of that importance, for refusals can vary in importance. Some may involve a risk to life or of irreparable damage to health. Others may not.'

2.4   The question that Mr Justice Thorpe held to be most salient was 'whether it has been established that Mr C's mental capacity is so reduced by his chronic mental illness that he does not sufficiently understand the nature, purpose and effects of the preferred amputation'. The test is paraphrased in the headnote thus: 'The decision-making process could be analysed in three stages: (i) comprehending and retaining treatment information; (ii) believing it; and (iii) weighing it in the balance to arrive at a choice'. The judgment is also authority for the availability of declaratory or injunctive relief in the exercise of its inherent jurisdiction.

2.5   Notwithstanding the time that the above test has been in existence, there is still confusion as to the test for capacity in respect of patients on the part of practitioners unfamiliar with this area. It is also noteworthy that this judgment presaged subsequent authorities which have emphasised the fluctuating nature of capacity, and the need to decide the issue of capacity in the specific context of the decision being made.

2.6   The test was re-stated in *Re MB (Medical Treatment)* [1997] 2 FLR 426 as follows:

'[437D–437H] A person lacks capacity if some impairment or disturbance of mental functioning renders the person unable to make a decision whether to consent or to refuse treatment. That inability to make a decision will occur when: (a) the patient is unable to comprehend and retain the information which is material to the decision, especially as to the likely consequences of having or not having the treatment in question; (b) the patient is unable to use the information and weigh it in the balance as part of the process of arriving at the decision. If, as Thorpe J observed in *Re C* (above) a compulsive disorder or phobia from which the patient suffers stifles belief in the information presented ... then the decision may not be a true one ... The temporary factors mentioned by Lord Donaldson MR in *Re T* (above) (confusion, shock, fatigue, pain or drugs) may completely erode capacity but those concerned must be satisfied that such factors are operating to such a degree that the ability to decide is absent ... Another such influence may be panic induced by fear. Again, careful scrutiny of the evidence is necessary because fear of an operation may be a rational reason for refusal to undergo it. Fear may also, however, paralyse the will and thus destroy the capacity to make a decision.'

2.7 The point is made at greater length in *Masterman-Lister v Brutton & Co (1) and Jewell and Home Counties Dairies (2)* [2002] EWCA Civ 1889, [2004] 7 CCLR 5. Whether or not an individual is incapable of managing his own affairs is a matter for judicial determination, based upon evidence. It is not a decision (within the context of litigation) that can be made either administratively, or without evidence. The definition of a patient (either as defined at s 1(2) of MHA 1983, or s 94(2)) may not be of great assistance. The test of capacity must be specific to the issue in question (it might be in respect of litigation, it might be in respect of financial matters, it might be in respect of medical treatment). The same test was adopted as set out in *Re C*. The Civil Procedure Rules (CPR 21.1) emphasise the need to focus on litigation rather than the ability to manage business affairs. The burden of proof is upon whomsoever wishes to establish a lack of capacity, based upon medical evidence. Incapacity does not depend upon rashness or irresponsibility.

2.8 A similar issue was the subject of judicial determination in *Re E (An Alleged Patient); Sheffield City Council v E & S* [2004] EWHC 2808 (Fam), [2005] 1 FLR 965, [2005] 2 WLR 953. Although *prima facie* the case was on the issue of protection of a vulnerable adult who wished to marry, the judgment concentrates upon the specific issue of capacity to consent within the context of a contract of marriage ('subject matter capacity'), and the capacity to litigate generally. The judgment is extensive, and provides a thorough review of all the authorities on the subject of capacity generally, and the contract of marriage specifically. The following propositions can be extracted. First, as regards the contract of marriage, there must be an understanding of the actual purpose and nature of the act – that is to say, an appreciation of the consequences in terms of duties and responsibilities which flow from entering into such a contract. Secondly, the test was general to the issue of a capacity to consent (that is to say, it did not depend upon the person to whom the alleged patient wished to marry, and whether the choice of that partner was itself an unwise choice). Thirdly, the test of 'best interests' was irrelevant to the issue of capacity to marry, since the court could not supply consent on behalf of someone who lacked capacity to marry, and if capacity to marry existed, then the involvement of the court was otiose. Fourthly, any analogies with consent to medical treatment were unhelpful (since expert evidence would undoubtedly inform the correct path, whereas the contract of marriage was in itself simple). Fifthly, there is a distinction between 'litigation capacity' (cf *Masterman-Lister*) and 'subject-matter capacity'. An individual who lacked litigation capacity (that is to say, who could not conduct litigation on his own behalf) may not necessarily lack 'subject matter capacity' (that is to say, the subject matter of the litigation itself). However, it was held to be unlikely that where someone lacked subject matter capacity, they would have litigation capacity.

2.9   Within the context of the Court of Protection, and the inherent jurisdiction, the test for capacity was also considered in *LBL v RYJ and VJ* [2010] EWHC 2665 (COP), [2011] 1 FLR 1279. The case was brought by way of invoking the inherent jurisdiction of the High Court and in part the decision relates to the competing jurisdictions (ie between the inherent jurisdiction and the Court of Protection). The local authority sought a declaration that a vulnerable adult lacked capacity to make decisions about her daily life, but that if she did have capacity, the Court should nevertheless make a decision upon her behalf by way of a 'best interests' declaration. Upon the evidence heard, Macur J found that the presumption of capacity was not displaced. She referred to s 2(1) of the Mental Capacity Act 2005, and that:

> '[25] I read the phrase "to a matter if at the material time he is unable to make a decision for himself in relation to the matter" ... to mean that capacity is to be assessed in relation to the particular type of decision at the time the decision needs to be made and not the person's ability to make decisions generally or in abstract.'

She went on to find, that in this particular case:

> '[33] inadequate regard [has been] paid to [the] potential tendency to teenage ennui, manipulation and fickleness which are traits not confined to those lacking capacity ... [49] ... the fact of inconsistency is not necessarily a sign of confusion. Equally, confusion is not necessarily an indication of incapacity.'

There was also implied criticism of the manner in which the views of the adults were elicited. The application for a declaration to be made was dismissed. Finally, in *PH v A Local Authority & Z Ltd & R* [2011] EWHC 1704 (Fam) Baker J set out a definitive analysis of the nature of the test, which is self-explanatory, and very helpful. For this reason, it is set out below in full.

> '[16] When addressing questions of capacity, the Court must apply the following principles.

> (i)   A person must be assumed to have capacity unless it is established that he lacks capacity: section 1 (2). The burden of proof therefore lies on the party asserting that P does not have capacity.
>
> (ii)   The standard of proof is the balance of probabilities: section 2(4).
>
> (iii)   A person is not to be treated as unable to make a decision unless all practicable steps to help him to do so have been taken without success: section 1(3). As paragraph 4.6 of the Mental Capacity Act 2005 Code of Practice makes clear, 'it is important to assess people when they are in the best state to make the decision, if possible".
>
> (iv)   A person is not to be treated as unable to make a decision merely because he makes an unwise decision: section 1(4).
>
> (v)   a person lacks capacity in relation to a matter if at the material time he is unable to make a decision for himself in relation to the matter because of an impairment of, or disturbance in the functioning of, the mind or brain: section 2(1). The first question is sometimes called "the diagnostic test".
>
> (vi)   For the purposes of section 2, a person is unable to make a decision for himself if he is unable to (a) to understand the information relevant to the

decision; (b) to retain that information; (c) to use or weigh that information as part of the process of making the decision, or (d) to communicate his decision whether by talking, using sign language or any other means: section 3(1). These four factors comprise the second question which is sometimes called the "functional test".

(vii) The Code of Practice gives guidance as to the meaning of the four factors in the functional test. Thus, so far as the first factor is concerned – understanding information about the decision to be made – paragraph 4.16 provides: "It is important not to assess someone's understanding before they have been given the relevant information about a decision. Every effort must be made to provide information in a way that is most appropriate to help the person understand".

(viii) The Code also gives guidance concerning the third of the four factors – using or weighing information as part of the decision-making process. Paragraph 4.21 provides "for someone to have capacity, they must have the ability to weigh up information and use it to arrive at a decision. Sometimes people can understand information, but an impairment or a disturbance stops them using it. In other cases, the impairment or disturbance leads to a person making a specific decision without understanding or using the information they have been given".

(ix) Further helpful guidance as to the interpretation of the functional test is given by Macur J in *LBL v RYJ* [2010] EWHC 2664 (Fam). At paragraph 24 of the judgment, the learned judge said: "I read section 3 to convey, amongst other detail, that it is envisaged that it may be necessary to use a variety of means to communicate relevant information, that it is not always necessary for a person to comprehend all peripheral detail and that it is recognised that different individuals may give different weight to different factors".

(x) Later, at paragraph 58 of the judgment, the learned judge indicated that she agreed with the interpretation of the section 3 test advanced by the expert in that case ... namely that it is "to the effect that the person under review must comprehend and weigh the salient details relevant to the decision to be made".

(xi) In *Sheffield City Council v E* [2004] EWHC 2808 (Fam) (a case concerning the capacity to marry decided before the implementation of the 2005 Act) Munby J (as he then was) said (at paragraph 144): "we must be careful not to set the test of capacity to marry too high, lest it operate as an unfair, unnecessary and indeed discriminatory bar against the mentally disabled". Although the observations concerned the capacity to marry, I agree with the submission made by Miss Morris on behalf of the Official Solicitor in this case that it should be applied to other questions of capacity. In other words, courts must guard against imposing too high a test of capacity to decide issues such as residence because to do so would run the risk of discriminating against persons suffering from a mental disability. In my judgment, the carefully drafted provisions of the 2005 Act and the Code of Practice are consistent with this approach.

(xii) The 2005 Act generally, and the DOLS in particular, are compliant with Article 5 of the European Convention of Human Rights and Fundamental Freedoms – see my earlier decision in *G v E* [2010] EWHC 621 upheld by the Court of Appeal at [2010] EWCA Civ 822 and in particular paragraphs 24–25 and 57 of the judgment of Sir Nicholas Wall P in the Court of Appeal. Just as there is no justification for imposing any threshold conditions before a best interests assessment under the DOLS can be carried out (the point taken up unsuccessfully by the appellants in *G v E*) so in my judgment there is no reason for adopting the approach advocated by Miss Morris on behalf of the Official Solicitor in this case, namely that a finding of a lack of capacity should only be made where the quality of the evidence in support of such a finding is "compelling". Equally, it is unnecessary for the court to adopt an approach, also advanced by Miss Morris on behalf of the Official Solicitor, that the statutory test should be construed "narrowly". The statutory scheme is, as I have already observed, carefully crafted. I agree with the submission made upon behalf of Z Limited … that the question of incapacity must be construed in accordance with the statutory test – "no more and no less".

(xiii) In assessing the question of capacity, the court must consider all the relevant evidence. Clearly, the opinion of an independently instructed expert will be likely to be of very considerable importance, but in many cases the evidence of other clinicians and professionals who have experience of treating and working with P will be just as important and in some cases more important. In assessing that evidence, the court must be aware of the difficulties which may arise as a result of the close professional relationship between the clinicians treating, and the key professionals working with, P. In *Oldham MBC v GW and PW* [2007] EWHC 136 (Fam) [2007] 2 FLR 597, a case brought under Part IV of the Children Act 1989, Ryder J referred to a "child protection imperative" meaning "the need to protect a vulnerable child" that for perfectly understandable reasons may lead to a lack of objectivity on the part of a treating clinician or other professional involved in caring for the child. Equally, in cases of vulnerable adults, there is a risk that all professionals involved with treating and helping that person – including, of course, a judge in the Court of Protection – may feel drawn towards an outcome that is more protective of the adult and thus, in certain circumstances, fail to carry out an assessment of capacity that is detached and objective. Having identified that hypothetical risk, however, I add that I have seen no evidence of any lack of objectivity on the part of the treating clinicians and social worker who gave evidence in this case.'

SUBJECT SPECIFIC CAPACITY

Capacity and medical treatment

2.10 Whilst it is beyond the range of this text to consider all of the material which exists within the context of medical treatment, the following cases illustrate the salient issues.

2.11 In *R v Collins, Pathfinder Mental Health Services NHS Trust and St George's Healthcare NHS Trust ex p S* [1998] 1 CCLR 410, [1998] 2 FLR 728, an adult woman was detained under MHA 1983. She was pregnant and wished to give birth naturally. The social worker (an Approved Social Worker (ASW)) applied for the woman to be admitted for assessment pursuant to s 2 of MHA 1983, as there were concerns about her mental health, and the risk that might be posed to both her and the unborn child. It was held that if an adult of sound mind rejected treatment, then no power of compulsion existed. The Mental Health Act could not be used to compel treatment unconnected with the reasons for detention. Merely illogical or bizarre thought processes would be insufficient in any event. The sequence of events set in train by the ASW were all vitiated by unlawfulness, and the declaration made *ex parte* was set aside. Guidelines were set down for situations when surgical or invasive treatment may be needed by a male or female patient who does not consent to that treatment. Those guidelines are set out below.

R v Collins, Pathfinder Mental Health Services NHS Trust and St George's Healthcare NHS Trust ex p S

The case highlighted some major problems which could arise for hospital authorities when a pregnant woman presented at hospital, the possible need for Caesarean surgery was diagnosed, and there was serious doubt about the patient's capacity to accept or decline treatment. To avoid any recurrence of the unsatisfactory events recorded in this judgment, and after consultation with the President of the Family Division and the Official Solicitor, and in the light of written submissions from Mr Havers and Mr Gordon, we shall attempt to repeat and expand the advice given in *Re MB (Medical Treatment)* [1997] 2 FLR 426. This advice also applies to any cases involving capacity when surgical or invasive treatment may be needed by a patient, whether female or male. References to "she" and "he" should be read accordingly. It also extends, where relevant, to medical practitioners and health practitioners generally as well as to hospital authorities.

The guidelines depend upon basic legal principles which we can summarise:

(i)   They have no application where the patient is competent to accept or refuse treatment. In principle a patient may remain competent notwithstanding detention under the Mental Health Act.

(ii)   If the patient is competent and refuses consent to the treatment an application to the High Court for a declaration would be pointless. In this situation the advice given to the patient should be recorded. For their own protection hospital authorities should seek unequivocal assurances from the patient (to be recorded in writing) that the refusal represents an informed decision: that is, that she understands the nature of and reasons for the proposed treatment, and the risks and likely prognosis involved in the decision to refuse or accept it. If the patient is unwilling to sign a written indication of this refusal, this too should be noted in writing. Such a written indication is merely a record for evidential purposes. It should not be confused with or regarded as a disclaimer.

(iii) If the patient is incapable of giving or refusing consent, either in the long term or temporarily (e g due to unconsciousness), the patient must be cared for according to the authority's judgment of the patient's best interests. Where the patient has given an advance directive, before becoming incapable, treatment and care should normally be subject to the advance directive. However, if there is reason to doubt the reliability of the advance directive, (for example it may sensibly be thought not to apply to the circumstances which have arisen) then an application for a declaration may be made.

Concern over capacity

(iv)   The authority should identify as soon as possible whether there is concern about a patient's competence to consent to or refuse treatment.

(v)   If the capacity of the patient is seriously in doubt it should be assessed as a matter of priority. In many such cases the patient's general practitioner or other responsible doctor may be sufficiently qualified to make the necessary assessment, but in serious or complex cases involving difficult issues about the future health and well-being or even life of the patient, the issue of capacity should be examined by an independent psychiatrist, ideally one approved under s 12(2) of the Mental Health Act. If following this assessment there remains a serious doubt about the patient's competence, and the seriousness or complexity of the issues in the particular case may require the involvement of the court, the psychiatrist should further consider whether the patient is incapable by reason of mental disorder of managing her property or affairs. If so the patient may be unable to instruct a solicitor and will require a guardian ad litem in any court proceedings. The authority should seek legal advice as quickly as possible. If a declaration is to be sought the patient's solicitors should be informed immediately and if practicable they should have a proper opportunity to take instructions and apply for legal aid where necessary. Potential witnesses for the authority should be made aware of the criteria laid down in *Re MB* and this case, together with any guidance issued by the Department of Health, and the British Medical Association.

(vi)   If the patient is unwilling to instruct solicitors, or is believed to be incapable of doing so, the authority or its legal advisors must notify the Official Solicitor and invite him to act as guardian ad litem. If the Official Solicitor agrees he will no doubt wish, if possible, to arrange for the patient to be interviewed to ascertain her wishes and to explore the reasons for any refusal of treatment. The Official Solicitor can be contacted through the Urgent Court Business Officer out of office hours on 0171 936 6000.

The hearing

(vii) The hearing before the judge should be inter partes. As the order made in her absence will not be binding on the patient unless she is represented either by a guardian ad litem (if incapable of giving instructions) or (if capable) by counsel or solicitor, a declaration granted ex parte is of no assistance to the authority. Although the Official Solicitor will not act for a patient if she is capable of instructing a solicitor, the court may in any event call on the Official Solicitor (who has considerable expertise in these matters) to assist as an amicus curiae.

(viii) It is axiomatic that the judge must be provided with accurate and all the relevant information. This should include the reasons for the proposed treatment, the risks involved in the proposed treatment, and in not proceeding with it, whether any alternative treatment exists, and the reason, if ascertainable, why the patient is refusing the proposed treatment. The judge will need sufficient information to reach informed conclusion about the patient's capacity, and, where it arises, the issue of best interest.

(ix)   The precise terms of any order should be recorded and approved by the judge before its terms are transmitted to the authority. The patient should be accurately informed of the precise terms.

(x) Applicants for emergency orders from the High Court made without first issuing and serving the relevant applications and evidence in support have a duty to comply with the procedural requirements (and pay the court fees) as soon as possible after the emergency hearing.

Conclusion

There may be occasions when, assuming a serious question arises about the competence of the patient, the situation facing the authority may be so urgent and the consequences so desperate that is impracticable to attempt to comply with these guidelines. The guidelines should be approached for what they are, that is, guidelines. Where delay may itself cause serious damage to the patient's health or put her life at risk then formulaic compliance with these guidelines would be inappropriate.

2.12 In summary, if the patient is competent then there can be no application. A patient may be competent though detained under MHA 1983. If there is a concern over capacity, then this should be addressed as a matter of urgency by a psychiatrist. This may in turn then lead to the need for the involvement of either any solicitors who might have been involved with the patient or the Official Solicitor. Hearings should be inter partes. In a very short judgment given within the Court of Protection (*DH NHS Foundation Trust v PS* [2010] EWHC 1217 (Fam), [2010] 2 FLR 1236) the issue of medical treatment for an adult who lacked capacity in respect of an operation without which she would have died was considered. The Trust sought declarations that it could use reasonable force and sedation to take the patient to hospital, and keep he there afterwards during the period required for recovery. The Court was satisfied: (a) that the operation was necessary (ie there was no alternative treatment); and (b) that it was in her bests interests not only to have the operation, but also that should persuasion fail, it was also in her best interests for her to be sedated and/or that reasonable force could be used. Thus, the Court of Protection now has exclusive jurisdiction over such matters, and the remedies available to it in order that medical treatment should take place. Practice Direction E governs the procedure for applications relating to serious medical treatment, and once an application has been made, then s 4B of the MCA 2005 permits deprivation of liberty in order to give the patient life sustaining treatment or the doing of 'any vital act'. A 'vital act' is 'any act which the person doing it reasonably believes to be necessary to prevent a serious deterioration in P's condition' (s 4B(5)). In other words, once an *application* has been made, there is no need to wait for a decision from the Court, whilst a decision is awaited (s 4B(1)).

2.13 In *R (on the Application of Burke) v General Medical Council* [2005] EWCA Civ 1003, [2005] 8 CCLR 463, it was held that whilst a competent patient can refuse treatment, it does not follow that he can demand it. If artificial nutrition and hydration is necessary to keep a patient alive a doctor's duty of care will generally result in it being required, irrespective of the desire of the patient. Exceptions to this may arise where either the patient is competent and does not wish to live, or where the patient is incompetent and it is not in his best interests to be kept alive. The Guidance provided by the

General Medical Council was not unlawful. The fact that a patient identified his best interests as being one particular course did not require a doctor to conform to this if he did not believe that this was clinically indicated. In respect of the best interests of an incompetent patient, it is not possible to apply a single test appropriate in all circumstances. An example of the manner in which the Court of Protection has deal with a similar issue is illustrated in *AVS (by his litigation friend, CS) v NHS Foundation Trust and B PCT* [2011] EWCA Civ 7, [2011] 2 FLR 1 967. In this instance, a capacitous decision was made (via a lasting power of attorney in favour of his brother) that all efforts should be made to prolong his life. When he lost capacity, a conflict arose between the treating clinicians and the brother as to whether further steps should be taken to prolong his life. The treatment proposed by the brother involved surgery, and the hospital refused to undertake such an operation (on the basis that it was not in his best interests). The brother was eventually able to find a clinician who was prepared to carry out the operation. He had asked the Court to make a declaration that it was in the interests of AVS to have such an operation. The Court dismissed the application upon the following basis:

> '[37] ... although [the clinicians] are willing to [treat AVS] ... there is no evidence of their current ability to do so. No hospital has been identified where that surgery can be undertaken...What the Court is being invited to do is no more nor less than to declare that if a medical practitioner is ready, willing and able to operate ... then it would be in the best interests of the patient to do so ... a declaration of the kind sought will not force the respondent hospital to provide treatment against their clinicians' judgment. To use a declaration of the court to twist the arm of some other clinician, as yet unidentified, to carry out these procedures or to put pressure on the Secretary of State to provide a hospital where these procedures may be undertaken is an abuse of the process of the court and should not be tolerated.'

In other words, declarations would not be made as a method of trying to force a clinician to do something which was objected to on sound grounds, and if a clinician was able and ready to treat a patient, then the requirement for a declaration to that effect was otiose. However, the most recent authority on case involving treatment to those in respect of whom the consequences of the declaration being sought from the Court will lead to either life or death is *M, Re* [2011] EWHC 2443 (Fam). The patient suffered from 'minimally conscious state' (MCS), as opposed to Persistent Vegetative State (PVS) which was the condition from which Mr Bland had been found to be suffering. Baker J carried out a review of all of the case law in this area, from *Bland* to the present day (including a review of the origins of the declaratory jurisdiction, and its current place within the Court of Protection cf paras [57]-[97]). The central issue was whether, if a patient with MCS is clinically stable, whether it can ever be in that person's best interests to withdraw and/or withhold life sustaining treatment, and whether to do so this would be unlawful, and if done intentionally, would amount to unlawful killing and murder, together with a breach of the rights of the patient pursuant to Arts 2, 3, 8, 13 and 14 of the ECHR. The professional evidence in the case was extensive as to the advantages and disadvantages for the patient, should the application have succeeded (which was for treatment to cease). Having analysed both (at paras [247] and [248]) the Court concluded that on the facts, the balance fell in favour of preserving life, this being the 'decisive factor' [249]. The Court did, however, make a declaration that the 'Do Not Resuscitate' order should continue (so that should there be a deterioration in certain specific circumstances, the treating physicians would lawfully be permitted to let the patient die). Four other procedural matters emerged. The first was the importance if using formal assessment procedure (described as SMART and WHIM tests) in order to provide an accurate diagnosis of MCS. Secondly, a call that public funding should be made available for such applications (there having been none available for the applicants, leading the case having been conducted *pro bono*. Thirdly, that all such cases must be made before a judge of the High Court. Fourthly, it was important for such cases to be heard in public, so that the decisions of the Court in respect of such important matters can be made more widely known provided that 'due respect is paid to the wishes of the family to protect their privacy' [261].

Capacity and adult contact/residence disputes

2.14 It is very often a local authority who will be responsible (via its adult social services) for making applications in respect of disputes involving those without capacity and family members (or others). The Court of Protection should be the venue for most of such applications (Mental Capacity Act 2005) although as is illustrated below in respect of those who may be vulnerable, but not lacking capacity this is not exclusively the case.

2.15 In *Cambridgeshire County Council v R (An Adult)* [1995] 1 FLR 50 the local authority had had responsibility for a woman with learning disabilities during her minority (having taken her into care at the age of 10). She remained in local authority accommodation. Perhaps the most interesting aspect of the case is the *per curiam* observations that:

> '... the ancient power derived from the royal prerogative to make orders relating to the person, as opposed to the property and affairs, of people unable to look after themselves was revoked when the new system of guardianship was introduced by the Mental Health Act 1959, designed to place all the necessary features of the prerogative jurisdiction on a statutory footing. It was clear however, from the circumstances of the present case that there existed no wholly appropriate legal mechanism for investigating the issues and providing suitable protection, It was to be hoped that Parliament would turn its attention to the matter.'

The application for injunctive relief was refused on the basis that: (a) there was no demonstrable threat to the woman by association with her family; and (b) there was no evidence to suggest that she was not competent to make decisions about this herself; and (c) there was no mechanism within declaratory relief for a review; and (d) that an order pursuant to s 7 of MHA 1983 would have been more appropriate. The *per curiam* observations, of course, are a reference to the need for a statutory regime to cover litigation involving those who lack capacity, and which has led to the jurisdiction of the Court of Protection. The existence of this Court is the most significant development in the law in this area since the Mental Health Act 1959, and has had a very direct and large impact upon local authorities, as some have discovered to their cost.

2.16 In *Re S (Adult Patient) (Inherent Jurisdiction: Family Life)* [2002] EWHC 2278 (Fam), [2003] 1 FLR 292, an adult who lacked capacity had always lived with his father. He had provided a 'good enough' level of care to his son, but one incident has caused the local authority to remove him from the care of his son. The local authority wished for a declaration that it was lawful to remove the son from the care of his father (who wished to continue to care for him). It was held that even though a child had reached majority, the relationship with a parent did not end at that point. Although parents lost their surrogate decision-making powers at that age (with an adult who lacked capacity) they could continue so to do by virtue of the doctrine of necessity. The father had rights under Art 8, as did the son. The local authority had a positive obligation to intervene. Any conflict had to be determined in accordance with the best interests of the son. The starting point was the normal assumption that a mentally incapacitated adult would be better off with his family. The Court had the jurisdiction to grant declaratory relief. This might be that a third party was able to act as the surrogate decision maker. On the facts in the case it was held that the best interests of the adult would be to move to accommodation suggested by the local authority.

2.17 In *Re S (Adult's Lack of Capacity: Carer and Residence)* [2003] EWHC 1909 (Fam), [2003] 2 FLR 1235, a similar situation arose. An adult woman who had been cared for by her father was removed by the local authority. It was held that once a Court was seized of the matter it would determine the outcome in accordance with the best interests of the incapacitated adult. This might involve deciding on disputed issues of fact. The four questions to be asked were: (1) Was mental incapacity established? (2) Was there a serious justiciable issue relating to welfare? (3) What was that issue? (4) What were the factors which must be balanced in order to decide which course of action was in the best interests of the mentally incapacitated adult? On the facts in the case, the relief sought by the local authority was granted.

2.18 In *B Borough Council v Mr S* [2006] EWHC 2584 (Fam), [2006] 9 CCLR 596, [2007] 1 FLR 1600, a man in his 90s was admitted to a nursing home. He lacked capacity. The nursing home determined that it could not cope with the needs of Mr S. The local authority wished to move him to a hospital. It obtained ex parte injunctions against his wife forbidding her from preventing the move, removing him from hospital and restricting her contact with him to being supervised by the local authority. It was held that in the circumstances of this case, an ex parte application had been justified (despite the exceptional nature of such applications).

2.19 Over recent years, and in accordance with the policy of central government, there has rightly been an emphasis on the need for those who may either be vulnerable adults, or who lack capacity (or both) to have their opportunities for independent living maximised. This is sometimes referred to within the general context of personalisation of services. However, in *AH v Hertfordshire Partnership NHS Foundation Trust* [2011] EWHC 276 (COP) the claimant had been living for a number of years in a unit devoted to the needs of a small number of individuals with similar requirements. There was no evidence other than that this placement suited the needs of AH perfectly, and was in his best interests. This applied to the other residents, each of whom had programmes which were individually suited to them. However, the local authority wished to implement its policy of 'care in the community' rather than for AH to remain in the specialist unit. It wished to move him to a flat, with his own self-contained accommodation, albeit with 1:1 staffing for support. It also included assistive technology (ie sensors) to provide him with further protection. The move would have disrupted all of the relationships he had formed whilst at the specialist unit (including those with staff members who had looked after him for many years). It was also in a rural location (to which he had become accustomed) whereas the flat was on a busy main road. His own learning difficulties and autism made it particularly important that his routines were not disrupted, and he had little or no concept of road safety. The evidence before the Court was that a move would destabilise him, cause him to self-harm, expose him to danger from traffic, and possibly lead to such a deterioration in his condition that might have led him to be detained under the Mental Health Act 1983. Jackson J held that AH should remain where he had lived since 2001, and that it was not in his best interests to be moved. He emphasised that the policies to which the local authority had referred were guidelines only, and that a move would in fact deprive AH of choice rather than optimise that choice. The community within which he lived at the specialist unit, although unusual, represented what was in his best interests. The significance of this authority is that in making plans for the movement of incapacitous adults (or indeed providing services to them), local government must consider the needs of those individuals, and not feel obliged to implement blanket guidance issued by central government without regard to those individual needs. This might appear to be stating no more than the obvious, but as this case illustrates, adherence to the obvious is not necessarily what always happens.

Capacity and marriage

2.20 The issue of marriage and capacity has been considered: (a) in the context of litigation capacity and subject matter capacity; and (b) in the context of protection of a vulnerable adult (who did possess subject matter capacity). In *M v B, A and S (by the Official Solicitor)* [2005] EWHC 1681 (Fam), [2006] 1 FLR 117, the Court considered the issue of restricting the removal from the jurisdiction of an adult who lacked capacity for the purposes of an arranged marriage. It was held that in the factual circumstances of the case (where there was a vulnerable adult who lacked capacity to enter into a contract of marriage) the 'best interests' test *was* to be applied. Injunctive and declaratory relief was granted. The procedure to be used was CPR Part 8, but with the hearings conducted in the Family Division (notwithstanding that there might be substantial issues of fact). The latter aspect of the judgment is of limited assistance in respect of procedure relating to applications using the Mental Capacity Act 2005 since this is precisely the type of case which would now be heard by the Court of Protection (which also has its own Rules effective as of 1 October 2007). A further analysis of the law in respect of capacity to enter into a contract of marriage is contained in *Re P (Forced Marriage)* [2011] EWHC 3467 (Fam), [2011] 1 FLR 2060.

Capacity and choice of residence

2.21   The facts in the following case (*Re F (Adult Patient)* [2000] 3 CCLR 210; *Re F (Adult: Court's Jurisdiction* [2000] 2 FLR 512) were that an adult (functioning at the level of a child between 5 and 8) was alleged to be living in conditions of extreme squalor and at considerable risk from her natural family. The local authority asked for declaratory relief in order that the best interests of the woman be determined (by declaring that she should live in local authority accommodation). It was held that the Court had the jurisdiction to grant such relief, and it arose out of the doctrine of necessity. It was also held that social services had the power (again arising out of the doctrine of necessity) to provide care and restraint where it was required in the best interests of an adult who lacked capacity. An interim declaration could be granted, and this was sufficiently flexible to be altered or modified.

2.22   This authority was re-visited in *City of Westminster v IC (by his friend the Official Solicitor) and KC and NN* [2008] EWCA Civ 198, [2008] 2 FLR 267. By the time the Court was obliged to consider the powers that it possessed on the facts in this case, the Mental Capacity Act 2005 was in force. IC himself lacked capacity to litigate, to consent to either marriage or sexual relations, to circumcision, and an order had been made preventing his removal from the jurisdiction. The judgment provides an extensive analysis of whether a marriage that has been entered into by someone who lacks capacity is voidable, or void *ab initio* (it being held that is is voidable), but for the purposes of determining the powers of the Court in terms of deciding where an adult should live, it is the decision of Wall LJ at [54] which is of significance:

> 'I am in no doubt at all that the inherent jurisdiction of the High Court to protect the welfare of incapable adults, confirmed in this court in *Re F* [*supra*] survives, albeit that it is now reinforced by the provisions of the Mental Capacity Act 2005 (the 2005 Act). I am also in no doubt that a combination of the inherent jurisdiction and the provisions of the 2005 Act is apt to confer jurisdiction on the High Court to make orders about where IC should live, including the decision as to whether it is in his best interests to go and live in Bangladesh.'

For the avoidance of doubt, Thorpe LJ confirmed that:

> '[13] Of obvious relevance is s 17(1)(a) ... that clearly empowers the judge to prevent an exeat to Bangladesh, where, as some of the evidence here suggests, it would be contrary to the health and welfare of the vulnerable adult.'

Judicial review of decisions made by local authorities vs welfare decisions

2.23 As the case law in this area has developed, it has become increasingly apparent that applications are made to the Court of Protection that are, in truth, judicial reviews, and that applications that are made to the Administrative Court, are, in truth, really applications that should be made to the Court of Protection. It is also correct to say that sometimes it can be very difficult to determine where a 'welfare' decision ends, and a public law case begins. There is also often an overlap between the two separate jurisdictions (ie between COP and the Administrative Court). In *A v A Health Authority and linked applications: Re J and linked applications* [2001] EWHC Fam/Admin 18, [2002] 5 CCLR 165, the Court was concerned with the function of the exercise of its jurisdiction to establish the best interests of an adult who lacked capacity. The adult in question was provided with accommodation by the local authority pursuant to s 21 of the National Assistance Act 1948. For a short while, he was admitted to hospital. Thereafter there was a dispute between the local authority and his father as to whether he should return to his original accommodation, or be placed elsewhere (in accordance with the wishes of his father). It was held that certain of the issues fell within the ambit of the Family Division, and determination of best interests. These were: (a) a dispute as to residence; (b) arguments over contact; (c) the need to give the adult a genuine choice as to accommodation; and (d) the preference of the adult and his carers. However, any challenge to the community care assessments completed by the local authority needed a judicial review of that process (which was not determined by the best interests test). A declaration as to where it would be best for the adult to reside would not be made, since this would be to control the decision-making process of the local authority, which required judicial review. There can be no doubt that this type of case (in terms of decisions to be made about the best interests of a patient as to where he should live, and who he should see) would now be heard by the Court of Protection. Similarly, the Court of Protection is not the venue for a collateral challenge to the community care assessments of a patient. That is purely a matter for the Administrative Court. However, it is by no means impossible for both Courts to sit at the same time, if the judge is able so to do. Furthermore CPR 30.5(1) and 54.20 both provide the mechanism for a transfer as between the jurisdictions. Finally, s 15(1)(c) of the MCA 2005 enable the Court to make a declaration as to the lawfulness or otherwise of any act done, or yet to be done, in relation to a patient. Thus, for example, a care plan was being considered within the Court of Protection, and it was declared to be *unlawful* it is difficult to envisage how this end would be achieved without considering public law principles. However, unlike a hearing in the Administrative Court, this would be the end of the jurisdiction. This point is made in the case referred to below.

2.24 In *A Local Authority v PB* [2011] EWHC 502 (COP) this issue was considered by Charles J. The central dispute was about where an adult should live, and the care afforded to him by his mother (the local authority arguing that her care was inadequate). Prima facie, therefore, this would have appeared to be a typical case for the Court of Protection to consider on a welfare basis. However, the case advanced by the mother was that the local authority had failed to properly consider what package of care could be made available to her, in order for her to care for her son at home. This, of course, is more akin to an argument before the Administrative Court. Further, the remedies available to the Court of Protection are different in kind and effect to those available in the Administrative Court. For example, the types of order that may be made in the Court of Protection (in cases such as this) would amount to a declaration that Plan A or Plan B, was or was not in the best interests of incapacitous adult. This would not force a local authority to change its care plan – only the remedies available in the Administrative Court could cause that to happen. In this particular case, the hearing was adjourned in order that the parties could formulate their respective cases with greater precision. In particular, it was observed that it was not for the Court of Protection to put pressure on a local authority to provide support which it might not be obliged to provide within the range of its statutory duties in this area of law (ie community care legislation in this instance).

2.25 A similar and illustrative issue arose in *R (on the application of W) v Croydon LBC* [2011] EWHC 696 (Admin) in which a decision had been made to terminate a placement for an adult who lacked capacity. The local authority had determined that the placement was (in effect) too expensive and convened a 'best interests' meeting at which this conclusion was explained to the parents. Neither, it transpired, had there been any consultation with the care providers for the adult. There was an overlap in this case between what might be described as a 'welfare decision' and a case that comes within the Administrative Court. However, it is also clearly a case which belongs within the latter jurisdiction. The remedies sought were granted, not only upon the basis that there had been a failure to consult, but also that the decision made was vitiated by a failure to adhere to the Community Care Assessment Directions 2004, s 4 of the Mental Capacity Act 2005, and the National Assistance Act (Choice of Accommodation) Directions 2004.

Capacity and sexual relationships/contraception

2.26 There have been quite a number of decisions in respect of this area of capacity. They tend to include other areas referred to above (eg capacity to marry) and also capacity to certain types of medical intervention to prevent conception. One of the earliest of these is *Re SK; A London Borough Council v KS and LU* [2008] EWHC 636 (Fam), [2008] 2 FLR 720. It was held that the combination of the learning disability and mental illness in SK amounted to 'an impairment of, or a disturbance in the functioning of, the mind and brain' (s 2(1) Mental Capacity Act 2005) such that she lacked capacity to consent to medical treatment. The medical treatment was for contraception, but due to her fierce opposition to contraception this could not amount to the insertion of a contraceptive device. In terms of her capacity to consent to sexual intercourse,

Wood J relied upon *Local Authority X v MM (by her litigation friend the Official Solicitor) & KM* [2007] EWHC 2003, [2009] 1 FLR 443 which is set out below.

2.27   The judgment in this *MM* is of particular use as it is one of the first decisions that takes into account the change between the common law principles to which reference has been made earlier in this chapter, and the current statutory framework. The facts of the case arose out of the relationship that the patient had with her long-term partner, and which had had an adverse effect upon all aspects of her life. The relief sought from the court upon her behalf was for declarations that she lacked capacity to litigate; decide where she should live; decide with whom she should have contact; manage her finances, and enter into a contract of marriage. It was held that the test for capacity was now that set out in s 3 of the Mental Capacity Act 2005 (which represented the statutory version of the test in *MB* referred to at **2.6** above) and that this test was not confined to the Court of Protection, but could be used in any jurisdiction where capacity was an issue. In respect of capacity to have sexual intercourse, this was specific to that subject, and was not connected with the partner with whom sexual intercourse might take place:

> '[87] A woman either has capacity, for example, to consent to "normal" penetrative vaginal intercourse, or she does not. It is difficult to see how it can sensibly be said that she has capacity to consent to a particular sex act with Y whilst at the same time lacking capacity to consent to precisely the same sexual act with Z. So capacity to consent to sexual intercourse depends upon a person having sufficient knowledge and understanding of the nature and character – the sexual nature and character – of the act of sexual intercourse, and of the reasonably foreseeable consequences of sexual intercourse, to have the capacity to choose whether or not to engage in it, the capacity to give or withhold consent to sexual intercourse ... It does not depend upon an understanding of the consequences of sexual intercourse with a particular person. Put shortly, capacity to consent to sexual relations is issue specific; it is not person specific.'

2.28   The same case also made some important observations upon the role of a local authority in such cases when intervening in the life of a vulnerable adult. In particular, Munby J held that:

> '[118–120] The Court should intervene only where there is a need to protect a vulnerable adult from abuse or the real possibility of abuse ... the Court must be careful to ensure that in rescuing a vulnerable adult from one type of abuse it does not expose her to the risk of treatment at the hands of the State which, however well intentioned, can itself end up being abusive of her dignity, her happiness and indeed her human rights ... what good is making someone safer if it merely makes them miserable.'

This theme is one that has emerged during the lifetime of the Court of Protection, and is referred to elsewhere in this chapter. Its essence is that any intervention in the life of an adult who requires protection should be the one that involves the most minimal restriction on autonomy, and where the local authority is taking steps which will lead to such a restriction or breach of the ECHR that before it does so it:

'[163 and 165] must either desist from what it is doing or take such additional (positive) steps as to ensure that there is no breach ... the local authority in this connection cannot seek to avoid its positive obligations by seeking to toll the bell of scarce resources ... the right in play (Article 8) here is, to repeat, too important, too precious in human terms, to be swept aside by such purely fiscal considerations.'

Upon that basis, and upon the basis that it was determined that MM did have capacity to consent to sexual relations, and that the care plan which was being proposed prevented MM from continuing her relationship with her partner(which was a disproportionate response to the risk he posed) that aspect of the relief sought by the local authority was refused. The case was revisited in what is described as a '*coda*' (*Re MM (An Adult)* [2007] EWHC 2689 (Fam), [2009] 1 FLR 487) by which time the local authority had adjusted its plan accordingly, and which enabled MM to continue her sexual relationship with her partner. It is to be noted that the case was decided *before* the Mental Capacity Act 2005 came into force (but only just) and the Court made its decisions within the inherent jurisdiction.

2.29 In *D Borough Council v AB* [2011] EWHC 101 (COP), [2011] 2 FLR 72, *MM* was revisited. In particular, it observes that even though the case was decided prior to the Mental Capacity Act 2005 coming into force, neither that fact, nor the *Code of Practice* had altered the test as explained above. It held that:

'[22] the test is really very simple, and is set at a relatively low level: "does she have sufficiently rudimentary knowledge of what the act comprises and of its sexual character to enable her to decide whether to give or withhold consent?" The simplicity and low level of this test is set consistently with the equivalently low test for capacity to marry.'

Mostyn J concluded that the capacity to consent to sex:

'[42] remains act-specific and requires a full understanding of the mechanics of the act; that there are health risks involved, particularly the acquisition of sexually transmitted and sexually transmissible infections; that sex between a man and a woman may result in the woman becoming pregnant.'

Finally, given that the interim steps taken by the local authority had prevented AB from having sex, it was held that 'the court must tread especially carefully where an organ of the state proposes that a citizen's ability to perform, in a non-abusive way, the sex function should be abrogated or curtailed. It involves very profound aspects of civil liberties and personal autonomy' [11] and that in the circumstance of this case, the Court was not prepared to make the declarations sought without it being satisfied that 'sufficient practical steps have [...] been taken to see if Alan can have sex, with the result that the present regime of deprivation of liberty can be lifted' [51].

Contraception

2.30 A similar topic to that set out above, with reassuringly similar conclusions in respect of the intervention of the state in the life of an individual without capacity, was considered in *A Local Authority v MRS A (Test for Capacity as to Contraception)* [2010] EWHC 1549 (COP), [2011] 1 FLR 26. The history of Mrs A had involved having children, all of whom were removed from her at birth. She had subsequently married another man (and had capacity to enter into a contract of marriage). The local authority became concerned about the nature of the relationship, and in particular what it alleged were coercive and violent elements of the marriage upon the part of the husband towards his wife. Specifically, there were concerns that she was being coerced into ceasing to use contraception by her husband. Consequently, it made an application to the Court of Protection for the purposes of obtaining a declaration that: (a) it was in her best interests to receive contraception; and that (b) it might be in her best interests for force to be used to administer contraception. On the evidence, the Court did determine that she lacked capacity to consent to contraception. The test to be applied is:

> '[64] the ability to understand and weigh up the immediate medical issues surrounding contraceptive treatment ... including
>
> (i)   the reason for contraception and what it does (which includes the likelihood of pregnancy if it is not in use during sexual intercourse);
> (ii)   the types available and how each is used;
> (iii) the advantages and disadvantages of each type;
> (iv)   the possible side-effects of each and how they can be dealt with;
> (v)   how easily each type can be changed; and
> (vi)   the generally accepted effectiveness of each.
>
> I do not consider that questions need to be asked as to the woman's understanding of what bringing up a child would be like in practice; nor any opinion attempted as to how she would be likely to get on; nor whether any child would be likely to be removed from her care.'

However the matter did not end at that point, as the Court still had to factor in whether the coercion of the husband vitiated her capacity to make a decision on this point. Bodey J cross-referred this to s 1(3)(a)-(c) of the Mental Capacity Act 2005, including her ability to understand, retain, use and weigh 'the information relevant to the decision'. He also relied upon whether 'the influence of Mr A over Mrs A has been so overpowering as to leave her unable to weigh up the information and take a decision of her own free will' [66]. Upon the basis of the information and evidence from and about Mr A, he held that she lacked capacity as a result of the effect of that coercion by him. However, nor was he prepared to make a declaration that contraception was in her best interests. This was due to two factors. The first was that there was no evidence that one of the possible consequences of not using contraception (pregnancy and birth) had ever adversely effected Mrs A. Nor would it be appropriate to make an order that permitted force to be used. The judge held that:

> '[75] In such a sensitive area, it is difficult if not impossible to envisage any acceptable way forward on these particular facts, other than by an attempt to achieve a capacitated decision from Mrs A, through "ability appropriate" help and discussion without undue contrary pressure from Mr A.'

Finally:

> '[77] any step towards long-term court-imposed contraception by way of physical coercion, with its affinity to enforced sterilisation and shades of social engineering, would raise profound questions about State intervention in private and family life. Whilst the issue of force has not been argued out at this hearing I cannot, on these facts, presently see how it could be acceptable.'

2.31   Upon the basis of the development of this area of law (that is to say the intervention in the most basic of human rights) the Court has been so far extremely resistant to permitting itself to make orders that either by force or otherwise permit the State to interfere with those rights. As will be seen in respect of the *defence* of such rights (and particularly the right to liberty and security of the person) the Courts have been alert to prevent local authorities from depriving those without capacity from being deprived of those rights.

Capacity to enter into tenancy agreements

2.32   There have been a number of occasions when either it has emerged that an adult without capacity has purportedly entered in to a contract for a tenancy agreement, or where it has become necessary for the Court of Protection to consider what the process should be if there is a need for a tenancy to exist in respect of that adult. There is no case law on this point at the moment, although it is likely that there will be in the foreseeable future. In the meantime, some guidance has been produced, with the approval of the Senior Judge of the Court of Protection. This is set out below.

Court of Protection Guidance on Tenancy Agreements (Elder Law Journal, 3 Eld L J [2011] 338

Introduction

The Association of Public Authority Deputies (APAD), and a number of other court users, have asked the court for guidance on how to make applications in relation to signing or terminating tenancy agreements on behalf of adults who lack the mental capacity to understand or sign the agreement themselves. The situation arises mainly where adults with learning disabilities are moved from hospital or care home settings into supported living arrangements in the community, that allow greater autonomy and independent decision making. Many of the adults will have the capacity to make certain decisions, such as dealing with social security benefit payments, but will lack the capacity deal with the tenancy arrangement.

The policy of assessing clients to support a move to supported living could affect several hundred adults per year across England and Wales. This guidance has been drawn up with the approval of the Senior Judge of the Court of Protection, and sets out: the circumstances when it is necessary to make an application; the court's requirements for such applications; and puts in place streamlined procedures for receiving applications in bulk, thereby simplifying some parts of the court procedure.

Is it Necessary to Apply to Court for Authority to Sign or Terminate the Tenancy Agreement?

If a person lacks the mental capacity to sign the tenancy agreement or terminate it, then anyone intending to sign on the person's behalf can only do so if they are authorised to do so by the Court of Protection (unless the person had capacity to make a power of attorney and has done so). Section 5 of the Mental Capacity Act 2005 makes provision for carers and health and social care professionals to make certain decisions on behalf of another in relation to care and treatment, without the need to obtain any formal authority to act. However, this does not cover signing legal documents, such as tenancy agreements, or any other decisions in relation to the person's property and affairs. This means that the court's authority must be sought in relation to signing or terminating a tenancy agreement.

In some cases, the landlord of the property that is the subject of the tenancy may not require a signature on the agreement. Although this would allow the adult to move without having to wait for formal authorisation, the court discourages such practice, as it could make the tenancy agreement unenforceable and put the adult's living arrangements at risk.

There may be some cases where moves have already taken place without the correct formalities having been followed. Where this is the case, the procedure outlined here may be used to ratify arrangements that are already in place.

Can a Deputy Sign or Terminate the Tenancy Agreement?

If an adult service user already has a deputy appointed to make decisions on their behalf, then the deputy can terminate or enter into a tenancy agreement without further authorisation from the court. Please note, however that deputies acting under an old style short order or receivership order made before the Mental Capacity Act came into force, may not have sufficient authority to sign the agreement, and it may be necessary to apply for 'reappointment' with the full powers of a deputy.

Does a Deputy Need to be Appointed in All Cases?

No, if the sole purpose of the application is to sign or terminate the tenancy, then the application should be for an order that specifically deals with the tenancy matter (see how to make an application, below). If, however, the adult lacks capacity to manage other aspects of their property and affairs and they have assets and income other than social security benefits then it will usually be necessary to appoint a deputy to deal with all these decisions.

Before Making an Application

It would assist the court in dealing with applications if you would contact us by telephone or email before making an application. This is so we can arrange to receive your application and to ensure it is dealt with in accordance with the procedure set out below.

If you do not contact us beforehand, there is a risk that applications will be rejected as incomplete and may be returned.

See contacts below.

How to Make an Application

The court is prepared to deal with all of the adults required to sign the tenancy agreement(s) in a single bulk application. This is on the understanding that the only order required from the court relates to the tenancy agreement and no further directions, for example the appointment of a deputy, are necessary.

The court will require:

- A single COP1 Application form setting out the order or declaration required with a list of all the adults required to sign the agreement annexed;
- A COP3 Assessment of capacity for each adult. The assessment should deal specifically with the adult's capacity to sign or terminate the agreement;
- A COP24 Witness statement setting out the circumstances behind the moves and confirming that a best interests assessment has been carried out, including consultation with close family members, or people in close contact with the person, where applicable.
- An application fee.

The application form should request the court to make a single order or declaration that it is in all the adult service users' best interests for the tenancy arrangement to be signed or terminated on their behalf.

The procedure above can also be used for applications relating to individuals.

How Will the Court Deal With the Application?

When the court issues the application, the applicant will notify each adult personally using form COP14 and provide evidence that they have done on form COP20A. Once notified, the person will have 21 days to object or respond to the application.

If the court receives an objection to the application it will deal with it as a discrete issue, in accordance with the usual procedure.

Once the 21 day time limit expires, the court will issue a single order that deals with the tenancy matter for all the service users.

Will the Court Remit the Fee?

No. The court is only charging a single fee for an application that relates to more than one person and will not remit fees in relation to bulk applications. The applicant is responsible for paying the fee, which must accompany the application.

If the application relates to a single individual only, then the usual policy on fee remissions and exemption will apply.

2.33   There is also no definitive authority on the issue as to whether or not when an adult has entered into a contact for a tenancy, it is voidable or void. The standard texts on this point suggest that it is voidable. The general rule, other than in relation to 'necessaries' such as food, is that a person suffering a mental disability is bound by contracts he enters into and the burden of proving that he lacked the capacity to do so rests on the person alleging this lack of capacity. In particular, the latter must show both a lack of understanding on the part of the person allegedly lacking capacity and that the other person knew of the lack of capacity. Where these two conditions are satisfied, the contract becomes voidable at the option of the mentally incapacitated person. In other words, it is for the Claimant to rescind the contract and until that point it has full legal effect. If the tenancy agreement is rescinded, then the security and protection afforded by it is lost. The apparent unfairness of the transaction does not itself provide grounds to set aside that transaction, although it may be important background material where an allegation of fraud or undue influence in equity is advanced. In terms of judging the capacity of WD to enter the Tenancy Agreement it might be said that it is only necessary to show that he had a general understanding of what he was entering into, ie an agreement to occupy premises at a fixed rate, and for a fixed period, and with exclusive occupation and subject to certain conditions. The threshold for capacity is not high ('The common law presumes that every person has capacity until the contrary is shown and the threshold for capacity is not a demanding one. These principles have recently been confirmed by Parliament in the Mental Capacity Act 2005' Baroness Hale at [26] *R (MH) v Secretary of State for Health* [2005] UKHL 60). The changes introduced by the MCA 2005 do not seem to have a significant impact on the correct analysis in this instance. In particular s 7 of the 2005 Act provides that:

'If necessary goods or services are supplied to a person who lacks the capacity to contract for the supply, he must pay a reasonable price for them.'

2.34   However, in *Wychavon District Council v EM (HB)* [2011] UKUT 144 (AAC), the opposite conclusion was reached. The Upper Tribunal were considering a case in which there had been a claim for housing benefit (in respect of a tenancy agreement with someone who lacked capacity). Clearly, if there is no valid tenancy, then there could have been no claim for housing benefit. This is not an insignificant issue for many supported living arrangements, where those who lack capacity may be party to such agreements, and where housing benefit is being claimed in respect of those 'tenancies'. In this instance it was held that there never had been a tenancy at all. This was upon the basis that the father of the claimant (who had been responsible for making all of the arrangements) must have known that his daughter could not have entered into such a contract. It was not, therefore, a voidable contract, as such a contract could never have existed at all, *ab initio*. It remains to be seen which analysis prevails, when the matter is addressed within the Court of Protection.

Capacity and transfer outside UK

2.35   The adult in this case (which was the subject of a determination within the inherent jurisdiction and pre-dated the Mental Capacity Act 2005 by just under 12 months) lacked capacity to make decisions about his care, residence and contact with others (*Re ST (Adult Patient)* [2006] EWHC 3458 (Fam), [2008] 1 FLR 111). The sole issue was whether it was in his best interests to move from the UK to Germany. Investigations were carried out into what arrangements would be made for his care in Germany, and the results, although not in the same format as would be expected in this jurisdiction, led to the conclusion that the standard of care that he would receive there would be commensurate with that in England. The simple but important proposition that emerges as between countries in Europe, is that:

> '[12] We are all members now of the European family of nations. This country and Germany are members of the European Union. We are both signatories to the European Convention for the Protection of Human Rights and Fundamental Freedoms 1950. My assumption will always be that, in a case such as this, someone in ST's position will receive the same standard of care in Germany (or, for that matter in France, in any of the Benelux countries and in many other countries in Europe) as he would receive in this country. That is not something which, as it seems to me, needs to be proved. It is the assumption which the Court can and should make unless and until the contrary is established.'

Capacity and abduction

2.36   A vulnerable adult (who lacked capacity) was removed in contravention of a court order to Israel. Whilst this is a case that post-dates the Mental Capacity Act 2005, Munby J lamented the fact that in respect of vulnerable adults, and the risk of their abduction, there was limited protection available to them (in contrast, for example, to the law in respect of abducted children). However, he also affirmed that:

> '[45] In my judgment and consistently with previous authority, the court has exactly the same power to make orders ... when it is concerned with an adult who lacks capacity as it undoubtedly has when concerned with a child. In particular, the court has exactly the same powers when it is concerned to locate the whereabouts of a missing or abducted adult lacking capacity as it has when

concerned to locate the whereabouts of a missing or abducted child.'
(*Re HM (Vulnerable Adult:Abduction)* [2010] EWHC 870 (Fam), [2010] 2 FLR 1057)

The orders to which he referred (and which had been made) amongst others included injunctions to return to the UK; orders inviting the authorities in the foreign jurisdiction to assist in tracing the adult; orders as against banks, travel agents, email service providers and telephone service providers to disclose information; orders freezing assets; orders disclosing information from the DVLA; orders permitting funds that had been frozen to be used for the purposes of litigation in the foreign jurisdiction and orders for disclosure from an airline company. In other words, all those remedies that are available and have been used in all other cases of abduction are available to the Court to locate and return an abducted adult who lacks capacity.

2.37 Although not relevant within this case, there is also the offence of ill treatment or neglect created by the Mental Capacity Act 2005 (s 44) which should engage the assistance of the relevant Chief Constable, if the abduction (or indeed any other act) might involve the commission of this offence. However, even if it does not, there is no reason to anticipate that the Court could not expect to receive assistance from the police in such circumstances, as it would where a child was abducted.

Capacity and deprivation of liberty

2.38 The issue of deprivation of liberty (and in particular as it applies to local authorities) has proved to be the most controversial and complex area of litigation that has developed over recent years. In order to understand how this has developed, it is necessary to look at the origins of the involvement of the Courts with considering those who lack capacity and are deprived of their liberty, to the manner in which Parliament has tried to remedy the problem (through what are known as Deprivation of Liberty Safeguards) to the interpretation by the Courts of what those safeguards means in practice, and indeed, what can amount to a deprivation of liberty. Throughout this Chapter, the abbreviation 'DOLS' will be used to refer to the statutory regime (Deprivation of Liberty Safeguards) but all other consideration of the matter will be referred to by reference to the more traditional and commonplace term 'deprivation of liberty'.

The Bournewood Gap

2.39 This area of law and capacity and its extension to the issue of deprivation of liberty has come to be of central importance to the role of the local authority. The origins of the law is commonly known as 'The Bournewood Gap'. It is worth summarising the legal and factual predicament that existed in relation to L (who was the patient in the case of *Bournewood*). He was autistic, and lacked capacity. He was admitted to hospital, informally, upon the basis of what the hospital decided was in his 'best interests'. He was the subject of continual control by the hospital, which included determining when and if he should see other individuals. The decisions which the hospital made were challenged by L's carers. The problem can be summarised as follows. L had no capacity to seek to challenge any of the decisions that were made upon his behalf (and, for example to consider whether they were, as a matter of fact, in his best interests). The hospital had no legal authority to make those decisions, or to keep him in the hospital, or to regulate who he should see, and when. The carers had no forum within which they could easily challenge the decisions made by the hospital (for example, had be been detained by way of the Mental Health Act 1983, he would have come within the jurisdiction of what was at that time the Mental Health Review Tribunal, within which the decision to detain him *could* have been challenged). It is this lacuna that is called 'the Bournewood Gap', that is to say, the gap in the law which is created when an adult who lacks capacity is deprived of his liberty (whether he 'consents' or not), and a public body is making a decision on his behalf in respect of his liberty, and there is no automatic recourse to an independent tribunal or court to consider the deprivation of liberty that arises from the decisions made by that public body.

2.40   The leading authority was *Re L (by his next friend GE)* [1998] 1 CCLR 390, [1999] AC 458. The provision within the legislation that created the anomaly is s 131(1) of MHA 1983. This permits admission of patients who lack capacity to consent, and do not positively object to admission. The House of Lords held that the detention of such individuals was justified in accordance with their best interests, the doctrine of necessity, and the duty of care owed to the patients by the hospital. Unfortunately, this decision also had the effect of depriving this category of patients from any formal method of access to an independent body to decide whether detention was justified. The matter was re-considered by the European Court of Human Rights (*HL v United Kingdom* App No 45508/99, [2004] 7 CCLR 498) in which it was held that: (a) it was the fact that the patient had been completely deprived of his liberty that was of the utmost significance; (b) the UK had shown that the patient required detention; (c) the legal basis of the doctrine of necessity could accommodate the minimum conditions for unsoundness of mind, but it is necessary to show that detention is not arbitrary. The lack of any fixed procedural rules, or review of the need for detention meant that the detaining authority had total power over the patient. Consequently there was a breach of Art 5(1); (d) the remedy of habeas corpus and judicial review were not sufficient for the purposes of Art 5(4). Thus, the UK was found to be in breach of Art 5(1) and (4). Thus, in essence, the factual basis upon which Bournewood is predicated is in effect where an adult who lacks capacity is admitted to a hospital or placed in a care home, and does not resist such admission. He is then prevented from leaving (or at least, if either he or someone else attempted to get him to leave, then this would be prevented).

2.41 The consequence of the judgment in the European Court of Human Rights was that amendments to the Mental Capacity Act 2005 were introduced by the Mental Health Act 2007. These amendments (DOLS) came into force on 1 April 2009. Fennel comments:

'**1.12** ... The MHA 2007 repeals the prohibition on deprivation of liberty under the MCA 2005 ... providing a complex procedure to authorise deprivations of liberty of mentally incapacitated adults. This will allow deprivation of liberty to be authorised not just in hospital but also in a privately run residential care home, and even in a private residence.'

He further comments:

'**1.29** ... If a person with a mental disorder needs treatment for mental disorder in their own best interests, and they lack capacity to consent to in-patient admission, their care is more likely to be managed under the Mental Capacity Act 2005...'

Section 50 of the Mental Health Act 2007 amends the Mental Capacity Act 2005 to authorise deprivation of liberty. It does this by inserting a new ss 4A, 4B and 16A into the Mental Capacity Act 2005 and by reference to new Schs A1 and 1A to the 2005 Act.

4A Restriction on deprivation of liberty

(1) This Act does not authorise any person ("D") to deprive any other person ("P") of his liberty.

(2) But that is subject to –

    (a)   the following provisions of this section, and
    (b)   section 4B.

(3) D may deprive P of his liberty if, by doing so, D is giving effect to a relevant decision of the court.

(4) A relevant decision of the court is a decision made by an order under section 16(2)(a) in relation to a matter concerning P's personal welfare.

(5) D may deprive P of his liberty if the deprivation is authorised by Schedule A1 (hospital and care home residents: deprivation of liberty).

4B Deprivation of liberty necessary for life-sustaining treatment etc

(1) If the following conditions are met, D is authorised to deprive P of his liberty while a decision as respects any relevant issue is sought from the court.

(2) The first condition is that there is a question about whether D is authorised to deprive P of his liberty under section 4A.

(3) The second condition is that the deprivation of liberty –

    (a)   is wholly or partly for the purpose of –
        (i)   giving P life-sustaining treatment, or
        (ii)   doing any vital act, or
    (b)   consists wholly or partly of –
        (i)   giving P life-sustaining treatment, or

(ii)   doing any vital act.

(4) The third condition is that the deprivation of liberty is necessary in order to –

(a)   give the life-sustaining treatment, or
(b)   do the vital act.

(5) A vital act is any act which the person doing it reasonably believes to be necessary to prevent a serious deterioration in P's condition.

16A Section 16 powers: Mental Health Act patients etc

(1) If a person is ineligible to be deprived of liberty by this Act, the court may not include in a welfare order provision which authorises the person to be deprived of his liberty.

(2) If –

(a)   a welfare order includes provision which authorises a person to be deprived of his liberty, and
(b)   that person becomes ineligible to be deprived of liberty by this Act,

the provision ceases to have effect for as long as the person remains ineligible.

(3) Nothing in subsection (2) affects the power of the court under section 16(7) to vary or discharge the welfare order.

(4) For the purposes of this section –

(a)   Schedule 1A applies for determining whether or not P is ineligible to be deprived of liberty by this Act;
(b)   "welfare order" means an order under section 16(2)(a).

The safeguards for deprivation of liberty are as follows:

'**6.41** Section 50 of the MHA 2007 amends the MCA 2005 to add provisions for the lawful deprivation of liberty of a person with a mental disorder, who lacks capacity to consent, if it is in that person's best interests. Section 50(2) inserts two new ss, 4A and 4B, into the MCA 2005. The effect of these will be that deprivation of liberty may only take place under the MCA in one of three situations. These are where:

(1)   the deprivation is authorised by a personal welfare decision of the Court of Protection under s 16(2)(a) of the MCA 2005; or
(2)   the deprivation is authorised in accordance with the deprivation of liberty procedures set out in Sch A1; or
(3)   the deprivation is carried out because it is necessary in order to give life sustaining treatment or to carry out a vital act to prevent serious deterioration in the person's condition "while a decision as respects any relevant issue is sought from the court" (MCA 2005, s 4B).' (Philip Fennell, *Mental Health – The New Law* (Jordan Publishing, 2007).

Deprivation of Liberty Safeguards – Code of Practice

2.42   It is the DOLS regime introduced by Sch A1 that has caused the greatest difficulties for local authorities, and for the Courts. The implications of the

DOLS regime is still relatively unknown to some local authorities, even though it has been in force since April 2009. It is likely that many steps that have been taken since that date by a local authority which may be unlawful, have yet to be discovered, and will be considered by the Courts in due course. However, the Code of Practice (DOLS) is a vital reference source for any person who is involved in this area of practice. It was issued on 26 August 2008 (pursuant to ss 42 and 43 of the Mental Capacity Act 2005) and remains in an unrevised edition. It will presumably be revised in due course in order to include the recent developments in the law. As with the main Code of Practice (for the Mental Capacity Act 2005, issued on 23 April 2007, and also unrevised) it is an extremely well written document, and very accessible and lucid. It contains many 'case studies' which are intended to illustrate the sorts of situations which DOLS may cover. The legal status of the Codes are enhanced by virtue of s 42(4) to the extent that 'it is the duty of a person to have regard to the relevant Code if he is acting in relation to a person who lacks capacity ...'. Thus, professionals in this area of law who are so acting are expected to follow the Code, and be familiar with its contents. Given the high quality of the contents, this should not be an onerous burden. The Code of Practice (DOLS) runs to 11 separate Chapters, and is 114 pages in length (including appendices). It is available via the Department of Health website, as well as in hard copy from TSO.

2.43 Parts of the specific interactions between Sch 1A and Sch A1 are considered below, but some of the fundamentals and general principles of DOLS are as follows;

(a) DOLS only apply if P is deprived of his liberty in a care home or a hospital;

(b) DOLS only apply if P is over the age of 18;

(c) the necessary assessments have been carried out in respect of P (which will include determination of whether P has a mental disorder and lacks capacity to consent to the arrangements made for their care or treatment);

(d) it is in the best interests of P to be deprived of his liberty in order to protect him from harm, and that the deprivation is a proportionate response to the seriousness of the harm, and that there is no less restrictive alternative;

(e) the authorisation must not be used as a punishment;

(f) DOLS are only a supplement to the MCA 2005, and are governed by its principles;

(g) restraint may fall short of deprivation of liberty (s 6(4) particularly in an emergency or for a very short period of time (eg preventing P from walking into traffic);

(h) where there is a deprivation of liberty, it is unlawful to do so without a lawful authority (which will be either via DOLS or an order of the Court of Protection);

(i) an urgent authorisation can be made, but this is up to a maximum of 7 days only;

(j) written records of all applications (by a managing authority) and decisions made (by a supervising authority) must be kept. These are records are kept in a standard format;

(k) anyone involved in the care or welfare of P should be kept informed;

(l) in certain circumstances an IMCA (Independent Mental Capacity Advocate) must be involved;

(m) there are specific and detailed requirements as to which people can and cannot be assessors for the purposes of deciding whether there should be a deprivation of liberty;

(n) there are 6 assessments:

  (1) age (18+);
  (2) no refusals (no conflict with other authority for deprivation of liberty in existence, e g advance decision to refuse treatment);
  (3) mental capacity assessment;
  (4) mental health assessment (mental disorder within the meaning of the MHA 1983, but **not** an assessment for the purposes of detention under MHA 1983);
  (5) eligibility assessment (are they *ineligible* to be deprived of their liberty by the MCA 2005);
  (6) best interests assessment;

(o) the authorisation may be refused or if granted, challenged in the Court of Protection;

(p) if any one of the assessment concludes that the conditions are not met, then the assessments should cease;

(q) a 'relevant person's representative' must be appointed, whose duties involve monitoring the situation, and if required, to challenge the authorisation whether by way of a review or by application to the Court of Protection. This person must be independent of the commissioners and providers of the service that is being provided;

(r) to bring an end to any authorisation as swiftly as possible (by way of review or other method – the authorisation is permissive only).

2.44   The authorisation for a DOL (Deprivation of Liberty) will be sought by a 'managing authority' (ie a care home or a hospital) from a 'supervisory body' (ie a local authority or a primary care trust). Some areas have pooled responsibility between primary care trusts and local authorities in order to co-ordinate and regulate the granting of an application to deprive someone of their liberty. A DOL cannot last for more than 12 months, and cannot last any longer than the period recommended by the 'Best Interests Assessor'. As it is a matter of liberty, such period should be of short a duration as possible, and as limited in scope as possible. Moreover, if there is a change in circumstances, then there should be a review of the authority, and in any event, if there is a change in residence, the authority does not travel – it will only provide lawful authority to deprive P of his liberty in the location for which it was granted. Whether P is being treated for a physical or mental disorder, and is being deprived of their liberty, a DOLS authorisation is required. The authorisation for deprivation of liberty does only that – it does **not** authorise the treatment itself, which is an entirely separate matter. If there is treatment for a mental disorder, then this must come within the Mental Health Act 1983. For treatment to take place lawfully, their must either be capacitous consent, or in accordance with the Code of Practice (MCA 2005). As with all of these procedures, the ultimate arbiter in the case of a dispute is a judge sitting in the Court of Protection. Disputes arising out of DOLS are currently reserved to the High Court. It is at the very least arguable that if an authorisation is granted, and the requirements are not met in accordance with the DOLS Code of Practice, then that authorisation is vitiated, in which case it will not amount to a lawful deprivation of liberty. If so, if follows that P will have been unlawfully deprived of his liberty. The consequences of this in terms of remedies is set out at **2.100**, **2.102** and **2.103** below.

2.45   The issue of interaction and distinction between Schs A1 and 1A were considered at length in *GJ v (1) Foundation Trust; (2) PCT; (3) Secretary of State for Health* [2009] EWHC 2972 (Fam), [2010] 1 FLR 1251. It is not possible within a work of this scope to set out the relevant schedules in their entirety (for example, Sch A1 runs to 188 different sections). However, the facts in this case illustrate the difference between the different principles which are to be applied. P himself suffered from Korsakoff's syndrome, and vascular dementia (either of which would have brought him within the Mental Health Act 1983, or the Mental Capacity Act 2005). He did not have capacity to litigate, or to make decisions about his care, treatment or residence. He also suffered from diabetes. His mental disorder meant that he was unable to control his diabetes. This failure led to a worsening of his condition, such that he was assessed as being suitable for detention under s 2 and then s 3 of the Mental Health Act 1983. He was subsequently deprived of his liberty (via a DOLS authorisation) in a clinic, where he was being treated for his mental disorder. He objected to treatment for his mental disorder. The ratio of the judgment by Charles J may be explained as follows. If a patient either should be (or actually is) detained under the Mental Health Act 1983, then he is ineligible to be deprived of his liberty via the Mental Capacity Act 2005. In particular, he is ineligible if already detained under the MHA 1983, or meets the criteria for such detention and objects to some or all of the treatment for the mental disorder from which he suffers. In those circumstances, the MHA 1983 must be used, and not the MCA 2005. There is no jurisdiction within the MCA 2005. The main propositions that emerge are that: (a) the MHA 1983 has primacy in such situations; (b) there is no jurisdiction at all within the MCA 2005 if P falls outside the provision, and only if P is *not ineligible* to be deprived of his liberty can such authorisation be provided either by the Court or by way of a DOLS authorisation; (c) the starting point should be to look at the facts and reality of the case in terms of what is actually the purpose of the deprivation of liberty, and that this could be done by applying a 'but for' test, e g is the reason for the detention in hospital for physical treatment for a matter unconnected with his mental health. If (as a matter of fact) it was apparent from this analysis that the deprivation of liberty was for treatment for a mental disorder, it was not possible for the decision maker to opt for a deprivation of liberty authorisation to treat his physical disorder, as this was clearly not the prime reason for the need to detain him. Roderic Wood J was faced with a similar issue in *W Primary Care Trust v (1) TB (An Adult by her litigation friend the Official Solicitor); (2) V & S Metropolitan Borough Council (3) C & W Partnership NHS Foundation Trust (4) W Metropolitan Borough Council* [2009] EWHC 1737 (Fam), [2010] 1 FLR 682 (COP), albeit the solution was simpler, since upon the facts in the case, the Mental Health Act 1983 could not have applied, as the placement in issue was a care home, and not a hospital.

2.46 There has also been consideration of the *manner* in which authorisations have been granted, in circumstances where a lapse of that authority has been permitted to occur. In *A County Council v MB,JB and a Residential Home* [2010] EWHC 2508 (COP), [2011] 1 FLR 790 a standard authorisation had been obtained. As is in keeping with the Code of Practice, shortly before this was due to expire, there was consideration given as to whether a second standard authorisation should be granted. However, the best interests assessor determined that such an authority would not be in P's best interests. However, she had no other place to go, than the placement in which she was deprived of her liberty. Without any authority, she would have been unlawfully deprived of her liberty. Consequently a DOL authorisation was made on an urgent basis (with a life span of 7 days) but this was invalid as it contained no indication as to when it actually ended. An application was made to the Court of Protection, but this caused a 2 week delay, during which there was no lawful authority for her deprivation of liberty. In addition to making a declaration that there had been a breach of Art 5, extensive guidance was given in respect of the precise manner in which DOLS authorisations should be documented. In summary this is that:

(a)   a record of the precise time at which an urgent DOL came into force should be kept;

(b)   the maximum period for a standard authorisation should also be calculated exactly;

(c)   only one urgent authorisation is permissible, and thus if there can be no implementation of the DOLS regime then only a Court can provide that lawful authority, and an application to the Court must be made;

(d)   if there was a serious issue for a best interests assessor to consider, such as in the circumstances of this case where it was concluded that a standard authorisation was not appropriate, it might remain in the best interests of P for there to be a short standard authorisation (given the practical alternatives on the facts in this case);

(e)   that the fact that the local authority made an application to the Court swiftly, and had been acting in the best interests of P, did not prevent there being a breach of Art 5. A failure to act in accordance with the Mental Capacity Act 2005 was a breach of domestic law.

Role of local authority when DOLS regime cannot be applied

2.47   It may be worth noting that prior to the DOLS regime coming into force, the High Court had been obliged to consider what safeguards should exist where an adult without capacity was being deprived of his liberty, and had established certain principles. For example For example in *Salford City Council v GJ, NJ and BJ (by their respective litigation friends)* [2008] EWHC 1097 (Fam), [2008] 2 FLR 1295 the local authority were clearly aware of its obligations pursuant to Art 5(4) when placing adults with no capacity, and requiring authorisation of the Court so to do. General guidance was given by Munby J as to how to regulate such deprivation of liberty in a non-statutory situation (ie where there is no regime provided for by Parliament to render lawful the deprivation of liberty). This is still of great significance, as DOLS only applies to care homes and hospitals, and, of course, there are situations where those without capacity may be deprived of their liberty outside of either of those environments. As will be seen, local authorities still have an obligation to manage situations that arise where either an adult *or* child may be being deprived of his liberty outside either a care home, or a hospital. In summary, the procedure should be as follows:

(a)   authority should be obtained *before* the deprivation of liberty took place;

(b)   the Official Solicitor (in the absence of any other) should act as litigation friend;

(c)   the litigation friend should be supplied with up to date material at the earliest possible date;

(d)   an interim order should last for no more than 4 weeks as a general practice;

(e)   during the interim period the local authority should hold regular reviews (of between 4–6 weeks, depending upon the circumstances);

(f)   the dates of the reviews should be set out, and the litigation friend invited to attend;

(g)   after a final hearing, there should be regular reviews by the Court, at about 12 months after the final order, and the litigation friend to remain involved;

(h)   the first review would be oral, but thereafter could be in the absence of a hearing, subject to confirmation and agreement that there was no change in the circumstances of P;

(i)   there must be a clear timetable leading up to the hearing, with provision of all documents to all parties, and a multidisciplinary meeting at least 28 days prior to the Court hearing;

(j)   there should be judicial continuity, if possible;

(k)   during the 12 month period, there should be internal reviews of about once every 8–10 weeks, and at each review the local authority should consider both the issues of capacity, and what was in the best interests of P;

(l)   there would be no need for independent expert evidence to be available at the internal reviews, but the interests of P must be represented by an independent person.

This judgment was made approximately 11 months prior to the DOLS regime coming into force, and Munby J was clearly taking into account the main features of that regime in setting out the general guidance listed above. It should be stressed that he intended this as general guidance only, and that each case might require adjustment (particularly in terms of time frames). However, the fundamental principles are set out – frequent reviews; independent representation; minimum interference; access to a Court. In the actual review in this case (*Re BJ (Incapacitated Adult)* [2009] EWHC 3310 (Fam), [2010] 1 FLR 1373) the DOLS regime could not have applied to him (since the accommodation was neither a care home, nor a hospital). Munby J re-iterated that Sch A1 (see above) provided important guidance as to how reviews should be conducted, and how the Court itself should review such cases. The point is a simple one. Parliament has produced a definitive system (through DOLS) which regulates the position where an incapacitated adult is deprived of their liberty, but only when the building in which that takes place is defined as a care home, or a hospital. If an incapacitated adult is deprived of his liberty outside such a defined location, the local authority (if involved) can use the DOLS regime as its gold standard, or at least, as the starting point for ensuring that the Art 5 rights of the incapacitated adult are not breached. It may also be worth noting that the purpose of the DOLS regime was to remedy a lacuna in the law arising out of Art 5 only. However, there are many instances where it is used to regulate the life of a patient which goes beyond this (typically, involving interference in Art 8 rights). This, it may be argued with some force, is a matter for an order of the Court of Protection, and not a matter that was ever contemplated as being within the purview of DOLS.

2.48 The significance of the above is particularly apparent in considering a important later case, also decided by Munby LJ (as he had become by that time). This is the authority of *Re A and C (Equality and Human Rights Commission Intervening)* [2010] EWHC 978 (Fam), [2010] 2 FLR 1363. There are some difficulties with the ratio in this case, as in part it relied upon an earlier judgment by Parker J (*Re MIG & MEG* [2010] EWHC 785 (Fam)) which was subsequently appealed. However, the consequences of that appeal are not relevant for the principles it established, and which are binding on local authorities. The issues in the case were stated to be:

> '[3] Do the circumstances of their [the claimants] domestic care by their families in the family home involve a deprivation of liberty engaging the protection of Article 5 of the European Convention for the Protection of Human Rights and Fundamental Freedoms? And what, if any, role does the local authority have in such cases?'

Article 5 is set out below in it entirety for ease of reference. Munby LJ summarised the different statutes and common law obligations that might lead to a connection between a local authority, and an individual lacking capacity (or merely a vulnerable adult). These are all referred to elsewhere in this textbook, but include the National Health Service and Community Care Act 1990, the National Assistance Act 1948, the Chronically Sick and Disabled Persons Act 1970, the National Health Service Act 2006, and s 117 of the Mental Health Act 1983. All of these merely provide the local authority with powers and/or duties to provide services. They do not have any coercive effect [66] He affirms that for any coercive power to be lawful, then an order under the inherent jurisdiction is required (in the absence of the jurisdiction of the Court of Protection) [68]. He also refers to the judgment of Hedley J in *Re Z* with approval, which is considered in Chapter 3 (at **3.93**) in relation to the protection of vulnerable adults generally. His conclusions in respect of the duties of the local authority are as follows:

> '[95] Where the State – here, a local authority – knows or ought to know that a **vulnerable child or adult** [emphasis added] is subject to restrictions on their liberty by a **private individual** [emphasis added] that arguably give rise to a deprivation of liberty, then its positive obligations under Article 5 will be triggered.
>
> (i)   These will include the duty to investigate, as as to determine whether there is, in fact, a deprivation of liberty. In this context the local authority will need to consider all the factors relevant to the objective and subjective elements referred to in paragraph [48] above.
>
> (ii) If, having carried out its investigation, the local authority is satisfied that the objective element is not present , so there is no deprivation of liberty, the local authority will have discharged its immediate obligations. However, its

positive obligations may in an appropriate case require the local authority to continue to monitor the situation in the event that circumstances should change;

(iii) If, however, the local authority concludes that the measures imposed do **or may** [emphasis added] constitute a deprivation of liberty, then it will be under a positive obligation, both under Article 5 alone and taken together with Article 14, to take reasonable and proportionate measures to bring that state of affairs to an end. What is reasonable and proportionate in the circumstances will, of course, depend upon the context, but it might require for example ... the local authority to exercise its statutory powers and duties so as to provide support services for the carers that will enable inappropriate restrictions to be ended, or at least minimised.

(iv) If, however, there are no reasonable measures that the local authority can take to bring the deprivation of liberty to and end, or if the measures it proposes are objected to by the individual or his family, then it may be necessary for the local authority to seek the assistance of the Court in determining whether there is, in fact, a deprivation of liberty and, if there is, obtaining authorisation for its continuance.'

2.49 The reference to the *objective and subjective* tests will be considered below, when examining what the Courts have struggled to define as what actually constitutes (as a matter of fact) a deprivation of liberty. What is very important about this decision is that;

(a) it extends the obligations of the local authority to children and vulnerable adults (ie not just those who lack capacity);

(b) Children are not within the DOLS regime at all, and the Mental Capacity Act 2005 only applies to those over the age of 16;

(c) It extends the obligation of local authorities to *private individuals* (ie not just public bodies, whether these may be hospitals or care homes, or any other similar organisation).

This means that a local authority has upon its shoulders an obligation to a far wider section of the population that either the DOLS regime or the Mental Capacity Act envisaged. This in turn means that a local authority will need to look to both of these regimes, and the case law which has been created as a result, in order to decide what it should do, and how it should do it, and when. One option that is not available to a local authority is to do nothing. It must act upon behalf of either incapacitous or vulnerable adults or children to protect their rights under Art 5.

Article 5

Right to liberty and security

1. Everyone has the right to liberty and security of person. No one shall be deprived of his liberty save in the following cases and in accordance with a procedure prescribed by law:

(a)   the lawful detention of a person after conviction by a competent court;

(b)   the lawful arrest or detention of a person for non-compliance with the lawful order of a court or in order to secure the fulfilment of any obligation prescribed by law;

(c)   the lawful arrest or detention of a person effected for the purpose of bringing him before the competent legal authority on reasonable suspicion of having committed an offence or when it is reasonably considered necessary to prevent his committing an offence or fleeing after having done so;

(d)   the detention of a minor by lawful order for the purpose of educational supervision or his lawful detention for the purpose of bringing him before the competent legal authority;

(e)   the lawful detention of persons for the prevention of the spreading of infectious diseases, of persons of unsound mind, alcoholics or drug addicts or vagrants;

(f)   the lawful arrest or detention of a person to prevent his effecting an unauthorised entry into the country or of a person against whom action is being taken with a view to deportation or extradition.

2. Everyone who is arrested shall be informed promptly, in a language which he understands, of the reasons for his arrest and of any charge against him.

3. Everyone arrested or detained in accordance with the provisions of paragraph 1(c) of this Article shall be brought promptly before a judge or other officer authorised by law to exercise judicial power and shall be entitled to trial within a reasonable time or to release pending trial. Release may be conditioned by guarantees to appear for trial.

4. Everyone who is deprived of his liberty by arrest or detention shall be entitled to take proceedings by which the lawfulness of his detention shall be decided speedily by a court and his release ordered if the detention is not lawful.

5. Everyone who has been the victim of arrest or detention in contravention of the provisions of this Article shall have an enforceable right to compensation.

2.50   Lady Hale has commented on the apparent causes of a reluctance to use DOLS (even when they do apply) as:

'(1) Ignorance of the law: "It always used to be legal to do this (well, it was under Bournewood, though not under the Mental Capacity Act 2005) so let's carry on as normal"; (2) Fear of the law: "formalities of all kinds are a barrier to doing what is best for the patient or resident so let's ignore them". The more burdensome and cumbersome the formalities, the worse the problem. (3) Uncertainty about what the law requires: the problems identified so far relate to what amounts to a deprivation of liberty (so, "when are safeguards required?") and what is the relationship between the Mental Capacity Act and the Mental Health Act (so "when is the person concerned eligible for the DOLS?").'
[2010] 13 CCLR 7 (text of a presentation given to a seminar on 3 December 2009).

Ignorance, fear and uncertainty appear to have been the three areas which have caused difficulties for local authorities in implementing the DOLS regime. Amongst the most intractable of these problems has been deciding whether (as a matter of fact) there actually *is* a deprivation of liberty, and also to what extent the DOLS regime should be used when there is an intractable dispute, and whether an immediate application to the Court of Protection is the simplest and safest route in order to protect the Art 5 rights of P. Further, it may be that the problems that this regime is being used to address actually go much further than the purpose for which it was designed (e.g regulating contact arrangements with family members).

What is deprivation of liberty?

2.51 In *Re A and C (Equality and Human Rights Commission Intervening)* [2010] EWHC 978 (Fam), [2010] 2 FLR 1363 Munby J summarised the three conditions that must exist for there to be a deprivation of liberty. It is to be noted that a deprivation of liberty does not necessarily equate to false imprisonment. Relying on *Storck v Germany* (2005) 43 EHRR 96 he stated the law to be thus:

> '[48] (i) an objective element of a "person's confinement to a certain limited place for a not negligible length of time"; (ii) a subjective element, namely that the person has not "validly consented to the confinement in question" and (iii) the deprivation of liberty must be one for which the State is responsible.'

Thus, it should be fairly simple to establish whether the objective element is in existence. Is P prevented from leaving a particular location or not? For how long has P been prevented from so leaving? In respect of (ii), if there is a lack of capacity as to the ability to decide where to live, or stay, then there cannot have been a valid consent to that course of action. In respect of (iii), in this context, this refers to a local authority. This basic formula is extremely helpful, but the Courts have grappled with the finer points of this starting point, and in particular by reference to the many variants on individual facts in each case. It has proved very difficult, in practice, to decide what is a deprivation of liberty, and what does not.

2.52 The Code of Practice (DOLS) provides a summary of the law up until 26 August 2008 as to what might be a deprivation of liberty. The relevant parts of the Code are set out below.

DOLS CODE OF PRACTICE

2.1 The European Court of Human Rights (ECtHR) has drawn a distinction between the deprivation of liberty of an individual (which is unlawful, unless authorised) and restrictions on the liberty of movement of an individual.

2.2 The ECtHR made it clear that the question of whether someone has been deprived of liberty depends on the particular circumstances of the case. Specifically, the ECtHR said in its October 2004 judgment in *HL v the United Kingdom*:

> 'to determine whether there has been a deprivation of liberty, the starting-point must be the specific situation of the individual concerned and account must be taken of a whole range of factors arising in a particular

case such as the type, duration, effects and manner of implementation of the measure in question. The distinction between a deprivation of, and restriction upon, liberty is merely one of degree or intensity and not one of nature or substance.'

2.3 The difference between deprivation of liberty and restriction upon liberty is one of degree or intensity. It may therefore be helpful to envisage a scale, which moves from 'restraint' or 'restriction' to 'deprivation of liberty'. Where an individual is on the scale will depend on the concrete circumstances of the individual and may change over time. For more information on how the Act defines restraint, see paragraphs 2.8–2.12.

2.4 Although the guidance in this chapter includes descriptions of past decisions of the courts, which should be used to help evaluate whether deprivation of liberty may be occurring, each individual case must be assessed on its own circumstances. No two cases are likely to be identical, so it is important to be aware of previous court judgments and the factors that the courts have identified as important.

2.5 The ECtHR and UK courts have determined a number of cases about deprivation of liberty. Their judgments indicate that the following factors can be relevant to identifying whether steps taken involve more than restraint and amount to a deprivation of liberty. It is important to remember that this list is not exclusive; other factors may arise in future in particular cases.

- Restraint is used, including sedation, to admit a person to an institution where that person is resisting admission.
- Staff exercise complete and effective control over the care and movement of a person for a significant period.
- Staff exercise control over assessments, treatment, contacts and residence.
- A decision has been taken by the institution that the person will not be released into the care of others, or permitted to live elsewhere, unless the staff in the institution consider it appropriate.
- A request by carers for a person to be discharged to their care is refused.
- The person is unable to maintain social contacts because of restrictions placed on their access to other people.
- The person loses autonomy because they are under continuous supervision and control.

There is more information on some relevant cases at the end of this chapter (paragraphs 2.17–2.23).

How can deprivation of liberty be identified?

2.6 In determining whether deprivation of liberty has occurred, or is likely to occur, decision-makers need to consider all the facts in a particular case. There is unlikely to be any simple definition that can be applied in every case, and it is probable that no single factor will, in itself, determine whether the overall set of steps being taken in relation to the relevant person amount to a deprivation of liberty. In general, the decision-maker should always consider the following:

- All the circumstances of each and every case.

- What measures are being taken in relation to the individual? When are they required? For what period do they endure? What are the effects of any restraints or restrictions on the individual? Why are they necessary? What aim do they seek to meet?
- What are the views of the relevant person, their family or carers? Do any of them object to the measures?
- How are any restraints or restrictions implemented? Do any of the constraints on the individual's personal freedom go beyond 'restraint' or 'restriction' to the extent that they constitute a deprivation of liberty?
- Are there any less restrictive options for delivering care or treatment that avoid deprivation of liberty altogether?
- Does the cumulative effect of all the restrictions imposed on the person amount to a deprivation of liberty, even if individually they would not?

What practical steps can be taken to reduce the risk of deprivation of liberty occurring?

2.7 There are many ways in which providers and commissioners of care can reduce the risk of taking steps that amount to a deprivation of liberty, by minimising the restrictions imposed and ensuring that decisions are taken with the involvement of the relevant person and their family, friends and carers. The processes for staff to follow are:

- Make sure that all decisions are taken (and reviewed) in a structured way, and reasons for decisions recorded.
- Follow established good practice for care planning.
- Make a proper assessment of whether the person lacks capacity to decide whether or not to accept the care or treatment proposed, in line with the principles of the Act (see chapter 3 of the main Code for further guidance).
- Before admitting a person to hospital or residential care in circumstances that may amount to a deprivation of liberty, consider whether the person's needs could be met in a less restrictive way. Any restrictions placed on the person while in hospital or in a care home must be kept to the minimum necessary, and should be in place for the shortest possible period.
- Take proper steps to help the relevant person retain contact with family, friends and carers. Where local advocacy services are available, their involvement should be encouraged to support the person and their family, friends and carers.
- Review the care plan on an ongoing basis. It may well be helpful to include an independent element, possibly via an advocacy service, in the review.

What does the Act mean by 'restraint'?

2.8 Section 6(4) of the Act states that someone is using restraint if they:

- use force – or threaten to use force – to make someone do something that they are resisting, or
- restrict a person's freedom of movement, whether they are resisting or not.

2.9 Paragraphs 6.40 to 6.48 of the main Code contain guidance about the appropriate use of restraint. Restraint is appropriate when it is used to prevent harm to the person who lacks capacity and it is a proportionate response to the likelihood and seriousness of harm. Appropriate use of restraint falls short of deprivation of liberty.

2.10 Preventing a person from leaving a care home or hospital unaccompanied because there is a risk that they would try to cross a road in a dangerous way, for example, is likely to be seen as a proportionate restriction or restraint to prevent the person from coming to harm. That would be unlikely, in itself, to constitute a deprivation of liberty. Similarly, locking a door to guard against immediate harm is unlikely, in itself, to amount to a deprivation of liberty.

2.11 The ECtHR has also indicated that the duration of any restrictions is a relevant factor when considering whether or not a person is deprived of their liberty. This suggests that actions that are immediately necessary to prevent harm may not, in themselves, constitute a deprivation of liberty.

2.12 However, where the restriction or restraint is frequent, cumulative and ongoing, or if there are other factors present, then care providers should consider whether this has gone beyond permissible restraint, as defined in the Act. If so, then they must either apply for authorisation under the deprivation of liberty safeguards (as explained in chapter 3) or change their care provision to reduce the level of restraint.

2.53 The first substantial case where this question (amongst others) was addressed was *G v E, A Local Authority and F* [2010] EWHC 621 (Fam), [2010] 2 FLR 294. In his exhaustive analysis of the development of the law, Baker J fastens upon s 64(5) of the Mental Capacity Act 2005 which is as follows:

'Section 64(5) in this Act, references to deprivation of a person's liberty have the same meaning as in Article 5 (1) of the Human Rights Convention.'

He then adds that:

'[77] any analysis of whether E has been in fact deprived of his liberty must have close regard to the jurisprudence of the European Court and of English courts on the interpretation of that Article.'

He then cites the same extract from *Storck* as referred to by Munby LJ and as contained at **2.51** above. His gloss on those criteria is as follows:

'[77] the starting point is to examine the concrete situation of the individual concerned and account must be taken of a whole range of criteria such as the type, duration, effects and manner of implementation of the measure in question. The distinction between a deprivation of and a restriction of liberty is merely one of degree or intensity and not one of nature or substance ... the key factor is whether the person is, or is not, free to leave. This may be tested by determining whether those treating and managing the person exercise complete and effective control over the person's care and movements ... So far as the subjective element is concerned, whilst there is no deprivation of liberty if a person gives a valid consent to their confinement, such consent can only be valid if a person has capacity to give it ... So far as the third element is concerned, regardless of whether the confinement is effected by a private individual or institution, it is necessary to show that it is imputable to the state. This may happen by the direct involvement of public authorities, or by order of the court.'

2.54 On the facts in this case, the following pointed towards (and were conclusive of a factual deprivation of liberty):

• complete control over care and movement; assessments; treatment; contacts and residence;

• no private space within the residence;

• confined to residence except when on escorted trips elsewhere;

• restrictions on social and family contacts;

• medication (haloperidol) to reduce agitation, and over the administration of which P has no control [78].

2.55 There was no lawful authority for the above (and, on the facts there could have been, as the placement was a care home and so DOLS could have been used, although as can be seen, this may make no difference to a breach of Art 5). A declaration was made to this effect. There was also a declaration that there had been a breach of Art 8, in that little or no consultation with family members and others who were interested in the welfare of P had been carried out (in addition to the restrictions placed upon P's contact with family and others). The decision (although not on this point) was the subject of an unsuccessful appeal (*G v E (by his litigation friend the Official Solicitor), a local authority, F* [2010] EWCA Civ 822, [2011] 1 FLR 239). A similar conclusion as the deprivation of liberty of an individual was reached by Hedley J in *PCT v P, AH and the Local Authority* [2011] 1 FLR 287, notwithstanding the fact that the accommodation in which he was placed was described as independent living within a flat. Mr Justice Hedley referred to:

'[73] the degree of control to be exercised by staff ... the constraint on P leaving ... the power to refuse a request ... for discharge of P... restraints on contact between P and [mother] ... a fairly high degree of supervision and control within the placement.'

2.56 The case of *Re MIG & MEG* [2010] EWHC 785 (Fam) was referred to above, as having been the subject of an appeal. This is *P (otherwise known as MIG) and Q (otherwise known as MEG, by the Official Solicitor, their litigation friend v Surrey County Council, CA, LA and Equality and Human Rights Commission (Intervener)* [2011] EWCA Civ 190, [2011] 14 CCLR 209, which will be referred to as '*P&Q*'. Wilson LJ also re-visited *Storck* [17]. In the part of the judgment entitled 'General Discussion' a number of additional considerations were canvassed:

'[24–25] a person's happiness, as such, is not relevant to whether she is deprived of her liberty. Its relevance is as to whether any such deprivation is in her best interests: see section 4(6)(a) of the Mental Capacity Act 2005. Such is a necessary condition of it being 'lawful' and thus of its not infringing Article 5 ... but the overlapping feature which in my view is relevant to the enquiry is whether the person **objects** to the confinement which is imposed upon her ... If a person objects to the confinement, the consequence will be conflict. At the very least there will be arguments and she will suffer the stress of having her objections overruled ... This level of conflict inherent in overruled objections seems to me to be highly relevant in the objective element. Equally, however, the absence of objections generates an absence of conflict and thus a peaceful life, which seems to me to be capable of substantial relevance in the opposite direction.'

He also commented on the use of medication as an ingredient in the mix in these terms:

'[26] From the relevance of objections and also lack of them, it is logical to move to the relevance of **medication** and also the lack of it. In my view, the administration to a person of medication, at any rate of antipsychotic drugs and other tranquillisers, is always a pointer towards the existence of the objective element: for it suppresses her liberty to express herself as she would otherwise wish. Indeed, if the administration is attended by force, its relevance is increased. Furthermore, in that objections may be highly relevant, medication which has the effect of suppressing them may be relevant to an equally high degree. But again, conversely, the absence of medication is a pointer in the other direction.'

2.57 He also considered the issue of 'normality' (ie how close to a normal family home was the environment in which P was purportedly being deprived of her liberty?). In particular he observed that:

'[29] Of potentially great relevance in the case of children and young adults is whether ... they go out to some sort of school or college; and in the case of adults, whether they go out to a college or to a day centre or indeed to pursue some form of occupation.'

What follows in the judgment is a listing of all those factors, which on the specific facts of the case, tended to point one way or the other as to whether, as a matter of fact, there was a deprivation of liberty or not. Those factors which pointed *towards* deprivation of liberty were as follows:

• neither were free to leave their accommodation;

• they were under supervision and control for their daily care needs;

• in the case of P, her social life was very limited;

• in the case of Q she was not living in a family home;

• in the case of Q she sometimes required physical restraint.

Those factors which pointed *away* from deprivation of liberty were as follows:

- neither objected to the placement (and therefore did not require restraint);

- they each had their own private bedrooms;

- they were not under close confinement;

- they went out each day for education;

- they went out on other outings;

- they had good and regular contact with family members;

- all of the features of confinement, supervision and control were likely to be permanent;

- in respect of P she was living in a family home and she was not in receipt of medication;

- in respect of Q although not in a family home she was in a small 'home' with only four other residents;

- in respect of Q, her medication was not forcibly administered, and its effect was not to to restrain her from leaving the home.

It followed that the finding was that although in the case of Q, she was perhaps closer to the borderline of deprivation of liberty, that as a matter of factual interpretation, there had been no deprivation of liberty.

2.58 The concepts referred to above have become frequently contested territory, and four recent authorities have all considered various aspects of those concepts. The first is *The London Borough of Hillingdon v Steven Neary (by his litigation friend the Official Solicitor & Mark Neary* [2011] EWHC 1377 (COP). This will be referred to as the '*Neary*' case. Mr Justice Peter Jackson identified a number of salient features in a case where a local authority sought to deprive an incapacitous adult of his liberty. He stated:

> '[22] If a local authority seeks to regulate, control, compel, restrain, confine or coerce it must, except in an emergency, point to a specific statutory authority for what is doing or else obtain the appropriate sanction of the court ... [23] The origin of the basic legal principle is to be found in an era long before the invention of local authorities as we know them. Chapter 29 of Magna Carta 1297 provides that "No freeman shall be taken or imprisoned, or disseised of his freehold, or liberties, or free customs, or outlawed, or exiled, or any otherwise destroyed; nor will we not pass upon him, nor condemn him, but by lawful judgment of his peers, or by the law the land".'

On the facts of the case, such purported legal authority had been under the DOLS regime (by way of a number of standard authorisations). However, within the judgment Mr Justice Peter Jackson analyses in great detail the flaws in the authorisation procedure (which of course **have** to adhere to the Code of Practice, and the MCA 2005 in order for them to be valid). He found that the substantial and many flaws vitiated their lawfulness, and that therefore it followed that P had been deprived of his liberty unlawfully. In particular, the local authority were found liable for having: (a) failed to bring the matter before the Court of Protection sooner rather than later; (b) failing to appoint and IMCA sooner rather than later; (c) failing to conduct an effective review of the DOL best interest assessments. All of these failures amounted to a breach of Art 5(4). In addition, there was also found to have been a breach of Art 8. In respect of the function of DOL authorisations he had this to say:

> '[33] Significant welfare issues that cannot be resolved by discussion should be placed before the Court of Protection, where decisions can be taken as a matter of urgency. Where stringent conditions are met, it [the DOLs regime – parentheses added] allows a managing authority to deprive a person of liberty at a particular place. It is **not** to be used by a local authority as a means of getting its own way on the question of whether it is in the person's best interests to be in the place at all. Using the DOL regime in that way turns the spirit of the Mental Capacity Act 2005 on its head, with a code designed to protect the liberty of vulnerable people being used instead as an instrument of confinement. In this case, far from being a safeguard, the way in which the DOL process was used masked the real deprivation of liberty, which was the refusal to allow Steven to go home.'

He also criticised the local authority for failing to independently scrutinise the granting of standard authorisations with sufficient thoroughness and independence. Although not a part of the judgment, it is to be observed that the system devised by DOLS might almost inevitably lead to a lack of independence, since more often than not, it will be the local authority scrutinising and endorsing its own plan, leading to a fundamental breach of one of the principles of natural justice (*nemo debet esse judex in propria causa – no one can be a judge in his own cause*). In particular he held that 'no attempt was made at the outset to carry out a genuinely balanced best interests assessment, nor was one attempted subsequently' [155]. It is to be noted that some local authorities adopt a practice of using a best interest assessor from outside its own ranks, in order to ensure impartiality, which is a sensible and practical solution to this problem. It is, of course, also why the involvement of an IMCA is so important.

2.59 In terms of the specific facts of the case, and adopting the approach in *P&Q*, the following features were selected as establishing a deprivation of liberty:

- Steven objected to being at the care home and wished to go home;

- his father's request that he be discharged was refused;

- a programme of assessment was embarked upon which controlled and recorded all of Steven's behaviour;

- he was prevented from having contact with his father for substantial periods of time, and for other periods of time his contact was regulated and limited;

- he was physically restrained from time to time;

- he was under close supervision and control;

- he took medication (including anti-psychotic medication) albeit voluntarily;

- the house was locked;

- he was not allowed to leave on his own [160].

2.60 Cheshire West and Chester Council (CWAC) fell foul of the same, or similar problems in *Cheshire West and Chester Council v P & M* [2011] EWHC 1330 (Fam). In this instance, CWAC did make an application to the Court of Protection very shortly after taking M into emergency respite care, and an order was made which rendered his placement lawful. However, the measures taken to control his behaviour within that placement came under close scrutiny from the Official Solicitor. There was also evidence during the course of the proceedings that documents had been altered in order to efface any suggestion of wrongdoing (as a result of which staff were dismissed for gross misconduct). Mr Justice Baker re-visited all of the authorities to which he referred in his judgment in *G v E, A Local Authority and F* [2010] EWHC 621 (Fam), [2010] 2 FLR 294. In particular he referred to para 2.5 of the Code of Practice (see **2.52** above) for a non-exhaustive list of factors that pointed towards there being a deprivation of liberty. CWAC argued that there was no objective evidence of a deprivation of liberty. It identified twelve points (drawing on the law so far established in this area) to argue that he was not deprived of his liberty. All of the points raised are entirely legitimate indicators that he was **not** deprived of his liberty. Nine points were raised that pointed towards a deprivation of liberty. These included continual supervision and control; being obliged to stay in his placement; not being permitted to leave without an escort; little privacy; restraint used (including being strapped into a wheelchair); wearing of a body suit. He was found to have been deprived of his liberty within the meaning of Art 5 and the Mental Capacity Act 2005. There was also an order for costs as against CWAC and that the decision should specifically identify Chester West and Chester Council (the same consequence followed in the *Neary* case). A successful appeal was made in respect of this decision, the consequences of which will have a substantial impact in this area of law. For this reason, the analysis of the law is set out in some detail at this point. Munby LJ framed a part of the issue in the appeal as 'whether P is entitled to the important procedural protections of Article 5(4) and in particular, to the regular ongoing reviews of his detention (if such it be) mandated by Article 5' [4]. The facts of the physical circumstances of P are set out (and as summarised above), and therefore 'the question in dispute, accordingly, was (and is) whether his circumstances objectively amount to a deprivation of liberty' [17]. An exegesis on Art 5 is carried out by the Court in the following terms:

'[22] Examining the language and structure of Article 5, and comparing it with Article 2 of Protocol 4, four things are apparent.

[23] The first point is that to be "deprived of liberty" as that expression is used in Article 5 is to be distinguished from being "restricted" in "liberty of movement" as that expression is used in Article 2 of Protocol 4. As the Strasbourg Court said in *Guzzardi v Italy* (1981) 3 EHRR 333 para [92], repeating what it had earlier said in *Engel and Others v The Netherlands (No 1)* (1976) 1 EHRR 647 para [58], Article 5 "is not concerned with mere restrictions on liberty of movement: such restrictions are governed by Article 2 of Protocol No 4". In the same way, to be "deprived of liberty" as that expression is used in Article 5 is to be distinguished from being "restricted" in "freedom to choose [one's] residence" as that expression is used in Article 2 of Protocol 4. Hence, as Baroness Hale of Richmond said in *Secretary of State for the Home Department v JJ and others* [2007] UKHL 45 [2008] 1 AC 385 para 57, "merely being required to live at a particular address ... does not, without more, amount to a deprivation of liberty". Similarly, restraint must be distinguished from deprivation of liberty. In extreme cases, no doubt, restraint may be so pervasive as to constitute a deprivation of liberty, but restraint by itself is not deprivation of liberty. In short, as Lord Hope of Craighead said in *Austen and another v Commissioner of Police for the Metropolis* [2009] UKHL 5 [2009] 1 AC 564 para [15], Article 2 of Protocol 4 helps to put the ambit of Article 5 in its proper perspective.

[24] The second point is that Article 5 distinguishes between those deprivations of liberty which involve a breach of Article 5 in all circumstances and those deprivations of liberty, defined in paragraphs 1 (a)-(f), which, subject to compliance with the other requirements of Article 5, are capable of being lawful.Paragraphs 1 (a)-(f) exhaustively list the circumstances in which the State has the right to arrest or detain individuals and these paragraphs are to be narrowly interpreted: *Austin and another v Commissioner of Police for the Metropolis* ... Thus in *Guzzardi* where the relegation of a suspected Mafioso to a limited area of a small island was held to constitute a deprivation of liberty, the Strasbourg court went on to hold (paras [96]-[103]) that it could not be justified under any of paragraphs 1 (a)-(f). Likewise, as Lord Neuberger of Abbotsbury pointed out in *Austen*, para [64], in the case of crowd control measures ("kettling") undertaken by the police to preserve public order. And so too in the 'control order' cases: see Lord Brown of Eaton-under-Heywood in *Secretary of State for the Home Department v JJ and others* [2007] UKHL 45, [2008] 1 AC 385 para [90].

[25] The third point to be noted is the comparatively limited ambit of the exceptions recognised in paragraphs 1(a)-(f). Apart from the fairly obvious exceptions listed in paragraphs (a)-(c) and (f), the **only** circumstances in which a deprivation of liberty is capable of being justified are in relation to children (and even then only in the very limited circumstances referred to in paragraph 1(d) or in relation to those described in paragraph 1 (e) ... There is nothing in Article 5 comparable with the potential justifications under Article 2 (3) of Protocol 4,

where restrictions, in accordance with law and necessary in a democratic society, may be imposed "in the interests of national security or public safety, for the maintenance of **ordre public**, for the prevention of crime, for the protection of health or morals, or for the protection of the rights and freedoms of others".

[26] Putting the same point the other way around, it is revealing to note what is **not** included in paragraphs 1 (a)-(f)...The conclusion can only be that the framers did not see the exercise of police power in such circumstances as involving deprivation as opposed to restriction of liberty ...

[27] The drafting of paragraph 1 (d) is also striking for what it does **not** say. A child can be deprived of his liberty only for the purpose of "educational supervision" or "for the purpose of bringing him before the competent legal authority". The framers of the convention must have had very clearly in mind the close and pervasive supervision and control exercised by parents, at least in respect of children who had not reached the age of discretion, yet it finds no reference in Article 5. The conclusion must surely be that the framers did not see the exercise of such parental powers as involving deprivation of liberty. I must return to this point, which seems to me to lie at or near the heart of the issues we have to grapple with ...

[29] The fourth point is that whereas paragraphs 1 (a)-(f) by and large permit arrest or detention in circumstances where the public interest or the interests of other people are engaged, paragraphs 1 (d) and 1 (e) are at least in part contemplate the legitimacy of detention exclusively in the interests of the person being detained.'

Having scrutinised the range and purpose of Article 5, there follows a further analysis of the extensive jurisprudence in respect of the basic principles of deprivation of liberty which in part leads to the conclusion that 'the context is crucial' [34] and that 'no one factor is likely to be determinative' [35] and that 'account must be taken of an individual's whole situation' [35]. The context and variety of factors that may lead to a conclusion that there has been a deprivation of liberty are two principles which all the decisions have been consistent in stressing as important. What constitutes an important departure from previous case law is what is termed 'Context and Comparator'. Lord Justice Munby expresses the concept thus:

'[40] The unspoken assumption most of the time, I suspect, is that the relevant comparator is the ordinary adult enjoying ... "liberty to do those things which in this country free men are entitled to do".'

He provides the following and graphically illustrative example of the point:

'[42] If, perish the thought, Mr Gordon were to find himself locked in a police cell ... he would indubitably be deprived of his liberty. That unhappy state of affairs might be lawful in accordance with Article 5(1)(c), but that is not the point ... But suppose a one year old child is placed for three hours in a playpen, behind bars (albeit of wood rather than steel) and in a space proportionately even smaller than a police cell. The idea that Article 5 could be engaged, the idea that the child is being deprived of her liberty, is preposterous ...'

The judgment moves from this hypothetical example to consider what role the *purpose* of the actions of an individual in these sort of circumstances might be in deciding whether there is a deprivation of liberty. In the two further examples given, what emerges is the 'reason, purpose and motive' [47] for the actions of those individuals. In the one case (that of a husband imprisoning his wife in the family home for the purpose of restoring his conjugal rights (*R v Jackson* [1891] 1 QB 671) the reason for the act was that the wife was 'disobeying the decree for restitution of conjugal rights' [47] and his purpose was to 'induce his wife to restore conjugal rights' [47]. In the other (hypothetical) case, a husband was keeping his wife in the house, in order to prevent harm happening to her as the result of dementia. His motive was 'to further his wife's best interests, acting out of love, and, it may be, his sense of obligation as a husband' [47]. At para 57, and in respect of the latter example, he concludes 'it would be absurd to say that she is being deprived of her liberty' but that 'matters are, of course, very different where a person has somewhere else to go and wants to live there but is prevented from doing so by a coercive exercise of public authority' [58]. He relies on the judgment of Parker J in *Re MIG and MEG* to the effect that:

> 'In my judgment, if a person is living what is for them a normal life in a family home, and would not be living any different life in any other setting including in their own family home, then it is very difficult to see how they can be objectively confined, simply because they lack the capacity to consent to that placement.'

Lord Justice Munby sets in combination the factors of purpose, motive and intention, with that of normality. By reference not only to *Re MIG and MEG* but also *Austen* he held that:

> '[71] bad faith, deception, improper motives or other forms of arbitrary behaviour may have the effect that what would otherwise not be a deprivation of liberty is in fact and for that very reason, a deprivation. This is a very different proposition from some general proposition that good intentions can render innocuous what would otherwise be a deprivation of liberty.'

He added:

> '[76] Putting the same point another way, good intentions are essentially neutral. At most they merely negative the existence of some improper motive or intention. That is all.'

In terms of the concept of normality and relative normality, the judgment returns to the idea of a comparator (ie what is compared to what, and that like should be compared to like). He illustrates the point by reference to *Engel* (where the court was considering whether military personnel had been deprived of their liberty) and extrapolates the following:

> '[81] when considering whether or not some disciplinary measure imposed on a soldier involves a deprivation of liberty, the relevant comparator is not a civilian but another soldier who is not subject to that measure.'

So, when considering whether P is deprived of liberty, the comparator is not the ordinary adult, but someone who is like P. He held that:

> '[88] In the case of children we are dealing with people who are not adults. In such a case as this we are dealing with an adult with disabilities, in the present case an adult with significant physical and learning disabilities ... the relevant comparator in the case of a child is not an adult, but another child of the same age and development. In the case of an adult with disabilities, the relevant comparator is an adult of similar age with the same capacities and affected by the same condition or suffering the same inherent mental and physical disabilities and limitations.'

In so doing, the Court explicitly cross-referred its decision to the reasoning in *P and Q v Surrey County Council* which has been discussed above (at **2.56–2.57**). He concluded that:

> '[97] In agreement with Smith LJ I would hold that, when evaluating and assessing the 'relative normality' (or otherwise) of X's concrete situation in a case such as this, the contrast is not with the previous life led by X (nor with some future life that X might lead), nor with the life of the able-bodied man on the Clapham omnibus, but with the kind of lives that people like X would normally be expected to lead. The comparator, in other words, is an adult of similar age with the same capabilities as X, affected by the same condition or suffering the same inherent mental and physical disabilities and limitations (call them what you will) as X. Likewise, in the case of a child, the comparator is a child of the same age and development as X.'

So, in future, rather than conduct a minute forensic examination of each of the specific indicia for deprivation of liberty, the courts will be considering purpose, motive and reason (merely to identify and exclude *male fides*), the context of the deprivation, and P (whose liberty has been compromised) will be compared not with Richard Gordon QC, but with another P of a similar type. Lord Justice Munby sets out a review of all of the cases so far (at para 99) and summarises the conclusions in respect of each. In *Re A & C* [2010] EWHC 978 (Fam), [2010] 2 FLR 1363 where the context was a family home, there was no deprivation of liberty. In *Re MIG & MEG* where the context was foster care and sheltered accommodation, there was no deprivation of liberty. In *Re RK (Minor: Deprivation of Liberty)* [2010] EWHC 3355 (COP) where the context was a children's home, there was no deprivation of liberty. This case is being considered by the Court of Appeal and the decision was not available to Lord Justice Munby at the time of his decision (and was not available as at the date of this publication). In *LLBC v TG, JG and KR* [2007] EWHC 2640; [2009] 1 FLR 414, in the context of an 'ordinary' care home, there was no deprivation of liberty. Only in two cases has there been a finding that there was a deprivation of liberty. The first is *Neary* (see above at **2.58** and **2.59**) and the second is considered below (at **2.61**). Lord Justice Munby sets out the conclusions at para 102 of his judgment in allowing the appeal and determining that P had not been deprived of his liberty. Those conclusions encompass all the aspects referred to above.

2.61 In *C (by his litigation friend the Official Solicitor) v A Local Authority & LM & LPM & the PCT & An Organisation* [2011] EWHC 1539 (Admin), [2011] 14 CCLR 1539 very many of the same points were considered in respect of C. In addition, this case illustrates the difficulties and the interplay between not only different statutory regimes as they apply to children, but also how the Administrative Court and the Court of Protection can sit simultaneously. Further reference to this area of law and how it effects children is dealt with at **2.107–2.111.** C himself lived in a residential school. The agreed facts were that C was unable to leave the school; he was unable to leave the locked corridor on which his bedroom, bathing and other facilities were located; he was placed in seclusion ('the blue room'); there was no lawful authority for any of this between his 16th birthday and the first order of the Court; if he attempted to leave he would be prevented; he is under constant supervision and control; his only access to the community is by organised trips; there were daily restraints in addition to the use of the 'blue room'; he had no control over the use of his own accommodation by others. The DOLS could not have applied due to the fact that the placement was a school and not a care home or a hospital (but the DOLS Code of Practice could have been used as a way of determining his best interests). Clearly, it followed that not only was C deprived of his liberty as a matter of fact, but there was no lawful authority for that action. The issue of whether his rights under Art 3 (Prohibition of Torture – this being a reference to the conditions in the 'blue room') and Art 8, together with the issue of damages, was not determined at this part of the hearing. Finally, in *RK v BCC (1); YB (2); AK(3)* [2011] EWCA Civ 1305, the issue arose as to: (a) whether a child who had been accommodated by a local authority (with the consent of his parents, pursuant to s 20 of the Children Act 1989); and (b) whether the restrictions imposed by the parents as a part of that voluntary arrangement could amount to detention. The key aspect of s 20 is that in the absence of agreement, the child can be removed by any person with parental responsibility (s 20(8)). The Court of Appeal upheld the 'trenchant' judgment of Mostyn J on this point to the effect that:

> '[26] I find it impossible to say, quite apart from section 20(8) Children Act 1989, that these factual circumstances amount to a "deprivation of liberty". Indeed it is an abuse of language to suggest it. To suggest that taking steps to prevent RK attacking others amounts to "restraints" signifying confinement is untenable. Equally, to suggest that petty sanctions I have identified signifies confinement is untenable. The supervision that is supplied is understandably necessary to keep RK safe and to discharge the duty of care. The same is true of the need to ensure that RK takes her medicine. None of these things whether taken individually or collectively comes remotely close to crossing the line marked "deprivation of liberty".'

Thus, the current law in respect of deprivation of liberty, as set out in this decision and the *Chester* case is clear in that the bar for engagement of Art 5 has now been raised substantially.

2.62 It is possible to extrapolate a series of factors that will be called into account when a Court is asked to decide whether there has been a deprivation of liberty or not. However, it should not really have to be a Court which decides these matters – it is a local authority employee who has the obligation to make a decision, and then to act accordingly. As can be seen from the above three cases (all judgments given within a matter of days of each other in June 2011) social work practice is still often very poor indeed (although the Courts have all been at pains to point out that at no stage has there been anything other than genuine attempts to try and serve the best interests of the adults who have lacked capacity). The factors that can be drawn from the legal authorities, and the Codes of Practice are, perhaps, as follows:

Category of accommodation

Is it a family home? Is it a quasi-domestic placement? Is it a 'supported living' environment? Is is it a care home? Is it a hospital? The closer to an 'institution' the more likely it is to be an indicator of a deprivation of liberty.

Specific Social Contacts

With whom does P have contact? Are there any restrictions on P's contact? Are there no restrictions on contact? The more restrictions, the more likely it is that there is a deprivation of liberty.

Restrictions on staying in accommodation

Can P leave when she wants? If there are restrictions, what are the reasons for those restrictions? Is P free to leave or not?

Within accommodation

Does P have her own room? Does she have her own keys to the room? Can P exclude anyone from her room? Is she under close confinement in the accommodation (e g by being under continuous observation?). Lack of privacy is a key indicator for a deprivation of liberty.

Wishes of P

Has she expressed discontent with any of the restrictions? Is there no discontent expressed to any restrictions? Is she happy?

Restrictions

If there are restrictions, how they are implemented? What is the lawful authority for such restrictions?

Remedies

If P refuses to abide by the restrictions, what is done to impose restrictions? Is force used, or persuasion? If persuasion is used, what kind of persuasion?

Social & Educational

What are the educational arrangements for P? What arrangements are made for social outings, holidays etc? The more extensive these are, the less likely there is to be a deprivation of liberty.

Supervision/Control

Who does this and how often and why? Is it a deprivation of liberty, or a restriction? What is the reason for the supervision and control? What is the purpose or aim of the supervision and control? Good intentions are essentially neutral in deciding whether there is a deprivation of liberty.

Medication

What type and for what mental/medical condition? Is medication forcibly administered? Is the *effect* of medication to suppress liberty to express herself? Is the *purpose* of medication to suppress liberty to express herself? Is purpose of medication to suppress liberty?

Duration of Restrictions

What is likely length of all or any of the above? Is is for a very short period and a 'one off' or for the rest of P's life? What is the 'relative normality' of the life that P leads? With whom could the life of P be compared ? (e g it has to be a comparison of 'like with like').

Behavioural

Does the condition of P (physical or mental) lead to conflict with other people? If so what? Is restraint required? If so what and by whom? The same 'comparator' principles would apply.

MENTAL CAPACITY ACT 2005 AND THE COURT OF PROTECTION

2.63 The basis of the law in respect of most matters which would come within the ambit of the Mental Capacity Act 2005 is set out above. For the purposes of this textbook the most significant development is a new jurisdiction of the Court of Protection (which bears little or no resemblance to the old Court of Protection). At the risk of stating the obvious, this Act only applies where there is a lack of capacity (or an issue as to lack of capacity). In the foreword to the Court of Protection: 2009 Report, the Senior Judge of the Court of Protection (Denzil Lush) made the following candid observations as to how it was working. In particular he commented on the 'volume of work … and the overall burden it would place on the judges and staff … in addition, there have been insufficient judges in the court's central registry at Archway Tower to be able to cope with this demand … service users have complained that the Court's procedures have become more bureaucratic and time consuming than they used to be. I agree.' One of the advantages of the new system was to have been the creation of regional Courts, and this has been done. However, the problems indentified in 2009 still prevail. Despite the more optimistic tone of the 'Court of Protection Report 2010' there are still insufficient judges, the processing of all applications in London prior to transfer to the regional centres, and the paperwork that has to be completed all tend to lead to delay, and confusion. Given the enormous increase in the applications, together with the likelihood that these will grow rather than diminish, the Court of Protection remains very much the Cinderella of the courts service (compared, for example with the Criminal, Civil and Family jurisdiction).

2.64   In terms of what the Court of Protection does, and can do (by way of protecting and regulating the lives of those who lack capacity) it is very far reaching, and can be extraordinarily complex. Lord Justice Munby has commented (in an extra judicial capacity) on the general implications of this area of law in '*What Price Dignity?*' [Keynote address to the LAG Community Care Conference *Protecting Liberties* 14 July 2010 [2010] 13 CCLR 305]. This is vital reading for any local authority employee who is considering making an application to the Court of Protection. He stated that '... in this type of case public authority (whether the local authority or the court) is exercising an essentially **protective** jurisdiction' and in particular, he comments that:

> 'the starting point should be the normal assumption that incapacitated adults will be better off if they live with a family rather than in an institution ... we have to be conscious of the limited ability of public authorities to improve on nature. We need to be careful not to embark upon 'social engineering'. And we should not lightly interfere with family life ... if the state is to justify removing vulnerable adults from their relatives, partners, friends or carers it can only be on the basis that the state is going to provide a better quality of care than that which they have hitherto been receiving.'

In respect of capacity of those who come before the courts, he said:

> 'the nearer to the borderline [of capacity] the more weight must in principle be attached to P's wishes and feelings, because the greater the distress, the humiliation and indeed it may even be the anger she is likely to feel.'

He stated that there has to be a consideration of:

> 'the strength and consistency of the views being expressed by P; the possible impact on P that her wishes and feelings are not being given effect to; the extent to which P's wishes and feelings are, or are not, rational, sensible, responsible and pragmatically capable of sensible implementation in the particular circumstances; and crucially, the extent to which P's wishes and feelings, if given effect to, can properly be accommodated within our overall assessment of what is in her best interests.'

Finally, of local authorities themselves, he reminds us that 'The state, the local authority, is the servant of those in need of its support and assistance, not their master'.

Principles of the Act

2.65 The Code identifies five statutory principles. These are that: (1) a person must be assumed to have capacity unless it is established that he lacks capacity (s 1(2)); (2) a person is not to be treated as unable to make a decision unless all practicable steps to help him to do so have been taken without success (s 1(3)); (3) a person is not to be treated as unable to make a decision merely because he makes an unwise decision (s 1(4)); (4) an act done, or decision made, under this Act for or on behalf of a person who lacks capacity must be done, or made, in his best interests (s 1(5)); and (5) before the act is done, or the decision made, regard must be had to whether the purpose for which it is needed can be as effectively achieved in a way that is less restrictive of the person's rights and freedom of action (s 1(6)).

Capacity

2.66 In respect of the determination of the issue of capacity, there are three authorities that touch upon this point from a procedural (as opposed to subsantive) perspective. The first is in relation to an application to the Court of Protection, and the evidence that is required in order for the presumption of capacity to be displaced. In *Re F (Mental Capacity: Interim Jurisdiction)* [2009] EWHC B30 (Fam), [2010] 2 FLR 28, the general principle of the power of the High Court within the inherent jurisdiction to make interim declarations was imported into the Court of Protection. Using s 48 of the Mental Capacity Act 2005, an interim declaration was made that P lacked capacity. HHJ Marshall QC held that:

> '[45 and 46] F's GP plainly regarded the issue of capacity as a difficult question … Dr M's opinion was tentative and in reality was undecided … Mr Rook's evidence supported the view that F lacked capacity in respect of litigation … to my mind, the unclear situation certainly suggested a serious possibility that F **might** lack capacity … that possibility was also … clearly sufficiently serious, or real, that the Court was entitled to take jurisdiction under section 48.'

Therefore, all that is required for an interim hearing is sufficient evidence that there is a genuine issue as to capacity. By the same token, in *SMBC v WMP, RG and CG (by their litigation friend the Official Solicitor), HSG, SK and SKG* [2011] 14 CCLR 413 where an interim order had been made, it would not be discharged where the expert had identified gaps in the evidence, and remained of the view that there was still good cause to suggest that capacity was absent.

2.67 The second authority deals with the assessment of capacity by a local authority, when it is making decisions of the type referred to by Lord Justice Munby at **2.64**. On the facts in the case, contact had been prevented between P and a man with whom she had been cohabiting for 4 years. The period during which contact had been prevented was 2 years. The local authority did not seek a declaration from the Court until the end of that 2 year period, and had delayed carrying out an assessment of her capacity for a period of 10 months. HHJ Moir (*Re MM* [2011] 1 FLR 712) held that:

'[18 and 20] Where the capacity is in issue and it has been determined that a medical opinion is necessary before taking any action or steps in relation of determining either the Article 8 rights or the best interests of that person, then it is incumbent on the local authority to act with all expediency in securing the determination of that capacity ... It is regrettable that there was no policy, procedure or service agreement in place between the local authority and local NHS Trust in respect of securing an assessment of capacity of a person for whom the local authority were responsible.'

So, where a local authority is dealing with an individual who may or does lack capacity, it needs to ensure the information is available rapidly, or stand the risk of being in breach of Art 8. Evidence in respect of capacity, is, after all, one of the most fundamental parts of this area of law. It is also worth observing that once an application has been made to the court, it has the power (s 49) to call for reports, and this may of course include reports on capacity.

2.68 The third authority (*RT v LT and a Local Authority* [2010] EWHC 1910 (Fam), [2011] 1 FLR 594) cautioned against the use of case law which pre-dated the Mental Capacity Act 2005, and the statutory test for capacity. It encouraged the application of the plain words of the Act, and applying them to the particular facts of each case. Wall LJ held that in respect of the individual capacities set out at s 3(1) a person lacked capacity if any one of the sub-sections applied – they were disjunctive and not cumulative.

Private/public hearings

2.69 Generally, hearings will be in private (Part 13 of the Court of Protection Rules 2007, rr 90–93) although either the whole or part of the hearing may be held in public. However, this is one area that has received substantial judicial scrutiny, particularly in the light of the debate about more 'open justice'. This area of law is set out within the commentary on rr 90–93, below at **2.96**

Interaction with Mental Health Act 1983

2.70 The main difference between the Mental Capacity Act 2005 (MCA 2005) and MHA 1983 is the power to detain (and in certain circumstances to treat without consent). Although in theory it may be possible for MCA 2005 to be used to direct that someone lives in a particular place, if it is not possible to give the person the care and treatment that they need (but only for a mental disorder as defined by MHA 1983), then MHA 1983 is more likely to be used than MCA 2005. There may also be issues of public protection, or safety, that requires the use of MHA 1983. MCA 2005 applies to a patient subject to MHA 1983 with four exceptions. First, 'if someone is detained under the MHA, decision makers cannot normally rely on the MCA to give treatment for mental disorder or make decisions about that treatment on that persons behalf'. Secondly, 'if somebody can be treated for their mental disorder without their consent because they are detained under the MHA, healthcare staff can treat them even if it goes against an advance decision to refuse that treatment'. Thirdly, 'if a person is subject to guardianship, the guardian has the exclusive right to take certain decisions, including where the person is to live'. Fourthly, 'Independent Mental Health Advocates do not have to be involved in decisions about serious medical treatment or accommodation, if those decisions are made under the MHA' (Chapter 13, Code of Practice). There is no requirement to seek the approval of the Court of Protection to use MHA 1983 in respect of someone who lacks capacity. It must also be remembered that it is a common fallacy that someone detained under MHA 1983 lacks capacity. This is not the case at all – someone who is detained under MHA 1983 must fit the criteria for detention, and these do not mention the issue of capacity. For the specific case law on the overlap between DOLS and the Mental Capacity Act 2005 and the Mental Health Act 1983, refer to **2.45**.

2.71   In particular some of the coercive powers available with the Mental Health Act 1983 are not so readily available under the Mental Capacity Act 2005. By way of illustration, it is possible to obtain an authority from the Court that P can be removed from his home, and that reasonable force and restraint deployed for that purpose (*LBH v GP & MP* [2010] 13 CCLR 171). Without such an authority, such an action would be unlawful, save for situations in which there was an emergency. The issue in this case was the amount of force used (police officers in riot gear had attended, and handcuffs were used). The guidance arising from this case suggests that such removal should be planned more carefully in advance, and that where there is a dispute as to the correct method, the police may have to be invited to attend the hearing to adjudicate on the issue. If a situation arose whereby an offence was being committed under s 44 (ill treatment or neglect), then the police may sufficient grounds to enter the premises in order to arrest an offender.

After-care

2.72   There is no provision for after-care within MCA 2005, whereas this does apply with MHA 1983 (see Chapter 1).

Definition of aims of Court of Protection

2.73   The Code of Practice (at para 8.1) describes the Court in the following terms:

> 'Section 45 of the Act sets up a specialist Court, the Court of Protection, to deal with decision making for adults (and children in a few cases) who may lack capacity to make specific decisions for themselves. The new Court of Protection replaces the old court of the same name, which only dealt with decisions about the property and financial affairs of people lacking capacity to manage their own affairs. As well as property and affairs, the new court also deals with serious decisions affecting health care and personal welfare matters. These were previously dealt with by the High Court under its inherent jurisdiction.'

The principles developed by the High Court will hold good before the new Court. The Code continues to describe the Court as 'a superior court of record and is able to establish precedent ... when reaching any decision, the court must apply all the statutory principles set out in Section 1 of the Act. In particular, it must make a decision in the best interests of the person who lacks capacity to make a specific decision' (para 8.2). This includes decisions about financial matters.

Powers of Court

2.74   The Court can make declarations, and decisions and orders on all aspects of financial and welfare issues which are linked to the lack of capacity (including the granting of injunctive relief). In respect of the latter, care should be taken if the injunctive relief is to be ordered against someone who themselves lacks capacity, since this may render the order unenforceable if that individual lacks capacity to understand the order). It can appoint a 'deputy' to make those decisions upon behalf of those who lack capacity. It can remove a deputy who acts inappropriately. A deputy is likely to be required where there is a need for a continued management of the life of the individual who lacks capacity (for example, in financial cases). It is less likely that a deputy would be required in welfare and healthcare decisions, although this would depend upon the facts of the case. There is also a provision for the appointment of joint deputies (who must, however, act together). Paid care workers should not agree to become deputies (as there is a possibility of a conflict of interest). It also has the power to summarily dismiss an application (*KD & LD v Havering London Borough Council* [2010] 1 FLR 1393) but not if there were questions regarding the disposal and management of the case, and nor where the outcome of an expert social report was awaited, and nor when there were also issues as to deprivation of liberty and/or Art 5 matters to consider.

Persons who lack capacity

2.75   The complete scope of this Act is outside the range of this book. For a full exposition, the reader is directed to *Court of Protection Practice* (Jordan Publishing). This book concerns itself with all aspects of the substantive and procedural law in this area.

Mental Capacity Act 2005

1 The principles

(1) The following principles apply for the purposes of this Act.

(2) A person must be assumed to have capacity unless it is established that he lacks capacity.

(3) A person is not to be treated as unable to make a decision unless all practicable steps to help him to do so have been taken without success.

(4) A person is not to be treated as unable to make a decision merely because he makes an unwise decision.

(5) An act done, or decision made, under this Act for or on behalf of a person who lacks capacity must be done, or made, in his best interests.

(6) Before the act is done, or the decision is made, regard must be had to whether the purpose for which it is needed can be as effectively achieved in a way that is less restrictive of the person's rights and freedom of action.

2.76   As can be seen from the above, the Act incorporates into it the principles set out in the case law summarised above. In particular it incorporates the law of a presumption of capacity, that an unwise decision does not equate with a lack of capacity, that assistance may be required in making a decision, and that if there is a lack of capacity, then the test to be applied is that of 'best interests'.

2 People who lack capacity

(1) For the purposes of this Act, a person lacks capacity in relation to a matter if at the material time he is unable to make a decision for himself in relation to the matter because of an impairment of, or a disturbance in the functioning of, the mind or brain.

(2) It does not matter whether the impairment or disturbance is permanent or temporary.

(3) A lack of capacity cannot be established merely by reference to –

    (a)   a person's age or appearance, or

    (b)   a condition of his, or an aspect of his behaviour, which might lead others to make unjustified assumptions about his capacity.

(4) In proceedings under this Act or any other enactment, any question whether a person lacks capacity within the meaning of this Act must be decided on the balance of probabilities.

(5) No power which a person ("D") may exercise under this Act –

    (a)   in relation to a person who lacks capacity, or

    (b)   where D reasonably thinks that a person lacks capacity,

is exercisable in relation to a person under 16.

(6) Subsection (5) is subject to section 18(3).

2.77   This provides for a situation whereby a lack of capacity may be temporary, and links it to a specific diagnosis. It also emphasises the requirement not to use age, appearance, behaviour or a condition to make assumptions about capacity. The standard of proof is that of a balance of probabilities (and it will be upon the individual or body who seeks to prove lack of capacity to prove it to that standard).

3 Inability to make decisions

(1) For the purposes of section 2, a person is unable to make a decision for himself if he is unable –

    (a)   to understand the information relevant to the decision,

    (b)   to retain that information,

    (c)   to use or weigh that information as part of the process of making the decision, or

    (d)   to communicate his decision (whether by talking, using sign language or any other means).

(2) A person is not to be regarded as unable to understand the information relevant to a decision if he is able to understand an explanation of it given to him in away that is appropriate to his circumstances (using simple language, visual aids or any other means).

(3) The fact that a person is able to retain the information relevant to a decision for a short period only does not prevent him from being regarded as able to make the decision.

(4) The information relevant to a decision includes information about the reasonably foreseeable consequences of –

(a)   deciding one way or another, or
(b)   failing to make the decision.

2.78   This sets out in statutory form the common law described above. It also, however, adds weight to the necessity to ensure that information to enable a decision to be made is conveyed in an appropriate manner. It also adds that an ability to retain information for a short period only does not compromise the validity of a decision made. A consideration of the provisions for formal assessments of capacity, and interim capacity, and the application of this section in particular, are contained in **2.9** and **2.65–2.68**.

4 Best interests

(1) In determining for the purposes of this Act what is in a person's best interests, the person making the determination must not make it merely on the basis of –

(a)   the person's age or appearance, or
(b)   a condition of his, or an aspect of his behaviour, which might lead others to make unjustified assumptions about what might be in his best interests.

(2) The person making the determination must consider all the relevant circumstances and, in particular, take the following steps.

(3) He must consider –

(a)   whether it is likely that the person will at some time have capacity in relation to the matter in question, and
(b)   if it appears likely that he will, when that is likely to be.

(4) He must, so far as reasonably practicable, permit and encourage the person to participate, or to improve his ability to participate, as fully as possible in any act done for him and any decision affecting him.

(5) Where the determination relates to life-sustaining treatment he must not, in considering whether the treatment is in the best interests of the person concerned, be motivated by a desire to bring about his death.

(6) He must consider, so far as is reasonably ascertainable –

(a)   the person's past and present wishes and feelings (and, in particular, any relevant written statement made by him when he had capacity),
(b)   the beliefs and values that would be likely to influence his decision if he had capacity, and

(c)   the other factors that he would be likely to consider if he were able to do so.

(7) He must take into account, if it is practicable and appropriate to consult them, the views of –

(a)   anyone named by the person as someone to be consulted on the matter in question or on matters of that kind,

(b)   anyone engaged in caring for the person or interested in his welfare,

(c)   any donee of a lasting power of attorney granted by the person, and

(d)   any deputy appointed for the person by the court,
as to what would be in the person's best interests and, in particular, as to the matters mentioned in subsection (6).

(8) The duties imposed by subsections (1) to (7) also apply in relation to the exercise of any powers which –

(a)   are exercisable under a lasting power of attorney, or

(b)   are exercisable by a person under this Act where he reasonably believes that another person lacks capacity.

(9) In the case of an act done, or a decision made, by a person other than the court, there is sufficient compliance with this section if (having complied with the requirements of subsections (1) to (7)) he reasonably believes that what he does or decides is in the best interests of the person concerned.

(10) "Life-sustaining treatment" means treatment which in the view of a person providing health care for the person concerned is necessary to sustain life.

(11) "Relevant circumstances" are those –

(a)   of which the person making the determination is aware, and

(b)   which it would be reasonable to regard as relevant.

2.79 This provides (for the first time) a checklist of factors that are to be taken into account when deciding what is in the best interests of an adult who lacks capacity. It obliges a consideration of the duration of the period of incapacity. It encourages the consideration of what limited autonomy the individual might have in participating in any decisions made. It takes into account the potential of *male fides* in considering the issue of life-sustaining treatment. It also requires a consideration of any past expressions of wishes (and any documentation in existence to support those wishes). Finally, it may be that the subject held beliefs (religious or otherwise) that would have influenced his wishes and choices prior to losing capacity, and these may be taken into account when a decision is made about the most appropriate way forward. There is a requirement to take into account any formally or informally appointed individuals who might shed light on the issue in question.

5 Acts in connection with care or treatment

(1) If a person ("D") does an act in connection with the care or treatment of another person ("P"), the act is one to which this section applies if –

(a)   before doing the act, D takes reasonable steps to establish whether P lacks capacity in relation to the matter in question, and

(b)   when doing the act, D reasonably believes –

(i)   that P lacks capacity in relation to the matter, and

(ii)   that it will be in P's best interests for the act to be done.

(2) D does not incur any liability in relation to the act that he would not have incurred if P –

(a)   had had capacity to consent in relation to the matter, and

(b)   had consented to D's doing the act.

(3) Nothing in this section excludes a person's civil liability for loss or damage, or his criminal liability, resulting from his negligence in doing the act.

(4) Nothing in this section affects the operation of sections 24 to 26 (advance decisions to refuse treatment).

6 Section 5 acts: limitations

(1) If D does an act that is intended to restrain P, it is not an act to which section 5 applies unless two further conditions are satisfied.

(2) The first condition is that D reasonably believes that it is necessary to do the act in order to prevent harm to P.

(3) The second is that the act is a proportionate response to –

(a)   the likelihood of P's suffering harm, and

(b)   the seriousness of that harm.

(4) For the purposes of this section D restrains P if he –

(a)   uses, or threatens to use, force to secure the doing of an act which P resists, or

(b)   restricts P's liberty of movement, whether or not P resists.

(5) But D does more than merely restrain P if he deprives P of his liberty within the meaning of Article 5(1) of the Human Rights Convention (whether or not D is a public authority).

(6) Section 5 does not authorise a person to do an act which conflicts with a decision made, within the scope of his authority and in accordance with this Part, by –

(a)   a donee of a lasting power of attorney granted by P, or

(b)   a deputy appointed for P by the court.

(7) But nothing in subsection (6) stops a person –

(a)   providing life-sustaining treatment, or

(b)   doing any act which he reasonably believes to be necessary to prevent a serious deterioration in P's condition,

while a decision as respects any relevant issue is sought from the court.

2.80   The significance is that there is now a codification of the concept of the doctrine of necessity. It also provides a statutory definition of what is meant by 'restraint' and when such restraint may be used. This is of significance where a local authority is taking action on (in effect) an emergency basis (although this is not a word used in the statute). It is not a substitute for an authority from the Court where the problem is more than transient, or where it is linked to a deprivation of liberty of a more substantial nature, or where there is a serious dispute involved in the plans for P. The 'Court of Protection Report 2010' (at p 7) comments that:

> 'section 5 of the MCA confers a general authority for someone to make decisions in connection with another's care or treatment, without formal authorisation, provided: that P lacks capacity in relation to the decision; and it would be in P's best interests for the act to be done.'

Mention has already been made of s 4B, which governs the power to deprive P of his liberty whilst a decision is awaited in respect of serious medical treatment.

7 Payment for necessary goods and services

(1) If necessary goods or services are supplied to a person who lacks capacity to contract for the supply, he must pay a reasonable price for them.

(2) "Necessary" means suitable to a person's condition in life and to his actual requirements at the time when the goods or services are supplied.

2.81 This part of the Act makes provision for payments for goods and services, and is important for the capacity of P to enter into contracts (see **2.33**).

15 Power to make declarations

(1) The court may make declarations as to –

    (a)   whether a person has or lacks capacity to make a decision specified in the declaration;

    (b)   whether a person has or lacks capacity to make decisions on such matters as are described in the declaration;

    (c)   the lawfulness or otherwise of any act done, or yet to be done, in relation to that person.

(2) "Act" includes an omission and a course of conduct.

2.82 This section codifies the current power of the High Court to make declarations, and particularly as to the lawfulness of any future course of action. It includes the power to make interim declarations.

16 Powers to make decisions and appoint deputies: general

(1) This section applies if a person ("P") lacks capacity in relation to a matter or matters concerning –

    (a)   P's personal welfare, or

    (b)   P's property and affairs.

(2) The court may –

    (a)   by making an order, make the decision or decisions on P's behalf in relation to the matter or matters, or

(b)   appoint a person (a "deputy") to make decisions on P's behalf in relation to the matter or matters.

(3) The powers of the court under this section are subject to the provisions of this Act and, in particular, to sections 1 (the principles) and 4 (best interests).

(4) When deciding whether it is in P's best interests to appoint a deputy, the court must have regard (in addition to the matters mentioned in section 4) to the principles that –

(a)   a decision by the court is to be preferred to the appointment of a deputy to make a decision, and
(b)   the powers conferred on a deputy should be as limited in scope and duration as is reasonably practicable in the circumstances.

(5) The court may make such further orders or give such directions, and confer on a deputy such powers or impose on him such duties, as it thinks necessary or expedient for giving effect to, or otherwise in connection with, an order or appointment made by it under subsection (2).

(6) Without prejudice to section 4, the court may make the order, give the directions or make the appointment on such terms as it considers are in P's best interests, even though no application is before the court for an order, directions or an appointment on those terms.

(7) An order of the court may be varied or discharged by a subsequent order.

(8) The court may, in particular, revoke the appointment of a deputy or vary the powers conferred on him if it is satisfied that the deputy –

(a)   has behaved, or is behaving, in a way that contravenes the authority conferred on him by the court or is not in P's best interests, or
(b)   proposes to behave in a way that would contravene that authority or would not be in P's best interests.

2.83 If a third party is appointed to make decisions upon behalf of an individual, then this is to be hedged about with limitations both in terms of scope and duration. Moreover, it is not the preferred option (which is that a Court should make the decision). In respect of the appointment of deputies, the case law has supported the statute in the following manner. In *G v (1) (E) (by his litigation friend, the Official Solicitor) (2) Manchester City Council (3) F* [2010] EWHC 2512 (Fam), [2010] 13 CCLR 610) Mr Justice Baker considered an application for the appointment of deputies (as well as litigation friends). The judgment rejected the application (for family members to act as both welfare and property and affairs deputies). The welfare issues were matters of routine day to day care of P, and should be decided collaboratively. Any medical issues should be determined by treating clinicians in consultation with family members, and if there was a serious issue, the matter could be placed before the Court, as could any decisions about who might look after P in the future (if this ever arose). The finance and property of P consisted of state benefits, and a savings of £1000. His individual budget was managed via the direct payments scheme. None of this merited the appointment of a finance and property deputy. If P came into a substantial amount of money (by way of a pending claim for damages against Manchester City Council) then the application could be renewed. It also distinguished the judgment of Mr Justice Hedley in *Re P (Vulnerable Adults:Deputies)* [2010] EWHC 1592, [2010] 2 FLR 1712) in that Mr Justice Baker interpreted this as being addressed to the issue of who should be appointed deputy, rather than whether any deputy should be appointed. If a family member could demonstrate impartiality, and the appointment was necessary, then 'members of the family, where they are willing and able to do so' should 'take first place' [8]. It is rarely appropriate for a property and welfare deputy to be involved when P is in receipt of state benefits. If there is a dispute as to mismanagement of such funds, then an appointeeship via the Department of Work and Pensions is the more appropriate route. This aspect was not considered by the Court in *G*.

17 Section 16 powers: personal welfare

(1) The powers under section 16 as respects P's personal welfare extend in particular to –

   (a)   deciding where P is to live;
   (b)   deciding what contact, if any, P is to have with any specified persons;
   (c)   making an order prohibiting a named person from having contact with P;
   (d)   giving or refusing consent to the carrying out or continuation of a treatment by a person providing health care for P;
   (e)   giving a direction that a person responsible for P's health care allow a different person to take over that responsibility.

(2) Subsection (1) is subject to section 20 (restrictions on deputies).

2.84   This incorporates the powers currently permitted within the inherent jurisdiction (residence; contact with others; prohibition on contact with others; treatment).

18 Section 16 powers: property and affairs

(1) The powers under section 16 as respects P's property and affairs extend in particular to –

   (a)   the control and management of P's property;
   (b)   the sale, exchange, charging, gift or other disposition of P's property;
   (c)   the acquisition of property in P's name or on P's behalf;
   (d)   the carrying on, on P's behalf, of any profession, trade or business;
   (e)   the taking of a decision which will have the effect of dissolving a partnership of which P is a member;
   (f)   the carrying out of any contract entered into by P;
   (g)   the discharge of P's debts and of any of P's obligations, whether legally enforceable or not;
   (h)   the settlement of any of P's property, whether for P's benefit or for the benefit of others;
   (i)   the execution for P of a will;
   (j)   the exercise of any power (including a power to consent) vested in P whether beneficially or as trustee or otherwise;
   (k)   the conduct of legal proceedings in P's name or on P's behalf.

(2) No will may be made under subsection (1)(i) at a time when P has not reached 18.

(3) The powers under section 16 as respects any other matter relating to P's property and affairs may be exercised even though P has not reached 16, if the court considers it likely that P will still lack capacity to make decisions in respect of that matter when he reaches 18.

(4) Schedule 2 supplements the provisions of this section.

(5) Section 16(7) (variation and discharge of court orders) is subject to paragraph 6 of Schedule 2.

(6) Subsection (1) is subject to section 20 (restrictions on deputies).

19 Appointment of deputies

(1) A deputy appointed by the court must be –

  (a)   an individual who has reached 18, or
  (b)   as respects powers in relation to property and affairs, an individual who has reached 18 or a trust corporation.

(2) The court may appoint an individual by appointing the holder for the time being of a specified office or position.

(3) A person may not be appointed as a deputy without his consent.

(4) The court may appoint two or more deputies to act –

  (a)   jointly,
  (b)   jointly and severally, or
  (c)   jointly in respect of some matters and jointly and severally in respect of others.

(5) When appointing a deputy or deputies, the court may at the same time appoint one or more other persons to succeed the existing deputy or those deputies –

  (a)   in such circumstances, or on the happening of such events, as may be specified by the court;
  (b)   for such period as may be so specified.

(6) A deputy is to be treated as P's agent in relation to anything done or decided by him within the scope of his appointment and in accordance with this Part.

(7) The deputy is entitled –

  (a)   to be reimbursed out of P's property for his reasonable expenses in discharging his functions, and
  (b)   if the court so directs when appointing him, to remuneration out of P's property for discharging them.

(8) The court may confer on a deputy powers to –

  (a)   take possession or control of all or any specified part of P's property;
  (b)   exercise all or any specified powers in respect of it, including such powers of investment as the court may determine.

(9) The court may require a deputy –

(a)   to give to the Public Guardian such security as the court thinks fit for the due discharge of his functions, and

(b)   to submit to the Public Guardian such reports at such times or at such intervals as the court may direct.

2.85 It is sometimes the case that a local authority may wish to be the property and affairs deputy for P, but this may raise the issue of a conflict of interest, and also if the sums of money are substantial, then there may be an understandable reluctance. In such circumstances, a panel deputy is likely to be the solution.

21A Powers of court in relation to Schedule A1

(1) This section applies if either of the following has been given under Schedule A1 –

(a)   a standard authorisation;
(b)   an urgent authorisation.

(2) Where a standard authorisation has been given, the court may determine any question relating to any of the following matters –

(a)   whether the relevant person meets one or more of the qualifying requirements;
(b)   the period during which the standard authorisation is to be in force;
(c)   the purpose for which the standard authorisation is given;
(d)   the conditions subject to which the standard authorisation is given.

(3) If the court determines any question under subsection (2), the court may make an order –

(a)   varying or terminating the standard authorisation, or
(b)   directing the supervisory body to vary or terminate the standard authorisation.

(4) Where an urgent authorisation has been given, the court may determine any question relating to any of the following matters –

(a)   whether the urgent authorisation should have been given;
(b)   the period during which the urgent authorisation is to be in force;
(c)   the purpose for which the urgent authorisation is given.

(5) Where the court determines any question under subsection (4), the court may make an order –

(a)   varying or terminating the urgent authorisation, or
(b)   directing the managing authority of the relevant hospital or care home to vary or terminate the urgent authorisation.

(6) Where the court makes an order under subsection (3) or (5), the court may make an order about a person's liability for any act done in connection with the standard or urgent authorisation before its variation or termination.

(7) An order under subsection (6) may, in particular, exclude a person from liability.

2.86   The significance of this section has been considered in the context of DOLS (at **2.42–2.46**).

35 Appointment of independent mental capacity advocates

(1) The appropriate authority must make such arrangements as it considers reasonable to enable persons ("independent mental capacity advocates") to be available to represent and support persons to whom acts or decisions proposed under sections 37, 38 and 39 relate or persons who fall within section 39A, 39C or 39D.

(2) The appropriate authority may make regulations as to the appointment of independent mental capacity advocates.

(3) The regulations may, in particular, provide –

  (a)   that a person may act as an independent mental capacity advocate only in such circumstances, or only subject to such conditions, as may be prescribed;

  (b)   for the appointment of a person as an independent mental capacity advocate to be subject to approval in accordance with the regulations.

(4) In making arrangements under subsection (1), the appropriate authority must have regard to the principle that a person to whom a proposed act or decision relates should, so far as practicable, be represented and supported by a person who is independent of any person who will be responsible for the act or decision.

(5) The arrangements may include provision for payments to be made to, or in relation to, persons carrying out functions in accordance with the arrangements.

(6) For the purpose of enabling him to carry out his functions, an independent mental capacity advocate –

  (a)   may interview in private the person whom he has been instructed to represent, and

  (b)   may, at all reasonable times, examine and take copies of –
    (i)   any health record,
    (ii)   any record of, or held by, a local authority and compiled in connection with a social services function, and
    (iii) any record held by a person registered under Part 2 of the Care Standards Act 2000 (c 14),

which the person holding the record considers may be relevant to the independent mental capacity advocate's investigation.

(7) In this section, section 36 and section 37, "the appropriate authority" means –
    (a)   in relation to the provision of the services of independent mental capacity advocates in England, the Secretary of State, and
    (b)   in relation to the provision of the services of independent mental capacity advocates in Wales, the National Assembly for Wales.

36 Functions of independent mental capacity advocates

(1) The appropriate authority may make regulations as to the functions of independent mental capacity advocates.

(2) The regulations may, in particular, make provision requiring an advocate to take such steps as may be prescribed for the purpose of –

(a)   providing support to the person whom he has been instructed to represent ("P") so that P may participate as fully as possible in any relevant decision;

(b)   obtaining and evaluating relevant information;

(c)   ascertaining what P's wishes and feelings would be likely to be, and the beliefs and values that would be likely to influence P, if he had capacity;

(d)   ascertaining what alternative courses of action are available in relation to P;

(e)   obtaining a further medical opinion where treatment is proposed and the advocate thinks that one should be obtained.

(3) The regulations may also make provision as to circumstances in which the advocate may challenge, or provide assistance for the purpose of challenging, any relevant decision.

39 Provision of accommodation by local authority

(1) This section applies if a local authority propose to make arrangements –

(a)   for the provision of residential accommodation for a person ("P") who lacks capacity to agree to the arrangements, or

(b)   for a change in P's residential accommodation,

and are satisfied that there is no person, other than one engaged in providing care or treatment for P in a professional capacity or for remuneration, whom it would be appropriate for them to consult in determining what would be in P's best interests.

(2) But this section applies only if the accommodation is to be provided in accordance with –

(a)   section 21 or 29 of the National Assistance Act 1948 (c 29), or

(b)   section 117 of the Mental Health Act,

as the result of a decision taken by the local authority under section 47 of the National Health Service and Community Care Act 1990 (c 19).

(3) This section does not apply if P is accommodated as a result of an obligation imposed on him under the Mental Health Act.

(3A) And this section does not apply if –

(a)   an independent mental capacity advocate must be appointed under section 39A or 39C (whether or not by the local authority) to represent P, and

(b)   the place in which P is to be accommodated under the arrangements referred to in this section is the relevant hospital or care home under the authorisation referred to in that section.

(4) Before making the arrangements, the local authority must instruct an independent mental capacity advocate to represent P unless they are satisfied that –

(a)   the accommodation is likely to be provided for a continuous period of less than 8 weeks, or

(b)   the arrangements need to be made as a matter of urgency.

(5) If the local authority –

(a)   did not instruct an independent mental capacity advocate to represent P before making the arrangements because they were satisfied that subsection (4)(a) or (b) applied, but

(b)   subsequently have reason to believe that the accommodation is likely to be provided for a continuous period that will end 8 weeks or more after the day on which accommodation was first provided in accordance with the arrangements,

they must instruct an independent mental capacity advocate to represent P.

(6) The local authority must, in deciding what arrangements to make for P, take into account any information given, or submissions made, by the independent mental capacity advocate.

(7) For the purposes of subsection (1), a person appointed under Part 10 of Schedule A1 to be P's representative is not, by virtue of that appointment, engaged in providing care or treatment for P in a professional capacity or for remuneration.

Independent Mental Capacity Advocate (IMCA)

2.87 Greater details in respect of the Act may be found in the Mental Capacity Act 2005 Code of Practice (Department of Constitutional Affairs). In respect of Independent Mental Capacity Advocates (IMCAs) Chapter 10 of the Code of Practice is the most helpful. The circumstances in which a local authority will become involved is when it is proposing to arrange accommodation or a change of accommodation in a hospital or care home (if the local authority has carried out an assessment under s 47 of the NHS and Community Care Act 1990, or has accommodated the individual pursuant to s 21 or 29 of the NAA 1948, or s 117 of MHA 1983). If a hospital is involved, then the period must be for more than 28 days, and if a care home, then more than 8 weeks. If there is no one else available (other than paid staff) to support or represent them, or be consulted, then the local authority *must* appoint an IMCA. There is a discretion to appoint an IMCA if decisions being made concern care reviews, or adult protection cases (whether or not family or friends are available). An IMCA provides safeguards for those who lack capacity to make a specified decision, ie those who are facing a decision about a long-term move or serious medical treatment, where there is nobody else to represent them or where there is a need for someone to work out their best interests. If a person is required to live in accommodation under MHA 1983, an IMCA will not be needed, since the safeguards already exist under that Act. LAC 2006 (15) (dated 1 November 2006) gives some information to local authorities about the resources to be made available, and the duties imposed upon them to appoint an IMCA in certain circumstances. The role of an IMCA can be vital in safeguarding the interests of P.

44 Ill-treatment or neglect

(1) Subsection (2) applies if a person ("D") –

(a)   has the care of a person ("P") who lacks, or whom D reasonably believes to lack, capacity, (b)　is the donee of a lasting power of attorney, or an enduring power of attorney (within the meaning of Schedule 4), created by P, or

(c)　is a deputy appointed by the court for P.

(2) D is guilty of an offence if he ill-treats or wilfully neglects P.

(3) A person guilty of an offence under this section is liable –

(a)　on summary conviction, to imprisonment for a term not exceeding 12 months or a fine not exceeding the statutory maximum or both;

(b)　on conviction on indictment, to imprisonment for a term not exceeding 5 years or a fine or both.

2.88 This creates a new offence, for which enhances the powers and obligations of local authorities (and any others involved in safeguarding, including the police).

48　Interim orders and directions

The court may, pending the determination of an application to it in relation to a person ("P"), make an order or give directions in respect of any matter if –

(a)　there is reason to believe that P lacks capacity in relation to the matter,

(b)　the matter is one to which its powers under this Act extend, and

(c)　it is in P's best interests to make the order, or give the directions, without delay.

2.89 Most of the orders made by the Court of Protection at a first hearing are by way of s 48, and it include interim declarations (see **2.66**).

49　Power to call for reports

(1) This section applies where, in proceedings brought in respect of a person ("P") under Part 1, the court is considering a question relating to P.

(2) The court may require a report to be made to it by the Public Guardian or by a Court of Protection Visitor.

(3) The court may require a local authority, or an NHS body, to arrange for a report to be made –

(a)　by one of its officers or employees, or

(b)　by such other person (other than the Public Guardian or a Court of Protection Visitor) as the authority, or the NHS body, considers appropriate.

(4) The report must deal with such matters relating to P as the court may direct.

(5) Court of Protection Rules may specify matters which, unless the court directs otherwise, must also be dealt with in the report.

(6) The report may be made in writing or orally, as the court may direct.

(7) In complying with a requirement, the Public Guardian or a Court of Protection Visitor may, at all reasonable times, examine and take copies of –

(a)　any health record,

(b)   any record of, or held by, a local authority and compiled in connection with a social services function, and

(c)   any record held by a person registered under Part 2 of the Care Standards Act 2000 or Chapter 2 of Part 1 of the Health and Social Care Act 2008,

so far as the record relates to P.

(8) If the Public Guardian or a Court of Protection Visitor is making a visit in the course of complying with a requirement, he may interview P in private.

(9) If a Court of Protection Visitor who is a Special Visitor is making a visit in the course of complying with a requirement, he may if the court so directs carry out in private a medical, psychiatric or psychological examination of P's capacity and condition.

(10) "NHS body" has the meaning given in section 148 of the Health and Social Care (Community Health and Standards) Act 2003.

(11) "Requirement" means a requirement imposed under subsection (2) or (3).

2.90   This is a useful method of obtaining evidence on capacity, where there has already been substantial involvement with P by an NHS body, and can often save time and money in obtaining information (see, for example **2.67**).

Procedure and the Court of Protection Rules

2.91   Local authorities have inevitably become involved in using the Court of Protection in resolving the range of issues that hitherto have been dealt with via the inherent jurisdiction of the High Court. The statute sets out that jurisdiction, and the manner in which applications should be made. In terms of the applicant, then:

'8.8 If social care staff are concerned about a decision that affects the welfare of a person who lacks capacity, the relevant local authority should make the application.'

However, it is within the Rules that the specific conduct of each and every aspect of the new jurisdiction is regulated. These came into force on 1 October 2007. The interpretation section refers to a new term of art ('P') which is defined as follows:

'P means any person (other than a protected party) who lacks or, so far as consistent with the context, is alleged to lack capacity to make a decision or decisions in relation to any matter that is the subject of an application to the Court and references to a person who lacks capacity are to be construed in accordance with the Act.'

Applications and notification of P

2.92   Rules 40–49 deal with the general requirement to notify P of an application. 'Practice Direction A – Notifying P' accompanies these Rules. P must be notified of all matters in rr 42–45 unless the Court directs otherwise. If a notice is issued in accordance with Part 10 (applications within existing proceedings, e g urgent and/or interim remedies) then the applicant may notify P but is not obliged to do so unless it is felt appropriate. Applications where notification may not be appropriate is where P is in a permanent vegetative state, or a minimally conscious state, or where it is likely to cause significant and disproportionate distress to P.

40 General

(1) Subject to paragraphs (2) and (3), the rules in this Part apply where P is to be given notice of any matter or document, or is to be provided with any document, either under the Rules or in accordance with an order or direction of the court.

(2) If P becomes a party, the rules in this Part do not apply and service is to be effected in accordance with Part 6 or as directed by the court.

(3) In any case the court may, either on its own initiative or on application, direct that P must not be notified of any matter or document, or provided with any document, whether in accordance with this Part or at all.

41 Who is to notify P

(1) Where P is to be notified under this Part, notification must be effected by –

    (a)   the applicant;
    (b)   the appellant (where the matter relates to an appeal);
    (c)   an agent duly appointed by the applicant or the appellant; or
    (d)   such other person as the court may direct.

(2) The person within paragraph (1) is referred to in this Part as "the person effecting notification".

Circumstances in which P must be notified

42 Application forms

(1) P must be notified –

    (a)   that an application form has been issued by the court;
    (b)   that an application form has been withdrawn; and
    (c)   of the date on which a hearing is to be held in relation to the matter, where that hearing is for disposing of the application.

(2) Where P is to be notified that an application form has been issued, the person effecting notification must explain to P –

    (a)   who the applicant is;
    (b)   that the application raises the question of whether P lacks capacity in relation to a matter or matters, and what that means;
    (c)   what will happen if the court makes the order or direction that has been applied for; and
    (d)   where the application contains a proposal for the appointment of a person to make decisions on P's behalf in relation to the matter to which the application relates, details of who that person is.

(3) Where P is to be notified that an application form has been withdrawn, the person effecting notification must explain to P –

  (a)   that the application form has been withdrawn; and
  (b)   the consequences of that withdrawal.

(4) The person effecting notification must also inform P that he may seek advice and assistance in relation to any matter of which he is notified.

Permission and forms

2.93   The application forms referred to (and indeed all the relevant forms) can be found via the Public Guardian's Office and downloaded. A local authority will require permission to make an application. 'Practice Note A – Permission' accompanies these Rules. If the applicant is unable to complete an assessment of capacity form (where for example P does not reside with the applicant and the applicant is unable to take P to a doctor, or where P refuses to undergo an assessment), then a witness statement is required explaining the circumstances, and the attempts that have been made to get an assessment of capacity, and the basis for believing that capacity is absent in relation to the relevant decision.

50 General

Subject to these Rules and to section 50(1) of, and paragraph 20 of Schedule 3 to, the Act, the applicant must apply for permission to start proceedings under the Act.

(Section 50(1) of the Act specifies persons who do not need to apply for permission. Paragraph 20 of Schedule 3 to the Act specifies an application for which permission is not needed.)

54 Application for permission

The applicant must apply for permission by filing a permission form and must file with it –

  (a)   any information or documents specified in the relevant practice direction;
  (b)   a draft of the application form which he seeks permission to have issued; and
  (c)   an assessment of capacity form, where this is required by the relevant practice direction.

55 What the court will do when an application for permission to start proceedings is filed

Within 14 days of a permission form being filed, the court will issue it and –

  (a)   grant the application in whole or in part, or subject to conditions, without a hearing and may give directions in connection with the issue of the application form;
  (b)   refuse the application without a hearing; or
  (c)   fix a date for the hearing of the application.

56 Persons to be notified of the hearing of an application for permission

(1) Where the court fixes a date for a hearing under rule 55(c), it will notify the applicant and such other persons as it thinks fit, and provide them with –

(a)   subject to paragraph (2), the documents mentioned in rule 54; and
(b)   a form for acknowledging notification.

(2) The court may direct that any document is to be provided on an edited basis.

57 Acknowledgment of notification of permission application

(1) Any person who is notified of an application for permission and who wishes to take part in the permission hearing must file an acknowledgment of notification in accordance with the following provisions of this rule.

(2) The acknowledgment of notification must be filed not more than 21 days after notice of the application was given.

(3) The court will serve the acknowledgment of notification on the applicant and on any other person who has filed such an acknowledgment.

(4) The acknowledgment of notification must –

(a)   state whether the person acknowledging notification consents to the application for permission;
(b)   state whether he opposes the application for permission, and if so, set out the grounds for doing so;
(c)   state whether he proposes that permission should be granted to make an application for a different order, and if so, set out what that order is;
(d)   provide an address for service, which must be within the jurisdiction of the court; and
(e)   be signed by him or his legal representative.

(5) The acknowledgment of notification may include or be accompanied by an application for directions.

(6) Subject to rules 120 and 123 (restrictions on filing an expert's report and court's power to restrict expert evidence), where a person opposes the application for permission or proposes that permission is granted for a different order, the acknowledgment of notification must be accompanied by a witness statement containing any evidence upon which that person intends to rely.

How to start proceedings

2.94 Commencement of proceedings is regulated from r 61 onwards. Those which are applicable to a local authority are set out below. 'Practice Note A – The Application Form' accompanies these Rules. In respect of r 70, the applicant should seek to identify at least three persons who are likely to have an interest in being notified that an application form has been issued. Examples given are members of close family (eg spouse, civil partner, parents and children). That presumption can be displaced if the applicant is aware of circumstances which contra-indicate such notification (eg if the relative has had little or no involvement in P's life and has shown no inclination to do so, or where non-relatives have a closer relationship with P than relatives). The

Direction provides a list of family members that is similar to that in s 26 of MHA 1983 (as amended). It is as follows:

(a)   spouse or civil partner;

(b)   person who is not a spouse or a civil partner but who has been living with P as if they were;

(c)   parent or guardian;

(d)   child;

(e)   brother or sister;

(f)   grandparent or grandchild;

(g)   aunt or uncle;

(h)   child of a person falling within subparagraph (e);

(i)   step-parent;

(j)   half-brother or half-sister.

In addition, the following persons must be notified where appropriate:

(a)   where P is under 18, anyone with parental responsibility;

(b)   any legal or natural person likely to be affected by the outcome of the application (for example, where there is an organisation responsible for the care of P and the application relates to provision/withdrawal of treatment or accommodation);

(c)   any deputy, attorney or donee;

(d)   any other person who might reasonably be interested, for example a close friend who has provided care on an informal basis.

There should be notification of all those who fall within each of the categories (for example, it there are four siblings), unless there is good reason not to. If a decision is made not to notify a person in the list, then evidence must be provided to say why they have not been notified.

63 Contents of the application form

The application form must –

    (a)   state the matter which the applicant wants the court to decide;

    (b)   state the order which the applicant is seeking;

    (c)   name –

> (i) the applicant;
>
> (ii) P;
>
> (iii) as a respondent, any person (other than P) whom the applicant reasonably believes to have an interest which means that he ought to be heard in relation to the application (as opposed to being notified of it in accordance with rule 70); and
>
> (iv) any person whom the applicant intends to notify in accordance with rule 70; and

(d) if the applicant is applying in a representative capacity, state what that capacity is.

64 Documents to be filed with the application form

When an applicant files his application form with the court, he must also file –

(a) in accordance with the relevant practice direction, any evidence upon which he intends to rely;

(b) if permission was required to make the application, a copy of the court's order granting permission;

(c) an assessment of capacity form, where this is required by the relevant practice direction;

(d) any other documents referred to in the application form; and

(e) such other information and material as may be set out in a practice direction.

Steps following issue of application form

66 Applicant to serve the application form on named respondents

(1) As soon as practicable and in any event within 21 days of the date on which the application form was issued, the applicant must serve a copy of the application form on any person who is named as a respondent in the application form, together with copies of any documents filed in accordance with rule 64 and a form for acknowledging service.

(2) The applicant must file a certificate of service within 7 days beginning with the date on which the documents were served.

69 Applicant to notify P of an application

P must be notified in accordance with Part 7 that an application form has been issued, unless the requirement to do so has been dispensed with under rule 49.

70 Applicant to notify other persons of an application

(1) As soon as practicable and in any event within 21 days of the date on which the application form was issued, the applicant must notify the persons specified in the relevant practice direction –

(a) that an application form has been issued;

(b) whether it relates to the exercise of the court's jurisdiction in relation to P's property and affairs, or his personal welfare, or to both; and

(c) of the order or orders sought.

(2) Notification of the issue of the application form must be accompanied by a form for acknowledging notification.

(3) The applicant must file a certificate of notification within 7 days beginning with the date on which notification was given.

The parties to the proceedings

73 Parties to the proceedings

(1) Unless the court otherwise directs, the parties to any proceedings are –

    (a)   the applicant; and

    (b)   any person who is named as a respondent in the application form and who files an acknowledgment of service in respect of the application form.

(2) The court may order a person to be joined as a party if it considers that it is desirable to do so for the purpose of dealing with the application.

(3) The court may at any time direct that any person who is a party to the proceedings is to be removed as a party.

(4) Unless the court orders otherwise, P shall not be named as a respondent to any proceedings.

(5) A party to the proceedings is bound by any order or direction of the court made in the course of those proceedings.

74 Persons to be bound as if parties

(1) The persons mentioned in paragraph (2) shall be bound by any order made or directions given by the court in the same way that a party to the proceedings is so bound.

(2) The persons referred to in paragraph (1) are –

    (a)   P; and

    (b)   any person who has been served with or notified of an application form in accordance with these Rules.

75 Application to be joined as a party

(1) Any person with sufficient interest may apply to the court to be joined as a party to the proceedings.

(2) An application to be joined as a party must be made by filing an application notice in accordance with Part 10 which must –

    (a)   state the full name and address of the person seeking to be joined as a party to the proceedings;

    (b)   state his interest in the proceedings;

    (c)   state whether he consents to the application;

    (d)   state whether he opposes the application and, if so, set out the grounds for doing so;

    (e)   state whether he proposes that an order different from that set out in the application form should be made and, if so, set out what that order is;

(f)   provide an address for service, which must be within the jurisdiction of the court; and

(g)   be signed by him or his legal representative.

(3) Subject to rules 120 and 123 (restriction on filing an expert's report and court's power to restrict expert evidence), an application to be joined must be accompanied by –

(a)   a witness statement containing evidence of his interest in the proceedings and, if he proposes that an order different from that set out in the application form should be made, the evidence on which he intends to rely; and

(b)   a sufficient number of copies of the application notice to enable service of the application on every other party to the proceedings.

(4) The court will serve the application notice and any accompanying documents on all parties to the proceedings.

(5) The court will consider whether to join a person applying under this rule as a party to the proceedings and, if it decides to do so, will make an order to that effect.

Applications within proceedings (including emergency and ex parte applications)

2.95   There is also a provision for applications to be made either within existing proceedings, or on an emergency basis (including ex parte or 'without notice' applications). Part 10 of the Rules are accompanied by two practice directions. The first is 'Applications within Proceedings'. The second is 'Urgent and Interim Applications'. Concern is expressed that urgent applications have been made in the past simply due to delay in the first place. If a judge is concerned that the process is being abused, there may be a requirement for the applicant to attend Court and to provide an explanation as to that delay. Steps should be taken to notify the respondent of the application, unless justice would be defeated by so doing. Any orders made must be served as soon as practicable, or as ordered. If the matter is exceptionally urgent, then an oral application is permissible. Telephone applications should be recorded, and a transcript made available. Where the application relates to serious medical treatment, Practice Direction 9E applies.

Interim remedies

82 Orders for interim remedies

(1) The court may grant the following interim remedies –

(a)   an interim injunction;

(b)   an interim declaration; or

(c)   any other interim order it considers appropriate.

(2) Unless the court orders otherwise, a person on whom an application form is served under Part 9, or who is given notice of such an application, may not apply for an interim remedy before he has filed an acknowledgment of service or notification in accordance with Part 9.

(3) This rule does not limit any other power of the court to grant interim relief.

Private and public hearings

90 General rule–hearing to be in private

(1) The general rule is that a hearing is to be held in private.

(2) A private hearing is a hearing which only the following persons are entitled to attend –

    (a)   the parties;
    (b)   P (whether or not a party);
    (c)   any person acting in the proceedings as a litigation friend;
    (d)   any legal representative of a person specified in any of sub-paragraphs (a) to (c); and
    (e)   any court officer.

(3) In relation to a private hearing, the court may make an order–

    (a)   authorising any person, or class of persons, to attend the hearing or a part of it; or
    (b)   excluding any person, or class of persons, from attending the hearing or a part of it.

91 Court's general power to authorise publication of information about proceedings

(1) For the purposes of the law relating to contempt of court, information relating to proceedings held in private may be published where the court makes an order under paragraph (2).

(2) The court may make an order authorising –

    (a)   the publication of such information relating to the proceedings as it may specify; or
    (b)   the publication of the text or a summary of the whole or part of a judgment or order made by the court.

(3) Where the court makes an order under paragraph (2) it may do so on such terms as it thinks fit, and in particular may –

    (a)   impose restrictions on the publication of the identity of –
        (i)   any party;
        (ii)   P (whether or not a party);
        (iii)   any witness; or
        (iv)   any other person;
    (b)   prohibit the publication of any information that may lead to any such person being identified;
    (c)   prohibit the further publication of any information relating to the proceedings from such date as the court may specify; or

(d)   impose such other restrictions on the publication of information relating to the proceedings as the court may specify.

92 Court's power to order that a hearing be held in public

(1) The court may make an order –

(a)   for a hearing to be held in public;
(b)   for a part of a hearing to be held in public; or
(c)   excluding any person, or class of persons, from attending a public hearing or a part of it.

(2) Where the court makes an order under paragraph (1), it may in the same order or by a subsequent order –

(a)   impose restrictions on the publication of the identity of –
        (i)   any party;
        (ii)   P (whether or not a party);
        (iii)   any witness; or
        (iv)   any other person;
(b)   prohibit the publication of any information that may lead to any such person being identified;
(c)   prohibit the further publication of any information relating to the proceedings from such date as the court may specify; or
(d)   impose such other restrictions on the publication of information relating to the proceedings as the court may specify.

93 Supplementary provisions relating to public or private hearings

(1) An order under rule 90, 91 or 92 may be made –

(a)   only where it appears to the court that there is good reason for making the order;
(b)   at any time; and
(c)   either on the court's own initiative or on an application made by any person in accordance with Part 10.

(2) A practice direction may make further provision in connection with –

(a)   private hearings;
(b)   public hearings; or
(c)   the publication of information about any proceedings.

2.96   The leading authority on this is *Independent News & Media v A* [2010] EWCA Civ 343, [2010] 2 FLR 1290. Essentially, the conflict is between Art 8 and Art 10. The presumption in the Rules is for privacy. That protects the Art 8 rights of P. However, it may be in the public interest that the details of the case are made known, which may (but not necessarily) conflict with those rights. The procedure for permitting a hearing to be in public was set out as follows. Rule 90(3) permits others to attend a hearing. Rule 91(1)–(3) permits information to be released. Rule 92 permits a hearing to be in public, completely. The first step is to decide whether there is a good reason for any of the steps away from privacy to be taken. If there was, then there had to be a balancing exercise as to whether there were more compelling reasons not to take steps away from a private hearing. Those would tend to be the impact on P and his family life. In the case that was being considered, a significant amount of information about P was already in the public domain. This, together with the importance of a small number of representatives of the media being permitted access for the purposes of demonstrating how the Court of Protection operated, led to the conclusion that the balancing exercise pointed towards the hearing being public to that extent. This was also the case in *London Borough of Hillingdon v Steven Neary (by his litigation friend the Official Solicitor) and Mark Neary* [2011] EWHC 413 (COP), [2011] 14 CCLR 239 (where a substantial amount of material was already in the public domain). This has particular significance for local authorities, as the media will be interested in any cases where things have (arguably) been done in a manner which is not in accordance with the law. This was the reason for the revealing of the identity of the local authority in *Cheshire West and Chester Council v P & M* [2011] EWHC 1330 (Fam) (see **2.60**) and the use of r 91(2)(b) and (3) to permit this to happen. Where there are significant criticisms to be made of a local authority, then this is likely to happen again. The reverse happened in *W (by her litigation friend, B) v M (by the Official Solicitor) and S* [2011] EWHC 1197 (COP), [2011] 2 FLR 1143, where it was held that the vulnerability of P and her family was such that injunctions were required to prevent the media from disclosing information. The power to make such an injunction lay within s 47(1) of the Mental Capacity Act 2005. It is to be noted that Mr Justice Baker was also concerned that press coverage might also lead to a breach of Art 6.

Expert evidence (rr 119–131)

2.97   Plainly, the extent of expert evidence in cases will be significant. None of the directions contained in Part 15 of the Court of Protection Rules 2007 will come as a surprise to any practitioner who has experience in the field of the Children Act 1989. The Rules on this aspect are particularly extensive, and are not set out fully below. 'Practice Direction A – Expert Evidence' supplements Part 15 of the Rules. It is intended to limit expert evidence. If an expert changes his mind, then this should be notified to the parties and when appropriate to the Court. Any questions put to the expert should be in writing within 28 days after service of the report, and copies of the questions should be sent to other parties. In *Re SK (Local Authority: Expert Evidence)* [2007] EWHC 3289 (Fam), [2008] 2 FLR 707 the issue of permitting further reports when there had been a joint instruction was considered. It was held that a second report would only be permitted if: (a) it could be established that the report was substantially flawed; and (b) if it was not, then how pivotal that report was to determining the best interests of P.

Disclosure

2.98   Part 16 deals with the issue of disclosure. Again, the Rules are in keeping with common practice (and provide for orders for disclosure, and an ongoing duty for disclosure, inspection of documents, and claims concerning withholding of disclosure, and the consequences of a failure to disclose). In *Enfield London Borough Council v SA (by her litigation friend, the Official*

Solicitor) FA & KA [2010] EWHC 196 (Admin), [2010] 1 FLR 1836, the issue of the extent of the duty to disclose was considered (amongst other matters). The local authority had failed to disclose an important item of evidence which went to the heart of allegations in respect of abuse of P. It was held that in future, in cases such as this, there would be a direction for 'full and frank disclosure' (the current rules being silent on this point).

Litigation friend

2.99 Part 17 sets out the requirements for a litigation friend. Within the context of the Court of Protection, this is an important aspect of procedure. 'Practice Direction A – Litigation Friend' supplements Part 17 of the Rules. Generally speaking, evidence is required of the suitability to act as a litigation friend, and for any major steps taken (for example to change the litigation friend, or to cease litigation). In *RP v Nottingham City Council and the Official Solicitor (Mental Capacity of Parent)* [2008] EWCA Civ 462, [2008] 2 FLR 1516 the probity of the legal representatives of a mother were (unreasonably) called into question. The judgment identifies the need for lawyers acting for P to speedily act if they considered that a client lacked capacity. The appointment of a litigation friend did not breach Art 6. In *G v (1) (E) (by his litigation friend, the Official Solicitor) (2) Manchester City Council (3) F* [2010] EWHC 2512 (Fam), [2010] 13 CCLR 610) an application was made to replace the Official Solicitor on the basis that there was a potential claim for damages against him. The basis of this claim was without foundation. The general rule is that the Official Solicitor will be appointed to represent the interests of those who lack capacity. On a similar point, the role of a McKenzie friend was considered in *HBCC v LC (by her litigation friend the Official Solicitor), JG and SG* [2010] EWHC 1527 (Fam), [2011] 1 FLR 463. In this instance, an elected representative of one of the parties had acted as McKenzie friend, but had opted to take up her cause directly against the local authority. Eleanor King J held that by adopting such a position, he became in danger of creating a conflict of interest, and if so, should withdraw. He also put himself in danger of being in contempt of court, and also was failing to adhere to *President's Guidance: McKenzie Friends* [2008] 2 FLR 110 by acting as the agent of the party.

Litigation Friend

140 Who may act as a litigation friend

(1) A person may act as a litigation friend on behalf of a person mentioned in paragraph (2) if he –

    (a)   can fairly and competently conduct proceedings on behalf of that person; and

    (b)   has no interests adverse to those of that person.

(2) The persons for whom a litigation friend may act are –

    (a)   P;

    (b)   a child; or

(c)   a protected party.

141 Requirement for a litigation friend

(1) Subject to rule 147, P (if a party to proceedings) must have a litigation friend.

(2) A protected party (if a party to the proceedings) must have a litigation friend.

(3) A child (if a party to proceedings) must have a litigation friend to conduct those proceedings on his behalf unless the court makes an order under paragraph (4).

(4) The court may make an order permitting the child to conduct proceedings without a litigation friend.

(5) An application for an order under paragraph (4) –

(a)   may be made by the child;
(b)   if the child already has a litigation friend, must be made on notice to the litigation friend; and
(c)   if the child has no litigation friend, may be made without notice.

(6) Where—

(a)   the court has made an order under paragraph (4); and
(b)   it subsequently appears to the court that it is desirable for a litigation friend to conduct the proceedings on behalf of the child,

the court may appoint a person to be the child's litigation friend.

142 Litigation friend without a court order

(1) This rule does not apply –

(a)   in relation to P;
(b)   where the court has appointed a person under rule 143 or 144; or
(c)   where the Official Solicitor is to act as litigation friend.

(2) A deputy with the power to conduct legal proceedings in the name of the protected party or on the protected party's behalf is entitled to be a litigation friend of the protected party in any proceedings to which his power relates.

(3) If no one has been appointed by the court, or in the case of a protected party, there is no deputy with the power to conduct proceedings, a person who wishes to act as a litigation friend must –

(a)   file a certificate of suitability stating that he satisfies the conditions specified in rule 140(1); and
(b)   serve the certificate of suitability on –
    (i)   the person on whom an application form is to be served in accordance with rule 32 (service on children and protected parties); and
    (ii)   every other person who is a party to the proceedings.

(4) If the person referred to in paragraph (2) wishes to act as a litigation friend for the protected party, he must file and serve a copy of the court order which appointed him on those persons mentioned in paragraph (3)(b).

143 Litigation friend by court order

(1) The court may make an order appointing –

(a)   the Official Solicitor; or
(b)   some other person to act as a litigation friend.

(2) The court may act under paragraph (1) –

(a)   either on its own initiative or on the application of any person; but
(b)   only with the consent of the person to be appointed.

(3) An application for an order under paragraph (1) must be supported by evidence.

(4) The court may not appoint a litigation friend under this rule unless it is satisfied that the person to be appointed satisfies the conditions specified in rule 140(1).

(5) The court may at any stage of the proceedings give directions as to the appointment of a litigation friend.

144 Court's power to prevent a person from acting as litigation friend or to order change

(1) The court may either on its own initiative or on the application of any person –

(a)   direct that a person may not act as a litigation friend;
(b)   terminate a litigation friend's appointment; or
(c)   appoint a new litigation friend in place of an existing one.

(2) An application for an order under paragraph (1) must be supported by evidence.

(3) The court may not appoint a litigation friend under this rule unless it is satisfied that the person to be appointed satisfies the conditions specified in rule 140(1).

145 Appointment of litigation friend by court order – supplementary

The applicant must serve a copy of an application for an order under rule 143 or 144 on –

(a)   the person on whom an application form is to be served in accordance with rule 32 (service on children and protected parties);
(b)   every other person who is a party to the proceedings;
(c)   any person who is the litigation friend, or who is purporting to act as the litigation friend, when the application is made; and
(d)   unless he is the applicant, the person who it is proposed should be the litigation friend,

as soon as practicable and in any event within 21 days of the date on which it was issued.

Costs (rr 156–160)

2.100 The issue of costs has become of greater significance in recent years, particularly if a local authority has acted in a manner which is open to criticism. In *EG v RS, JS and BEN PCT* [2010] EWHC 3073 (COP) an order for costs was made against a professional deputy who became too closely identified with the cause of one of the litigants. Of greater relevance to local authorities specifically, the matter was considered at greater length in *G v E (Costs)* [2010] EWHC 3385 (Fam), [2011] 1 FLR 1566. The argument that all the litigation in many such cases would be borne by the public purse in one guise or another carried no weight. A departure from the general rule (r 156) and departure from it (r 159), together with the CPR (on the matter of indemnity costs) all mean that it is possible for a local authority to face an order for costs. However, such orders would be reserved for such cases as *G* where a local authority had broken the law or had been guilty of misconduct. Manchester City Council had been guilty of such misconduct, including being unreasonable in the conduct of the litigation itself. This was the subject of an appeal (reported at [2011] EWCA Civ 939) which failed in its entirety. In effect, where there is bad faith on the part of a litigant, then this will justify departure from the general rule (*Re RC (Deceased)* [2011] 1 FLR 1447).

156 Property and affairs – the general rule

Where the proceedings concern P's property and affairs the general rule is that the costs of the proceedings or of that part of the proceedings that concerns P's property and affairs, shall be paid by P or charged to his estate.

157 Personal welfare – the general rule

Where the proceedings concern P's personal welfare the general rule is that there will be no order as to the costs of the proceedings or of that part of the proceedings that concerns P's personal welfare.

158 Apportioning costs – the general rule

Where the proceedings concern both property and affairs and personal welfare the court, insofar as practicable, will apportion the costs as between the respective issues.

159 Departing from the general rule

(1) The court may depart from rules 156 to 158 if the circumstances so justify, and in deciding whether departure is justified the court will have regard to all the circumstances, including –

    (a)   the conduct of the parties;
    (b)   whether a party has succeeded on part of his case, even if he has not been wholly successful; and
    (c)   the role of any public body involved in the proceedings.

(2) The conduct of the parties includes –

    (a)   conduct before, as well as during, the proceedings;

(b) whether it was reasonable for a party to raise, pursue or contest a particular issue;

(c) the manner in which a party has made or responded to an application or a particular issue; and

(d) whether a party who has succeeded in his application or response to an application, in whole or in part, exaggerated any matter contained in his application or response.

(3) Without prejudice to rules 156 to 158 and the foregoing provisions of this rule, the court may permit a party to recover their fixed costs in accordance with the relevant practice direction.

Practice Directions

2.101 The procedures relating to the Court of Protection are subject to Practice Directions. At the date of publication, there are 35 of these, and a partial summary of some of the most relevant are set out above. All of them can be obtained from the website of the Public Guardian's Office. Practice Direction 9E (Applications relating to serious medical treatment) is reproduced below, since this relates to the most substantive of applications (rather than the procedural aspects referred to above).

Practice Direction – How to Start Proceedings

This practice direction supplements Part 9 of the Court of Protection Rules 2007

Practice Direction E – Applications Relating to Serious Medical Treatment

General

1. Rule 71 enables a practice direction to make additional or different provision in relation to specified applications.

Applications to which this practice direction applies

2. This practice direction sets out the procedure to be followed where the application concerns serious medical treatment in relation to P.

Meaning of "serious medical treatment" in relation to the Rules and this practice direction

3. Serious medical treatment means treatment which involves providing, withdrawing or withholding treatment in circumstances where:

(a) in a case where a single treatment is being proposed, there is a fine balance between its benefits to P and the burdens and risks it is likely to entail for him;

(b) in a case where there is a choice of treatments, a decision as to which one to use is finely balanced; or

(c) the treatment, procedure or investigation proposed would be likely to involve serious consequences for P.

4. "Serious consequences" are those which could have a serious impact on P, either from the effects of the treatment, procedure or investigation itself or its wider implications. This may include treatments, procedures or investigations which:

    (a)   cause, or may cause, serious and prolonged pain, distress or side effects;

    (b)   have potentially major consequences for P; or

    (c)   have a serious impact on P's future life choices.

Matters which should be brought to the court

5. Cases involving any of the following decisions should be regarded as serious medical treatment for the purpose of the Rules and this practice direction, and should be brought to the court:

    (a)   decisions about the proposed withholding or withdrawal of artificial nutrition and hydration from a person in a permanent vegetative state or a minimally conscious state;

    (b)   cases involving organ or bone marrow donation by a person who lacks capacity to consent; and

    (c)   cases involving non-therapeutic sterilisation of a person who lacks capacity to consent.

6. Examples of serious medical treatment may include:

    (a)   certain terminations of pregnancy in relation to a person who lacks capacity to consent to such a procedure;

    (b)   a medical procedure performed on a person who lacks capacity to consent to it, where the procedure is for the purpose of a donation to another person;

    (c)   a medical procedure or treatment to be carried out on a person who lacks capacity to consent to it, where that procedure or treatment must be carried out using a degree of force to restrain the person concerned;

    (d)   an experimental or innovative treatment for the benefit of a person who lacks capacity to consent to such treatment; and

    (e)   a case involving an ethical dilemma in an untested area.

7. There may be other procedures or treatments not contained in the list in paragraphs 5 and 6 above which can be regarded as serious medical treatment. Whether or not a procedure is regarded as serious medical treatment will depend on the circumstances and the consequences for the patient.

Consultation with the Official Solicitor

8. Members of the Official Solicitor's staff are prepared to discuss applications in relation to serious medical treatment before an application is made. Any enquiries about adult medical and welfare cases should be addressed to a family and medical litigation lawyer at the Office of the Official Solicitor, 81 Chancery Lane, London WC2A IDD, ph: 020 7911 7127, fax: 020 7911 7105, email: enquiries@offsol.gsi.gov.uk.

Parties to proceedings

9. The person bringing the application will always be a party to proceedings, as will a respondent named in the application form who files an acknowledgment of service. In cases involving issues as to serious medical treatment, an organisation

which is, or will be, responsible for providing clinical or caring services to P should usually be named as a respondent in the application form (where it is not already the applicant in the proceedings).

(Practice direction B accompanying Part 9 sets out the persons who are to be notified that an application form has been issued)

10. The court will consider whether anyone not already a party should be joined as a party to the proceedings. Other persons with sufficient interest may apply to be joined as parties to the proceedings and the court has a duty to identify at as early a stage as possible who the parties to the proceedings should be.

Allocation of the case

11. Where an application is made to the court in relation to:

(a) the lawfulness of withholding or withdrawing artificial nutrition and hydration from a person in a permanent vegetative state, or a minimally conscious state; or

(b) a case involving an ethical dilemma in an untested area,

the proceedings (including permission, the giving of any directions, and any hearing) must be conducted by the President of the Court of Protection or by another judge nominated by the President.

12. Where an application is made to the court in relation to serious medical treatment (other than that outlined in paragraph 11) the proceedings (including permission, the giving of any directions, and any hearing) must be conducted by a judge of the court who has been nominated as such by virtue of section 46(2)(a) to (c) of the Act (i.e. the President of the Family Division, the Chancellor or a puisne judge of the High Court).

Matters to be considered at the first directions hearing

13. Unless the matter is one which needs to be disposed of urgently, the court will list it for a first directions hearing.

(Practice direction B accompanying Part 10 sets out the procedure to be followed for urgent applications.)

14. The court may give such directions as it considers appropriate. If the court has not already done so, it should in particular consider whether to do any or all of the following at the first directions hearing:

(a) decide whether P should be joined as party to the proceedings, and give directions to that effect;

(b) if P is to be joined as a party to the proceedings, decide whether the Official Solicitor should be invited to act as a litigation friend or whether some other person should be appointed as a litigation friend;

(c) identify anyone else who has been notified of the proceedings and who has filed an acknowledgment and applied to be joined as a party to proceedings, and consider that application; and

(d) set a timetable for the proceedings including, where possible, a date for the final hearing.

15. The court should also consider whether to give any of the other directions listed in rule 85(2).

16. The court will ordinarily make an order pursuant to rule 92 that any hearing shall be held in public, with restrictions to be imposed in relation to publication of information about the proceedings.

Declarations

17. Where a declaration is needed, the order sought should be in the following or similar terms:

- That P lacks capacity to make a decision in relation to the (proposed medical treatment or procedure).

E.g. 'That P lacks capacity to make a decision in relation to sterilisation by vasectomy'; and

- That, having regard to the best interests of P, it is lawful for the (proposed medical treatment or procedure) to be carried out by (proposed healthcare provider).

18. Where the application is for the withdrawal of life-sustaining treatment, the order sought should be in the following or similar terms:

- That P lacks capacity to consent to continued life-sustaining treatment measures (and specify what these are); and
- That, having regard to the best interests of P, it is lawful for (name of healthcare provider) to withdraw the life-sustaining treatment from P.

Damages

2.102   The issue of whether the Court of Protection has the jurisdiction to make an award of damages was considered in *YA (F) v A Local Authority* [2010] EWHC 2770 (COP), [2011] 1 FLR 2007. The jurisdiction for an award of damages arises out of s 8 of the Human Rights Act 1998.

8   Judicial remedies

(1) In relation to any act (or proposed act) of a public authority which the court finds is (or would be) unlawful, it may grant such relief or remedy, or make such order, within its powers as it considers just and appropriate.

(2) But damages may be awarded only by a court which has power to award damages, or to order the payment of compensation, in civil proceedings.

(3) No award of damages is to be made unless, taking account of all the circumstances of the case, including –

(a)   any other relief or remedy granted, or order made, in relation to the act in question (by that or any other court), and

(b)   the consequences of any decision (of that or any other court) in respect of that act,

the court is satisfied that the award is necessary to afford just satisfaction to the person in whose favour it is made.

(4) In determining –

(a)   whether to award damages, or

(b)   the amount of an award,

the court must take into account the principles applied by the European Court of Human Rights in relation to the award of compensation under Article 41 of the Convention.

(5) A public authority against which damages are awarded is to be treated –

   (a)   in Scotland, for the purposes of section 3 of the Law Reform (Miscellaneous Provisions) (Scotland) Act 1940 as if the award were made in an action of damages in which the authority has been found liable in respect of loss or damage to the person to whom the award is made;

   (b)   for the purposes of the Civil Liability (Contribution) Act 1978 as liable in respect of damage suffered by the person to whom the award is made.

(6) In this section –

   "court" includes a tribunal;
   "damages" means damages for an unlawful act of a public authority; and
   "unlawful" means unlawful under section 6(1).

The decision of Charles J was that the Court of Protection was a court that had the power to make such an order, but that:

> '[35] damages are not recoverable as of right as, for example in tort or breach of contract, but are to give just satisfaction if, applying and equitable approach, the court considers that to be the right result.'

2.103   It is difficult to be precise about the level of damages that a Court might award, since this will depend very much upon the breach, and the circumstances in which it occurred. Certainly in *Anufrijeva* [2003] EWCA Civ 1406, [2004] 1 FLR 8 (cited by Charles J) the general outcome was that damages were a remedy of last resort, and that an award must strike a balance between the rights of the individual and the public as a whole. In respect of a breach of Art 5(4), the general principle is that there is a requirement for causation between the breach and any alleged harm arising from that violation (*Hussain v UK (1996)* 2 EHRR 1). Even in the seminal case of *Bournewood* a nominal award of £1.00 was made ([1998] 2 WLR at [778]). The ECHR upheld this decision, and adjudicated that a violation of both Arts 5 and 8 was sufficiently met with a declaration that there had been such a violation (*HL v UK* [2004] ECHR 471). Similarly in *R (on the application of Michael Degainis) v SoS for Justice* [2010] EWHC 137 (Admin) and apology and admission of a breach of Art 5(4) was sufficient in respect of a prisoner whose period in custody had not been extended by the breach, and nor was there any demonstrable frustration or anxiety that might be associated with that breach. The corollary of this, of course, that if there is demonstrable frustration, anxiety, or worse, then it is most likely that an award would be made. A delay in achieving a hearing (in the context of Mental Health Review Tribunals) led to awards of between £750–£4000, but that such claims needed to be substantiated by medical evidence that the delay had impacted upon the claimants (*R (KB) v MHRT* [2003] EWHC 193 (Admin). Further, the Court was entitled to take into account not only the extent to which the claimant realised that they had been illegally detained (*R v SSHD ex parte Naughton* [1997] 1 WLR 118). An apology from a local authority may be sufficient in itself. Further, if the breach of Art 5 would have made no difference had the matter been brought before a Court, then damages may be nominal only (*R (on the application of S) v SoS for the Home Department & Ors* [2011] EWHC 2120 (Admin). A similar decision was reached in *R (on the application of Betteridge) v Parole Board* [2009] EWHC 1638 (Admin). In terms of assessing damages, the domestic courts are enjoined to look at past decisions within the European Court of Human Rights (*R (on the application of Pennington) v Parole Board* [2010] EWHC 78 (Admin)). It will be the case that if the circumstances are particularly compelling, then a much higher award of damages may be appropriate. For example, in *Rakevich v Russia* [2003] ECHR 558 an award of €3000 was made where there had been a breach of Art 5 and the applicant had been detained in a psychiatric institution where she had suffered emotional stress and anxiety caused by the detention, and had also experienced frustration over what is described as 'many days'. The initial claim had been for €10,000. In terms of heads of damages, in *R (on the application of Daniel Falkner) v SoS for Justice (1) Parole Board (2)* [2011] EWCA Civ 349 it was held that it was not appropriate to make an award for distress and anxiety separately from damages for loss of liberty where there was a breach of Art 5(4). In respect of Art 8, in the case of *R (on the application of Bernard) v Enfield LBC* [2002] EWHC 2282 (Admin) an award of £10,000 was made. The breach had the effect of leaving the family living in the most appalling physical conditions for 2 years.

Ordinary residence

2.104 *Ordinary Residence: Guidance on the identification of the ordinary residence of people in need of community services, England* (DoH April 2011) contains specific information about those who lack capacity (paras 27–43 and 167–178). In effect, if a person lacks capacity and was totally dependent upon a parent or guardian then she could have no independent ordinary residence of her own. However this test (the *Vale* test) is to be qualified if it involves an older person whose parents have died, and who has lived in the area for some time, or people who have lived in an area for some time and then lost capacity, or younger people who have lived independently of their parents prior to losing capacity (paras 31 and 33). The alternative approach suggested is the test for ordinary residence as it would apply to someone who had capacity, albeit without the requirement for them to have adopted that residence voluntarily [34].

2.105 Paragraphs 167–178 concern themselves with DOLS. Where a person is to be deprived of their liberty in a care home, the supervisory body is **always** the local authority in which the person is ordinarily resident (para 170). However, if the person is self-funding, they will acquire the ordinary residence of the location of the care home (para 171). If of no settled residence, the same applies (para 171). Paragraph 183 of Sch A1 of the Mental Capacity Act 2005 means that the deeming provisions of the 1948 Act apply. This means that the placing authority would be the supervisory body (para 172). If the DOLS is in a hospital, then they are ordinarily resident in the area where they lived immediately prior to being admitted (para 173). This means that the local authority for that area will be the supervisory body. The arrangements in respect of those who fall outside this more straightforward situation are contained in paras 174–178, which are set out below.

174. If the person does not require the local authority to make arrangements on their behalf under section 21 of the 1948 Act and enters that home as a self-funder (usually a deputy would enter into a contract with the care home on their behalf), they would generally acquire an ordinary residence in the area in which their care home is located. However, if the person has not entered the care home at the point when the MCA DOLS application is made, they cannot be ordinarily resident in that local authority, despite any imminent plans to move there. Whilst the person remains in hospital, the section 24(6) deeming provision applies making them ordinarily resident in their previous local authority until they are discharged from hospital. It is likely that the self-funder would become ordinarily resident in the local authority in which their care home is located as soon as their move takes place but their supervisory body under the MCA DOLS would be their previous local authority. The scenario on page 59 below provides more guidance on how ordinary residence is determined when a person moves to a care home in a new local authority area under a MCA DOLS authorisation.

175. Section 24(6) of the 1948 Act applies to all NHS accommodation and not just hospitals (see paragraphs 60–65). This means that where a person is placed in a care home "out of area" by a PCT under NHS CHC arrangements they remain ordinarily resident in the area in which they were ordinarily resident before being provided with NHS CHC. Therefore, if the person in receipt of NHS CHC subsequently needs to be deprived of their liberty, it is the local authority in which they were ordinarily resident immediately before being provided with NHS CHC that is responsible for performing the supervisory body role.

176. Where two or more local authorities fall into dispute over a person's ordinary residence in respect of which authority should exercise the supervisory body role, the 2005 Act provides that disputes may be determined by the Secretary of State or by the Welsh Ministers where they cannot be resolved locally. Cross-border arrangements made under paragraph 183(4) of Schedule A1 to the 2005 Act set out which cases are to be determined by the Secretary of State and which are to be determined by Welsh Ministers.

177. It should be noted that a determination under the 2005 Act can only be sought in relation to ordinary residence disputes that arise in connection with which local authority should take on the role of supervisory body for the purpose of granting (and reviewing) a deprivation of liberty authorisation. Where ordinary residence disputes occur in relation to the general provision of social care accommodation or services, determinations should be sought under section 32(3) of the 1948 Act.

178. Regulations made under the 2005 Act put in place arrangements for when disputes occur between local authorities over the ordinary residence of a person who needs to be deprived of liberty. They set out that, in the event of a dispute occurring, the local authority which receives the request for a deprivation of

liberty authorisation must act as the supervisory body until the dispute is resolved, unless another local authority agrees to perform this role.

2.106   The provisions for referring the matter to the Secretary of State in the event of a dispute are set out in the Ordinary Residence Disputes (Mental Capacity Act 2005) Directions 2010.

Children and the Court of Protection

2.107   The Court of Protection only applies to those over the age of 16 (s 2(5) Mental Capacity Act 2005). DOLS only apply to those over the age of 18. Thus, if under the age of 16, and there are matters relating to a child and capacity, then a statutory lacuna exists if the best interests of that child cannot be dealt with by way (principally) of the Children Act 1989. If a child is between the age of 16 and 18, and there is a need to deprive her of her liberty, then DOLS cannot be used to effect this end, and an order of the Court of Protection would be required. Deprivation of liberty between 16 and 18 without an order of the court remains unlawful. If a child falls outside the provisions of either the Children Act 1989, or the Mental Capacity Act 2005, then the inherent jurisdiction of the High Court remains as an option, or, rarely, wardship.

2.108   It is not uncommon for there to have been proceedings in existence under Part IV of the Children Act 1989 (or s 25 of the Children Act 1989 for a secure accommodation order), and sometimes for there to have been detention under the Mental Health Act 1983, although there cannot be a s 25 order if there is an order pursuant to the Mental Health Act 1983. It will also be noted that there is no lower age limit for detention under either s 2 or 3 of the Mental Health Act 1983, but there is, for example, for reception for Guardianship under s 7(16)). It is also not uncommon for that child to be either approaching the age of 17 (beyond which a care order cannot be made) or approaching 18 (at which point a care order ceases to have effect). It is also common for there to have been no liaison between the children's social services department and the adult social services department. This need for co-ordination is more acute where there has been a long involvement between the child and children's services (which more often than not, there will have been). If the child has either been accommodated or has been in care or otherwise comes within the provisions of the Children (Leaving Care) Act 2000 then a pathway plan will be required (see Chapter 5). If the child has been detained under s 3 of the Mental Health Act 1983, then an after care plan may be required in which the local authority will be involved (and this may be a **different** local authority). Matters arising from s 117 of the Mental Health Act 1983 are set out in Chapter 1. If a child is in care, and detained under the Mental Health Act 1983, then the local authority becomes the nearest relative for the purposes of that Act (s 27). The Code of Practice (Mental Health Act 1983) has a chapter devoted to children although parts of it are somewhat opaque. A fuller consideration of children who are detained under the Mental Health Act is set out in *Mental Health Tribunals: Law, Practice and Procedure, Jonathan Butler* (Jordans, 2009). In addition, the National Institute for Mental Health in England have published *The Legal Aspects of the Care and Treatment of Children and Young People with Mental Disorder* (January 2009) and Anthony Harbour is the author of *Children with Mental Disorder and the Law: A Guide to Law and Practice* (Jessica Kingsley, 2008).

2.109 There is a provision for transferring proceedings between the Family Division and the Court of Protection, and vice versa. For the sake of convenience, this is set out below.

Mental Capacity Act 2005 (Transfer of Proceedings) Order 2007, SI 2007/1899

Citation and commencement

1 (1) This Order may be cited as the Mental Capacity Act 2005 (Transfer of Proceedings)

Order 2007.

(2) This Order shall come into force on 1st October 2007.

(3) In this Order "the Children Act" means the Children Act 1989(**2**).

Transfers from the Court of Protection to a court having jurisdiction under the Children Act

2 (1) This article applies to any proceedings in the Court of Protection which relate to a person under 18.

(2) The Court of Protection may direct the transfer of the whole or part of the proceedings to a court having jurisdiction under the Children Act where it considers that in all the circumstances, it is just and convenient to transfer the proceedings.

(3) In making a determination, the Court of Protection must have regard to –

(a) whether the proceedings should be heard together with other proceedings that are pending in a court having jurisdiction under the Children Act;

(b) whether any order that may be made by a court having jurisdiction under that Act is likely to be a more appropriate way of dealing with the proceedings;

(c) the need to meet any requirements that would apply if the proceedings had been started in a court having jurisdiction under the Children Act; and

(d) any other matter that the court considers relevant.

(4) The Court of Protection –

(a) may exercise the power to make an order under paragraph (2) on an application or on its own initiative; and

(b) where it orders a transfer, must give reasons for its decision.

(5) Any proceedings transferred under this article –

(a)   are to be treated for all purposes as if they were proceedings under the Children Act which had been started in a court having jurisdiction under that Act; and

(b)   are to be dealt with after the transfer in accordance with directions given by a court having jurisdiction under that Act.

Transfers from a court having jurisdiction under the Children Act to the Court of Protection

3 (1) This article applies to any proceedings in a court having jurisdiction under the Children Act which relate to a person under 18.

(2) A court having jurisdiction under the Children Act may direct the transfer of the whole or part of the proceedings to the Court of Protection where it considers that in all circumstances, it is just and convenient to transfer the proceedings.

(3) In making a determination, the court having jurisdiction under the Children Act must have regard to –

(a)   whether the proceedings should be heard together with other proceedings that are pending in the Court of Protection;

(b)   whether any order that may be made by the Court of Protection is likely to be a more appropriate way of dealing with the proceedings;

(c)   the extent to which any order made as respects a person who lacks capacity is likely to continue to have effect when that person reaches 18; and

(d)   any other matter that the court considers relevant.

(4) A court having jurisdiction under the Children Act –

(a)   may exercise the power to make an order under paragraph (2) on an application or on its own initiative; and

(b)   where it orders a transfer, must give reasons for its decision.

(5) Any proceedings transferred under this article –

(a)   are to be treated for all purposes as if they were proceedings under the Mental Capacity Act 2005 which had been started in the Court of Protection; and

(b)   are to be dealt with after the transfer in accordance with directions given by the Court of Protection.

Avoidance of double liability for fees

4 Any fee paid for the purpose of starting any proceedings that are transferred under article 2 or 3 is to be treated as if it were the fee that would have been payable if the proceedings had started in the court to which the transfer is made.

2.110 Mr Justice Hedley (in *B (A Local Authority) v RM, MM and AM* [2011] 1 FLR 1635) considered just such a case. The child was 17 at the date of the hearing, and had been the subject of wardship proceedings. The local authority had applied for a care order, even though this would have lasted for less than a year. The mental health and/or capacity issues would be lifelong. The Court itself raised the point about whether the Children Act 1989 was the appropriate statute to deal with the matter, and whether there should be a transfer to the Court of Protection from the Family Division. The criteria for transfer were considered (although the judgment is described as *ex tempore* and does not purport to be an exhaustive analysis):

> '[28] a number of matters suggest themselves, matters which may often be relevant in the relatively small number of cases in which this issue is likely to arise. One, is the child over 16? Otherwise, of course, there is no power. Two, does the child manifestly lack capacity in respect of the principal decisions which are to be made in the Children Act proceedings? Three, are the disabilities which give rise to lack of capacity lifelong or at least long-term? Four, can the decisions which arise in respect of the child's welfare all be taken and all issues resolved during the child's minority? Five, does the Court of Protection have powers or procedures more appropriate to the resolution of outstanding issues than are available under the Children Act? Six, can the child's welfare needs be fully met by the exercise of Court of Protection powers? These provisional thoughts are intended to put some flesh on to the provisions of Article (3)(3) ... the essential thrust, however, is whether looking at the individual needs of the specific person, it can be said that their welfare will be better safeguarded within the Court of Protection than it would be under the Children Act.'

It should be noted that it is also possible for the Court of Protection to sit at the same time as the Family Division, and before the same judge.

2.111 Finally, in *C (by his litigation friend the Official Solicitor) v (1) A Local Authority (2) LM (3) LPM (4) the PCT (4) An Organisation* [2011] EWHC 1539 (Admin); [2011] 14 CCLR 471 Ryder J (sitting as a judge of the Court of Protection and as a judge of the Administrative Court) was obliged to unravel and consider the relevant provisions arising out of various fragments of legislation falling outside the Mental Capacity Act 2005 in respect of a man who was 18 at the date of the hearing. He had been moved to a residential school when aged 16. Between the ages of 6–18 he had been accommodated pursuant to s 20 of the Children Act 1989. The Local Authority had never sought to use or make an application to the Court via s 25 of the Children Act 1989 (secure accommodation order). Once the claim for judicial review commenced, the local authority did make an application to the Court of Protection for a declaration as to the legality of the deprivation of the liberty of C. A DOLs authorisation could not have been granted, as the accommodation was neither a care home, nor a hospital (and could not have applied prior to his 18th birthday in any event). As a result of his status as a 'looked after child' he became eligible for a pathway plan Children (Leaving Care) Act 2000 (see Chapter 5). This obligation would have continued until the age of 21. The absence of such a plan was one feature of the claim for judicial review. As an adult, he came within the ambit of the Chronically Sick and Disabled Persons Act 1970, ss 21 and 29 of the National Assistance Act 1948, and s 47 of the National Health Service and Community Care Act 1990 (see Chapter 3). He would also have come within the Chronically Sick and Disabled Persons Act 1970 whilst a child by virtue of s 28A. There was an attempt to argue that the Mental Health Act Code of Practice should have been taken into account whilst C was 'detained' although during the proceedings, he was not detained under the Mental Health Act 1983, but a afternote to the judgment it is apparent that he was subsequently detained under s 2 of the Mental Health Act 1983, and removed from his school. This authority would only last for a maximum of 28 days, unless altered to a detention under s 3 (which would then in turn trigger the requirement for preparation for an aftercare plan under s 117 of the Mental Health Act 1983). The claim for judicial review highlighted the lack of co-ordination between children and adult social services department (which is a familiar problem) in that there had been no pathway plan produced, and no transition plan from a move from a school to an adult placement. This lack of co-ordination seems to have been justified by the subsequent decision to use the Mental Health Act 1983. This case illustrates perfectly the need for local authorities who are involved with children (typically in the 16–18 age range) to be aware of *all* their statutory obligations when before either the Court of Protection, or when considering what steps to take prior to any such application.

Chapter 3

ASSESSMENT OF COMMUNITY CARE NEEDS FOR ADULTS

GENERAL

3.1 This chapter concerns itself with the legislation which governs the assessment of those adults who are disabled or in need of community services or both. It considers the extent to which local authorities are obliged to provide such services. In particular, it will also consider the need for the protection of vulnerable adults (that is to say, adult with capacity and who therefore fall outside the provisions of the Mental Capacity Act 2005). It is a developing area of law, in part due to the demographic of the section of the population to which it applies (ie generally older adults). It has also seen the resurgence in the use of applications to the High Court (Inherent Jurisdiction).

Putting People First

3.2 The case-law that has arisen out of this area is considered below. The Department of Health had issued guidance as to eligibility criteria for what it describes as 'social care' (*Fair Access to Care Services – Guidance on Eligibility Criteria for Adult Social Care*). It was published on 28 May 2002 (LAC (2002) 13) pursuant to s 7(1) of the Local Authority Social Services Act 1970, but was replaced on 25 February 2010 with *Prioritising need in the context of Putting People First: A whole system approach for eligibility for social care*. It was also issued pursuant to s 7(1), and is subtitled *Guidance on Eligibility Criteria for Adult Social Care, England 2010*. It has been applicable since April 2010. It is referred to as '*The Guidance*' and internal references are by paragraph numbers.

Local Authority Social Services Act 1970

7 Local authorities to exercise social services functions under guidance of Secretary of State

(1) Local authorities shall, in the exercise of their social services functions, including the exercise of any discretion conferred by any relevant enactment, act under the general guidance of the Secretary of State.

(2), (3) ...

7A Directions by the Secretary of State as to exercise of social services functions

(1) Without prejudice to section 7 of this Act, every local authority shall exercise their social services functions in accordance with such directions as may be given to them under this section by the Secretary of State.

(2) Directions under this section –

    (a)   shall be given in writing; and

    (b)   may be given to a particular authority, or to authorities of a particular class, or to authorities generally.

3.3   The significance of the wording of the statute was considered in *R v Islington LBC ex p Rixon (Jonathan)* [1998] 1 CCLR 119, (1996) *Times* 17 April. Mr Justice Sedley (as he then was) held that:

> '[123J–123K] ... in my view Parliament by Section 7(1) has required Local Authorities to follow the path chartered by the Secretary of State's Guidance, with liberty to deviate from it where the Local Authority judges on admissible grounds that there is good reason to do so, but without freedom to take a substantially different course ... [125I–125J] a failure to comply with the statutory policy guidance is unlawful and can be corrected by means of judicial review.'

It follows that where Guidance (any Guidance) has been issued pursuant to this section, a local authority is obliged to pay very close attention to its content. The statutes to which it refers will be familiar, but they are the National Assistance Act 1948, Health Services and Public Health Act 1968, Chronically Sick and Disabled Persons Act 1970, National Health Service Act 2006, Mental Health Act 1983. To all intents and purposes, to this list can be added the Disabled Persons (Services, Consultation and Representation) Act 1986,, the Carers (Recognition and Services) Act 1995 and the Carers and Disabled Children Act 2000. The aim of the Guidance 'is to assist councils with adult social services responsibilities (CASSRs) to determine eligibility for adult social care, in a way that is fair, transparent and consistent, accounting for the needs of their local community as a whole as well as individuals' need for support ... [14] ... The revised guidance aims to set social care eligibility criteria firmly within the context of both the new direction of policy established by 'Putting People First', and more generally within a broader theme of public service reform'. One main part of this envisaged reform is set out in the Law Commission – Adult Social Care (Law Com No 326 10 May 2011) and to which further reference will be made. The policy document Putting People First: A shared vision and commitment to the transformation of Adult Social Care (produced in 2007) was not issued pursuant to s 7 of the Local Authority Social Services Act 1970. The latter contains a reference to the creation of '*A personalised Adult Social Care System*'. Before considering the consequences of the Guidance, it is worth analysing the current law (from a general and historical perspective) in order to understand how it operates at the moment.

Historical development

3.4   The most recent case law in this area is *R (on the application of McDonald) (Appellant) v Royal London Borough of Kensington & Chelsea (Respondent)* [2011] UKSC 33, [2011] 14 CCLR 341. In dissenting from the majority the judgment of Baroness Hale sets out with customary clarity the rationale behind the requirement for the provision of services of this type within 'a civilised society' [79]. It is not possible to improve upon this summary, and the relevant extracts from it are therefore set out. The statutes to which the authority refers are all set out within this Chapter, or elsewhere in the text.

> '[62] Since the foundation of the welfare state in the post war years, local authorities have had power to provide a range of social services for adults who need them, usually because of age, ill-health or disability. It is, perhaps, unlikely that the original framers of the legislation envisaged that any of these powers would give rise to an individual entitlement to be provided for a particular service: they were framed in terms of devising schemes to provide such services which would be approved by the Minister. Means tested benefits, on the other hand, became available to fund accommodation in residential care. More and more public money was being spent on old and other vulnerable people living in private or voluntary nursing or care homes without any professional assessment of whether they actually needed to be there. This was not only wasteful and inefficient; it was also inconsistent with the policy aim of enabling people to live independent lives in their own homes for as long as possible. The system was changed following reports from the Audit Commission ... Local social services authorities were to be given the task of assessing people's needs and either providing or arranging appropriate services for those who needed them to do so.'

It is within this historical context, and the move towards encouraging and promoting greater autonomy that the current policy documents (which are merely that, statement of government policy) and guidance, now fit.

Individual entitlement and the obligations of the local authority (*needs versus provision*)

3.5   The judgment of Baroness Hale continues:

> '[63] Thus, section 47(1)(a) of the National Health Service and Community Care Act 1990 requires a local authority to carry out an assessment if it appears that any person for whom they have power to provide or arrange community care services may be in need of them. Section 46(3) of the 1990 Act defines "community care services" as those which a local authority may provide or arrange under four different statutory regimes, all of which pre-dated the 1990 Act ...
>
> [64] But are these merely "target" duties, owed towards the relevant population as a whole, or do they give rise to individual rights? It was held in *R v Sefton Metropolitan Borough Council Ex p Help the Aged* [1997] 4 All ER 532, that s 21(1)(a) of the 1948 Act does give rise to an individual entitlement once the local authority have decided that the individual fulfils the statutory criteria. No-one has

challenged that decision and, indeed, it has been assumed to be correct in more than one decision of the House of Lords: see *R (M) v Slough Borough Council* [2008] UKHL 52 ...

[66] ... it is quite clear that section 2(1) of the Chronically Sick and Disabled Persons Act 1970 was intended to create an individual right to services if its criteria were met ...

[67] ...The 1970 Act ... specified services which had to be provided for disabled people who needed them under s 29 [National Assistance Act 1948] and gave those people an enforceable right to those services. Implicit in that right was a right to have one's needs assessed, at least if the local authority were asked to do so. But the matter was put beyond doubt by section 4 of the Disabled Persons (Services, Consultation and Representation) Act 1986 ... [the] ... wording draws a clear distinction between "the needs of the disabled person" and the services which should be provided in response.

[68] ... the duty in section 4 of the 1986 Act remains in force despite the enactment of the more comprehensive duty in section 47(1) of the 1990 Act. As section 2(1) services are provided in the exercise of the authority's functions under section 29 of the 1948 Act, it has been held that they are also included in the definition of community care services" in section 46 of the 1990 Act and thus within the duty to assess the need for them in section 47(1): see *R v Kirklees Metropolitan Borough Council, Ex p Daykin* (1996) 1 CCLR 512. Having carried out an assessment under section 47(1)(a) , section 47(1)(b) requires that the authority "having regard to the results of that assessment, shall then decide whether his needs call for the provision by them of any such services". But not all community care services are a right, so section 47(2) of the 1990 Act expressly preserves the special position of disabled people who are entitled to services under s 2(1) of the 1970 Act. If at any time during an assessment of needs under s 47(1)(a) it appears that the client is a disabled person, then the authority must proceed to make a decision as to the services which he requires under the 1970 Act without being requested so to do. This underlines the fact that Parliament intended to treat the needs of disabled people as a special case. Otherwise, it is hard to see why they did not simply subsume the former provisions in the new.

[69] In sum, disabled people have an individual right to certain services under section 2(1) of the 1970 Act and a right to have their entitlement to such services assessed and a decision made under both section 4 of the 1986 Act and section 47 of the 1990 Act. Clearly, it is for the local authority and not the court to make that assessment. It is for the local authority to be satisfied that the criteria are met. But in doing so they have to ask themselves the right questions and provide rational answers. **The key question is what is meant by "necessary to meet the needs" of the disabled person in section 2(1) of the 1970 Act. These words contain two separate questions: first, what are the needs of the disabled person; and second, what is necessary to meet those needs? The second question is then supplemented by a third: having decided what is necessary to meet those needs, is it necessary for the local authority to arrange it?** [emphasis added] ...

[71] ... The subsequent Guidance on Adult Social Care, *Fair Access to Care Services, Guidance on Eligibility Criteria for Adult Social Care (2003)* **sought to make sense of the distinction which which the House of Lords had elided. Thus is**

distinguished between a person's "presenting needs" and her "eligible needs": ... the presenting needs were those which the client actually had. The eligible needs were those which the authority were prepared to meet. This depended upon whether they were assessed as being "critical"; "substantial"; "moderate" or "low"... the lesson that I learn from this guidance (and from its replacement, *Prioritising Need in the Context of Putting People First: A Whole System Approach to Eligibility for Social Care (2010)* is that there is an obvious distinction between what people need and what the authorities are prepared to do to meet that need.' [emphasis added].

The current Guidance, and commentary upon it, follows below.

Determining eligibility

3.6   At para 47, the Guidance defines its terms as follows. It states that 'the issues and support needs that are identified when individuals approach, or are referred to, councils seeking social care support are defined as '**presenting needs**'. Those presenting needs for which a council will provide help because they fall within the council's eligibility criteria, are defined as '**eligible needs**'. It continues (at para 52) to state that 'Once eligible needs are identified, councils should take steps to meet those needs in a way that supports the individual's aspirations and outcomes that they want to achieve'. The eligibility framework is set out in four bands, which are familiar.

Eligibility Framework

54. The eligibility framework is graded into four bands, which describe the seriousness of the risk to independence and well-being or other consequences if needs are not addressed. The four bands are as follows:

Critical – when

- life is, or will be, threatened; and/or
- significant health problems have developed or will develop; and/or
- there is, or will be, little or no choice and control over vital aspects of the immediate environment; and/or
- serious abuse or neglect has occurred or will occur; and/or
- there is, or will be, an inability to carry out vital personal care or domestic routines; and/or
- vital involvement in work, education or learning cannot or will not be sustained; and/or
- vital social support systems and relationships cannot or will not be sustained; and/or
- vital family and other social roles and responsibilities cannot or will not be undertaken.

Substantial – when

- there is, or will be, only partial choice and control over the immediate environment; and/or
- abuse or neglect has occurred or will occur; and/or

- there is, or will be, an inability to carry out the majority of personal care or domestic routines; and/or
- involvement in many aspects of work, education or learning cannot or will not be sustained; and/or
- the majority of social support systems and relationships cannot or will not be sustained; and/or
- the majority of family and other social roles and responsibilities cannot or will not be undertaken.

Moderate – when

- there is, or will be, an inability to carry out several personal care or domestic routines; and/or
- involvement in several aspects of work, education or learning cannot or will not be sustained; and/or
- several social support systems and relationships cannot or will not be sustained; and/or
- several family and other social roles and responsibilities cannot or will not be undertaken.

Low – when

- there is, or will be, an inability to carry out one or two personal care or domestic routines; and/or
- involvement in one or two aspects of work, education or learning cannot or will not be sustained; and/or
- one or two social support systems and relationships cannot or will not sustained; and/or
- one or two family and other social roles and responsibilities cannot or will not be undertaken.

3.7   The general tenor of the Guidance is to encourage autonomy and independence and control and choice on the part of the user of services. There has been a substantial amount of litigation arising out of the attempts by Local Authorities to restrict themselves to applying only certain bands. The most recent of these is *R (on the application of JM and NT) v Isle of Wight Council* [2011] EWHC 2911 (Admin). This contains a summary of all the law in this area (all of which is referred to elsewhere in this book at various points when considering the eligible needs of community care services for adults). In the *Wight* case, the claim turned in part of s 49A of the Disability Discrimination Act 1995 (but newer cases have considered the same issues arising out of s 149 of the Equality Act 2010). In short, in this particular case, the Council were held to have acted unlawfully by failing to carry out an adequate impact assessment in terms of the DDA, and that so its decision to restrict services only to the critical band was quashed. Mrs Justice Land refers to the helpful summary of the legislative framework to be found in *R v McDonald v Kensington and Chelsea RLBC* (at **3.46** et seq below) and for the law on needs and resources (at **3.37–3.45** and **4.7–4.8**), as well as the specific case law on restricting services to particular bandings (eg at **3.64**). In *Chavda v Harrow* [2007] EWHC 3064, for example, a decision to limit the eligibility criteria to 'critical' only was also quashed, whereas in *JG and MB v Lancashire County Council* [2011] EWHC 2295 (Admin), a decision to limit eligibility criteria to substantial and critical needs was lawful in that the Council had not made a final decision to cut funding, and would not do so until an equality impact assessment had taken place. In *R (on the application of W, M and others) v Birmingham CC* [2011] EWHC 1147 (Admin) there had been an unlawful decision, as the Council had not taken into account the provisions of the Equality Act 2010 (at **3.64–3.65**).

Resources and assessment to pay

3.8   The Guidance observes:

> '68 Decisions as to who gets local authority support should be made **after** an assessment ...
>
> 71 Once an individual's needs, and those of their carer(s) where appropriate, have been assessed and a decision made about the support to be provided, an assessment of the individual's ability to pay charges should be carried out promptly, and written information about any charges or contributions payable, and how they have been calculated, should be communicated to the individual. This means that once a person has been identified as having an eligible need, councils should take steps to ensure those needs are met, regardless of the person's ability to contribute to the cost of those services. An assessment of the person's ability to pay for services should therefore only take place after they have been assessed as having eligible needs.'

3.9   There is separate Guidance (issued pursuant to s 7 of the Local Authority Social Services Act 1970) *Fairer Charging Policies for Home Care and other Non-Residential Services – Guidance for Councils with Social Services Responsibilities* which was issued in September 2003. Greater consideration is given to this Guidance in Chapter 7, but the service for which charges may be made are meals at home, or in day care, day care, domestic help, personal home care, and 'other support from social services eg transport, equipment and housing adaptations not provided through Disabled Facilities Grants'. Close reading of this Guidance is required in order that those in receipt of services are not charged unlawfully for those services. An example of an error of a similar nature can be found in *R (on the application of B) v Cornwall County Council and the Brandon Trust* [2009] EWHC 491 (Admin), [2009] 12 CCLR 381. The local authority (in respect of a service user whose needs had hitherto been met by an NHS Trust) had initially assessed his contribution to pay for services as nil (having taken into account his disability related expenditure). This assessment did involve his parents, but a subsequent assessment did not, and erroneously concluded that he should make a contribution. An application for judicial review succeeded upon the basis that: (a) there had been a failure to consult with parents; (b) it had fettered its own discretion in determining that certain matters could never be regarded as disability related expenditure; and

(c) had abrogated its duty to make a lawful assessment of his eligible needs. The failure to consult, of course, was linked to the Community Care Assessment Directions 2004.

3.10   Should a local authority be in the position to offer personal budgets, then it will have to do so in accordance with yet further Guidance (also issued pursuant to s 7 of the Local Authority Social Services Act 1970) *Fairer Contributions Guidance 2010 – Calculating an Individual's Contribution to their Personal Budget'* (November 2010). This is also considered in Chapter 7.

The assessment process

3.11   The Guidance warns 'Councils should, however, be aware of the risks of screening people out of the assessment process before sufficient information is known about them. Removing people from the process too early could have a significant impact upon their well being as well as potential economic costs, as it may well lead to them re-entering the system at a later date with a higher level of need' (para 76).

3.12   It also reminds local authorities of its obligation to consult the person being assessed (together with carers, where appropriate) and in accordance generally with the Community Care Assessment Directions 2004.

The Community Care Assessment Directions 2004

The Secretary of State for Health, in exercise of the powers conferred on him by section 47(4) of the National Health Service and Community Care Act 1990 hereby makes the following Directions:

Commencement, application and interpretation

1 (1) These Directions come into force on 1 September 2004 and apply to every local authority in England.

(2) In these Directions –

> "the Act" means the National Health Service and Community Care Act 1990;
> "community care services" has the same meaning as in section 46(3) of the Act;
> "local authority" has the same meaning as in section 46(3) of the Act.

Manner and form of assessment of needs for community care services

2 (1) In assessing the needs of a person under section 47(1) of the Act a local authority must comply with paragraphs (2) to (4).

(2) The local authority must consult the person, consider whether the person has any carers and, where they think it appropriate, consult those carers.

(3) The local authority must take all reasonable steps to reach agreement with the person and, where they think it appropriate, any carers of that person, on the community care services which they are considering providing to him to meet his needs.

(4) The local authority must provide information to the person and, where they think it appropriate, any carers of that person, about the amount of the payment (if any) which the person will be liable to make in respect of the community care services which they are considering providing to him.

A failure to adhere to these Directions may (but not always, as can be seen in *R (on the application of McDonald) (Appellant) v Royal London Borough of Kensington & Chelsea (Respondent)* [2011] UKSC 33) lead to a successful judicial review. In *R (on the application of W) v Croydon LBC* [2011] EWHC 696 (Admin), [2011] 14 CCLR 247 a decision was made to change the residential placement of an adult (who lacked capacity) without any form of adequate consultation. The application for judicial review was successful upon the basis of a lack of consultation.

Mental capacity

3.13 It also identifies the 'unique position of adults who lack capacity' and suggests that access to an 'independent advocate' may be appropriate in order to attempt to ensure that the individual is able to 'communicate their needs and aspirations' (para 89). This message is reinforced as follows:

> '146 Adults lacking capacity are likely to need more frequent monitoring arrangements than other service users … regulations enabling local authorities to make direct payments to adults lacking capacity came into force in November 2009. If the person lacking capacity has a direct payment or other form of personal budget, councils will wish to be satisfied that arrangements for the management of the personal budget on that person's behalf are meeting their needs and supporting the best interests of the person lacking capacity. Councils should consider involving other people known to the person lacking capacity in the review, as well as independent advocates where appropriate. The Mental Capacity Act Code of Practice specifies that Independent Mental Capacity Advocates (IMCA's) can be used in care reviews where the person concerned has no-one else to be consulted.'

Assessing the needs of carers

3.14 The statutory underpinning for the assessment of some carers is contained in the Carers (Recognition and Services) Act 1995, and the Carers and Disabled Children Act 2000. The first is considered in this Chapter, and the second in Chapter 5.

Ineligible for support

3.15 If a local authority reaches the conclusion that someone is ineligible for support, then 'the council should have satisfied itself that the person's needs would not significantly worsen or increase in the foreseeable future because of a lack of help, and thereby compromise key aspects of independence and/or well being (para 105). Furthermore, such reasons should be 'in writing, and make a written record available to the individual. Councils should tell individuals who are found ineligible for help that they should come back if their circumstances change, at which point their needs may be re-assessed' (para 106).

Withdrawal of support

3.16 The Guidance merely warns a local authority to 'exercise caution and sensitivity when considering the withdrawal of support. In some individual cases, it may not appear practicable or safe to withdraw support, even though needs may initially appear to fall outside eligibility criteria ... if, following a review, councils do withdraw support ... they should be certain that needs will not worsen or increase in the short term and the individual become eligible for help again as independence and/or well being are undermined' (para 109).

Commissioning

3.17 The Guidance provides general observations on this aspect of care services, which tends to replicate the aspirational language of the policy documents. For example, it states that:

> '114 Extending choice through personal budgets should be accompanied by commissioning strategies that put people at the centre. Services should be commissioned to more flexible, outcome-focused specifications to ensure that they are fully integrated around the needs of the individual.'

In essence, as has been the case for some time, this merely means that the duty created by s 47 may be discharged by commissioning services from a provider.

Contents of support plan

3.18 In terms of the content of a support plan, the Guidance suggests that the following should be included (para 121):

> '–   a note of the eligible needs identified during the assessment
> –   agreed outcomes and how support will be organised to meet those outcomes
> –   a risk assessment including any actions to be taken to manage identified risks
> –   contingency plans to manage emergency changes
> –   any financial contributions the individual is assessed to pay
> –   support which carers and others are willing and able to provide
> –   support to be provided to address needs identified through the carers assessment, where appropriate and
> –   a review date.'

3.19 There is no standard format for an assessment. The fault of many support plans is that they fail to address this list, or simply fail to record what is actually going to be done (or not done). Some local authorities have a 'tick box' format which appears to encourage a cursory and superficial record of the support to be provided (and thus works against the concept of 'personalisation' to which the policy and Guidance aspire). Criticism of the manner in which local authorities prepare their plans has been set out in another context (see **5.20** and **5.33–5.36**). In summary, for a plan to make sense, it must state precisely what is going to be provided, and when, and by whom, and why. Sadly, many plans fail to come anywhere near this basic standard, and are frequently riddled with jargon. None of this assists in providing proper community care services, and in many instances it will lead to litigation against the local authority. However, if an attack on the contents of a care plan was merely based upon the assertion that it failed to address each of the above, or was in a 'tick box' format as long as it nevertheless achieved the aim of providing an assessment of eligible needs, then this would not found a claim (*R (on the application of F, J, S, R) v Wirral Borough Council* [2009] EWHC 1626 (Admin), [2009] 12 CCLR 452).

3.20 The previous Guidance (FACS) stated that the *minimum* recorded contents of a care plan should include:

(a)   a note of the eligible needs and risks;

(b)   the preferred outcome in terms of service provision;

(c)   contingency plans for emergencies;

(d)   details of the services to be provided and any charges the individual has been assessed to pay, or if direct payments have been agreed;

(e)   contributions to care that might be made by carers and others;

(f)   a date upon which the plan will be reviewed.

This should be within 3 months (para 47). The review should:

(a)   establish how far the services provided have achieved the outcome set out in the original care plan;

(b)   re-assess the needs and circumstances of the service user;

(c)   help to determine the service user's continued eligibility;

(d)   confirm or amend the care plan, or its closure;

(e)   comment on the effectiveness of direct payments.

The review should involve all key individuals and agencies involved in the life of the service user. A copy of the plan should be provided to the service user, and its contents should be agreed if possible (para 58). Whilst this has now been superseded the general aims of a care plan (and a review of such a plan) are still valid.

Reviews of plans

3.21　There is no fixed date upon which a review should be carried out (other than the suggestion that those who lack capacity will require greater attention in that regard), and that 'as individual needs are likely to change over time, councils should therefore ensure that arrangements are put in place for regular reviews of support plans. The projected timing of the review should be established with the service user, and their carer(s) where appropriate, at the outset (para 141). Like initial assessments, reviews should be focused on outcomes rather than services (para 142).

3.22　The emphasis on personal involvement in devising support plans has also led to yet further Guidance being created (*Independence, choice and risk: a guide to best practice in supported decision making* (May 2007)). This is **not** issued pursuant to s 7 of the Local Authority Social Services Act 1970. It defines personalisation and care planning as:

> '2.12 systems and those working within them treat each person as an individual ...
>
> 2.13 Person-centred planning is an approach which helps to identify what is important to a person from his or her own perspective, and identifies personalised solutions.'

Personal budgets

3.23　The policy document (Putting People First) is cited as the basis for the proposition that:

> '127 envisages the availability of personal budgets for everyone eligible for publicly funded social care support. Councils should therefore support all individuals with eligible needs to draw on the benefits of self-directed support. This includes making sure people who use services and their carers understand the options available for using personal budgets, either as direct payments or as a notional budget to be held on their behalf by the council or a third party.'

In the latter case, this is likely to be in circumstances where an individual lacks capacity to manage their own finances. For the arrangements that might be made in these circumstances, refer to Chapters 2 and 6.

> '128 The way in which a personal budget might be achieved is via the exploration of "resource allocation systems" (RAS) as a way of determining how much money a person should get in their personal budget to meet their needs.
>
> 129 The aim of the RAS should be to provide a transparent system for the allocation of resources, linking money to outcomes while taking account of the

different levels of support people need to achieve their goals. It allows people to know how much money they have available to spend so that they can make choices and direct the way their support is provided.

130 **Calculating what resources should be made available to individuals should not detract from a council's duty to determine eligibility following assessment and to meet eligible needs. Rather a RAS should be applied as a means of giving an approximate indication of what it might reasonably cost to meet a person's particular needs according to their individual circumstances'** [emphasis added].

It is important that a council does not conflate the requirement for a transparent personal budget with an assessment as to what a service user might have to pay for – if it fell into this error, then it would run the risk of levying charges unlawfully.

Use of resource allocation systems

3.24   A different but related point arose in *R (on the application of Savva) v Royal Borough of Kensington & Chelsea* [2010] EWCA Civ 1209. The Court observed the role of central government (the Department of Health) was in encouraging 'local authorities to discharge the duty (s 2 CSDPA 1970) by providing a disabled person with money in the form of a personal budget, thereby enabling the person to purchase the services required to meet his or her eligible needs. This is thought to enhance personal autonomy' [2]. Mr Justice Kay then continued (by reference to provisions for the making of direct payments, which are considered in Chapter 7) to the Guidance set out above. He stated:

'[6–7] First, there is an emphasis on "transparency" in the decision making process – "clear, upfront allocation of funding", providing recipients with clarity on how decisions are made. Secondly, there is encouragement of the use of resource allocation systems (RAS). No single RAS is prescribed. Several are described. It is clear that they are not seen as being in themselves precise methods of producing a definitive personal budget in an individual case. They produce a provisional or indicative figure. Thus the Department of Health's *Guidance on Direct Payments – for Community Care, Services for Carers and Children's Services* ... states that an RAS "should **be** applied as a means of giving an approximate indication of what it may reasonably cost to meet a person's particular needs according to their individual circumstances. It is important for councils to ensure that their resource allocation process is sufficiently flexible to allow for someone's individual circumstances to be taken into account when determining the amount of resources he or she is allocated in a personal budget." It is axiomatic that local authorities do not have a bottomless pit of funds at their disposal. It is permissible for them to take account of the relative severity of the individual's needs and the availability of resources when determining whether it is necessary to make arrangements to meet an individual's needs. However, once a local authority has decided that it is necessary to make such arrangements, it has an absolute duty to provide the individual with the services or the personal budget with which to meet the assessed needs.'

On the facts in the case, there was no evidence to suggest that:

'[18] the Council ever lost sight of the fact that, once Mrs Savva's eligible needs had been assessed, it was under an absolute duty to provide her with the services that would meet those needs or a personal budget with which to purchase them.'

In short, as long as a council does not permit itself into being misled into either believing or using personal budgets to avoid its obligations and duties to fulfil the needs which have been identified, then it is permissible to adopt an approach using the Guidance, which in itself allows a number of different approaches as to how these budgets may (or may not) be used. Thus, as the law stands at the moment, it would be difficult to challenge a local authority that made a decision which included the latitude afforded to it by policy and Guidance.

3.25   In *R (on the application of Broster & Ors) v Wirral Metropolitan Borough Council and Salisbury Independent Living* [2010] EWHC 3086 (Admin), a claim for judicial review was made (in part) upon the basis that there had been a refusal to make a provision for personal budgets for a number of individuals. The judgment also includes observations upon the interaction of this area of law with the disability discrimination legislation (which is considered later in this Chapter). What Mr Justice Langstaff has to say in respect of the idea of personal budgets is of great interest. He refers in detail to paras 119, 120, and 133 of the Guidance. Paragraphs 119 and 120 are set out thus:

'119 If an individual is eligible for help then the council should work with that individual to develop a plan for their care and support. *Putting People First* sets out a vision where all people in receipt of social care support and their carers should be in control of their own lives, using personal budgets to direct the funding available to them to meet their needs in the way that suits them best. **The Care and Support Green Paper confirmed this direction of travel.** [emphasis added]

120 The success of self-directed support initiatives will therefore depend upon effective support planning. This should be person centred, exploring what is important to the individual concerned and how they can spend their personal budget to organise and create support in order to achieve their aims. In local authorities where personal budgets have not yet been implemented, choice and control should also be available to people receiving directly managed services to help identify personalised solutions to meet their outcomes. In this way a support plan will reflect the decisions made by the individual, supported by anyone they have chosen to assist them in this planning.'

He held that:

'[12] It is worth noting that the guidance which I have set out at paragraphs 119 and 120 falls short of requiring a local authority to provide a personal budget unless there are good reasons not to. This emerges from the closing sentence of section 119 which describes the move from commissioned services to personal budgets as "a direction of travel". This indicates a policy emphasis on ensuring that an individual has greater control over decisions made in respect of his or her life, including decisions which involve finance, and it is easy to see that possession of control over finance allows and individual potentially to have greater control over that which is provided for his or her benefit ... [14] the balance of the chapter in the Guidance beyond para 120 is concerned with urging local authorities to offer a greater degree of personal choice, whether in respect of a commissioned service or one provided through a personal budget, even where it involves some risk.'

3.26 The substance of the claim (to the effect that the refusal to make personal budgets available to some individuals) was found to be without justification:

'[51] The exercise of discretion in the same way in respect of a number of people at the same time is not to be confused with a blanket policy that takes no account of an makes no intentional allowance for individual circumstances. It all depends upon the context and why the discretion is exercised as it is.'

OLDER PEOPLE

3.27 There is a developing awareness of the need for separate assessment of the needs of older people. There is an overlap between this area, and the law in respect of protection of older people from abuse (or, at least, vulnerable adults from abuse, since it is more likely that older people will form a larger part of the population who may be subject to abuse). The latter is considered at greater length below.

National Service Framework for Older People (NSF)

Rationale behind NSF

3.28 In March 2001 the Department of Health produced a document entitled 'Modern Standards and Service Models – Older People – National Service Framework for Older People'. It contains 194 pages of information about the rationale behind the concern of central government in respect of an ageing population. Significantly it starts with an analysis of the statistics and concludes that:

'Between 1995 and 2025 the number of people over the age of 80 is set to increase by almost a half and the number of people over 90 will double ... in 1998/99 ... social services spent nearly 50% of their budget on the over 65s, some £5.2 billion.'

Different categories within older people

3.29 The NSF identified the following groups within the general category of those who might require assistance:

(a) black and minority ethnic communities;

(b) disabled people;

(c)   those with learning difficulties;

(d)   prisoners.

Standards within NSF

3.30   The NSF has eight 'standards'. These are:

(1)   rooting out age discrimination in respect of the provision of social care services;

(2)   the provision of 'person-centred care' which means the provision of care for their individual needs regardless of any division between health and social service boundaries (and this should include a single assessment process so that there is a coordination between the two areas);

(3)   intermediate care (to prevent admission to hospitals or early discharge from hospitals or to prevent inappropriate admission to residential care);

(4)   general hospital care (which will include a discharge plan which contains information about what social care needs might be required);

(5)   strokes;

(6)   falls;

(7)   mental health;

(8)   promotion of health and active life in older age (led by the NHS with support from councils).

Mental health in older people

3.31   Of the above standards, this is the area that is most likely to be one that involves local authorities (Chapter 1). The NSF states:

'7.9 Mental health services for older people should be community-orientated and provide seamless packages of care and support for older people and their carers ...

7.13 Older people with mental health problems are a particularly vulnerable group who may come into contact with a number of health and social care services. These agencies should have systems in place to communicate with one another, share information, to understand how and when to refer people on to appropriate services, and to review the older person's needs as changes or conditions arise ...

7.19 The NHS and local councils should work with care home providers in their areas to develop a range of services to meet the needs of older people with mental health problems, including specialist residential care places for older people with dementia.'

The statistics in relation to the latter make rather grim reading:

> '7.34 Approximately 600,000 people in the UK have dementia. This represents 5% of the total population aged 65 and over, rising to 20% of the population aged 80 and over. Dementia can also occur before the age of 65; there are about 17,000 people with dementia in younger age groups in the UK ... it is estimated that by 2026 there will be 840,000 people with dementia in the UK, rising to 1.2 million by 2025.'

3.32 These statistics may ultimately have an impact upon applications for guardianship under s 7 of the Mental Health Act 1983 (MHA 1983), for example, or indeed s 3 or under the Mental Capacity Act 2005 (MCA 2005) (see Chapters 1 and 2). The action recommended in NSF is for local authorities and the NHS to review: (a) mental health services for older people; (b) arrangements for the management of depression and dementia; (c) review arrangements for the management of dementia in younger people.

Progress of the NSF

3.33 The Department of Health (*Modernising Adult Social Care – what's working'*, 22 June 2007) refers to the 'Single Assessment Process' (SAP) that was promulgated within the NSF. There is no completed evaluation of the SAP. The early results of the evaluation (insofar as they involve local authorities) are: (a) a greater involvement by the local authority and primary care services than acute hospital sectors; and (b) dissatisfaction by service users of the care planning and delivery of services (pp 50–51). An earlier Department of Health report ('A new ambition for old age – next steps in implementing the national service framework for older people', April 2006) purports to provide information about progress. Guidance for local authorities as to the implementation of the SAP was provided in HSC 2002/001: LAC (2002) 1 (on 28 January 2002).

PARENTS WITH LEARNING DISABILITIES

3.34 This area of assessment is to a certain extent the mirror image of legislation designed to assist parents with disabled children (Chapter 5).

The Chronically Sick and Disabled Persons Act 1970

2 Provision of welfare services

(1) Where a local authority having functions under section 29 of the National Assistance Act 1948 are satisfied in the case of any person to whom that section applies who is ordinarily resident in their area that it is necessary in order to meet the needs of that person for that authority to make arrangements for all or any of the following matters, namely –

    (a)   the provision of practical assistance for that person in his home;

    (b)   the provision for that person of, or assistance to that person in obtaining, wireless, television, library or similar recreational facilities;

(c)   the provision for that person of lectures, games, outings or other recreational facilities outside his home or assistance to that person in taking advantage of educational facilities available to him;

(d)   the provision for that person of facilities for, or assistance in, travelling to and from his home for the purpose of participating in any services provided under arrangements made by the authority under the said section 29 or, with the approval of the authority, in any services provided otherwise than as aforesaid which are similar to services which could be provided under such arrangements;

(e)   the provision of assistance for that person in arranging for the carrying out of any works of adaptation in his home or the provision of any additional facilities designed to secure his greater safety, comfort or convenience;

(f)   facilitating the taking of holidays by that person, whether at holiday homes or otherwise and whether provided under arrangements made by the authority or otherwise;

(g)   the provision of meals for that person whether in his home or elsewhere;

(h)   the provision for that person of, or assistance to that person in obtaining, a telephone and any special equipment necessary to enable him to use a telephone,

then ... subject ... to the provisions of section 7(1) of the Local Authority Social Services Act 1970 (which requires local authorities in the exercise of certain functions, including functions under the said section 29, to act under the general guidance of the Secretary of State) and to the provisions of section 7A of that Act (which requires local authorities to exercise their social services functions in accordance with directions given by the Secretary of State), it shall be the duty of that authority to make those arrangements in exercise of their functions under the said section 29.

(2) ...

28A Application of Act to authorities having functions under the Children Act 1989

This Act applies with respect to disabled children in relation to whom a local authority have functions under Part III of the Children Act 1989 as it applies in relation to persons to whom section 29 of the National Assistance Act 1948 applies.

Ordinary residence

3.35   The provision of services under s 2 of the Chronically Sick and Disabled Persons Act 1970 (CSDPA 1970) will only be to those service users who are ordinarily resident within the jurisdiction of the relevant local authority. The concept of ordinary residence is identical to that of the National Assistance Act 1948 (NAA 1948). There is no facility for deciding the matter by way of a reference to the Secretary of State however (as there is if there is a dispute arising out of ordinary residence pursuant to NAA 1948 falls to be considered via s 32(3)) together with the *Ordinary Residence Disputes (National Assistance Act 1948) Directions* which must be followed in providing the information to the Secretary of State for the purposes of his adjudication. Thus, if there is a dispute, then it will be decided by the Court, based on the facts, and in accordance with the assistance of the case-law as to ordinary residence (*R v Kent CC and Salisbury and Pierre* [2000] 3 CCLR 38).

Ordinary residence and children

3.36 The concept of ordinary residence and children (which is relevant because of s 28A) is a different one than that which applies to adults. This makes reference to Part III of the Children Act 1989 only (ie ss 17 and 20, in this context). A different test again is applied if there is an issue arising under Part IV of the Act. The test in respect of both s 17 and s 20 (children in need, and accommodation, respectively) refers to children 'within their area'. Unfortunately, the same section of the statute (ss 20(2), 21(3), 29(7), 29(9)) places financial responsibility for accommodation upon the local authority where the child is 'ordinarily resident'. In terms of the expression 'within their area' it has been held that this simply means physical presence (which will in turn be a matter of fact) (*R (on the application of Stewart) v Wandsworth LBC, Hammersmith and Fulham LBC and Lambeth LBC* [2001] EWHC 709 (Admin), [2001] 4 CCLR 446 and *R (on the application of M) v Barking and Dagenham LBC and Westminster LBC* [2002] EWHC 2663 (Admin), [2003] 6 CCLR 68). It should also be noted that there is a provision (at s 20(2) of the Children Act 1989) for local authorities to take over provision of responsibilities as between each others' jurisdiction. The law in respect of care leavers has been simplified by the Children (Leaving Care) Act 2000 (which is considered in more detail in Chapter 5, at **5.9** and **5.28**). Unless there is a dispute as to ordinary residence for the purpose of designation for a care order (pursuant to Part IV of the Children Act 1989) in which case a different test again applies, the issue of ordinary residence will be determined in accordance with the common law. In broad terms, where a child is concerned, this will be decided in accordance with the ordinary residence of his parents. If there is no resolution, then s 30(2) of the Children Act 1989 may be used, which is similar to s 32(3) of NAA 1948.

Needs

3.37 The statute refers back to s 29 of NAA 1948, but the expression 'necessary in order to meet the needs of that person for that authority to make arrangements' has given rise to a plethora of litigation, the most well-known of which is *R v Gloucestershire County Council ex parte Barry* [1997] 1 CCLR 40, [1997] 2 WLR 459, HL. Although this is the leading case on the matter, and should be definitive and well understood, the concepts that it considers are still causing difficulties for those who carry out an assessment of the needs. It is therefore worth looking at in some detail. It should also be noted that the principles established have consequences for assessments in respect of other statutes (for example, the National Health Service and Community Care Act 1990). The principal debate was to what extent (if any) a local authority can take into account the resources that are available to it when deciding whether or not to provide for the needs of an individual who came within the scope of the statute. The facts of the case itself are unremarkable and quotidian. A disabled man had been assessed as needing assistance at home. This included cleaning and laundry services. The local authority withdrew the services, citing a lack of financial resources as the reason for cessation of the services.

Relevance of resources in considering needs

3.38 The majority decision in *Barry* (Lord Nicholls, Lord Clyde and Lord Hoffmann) held that a local authority was entitled to have regard to costs and resources when deciding what services should be provided. The question was framed by Lord Nicholls thus: 'Can a Local Authority properly take into account its own financial resources when assessing the needs of a disabled person under section 2(1)?' [49B–49C]. It should be noted that it is lawful for a local authority to have waiting lists for assessments in the first place, as long as the delay is not excessive.

3.39 The answer provided was 'needs for services cannot sensibly be assessed without having some regard to the cost of providing them. A person's need for a particular type or level of service cannot be decided in a vacuum from which all considerations of cost have been expelled' [49E–49F]. The individual who will make the decision as to a judgment of needs will be a social worker, who in turn will use criteria that have been established by the local authority (via its social services committee). The local authority should have regard to the cost of providing the service:

> '[50A–50B] The relative cost will be balanced against the relative benefit and the relative need for that benefit.'

However:

> '[50C–50D] Once it is accepted ... that cost is a relevant factor in assessing a person's needs for the services listed in Section 2(1), then in deciding how much weight is to be attached to cost some evaluation or assumption has to be made about the impact which the cost will have upon the authority ... [50G–50H] A local authority must carry out its functions under Section 2(1) in a responsible fashion. In the event of a local authority acting with Wednesbury unreasonableness, a disabled person would have a remedy ... [50I–50J] when assessing needs under Section 2(1) a local authority may take its resources into account.'

Lord Clyde held:

> '[55B–55D] In the framing of the criteria to be applied it seems to me that the severity of a condition may have to be matched against the availability of resources. Such an exercise indeed accords with everyday domestic experience in relation to things that we do not have. If my resources are limited I have to need the thing very much before I am satisfied that it is necessary to purchase it ... [55D] It is not necessary to hold that cost and resources are always an element in determining necessity. It is enough for the purposes of the present case to recognise that they may be a proper consideration.'

As a consequence of this (and other judgments) Local Authorities Social Services Letter (97) 13 was issued by the Department of Health on 11 December 1997 (LASSL (97) 13). It states:

'... the judgment does not give authorities a licence to take decisions on the basis of resources alone. Authorities must still take account of all other relevant factors. Pressure on resources cannot be used as an excuse for taking arbitrary or unreasonable decisions. In particular it was confirmed in the course of the judicial review cases that an authority cannot arbitrarily change the services which it is arranging for a disabled person merely because its own resource position has changed. It needs to reconsider what needs it will meet (ie what its eligibility criteria will be) and re-assess the individual against those redcfiued needs – nor does the judgment mean that local authorities are not under any duty towards disabled people. Once a local authority has decided that it is necessary, in order to meet the needs of a disabled person, for it to arrange a service listed in section 2, then it is under a duty to arrange it.'

This letter fits almost seamlessly into the analysis of Lord Browne-Wilkinson as set out below in the case of *Tandy*.

3.40   The decision in *Barry* was re-considered in *R v East Sussex County Council ex parte Tandy* [1998] 2 All ER 769; *Re T (A Minor)* [1998] 1 CCLR 352. Specifically, it referred to the dicta of Lord Nicholls (as referred to above). Lord Browne-Wilkinson noted the difference between the two statutes under consideration as well as the similarity (the issue in *Tandy* related to education) and stated that the similarity was 'the extent to which a local authority can take account of its lack of resources in carrying out a statutory duty' [359F].

3.41   Lord Browne-Wilkinson drew attention to the dicta of Lord Clyde thus:

'[359H–359I] He apparently accepted that the local authority's resources were not relevant to deciding what were the needs of the applicant but held that they were relevant to the decision whether it was "necessary" to make arrangements to meet those needs: he accepted that there might be in one sense "unmet needs" if the local authority decided, in the light of its financial circumstances, that there was no necessity to meet those needs.'

In other words, it was only at the stage where the provision of services was to be decided that the issue of resources might be relevant. At the stage where the needs were judged, resources were not relevant.

3.42   Although Lord Browne-Wilkinson specifically stated that *Barry* did not affect the decision in *Tandy* he held in respect of the matter of resources as follows:

'[360E–360I] The argument is not one of insufficient resources to discharge the duty but of a preference for using the money for other purposes. To permit a local authority to avoid performing a statutory duty on the ground that it prefers to spend the money in other ways is to downgrade a statutory duty to a discretionary power. A similar argument was put forward in the *Barry* case but dismissed by

Lord Nicholls ... on the ground that the complainant could control the failure of a local authority to carry out its statutory duty by showing that it was acting in a way which was Wednesbury unreasonable in failing to allocate the necessary resources. But with respect this is a very doubtful form of protection. Once the reasonableness of the actions of a local authority depends upon its decision how to apply scarce financial resources, the local authority's decision becomes extremely difficult to review. The court cannot second guess the local authority in the way in which it spends its limited resources ... Parliament has chosen to impose a statutory duty, as opposed to a power, requiring the local authority to do certain things. In my judgment the courts should be slow to downgrade such duties into what are, in effect, mere discretions over which the court would have very little real control.'

3.43   The judgment of Lord Clyde was also cited with approval in *R v South Lanarkshire County Council ex p MacGregor* (Court of Session, Outer House) [2001] 4 CCLR 188. An elderly man had been assessed as requiring nursing care to meet his needs. This was not provided due to a shortage of funds. It was held that when assessing needs, resources were irrelevant. When deciding what provision was to be made, resources were relevant, but the local authority had to act – it could not simply state that resources were inadequate and then do nothing. Lord Hardie cited Lord Clyde with approval thus:

'[194G–194H] The right given to a person by section 2(1) of the Act of 1970 was a right to have the arrangements made by which the local authority was satisfied were necessary to meet his needs. The duty only arises if or when the local authority is so satisfied. But when it does arise then it is clear that a shortage of resources will not excuse a failure in the performance of the duty.'

3.44   To a certain extent, the judgment of Lord Browne-Wilkinson is similar to the dissenting judgment of Lord Lloyd of Berwick in *Barry*. He held that:

'[43E–43F] This section contemplates three separate stages. The Council must first assess the individual needs of each person to whom section 29 of the Act of 1948 applies. Having identified those needs, the council must then decide whether it is necessary to make arrangements to meet those needs ... [43G] if there is no other way of meeting the individual's needs, as assessed, and the Council are therefore satisfied that it is necessary for them to make arrangements to meet those needs, then the Council are under a duty to make those arrangements ... [44F–44G] in other words, the Council cannot escape their duty to make arrangements to meet the need by saying that they do not have the money [43H–43I] ... resources can, of course, operate to impose a cash limit on what is provided. But how can resources help to measure the need?'

3.45   For the avoidance of doubt, Lord Lloyd of Berwick also highlighted the difference between s 29 of NAA 1948 (which confers a mere power on local authorities to promote the welfare of the blind, deaf or dumb and other persons who are substantially and permanently handicapped by illness, injury, congenital deformities or other disabilities) and the Chronically Sick and Disabled Persons Act 1970 which imposed a positive duty for such provision:

'[46A–46B] It seems plain enough that the legislative purpose behind sections 1 and 2 was to impose a duty towards the disabled where hitherto there had been no more than a power.'

3.46 To this line of reasoning must be added *R (on the application of McDonald) (Appellant) v Royal Borough of Kensington and Chelsea (Respondent)* [2011] UKSC 33, [2011] 14 CCLR 341 (from which extracts of the dissenting judgment of Baroness Hale are provided at the beginning of this Chapter for an analysis of the law and the historical background to the entire debate). On the simple but stark facts of the case, the Court was deliberating whether it was lawful for the local authority to substitute incontinence pads for a night-time carer (the former being the cheaper option). The night-time carer had assisted the Appellant to use a commode. Without such assistance, she would be unable to use a commode, and would be obliged to use incontinence pads. She argued not only that this was unlawful but also that it breached her rights pursuant to Art 8, and also s 21E of the Disability Discrimination Act 1995, as inserted by s 2 of the Disability Discrimination Act 2005. The Court also considered the interrelationship between the National Health Service and Community Care Act 1990, s 29(1) of the National Assistance Act 1948, and the Chronically Sick and Disabled Persons Act 1970. It was also obliged to consider FACS (and the Guidance now in existence) together with the Community Care Assessment Directions 2004.

3.47 The criticism of the assessment(s) that had taken place was that a later assessment had concluded that assistance to use a commode during the night was no longer a 'need', but merely what she wanted. The 'need' was for management of nocturnal toileting. That 'need' could be met by the use of incontinence pads (even though Ms McDonald was not incontinent). The suggestion that Ms McDonald had not been involved in the production of the care plan was dismissed (the council had on the facts complied with the Community Care Assessment Directions). The Art 8 claim was also dismissed as there was no 'direct and immediate link between the measures sought by an applicant and the latter's private life – *Botta v Italy* (1998) 26 EHRR 241 paras 34 and 35 and [no] special link between the situation complained of and the particular needs of the [applicant's] private life': *Sentges v The Netherlands* (2003) 6 CCLR 400, 405 [15].

3.48 Although repealed, the relevant sections of the Disability Discrimination Act are set out below, in this Chapter, at **3.64** as they are still required to make sense of the continuing debate in this area of law. The arguments in respect of ss 21 and 21D(5) were described as 'hopeless' [22]. Lord Brown stated:

'[22] In the first place I find it impossible to regard the respondents' decision in this case as the manifestation or application of anything that can properly be characterised as a "practice, policy or procedure" within the meaning of the legislation. Rather, in taking the impugned decision, the respondents were doing no more and no less than their statutory duty ... even if that were not so , it follows from all that I have said (not least with respect to Article 8(2)) that the respondents' acts here must be regarded as constituting 'a proportionate means of achieving a legitimate aim' within the meaning of section 21D(5).'

3.49 In respect of s 49A, Lord Brown also described this argument as 'hopeless' [24] and that:

> '[24] Where, as here, the person concerned is ex-hypothesi disabled and the public authority is discharging its functions under statutes which expressly direct their attention to the needs of disabled persons, it may be entirely superfluous to make express reference to section 49A and absurd to infer from an omission to do so a failure on the authority's part to have regard to their general duty under that section. That, I am satisfied, is the position here. The question is one of substance, not of form. This case is wholly unlike *Pieretti v Enfield London Borough Council* [2010] EWCA Civ 1104 (which held that the section 49A duty complements a housing authority's duty to the homeless under Part 7 of the Housing Act 1996).'

The relevant sections of the Disability Discrimination Act 'have now been superseded by broadly comparable provisions in the Equality Act 2010' [25].

CHRONICALLY SICK AND DISABLED PERSONS ACT 1970, S 1

Assessments

3.50 Local authorities can, of course, review the needs of individuals (and indeed in most circumstances are obliged so to do). Difficulties may arise where such re-assessments are flawed by way of reference to an erroneous reliance on previous assessments. In *R v Haringey LBC ex p Norton* [1998] 1 CCLR 168 the Court considered this issue as well as resources versus needs. On the facts in the case, the local authority had funded the provision of substantial support of a disabled man (24 hours per day). It then altered its position to one whereby it asserted that the assessment of needs indicated only 5 hours per day practical assistance, together with various other provision. It based its decision to reduce provision on lack of resources. In effect, the local authority was held to have acted unlawfully in that it failed to give appropriate weight to the original assessment (for 24-hour support) which demonstrated that 24-hour care had been desirable and at reasonable cost, and that it had carried out its subsequent assessment which put social, recreational and leisure needs to one side, and did not follow the guidance in *The Care and Management Assessment: A Practitioner's Guide* and in particular para 16, which reflects the true effect of the statute. This reads:

> 'Need is a multi-faceted concept which, for the purpose of this guidance, is sub-divided into six broad categories, each of which should be covered in a comprehensive assessment of need: personal/social care; health care; accommodation; finance; education/employment/leisure; transport/access.'

The case also explored the extent to which it is permissible for a local authority to attempt to admit affidavit evidence to supplement, amend or impugn assessments that were being challenged (*R v Westminster CC ex parte Ermakov* [1996] 2 All ER 302).

3.51 Flaws in assessments themselves will be of limited relevance where a local authority has conceded that it ought to provide the service requested, but has not done so due to shortage of physical resources (*R v Lambeth LBC ex p A1 and A2* [1998] 1 CCLR 336). In *R (on the Application of Heffernan) v Sheffield CC* [2004] EWHC 1377 (Admin), [2004] 7 CCLR 350, a local authority was obliged to provide services (pursuant to s 29 of the NAA 1948 and the CSDPA 1970), and as a result of its assessment provided those services. A challenge was made to the provision, based in part upon a privately commissioned report which concluded that greater provision was required, and in part upon an alleged failure to adhere to the procedure and guidance contained in *Fair Access to Care Services* (Circular LAC (2002) 13). The judgment considered the eligibility framework (critical, substantial, moderate, low) and confirmed that resources could be taken into account in determining which of the four bands to fund. The manner in which the eligibility criteria had been applied on the facts in this specific case led to it being held that the care plan should be reconsidered, but was not in itself perverse. Mr Justice Collins concluded:

> '[360D–360E] I appreciate that this judgment may not be regarded as particularly helpful to either party, but this court is not the best tribunal to decide what are essentially issues of judgment based on a factual assessment. In all the circumstances, I am not prepared to say that the Care Plan is perverse, albeit I think that it must be reconsidered.'

3.52 A claim framed in tort against a local authority for failure to deliver equipment once an assessment had been carried out (within a reasonable time) failed, on the basis that there arose no private law right of action arising out of either s 29 of the National Assistance Act 1948 or s 2 of the Chronically Sick and Disabled Persons Act 1970 (*Sandford and Scherer v Waltham Forest LBC* [2008] EWHC 1106 (QB), [2008] 11 CCLR 480. It is interesting to note that this case was decided on 21 May 2008, and that *AK v Central and North West London Mental Health NHS Trust and Royal London Borough of Kensington and Chelsea* [2008] EWHC 1217 (QB), [2008] 11 CCLR 543 (see Chapter 1) was decided on 30 May 2008, and yet reached the opposite conclusion, albeit in respect of s 117 of the Mental Health Act 1983.

DISABLED CHILDREN

3.53 The implications for s 28A are considered in Chapter 5.

Disabled Persons (Services, Consultation and Representation) Act 1986

3.54 One of the predictable paradoxes involved in the duties that a local authority has towards disabled adults is that the very section of the community towards which the legislation is aimed may be unable to access the relevant information. To this end, a number of statutes have been enacted that attempt to remedy the problem. The first was the Disabled Persons (Services, Consultation and Representation) Act 1986. In essence, it provides that a disabled person may either appoint someone as his representative, or have someone appointed as his representative. The purpose of such an appointment (in broad terms) is to ensure access to information, and a degree of representation. It is also supplemented by Circular No 87 (6) (March 1987). The ratio of Baroness Hale in respect of s 4 of the Act (cited above) are also of assistance in understanding the continuing significance of the statute.

Disabled Persons (Services, Consultation and Representation) Act 1986

1 Appointment of authorised representatives of disabled persons

(1) In this Act "authorised representative", in relation to a disabled person, means a person for the time being appointed by or on behalf of that disabled person (in accordance with regulations made under this section) to act as his authorised representative for the purposes of this Act.

(2) The Secretary of State may by regulations make provision with respect to the appointment of persons to act as the authorised representatives of disabled persons, including provision –

    (a)   for the manner in which the appointment of a person as an authorised representative is to be made; and

    (b)   for any such appointment to be notified to the relevant local authority (as defined in the regulations) if made otherwise than by that authority.

(3) Any such regulations –

    (a)   may provide for –
        (i)   the parent of a disabled person under the age of sixteen, or
        (ii)   any other person who is not a parent of his but who has parental responsibility for him

to appoint himself or some other person as the authorised representative of the disabled person (but shall not permit a person under that age himself to appoint a person as his authorised representative);

    (b)   may provide for the appointment of a person as the authorised representative of a disabled person who is a child looked after by a local authority to be made by that authority in such circumstances as may be specified in the regulations;

    (c)   may, in accordance with subsection (4), provide for the appointment of a person as the authorised representative of a disabled person to be made by, or under arrangements made by, a local authority in a case where the disabled person appears to the authority to be unable to appoint a person as his authorised representative by reason of any mental or physical incapacity;

(d)   may contain such incidental or supplementary provisions as the Secretary of State thinks fit.

(4) Regulations under paragraph (c) of subsection (3) may make provision –

(a)   for requiring a local authority, for the purpose of enabling them to determine whether a disabled person is unable to appoint a person as his authorised representative as mentioned in that paragraph, to obtain the opinion of a registered medical practitioner;

(b)   for authorising a local authority, where they determine that a disabled person is so unable, either –

(i)   themselves to appoint a person as the disabled person's authorised representative, or

(ii)   to make with any voluntary organisation, person or persons approved by them for the purpose such arrangements as they think fit for such an appointment to be made by the organisation, person or persons concerned;

(c)   for requiring or authorising a local authority, before determining the question specified in paragraph (a), or (as the case may be) before making any appointment of an authorised representative, or any arrangements, in pursuance of paragraph (b), to consult any of the following, namely –

(i)   a person or persons appointed by them for the purpose, or

(ii)   a person or persons falling within any class or description specified in the regulations;

(d)   for requiring a local authority, in such circumstances as may be specified in the regulations, to review the case of a disabled person whose authorised representative has been appointed in pursuance of paragraph (b) (whether by the local authority or under any arrangements made by them) for the purpose of determining whether he is still unable to appoint a person as his authorised representative as mentioned in subsection (3)(c).

(5) Subsections (2) to (4) shall apply, with any necessary modifications, in relation to the termination of the appointment of a person as an authorised representative as they apply in relation to the making of such an appointment.

(6) It is hereby declared that any person exercising under Part II of the 1983 Act or Parts 5, 6 and 7 of the 2003 Act –

(a)   the functions of the nearest relative of a disabled person, or

(b)   the functions of the guardian of a disabled person received into guardianship under that Part of that Act,

may, if appointed as such in accordance with this section, also act as that person's authorised representative.

2 Rights of authorised representatives of disabled persons

(1) A local authority shall permit the authorised representative of a disabled person, if so requested by the disabled person –

(a)   to act as the representative of the disabled person in connection with the provision by the authority of any services for him in the exercise of any of their functions under the welfare enactments, or

(b)   to accompany the disabled person (otherwise than as his representative) to any meeting or interview held by or on behalf of the authority in connection with the provision by them of any such services.

(2) For the purpose of assisting the authorised representative of a disabled person to do any of the things mentioned in subsection (1)(a) and (b) a local authority shall, if so requested by the disabled person –

(a)   supply to the authorised representative any information, and

(b)   make available for his inspection any documents,

that the disabled person would be entitled to require the authority to supply to him or (as the case may be) to make available for his inspection.

(3) In relation to a disabled person whose authorised representative has been appointed by virtue of subsection (3) of section 1, subsections (1) and (2) above shall each have effect as follows –

(a)   if the appointment was made by virtue of subsection (3)(a) of that section, for the words "if so requested by the disabled person" there shall be substituted "if so requested by any person mentioned in section 1(3)(a)(i) or (ii)"; and

(b)   if the appointment was made by virtue of subsection (3)(b) or (c) of that section, the words "if so requested by the disabled person" shall be omitted.

(4) A local authority shall not be required by virtue of subsection (1) or (2) –

(a)   to permit an authorised representative to be present at any meeting or interview or part of a meeting or interview, or

(b)   to supply any information to an authorised representative or to make any documents available for the inspection of an authorised representative,

if the authority are satisfied that to do so would be likely to be harmful to the interests of the disabled person by whom or on whose behalf the representative has been appointed; and in determining that matter the authority shall have regard to any wishes expressed by the disabled person.

(5) Where a disabled person is residing –

(a)   in hospital accommodation provided by the Welsh Ministers under section 3(1)(a) of the National Health Service (Wales) Act 2006, by the Secretary of State under section 3(1)(a) of the National Health Service Act 2006, by a Primary Care Trust established under that Act, by a National Health Service Trust established under that Act or the National Health Service (Wales) Act 2006 or by an NHS foundation trust or, in Scotland, in hospital accommodation (other than accommodation at a State hospital) provided by the Secretary of State under section 36(1)(a) of the 1978 Act or by a National Health Service trust established under that Act, or

(b)   in accommodation provided by a local authority under Part III of the 1948 Act or Schedule 8 to the 1977 Act or, in Scotland, under Part IV of the 1968 Act or section 25 of the 2003 Act, or (bb) in accommodation provided by or on behalf of a local authority under Part III of the Children Act 1989, or

(bc) in Scotland, in accommodation provided by or on behalf of a local authority under Chapter 1 of Part II of the Children (Scotland) Act 1995, or

(c) in accommodation provided by a voluntary organisation or other person in accordance with arrangements made by a local authority under section 26 of the 1948 Act or, in Scotland, provided by a voluntary organisation or other persons in accordance with arrangements made by a local authority under section 59(2)(c) of the 1968 Act, or

(cc) in accommodation provided by a voluntary organisation or other person in accordance with arrangements made by a local authority under section 17 of the Children Act 1989, or

(d) in a care home within the meaning of the Care Standards Act 2000 or, in Scotland, provided by a care home service within the meaning of the Regulation of Care (Scotland) Act 2001 (asp 8), or

(dd) in accommodation provided by any educational establishment,

(e) at any place specified by a person having the guardianship of the disabled person under Part II of the 1983 Act or Parts 5, 6 and 7 of the 2003 Act,

the disabled person's authorised representative may at any reasonable time visit him there and interview him in private.

(6) In paragraph (c) of subsection (5) "voluntary organisation" in relation to England and Wales includes a housing association within the meaning of the Housing Associations Act 1985.

(7) The Secretary of State may, after consulting such bodies representing health authorities or local authorities as appear to him to be appropriate and such other bodies as appear to him to be concerned, provide by order for any of the preceding provisions of this section to have effect (with such modifications as may be prescribed by the order) in relation to –

(a) the provision of services by health authorities in the exercise of such of their functions under the 2006 Act or the National Health Service (Wales) Act 2006 or the 1978 Act as may be prescribed by the order, or

(b) the provisions of services by local authorities in the exercise of such of their functions as may be so prescribed.

(8) An order under subsection (7) may provide for any provision of regulations made under section 1 to have effect for the purposes of the order with such modifications as may be prescribed by the order, and in that event the reference in subsection (1) of that section to regulations made under that section shall be read as a reference to any such regulations as they have effect in accordance with the order.

(9) In subsection (7) –

"health authority" –
(a) in relation to England, means a Strategic Health Authority, a Special Health Authority or a Primary Care Trust,

(aa) in relation to Wales, means a Local Health Board or a Special Health Authority, and

(b) in relation to Scotland, means a Health Board; and

"local authority" –

(a)   in relation to England and Wales, has the meaning given by section 270(1) of the Local Government Act 1972; and

(b)   in relation to Scotland, means a council constituted under section 2 of the Local Government etc (Scotland) Act 1994.

3 Assessment by local authorities of needs of disabled persons

(1) Where –

(a)   on any assessment carried out by them in pursuance of any provision of this Act, or

(b)   on any other occasion,

it falls to a local authority to decide whether the needs of a disabled person call for the provision by the authority (in accordance with any of the welfare enactments) of any statutory services for that person, the authority shall afford an opportunity to the disabled person or his authorised representative to make, within such reasonable period as the authority may allow for the purpose, representations to an officer of the authority as to any needs of the disabled person calling for the provision by the authority (in accordance with any of those enactments) of any statutory services for him.

(2) Where any such representations have been made to a local authority in accordance with subsection (1) or the period mentioned in that subsection has expired without any such representations being made, and the authority have reached a decision on the question referred to in that subsection (having taken into account any representations made as mentioned above), the authority shall, if so requested by the disabled person or his authorised representative, supply the person making the request with a written statement –

(a)   either specifying –

(i)   any needs of the disabled person which in the opinion of the authority call for the provision by them of any statutory services, and

(ii)   in the case of each such need, the statutory services that they propose to provide to meet that need,

or stating that, in their opinion, the disabled person has no needs calling for the provision by them of any such services; and

(b)   giving an explanation of their decision; and

(c)   containing particulars of the right of the disabled person or his authorised representative to make representations with respect to the statement under subsection (4).

(3) Where the local authority do not propose to provide any statutory services to meet a particular need identified in any representations under subsection (1), any statement supplied under subsection (2) must state that fact together with the reasons why the authority do not propose to provide any such services.

(4) If the disabled person or his authorised representative is dissatisfied with any matter included in the statement supplied under subsection (2), that person may, within such reasonable period as the authority may allow for the purpose, make representations to an officer of the authority with respect to that matter.

(5) Where any such representations have been made to the authority in accordance with subsection (4), the authority shall –

    (a)   consider (or, as the case may be, reconsider) whether any, and (if so) what, statutory services should be provided by them for the disabled person to meet any need identified in the representations; and

    (b)   inform the disabled person or his authorised representative in writing of their decision on that question and their reasons for that decision.

(6) Where –

    (a)   the disabled person or his authorised representative is unable to communicate, or (as the case may be) be communicated with, orally or in writing (or in each of those ways) by reason of any mental or physical incapacity, or

    (b)   both of those persons are in that position (whether by reason of the same incapacity or not),

the local authority shall provide such services as, in their opinion, are necessary to ensure that any such incapacity does not –

        (i)   prevent the authority from discharging their functions under this section in relation to the disabled person, or

        (ii)   prevent the making of representations under this section by or on behalf of that person.

(7) In determining whether they are required to provide any services under subsection (6) to meet any need of the disabled person or his authorised representative, and (if so) what those services should be, the local authority shall have regard to any views expressed by either of those persons as to the necessity for any such services or (as appropriate) to any views so expressed as to the services which should be so provided.

(8) In this section "representations" means representations made orally or in writing (or both).

4 Services under s 2 of the 1970 Act: duty to consider needs of disabled persons

When requested to do so by –

    (a)   a disabled person,

    (b)   his authorised representative, or

    (c)   any person who provides care for him in the circumstances mentioned in section 8,

a local authority shall decide whether the needs of the disabled person call for the provision by the authority of any services in accordance with section 2(1) of the 1970 Act (provision of welfare services).

8 Duty of local authority to take into account abilities of carer

(1) Where –

    (a)   a disabled person is living at home and receiving a substantial amount of care on a regular basis from another person (who is not a person employed to provide such care by any body in the exercise of its functions under any enactment), and

(b)   it falls to a local authority to decide whether the disabled person's needs call for the provision by them of any services for him under any of the welfare enactments,

the local authority shall, in deciding that question, have regard to the ability of that other person to continue to provide such care on a regular basis.

(2) Where that other person is unable to communicate, or (as the case may be) be communicated with, orally or in writing (or in each of those ways) by reason of any mental or physical incapacity, the local authority shall provide such services as, in their opinion, are necessary to ensure that any such incapacity does not prevent the authority from being properly informed as to the ability of that person to continue to provide care as mentioned in subsection (1).

(3) Section 3(7) shall apply for the purposes of subsection (2) above as it applies for the purposes of section 3(6), but as if any reference to the disabled person or his authorised representative were a reference to the person mentioned in subsection (2).

CIRCULAR NO (87) 6 DISABLED PERSONS (SERVICES, CONSULTATION AND REPRESENTATION) ACT 1986

Section 4: Services under section 2 of the Chronically Sick and Disabled Persons Act 1970, duty to consider needs of disabled persons

2. Section 2(1) of the CSDP Act places a duty on local authorities to 'make arrangements' for all or any of specified matters (practical assistance in the home, recreational facilities, holidays, telephones etc) in the case of any disabled person who is ordinarily resident in their area where they are satisfied that this is necessary in order to meet the needs of that person.

3. However, Section 2(1) does not make it explicit whether a local authority has a duty to determine the needs of a disabled person. It was suggested in the course of debates in Parliament on the Disabled Persons (Services, Consultation and Representation) Bill that as the duty to 'make arrangements' could be interpreted as applying only after the local authority are satisfied that such arrangements are necessary in order to meet particular needs, local authorities might refuse to 'come to a view as to what those needs as a means avoiding the obligation to make arrangements'. It has never been the Government's view that Subsection 2(1) should be interpreted in that way, and it is clear that this is shared by the vast majority of local authorities. However, it was agreed that the matter should be put beyond doubt.

4. Section 4 of the 1986 Act accordingly makes it clear that local authorities have a duty to decide whether the needs of a disabled person call for the provision of services under section 2 of the 1970 Act, of they are requested to do so by a disabled person (Section 4(a)) or by anyone who provides care for him or her (Section 4(c)) in the circumstances mentioned in section 8 of the 1986 Act.

Section 8(1): Duty of the local authority to take into account the ability of the carer

5. Section 8(1) has effect where a disabled person is living at home, and is receiving a substantial amount of care on a regular basis from another person (other than a person employed to provide such care by any body by virtue of its statutory functions). In these circumstances, where it falls to a local authority to decide whether the disabled person's needs call for the provision of them of any services under the 'welfare enactments' (defined in Section 16 of the 1986 Act as Part III of the National Assistance Act 1948, section 2 of the CSDP Act 1970 or Schedule 8 to the National Health Services Act 1977), the authority is required in deciding that question, to have regard to the ability of the 'carer' to continue to provide such care on a regular basis.

6. Although the section places no specific requirement on the local authority to provide services or support for the carer, authorities will no doubt continue as part of normal good practice to have regard to the possible need for such services and to the desirability of enabling the disabled person to continue living at home for as long as possible if this is what he or she wishes to do.

Section 9: Information about services

7. Section 1(2)(b) of the 1970 CSDP Act requires local authority social services authorities to ensure that a disabled person who uses any welfare services is informed of any other of these services considered by the authority to be relevant to his needs. Section 9 of the 1986 Act extends the provisions of the 1970 Act to require authorities to provide information about other services provided by the same authority and about services provided by other organisations which it considers relevant to that persons needs, if the particulars are in the local authority's possession.

Section 10: Co-option to committees, etc, of persons representing interest of disabled person

8. Various enactments provide for the appointment of co-option to councils, committees and other bodies of a person or persons with special knowledge of the needs of disabled persons. These include the provisions of section 15 of the 1970 CSDP Act which refer to the desirability of appointing to Committees persons who may be disabled or have experience of their special needs. Section 10 provides that such appointments or co-option shall be made only after consultation with such organisation or organisations of disabled persons as may be appropriate in each case.

9. [...]

3.55 The majority of the statute is fairly straightforward, and the significance of particularly ss 3 and 4 should be self-evident. Section 4 specifically refers back to s 2 of CSDPA 1970. If either a disabled person, or his authorised representative (or any person specified under s 8) fulfils the relevant criteria then this triggers a mandatory requirement for the local authority to make a decision as to whether the needs of the disabled person call for the provision of an welfare services (as listed in CSDPA 1970). A response is therefore required, and the response must be in the form set out in s 3 (which also permits representations to be made to the local authority as to the needs of the disabled person). In effect, the response must say: (a) what needs exist; (b) how they are to be met; (c) if there are no needs, then providing an explanation as to that conclusion together with reasons. Any subsequent departure from this response used as the basis for a claim for judicial review would presumably be subject to the authority of *Ermakov*. Thus, although essentially an adjectival statute, the practical consequences for enforcement are of considerable potential significance for local authorities and those wishing to have access to local authority resources. A complaint against Liverpool City Council was upheld in respect of a failure to comply with s 4 (inter alia) in that it did not respond to a request or provide a comprehensive assessment (*Investigation into Complaint No 96/C/4315 against Liverpool CC* (20.8.98) [1999] 2 CCLR 128). The Local Government Ombudsman concluded:

> 'Social Services authorities ... have a duty to assess a person with disabilities on request and decide whether that person has a need for welfare services (Section 4). If they decide that welfare services are required, then those must be provided (DHSS Circular LAC (87)(6)) ... The law (Section 4) makes clear that a request from a person with disabilities should be met by a comprehensive assessment irrespective of the scale of need initially presented. A person with disabilities is entitled to expect a request to be met within a reasonable time. Social Services authorities have a duty to ensure that staffing is sufficient to enable the duty to assess to be carried out (Local Authority Social Services Act 1970 Section 6) ... Carers who provide a substantial amount of care on a regular basis have a statutory right to be involved in the assessment process (Section 8) ... Government guidance ("Caring for People" Department of Health) states that once the user's individual needs for care have been identified the next step will be to decide what services can be provided at the public expense, in the light of the resources available to the authority and the services obtainable in the public or independent sectors ... once an assessed need has been determined the council remains under a duty to provide it.'

National Health Service and Community Care Act 1990

3.56 The extension of planning for community care services, and the obligation to assess for those services, was further extended by this statute. It has generated substantial amounts of case-law, and almost inevitably those authorities also involve consideration of all or some of the other statutes considered hitherto.

National Health Service and Community Care Act 1990

46 Local authority plans for community care services

(1) Each local authority –

    (a)   shall, within such period after the day appointed for the coming into force of this section as the Secretary of State may direct, prepare and publish a plan for the provision of community care services in their area;

(b)   shall keep the plan prepared by them under paragraph (a) above and any further plans prepared by them under this section under review; and

(c)   shall, at such intervals as the Secretary of State may direct, prepare and publish modifications to the current plan, or if the case requires, a new plan.

(2) In carrying out any of their functions under paragraphs (a) to (c) of subsection (1) above, a local authority shall consult –

(a)   any Health Authority and any Local Health Board the whole or any part of whose area lies within the area of the local authority;

(b)   ...

(c)   in so far as any proposed plan, review or modifications of a plan may affect or be affected by the provision or availability of housing and the local authority is not itself a local housing authority, within the meaning of the Housing Act 1985, every such local housing authority whose area is within the area of the local authority;

(d)   such voluntary organisations as appear to the authority to represent the interests of persons who use or are likely to use any community care services within the area of the authority or the interests of private carers who, within that area, provide care to persons for whom, in the exercise of their social services functions, the local authority have a power or a duty to provide a service;

(e)   such voluntary housing agencies and other bodies as appear to the local authority to provide housing or community care services in their area; and

(f)   such other persons as the Secretary of State may direct.

(3) In this section –

"local authority" means the council of a county, a county borough, a metropolitan district or a London borough or the Common Council of the City of London;
"community care services" means services which a local authority may provide or arrange to be provided under any of the following provisions –

(a)   Part III of the National Assistance Act 1948;
(b)   section 45 of the Health Services and Public Health Act 1968;
(c)   section 254 of, and Schedule 20 to, the National Health Service Act 2006, and section 192 of, and Schedule 15 to, the National Health Service (Wales) Act 2006; and
(d)   section 117 of the Mental Health Act 1983; and

"private carer" means a person who is not employed to provide the care in question by any body in the exercise of its functions under any enactment.

Promotion and planning of services

3.57 Section 46 ensures that a local authority will plan and publish its provision for community care services. These are defined at s 46(3). The most significant are Part III of NAA 1948 (Local Authority Services: provision of accommodation (s 21); Charges to be made for accommodation (s 22); Management of premises in which accommodation provided (s 23); Liability for provision of accommodation (s 24); Provision of accommodation in premises maintained by voluntary organisations (s 26); Welfare Services (s 29);

Adjustments between authorities providing accommodation and authority of area of residence (s 32)). It also requires the local authority to consult with various voluntary agencies and private providers of services which the local authority have a power or duty to provide (s 46(2)(d)). All of these provisions mark the augmentation of the obligation of the local authority to be proactive in promoting accessibility of its services.

47 Assessment of needs for community care services

(1) Subject to subsections (5) and (6) below, where it appears to a local authority that any person for whom they may provide or arrange for the provision of community care services may be in need of any such services, the authority –

(a)   shall carry out an assessment of his needs for those services; and

(b)   having regard to the results of that assessment, shall then decide whether his needs call for the provision by them of any such services.

(2) If at any time during the assessment of the needs of any person under subsection (1)(a) above it appears to a local authority that he is a disabled person, the authority –

(a)   shall proceed to make such a decision as to the services he requires as is mentioned in section 4 of the Disabled Persons (Services, Consultation and Representation) Act 1986 without his requesting them to do so under that section; and

(b)   shall inform him that they will be doing so and of his rights under that Act.

(3) If at any time during the assessment of the needs of any person under subsection (1)(a) above, it appears to a local authority –

(a)   that there may be a need for the provision to that person by such Primary Care Trust or Health Authority as may be determined in accordance with regulations of any services under the National Health Service Act 2006 or the National Health Service (Wales) Act 2006, or

(b)   that there may be a need for the provision to him of any services which fall within the functions of a local housing authority (within the meaning of the Housing Act 1985) which is not the local authority carrying out the assessment,

the local authority shall notify that Primary Care Trust, Health Authority or local housing authority and invite them to assist, to such extent as is reasonable in the circumstances, in the making of the assessment; and, in making their decision as to the provision of the services needed for the person in question, the local authority shall take into account any services which are likely to be made available for him by that Primary Care Trust, Health Authority or local housing authority.

(4) The Secretary of State may give directions as to the manner in which an assessment under this section is to be carried out or the form it is to take but, subject to any such directions and to subsection (7) below, it shall be carried out in such manner and take such form as the local authority consider appropriate.

(5) Nothing in this section shall prevent a local authority from temporarily providing or arranging for the provision of community care services for any person without carrying out a prior assessment of his needs in accordance with

the preceding provisions of this section if, in the opinion of the authority, the condition of that person is such that he requires those services as a matter of urgency.

(6) If, by virtue of subsection (5) above, community care services have been provided temporarily for any person as a matter of urgency, then, as soon as practicable thereafter, an assessment of his needs shall be made in accordance with the preceding provisions of this section.

(7) This section is without prejudice to section 3 of the Disabled Persons (Services, Consultation and Representation) Act 1986.

(8) In this section –

"disabled person" has the same meaning as in that Act; and
"local authority" and "community care services" have the same meanings as in section 46 above.

Mandatory provision for assessment

3.58 Section 47 takes that promotion still further. Section 47(1) imposes a mandatory duty to assess the needs of any person for whom it *appears* to a local authority that community care services may be required. In other words, a request from an individual is not actually required. Once it so appears, it is mandatory that an assessment of the needs for those services is carried out, followed by a decision as to whether his needs call for the provision of the services. Further, if the person who has come to the attention of the local authority is disabled, then s 4 of the Disabled Persons (Services, Consultation and Representation) Act 1986 is triggered, *without* the requirement for a request for such an assessment being made (s 47(2)). On 1 September 2004 the Community Care Assessment Directions 2004 came into force which added provisions to s 47(1). These are that in assessing the needs of a person, the local authority:

'(2) … must consult the person, consider whether the person has any carers and, where they think it is appropriate, consult those carers

(3) … must take all reasonable steps to reach agreement with the person and, where they think it appropriate, any carers of that person, on the community care services which they are considering providing to him to meet his needs

(4) must provide information to the person and, where they think it appropriate, any carers of that person, about the amount of payment (if any) which the person will be liable to make in respect of the community care services which they are considering providing to him.'

However, it should be noted that a local authority does not have a duty to assess upon request, but only 'where they think that the person may be in need of services they provide' (Letter C1(92) 34 (Chief Inspector, Social Services Inspectorate 14.12.92)). The same letter suggests that published criteria for identifying disabled persons, and the type and level of assessment should be made available. The definition of a disabled person remains as at s 16 of that

Act (in England and Wales, someone to whom s 29 of NAA 1948 applies, and if under 18, someone who is disabled within the meaning of Part III of the Children Act 1989). Section 47(3) triggers a referral to either the relevant healthcare providers, or housing authority, if either of these are relevant.

Assessment of parents with learning disabilities

3.59   A subset of disabled adults will be those with learning disabilities or learning difficulties, who themselves have children. Those parents themselves may be entitled to an assessment under s 47 of the Act (and/or other statutory provisions set out in this book). The children may also be subject to assessments or proceedings under the Children Act 1989. The Department of Health has published *Good Practice Guidance on Working with Parents with a Learning Disability* (April 2006 published on 1 June 2007) which is intended to assist both adult and children's services. The stated reason for the requirement for such guidance is:

> 'Children whose parents have learning disabilities and who are in contact with children's social care services have high levels of needs; there is little evidence of effective joint working between adult and children's services. Children's services practitioners, and adult learning disability workers, rarely have a good working knowledge of the policy and legislative framework within each other are working.'

3.60   In addition it states:

> '1.1.3 Few parents with learning disabilities are aware of the support they may be entitled to from adult social care services. Attention should be given to providing information about their rights, as this may help to overcome the fear that an involvement with services as a parent with learning difficulties puts them at risk of losing their children into care.'

It also suggests that:

> '1.2.1 Adult and Children's services, and health and social care, should jointly agree local protocols for referrals, assessments and care pathways in order to respond appropriately and promptly to the need of both parents and children.'

The significance of early intervention and planning in advance should be self-evident where children are concerned, but this is stressed at para 1.2.3 thus: 'Identification of needs should start when a pregnancy is confirmed'. In terms of eligibility for services it 'should not be determined by general exclusions or based upon one type of criteria, such as IQ' (para 1.2.4). It cross-refers to FACS (albeit now superseded) for the provision of support at an early stage. In terms of child protection:

> '1.2.5 Whatever level of concern there is about children's welfare, practitioners need to be aware of parents with learning disabilities' entitlements to support under community care legislation, and to ensure that they receive the assessment and service response they are entitled to.'

VULNERABLE ADULT PARENTS

3.61 An additional feature of this area is that the learning disabled parent may also be classed as a vulnerable adult, and require protection themselves (para 2.2.5).

Eligibility thresholds

3.62 There may be a mismatch between thresholds for adult services and children' services:

> '2.2.10 This may mean that parents struggle to maintain improvements in their parenting capacity and they enter a "revolving door" of re-referrals which may [lead to] their children being looked after by the local authority. The involvement of both children's and adult services in providing services to members of the family will help to prevent this happening.'

Statistics

3.63 Estimates of the 'number of parents with learning disabilities in the United Kingdom vary widely, from 23,000 to 250,000'. The practical implications for parents are stark:

> 'In one local authority area, about a sixth of family court care proceedings concerned children with at least one parent who has learning disabilities and in about 75% of cases children were permanently removed from their family.'
> (Booth *et al*, 2005) (Appendix A of *Good Practice Guidance*).

Disability Discrimination Acts

3.64 This Disability Discrimination Acts have been repealed, and those sections set out below are retained purely for reference purposes. This is because the case law in this area has so far all turned upon the old statutes, and also because the 'replacement' statute (the Equality Act 2010) covers substantially the same area of law. To some extent, the old concepts have been considered in the judgment of Lord Brown set out at **3.48 and 3.49.** In that case, the arguments failed. However in *R(on the application of (1) Chavda (2) Fitzpatrick (by her daughter and litigation friend Pamela Fitzpatrick) (3) Maos) v Harrow LBC* [2007] EWHC 3064 (Admin), [2008] 11 CCLR 187 they did not fail. In this instance a decision had been taken to restrict adult services to those who fell within the 'critical needs' band only. However, in so doing the council had failed to take into account its obligations under s 49A of the Disability Discrimination Act 1995. Similarly in *R (on the application of W) v Birmingham City Council* [2011] EWHC 1147 (Admin), [2011] 14 CCLR 516 an application for judicial review was successful in similar circumstances (where a decision had been made by the council to provide for those with only critical needs). It was argued that this failed to accord with s 49A of the Disability Discrimination Act, and that the consultation process was itself unfair and rendered the decision unlawful. In making such decisions a local authority was to have due regard to the principles of disability equality. The equivalent to this (since April 2010) has been s 149 of the Equality Act 2010. It follows that any council who carried out a similar exercise without considering the equivalent implications under the Equality Act 2010 would fall foul of the same problem. A helpful analysis of the old law is to be found in the judgment of Langstaff J (in *R (on the Application of Broster & Ors) v Wirral MBC & Salisbury Independent Living* [2010] EWHC 3086 (Admin):

> '[64] A simple model of discrimination with which the Act is concerned is that people in like circumstances are treated in an unlike manner to their disadvantage, or people who are in like circumstances are treated in an unlike manner to their disadvantage, and that difference in treatment is because they possess some personal characteristic which is irrelevant to the decision in question. Such a characteristic might, it is well appreciated, be such as race, sex, gender, orientation or disability.'

It is this situation which would render the decision of a local authority unlawful, should it not adhere to the provisions of the Equality Act 2010.

Disability Discrimination Act 1995

21B Discrimination by public authorities

(1) It is unlawful for a public authority to discriminate against a disabled person in carrying out its functions.

(2) In this section, and sections 21D and 21E, "public authority" –

    (a)   includes any person certain of whose functions are functions of a public nature; but

    (b)   does not include any person mentioned in subsection (3).

(3) The persons are –

    (a)   either House of Parliament;

    (b)   a person exercising functions in connection with proceedings in Parliament;

    (c)   the Security Service;

    (d)   the Secret Intelligence Service;

    (e)   the Government Communications Headquarters; and

    (f)   a unit, or part of a unit, of any of the naval, military or air forces of the Crown which is for the time being required by the Secretary of State to assist the Government Communications Headquarters in carrying out its functions.

(4) In relation to a particular act, a person is not a public authority by virtue only of subsection (2)(a) if the nature of the act is private.

(5) Regulations may provide for a person of a prescribed description to be treated as not being a public authority for purposes of this section and sections 21D and 21E.

(6) In the case of an act which constitutes discrimination by virtue of section 55, subsection (1) of this section also applies to discrimination against a person who is not disabled.

(7) Subsection (1) –

- (a)   does not apply to anything which is unlawful under any provision of this Act other than subsection (1); and
- (b)   does not, subject to subsections (8) and (9), apply to anything which would be unlawful under any such provision but for the operation of any provision in or made under this Act.

(8) Subsection (1) does apply in relation to a public authority's function of appointing a person to, and in relation to a public authority's functions with respect to a person as holder of, an office or post if –

- (a)   none of the conditions specified in section 4C(3) is satisfied in relation to the office or post; and
- (b)   sections 4D and 4E would apply in relation to an appointment to the office or post if any of those conditions was satisfied.

(9) Subsection (1) does apply in relation to a public authority's functions with respect to a person as candidate or prospective candidate for election to, and in relation to a public authority's functions with respect to a person as elected holder of, an office or post if –

- (a)   the office or post is not membership of a House of Parliament, the Scottish Parliament, the National Assembly for Wales or an authority mentioned in section 15A(1);
- (b)   none of the conditions specified in section 4C(3) is satisfied in relation to the office or post; and
- (c)   sections 4D and 4E would apply in relation to an appointment to the office or post if –
- (i)   any of those conditions was satisfied, and
- (ii)   section 4F(1) (but not section 4C(5)) was omitted.

(10) Subsections (8) and (9) –

(a) shall not be taken to prejudice the generality of subsection (1); but
(b) are subject to section 21C(5).

21D Meaning of 'discrimination' in section 21B

(1) For the purposes of section 21B(1), a public authority discriminates against a disabled person if –

- (a)   for a reason which relates to the disabled person's disability, it treats him less favourably than it treats or would treat others to whom that reason does not or would not apply; and
- (b)   it cannot show that the treatment in question is justified under subsection (3), (5) or (7)(c).

(2) For the purposes of section 21B(1), a public authority also discriminates against a disabled person if –

- (a)   it fails to comply with a duty imposed on it by section 21E in circumstances in which the effect of that failure is to make it –
- (i)   impossible or unreasonably difficult for the disabled person to receive any benefit that is or may be conferred, or

    (ii)   unreasonably adverse for the disabled person to experience being subjected to any detriment to which a person is or may be subjected,

by the carrying-out of a function by the authority; and

    (b)   it cannot show that its failure to comply with that duty is justified under subsection (3), (5) or (7)(c).

(3) Treatment, or a failure to comply with a duty, is justified under this subsection if –

    (a)   in the opinion of the public authority, one or more of the conditions specified in subsection (4) are satisfied; and

    (b)   it is reasonable, in all the circumstances of the case, for it to hold that opinion.

(4) The conditions are –

    (a)   that the treatment, or non-compliance with the duty, is necessary in order not to endanger the health or safety of any person (which may include that of the disabled person);

    (b)   that the disabled person is incapable of entering into an enforceable agreement, or of giving an informed consent, and for that reason the treatment, or non-compliance with the duty, is reasonable in the particular case;

    (c)   that, in the case of treatment mentioned in subsection (1), treating the disabled person equally favourably would in the particular case involve substantial extra costs and, having regard to resources, the extra costs in that particular case would be too great;

    (d)   that the treatment, or non-compliance with the duty, is necessary for the protection of rights and freedoms of other persons.

(5) Treatment, or a failure to comply with a duty, is justified under this subsection if the acts of the public authority which give rise to the treatment or failure are a proportionate means of achieving a legitimate aim.

(6) Regulations may make provision, for purposes of this section, as to circumstances in which it is, or as to circumstances in which it is not, reasonable for a public authority to hold the opinion mentioned in subsection (3)(a).

(7) Regulations may –

    (a)   amend or omit a condition specified in subsection (4) or make provision for it not to apply in prescribed circumstances;

    (b)   amend or omit subsection (5) or make provision for it not to apply in prescribed circumstances;

    (c)   make provision for purposes of this section (in addition to any provision for the time being made by subsections (3) to (5)) as to circumstances in which treatment, or a failure to comply with a duty, is to be taken to be justified.

21E Duties for purposes of section 21D(2) to make adjustments

(1) Subsection (2) applies where a public authority has a practice, policy or procedure which makes it –

    (a)   impossible or unreasonably difficult for disabled persons to receive any benefit that is or may be conferred, or

(b)   unreasonably adverse for disabled persons to experience being subjected to any detriment to which a person is or may be subjected,

by the carrying-out of a function by the authority.

(2) It is the duty of the authority to take such steps as it is reasonable, in all the circumstances of the case, for the authority to have to take in order to change that practice, policy or procedure so that it no longer has that effect.

(3) Subsection (4) applies where a physical feature makes it –

(a)   impossible or unreasonably difficult for disabled persons to receive any benefit that is or may be conferred, or

(b)   unreasonably adverse for disabled persons to experience being subjected to any detriment to which a person is or may be subjected,

by the carrying-out of a function by a public authority.

(4) It is the duty of the authority to take such steps as it is reasonable, in all the circumstances of the case, for the authority to have to take in order to –

(a)   remove the feature;

(b)   alter it so that it no longer has that effect;

(c)   provide a reasonable means of avoiding the feature; or

(d)   adopt a reasonable alternative method of carrying out the function.

(5) Regulations may prescribe –

(a)   matters which are to be taken into account in determining whether any provision of a kind mentioned in subsection (4)(c) or (d) is reasonable;

(b)   categories of public authorities to whom subsection (4) does not apply.

(6) Subsection (7) applies where an auxiliary aid or service would –

(a)   enable disabled persons to receive, or facilitate the receiving by disabled persons of, any benefit that is or may be conferred, or

(b)   reduce the extent to which it is adverse for disabled persons to experience being subjected to any detriment to which a person is or may be subjected,

by the carrying-out of a function by a public authority.

(7) It is the duty of the authority to take such steps as it is reasonable, in all the circumstances of the case, for the authority to have to take in order to provide that auxiliary aid or service.

(8) Regulations may make provision, for purposes of this section –

(a)   as to circumstances in which it is, or as to circumstances in which it is not, reasonable for a public authority to have to take steps of a prescribed description;

(b)   as to steps which it is always, or as to steps which it is never, reasonable for a public authority to have to take;

(c)   as to what is, or as to what is not, to be included within the meaning of "practice, policy or procedure";

(d)   as to things which are, or as to things which are not, to be treated as physical features;

(e)   as to things which are, or as to things which are not, to be treated as auxiliary aids or services.

(9) Nothing in this section requires a public authority to take any steps which, apart from this section, it has no power to take.

(10) This section imposes duties only for the purposes of determining whether a public authority has, for the purposes of section 21B(1), discriminated against a disabled person; and accordingly a breach of any such duty is not actionable as such.

49A General duty

(1) Every public authority shall in carrying out its functions have due regard to –

  (a)   the need to eliminate discrimination that is unlawful under this Act;
  (b)   the need to eliminate harassment of disabled persons that is related to their disabilities;
  (c)   the need to promote equality of opportunity between disabled persons and other persons;
  (d)   the need to take steps to take account of disabled persons' disabilities, even where that involves treating disabled persons more favourably than other persons;
  (e)   the need to promote positive attitudes towards disabled persons; and
  (f)   the need to encourage participation by disabled persons in public life.

(2) Subsection (1) is without prejudice to any obligation of a public authority to comply with any other provision of this Act.

***

Equality Act 2010

Part 1
Socio-Economic Inequalities

1 Public sector duty regarding socio-economic inequalities

(1) An authority to which this section applies must, when making decisions of a strategic nature about how to exercise its functions, have due regard to the desirability of exercising them in a way that is designed to reduce the inequalities of outcome which result from socio-economic disadvantage.

(2) In deciding how to fulfil a duty to which it is subject under subsection (1), an authority must take into account any guidance issued by a Minister of the Crown.

(3) The authorities to which this section applies are –

  (a)   a Minister of the Crown;
  (b)   a government department other than the Security Service, the Secret Intelligence Service or the Government Communications Head-quarters;
  (c)   a county council or district council in England;
  (d)   the Greater London Authority;
  (e)   a London borough council;
  (f)   the Common Council of the City of London in its capacity as a local authority;
  (g)   the Council of the Isles of Scilly;

(h)   a Strategic Health Authority established under section 13 of the National Health Service Act 2006, or continued in existence by virtue of that section;

(i)   a Primary Care Trust established under section 18 of that Act, or continued in existence by virtue of that section;

(j)   a regional development agency established by the Regional Development Agencies Act 1998;

(k)   a police authority established for an area in England.

(4) This section also applies to an authority that –

(a)   is a partner authority in relation to a responsible local authority, and

(b)   does not fall within subsection (3),

but only in relation to its participation in the preparation or modification of a sustainable community strategy.

(5) In subsection (4) –

"partner authority" has the meaning given by section 104 of the Local Government and Public Involvement in Health Act 2007;

"responsible local authority" has the meaning given by section 103 of that Act;

"sustainable community strategy" means a strategy prepared under section 4 of the Local Government Act 2000.

(6) The reference to inequalities in subsection (1) does not include any inequalities experienced by a person as a result of being a person subject to immigration control within the meaning given by section 115(9) of the Immigration and Asylum Act 1999.

4 The protected characteristics

The following characteristics are protected characteristics –

age;
disability;
gender reassignment;
marriage and civil partnership;
pregnancy and maternity;
race;
religion or belief;
sex;
sexual orientation.

6 Disability

(1) A person (P) has a disability if –

(a)   P has a physical or mental impairment, and

(b)   the impairment has a substantial and long-term adverse effect on P's ability to carry out normal day-to-day activities.

(2) A reference to a disabled person is a reference to a person who has a disability.

(3) In relation to the protected characteristic of disability –

(a)   a reference to a person who has a particular protected characteristic is a reference to a person who has a particular disability;

(b)   a reference to persons who share a protected characteristic is a reference to persons who have the same disability.

(4) This Act (except Part 12 and section 190) applies in relation to a person who has had a disability as it applies in relation to a person who has the disability; accordingly (except in that Part and that section) –

(a)   a reference (however expressed) to a person who has a disability includes a reference to a person who has had the disability, and

(b)   a reference (however expressed) to a person who does not have a disability includes a reference to a person who has not had the disability.

(5) A Minister of the Crown may issue guidance about matters to be taken into account in deciding any question for the purposes of subsection (1).

(6) Schedule 1 (disability: supplementary provision) has effect.

Chapter 2

Prohibited Conduct
Discrimination

13 Direct discrimination

(1) A person (A) discriminates against another (B) if, because of a protected characteristic, A treats B less favourably than A treats or would treat others.

(2) If the protected characteristic is age, A does not discriminate against B if A can show A's treatment of B to be a proportionate means of achieving a legitimate aim.

(3) If the protected characteristic is disability, and B is not a disabled person, A does not discriminate against B only because A treats or would treat disabled persons more favourably than A treats B.

(4) If the protected characteristic is marriage and civil partnership, this section applies to a contravention of Part 5 (work) only if the treatment is because it is B who is married or a civil partner.

(5) If the protected characteristic is race, less favourable treatment includes segregating B from others.

(6) If the protected characteristic is sex –

(a)   less favourable treatment of a woman includes less favourable treatment of her because she is breast-feeding;

(b)   in a case where B is a man, no account is to be taken of special treatment afforded to a woman in connection with pregnancy or childbirth.

(7) Subsection (6)(a) does not apply for the purposes of Part 5 (work).

(8) This section is subject to sections 17(6) and 18(7).

14 Combined discrimination: dual characteristics

(1) A person (A) discriminates against another (B) if, because of a combination of two relevant protected characteristics, A treats B less favourably than A treats or would treat a person who does not share either of those characteristics.

(2) The relevant protected characteristics are –

    (a)   age;
    (b)   disability;
    (c)   gender reassignment;
    (d)   race
    (e)   religion or belief;
    (f)   sex;
    (g)   sexual orientation.

(3) For the purposes of establishing a contravention of this Act by virtue of subsection (1), B need not show that A's treatment of B is direct discrimination because of each of the characteristics in the combination (taken separately).

(4) But B cannot establish a contravention of this Act by virtue of subsection (1) if, in reliance on another provision of this Act or any other enactment, A shows that A's treatment of B is not direct discrimination because of either or both of the characteristics in the combination.

(5) Subsection (1) does not apply to a combination of characteristics that includes disability in circumstances where, if a claim of direct discrimination because of disability were to be brought, it would come within section 116 (special educational needs).

(6) A Minister of the Crown may by order amend this section so as to–

    (a)   make further provision about circumstances in which B can, or in which B cannot, establish a contravention of this Act by virtue of subsection (1);
    (b)   specify other circumstances in which subsection (1) does not apply.

(7) The references to direct discrimination are to a contravention of this Act by virtue of section 13.

15 Discrimination arising from disability

(1) A person (A) discriminates against a disabled person (B) if –

    (a)   A treats B unfavourably because of something arising in consequence of B's disability, and
    (b)   A cannot show that the treatment is a proportionate means of achieving a legitimate aim.

(2) Subsection (1) does not apply if A shows that A did not know, and could not reasonably have been expected to know, that B had the disability.

19 Indirect discrimination

(1) A person (A) discriminates against another (B) if A applies to B a provision, criterion or practice which is discriminatory in relation to a relevant protected characteristic of B's.

(2) For the purposes of subsection (1), a provision, criterion or practice is discriminatory in relation to a relevant protected characteristic of B's if –

   (a)   A applies, or would apply, it to persons with whom B does not share the characteristic,

   (b)   it puts, or would put, persons with whom B shares the characteristic at a particular disadvantage when compared with persons with whom B does not share it,

   (c)   it puts, or would put, B at that disadvantage, and

   (d)   A cannot show it to be a proportionate means of achieving a legitimate aim.

(3) The relevant protected characteristics are –

> age;
> disability;
> gender reassignment;
> marriage and civil partnership;
> race;
> religion or belief;
> sex;
> sexual orientation.

Adjustments for disabled persons

20 Duty to make adjustments

(1) Where this Act imposes a duty to make reasonable adjustments on a person, this section, sections 21 and 22 and the applicable Schedule apply; and for those purposes, a person on whom the duty is imposed is referred to as A.

(2) The duty comprises the following three requirements.

(3) The first requirement is a requirement, where a provision, criterion or practice of A's puts a disabled person at a substantial disadvantage in relation to a relevant matter in comparison with persons who are not disabled, to take such steps as it is reasonable to have to take to avoid the disadvantage.

(4) The second requirement is a requirement, where a physical feature puts a disabled person at a substantial disadvantage in relation to a relevant matter in comparison with persons who are not disabled, to take such steps as it is reasonable to have to take to avoid the disadvantage.

(5) The third requirement is a requirement, where a disabled person would, but for the provision of an auxiliary aid, be put at a substantial disadvantage in relation to a relevant matter in comparison with persons who are not disabled, to take such steps as it is reasonable to have to take to provide the auxiliary aid.

(6) Where the first or third requirement relates to the provision of information, the steps which it is reasonable for A to have to take include steps for ensuring that in the circumstances concerned the information is provided in an accessible format.

(7) A person (A) who is subject to a duty to make reasonable adjustments is not (subject to express provision to the contrary) entitled to require a disabled person, in relation to whom A is required to comply with the duty, to pay to any extent A's costs of complying with the duty.

(8) A reference in section 21 or 22 or an applicable Schedule to the first, second or third requirement is to be construed in accordance with this section.

(9) In relation to the second requirement, a reference in this section or an applicable Schedule to avoiding a substantial disadvantage includes a reference to –

(a) removing the physical feature in question,
(b) altering it, or
(c) providing a reasonable means of avoiding it.

(10) A reference in this section, section 21 or 22 or an applicable Schedule (apart from paragraphs 2 to 4 of Schedule 4) to a physical feature is a reference to –

(a) a feature arising from the design or construction of a building,
(b) a feature of an approach to, exit from or access to a building,
(c) a fixture or fitting, or furniture, furnishings, materials, equipment or other chattels, in or on premises, or
(d) any other physical element or quality.

(11) A reference in this section, section 21 or 22 or an applicable Schedule to an auxiliary aid includes a reference to an auxiliary service.

(12) A reference in this section or an applicable Schedule to chattels is to be read, in relation to Scotland, as a reference to moveable property.

(13) The applicable Schedule is, in relation to the Part of this Act specified in the first column of the Table, the Schedule specified in the second column.

Part of this Act	Applicable Schedule
Part 3 (services and public functions)	Schedule 2
Part 4 (premises)	Schedule 4
Part 5 (work)	Schedule 8
Part 6 (education)	Schedule 13
Part 7 (associations)	Schedule 15
Each of the Parts mentioned above	Schedule 21

21 Failure to comply with duty

(1) A failure to comply with the first, second or third requirement is a failure to comply with a duty to make reasonable adjustments.

(2) A discriminates against a disabled person if A fails to comply with that duty in relation to that person.

(3) A provision of an applicable Schedule which imposes a duty to comply with the first, second or third requirement applies only for the purpose of establishing whether A has contravened this Act by virtue of subsection (2); a failure to comply is, accordingly, not actionable by virtue of another provision of this Act or otherwise.

24 Irrelevance of alleged discriminator's characteristics

(1) For the purpose of establishing a contravention of this Act by virtue of section 13(1), it does not matter whether A has the protected characteristic.

(2) For the purpose of establishing a contravention of this Act by virtue of section 14(1), it does not matter –

(a)   whether A has one of the protected characteristics in the combination;
(b)   whether A has both.

25 References to particular strands of discrimination

(1) Age discrimination is –

(a)   discrimination within section 13 because of age;
(b)   discrimination within section 19 where the relevant protected characteristic is age.

(2) Disability discrimination is –

(a)   discrimination within section 13 because of disability;
(b)   discrimination within section 15;
(c)   discrimination within section 19 where the relevant protected characteristic is disability;
(d)   discrimination within section 21.

(3) Gender reassignment discrimination is –

(a)   discrimination within section 13 because of gender reassignment;
(b)   discrimination within section 16;
(c)   discrimination within section 19 where the relevant protected characteristic is gender reassignment.

(4) Marriage and civil partnership discrimination is –

(a)   discrimination within section 13 because of marriage and civil partnership;
(b)   discrimination within section 19 where the relevant protected characteristic is marriage and civil partnership.

(5) Pregnancy and maternity discrimination is discrimination within section 17 or 18.

(6) Race discrimination is –

(a)   discrimination within section 13 because of race;
(b)   discrimination within section 19 where the relevant protected characteristic is race.

(7) Religious or belief-related discrimination is –

(a)   discrimination within section 13 because of religion or belief;
(b)   discrimination within section 19 where the relevant protected characteristic is religion or belief.

(8) Sex discrimination is –

(a)   discrimination within section 13 because of sex;
(b)   discrimination within section 19 where the relevant protected characteristic is sex.

(9) Sexual orientation discrimination is –

(a)   discrimination within section 13 because of sexual orientation;

    (b)   discrimination within section 19 where the relevant protected characteristic is sexual orientation.

Part 11
Advancement of Equality

Chapter 1
Public Sector Equality Duty

149 Public sector equality duty

(1) A public authority must, in the exercise of its functions, have due regard to the need to –

    (a)   eliminate discrimination, harassment, victimisation and any other conduct that is prohibited by or under this Act;
    (b)   advance equality of opportunity between persons who share a relevant protected characteristic and persons who do not share it;
    (c)   foster good relations between persons who share a relevant protected characteristic and persons who do not share it.

(2) A person who is not a public authority but who exercises public functions must, in the exercise of those functions, have due regard to the matters mentioned in subsection (1).

(3) Having due regard to the need to advance equality of opportunity between persons who share a relevant protected characteristic and persons who do not share it involves having due regard, in particular, to the need to –

    (a)   remove or minimise disadvantages suffered by persons who share a relevant protected characteristic that are connected to that characteristic;
    (b)   take steps to meet the needs of persons who share a relevant protected characteristic that are different from the needs of persons who do not share it;
    (c)   encourage persons who share a relevant protected characteristic to participate in public life or in any other activity in which participation by such persons is disproportionately low.

(4) The steps involved in meeting the needs of disabled persons that are different from the needs of persons who are not disabled include, in particular, steps to take account of disabled persons' disabilities.

(5) Having due regard to the need to foster good relations between persons who share a relevant protected characteristic and persons who do not share it involves having due regard, in particular, to the need to –

    (a)   tackle prejudice, and
    (b)   promote understanding.

(6) Compliance with the duties in this section may involve treating some persons more favourably than others; but that is not to be taken as permitting conduct that would otherwise be prohibited by or under this Act.

(7) The relevant protected characteristics are –

    age;

disability;
gender reassignment;
pregnancy and maternity;
race;
religion or belief;
sex;
sexual orientation.

(8) A reference to conduct that is prohibited by or under this Act includes a reference to –

   (a)   a breach of an equality clause or rule;

   (b)   a breach of a non-discrimination rule.

(9) Schedule 18 (exceptions) has effect.

3.65 The remaining statute that needs considering, for the sake of completeness, is the Local Government Act 2000, which (subject to any restrictions imposed by other Acts) provides what appears to be a very wide discretion to promote the welfare of individuals, irrespective of their community care needs.

Local Government Act 2000

2 Promotion of well-being

(1) Every local authority are to have power to do anything which they consider is likely to achieve any one or more of the following objects –

   (a)   the promotion or improvement of the economic well-being of their area;

   (b)   the promotion or improvement of the social well-being of their area, and

   (c)   the promotion or improvement of the environmental well-being of their area.

(2) The power under subsection (1) may be exercised in relation to or for the benefit of –

   (a)   the whole or any part of a local authority's area, or

   (b)   all or any persons resident or present in a local authority's area.

(3) In determining whether or how to exercise the power under subsection (1), a local authority in England must have regard to their strategy under section 4.

(3A) But, in the case of an eligible parish council, that is subject to section 4A.

(3B) In determining whether or how to exercise the power under subsection (1), a local authority in Wales must have regard to the community strategy for its area published under section 39(4) of the Local Government (Wales) Measure 2009 or, where the strategy has been amended following a review under section 41 of that Measure, the strategy most recently published under section 41(6).

(3C) The community strategy for the area of a community council is the strategy referred to in subsection (3B) that is published by the county council or county borough council in whose area lies the community or communities for which the community council is established.

(4) The power under subsection (1) includes power for a local authority to –

(a)   incur expenditure,
(b)   give financial assistance to any person,
(c)   enter into arrangements or agreements with any person,
(d)   co-operate with, or facilitate or co-ordinate the activities of, any person,
(e)   exercise on behalf of any person any functions of that person, and
(f)   provide staff, goods, services or accommodation to any person.

(5) The power under subsection (1) includes power for a local authority to do anything in relation to, or for the benefit of, any person or area situated outside their area if they consider that it is likely to achieve any one or more of the objects in that subsection.

(6) Nothing in subsection (4) or (5) affects the generality of the power under subsection (1).

3 Limits on power to promote well-being

(1) The power under section 2(1) does not enable a local authority to do anything which they are unable to do by virtue of any prohibition, restriction or limitation on their powers which is contained in any enactment (whenever passed or made).

(2) The power under section 2(1) does not enable a local authority to raise money (whether by precepts, borrowing or otherwise).

(3) The Secretary of State may by order make provision preventing local authorities from doing, by virtue of section 2(1), anything which is specified, or is of a description specified, in the order.

(3A) The power under subsection (3) may be exercised in relation to –

(a)   all local authorities,
(b)   particular local authorities, or
(c)   particular descriptions of local authority.

(4) Subject to subsection (4A), before making an order under subsection (3), the Secretary of State must consult such representatives of local government and such other persons (if any) as he considers appropriate.

(4A) Subsection (4) does not apply to an order under this section which is made only for the purpose of amending an earlier order under this section –

(a)   so as to extend the earlier order, or any provision of the earlier order, to a particular authority or to authorities of a particular description, or
(b)   so that the earlier order, or any provision of the earlier order, ceases to apply to a particular authority or to authorities of a particular description.

(5) Before exercising the power under section 2(1), a local authority must have regard to any guidance for the time being issued by the Secretary of State about the exercise of that power.

(6) Before issuing any guidance under subsection (5), the Secretary of State must consult such representatives of local government and such other persons (if any) as he considers appropriate.

(7) In its application to Wales, this section has effect as if for any reference to the Secretary of State there were substituted a reference to the Welsh Ministers.

(8) In this section "enactment" includes an enactment comprised in subordinate legislation (within the meaning of the Interpretation Act 1978).

Ordinary residence and assessment

3.66   When a dispute arises as to the ordinary residence of an individual under NAA 1948, the mechanism for resolution is found in s 32(3), whereby any question arising under that part of the Act as to the ordinary residence of a person shall be determined by the relevant minister (together with compliance with the *Ordinary Residence Disputes (National Assistance Act 1948) Directions 2010)*. Where no such mechanism exists, then the Courts would have to decide the matter. The procedure for making such an application is contained in Part 5 (paras 190–213) of *Ordinary Residence: Guidance on the identification of the ordinary residence of people in need of community care services, England* (15 April 2011).It is probably convenient at this point to provide a brief summary of the provisions for ordinary residence and NAA 1948, as it applies to different categories. A local authority is responsible for providing accommodation to those who are ordinarily resident in its area (s 24(1)). A similar responsibility applies for welfare services (s 29). These are positive duties. There is a power to provide such services in other circumstances. The definition of ordinary residenceis as set out in *Ordinary Residence: Guidance on the identification of the ordinary residence of people in need of community care services, England* (see Chapter 1 at **1.15**). If a local authority has provided residential accommodation then he will remain ordinarily resident in the area in which he was resident prior to the accommodation having been provided (s 24(5)). Where he is in NHS care then he is resident in the area prior to admission (s 24(6)). The Guidance (on eligibility criteria) adds to this by stating the following:

> '48 Because local authorities have a **power** to provide services to people who live outside their area, the duty to assess is not limited to people who are ordinarily resident in the authority's area. This gives rise to the question of when it might appear that a person who is not ordinarily resident in an authority's area may be in need" of services.

> 49 Local authorities are already required to assess people who are about to be discharged from hospital and may need community care services under the delayed discharges legislation. The Courts have recognised that a pragmatic approach needs to be taken in similar circumstances. For example, it was held in the case of *R (on the application of B) v Camden LBC and Camden and Islington Mental Health and Social Care Trust* [2005] 1366 (Admin) that the words "a person ... may be in need of such services" refer to a person who may be in need at the time, or may be **about to be** in need ...

> 50 This pragmatic approach should also be taken in relation to people with firm plans to move to another local authority's area, for example, a person with a job offer who intends to take it up, subject to suitable community care services being available ... the person's move must be reasonably certain: local authorities would not be obliged to assess a person who was simply considering a move to an area.'

The self same words are to be found in paras 6–8 of the Ordinary Residence Guidance. Similar provisions exist in relation to a move from one form of accommodation to another (paras 92–106). The Guidance in respect of duties owed over the provision of accommodation are considered in Chapter 4.

No settled residence

3.67 Paragraphs 43–46 of the Ordinary Residence Guidance address this issue, and paras 43–45 are set out below.

> 43 Under section 24(3) of the 1948 Act, local authorities have a power to treat people of "no settled residence" as if they were ordinarily resident in their area and provide them with Part 3 accommodation.

> 44 Where doubts arise in respect of a person's ordinary residence, it is usually possible for local authorities to decide that the person has resided in one place long enough, or has sufficiently firm intentions in relation to that place, to have acquired an ordinary residence there. Therefore, it should only be in rare circumstances that local authorities conclude that someone is of no settled residence for the purpose of providing Part 3 accommodation. For example, if a person has clearly and intentionally left their previous residence and moved to stay elsewhere on a temporary basis during which time their circumstances change, a local authority may conclude the person to be of no settled residence. A local authority may also conclude that a person arriving from abroad is of no settled residence, including those people who are returning to England after a period of residing abroad and who have given up their previous home in this country, although note paragraph 22 of this guidance. For more details on people returning to England after a period of living abroad, see paragraphs 129–132 (*British citizens resuming permanent residence in England after a period abroad*).

> 45 The courts considered the application of section 24(3) in relation to the meaning of no settled residence in the case of *R v London Borough of Redbridge ex parte East Sussex County Council* (1992) *Times*, 31 December. In this case, the judge held that young twins with learning disabilities who had been placed in a residential school in East Sussex by the London Borough of Redbridge, where their parents had previously lived, were of no settled residence when their school closed. At this point, their parents had returned to Nigeria and were therefore no longer ordinarily resident in Redbridge. Consequently, applying the principles outlined in the *Vale* case the judge found that Redbridge no longer had any duty towards the twins and made a finding of no settled residence. However a duty to make provision fell on East Sussex County Council as the "local authority of the moment" because the twins were physically present in that county and were suffering from mental disorder.

3.68 In *R v Berkshire CC ex parte P* [1998] 1 CCLR 141 a dispute arose out of the issue of the ordinary residence of a seriously disabled man. However, this aspect of the case was dealt with by way of an agreement that the matter should be determined by the Secretary of State (as required by s 32(3) of NAA 1948). What remained in issue was the extent of the obligation of the local authority to assess (s 47(1) of the NHS and Community Care Act 1990 and s 29(1) of NAA 1948) at a point where there was had been no determination of the issue of ordinary residence. Laws J summarised the consequences of this as follows:

> '[146B] If there is an open question where he is ordinarily resident, he will have no rights under s 47(1) until that question is decided by the Secretary of State. Depending no doubt upon the particular conditions in which he is presently living, that may have very deleterious consequences.'

Further, he held that:

> '[146G–146I] If Parliament had intended the s 47(1) duty to be subject to a factual capacity in the authority itself to make provision within its existing arrangements, it could readily have so provided. Miss Richards in my judgment correctly relied on the fact that s 47(1) contemplates not only provision of community care services, but also arrangement by the authority for such provision; and in addition the terms of s 47(1)(b) show that once an assessment is made by the authority it is to decide whether the person's needs "call for the provision **by them** of any such services" [emphasis added] … [147G] the duty to assess arises where the local authority possesses the legal power to provide and arrange for the provision of community care services to the individual in question.'

On the construction of s 29(1) of NAA 1948, he held:

> '[148G–148H] In my judgment s 29(1) confers two distinct functions on local authorities; one permissive, the other mandatory. Within it is the **duty** to make arrangements is confined to cases where the Secretary of State has given a direction relating to persons ordinarily resident in the authority's area. The **power** to make arrangements is not so confined; it arises where the Secretary of State has given his approval to arrangements being made, and his approval may be given without regard to the place of residence of any potential beneficiary [emphasis added].'

3.69   In *R (on the Application of Greenwich LBC) v Secretary of State for Health and Bexley LBC* [2006] EWHC 2576 (Admin), [2007] 10 CCLR 60, an assessment had been made under the provisions of ss 46 and 47. The statute contains no mention of the matter of ordinary residence. The balance of the case turned on the issue of ordinary residence (under NAA 1948) and which local authority would be liable for the costs of accommodation thereafter. The Secretary of State had already determined (pursuant to s 32(3) of NAA 1948) that the service user was ordinarily resident in Greenwich. No arrangements had been made with the accommodation provider (s 26) and therefore the deeming provision of s 24(5) applied.

Inadequate care plans/assessments

3.70   In *R v Sutton LBC ex p Tucker* [1998] 1 CCLR 251, a dispute arose regarding the long-term care of a severely disabled woman, who had been cared for on NHS premises. It was held that the local authority had acted unlawfully and in breach of s 47(1)(b) in that it had not provided an option for the care of the service user more than 2 years after she had been fit to leave the NHS premises. It had also failed to provide a care plan, but had purported to use its discretion to make short-term decisions to replace the obligation to make long-term provision.

3.71 An assessment had taken place of the applicant, and a care plan produced. The care plan bore no relation to the assessment of the needs of the applicant. A second care plan was provided, as a result of which the claim for judicial review was withdrawn. The local authority was obliged to pay the costs of the proceedings upon the basis that the claim would have been likely to have succeeded (*R v Calderdale MBC ex P Houghton* [2000] 3 CCLR 228).

3.72 In *R (on the application of Ireneschild) v Lambeth LBC* [2007] EWCA Civ 234, [2007] 10 CCLR 243, a disabled adult was the subject of an assessment (her main concern being housing problems). An occupational therapist provided a report which established the concerns of the service user as being an eligible need. Subsequent to this, the medical housing adviser for the local authority had used different criteria for assessing the needs of the service user. A final assessment and care plan was produced which did not find any eligible needs arising from her housing situation. It was held that there was no failure to take into account the first report when formulating the conclusions of the assessment, and that proper weight had been given to both. It was also held that the Guidance set out in FACS had been followed. There had also been no procedural unfairness in failing to consult the service user on the findings contained in the second report, before concluding the assessment.

Refusal to assess/non-assessment

3.73 In *R v Bristol CC ex p Penfold (Alice)* [1998] 1 CCLR 315, a single parent (who suffered from anxiety and depression) had requested an assessment pursuant to s 47(1) (and an assessment of her dependent daughter under both the Children Act 1989 and the Carers (Recognition and Services) Act 1995). Mr Justice Scott Baker stated the issues to be thus:

> '[322B–322C] … whether in conducting the first stage of the exercise under Section 47(1), that is in deciding whether the Applicant may be in need, the Respondent is entitled to take into account resources.'

It was held that there was no discretion available to the local authority at this stage in the process (that is to say, those community care services which the local authority may provide or arrange for, and for services being those which the person *may* need). He stated:

> '[322G] As a matter of logic it is difficult to see how the existence or otherwise of resources to meet a need can determine whether or not that need exists … [322K] the mere fact of unavailability of resources to meet a need does not mean that there is no need to be met. Resource implications in my view play no part in the decision whether to carry out an assessment.'

He also held that 'normal' housing can be provided under the power to provide accommodation given by s 21 of NAA 1948, when a community care assessment has been carried out.

3.74 On a similar point (arising out of not only s 47, but also s 21 of NAA 1948), an issue arose as to the provision of accommodation for a mother and four children, three of whom were severely mentally handicapped and had behavioural problems. It was held that a local authority could take into account its resources in deciding what needs exist under s 21, but once it had accepted that the needs (for larger accommodation) existed, it could not refuse to perform that part of its duty upon the basis of a lack of resources (*R v Wigan MBC ex p Tammadge* [1998] 1 CCLR 581).

3.75 In a case associated with the closing and selling of a building owned by an NHS Trust used by community care service users, it was held that the local authority should have done more to re-assess the needs of those users. However, on the facts in the case (the closure was imminent; the sale was not unlawful; re-assessments had been agreed), there was nothing to be gained by an order being made against it (*R v Bath Mental Healthcare NHS Trust, Wiltshire Health Authority and Wiltshire CC ex p Beck, Pearce, Doran and Burden* [2000] 3 CCLR 5).

Delay in assessments/maladministration

3.76 In *Investigation into Complaint No 97/A2959 against Hackney LBC* (Local Government Ombudsman) [1999] 2 CCLR 67, there had been a delay in re-assessing the needs of persons with learning difficulties. The delay was for 22 months. The basis of the assessments was pursuant to s 47. The delay, and the manner in which the assessments had been carried out was found to amount to maladministration. Compensation of £1,500 was paid to the parents of two of the adults with learning difficulties.

3.77 In *R (on the application of Bernard) v Enfield LBC* [2002] EWHC 2282 (Admin), [2002] 5 CCLR 577, an assessment had been carried out in September 2000. Its conclusions as to the accommodation of the claimant were dire. Suitable accommodation was not provided until October 2002. A claim was made pursuant to the Human Rights Act 1998, both for damages and in respect of a breach of Arts 8 and 3. The claim under Art 3 failed, but not that which related to damages and Art 8. A total award of £10,000 was made. This case was referred to in the judgment of Lord Brown in the *McDonald* case and used to distinguish the situation of the Appellant from the Claimants in the circumstances of this case, which were appalling and over a significant period of time (hence the level of damages awarded).

Carers (Recognition and Services) Act 1995

3.78 This is the second piece of adjectival legislation which in part has the effect of triggering an assessment. It interlocks with the National Health

Service and Community Care Act 1990, the Chronically Sick and Disabled Persons Act 1970, the Children Act 1989 and the Carers and Disabled Children Act 2000 (see Chapter 5).

3.79 If the local authority carry out an assessment pursuant to s 47, and there is in addition a carer in existence for the individual who is the subject of that substantive assessment, then that carer can make his own request for an assessment of his own ability to provide the care to that individual. The assessment of the carer should take place before the local authority make its decision as to the needs of the subject of the s 47 assessment. Moreover, the assessment of the ability of the carer shall be taken into account when deciding what the needs of the assessed individual may be.

3.80 The same applies where the subject of an assessment is a disabled child.

3.81 If an assessment of either an adult or a child is taking place, and it appears to a local authority that a carer may be entitled to his own assessment, then the local authority must tell that carer that they are so entitled.

3.82 Individuals excluded from the legislation are those employed to care, or working as a volunteer for a voluntary organisation.

Carers (Recognition and Services) Act 1995

1 Assessment of ability of carers to provide care: England and Wales

(1) Subject to subsection (3) below, in any case where –

(a) a local authority carry out an assessment under section 47(1)(a) of the National Health Service and Community Care Act 1990 of the needs of a person ("the relevant person") for community care services, and

(b) an individual ("the carer") provides or intends to provide a substantial amount of care on a regular basis for the relevant person,

the carer may request the local authority, before they make their decision as to whether the needs of the relevant person call for the provision of any services, to carry out an assessment of his ability to provide and to continue to provide care for the relevant person; and if he makes such a request, the local authority shall carry out such an assessment and shall take into account the results of that assessment in making that decision.

(2) Subject to subsection (3) below, in any case where –

(a) a local authority assess the needs of a disabled child for the purposes of Part III of the Children Act 1989 or section 2 of the Chronically Sick and Disabled Persons Act 1970, and

(b) an individual ("the carer") provides or intends to provide a substantial amount of care on a regular basis for the disabled child,

the carer may request the local authority, before they make their decision as to whether the needs of the disabled child call for the provision of any services, to carry out an assessment of his ability to provide and to continue to provide care for the disabled child; and if he makes such a request, the local authority shall carry out such an assessment and shall take into account the results of that assessment in making that decision.

(2A) For the purposes of an assessment under subsection (1) or (2), the local authority may take into account, so far as it considers it to be material, an assessment under section 1 or 6 of the Carers and Disabled Children Act 2000.

(2B) In any case where –

    (a)   a local authority are carrying out an assessment mentioned in paragraph (a) of either subsection (1) or subsection (2) above in relation to the relevant person or (as the case may be) a disabled child, and

    (b)   it appears to the local authority that an individual may be entitled to request (but has not requested) an assessment under the subsection in question of his ability to provide and to continue to provide care for the relevant person or the disabled child,

the local authority must inform the individual that he may be so entitled before they make their decision as to the needs of the relevant person or the disabled child.

(2C) An assessment under subsection (1) or (2) above must include consideration of whether the carer –

    (a)   works or wishes to work,

    (b)   is undertaking, or wishes to undertake, education, training or any leisure activity.

(3) No request may be made under subsection (1) or (2) above by an individual who provides or will provide the care in question –

    (a)   by virtue of a contract of employment or other contract with any person; or

    (b)   as a volunteer for a voluntary organisation.

(4) The Secretary of State may give directions as to the manner in which an assessment under subsection (1) or (2) above is to be carried out or the form it is to take but, subject to any such directions, it shall be carried out in such manner and take such form as the local authority consider appropriate.

(5) Section 8 of the Disabled Persons (Services, Consultation and Representation) Act 1986 (duty of local authority to take into account ability of carers) shall not apply in any case where –

    (a)   an assessment is made under subsection (1) above in respect of an individual who provides the care in question for a disabled person; or

    (b)   an assessment is made under subsection (2) above.

(6) In this section –

> "community care services" has the meaning given by section 46(3) of the National Health Service and Community Care Act 1990;
> "child" means a person under the age of eighteen;
> "disabled child" means a child who is disabled within the meaning of Part III of the Children Act 1989;
> "disabled person" means a person to whom section 29 of the National Assistance Act 1948 applies;
> "local authority" has the meaning given by section 46(3) of the National Health Service and Community Care Act 1990; and

"voluntary organisation" has the same meaning as in the National Assistance Act 1948.

(7) ...

3.83   In *R v Kirklees MBC ex p Good* [1998] 1 CCLR 506, a dispute arose as to the provision of a housing grant to alter the property occupied by a family, the two eldest of which were looked after by two younger (adult) members. An attempt was made to argue that the terms of this statute (together with others) provided an obligation upon the local authority to make the required physical alterations to the property. Mr Justice Popplewell considered that the purpose of the statute was:

> '[508F] ... to ensure for instance a carer who is not living in such a condition that he or she is not able to carry out the duty of carer properly ... [508G–508I] it is clear that simply making an assessment does not get anyone anywhere. Unless there is a power under this Act to make the sort of provision which it is suggested should be made ... there is nothing in the Act which appears to me to require the Local Authority to give a grant ... The request ... has been made under the Carers Act. It is clear from Section 1 ... that the provisions related to community care services which have the meaning given by section 46(2) of the National Health Service and Community Care Act 1990. It is equally clear that those provisions mean services which may be made under the National Assistance Act, the Health Services and Public Health Act, National Health Service Act and the Mental Health Act. None of those are relevant to the instant application.'

It was held that an assessment did not require a local authority to take any action on the basis of an assessment, and that in any event there was no obligation imposed upon a local authority to provide carers with adaptations to their premises (pursuant to CSDPA 1970).

OLDER AND VULNERABLE ADULTS

Older adults

3.84   Some reference has already been made to this area and in particular the *National Service Framework for Older People*. The single assessment process for older people is a part of the overall framework in the NSF. Some guidance has been produced (HSC 2002/001: LAC (2002) 1). There is an overlap between this category and the other categories of adults set out above. However, there is currently no statute in existence which imposes upon a local authority specific obligations. The only statute that imposes some responsibilities is the Health Services and Public Health Act 1968 (s 45). This imposes a duty upon local authorities (subject to direction by the Secretary of State) to make arrangements to promote the welfare of old people. It excludes certain things (payment of money; accommodation pursuant to the National Health Service Act 2006; certain parts of the Immigration and Asylum Act 1999). If an old person were to be disabled, then CSDPA 1970 would be of greater relevance.

3.85 The Care Standards Act 2000 (Chapter 3) put in place 'a strong, independent regulatory system for care principally outside the NHS through the creation of the National Care Standards Commission, which was replaced by the Care Quality Commission (CQC). For example the CQC should ensure that all care homes for older people meet the relevant 'National Minimum Standards' (NSF, para 20). This statute removed most of the responsibility for regulating care homes from local authorities.

3.86 In 2006 the Department of Health produced *A New Ambition for Old Age – Next Steps in Implementing the National Service Framework for Older People*. On the whole, this tends to emphasise the role of healthcare, rather than specific involvement of local authorities.

Vulnerable adults

3.87 Greater steps have recently been taken to safeguard vulnerable adults (Safeguarding Vulnerable Groups Act 2006), and these are also considered in Chapter 4.

3.88 Guidance in respect of vulnerable adults (issued under s 7 of the Local Authority Social Services Act 1970) has been issued by the Department of Health and the Home Office (*No Secrets – Guidance on developing and implementing multi-agency policies and procedures to protect vulnerable adults from abuse*). It contains some definitions. A vulnerable adult is a person 'who is or may be in need of community care services by reason of mental or other disability, age or illness and who is or may be unable to take care of him or herself or unable to protect him or herself against significant harm or exploitation' (para 2.3). There has been some development since this was published in that in October 2008 the Department of Health carried out a national consultation on safeguarding adults from abuse, which has in turn led to some further guidance being produced (eg *Clinical Governance and Adult Safeguarding – An Integrated Process* (Department of Health, 10 February 2010). Also, since *No Secrets* the Mental Capacity Act 2005 has created a specific offence (s 44, see Chapter 2) of ill-treatment or neglect, although this is confined to those vulnerable adults who lack capacity.

Abuse

3.89 The term 'abuse' is 'a violation of an individual's human and civil rights by another person or persons' (para 2.5) and specifically 'physical abuse ... sexual abuse ... psychological abuse ... financial or material abuse ... neglect and acts of omission ... discriminatory abuse ...' (para 2.7). Abuse may be perpetrated by 'relatives and family members, professional staff, paid care workers, volunteers, other service users, neighbours, friends and associates, people who deliberately exploit vulnerable people and strangers' (para 2.9).

Inter-agency framework and policy

3.90 There are plainly a number of different agencies who will be involved in preventing abuse. Social Services are one of the main agencies (para 3.3). The Guidance suggests that a multi-agency management committee (adult protection) should be set up. A local authority should also have a policy in respect of the protection of vulnerable adults (s 4) together with a strategy for implementation (s 5). Similarly, its involvement will be integral to investigation of alleged abuse (s 6).

Protection of Vulnerable Adults Scheme

3.91 This was introduced in 2004, and guidance in the form of a practical guide was produced in May 2006 (*Protection of Vulnerable Adults Scheme in England and Wales for adult placements, domiciliary care agencies and care homes*). The origin of the scheme is the Care Standards Act 2000. This and the scheme is considered in more detail in Chapter 4. The role of local authorities is set out at paras 18–20a. These include references to the fact that a local authority may be a registered provider of adult placement schemes, care homes and domiciliary care agencies, and may also employ staff indirectly provided services to this group.

Health Select Committee's Inquiry into Elder Abuse

3.92 The Government provided a response to this Inquiry in June 2004 (*The Government's Response to the recommendations and conclusions of the Health Select Committee's Inquiry into Elder Abuse*). The Committee itself recommended that the definition of elder abuse should include those who do not require community care services. The Government rejected this recommendation. Therefore, local authority responsibility is confined only to those in receipt of some form of community care.

Duty of care by local authority towards vulnerable adults

3.93 The current extent of the duties of a local authority towards protecting vulnerable adults is contained in two authorities. The first is *Re Z (An Adult: Capacity)* [2005] 8 CCLR 146; *Re Z (Local Authority: Duty)* [2004] EWHC 2817 (Fam), [2005] 1 FLR 740. This was also relied upon by Munby LJ in partial support for the conclusion that he reached in respect of a local authority duty to those who might or were being deprived of their liberty (*Re A and C (Equality and Human Rights Commission Intervening)* [2010] EWHC 978 (Fam), [2010] 2 FLR 1363 para 2.48 Chapter 2). The facts of the case involved a woman with capacity who elected to die by way of assisted suicide (in Switzerland). Her husband had made the travel arrangements. Mr Justice Hedley held that:

> 'In my judgment in a case such as this the local authority incurred the following duties: (i) to investigate the position of a vulnerable adult to consider what was her

true position and intention; (ii) to consider whether she was legally competent to make and carry out her decision and intention; (iii) to consider whether any other (and if so, what) influence may be operating on her position and intention and to ensure that she has all relevant information and knows all available options; (iv) to consider whether she was legally competent to make and carry out her decision and intention; (v) to consider whether to invoke the inherent jurisdiction of the High Court so that the question of competence could be judicially investigated and determined; (vi) in the event of the adult not being competent, to provide all such assistance as may be reasonably required both to determine and give effect to her best interests; (vii) in the event of the adult being competent to allow her in any lawful way to give effect to her decision although that should not preclude the giving of advice or assistance in accordance with what are perceived to be her best interests; (viii) where there are reasonable grounds to suspect that the commission of a criminal offence may be involved, to draw that to the attention of the police; (ix) in very exceptional circumstances, to invoke the jurisdiction of the court under s 222 of the Local Government Act 1972.'

3.94 The second authority is *X v Hounslow London Borough Council* [2009] EWCA Civ 286, [2009] 2 FLR 262. The facts of the case involved a couple (both of whom were vulnerable adults). Both had regulars contacts with social workers. No blame was at any point laid at the door of the local authority in respect of the specific behaviour of any of these social workers. Through those social workers, there was an awareness on the part of the council that some youths had been exploiting the couple for some time, and that this was worsening. Steps were taken to provide them with alternative housing, but prior to that happening, they were imprisoned in their accommodation by the youths, and assaulted and abused by them in the presence of their own two children. The claim against the council was that: (a) there was a negligent failure to re-house the family; and (b) that failure was a breach of the duty of care towards the couple. On these facts, this is a very different situation to *Re Z*, of course. The court held that in circumstances such as this, there was **no** duty of care. The local authority had not created the danger. There was no element of supervision over those who did create the danger. The local authority had at no point assumed responsibility for the safety of the couple. Had there been any of these, then a duty of care might have existed, and the council might have been liable for the consequences that flowed from that negligence. *Per curiam,* the Court noted that:

'[92] in our judgment, there is an important difference between a case where children assert that a duty of care is owed to them and a case like this where the claimants are adults living in the community, albeit vulnerable adults. Although we do not take this point too far because the vulnerability of the respondents here is undoubtedly a relevant factor, local authorities have specific obligations in respect of children under the Children Act 1989 which are different from those which apply in respect of adults. For example, there are statutory duties to protect children from harm, which may lead to care proceedings and, indeed, to the local authority having parental responsibility.'

3.95 The couple did not lack capacity, but had they done so, it is arguable that the framework of the Mental Capacity Act 2005 *might* have created just that duty to protect from harm. However, the offence of ill-treatment is a matter that can be drawn to the attention of the police (and the police had declined to become involved in this case without a complaint from the couple, which had not been forthcoming). Further, as can be seen from **3.92** above, the Government itself has not been keen to extend the duty of care owed by councils towards vulnerable adults within the context of abuse of the elderly. The role of the High Court in using the inherent jurisdiction to protect vulnerable but capacitous adults is set out below.

Role of the inherent jurisdiction and vulnerable adults

3.96 In *A Local Authority v (1) MA (2) NA and (3) SA (by her children's guardian LJ)* [2005] EWHC 2942 (Fam), [2007] 10 CCLR 193, [2006] 1 FLR 867, the question of whether it was appropriate or not to use the inherent jurisdiction within the context of a local authority which wished to protect a young woman who had only just achieved her majority. Mr Justice Munby summarised the issues in the case thus:

> '[195I–195J] This case raises novel questions about the Court's inherent jurisdiction in relation to vulnerable adults. I have before me a vulnerable young woman who has just turned 18 and has therefore attained her majority. While she was still a child the court had exercised its inherent *parens patriae* and wardship jurisdiction to protect her from the risk of an unsuitable arranged marriage. The question is whether I have jurisdiction to continue that protection whilst she is an adult.'

3.97 The question that was peculiar to the facts of the case was that:

> '[195K–196B] ... this young woman, although undoubtedly vulnerable, equally undoubtedly has the capacity to marry. In other words the case raises the question of whether the inherent jurisdiction in relation to adults can be exercised for the protection of adults who do not, as such, lack capacity. In my judgment, the jurisdiction can be so exercised. And I propose to exercise the jurisdiction in this particular case, so that a young woman who remains just as vulnerable now as she did when she was a child should not suddenly be deprived of the protection which the court has hitherto felt it necessary to afford her and which I believe is very much required in her best interests.'

On the basis of this case, therefore, a local authority would have a basis for protection of a *competent* but vulnerable adult. Such protection would not be available via the Mental Capacity Act 2005 since this only affects those who lack capacity. The case can be contrasted with *M v B, A & S (by the Official Solicitor)* [2005] EWHC 1681 (Fam), [2006] 1 FLR 117 when the same jurisdiction was considered on the same subject matter, but where there was an absence of capacity.

3.98 There has been some dispute as to the extent of this use of the inherent jurisdiction, and it is an area of law that is still developing. In *A Local Authority v DL, RL and ML* [2010] EWHC 2675 (Fam), [2011] 1 FLR 957 the authority of *A Local Authority v (1) MA (2) NA and (3) SA (by her children's guardian LJ* was revisited. It also considered *Re Z* and the use of s 222 of the Local Government Act 1972. The facts of the case related to two elderly (and vulnerable) but capacitous adults about whom the council had legitimate concerns arising from the behaviour of their son. The council wished to take steps to protect the couple from him, and applied to the court for relief using (inter alia) the inherent jurisdiction of the High Court. Lord Justice Wall reached the conclusion that the decision in *A Local Authority v (1) MA (2) NA and (3) SA (by her children's guardian LJ* established the necessary basis for the jurisdiction, even though on the facts of that case there could have been no action taken by the vulnerable adult (whereas the couple in this case could have sought the assistance of the court themselves, but did not wish to do so). Lord Justice Wall was satisfied that the Court of Protection could not assist (as there was no lack of capacity), and neither would an ASBO or an ASBI. He held that:

> '[11] It is, I think, reasonably well established that the inherent jurisdiction of the High Court exists to remedy the lacunae left by the common law or statute. There is no doubt also, I think, that in the years leading up to the passing of MCA 2005 (and the plugging of the Bournewood Gap by means of the amendments to MCA 2005 by the Mental Health Act 2007) there was a considerable development in the High Court's jurisdiction over vulnerable adults who were not mentally ill within the Mental Health Act 1983, but who were in need of protection.'

He then proceeded to set out the law in this area which has already been considered in Chapter 2. Upon the basis that there was a lacuna in the law and upon the facts of the case, an injunction (non-molestation) was made against the son.

3.99 However, this order was made upon an ex parte basis, and the son resisted the continuation of the order, and sought to dispute that the inherent jurisdiction could be used in this situation. It should be noted that whilst Wall LJ did not consider that s 222 of the Local Government Act 1970 added to the powers under the inherent jurisdiction, it could, of course still (in theory) have been used entirely without the need of the inherent jurisdiction to have been invoked, although its purpose was never to have extended to cases such as this, and had generally been used to enforce (for example) Sunday trading laws. The matter returned before the Court (and Mrs Justice Theis) in *A Local Authority v DL* [2011] EWHC 1022 (Fam), [2011] 14 CCLR 443. The judgment contains a thorough review of all the law in this area (including a consideration of the MCA 2005, and the purpose for which it was intended). She held that:

> '[53(4)] Each case will, of course, have to be carefully considered on its own facts, but if there is evidence to suggest that an adult who does not suffer from any kind of mental incapacity that comes within the MCA 2005 but who is, or reasonably believed to be, incapacitated from making the relevant decision by reason of such things as constraint, coercion, undue influence or other vitiating factors they may be entitled to the protection of the inherent jurisdiction ... This may, or may not, include a vulnerable adult.'

She also held that:

> '[53(6)] ... the obligations on the State under the Convention and the HRA 1998 require the court to retain the inherent jurisdiction, as by refusing to exercise it in principle the court is, in effect, creating a new "Bournewood gap". Whilst it is correct that the cases to date regarding any positive obligation on the State (including the LA) arising under Article 8 have concerned cases involving children or adults who lack mental capacity that does not mean, in principle, such positive duties cannot arise in other circumstances. There may be a heightened positive duty in cases concerning children and adults who have mental incapacity. Much will depend on the circumstances of each case and what the proportionate response is considered to be by the LA.'

In summary, she confirmed that the inherent jurisdiction did exist to cover such situations as pertained in this case (ie where the Mental Capacity Act could not apply). Parliament had not sought to exclude the jurisdiction and its retention was important to prevent a new 'Bournewood Gap' from developing, and in particular so that a local authority can respond positively to its positive duties under (in this instance) Art 8. Finally, she held that although vulnerability was a factor in such cases, the inherent jurisdiction was not limited to this category alone. The intervention of the Court would be (in its effect) to permit the adult to make a decision in a situation that was free from 'constraint, coercion, undue influence or other vitiating factors'.

Chapter 4

PROVISION OF ACCOMMODATION

INTRODUCTION

4.1   There remain a number of areas in which the duties and powers of local authorities impact upon the provision of accommodation for adults over and above those which flow from a consequence of the type of assessments set out in Chapter 3. These are primarily:

(a)   the continued existence (or otherwise) of care or nursing homes still owned by a local authority;

(b)   an obligation to ensure the protection of vulnerable adults within accommodation arranged/financed by the local authority; and

(c)   the arrangements to make it possible for those who are accommodated to choose accommodation which meets with their preference.

(d)   accommodation of those who fall within s 21 of the National Assistance Act 1948.

There is plainly an overlap with many of the issues relating to the assessment of the community care needs for adults, as described in Chapter 3. Indeed, many of the problems in this area of law is distinguishing the need for accommodation, from other (or any) community care needs. This Chapter only concerns itself with provision of accommodation for adults.

BACKGROUND

4.2   A historical analysis of the legislation and its purpose has recently been provided by Baroness Hale in *YL (by her litigation friend the Official Solicitor) v Birmingham City Council* [2007] UKHL 27, [2007] 10 CCLR 505 (at 518–519). She held:

> '[50] Section 21(1)(a) of the National Assistance Act 1948 originally required each local authority to provide:
>
> > "residential accommodation for persons who by reason of age, infirmity or other circumstances are in need of care and attention which is not otherwise available to them".

Accommodation could be provided either in homes owned and run by the local authority, or by another local authority (s 21(4)), or by a voluntary organisation (s 26), but not by private persons. Residents were required to pay for their local authority accommodation according to their ability to pay (s 22). Where accommodation was arranged with a voluntary organisation, the local authority was liable to pay for it and could then recoup a means-tested contribution from the resident (s 26(2) and (3)). Schemes were later replaced with ministerial approval and directions (s 195(3) of the Local Government Act 1972) and the relevant words of s 21(1) amended to read: "... a local authority may with the approval of the Secretary of State, and to such extent as he may direct, shall make arrangements for providing ..." (1972 Act s 195(6), Sch 23 para 2(1)). Ministerial directions required that provision be made for people ordinarily resident in the area (DHSS Local Authority Circular 13/74).

[51] But supply was never able to match demand. Many older people were accommodated in private residential homes but paid for by the state, through the means tested benefit system rather than by local authorities. This was widely regarded as inefficient and expensive, because there was no professional assessment of whether the resident really needed this expensive form of care, rather than to be helped to remain in her own home, nor was there any systematic control of the cost ... The result was Part III of the National Health Service and Community Care Act 1990. Under this, each local authority must prepare and publish a strategic plan for the provision of community care services in their area (s 46). They were instructed to develop a "mixed economy of care" making use of voluntary, not for profit and private providers whenever this was most cost effective. They were to move away from the role of exclusive service providers and into the role of service arranger and procurer ... To this end section 26 of the 1948 Act was amended to allow them to place residents with private providers as well as with voluntary organisations. The charging arrangements remained broadly the same, primary liability remaining with the local authority.

[52] At the same time, local authorities were placed under a duty to carry out an assessment of the need for community care services of any person who might be in need of them (1990 Act s 47(1)(a)) and then to decide whether those needs called for the provision by them of any such services (s 47(1)(b)). "Community care services" include arranging or providing accommodation under Section 21(1) of the 1948 Act (s 46(3)) ... a large slice of the social security budget was transferred to local authorities to enable them to meet these responsibilities.'

4.3   The principal relevant statutes and sections in respect of the actual provision of accommodation are ss 21, 24, 26 and 29 of the National Assistance Act 1948 (NAA 1948) and s 54 of the Health and Social Care Act 2001. The principal statute in terms of the vestigial responsibility for service users placed in accommodation are contained in the the Safeguarding Vulnerable Groups Act 2006. In addition to the case-law, in respect of choice of accommodation, it is the National Assistance Act 1948 (Choice of Accommodation) Directions 1992 which are relevant (together with the Guidance provided by the Department of Health in Circular No LAC (2004) 20).

National Assistance Act 1948

4.4 The relevant text of the statute is set out below as is the relevant case law in respect of provision of accommodation. The ability of the local authority to charge for accommodation (s 22 of NAA 1948) is set out in Chapter 6.

National Assistance Act 1948

21 Duty of local authorities to provide accommodation

(1) Subject to and in accordance with the provisions of this Part of this Act, a local authority may with the approval of the Secretary of State, and to such extent as he may direct shall, make arrangements for providing –

   (a)   residential accommodation for persons aged eighteen or over who by reason of age, illness, disability or any other circumstances are in need of care and attention which is not otherwise available to them; and

   (aa) residential accommodation for expectant and nursing mothers who are in need of care and attention which is not otherwise available to them.

   (b) ...

(1A) A person to whom section 115 of the Immigration and Asylum Act 1999 (exclusion from benefits) applies may not be provided with residential accommodation under subsection (1)(a) if his need for care and attention has arisen solely –

   (a)   because he is destitute; or

   (b)   because of the physical effects, or anticipated physical effects, of his being destitute.

(1B) Subsections (3) and (5) to (8) of section 95 of the Immigration and Asylum Act 1999, and paragraph 2 of Schedule 8 to that Act, apply for the purposes of subsection (1A) as they apply for the purposes of that section, but for the references in subsections (5) and (7) of that section and in that paragraph to the Secretary of State substitute references to a local authority.

(2) In making any such arrangements a local authority shall have regard to the welfare of all persons for whom accommodation is provided, and in particular to the need for providing accommodation of different descriptions suited to different descriptions of such persons as are mentioned in the last foregoing subsection.

(2A) In determining for the purposes of paragraph (a) or (aa) of subsection (1) of this section whether care and attention are otherwise available to a person, a local authority shall disregard so much of the person''s resources as may be specified in, or determined in accordance with, regulations made by the Secretary of State for the purposes of this subsection.

(2B) In subsection (2A) of this section the reference to a person's resources is a reference to his resources within the meaning of regulations made for the purposes of that subsection.

(3) ...

(4) Subject to the provisions of section 26 of this Act accommodation provided by a local authority in the exercise of their functions under this section shall be provided in premises managed by the authority or, to such extent as may be determined in accordance with the arrangements under this section, in such

premises managed by another local authority as may be agreed between the two authorities and on such terms, including terms as to the reimbursement of expenditure incurred by the said other authority, as may be so agreed.

(5) References in this Act to accommodation provided under this Part thereof shall be construed as references to accommodation provided in accordance with this and the five next following sections, and as including references to board and other services, amenities and requisites provided in connection with the accommodation except where in the opinion of the authority managing the premises their provision is unnecessary.

(6) References in this Act to a local authority providing accommodation shall be construed, in any case where a local authority agree with another local authority for the provision of accommodation in premises managed by the said other authority, as references to the first-mentioned local authority.

(7) Without prejudice to the generality of the foregoing provisions of this section, a local authority may –

(a) provide, in such cases as they may consider appropriate, for the conveyance of persons to and from premises in which accommodation is provided for them under this Part of the Act;

(b) make arrangements for the provision on the premises in which accommodation is being provided of such other services as appear to the authority to be required.

...

(8) ... nothing in this section shall authorise or require a local authority to make any provision authorised or required to be made (whether by that or by any other authority) by or under any enactment not contained in this Part of this Act or authorised or required to be provided under the National Health Service Act 2006 or the National Health Service (Wales) Act 2006.

EXTENT OF NEEDS AND PROVISION FOR ACCOMMODATION/HOUSING

Psychological need

4.5 Avon CC had assessed a man suffering from Down's syndrome, who had formed a view that he needed to live in a particular residential home. The view that he had formed was due to the syndrome itself. He was assessed (s 47 of the National Health Service and Community Care Act 1990) and it was decided that he needed accommodation (to be provided as a result of s 21 of NAA 1948). It was held that the accommodation had to be appropriate to the needs of the service user, and part of the need in this instance was a psychological need for a residence at a preferred home (*R v Avon CC ex p M* [1999] 2 CCLR 185, [1994] 2 FLR 1006).

Reasonableness of need

4.6 The balance to be struck between the conduct of a service user and the extent of the duties of a local authority was considered in *R v Kensington and*

Chelsea RLBC ex p Kujtim [1999] 2 CCLR 340, [1999] 4 All ER 161. An asylum seeker had been assessed pursuant to s 47(1). That assessment identified a need for care and attention within the wording of s 21(1)(a) of NAA 1948 (for residential accommodation). The local authority had a duty to provide the accommodation, not a discretion. However, it was held that if a service user persistently and unequivocally refused to comply with the requirements of the local authority and coupled with a careful consideration of the changed circumstances and the reasons for any conduct on the part of the service user, it might regard its duty as discharged.

Needs and resources

4.7   In *R v Sefton MBC ex parte Help the Aged and Charlotte Blanchard* [1997] 1 CCLR 57, [1997] 4 All ER 532, there was a consideration of the principles established in *Barry* (see Chapter 3, at **3.37–3.48**). This is a significant case in interpreting and applying the consequences of *Barry* and the ratio of Lord Woolf rewards close reading. He stated the issues were as follows:

'[59A–59C] (1) Whether a local authority in deciding if an elderly person is in need of care and attention, in which case it will be required to make arrangements for residential accommodation to be made available to her, is entitled under Section 21(1) of the National Assistance Act 1948 ... to have regard to its limited financial resources (2) If its limited resources are relevant do they justify the policy which Sefton has adopted (3) Whether, in determining if "care and attention is not otherwise available to a person" an Authority is entitled to take the resources of that person into account even though that person's resources fall below the levels prescribed by Regulations for the purposes of Sections 22–26 of the 1948 Act.'

4.8   Further, he held that:

'[64/65K-65A] The *Barry* case was not concerned with Section 21(2) of the Act ... the issue in *Barry* was whether a local authority can properly take into account its own financial resources when assessing the needs of a disabled person under Section 2(1) of the 1970 Act. That is very much the same as the first issue which arises on this appeal.'

He then set out sections of the judgments of Lord Nicholls and Lord Clyde, and observed:

'[67–68D-K; A-F] Caution therefore has to be exercised before applying the interpretation of "needs" in Section 29 to Section 21. As Lord Clyde also stated:

"The words 'necessary' and 'needs' are both relative expressions, admitting in each case a considerable range of meaning."

This is important because there are undoubted difficulties in adopting the general approach as to the elasticity of "necessary" and "needs" referred to by Lord Nicholls and Lord Clyde to the words "in need of care and attention" which appear in Section 21(1) of the 1948 Act. Under Section 2(1) of the Act of 1970, the obligation of the Local Authority only arose if the authority were satisfied that not only would the services described in the Section meet the needs of the person concerned but that it was necessary for the services to be provided in order to meet those needs. In the case of Section 21 once the authority has come to the conclusion that the person concerned is in need of care and attention, which is not otherwise available to them, then the residential accommodation is to be provided ... While I fully accept in accordance with the decision in *Barry* that it is possible to perform a cost benefit analysis in relation to a person's needs for services listed in Section 2(1) and then decide if they are necessary, taking into account the resources of the local authority, I find it very much more difficult to perform the same exercise when deciding whether a person is in need of care and attention. However, having regard to the reasoning of Lord Nicholls and Lord Clyde I am compelled to conclude that there is a limited subjective element in making the assessment of whether the ailments of the person concerned do or do not collectively establish a need for care and attention. I therefore determine the issue in the affirmative. However, in this case it is clear from the evidence that Sefton accepted that Mrs Blanchard met its own threshold as a person in need of care and attention. What is was seeking to do was to say that because of its lack of resources notwithstanding this it was not prepared to meet the duty which was placed upon it by the Section. This it was not entitled to do. There is nothing in the speeches in the House of Lords in *Barry* to indicate to the contrary ... so here, the local authority was satisfied that Mrs Blanchard was "in need of care and attention" and that being so, unless it can rely on the words "which is not otherwise available to them" it was under an obligation to fulfil its duty and a lack of resources was no excuse. The second issue is therefore to be determined adversely to Sefton. Sefton cannot succeed because of the effect of its resources on the requirement of "need". Can it succeed because the accommodation has to be "not otherwise available to the individual seeking to rely on Section 21"? ... the statutory scheme rests upon the assumption that care and attention is not to be regarded as "otherwise available" if the person concerned is unable to pay for it according to a means tested regime provided for in Section 22. Section 22(5) requires Sefton to give effect to the Regulations and this Sefton has not done. So the third issue must also be decided adversely to Sefton.'

4.9   In *R (on the Application of Alloway) (by his father and litigation friend) v Bromley LBC* [2004] EWHC 2108 (Admin), [2005] 8 CCLR 61, an assessment pursuant to s 47 had taken place with a recommendation that the learning disabled service user be provided with a specific placement. No such placement was made. It was held that the local authority had ruled out the placement on the grounds of cost without even considering viable alternatives, or the comparative costs of such placement. The decision was unlawful.

4.10   An assessment of the applicant had been carried out by the local authority pursuant to s 47(1)(a), which concluded that there was a need for a change in accommodation. The local authority attempted to rely upon a lack of resources in refusing to provide such accommodation. It was held that once the assessment had been completed the duty to provide accommodation lay with the social services committee. The fact that the applicant had refused two offers of (inappropriate) accommodation did not absolve the local authority of that duty (*R (on the Application of Batantu) v Islington LBC* [2001] 4 CCLR 445).

Needs and housing

4.11   In *R (on the application of Wahid) v The Mayor and Burgesses of Tower Hamlets LBC* [2002] EWCA Civ 287, [2002] 5 CCLR 239, the Court reconsidered the extent of the duty of the local authority to provide accommodation pursuant to s 21 of NAA 1948. The argument was (in part) that the local authority were obliged to 'provide better accommodation for the applicant as a person in need of care and attention under Section 21(1)' ([1] at 240). Lord Justice Pill proceeded to analyse the statute, and in part relied upon Department of Health Circular No LAC (93) 10 (Appendix 1). On the basis of the assessment by the local authority·

> '[[24] at 246] ... the need for care and attention has not been accepted ... and the first issue is whether it should have been. Reliance is placed first on section 117 of the Mental Health Act 1983. I see no basis for the submission that the fact that after-care services were provided under Section 117 ... amounted to or necessarily required a finding that he was in need of care and attention under section 21.
>
> [[26] at 246] ... [the local authority] was entitled to conclude that the section 21 duty had not been triggered. An applicant may have housing needs without a duty to provide residential accommodation under section 21 arising. Moreover, the decision to be made upon behalf of the authority was properly left to ... a team leader.
>
> [[28] at 247]... Provision under Section 21 is a last resort; to treat it otherwise would be to distort the procedures and priorities under the Housing Act.'

Lady Justice Hale (as she then was) extrapolated further:

> '[[32] at 248] ... it does not follow that because residential accommodation can mean ordinary housing and the claimant is in need of ordinary housing, a duty arises to provide him with that housing under Section 21(1)(a). That duty is premised on an unmet need for "care and attention" (a "condition precedent" as this court put it in [*R v Westminster CC ex p M, P, A & X* (1997) 1 CCLR 85] ... ordinary housing is not in itself 'care and attention.'

Circular No LAC (93)(10) Appendix 1 (as referred to by Lord Justice Pill) is set out below.

CIRCULAR NO LAC (93)(10) APPENDIX 1

Commencement, interpretation and extent

(1)   These approvals and Directions shall come into force on 1 April 1993.

(2)   In these Approvals and Directions, unless the context otherwise requires, 'the Act' means the National Assistance Act 1948.

(3)   The Interpretation Act 1978 applies to these Approvals and Directions as it applies to an Act of Parliament.

(4)   The Approvals and Directions shall apply only to England and Wales.

Residential accommodation for persons in need of care and attention

(1)   The Secretary of State hereby –
   —   approves the making by local authorities of arrangements under
        section 21(1)(a) of the Act in relation to persons with no settled
        residence and, to such an extent as the authority may consider
        desirable, in relation to persons who are ordinarily resident in the area
        of another local authority, with the consent of that other authority;
        and
   —   directs local authorities to make arrangements under section 21(1)(a)
        of the Act in relation to persons who are ordinarily resident in their
        area and other persons who are in urgent need thereof.
   To provide residential accommodation for persons aged 18 or over who by
   reason of age, illness, disability or any other circumstances are in need of
   care and attention not otherwise available to them.

(2)   Without prejudice to the generality of sub-paragraph (1), the Secretary of
   State hereby directs local authorities to make arrangements under
   section 21(1)(a) of the Act to provide temporary accommodation for
   persons who are in urgent need thereof in circumstances where the need for
   that accommodation could not reasonably have been foreseen.

(3)   Without prejudice to the generality of sub-paragraph (1), the Secretary of
   State hereby directs local authorities to make arrangements under
   section 21(1)(a) of the Act to provide accommodation –
   (a)   in relation to persons who are or have been suffering from mental
          disorder, or
   (b)   for the purposes of the prevention of mental disorder,
   for person who are ordinarily resident in their area and for persons with no
   settled residence who are in the authority's area.

(4)   Without prejudice to the generality of sub-paragraph (1) and subject to
   section 24(4) of the Act, the Secretary of State hereby approves the making
   by local authorities of arrangements under section 21(1)(a) of the Act to
   provide residential accommodation –
   (a)   in relation to persons who are or have been suffering from mental
          disorder; or
   (b)   for the purposes of the prevention of mental disorder,
   for person who are ordinarily resident in the area of another local authority
   but who following discharge from hospital have become resident in the
   authority's area;

(5)   Without prejudice to the generality of sub-paragraph (1), the Secretary of
   State hereby approves the making by local authorities of arrangements
   under section 21(1)(a) of the Act to provide accommodation to meet the
   needs of persons for –
   (a)   the prevention of illness;
   (b)   the care of those suffering from illness; and
   (c)   the aftercare of those so suffering,

(6)   Without prejudice to the generality of sub-paragraph (1), the Secretary of
   State hereby approves the making by local authorities of arrangements
   under section 21(1)(a) of the Act specifically for persons who are alcoholic
   or drug-dependent.

Residential accommodation for expectant and nursing mothers

The Secretary of State hereby approves the making by local authorities of arrangements under section 21(1)(aa) of the Act to provide residential accommodation (in particular mother and baby homes) for expectant and nursing mothers (of any age) who are in need of care and attention which is not otherwise available to them.

Arrangements to provide services for residents

The Secretary of State hereby directs local authorities to make arrangements in relation to persons provided with accommodation under section 21(1) of the Act for all or any of the following purposes –

- For the welfare of all persons for whom accommodation is provided;
- For the supervision of the hygiene of the accommodation so provided;
- To enable persons for whom accommodation is provided to obtain –
  (i)   medical attention,
  (ii) nursing attention during illnesses of a kind which are ordinarily nursed at home, and
  (iii) the benefit of any services provided by the National Health Service of which they may from time to time be in need,
  but nothing in this paragraph shall require a local authority to make any provision authorised or required to be provided under the National Health Service Act 1977;
- For the provision of board and such other services, amenities and requisites provided in connection with the accommodation, except where in the opinion of the authority managing the premises their provisions are unnecessary;
- To review regularly the provision made under the arrangements and to make such improvements as the authority considers necessary.

Arrangements for the conveyance of residents

The Secretary of State hereby approves the making by local authorities of arrangements under section 21(1) of the Act to provide, in such cases as the authority considers appropriate, for the conveyance of persons to and from premises in which accommodation is provided for them under Part III of the Act.

Duties in respect of residents in transferred accommodation

(1)   Where a person is provided with accommodation pursuant to section 21(1) of the Act, and
      the residential accommodation is local authority accommodation provided pursuant to section 21(4) of the 1948 Act;
by local authority transfer the management of the residential accommodation to a voluntary organisation who
      (i)   manage it as a residential care home within the meaning of Part I of the Registered Homes Act 1984, and
      (ii) is registered under that Part or is not required to be so registered by virtue of being an exempt body; and

the person is accommodated in the residential accommodation immediately before and after the transfer,

While that person remains accommodated in that residential accommodation, the local authority shall remain under a duty to make arrangements to provide accommodation for him after any transfer to which paragraph (b) of this sub-paragraph refers.

(2)   For the purposes of paragraph (c) of sub-paragraph (1), a person shall be regarded as accommodated in residential accommodation if –
    (a)   he is temporarily absent from such accommodation (including circumstances in which he is in hospital or on holiday);
    (b)   before 1 April 1993, that accommodation was provided under paragraph 2(1) of Schedule 8 to the National Health Service Act 1977.
(3)   Where immediately before these Approvals and Directions come into force a local authority was under a duty to provide a person with accommodation by virtue of –
    (a)   the Secretary of State's former Directions under Section 21(1) of the National Assistance Act 1948 contained in Annex 1 of Department of Health Circular LAC (91)12; or
    (b)   the Secretary of State's former Directions under paragraph 2 of Schedule 8 to the National Health Service Act 1977 contained in Annex 2 of Department of Health Circular LAC (91)12,

While that person remains accommodated in that residential accommodation, the local authority shall remain under a duty to make arrangements to provide that person with accommodation from the date on which these Directions come into force.

Powers to make arrangements with other local authorities and voluntary organisations etc.

7. For the avoidance of doubt, these Approvals and Directions are without prejudice to any of the powers conferred on local authorities by section 21(4) and section 26(1) of the Act (arrangements with voluntary organisations etc.).

4.12   An assessment was made of the (complex) needs of a 91-year-old woman pursuant to s 47(1). Her needs were assessed as requiring a placement in a residential home where 24-hour care was provided. The alternative placement requested by the service user (for domestic accommodation) was not felt to be appropriate for her needs. Evidence was available to support the preference that she had requested. However, it was held that the assessment of the needs rested with the local authority, and it had not been shown that 'normal housing' was the answer to her community care needs. Consequently, although that route is available where the need to be met can be met within 'normal housing' (as in *Penfold*), it was not so in this instance (*Khana (by her litigation friend the Official Solicitor) v The Mayor and Burgesses of Southwark LBC* [2001] EWCA Civ 999, [2001] 4 CCLR 267).

4.13 The question of the extent of the duty of a council to provide accommodation (under s 21(1)(a) of the National Assistance Act 1948) was again considered in *R (on the application of M (FC)) v Slough Borough Council* [2008] UKHL 52, [2008] 11 CCLR 733. The facts of the case were that an application was made (by a visitor to the UK who had remained after the period of leave to remain as a visitor had expired and who had been diagnosed as HIV positive) for an assessment of his needs. The issue turned upon whether the local authority had correctly assessed him as having not eligible needs, and that even if he did have those needs, then any duty would be excluded by virtue of his own destitution (s 21(1A)).

4.14 The leading judgment is that of Baroness Hale, who provides a thorough analysis of the history of the relevant legislative provisions, together with policy decisions, from 1948 to the present day [7]-[29]. In particular, she identifies why it was that asylum seekers sought to rely on s 21(1)(a) 'with all other avenues of support and housing denied to them' [20], leading to 'an 'inverted and unseemly turf war between local and national government' [28]. She concluded that:

> '[31] accommodation may be arranged under section 21 (1)(a) without including either nursing or personal care. So the "care and attention" which is needed under section 21(1)(a) is a wider concept than "nursing or personal care". Section 21 accommodation may be provided for the purpose of preventing illness as well as caring for those who are ill ...

> [33] But "care and attention" must mean something more than "accommodation". Section 21(1)(a) is not a general power to provide housing. This is dealt with by other legislation entirely, with its own criteria for eligibility. If a simple need for housing, with or without the means of subsistence, were within section 21(1)(a), there would have been no need for the original section 21(1)(b). Furthermore, every homeless person who did not qualify for housing under the Housing Act 1996 would be able to turn to the local social services authority instead....I remain of the view which I expressed in *Wahid* ... that the natural and ordinary meaning of the words 'care and attention' in this context is "looking after". Looking after means doing something for the person being cared for which he cannot or should not be expected to do for himself: it might be household tasks which an old person can no longer perform or can only perform with great difficulty; it might be protection from risks which a mentally disturbed person cannot perceive; it might be personal care, such as feeding, washing or toileting ... the provision of medical care is expressly excluded.'

However, in this case, M 'Although ... HIV positive, his medical needs are being catered for by the National Health Service. So, even if they did amount to "a need for care and attention" within the meaning of section 21(1) (a) he would not qualify. But for the reasons given above, I do not think that they do amount to such a need ... As he does not fall within section 21(1)(a) it is unnecessary to decide whether he would be excluded by section 21(1A)' [36].

4.15 In effect, the needs of M were confined to: (a) medication; (b) medical checks, in addition to the quotidian needs of food and shelter. The mere presence of (a) and (b) (which were catered for by the NHS) did not bring him within the meaning of the phrase 'in need of care and attention'. This is one of a series of important decisions which focus upon the need for a close correlation between the phrasing of the statute, and the way in which the statutory power and/or obligation has developed. Nevertheless, it does not mean (as can be seen below) that a local authority can circumvent its obligations by arguing that the facts in this case will lead to a lack of an obligation under s 21(1)(a) when an individual is in need of care and attention.

4.16   The substance of this decision was re-visited in *R (on the application of Zarzour) v Hillngdon LBC & Secretary of State for Home Department (Interested Party)* [2009] EWCA Civ 1529, [2010] 13 CCLR 157. The judgment in *R (on the application of M (FC)) v Slough Borough Council* is described in terms that 'it firms up what is meant by an infirm asylum seeker' [18]. The claimant was blind, and also seeking asylum in the UK, and sought an assessment by the council. This assessment concluded with the decision that whilst he was insufficiently infirm to come within the definition of being 'in need of care and attention' and thus did not require the provision of accommodation, he did come within s 29 of the National Assistance Act 1948, and s 2(1) of the Chronically Sick and Disabled Persons Act 1970. For an analysis of the latter, see Chapter 2, and for the former, the statute is set out at **4.38** below. In summary, on the facts of this case the local authority had already determined (by virtue of the factual basis of its own assessment) the very extensive needs of the claimant. These stood in contrast to the needs of the claimant in *R (on the application of M (FC)) v Slough Borough Council*. It was not, therefore, open to argument on the part of the local authority that he did not stand 'in need of care and attention' as predicated by the exegesis in both cases where Baroness Hale had considered the meaning of the phrase. However, the Court of Appeal has also again had the opportunity to re-visited the same territory in *SL v Westminster City Council & The Medical Foundation/Mind (Intervening)* [2011] EWCA Civ 954. The issue was the 'proper interpretation and scope of section 21(1)(a) of the National Assistance Act 1948' [1]. The facts of the case revolved around an Iranian asylum seeker, who had been in receipt of some 'care and attention' from the council, but which it had argued was not care and attention within the meaning of the NAA 1948, and so in consequence owed him no duty to provide accommodation. In this instance, the Court also held (as in *Zarzour*) that the decision that the Claimant was not in need of 'care and attention' was in itself an unreasonable conclusion to have reached. The extent of the care and attention that he was receiving was substantially less than that in *Zarzour*. Laws LJ stated the broader question to be:

'[15] Must it be shown that the necessary care and attention cannot be given without the provision of residential accommodation? Or should the expression be construed as meaning that the provision of accommodation is reasonably required in order for care to be furnished in a way that fully meets the claimant's needs? ... Or are there other possible meanings?'

The issue of 'care and attention' was a matter of fact, determined upon individual factors in this case, it being the question of 'not otherwise available' which poses the more complex issue at law. Laws LJ summarised the development of the development of this area in the following terms:

> '[27] What has happened ... is that cases seem to have proceeded on the basis that all destitute persons are liable to be accommodated under section 21(1)(a) unless they are able bodied. Only the "able bodied" destitute are excluded by section 21(1A). There is, so to speak, no undistributed middle between the two subsections.'

He stated:

> '[34] *Zarzour* thus indicates a need to find at least some nexus between care and attention on the one hand and the provision of accommodation on the other. However in the same case I also stated:

>> "It is ... important to note that it has been accepted ... that the need of care and attention spoken of in section 21 was not such as necessarily to call for the provision of residential accommodation notwithstanding the fact that such provision is made by the statute the principal medium for meeting the need, and notwithstanding the further fact that, as other parts of Part III of the 1948 Act show, section 21 typically entails a move into local authority accommodation."

> ...

> [36] This test reflects, indeed exemplifies, the division of destitute asylum seekers into two mutually exclusive classes, able bodied and infirm. All member of the first class are covered by section 21(1A), and all members of the second by section 21(1)(a); there is no third class, no undistributed middle. And if all asylum seekers who are destitute and infirm are entitled to the benefit of section 21(1)(a), so are all other persons who are destitute and infirm.'

He concluded:

> '[39] the third meaning, that care and attention is not otherwise available unless it would be reasonably practicable and efficacious to supply it without the provision of accommodation, can in my judgment live with the existing authority. Indeed it is, I think, an implicit assumption made in the course of the learning's evolution.'

On the facts in this case, it was held that the care and attention could not be made available without the 'necessary basis of stable accommodation'. The consequence of the judgment should make it easier for not only asylum seekers, but all those who are in need of 'care and attention' to argue that such care and attention may not be made available without the basic requirement for accommodation. Thus, local authorities may find more claims for accommodation (albeit linked to the necessary pre-requisites in s 21) being made.

Needs and lack of re-assessment

4.17 In *R (on the application of S) (by her mother and next friend Sandra Branch) v Leicester CC* [2004] EWHC 533 (Admin), [2004] 7 CCLR 254, an assessment (in 1999) had determined that an adult suffering from autism was best placed in accommodation in Newcastle. The purpose of the placement was in part connected with education (which had ceased in 1998). There had been no formal re-assessment of her needs since 1999. The case follows the majority of decisions in this area, in that once there has been a determination of needs, and when the individual comes with the scope of s 21 of NAA 1948, and in this instance in the absence of any re-assessment, a decision to change accommodation arrangements without an assessed change in needs is unlawful.

24 Authority liable for provision of accommodation

(1) The local authority empowered under this Part of this Act to provide residential accommodation for any person shall subject to the following provisions of this Part of this Act be the authority in whose area the person is ordinarily resident.

(2) ...

(3) Where a person in the area of a local authority –

    (a)   is a person with no settled residence, or

    (b)   not being ordinarily resident in the area of the local authority, is in urgent need of residential accommodation under this Part of this Act,

the authority shall have the like power to provide residential accommodation for him as if he were ordinarily resident in their area.

(4) Subject to and in accordance with the arrangements under section twenty-one of this Act, a local authority shall have power, as respects a person ordinarily resident in the area of another local authority, with the consent of that other authority to provide residential accommodation for him in any case where the authority would have a duty to provide such accommodation if he were ordinarily resident in their area.

(5) Where a person is provided with residential accommodation under this Part of this Act, he shall be deemed for the purposes of this Act to continue to be ordinarily resident in the area in which he was ordinarily resident immediately before the residential accommodation was provided for him.

(6) For the purposes of the provision of residential accommodation under this Part of this Act, a patient in a hospital vested in the Secretary of State, a Primary Care Trust, an NHS trust or an NHS foundation trust shall be deemed to be ordinarily resident in the area, if any, in which he was ordinarily resident immediately before he was admitted as a patient to the hospital, whether or not he in fact continues to be ordinarily resident in that area.

(6A) In subsection (6) "NHS accommodation" means –

    (a)   accommodation (at a hospital or elsewhere) provided under the National Health Service Act 2006 or the National Health Service (Wales) Act 2006, or

(b) accommodation provided under section 117 of the Mental Health Act 1983 by a Primary Care Trust or Local Health Board, other than accommodation so provided jointly with a local authority.

(6B) The reference in subsection (6A)(b) to accommodation provided by a Primary Care Trust includes a reference to accommodation –

(a) in respect of which direct payments are made under regulations under section 12A(4) of the National Health Service Act 2006, and

(b) which would be provided under section 117 of the Mental Health Act 1983 apart from the regulations.

Ordinary residence

4.18 The Department of Health publication *Ordinary Residence: Guidance on the identification of the ordinary residence of people in need of community care services* (the Guidance) has been referred to elsewhere in this text in respect of other aspects of community care law. However, the largest portion of it is devoted to the question of deciding upon the ordinary residence of an individual within the context of the provision of accommodation. The statutory framework on ordinary residence in the National Assistance Act 1948 is set out in the Guidance as follows:

38 The statutory framework on ordinary residence is set out in sections 24, 29 and 32(3) to (5) of the 1948 Act, and the supporting directions.

39 Section 24 contains the key provisions on ordinary residence that relate to residential accommodation. These provisions set out where responsibility lies between local authorities for the provision of Part 3 accommodation for people with assessed needs:

- Section 24(1) provides that it is the local authority in which the person is ordinarily resident that has power to provide residential accommodation, and directions made under section 21 convert this power into a duty.
- Section 24(3) enables local authorities to treat those of "no settled residence" or "in urgent need" as if they are ordinarily resident in their area and provide them with residential accommodation. Directions made under section 21 convert this power into a duty in relation to people in urgent need (see paragraphs 43–50 for more details on the identification of those of "no settled residence" or "in urgent need").
- Section 24(4) provides local authorities with a power to provide residential accommodation for persons ordinarily resident in another local authority area, provided they have the consent of the other local authority to do so.
- Section 24(5) sets out the first of two provisions which disapply the normal approach to ordinary residence (referred to in this guidance as the "deeming provisions") and provides that where a person is provided with residential accommodation under Part 3, they are deemed to continue to be ordinarily resident in the area (if any) in which they were ordinarily resident immediately before the residential accommodation was provided.
- Section 24(6) sets out the second of the two deeming provisions and provides that a person who is in receipt of NHS accommodation is deemed to be ordinarily resident in the area (if any) in which they were ordinarily resident

immediately before they were provided with the NHS accommodation (see paragraphs 53–66 for more details on the two deeming provisions). **Section 24 applies to residential accommodation only. It does not apply to services provided under section 29 of the 1948 Act.**

40 Section 29(1) provides that it is the local authority in which a person is ordinarily resident that has a power to provide non-residential services, and directions made under this section convert this power into a duty.

4.19 The 'deeming provisions' set out in s 24(5) and s 24(6) are contained in paras 53–66:

53 The "deeming provisions" are found in sections 24(5) and 24(6) of the 1948 Act. If they apply, they affect the date at which a person's ordinary residence falls to be determined. Broadly, they set out that a person's prior ordinary residence is retained where that person is placed by a local authority in Part 3 accommodation in the area of another local authority, or is a person provided with NHS accommodation.

54 **The deeming provisions only apply in relation to the ordinary residence of people who are provided with Part 3 accommodation**. If a person is only provided with non-residential community care services, the deeming provisions do not apply.

55 Section 24(5) sets out that where a person is provided with residential accommodation under Part 3 of the Act, they are *deemed* to continue to be ordinarily resident in the area in which they were ordinarily resident (if any) immediately before the residential accommodation was provided. This means that where a local authority places a person in accommodation out of their area, they will retain the same responsibility for that person as if they were placed in accommodation within their own area.

56 There may be occasions where it is necessary for a local authority to place a person in accommodation in another local authority area. This may be because the person is in need of specialist accommodation that is only available in another local authority area or they have expressed a wish to live in a particular care home that is outside of the local authority boundary. In such cases, the person placed "out of area" is *deemed* to continue to be ordinarily resident in the area of the "placing" local authority and does not acquire an ordinary residence in the "host" local authority.

Any resolution of a dispute between local authorities by the Secretary of State is also subject to the *Ordinary Residence Disputes (National Assistance Act 1948) Directions 2010*.

4.20 However, in respect of s 24(5) specifically, Mr Justice Charles considered the matter of a dispute between two local authorities as to ordinary residence in *R (on the application of Greenwich LBC) v Secretary of State for Health and Bexley LBC* [2006] EWHC 2576 (Admin), [2007] 10 CCLR 60. As with the all cases in respect of ordinary residence, the Courts have consistently stressed that it is the individual facts of each case which tend to be the determinative factor. On the facts in this instance a service user was admitted to a residential care home (within the jurisdiction of Bexley) in May 2001. In May 2002 (having been re-assessed by Bexley) she was moved to a nursing home in Greenwich. She funded her own care, until June 2002, at which point her capital was reduced sufficiently to the extent that she no longer was obliged to pay for her own accommodation. Bexley made no arrangements for her care from that time onwards. Both local authorities agreed that she had been ordinarily resident in Bexley until May 2002. Neither local authority accepted that she had been ordinarily resident in either of their areas since June 2002. The consequence of such a determination would have meant that one of the local authorities would have been responsible for the funding of the accommodation. The dispute was referred to the Secretary of State (using s 32(3) of NAA 1948). It was held that in June 2002, one of the local authorities should have made arrangements under s 26 to make arrangements for the payment for accommodation. Where this should have happened (but did not) then s 24(5) applied (the deeming provision). A significant factor to be taken into account (on the facts in this case) was that in June 2002 she did not have any right to reside at a home in Bexley (however this was not in itself determinative of the issue). The decision of the Secretary of State (which was that she was ordinarily resident in Greenwich) was not incorrect (although criticised for being poorly expressed).

4.21 A claim arising *after* the Secretary of State had determined that an individual was ordinarily resident in Manchester was considered in *R (on the application of Manchester CC) v St Helens BC (PE interested party)* [2009] EWCA Civ 1348, [2010] 13 CCLR 48. A care package (funded by St Helens) had been arranged, and PE (who was the 'service user') had moved to Manchester under that care provision in 1999. St Helens continued to fund the care, until in 2006 it decided that PE was now ordinarily resident in Manchester. The Secretary of State agreed, and also stated that PE had, in fact, been ordinarily resident since 2000. Once this decision had been made by the SoS, St Helens ceased to fund the care package. Manchester then applied for permission to bring a claim by way of judicial review of that decision to cease the funding. The claim was unequivocally rejected. The first observation made by the court was that:

> '[1] it is not, in my view, satisfactory when two publicly funded authorities engage in expensive litigation to decide which of them should pay for the care in the home of a woman whose mental and psychological conditions require constant and expensive care.'

As the SoS had determined that PE was ordinarily resident in Manchester, then pursuant to s 29 of the National Assistance Act, then it had the statutory duty to her under that Act [14]. By virtue of the same status of PE as being ordinarily resident in Manchester, the same obligations arise through s 2 of the Chronically Sick and Disabled Persons Act 1970 [15]. Section 32(1) of the National Assistance Act placed the burden for paying for that care on Manchester [16]. The Court accepted that for the purposes of ordinary residence, there was no material difference between s 21 and s 29 [17] and the attention of the Court was drawn to the draft Guidelines in existence at that time (now in para 3 of the Guidance) to the effect that ordinary residence was central to whose duty it was to provide services. Lord Justice May held that:

> '[50] Section 29(1) of the 1948 Act, and the Secretary of State's directions, impose a statutory duty on local authorities to provide community care services for a person who is ordinarily resident in their area and whom they assess to be in need of community care services.'

4.22 The Guidance is extensive, and extremely helpful. The following parts of it are provided for reference only, as space does not permit replication of the entire document. It is readily obtainable from the website of the Department of Health. It covers:

(a) people who are self-funding in their residential care (paras 72–76);

(b) where arrangements are made by the Local Authority under s 21 of the National Assistance Act 1948 (and including funding issues) (paras 77–83);

(c) people who are accommodated under the 12 week property disregard (paras 84–86);

(d) people who are parties to a deferred payment agreement (paras 87–91);

(e) people moving into independent living accommodation who have mental capacity (paras 92–101);

(f) people moving into independent living accommodation who lack the mental capacity to decide where to live (paras 102–104);

(g) people moving from one local authority area to another of their own volition (paras 105–106);

(h) people leaving prison etc (paras 107–111);

(i) the effect of NHS Continuing Healthcare (paras 112–115b);

(j) joint packages on health and community care services (paras 116–119);

(k) Shared Lives Schemes (paras 120–128);

(l) British Citizens resuming permanent residence in England (paras 129–132);

(m) armed forces (paras 133–135);

(n) carers (paras 136–137);

(o) young people in transition (and see Chapter 5) (paras 138–158);

(p) determination of ordinary residence under the Community Care (Delayed Discharges etc) Act 2003; Mental Capacity Act 2005 (paras 159–178).

Some of the above have been considered in greater detail the relevant Chapters of this book. In respect of (e), (f) and (g) the issue of movement between one local authority area and another was considered in *Buckinghamshire County Council v Royal Borough of Kingston upon Thames and (1) SL (by her litigation friend the Official Solicitor), (2) The National Society for Epilepsy and (3) Secretary of State for Health) (Interested Parties)* [2011] EWCA Civ 457, [2011] 14 CCLR 426. The claimant was placed in accommodation under s 21 of the NAA 1948 (by Kingston) and were responsible for paying for that accommodation. However, there was a wish to move to 'supported living' and having assessed her needs, Kingston moved her to Buckinghamshire (and if she then became ordinarily resident there, then Buckinghamshire would become liable to pay for this arrangement). Buckinghamshire argued that there was an legal obligation for Kingston to have liaised with it prior to the move. The claim was dismissed – no such obligation arises out of such a move. However, observation of the new Guidance should avoid the necessity or possibility of such disputes arising as between councils where there is a move between two different local authorities.

CLOSURE OF HOMES/SALES OF HOMES/HOMES FOR LIFE AND PRIVATE CARE HOMES

Private care/public body

4.23 In *R v Servite Houses and Wandsworth LBC e p Goldsmith and Chatting* [2000] 3 CCLR 325, the issue of whether a housing association providing residential accommodation in a care home pursuant to arrangements with the local authority under s 26 National Assistance Act 1948 was exercising public law functions itself (by virtue of that arrangement) was considered. This was in the factual context of the closure of a home. The housing association had given an assurance to two residents that they would be able to remain in the premises for life. It subsequently decided to close the home for financial reasons. It was held that the housing association was not amenable to judicial review itself. It was not performing a public function. It was not the agent of the local authority. Once the local authority had made arrangements (by providing for residential accommodation with a voluntary organisation or other person) then it has discharged its obligation. Once so placed, the relationship between the local authority and the Housing Association was purely commercial. The need of the two residents was assessed that they required accommodation (and not accommodation at this particular location). The obligation of the local authority extended no further than to re-assess the needs of the two relevant residents once a decision had been made that they could not longer live in their chosen accommodation.

4.24   The same issue was considered in *YL (by her litigation friend the Official Solicitor) v Birmingham City Council* [2007] UKHL 27, [2007] 10 CCLR 505. Lord Scott held that:

> '[[25/26] at 513] Southern Cross is a company carrying on a socially useful business for profit ... It is operating in a commercial market with commercial competitors ... the fees charged by Southern Cross and paid by local or health authorities are charged and paid for a service. There is no element whatever of subsidy from public funds.
>
> [[34] at 515] ... I do not see how its nature could be thought to be anything other than private.
>
> [[104] at 536] In distinguishing between other legislation where it might be argued that a local authority stood in the shoes of a private contractor (and thus by analogy or extension a delegation of its functions as a public body) Lord Mance held "... no delegation of that sort exists in relation to the council's funds under section 21 of the 1948 Act".'

Therefore, a private care home used by a local authority pursuant to its duties was not a public authority within the meaning of s 6(3)(b) of the Human Rights Act 1998.

Sale of home/re-assessment

4.25   In *R (on the application of L) v Mayor and Burgesses of the London Borough of Barking and Dagenham* [2001] EWCA Civ 533, [2001] 2 FLR 763, [2001] 4 CCLR 196, the role of the local authority in respect of a residential home that it had previously directly owned and controlled was considered. The local authority had intended to sell its home to a housing association, which would then grant tenancies to the residents. The resident issued proceedings for judicial review, which were adjourned upon an undertaking that a new assessment of the needs would take place (s 47 of the National Health Service and Community Care Act 1990). It was alleged that the assessment was incomplete, and consequently, the proceedings were revived. She refused to agree to the draft contract, which principally related to a dispute over communal dining facilities. It was held that the dispute regarding dining facilities, and the rejection of the contract upon that basis, had not been reasonable. Further, it was held that whilst the actual detail arrangements for dining might be unreasonable, it was not for the Court to decide this aspect of the case, and that any complaint in that respect lay to the Secretary of State.

Promise of home for life

4.26   In *R v North and East Devon Health Authority ex p Coughlan and Secretary of State for Health and Royal College of Nursing* [1999] 2 CCLR 285, [2000] 2 WLR 622, an issue arose as to the transfer of obligations between a health authority and a local authority (and the division of responsibility as between health needs and community care needs the significance of which is considered separately in Chapter 7). On the facts of the case the patient had been given a express assurance if she moved to a particular facility, she could remain there for as long as she wished. That was a lawful promise which had produced an expectation upon her part and a benefit which was 'substantive, not simply procedural'. It was held that the decision of the Health Authority (within this statutory context) was unfair and not justified by an overriding public interest. In respect of local authority obligations, it was held that s 21(5) of NAA 1948 was wide enough to enable nursing services to be provided by a local authority, if it was in connection with the accommodation itself. Section 21(8) enables a local authority to provide this as a social or care service. Whether the local authority can provide nursing care is a question of fact and degree (which in turn will depend upon the substantive assessment carried out by the local authority). If the primary need is a health need, then the Health Authority remains responsible for health provision, even if the local authority has placed the resident under s 21. Otherwise, it can be provided by the local authority.

4.27 *Coughlan* was applied in *R (on the application of Bodimeade and others) v Camden LBC* [2001] EWHC Admin 271, [2001] 4 CCLR 246. Mr Justice Turner held:

'The starting point is the National Assistance Act 1948 which by Section 21 enables a Local Authority to make arrangements for "providing residential accommodation for persons over 18 who by reason of age or disability who are in need of care and attention which is not otherwise available to them" and comply with a direction made by the Secretary of State to the extent that he should direct. The National Health Service and Community Care Act 1990 requires a local authority which may provide care services to carry out assessments and where appropriate to decide whether the needs of the person assessed calls for the provision of any services in the nature of community care. It is common ground between the parties that such services include the provision of accommodation under Section 21 of the National Assistance Act 1948 ... Section 7 of the Local Authority Social Services Act 1970 requires Local Authorities when exercising social services functions including the provision of care services to act under the guidance of the secretary of state. Such guidance should be followed unless there is good reason not to do so; *R v Islington LBC ex p Rixon* [1998] 1 CCLR 119.'

4.28 In considering the expectations of the residents whose home was to be closed he cited the ratio of Lord Woolf thus:

'[256] (a) the Court may decide that the public authority is only required to bear in mind its previous policy or other representation, giving it the weight it thinks right, but no more, before deciding whether to change course. Here the Court is confined to reviewing the decision on *Wednesbury* grounds ... (b) on the other hand the Court may decide that the promise or practice induces a legitimate expectation of, for example, being consulted before a particular decision is taken. Here it is uncontentious that the Court itself will require the opportunity for consultation to be given unless there is an overriding reason to resile from it in which case the Court itself will judge the adequacy of the reason for the change of policy, taking into account what fairness requires (c) where the Court considers that a lawful promise ... has induced a legitimate expectation of a benefit that is substantive, not merely procedural, authority now establishes that here too the Court will in a proper case decide whether to frustrate the expectation is so unfair that to take a new and different course will amount to an abuse of power. Here, once the legitimacy of the expectation is established, the Court will have the task of weighing the requirements of fairness against any overwhelming interest relied upon for the change in policy.'

On the facts in this case, it was held that the assessments had not been carried out in accordance with the statutory guidance, or the relevant Practitioner's Guide. It had also failed to take into account a statement given to the residents that the accommodation was a 'home for life'. This in itself raised a legitimate expectation to that effect. The local authority was obliged to make a fresh decision in the light of the judgment, and the relevant considerations highlighted in *Coughlan*.

4.29   The converse was held in *R (on the Application of Collins) v Lincolnshire Health Authority* [2001] EWHC 685 (Admin), [2001] 4 CCLR 429 (although this is a case which did not turn on the responsibilities of a local authority). It was held that a decision to transfer a patient from long-stay care to the community (despite a promise of a 'home for life') had been carried out: (a) with a proper understanding of the relevant government policy, and upon a proper and full assessment of her needs; (b) resources had not played an improper part in the decision; (c) proper weight had been attached to the preference of the patient to stay where she was; and (d) *Coughlan* was distinguished on the facts of the case in that there was no financial consideration in making the decision to move, but it was acting in what it (fairly) considered to be her best interests and there was no clear and certain promise of a 'home for life'. The decision of the High Court was upheld in the Court of Appeal ([2001] EWCA Civ 1779), and a subsequent appeal to the European Court of Human Rights was held to be inadmissible (*Collins v United Kingdom* App no 11909/02, [2003] 6 CCLR 388).

Closure of Homes: Art 2

4.30   In *R (on the application of Hide) v Staffordshire County Council* [2007] EWCA Civ 860, [2008] 11 CCLR 28, it was alleged that the council had made a decision to close 22 care homes and 10 day centres. The council denied that it had made such a decision, and gave assurances to the contrary. Despite this, an application was made by way of judicial review, which was refused. Given that no decision was made, and assurances had been given on this point, it is perhaps not surprising that permission to issue a writ was refused, but nevertheless that decision was appealed, and that, also, failed. However, where a 'multi-staged' decision is in progress, it may not be premature to make an application whilst this procedure is continuing (see **4.42**).

4.31   A more substantive challenge to the closure of homes (but which also failed on not entirely dissimilar grounds) was considered in *R (on the application of Wilson v Coventry City Council); R (on the application of*

Thomas) v (1) Havering LBC (2) Secretary of State for Health [2008] EWHC 2300 (Admin), [2009] 12 CCLR 7. In this instance it was alleged that there was a demonstrable (but general) risk to the residents of death if they were to be obliged to move elsewhere upon closure (and that this engaged Art 2 'Right to Life'), and that only a general consideration had been given to that risk, and that therefore the decision to close had been made on a *Wednesbury* irrational basis as an individual assessment of the risks to each resident should have been carried out. The Court held that there was no requirement for an individual assessment, and relied in part upon *R (on the application of Cowl) v Plymouth City Council* for that proposition. *Cowl* is considered at **4.33** below – it will be noted that the resulting *draft* guidance for local authorities suggests exactly the opposite (that there should be such and individual assessment – Appendix Nine, 1((b)). In any event, the local authority did undertake such an assessment but after the decision to close had been made. This was to enable as smooth a transition as possible to another location. The increased risk of death had been drawn to the attention of the council, and this evidence was equivocal, and not determinative. It had been taken into account as such and could not form the basis of an attack upon the reasonableness of the decision to close the homes. The argument using Art 2 failed since the evidence of an increased risk of death was too general, and in any event the local authority was entitled when reaching a conclusion to decide what was a balance between the needs of the residents and that of the community. In addition, there was evidence that the local authority had planned the move carefully, with the intention of minimising the risk to the residents. In effect, it would appear that the local authorities *had* followed the guidance that emerged *post Cowl* (see below). Whether they had or not, it is clear from this case that if a local authority does wish to decide to close a care home, then it remains the fairest method of making that decision.

4.32 An almost identical argument was placed before the Court in *R (on the application of Rutter) v Stockton on Tees BC* [2008] EWHC 2651 (Admin), [2009] 12 CCLR 27, and which failed for almost precisely the same reasons. It was argued that the risk to the life of the sole remaining resident of a care home was such that the decision to close the home was vitiated by a failure to take that risk into account (ie Art 2). The Court accepted that at the time the decision had been made, insufficient weight may have been attached to this point, but that it subsequently *had* formed a part of the decision making process at a later stage. The evidence pointed to a small risk to the life of the claimant, and moreover, by the time the application had been made upon her behalf, all of the other residents had moved, and she was being supported by 19 members of staff at a cost of £7,400 per week.

Procedure for closure; alternatives to litigation

4.33 Similarly, in *R (on the application of Cowl and others) v Plymouth CC* [2001] 4 CCLR 475, [2001] EWHC 734 (where the local authority owned a care home), a decision was made to close the home in order to reduce its expenditure. First, it was held that there was insufficiently clear evidence of a promise of a 'home for life'. Secondly, the residents had been consulted, and the re-assessed needs of the residents suggested that these could be met in other accommodation. There was no imminent closure of the home in any event. Thirdly, a decision to close the home in order to reduce local authority expenditure was compatible with its statutory obligations. Finally, it was held that it had been unfortunate that the complaints procedure offered to the residents had not been used. The residents subsequently did so complain, and a report was prepared in respect of the decision to close (*Report and Findings of the Extraordinary Complaints Panel – Closure of Granby Way Residential Care Home for Older People, Plymouth – November 2002* [2003] 6 CCLR 393). In between the *Report*, the case was re-considered in part by the Court of Appeal ([2001] EWCA Civ 1935, [2002] 1 WLR 803). Lord Woolf CJ expressed concern about the manner in which the litigation had arisen in the first place and held:

> '[25] We do not single out either side's lawyer for particular criticism. What followed was due to the unfortunate culture in litigation of this nature of over-judicialising the processes which are involved. It is indeed unfortunate that, that process having started, instead of the parties focussing on the future they insisted on arguing about what had happened in the past.'

The agreement reached between the parties led to the report referred to above and set out below. This contains useful draft guidance for local authorities.

Report and findings of the Extraordinary Complaints Panel – Closure of Granby Way Residential Care Home for Older People, Plymouth – November 2002

12. OUR RECOMMENDATIONS

12.1 WE therefore make the following recommendations to the Council based on these findings and conclusions:

1. That the Council look again at the recommendation to close Granby Way Residential Home and that when they do so they consider specifically:

(a)   This report, particularly its findings and conclusions.
(b)   The evidence of Dr Jeffreys as to the likely effect of a move on each of the named residents.

2. That in its reconsiderations, the Council:

(a)   Weighs specifically the effect of a move on these individual residents against any perceived need for financial constraint.
(b)   Acknowledge the fact, as we find it, that notwithstanding that legally enforceable promises of a home for life were not made by any official of the council, there was a general expectation, fostered widely by some officials, that residents were unlikely to be moved from their homes save for medical reasons.

(c)   Accept that in the particular circumstances of these residents none of them should be moved to another residential home at any point in their lives without their freely given consent to an alternative placement acceptable to them.

3. That in future cases of possible closure the draft guidelines set out in Appendix Nine [reproduced below] should be followed.

His Honour Sir Jonathan Clarke, Mrs Annie Stevenson, Mr Brian Parrott, 4 November 2002.

APPENDIX NINE

Draft Guidelines for Local Authorities when considering and implementing the Closure of a Residential Care Home for Older People.

(His Honour Sir Jonathan Clarke, Mrs Annie Stevenson, Mr Brian Parrott, 4 November 2002)

These draft guidelines are intended to highlight specific issues about which a local authority should be mindful when faced with such a far-reaching decision as the closure of a care home. Elected members, senior managers and practitioners will all be aware of these issues. This paper is written to emphasise their importance at a time when decision-makers will be faced with conflicting pressures.

It must be remembered that the majority of residents of care homes will consider the home they have moved into to be their permanent home. The decision they made to move into the home may have been one of the most difficult and important decisions they have ever made, and they will not be expecting to have to move again. Many may be highly vulnerable people, physically and emotionally, and feel themselves to be quite powerless.

In consequence, any decision to close a care home must be made with the utmost sensitivity for those living in the home. The decision must take into account the impact the closure will have on each resident individually – physically, emotionally and psychologically, and each individual should be at the centre of the decision-making process. This should involve an individual assessment of each resident being made prior to any decision being taken so that those responsible for taking such onerous decisions do so with the full facts before them. From the individual's perspective, the closure of their home may be a major loss, tantamount to bereavement, with many of the emotions associated with death present in this context – such as denial, disbelief, anger, passive acceptance, immobilisation of feelings. It must be remembered too that staff working in the home, the residents' relatives and the home or care provider will all be affected by the closure. Those caught up in it may not be at their most receptive and thus there may be many blocks to effective communication. All those responsible for the well being of the residents should consider each of the residents as if they were their own close relatives.

It is acknowledged that local authorities have to make difficult decisions balancing the needs of one set of citizens with the overall needs of the population. Indeed it is the duty if the authority not to avoid making decisions which will increase the benefit to groups of people in need. Sometimes these decisions have to be made when those affected do not agree. However, if the following principles and guidelines are applied in the decision-making and implementation process, it is far more likely that those affected will be able to adjust to any change required of them, with the minimum of distress.

1 The process of consultation and decision-making should be as open and transparent as possible without hidden agendas. Residents and relatives must be involved throughout the process.

(a) *Consultation.* This should not be rushed and must be genuine with face-to-face contact explaining the reasons for closure. Residents should be offered an advocacy service (and access to legal advice) in addition to their key-worker, throughout the whole decision-making process.

(b) *Assessments.* These should be made taking into account the individual's life history and all their needs. They should cover the physical, emotional, psychological, social and cultural needs and wishes of each individual and the risks involved for them in any move of residential home. Residents should have copies of their assessments and care plans. Along with the resident, the care staff and relatives should be central to the assessments and be included in discussions. A copy of a resident's 'life story' to take with them to a new home could make a huge difference to aid a smooth transition.

(c) *Possible Groupings.* Careful consideration should be given as to whether residents wish to move singly or in groups, explicitly thinking how much significance the group has for them.

(d) *Timescales.* All residents, relatives and advocates should be given a simple project plan including timescales.

(e) *Involvement.* As far as possible in the proposed closure process, the residents should be entitled to be part of the process of change so they see gain for themselves and others. They should be involved in any plans for alternative provision.

2 Residents with dementia should be assessed to see what capacity they have for being consulted and meaningfully involved. Those without capacity must have an advocate to act for them. Those with a history of mental illness and those suffering from any form of dementia need to be assessed with particular attention given to the impact of a move on their total well-being.

3 If a decision is made to transfer a resident to another care home the local authority should consider if the care staff known to the resident should maintain contact with the resident in the new home to help with a smooth handover. In particular, details about individual preferences, subject to the resident's wishes for these to be communicated, can make a real difference to the resident's wishes for these to be communicated, can make a real difference to the resident's well being (as well as their written 'life-story'.)

4 The staff affected by a potential closure should be treated with special care. The way they are treated has a direct effect on the residents. They should also be genuinely consulted, have access to independent advice and the trade unions

should be consulted. They must have a written project plan and be kept well informed – not just for themselves, but so they can respond to concerns the residents and relatives may have.

5 The timing of breaking the news to residents is also critical. Using the analogy of bereavement, people must be allowed to go through the various stages such as shock, denial, anger and finally acceptance with skilled staff and others on hand to assist individuals through the process, Residents' families or close friends may also have feelings of guilt and anxiety and may need special attention. Building in enough time to work through the stages is crucial. The local authority should keep people well informed every step of the way, making sure the residents, advocates, relatives and staff are the first to know of any developments. They need to be told the facts in a straightforward way, without bad news being couched in language intended to soften the blow, which could be received as being patronising.

6 Finally, to avoid misunderstanding about whether or not a placement is promised as 'a home for life', whenever potential residents are shown around a care home prior to their admission they should not be assured that the building will be their permanent home for ever, however desirable this feels. Rather, they should be assured that their wishes and needs will be continually reviewed with them, with their relatives and any other significant people. If remaining in the care home becomes no longer appropriate or possible they should be reassured about the process by which a move to another setting would be considered and made.

Home for life; re-assessment; resources

4.34 In *R (on the Application of Phillips) (by her daughter and litigation friend) and Rowe (by her sister and litigation friend) v Walsall MBC* [2001] EWHC Admin 789, [2002] 5 CCLR 383, a similar issue was raised (and again, in respect of a residential care home owned by the local authority). A decision was made to close the home. On the evidence in the case, there was some doubt as to the credibility and provenance of the promise of a 'home for life' and on the facts the most that could be said was that the local authority had assumed a permanent responsibility to find a suitable placement. A decision to close did not itself import a necessity to re-assess the needs of the residents. That assessment would be required at the point when it might be necessary to move the resident elsewhere. The local authority had carried out an appropriate consultation process – it was not required to respond to each view expressed during that process. There was no breach of Art 8 by way of substituting one home for another. The local authority was entitled to consider its resources when deciding to close a home.

Inadequate consultation; Art 8

4.35 However, in *R (on the application of Madden) v Bury MBC* [2002] EWHC 1882 (Admin), [2002] 5 CCLR 622, a decision to close two residential homes (owned by the local authority) was quashed. This was because: (a) the consultation process was inadequate (the residents were not given the true reasons for the decision to close; and (b) insufficient consideration had been given to Art 8.

4.36 On a connected point (a decision by a local authority not to renew a contract with residential care homes) (*R (on the application of Haggerty and others) v St Helens Council* [2003] EWHC 803 (Admin), [2003] 6 CCLR 352) it was held that: (a) the local authority was entitled to take into consideration the increased fees demanded by the care homes in terms of its own resources; (b) the deadline set by the owners of the care homes for renewal of the contract had passed, and even if the claim had succeeded, it was likely that the homes would close. This went to the exercise of discretion in respect of any remedy that the Court might have granted. There was also held to have been no breach of either Art 2, 3 or 8 of the European Convention on Human Rights.

Movement of resident and flawed assessment

4.37 In *R (on the Application of Goldsmith) v Wandsworth LBC* [2004] EWCA Civ 1170, [2004] 7 CCLR 472, a decision had been made by the local authority that the appellant should move from a (private) residential care home to a nursing home. The local authority also had an agreement with the South West London Strategic Health Authority, which in turn relied upon guidance by the Department of Health on Nursing Care and Residential Accommodation. The decisions as to the type and level of care required by individuals was made by a joint health and social services panel. The panel met (and excluded the daughter of the appellant) and decided that nursing care was appropriate. Subsequent to this decision a community care assessment was carried out (a s 47 assessment) which reached the opposite conclusion in terms of needs to the panel. The private residential care home indicated that it would accept the appellant, subject to finance being provided by the local authority. A report was obtained by the local authority from a consultant geriatrician which confirmed the view of the panel. However, he was not provided with the s 47 assessment. It was held that the panel decision was vitiated by: (a) the absence of the daughter; and (b) before the s 47 assessment had taken place. Further, the instruction of the consultant geriatrician had been done in a manner which simply requested him to confirm the decision of the panel, and moreover he was also not shown the assessment. Finally, the decision was made predominantly on financial grounds, with no consideration of all the factors, or the well-being of the appellant. The decision to move the appellant was quashed.

Section 29 of the National Assistance Act 1948

4.38 Section 29 of NAA 1948 is reproduced below for the sake of completeness and convenience. However, it also forms the basis for much of the case-law set out in Chapter 3 in respect of both the Chronically Sick and Disabled Persons Act 1970, and the National Health Service and Community Care Act 1990 and is primarily of significance within that context.

29 Welfare arrangements for blind, deaf, dumb and crippled persons, etc

(1) A local authority may, with the approval of the Secretary of State, and to such extent as he may direct in relation to persons ordinarily resident in the area of the

local authority shall make arrangements for promoting the welfare of persons to whom this section applies, that is to say persons aged eighteen or over who are blind, deaf or dumb or who suffer from mental disorder of any description, and other persons aged eighteen or over who are substantially and permanently handicapped by illness, injury, or congenital deformity or such other disabilities as may be prescribed by the Minister.

(2), (3) ...

(4) Without prejudice to the generality of the provisions of subsection (1) of this section, arrangements may be made thereunder –

    (a)   for informing persons to whom arrangements under that subsection relate of the services available for them thereunder;

    (b)   for giving such persons instruction in their own homes or elsewhere in methods of overcoming the effects of their disabilities;

    (c)   for providing workshops where such persons may be engaged (whether under a contract of service or otherwise) in suitable work, and hostels where persons engaged in the workshops, and other persons to whom arrangements under subsection (1) of this section relate and for whom work or training is being provided in pursuance of the Disabled Persons (Employment) Act 1944 or the Employment and Training Act 1973 may live;

    (d)   for providing persons to whom arrangements under subsection (1) of this section relate with suitable work (whether under a contract of service or otherwise) in their own homes or elsewhere;

    (e)   for helping such persons in disposing of the produce of their work;

    (f)   for providing such persons with recreational facilities in their own homes or elsewhere;

    (g)   for compiling and maintaining classified registers of the persons to whom arrangements under subsection (1) of this section relate.

(4A) Where accommodation in a hostel is provided under paragraph (c) of subsection (4) of this section –

    (a)   if the hostel is managed by a local authority, section 22 of this Act shall apply as it applies where accommodation is provided under section 21;

    (b)   if the accommodation is provided in a hostel managed by a person other than a local authority under arrangements made with that person, subsections (2) to (4A) of section 26 of this Act shall apply as they apply where accommodation is provided under arrangements made by virtue of that section; and

    (c)   sections 32 and 43 of this Act shall apply as they apply where accommodation is provided under sections 21 to 26;

and in this subsection references to "accommodation" include references to board and other services, amenities and requisites provided in connection with the accommodation, except where in the opinion of the authority managing the premises or, in the case mentioned in paragraph (b) above, the authority making the arrangements their provision is unnecessary.

(5) ...

(6) Nothing in the foregoing provisions of this section shall authorise or require –

    (a)   the payment of money to persons to whom this section applies, other than persons for whom work is provided under arrangements made by virtue of paragraph (c) or paragraph (d) of subsection (4) of this section or who are engaged in work which they are enabled to perform in consequence of anything done in pursuance of arrangements made under this section; or

(b)   the provision of any accommodation or services required to be provided under the National Health Service Act 2006 or the National Health Service (Wales) Act 2006 ...

(7) A person engaged in work in a workshop provided under paragraph (c) of subsection (4) of this section, or a person in receipt of a superannuation allowance granted on his retirement from engagement in any such workshop, shall be deemed for the purposes of this Act to continue to be ordinarily resident in the area in which he was ordinarily resident immediately before he was accepted for work in that workshop; and for the purposes of this subsection a course of training in such a workshop shall be deemed to be work in that workshop.

4.39   Directions have been made pursuant to s 29(1) of NAA 1948 (Appendix 2 to Department of Health Circular No LAC (93) 10). This is set out below.

CIRCULAR NO LAC (93) 10 APPENDIX 2

Commencement, interpretation and extent

1. (1) These Approvals and Directions shall come into force on 1 April 2003.

(2) In these Approvals and Directions, unless the context otherwise requires, 'the Act' means the National Assistance Act 1948.

(3) The Interpretation Act 1978 applies to these Approvals and Directions as it applies to an Act of Parliament.

(4) These Approvals and Directions shall apply only to England and Wales.

Powers and duties to make welfare arrangements

2. (1) The Secretary of State hereby approves the making by local authorities of arrangements under section 29(1) of the Act for all persons to whom that subsection applies and directs local authorities to make arrangements under section 29(1) of the Act in relation to persons who are ordinarily resident in their area for all or any of the following purposes –

(a)   to provide a social work service and such advice and support as may be needed for people in their own homes or elsewhere;
(b)   to provide, whether at centres or elsewhere, facilities for social rehabilitation and adjustment to disability including assistance in overcoming limitations of mobility or communication;
(c)   to provide, whether at centres or elsewhere, facilities for occupational, social, cultural and recreational activities and, where appropriate, the making of payments to persons for work undertaken by them;

(2) The Secretary of State hereby directs local authorities to make the arrangements referred to in section 29(4)(g) of the Act (compiling and maintaining registers) in relation to persons who are ordinarily resident in their area.

(3) The Secretary of State hereby approves the making by local authorities of arrangements under section 29(1) of the Act for all persons to whom that subsection applies for the following purposes –

(a) to provide holiday homes;
(b) to provide free or subsidised travel for all or any persons who do not otherwise qualify for travel concessions, but only in respect of travel arrangements for which concessions are available;
(c) to assist a person in finding accommodation which will enable him to take advantage of any arrangements made under section 29(1) of the Act;
(d) to contribute to the cost of employing a warden on welfare functions in warden assisted housing schemes;
(e) to provide warden services for occupiers of private housing.

Save as is otherwise provided for under this paragraph, the Secretary of State hereby approves the making by local authorities of all or any of the arrangements referred to in section 29(4) of the Act (welfare arrangements etc) for all persons to whom section 29(1) applies.

Welfare arrangements with another local authority

3. The Secretary of State hereby approves the making by local authorities of arrangements under section 29(1) of the Act, where appropriate, with another local authority for the provision of any of the services referred to in these Approvals and Directions.

Welfare arrangements with voluntary organisations and otherwise

4. For the avoidance of doubt, these Approvals and Directions are without prejudice to the powers conferred on local authorities by section 30(1) of the Act (voluntary organisations for disabled persons welfare).

Sections 29 and 21 and eligible needs and resources

4.40 As will be appreciated, the interrelationship between not only different statutes within this area, but also between the different sections in the statutes themselves will often give rise to different obligations within the same factual context. *R (on the Application of Hughes) v Liverpool CC* [2005] EWHC 428 (Admin), [2005] 8 CCLR 243 is one of many examples of this. The case was initially founded on the (purported) obligation of the local authority to provide accommodation pursuant to s 21 of NAA 1948. As in *R (on the application of Wahid) v The Mayor and Burgesses of Tower Hamlets LBC* the Court relied upon Appendix 1 of Circular No LAC (93) 10. The local authority sought to argue that the housing needs of the applicant came merely within the Housing Act 1996. Mr Justice Mitting also relied upon Appendix 2 of Circular No LAC

(93) 10 and Circular No LAC (2002) 13 (referred to mainly in Chapter 3, and then known as *Fair Access to Care Services: Guidance on Eligibility Criteria for Adult Social Care*). It was argued upon behalf of Liverpool that:

> '[[26] at 251] ... no decision of the Courts has yet been made under section 29 of the 1948 Act to like effect as *ex p Help the Aged* [paragraphs 3.8. and 3.9 above] and *Kujtim* [paragraph 3.7 above] under section 21. That may be so, but there is in my judgment no difference of principle or practice between the approach that the court should adopt to the two sections. Section 2 of the Chronically Sick and Disabled Persons Act 1970 imposes on the local authority a duty to make arrangements for the provision of practical assistance in the home in the exercise of its functions under section 29. Section 29 imposes a duty to make arrangements for promoting the welfare of relevant persons to such an extent as the Secretary of State may direct. He has so directed in local authority circular 93/10 appendix 2 to provide "such support as may be needed for people in their own home". Section 7 of the Local Authority Social Services Act 1970 provides that the Secretary of State may give guidance to local authorities in the exercise of their functions under Section 29. Liverpool accept that they are obliged to follow the guidance of the Secretary of State in making those arrangements. The Secretary of State's Guidance provide that they should identify eligible needs and meet them; see paragraphs 3 and 43 of the Guidance.

> [[27] at 251] Resources, which are relevant to the setting of eligibility criteria, see paragraph 18, are not relevant in meeting identified eligible needs ...'

The consequence was that the local authority was held to have failed in its duty to provide appropriate accommodation, and that provisions under the Housing Act were not relevant where there was a requirement for specially adapted housing arising out of eligible needs.

4.41   The analysis as to what is a need, and what is not, is seen throughout the litigation in this area. There will always be a complex interrelationship not only between the different statutes, but perhaps more obviously, dependent on the facts in each case. The latter can be seen, for example, by contrasting *R (on the application of M (FC)) v Slough Borough Council* with *R (on the application of Zarzour) v Hillingdon LBC and the Secretary of State for the Home Department* (**4.13–4.16** above) and in the case below.

4.42   In *R (on the application of B) v Worcestershire CC* [2009] EWHC 2915 (Admin), [2010] 13 CCLR 13 issues arising out of s 29 of the NAA 1948, and s 47 of the National Health Service and Community Care Act 1990, and s 2 of the Chronically Sick and Disabled Persons Act 1970 were considered. Although this is not directly related to the provision of accommodation (but day services) the decision of the court is relevant to the law across the entire area, and illustrates the difficulty of dividing one part from another. The factual basis of the case involved the needs of physically and learning disabled adults. Those needs had included the use of a day centre specifically designed for those with profound and multiple learning disabilities. A report had been prepared that concluded that their needs could be met elsewhere, with significant financial savings to the local authority, and that the centre at which their day services could be provided could then be closed entirely. The actual decision making process was described as 'multi-staged' and a final decision had not actually been made. It was clear on the facts of this case that the assessment of the needs of the individuals was intrinsically bound up in the decision to close the day centre, and distribute them to other centres where it was said that those needs could be met. The decision making process was held to be irrational, in that the local authority had failed to provide to itself sufficient information as to whether the assessed needs of the individuals would be met at the alternative centres. In the light of *McDonald* (see **4.13** et seq above) and had the consultation process and assessment of the impact on the needs of the individuals been adequately considered, it seems unlikely now that any challenge to such a closure would be effective.

Ordinary residence/mandatory and permissive functions

4.43 The claimants were resident in the area of Essex County Council. They were provided with day care facilities elsewhere (by Southend Borough Council). Those facilities were withdrawn. It was held that it was the local authority where the claimants resided that owed them duties pursuant to s 29 of NAA 1948. One duty was mandatory (and this was owed to those ordinarily resident within its territory). The other was permissive (pursuant to s 47(1) of the National Health Service and Community Care Act 1990) which is 'where it appears to a local authority that any person for whom they may provide or arrange for the provision of community care services, the authority (a) shall carry out an assessment of his needs ... and ... shall then decide whether his needs call for the provision by them of any such services'. This also fell to Essex County Council. The decision by Southend Borough Council was neither unlawful, nor in breach of the claimant's rights under Art 8 of the European Convention on Human Rights.

Choice of accommodation

4.44 Directions were made by the Secretary of State (pursuant to s 7A of the Local Authority Social Services Act 1970). These directions are the National Assistance Act 1948 (Choice of Accommodation) Directions 1992. They are accompanied by Guidance (Department of Health Circular No LAC (2004) 20). These are set out below. Directions were also made in respect of cross-border choice (that is to say, between Scotland and England) in Circular No LAC (93) 18.

NATIONAL ASSISTANCE ACT 1948 (CHOICE OF ACCOMMODATION) DIRECTIONS 1992 (as amended)

The Secretary of State in exercise of the powers conferred by section 7A of the Local Authority Social Services Act 1970 and of all other powers enabling her in that behalf hereby makes the following Directions –

Citation, commencement and extent

1 (1) These Directions may be cited as the National Assistance Act 1948 (Choice of Accommodation) Directions 1992 and shall come into force on 1st April 1993.

(2) These Directions extend only to England.

Local authorities to provide preferred accommodation

2 Where a local authority have assessed a person under section 47 of the National Health Service and Community Care Act 1990 (assessment) and have decided that accommodation should be provided pursuant to section 21 of the National Assistance Act 1948 (provision of residential accommodation), the local authority shall, subject to paragraph 3 of these Directions, make arrangements for accommodation pursuant to section 21 for that person at the place of his choice within England and Wales (in these Directions called 'preferred accommodation') if he has indicated that he wishes to be accommodated in preferred accommodation.

Conditions for provision of preferred accommodation

3 Subject to paragraph 4 of these Directions the local authority shall only be required to make or continue to make arrangements for a person to be accommodated in his preferred accommodation if –

(a)   the preferred accommodation appears to the authority to be suitable in relation to his needs as assessed by them;

(b)   the cost of making arrangements for him at his preferred accommodation would not require the authority to pay more than they would usually expect to pay having regard to his assessed needs;

(c)   the preferred accommodation is available;

(d)   the persons in charge of the preferred accommodation provide it subject to the authority's usual terms and conditions, having regard to the nature of the accommodation, for providing accommodation for such a person under Part III of the National Assistance Act 1948.

Guidance

4.45   Circular No LAC (2004) 20 was issued on 14 October 2004, and was effective from that date. It provides guidance on both the Directions (referred to above) and on the National Assistance (Residential Accommodation) (Additional Payments and Assessment of Resources) (Amendment) (England) Regulations 2001, SI 2001/3441. They are intended to:

'... ensure that when councils with social services responsibilities ... make placements in care homes or care homes providing nursing care, that, within reason, individuals are able to exercise genuine choice over where they live. The Regulations give individuals the right to enter into more expensive accommodation than they would otherwise have been offered in certain circumstances.'

By way of summary only it provides assistance in respect of: suitability of accommodation (in accordance with the assessment by the local authority); the usual cost of the preferred accommodation; availability of accommodation and the manner in which local authorities might ensure availability; arrangement of terms and conditions between local authorities and the private sector; placement in more expensive accommodation; responsibility for the costs of accommodation by the local authority; local authority payment of difference between the extra cost of accommodation direct to the private sector; top-ups by the resident and/or a third party; the amount that the resident or third party pays by way of top-up; alteration in prices; the responsibilities of third parties and residents in making top-up payments and the consequences of failing to make those payments; the position of those already in residential care; lack of capacity by residents as to where they might prefer to live; block contracting.

The extracts from the guidance below do not include any aspects of financial arrangements which might affect choice of accommodation. These are included in Chapter 6.

CIRCULAR NO LAC (2004) 20

1. Summary

1.1 If, after an assessment of need, made in accordance with the General Principles of Assessment in LAC(2002)13 Fair Access to Care Services and, where applicable, in accordance with a specific assessment framework and discussion with the individual and their carers, a council decides to provide residential accommodation under section 21 of the National Assistance Act 1948 either permanently or temporarily (intermediate care or short term break or any interim care arrangement), it will make a placement on behalf of the individual in suitable accommodation. Nearly all placements under section 21 of the National Assistance Act 1948 are made in registered care homes. However, some adults are placed under section 21 of the National Assistance Act 1948 in unregistered settings where they need neither nursing care or personal care. While the detail of this guidance applies to registered care homes, the principles apply to adults placed in unregistered settings.

1.2 When the term 'residential care' is used in this guidance, it covers placements made on both a long-term and a temporary (which includes short-term care) basis to care homes, whether they provide nursing care or not.

1.3 If the individual concerned expresses a preference for particular accommodation ('preferred accommodation') within England and Wales, the council must arrange for care in that accommodation, provided:

- The accommodation is suitable in relation to the individual's assessed needs (see paragraphs 2.5.1 to 2.5.3)
- To do so would not cost the council more than what it would usually expect to pay for accommodation for someone with the individual's assessed needs see paragraphs 2.5.4 to 2.5.8). This is referred to throughout this guidance as the usual cost.

- The accommodation is available (see paragraphs 2.5.9 and 2.5.15)
- The provider of the accommodation is willing to provide accommodation subject to the council's usual terms and conditions for such accommodation (see paragraphs 2.5.16 to 2.5.17)

1.4 If an individual requests it, the council must also arrange for care in accommodation more expensive than it would usually fund provided a third party or, in certain circumstances, the resident, is willing and able to pay the difference between the cost the council would usually expect to pay and the actual cost of the accommodation (to 'top up'). These are the only circumstances where either a third party or the resident may be asked to top up (see paragraph 3).

2. Preferred Accommodation

2.1 As with all aspects of service provision, there should be a general presumption in favour of individuals being able to exercise reasonable choice over the service they receive. The limitations on councils' obligation to provide preferred accommodation set out in the Directions and the Regulations are not intended to deny individuals reasonable freedom of choice but to ensure that councils are able to fulfil their obligations for the quality of service provided and for value for money. The terms of the Directions and the Regulations are explained more fully below. Where, for any reason, a council decides not to arrange a place for someone in their preferred accommodation it must have a clear and reasonable justification for that decision which relates to the criteria of the Directions and is not in breach of the Regulations.

2.2 Arrangements under section 26(3A) of the National Assistance Act 1948 require the agreement of all parties. Individuals should not be refused their preferred accommodation without a full explanation from councils, in writing, of their reasons for doing so.

2.3 The location of the preferred accommodation need not be limited by the boundaries of the funding council. Councils are obliged to cater for placements falling within the Directions or the Regulations in any permitted care home within England or Wales. Any extension to this beyond England and Wales is subject to any future regulations governing cross-border placements (but see LAC(93)18 in respect of placements involving Scotland and the Department of Health/Welsh Assembly protocol on NHS funded nursing care for cross border placements).

2.4 Funding councils may refer to their own usual costs when making placements in another council's area. However, because costs vary from area to area, if in order to meet a resident's assessed need it is necessary to place an individual in another area at a higher rate than the funding council's usual costs, the placing council should meet the additional cost itself.

2.5 The Directions state that a council must arrange for care in an individual's preferred accommodation subject to four considerations:

(a) Suitability of accommodation

2.5.2 Accommodation provided in a care home will not necessarily be suitable for the individual's needs simply because it satisfies registration standards. On the other hand, accommodation will not necessarily be unsuitable simply because it fails to conform to the council's preferred model of provision, or to meet to the letter a standard service specification laid down by the council.

2.5.3 The Directions and Regulations do not affect Section 26(1A) of the National Assistance Act 1948 as amended by the Care Standards Act 2000. Arrangements should not be made for the provision of accommodation together with nursing or personal care in a care home unless the accommodation to be provided is managed by an organisation or person who is registered under Part II of the Care Standards Act 2000. Similarly, the Directions and the Regulations do not require a council to contract with any accommodation where for any other reason it is prevented by law from doing so.

(b) Cost

(c) Availability

2.5.9 Generally, good commissioning by councils should ensure there is sufficient capacity so individuals should not have to wait for their assessed (that is, eligible) needs to be met. However, waiting is occasionally inevitable, particularly when individuals have expressed a preference towards a particular care home where there are no current vacancies. Where individuals may need to wait at home or elsewhere, their access to the most appropriate (and possibly, preferred) service should be based solely on their assessed need, and councils should ensure that in the interim adequate alternative services are provided. Waiting for the preferred care home should not mean that the person's care needs are not met in the interim or that they wait in a setting unsuitable for their assessed needs, and this includes an acute hospital bed, until the most suitable or preferred accommodation becomes available. In view of the Community Care (Delayed Discharges etc.) Act 2003, councils should have contingency arrangements in place, that address the likelihood that an individual's preferred accommodation will not always be readily available. These arrangements should meet the needs of the individual and sustain or improve their level of independence. For some, the appropriate interim arrangement could be an enhanced care package at home.

2.5.10 Councils should give individuals an indication of the likely duration of the interim arrangement. Councils should place the individual on the waiting list of the preferred accommodation and aim to move them into that accommodation as soon as possible. Information about how the waiting list is handled should be clear and the individual should be kept informed of progress. If the duration of the interim arrangement exceeds a reasonable time period e g 12 weeks, the individual should be reassessed to ensure that the interim and preferred accommodation, are still able to meet the individual's assessed needs and to prevent any unnecessary moves between care homes that are unable to meet the individual's assessed needs. As part of this reassessment, individuals should also be asked if their preference is now to remain in the interim accommodation or whether they wish to continue waiting for their original preferred accommodation (see paragraph 2.5.14 for guidance on individuals who choose to remain in the interim accommodation).

2.5.12 Councils should take all reasonable steps to gain an individual's agreement to an interim care home or care package. Councils should make reasonable efforts to take account of the individual's desires and preferences. In doing this, councils should ascertain all relevant facts and take into account all the circumstances relevant to the person, and ensure that the individual (and their family or carers) understands the consequences of failing to come to an agreement. Where patients have been assessed as no longer requiring NHS continuing inpatient care, they do not have the right to occupy indefinitely an NHS bed. If an individual continues to unreasonably refuse the interim care home or care package, the council is entitled to consider that it has fulfilled its statutory duty to assess and offer services, and may then inform the individual, in writing, they will need to make their own arrangements. This position also applies to the unreasonable refusal of a permanent care home, not just the interim care home or care package. If at a later date further contact is made with social services regarding the individual, the council should re-open the care planning process, if it is satisfied that the individual's needs remain such to justify the provision of services and there is no longer reason to think that the individual will persist in refusing such services unreasonably. Councils should refer to Annex A of LAC(2003)21 – The Community Care (Delayed Discharges etc) Act 2003 Guidance for Implementation. Councils may wish to take their own legal advice in such circumstances.

DISPUTES BETWEEN LOCAL AUTHORITIES AND CARE HOME OWNERS (CHOICE OF CONTRACTORS)

4.46 *R v Cumbria CC ex p Cumbria Professional Care Ltd* [2000] 3 CCLR 79 is an authority which helpfully sets out (within the context of this book) the rationale behind the legislation, and the misapprehensions that have arisen on the part of the private sector as a result. A similar exegesis can be found in the judgment of Baroness Hale (cited in part at **4.2** above). It also demonstrates the difficulties that aggrieved private care home owners face when attempting to mount challenges to local authorities within the context of community care legislation. The dispute arose between a private care consortium and the local authority as to the manner in which the latter had promoted a 'mixed economy' of placements. The applicant was vexed by four decisions taken by the local authority:

'(1) not to contract with [the applicant] for the purchase from them of respite care placements ... whereas the council made contracts with its "in-house" service providers for block-booked placements; (2) the decision to make such contracts as is referred to in (1) above; (3) the decision to unfairly advantage its "in-house" homes at the expense of the homes run by the applicants; (4) the failure to fulfil its statutory duty to provide suitable (or sufficient) accommodation for those in need of community care services, so that homes owned by the applicant members were therefore deprived of potential residents.'

Legislative background to dispute

4.47 Mr Justice Turner summarised this as follows:

'[84B–84D] The seeds of this wide-ranging dispute were sown by the change from the method of direct state control of the payments of benefits to those in need of care services to the making of bulk grants by central government to local authorities who are now required to distribute grant to those in need according to the scale of their needs. The seminal legislation is the National Health Service and Community Care Act 1990 under which the local authorities became the licensing authorities for care homes, the purchasing authority for care services in both the private and public sector as well as being itself a service provider.'

Community care in the next decade and beyond (LASSA Guidance 1990)

4.48 Mr Justice Turner relied upon the significance of the above in a number of respects but in the this context attention is drawn to para 1.14 (quoted at 87F):

'The independent sector is essential to the development of a mixed economy, which can offer local authorities a wide range of options leading to a greater choice for service users.'

Choice of accommodation

4.49 In due course, the judgment links the legislative backdrop to the National Assistance Act 1948 (Choice of Accommodation) Directions 1992 (**4.44** above), and specifically paras 2 and 3. He held that:

'[89H–89J] ... one of the principal changes introduced ... was that the right of the user to exercise choice became an important factor which, in terms of the Choice of Accommodation Directions, had to be taken into account by local authorities ... the legislative framework concentrates on the user and confers no direct rights on any service provider whether they come from the private, voluntary or statutory sectors.'

Outcome

4.50 The claims failed (it being held that they were 'clearly inadmissible' [97K]) and that there had been no unlawfulness in the way in which Cumbria County Council had failed to block book respite care in the private sector.

Disputes between care home owners and local authorities (levels of charges)

4.51 Disputes have arisen between the owners of care homes and local authorities as to the correct level of fees that may be charged. Most of these have a quasi-contractual basis, and arise out of confusion as to what was agreed as a level of payment between the litigants. These are likely to found a cause of action based on *quantum meruit*. However, in *R (on the Application of Birmingham Care Consortium and others) v Birmingham CC* [2002] EWHC 2118 (Admin), [2002] 5 CCLR 600, the local authority had entered into contracts with a private consortium of nursing and care homes. At the end of the initial contractual period, the local authority offered an extension of the placements subject to a modest increase in the fees paid. The consortium sought to argue that this offer was inconsistent with the National Assistance Act (Choice of Accommodation) Directions 1992 in that the rates offered did not reflect the true cost of care, and would lead to the closure of the homes. The claim was dismissed on the basis that para 3(b) of the Directions 'did not require a local authority to determine whether the costs were fair or reasonable, but simply entitled it to refuse to comply with an indication of preferred accommodation if the cost of that accommodation was more than the local authority would usually expect to pay, having regard to assessed means'. On the evidence in the case, in any event the claimants had not established that the rates offered were less than fair.

Disputes regarding third party payments

4.52   In *R v East Sussex CC ex p Ward* [2000] 3 CCLR 132, a dispute arose as to the third party top-up provisions which exist in respect of preferred accommodation (the National Assistance Act (Choice of Accommodation) Directions 1992). All parties (including the daughter of the resident) had agreed that suitable accommodation had been located, and the local authority agreed to fund the placement. In due course it stated that the amount to be paid exceeded the amount that it would usually expect to pay (para 3(b)). It duly suggested that the resident should make up the difference. An agreement was reached in which the resident was described both as 'a client' and as 'a third party'. It was held that there are (under the relevant legislation, directions and regulations) three possibilities:

> '(a) that the resident can afford to pay, in which case the resident is obliged to reimburse the local authority pursuant to Section 26(3); (b) that the resident cannot afford to pay, in which case the amount which s/he could reasonably be required to pay is the amount assessed under the 1992 Regulations; or (c) the Directions can be invoked and either a relative or a third party pays, or the local authority agree to make up the difference.'

It was held that the agreement was therefore unlawful, since a resident himself could not be a third party.

Health and Social Care Act 2001

54 Funding by resident etc of more expensive accommodation

(1) Regulations may make provision for and in connection with the making, in respect of the provision of Part 3 accommodation, of additional payments –

    (a)   by persons for whom such accommodation is provided ("residents"); or
    (b)   by other persons

(2) In this section "additional payments", in relation to a resident, means payments which –

    (a)   are made for the purpose of meeting all or part of the difference between the actual cost of his Part 3 accommodation and the amount that the local authority providing it would usually expect to pay in order to provide Part 3 accommodation suitable for a person with the assessed needs of the resident; and

(b)   (in the case of additional payments by the resident) are made out of such of his resources as may be specified in, or determined in accordance with, regulations under subsection (1);

and for this purpose "resources" has the meaning given by such regulations.

(3) In this Part "Part 3 accommodation" means accommodation provided under sections 21 to 26 of the 1948 Act.

4.53   The above statutory provision provides for either residents in Part III accommodation or third parties to make additional payments so that they can live in more expensive accommodation than that for which the local authority would normally pay. The Regulations referred to at s 54(1) are summarised at **4.52** above. Section 42 of the National Assistance Act was repealed by the Health and Social Care Act 2008.

REGULATION OF ACCOMMODATION

General

4.54   The introduction of the Care Standards Act 2000 removed a substantial amount of responsibility from local authorities in respect of the regulation of standards within care homes. This was further reduced by the repeal of Part VII of the Act (Protection of Children and Vulnerable Adults*)* by the Safeguarding Vulnerable Groups Act 2006. There has also been a steady increase in the use of private sector accommodation by local authorities in discharging its obligations (under NAA 1948). This in itself is in part a consequence of the National Health Service and Community Care Act 1990 (as referred to above). It is of course via s 26 of NAA 1948 that a local authority is able to purchase services from the private sector.

4.55   A complete analysis of the law in respect of the regulation of care homes is outside the scope of this book. For a detailed treatment of the law relating to Care Homes see Ridout, *Care Standards: A Practical Guide* (Jordans, 2010). However, there are some aspects of the Care Standards Act 2000 which particularly have a direct relation to the responsibility of a local authority to protect vulnerable groups and in any event local government still plays a major role in the delivery of care.

Care Standards Act 2000

4.56   Despite repeals, the scope of the entire Act is very wide but the only significance within the context of the area of law described in this Chapter is that which relates to the definition of a care home.

Definition of care homes

4.57 A definition of a care home is found in s 3 of the Care Standards Act 2000.

Care Standards Act 2000

3 Care homes

(1) For the purposes of this Act, an establishment is a care home if it provides accommodation, together with nursing or personal care, for any of the following persons.

(2) They are –

    (a)   persons who are or have been ill;
    (b)   persons who have or have had a mental disorder;
    (c)   persons who are disabled or infirm;
    (d)   persons who are or have been dependent on alcohol or drugs.

(3) But an establishment is not a care home if it is –

    (a)   a hospital;
    (b)   an independent clinic; or
    (c)   a children's home,

or if it is of a description excepted by regulations.

(4) And an establishment in England is not a care home it it is –

    (a)   a hospital (within the meaning of the National Health Service Act 2006); or
    (b)   a children's home,

or if it is of a description excepted by regulations.

What constitutes a care home

4.58 The components required in order to determine whether or not accommodation at home providing nursing and personal care amounted to a care home, and whether the accommodation and care needs to be provided by the same person was considered in *R (on the application of Moore and others) v Care Standards Tribunal Commission* [2004] EWHC 2481 (Admin), [2005] 8 CCLR 91.

4.59 The significance of this case is that there was an attempt to de-register the care homes, in order to move to a 'supported living' model. The use of supported living is very prevalent as placements for those who come within the general ambit of community care services, by local authorities. Such arrangements are very often in tandem with tenancies. If the individual who has been placed lacks capacity, then as a matter of law, the tenancy may be voidable (see Chapter 2 for a discussion on this point). There may also be a dispute as to whether what is described as a tenancy is, as a matter of law, merely a licence (for example if there is no actual right to exclusive possession of the premises within the supported living placement, e g if the 'tenant' cannot exclude others from that part of the premises which he occupies under the tenancy agreement). As Sir William Aldous states:

'[11] I like the judge will assume that the claimants are assured tenants of Housing. That being so, they have a legal interest in the property and have the right to exclude others: (see *Street v Mountford* [1985] AC 809) ...

[17] The judge ... put forward this working definition of the word establishment as used in s 3 of the Act: "A place, including a building, in which organised activities are conducted" and "the conduct of organised activities in a place, including a building'. He went on in ... as follows:

"31. The 'establishment' or 'it' must provide accommodation together with 'nursing or personal care'. As far as accommodation is concerned, it is provided by a room and facilities within a building which the owner permits the resident to occupy and make use of. As far as nursing or personal care is concerned, they have to be provided by a person or persons. Accommodation and care must be provided 'together', but they need not be provided by the same company or individual. Although "person" is referred to in the singular in section 11(1), the Interpretation Act 1978 permits that singular to include the plural ...

32 Does the fact that the accommodation element as provided by means of an assured shorthold tenancy mean that the establishment ceases to be a care home within section 3? The answer is: not in principle".'

4.60 Consequently, the existence of a tenancy does not mean that the establishment is not a care home, and neither does it matter that the provision of the services are from different agencies matter either. It will still be a care home. If it is a care home, then it comes within the regime prescribed by DOLS (see Chapter 2) which is of immense significance in terms of a local authority obligation as a supervisory body in ensuring that there is no unlawful deprivation of liberty.

4.61 However, to add to the list of complications over what constitutes a care home may be added the consequences of the Health and Social Care Act 2008 and its accompanying Regulations (the Health and Social Care Act 2008 (Regulated Activities) Regulations 2010). According to reg 2, personal care means:

    (a)   physical assistance given to a person in connection with –
        (i)   eating or drinking (including the administration of parenteral nutrition
        (ii) toileting (including in relation to the process of menstruation)
        (iii) washing or bathing
        (iv) dressing
        (v) oral care, or
        (vi) the care of skin, hair and nails (with the exception of nail care provided by a chiropodist or podiatrist); or

    (b)   the prompting, together with supervision, or a person, in relation to the performance of any of the activities listed in paragraph (a), where that person is unable to make a decision for themselves in relation to performing such an activity without such prompting and supervision.

The Regulations came into force in April 2010.

4.62 As a result of the Health and Social Care Act 2008, establishments are no longer registered as care homes. What is registered are 'regulated activities' (s 8), and the Regulations set out what are those prescribed activities.

Schedule 1

Regulated Activities

Personal care

1 (1) Subject to sub-paragraphs (2) and (3), the provision of personal care for persons who, by reason of old age, illness or disability are unable to provide it for themselves, and which is provided in a place where those persons are living at the time the care is provided.

(2) This paragraph does not apply where paragraph 2 (accommodation for persons who require nursing or personal care) or paragraph 4 (accommodation and nursing or personal care in the further education sector) applies.

(3) The following types of provision are excepted from sub-paragraph (1) –

    (a)   the supply of carers to a service provider by an undertaking acting as an employment agency or employment business for the purposes of that provider carrying on a regulated activity;
    (b)   the introduction of carers to an individual (other than a service provider) by a person (including an employment agency or an employment business) having no ongoing role in the direction or control of the service provided to that individual;
    (c)   the services of a carer employed by an individual, without the involvement of an undertaking acting as an employment agency or employment business, and working wholly under the direction and control of that individual in order to meet that individual's own care requirements; and
    (d)   the provision of personal care by a person managing a prison or other similar custodial establishment (other than a hospital within the meaning of Part 2 of the 1983 Act).

(4) In sub-paragraph (3), "carer" means an individual who provides personal care to a person referred to in sub-paragraph (1).

Accommodation for persons who require nursing or personal care

2 (1) The provision of residential accommodation, together with nursing or personal care.

(2) Sub-paragraph (1) does not apply to the provision of accommodation –

(a)   to an individual by an adult placement carer under the terms of a carer agreement;

(b)   in a school; or

(c)   in an institution within the further education sector.

Accommodation for persons who require treatment for substance misuse

3 The provision of residential accommodation for a person, together with treatment for drug or alcohol misuse, where acceptance by the person of such treatment is a condition of the provision of the accommodation.

Accommodation and nursing or personal care in the further education sector

4 (1) Subject to sub-paragraph (2), the provision of residential accommodation together with nursing or personal care for persons in an institution within the further education sector.

(2) Sub-paragraph (1) only applies where the number of persons to whom nursing or personal care and accommodation are provided is more than one tenth of the number of students to whom both education and accommodation are provided.

Thus, as may well be the case with a large number of individuals who are in receipt of personal care (and who may lack capacity), if this is the case then that activity needs to have been registered. However, it also tends to further attenuate the statutory definition of a care home as set out in the Care Standards Act 2000. If where a person is living is an establishment, and within that establishment there is a tenancy by which the person occupies a part of the establishment, and they are receiving personal care that comes within the regulatory definition set out above, then the question may legitimately be asked, why is that establishment not a care home? In other words, placements which regard themselves as supported living may, as a matter of law, be care homes. There is currently no authority on this point, but it is unlikely to remain an unscrutinised area for very much longer. What is clear is that irrespective of the Health and Social Care Act 2008, and the Regulations, the definition in s 3 of the Care Standards Act 2000 still applies for the purposes of the Mental Capacity Act 2005.

Guidance to local authorities

4.63 The Department of Health has provided Guidance to local authorities with social services responsibilities (pursuant to s 7 of the Local Authority Social Services Act 1970) in respect of 'Supported Housing and Care Homes' (August 2002). Its main purpose is to explain when registration as a care home is required, and 'how to distinguish care homes from supported housing of various kinds' (Summary, para 6). Clearly, this has now been partially occluded by the Regulations referred to above, but there has been no replacement produced.

Personal care

4.64 It is suggested that this includes physical assistance with bodily functions (feeding, bathing, toileting, dressing, getting out of a bath); non-physical assistance (encouragement, advice, supervision of the foregoing); emotional and psychological support. This will only become relevant within the context of a requirement for registration of/as a care home when the physical or quasi-physical care is an integral part of the accommodation (paras 8 and 9). This should now be considered alongside the definition of personal care described above at **4.61** and **4.62**.

Care homes

4.65 There are two elements to a care home. The first is that there is accommodation and nursing care (for specific types of resident). The second is that assistance is provided with bodily functions. If such assistance cannot be provided, there would be no eligibility to register as a care home (paras 12–15). Again, this has to be considered alongside the commentary referred to above.

Domiciliary care

4.66 An individual providing personal care (on a paid basis) at home does not come within the ambit of the statute. However, personal care delivered in this manner will be covered by the Domiciliary Care Agency Regulations, to ensure that 'vulnerable people receiving care in their own homes will get the protection they need' (paras 16–18).

Housing and care schemes

4.67 Paragraphs 19–26 give a number of examples of 'extra care housing' whereby independence of the individual is encouraged. It is not intended that this type of accommodation should come within the Care Standards Act 2000. The same applies to housing and support for people with learning disabilities (paras 27–30). Paragraphs 31–41 give various examples of the type of accommodation that is not likely to require registration.

Capacity and choice of accommodation

4.68 For a fuller consideration of this aspect, refer to Chapter 2. However, within that context, the Guidance is as follows:

> '43 The aim should be to protect vulnerable persons, but not to inhibit self-determination. Due weight should always be given to the person's own wishes in relation to their care and accommodation, as part of a proper assessment of the person's needs and as a part of an individual care plan. Even when users have a limited understanding of the detail of tenancies and contracts, no assumption should be made that they cannot be supported to achieve the maximum degree of rights, choice, inclusion, and independence.'

Adult placements

4.69 This is taken to include short or long-term accommodation of between one to three adults. If a local authority manages an adult placement scheme it is responsible for recruiting, assessing, training and supporting the carers, and for taking referrals and matching and placing service users with those carers (paras 45–50).

Safeguarding Vulnerable Groups Act 2006

4.70 This statute creates two 'barred' lists. One is for adults, and the other for children. The relevant list in this context is the 'adults barred list'. The criteria for inclusion are (very broadly): (1) being cautioned for, or convicted of the most serious offences against vulnerable individuals; (2) engaging in behaviour which harms, attempts to harm, puts at risk or incites another to harm a vulnerable adult, involves inappropriate conduct involving violent pornography, or is of an inappropriate sexual nature involving a vulnerable adult.

Regulated activity

4.71 The statute only applies to regulated activities. In broad terms this is work (both paid and unpaid) which involves close contact with vulnerable adults. Section 5 sets out the definition of a regulated activity (Part 2, Sch 4, para 7(1)). In the context of this book, if the activity is:

(a)   any form of training, teaching or instruction provided wholly or mainly for vulnerable adults;

(b)   any form of care for or supervision of vulnerable adults;

(c)   any form of assistance, advice, guidance provided wholly or mainly for vulnerable adults;

(d)   any form of treatment or therapy provided for a vulnerable adult;

(e)   moderating a public electronic interactive communication service which is likely to be used wholly or mainly by vulnerable adults;

(f)   driving a vehicle which is being used only for the purpose of conveying vulnerable adults and any person caring for the vulnerable adults pursuant to arrangements made in prescribed circumstance;

(g)   anything done on behalf of a vulnerable adult in such circumstances as are prescribed.

Regulated activity provider

4.72 Section 6 sets out the definition of a regulated activity provider. Broadly, it includes anyone who is responsible for the management or control of a regulated activity, which would include care and support to an adult (which may include accommodation). It does not apply to private arrangements (which in turn means if the activity is for a member of the family, or a friend).

Controlled activity relating to vulnerable adults

4.73 These are set out at s 22, and subject to time limitations (carried out frequently or by the same person on more than 2 days in any period of 30 days) or the day-to-day management of the following; primary care services; hospital services; domiciliary care; arrangements in relation to an adult placement scheme; provision of community care services; making of payments under s 57 of the Health and Social Care Act 2001. The expression 'community care services' is the same as in s 46(3) of the National Health Service and Community Care Act 1990.

Local authority information and referrals

4.74 There is an obligation upon a local authority to provide the Independent Barring Board with prescribed information that it holds in relation to a person. The criteria are set out at s 39(1)–(7). A similar obligation is imposed on a local authority pursuant to s 40.

39 Local authorities: duty to refer

(1) A local authority must provide IBB with any prescribed information they hold relating to a person if the first and second conditions are satisfied.

(2) The first condition is that the local authority thinks –

    (a)   that paragraph 1, 2, 7 or 8 of Schedule 3 applies to the person,

    (b)   that the person has engaged in relevant conduct (within the meaning of paragraph 4 or 10 of Schedule 3) occurring after the commencement of this section, or

    (c)   that the harm test is satisfied.

(3) The harm test is that the person may-

    (a)   harm a child or vulnerable adult,

    (b)   cause a child or vulnerable adult to be harmed,

    (c)   put a child or vulnerable adult at risk of harm,

    (d)   attempt to harm a child or vulnerable adult, or

    (e)   incite another to harm a child or vulnerable adult.

(4) The second condition is that the local authority thinks-

    (a)   that the person is engaged or may engage in regulated activity or controlled activity, and

    (b)   (except in a case where paragraph 1, 2, 7 or 8 of Schedule 3 applies) that IBB may consider it appropriate for the person to be included in a barred list.

(5) A local authority may provide IBB with any prescribed information it holds relating to a person if –

    (a)   the local authority think that a person has engaged in relevant conduct (within the meaning of paragraph 4 or 10 of Schedule 3) occurring before the commencement of this section, and

    (b)   the condition in subsection (4) is satisfied.

(6) For the purposes of subsection (2)(b) or (5)(a), conduct is inappropriate if it appears to the local authority to be inappropriate having regard to the guidance issued by the Secretary of State under paragraph 4(6) or 10(6) of Schedule 3.

(7) "Local authority" has the same meaning as in section 1 of the Local Authorities (Goods and Services) Act 1970 (c. 39).

Definition of a vulnerable adult

4.75 This is set out in s 59 below.

59 Vulnerable adults

(1) A person is a vulnerable adult if he has attained the age of 18 and –

(a) he is in residential accommodation,
(b) he is in sheltered housing,
(c) he receives domiciliary care,
(d) he receives any form of health care,
(e) he is detained in lawful custody,
(f) he is by virtue of an order of a court under supervision by a person exercising functions for the purposes of Part 1 of the Criminal Justice and Court Services Act 2000 (c. 43),
(g) he receives a welfare service of a prescribed description,
(h) he receives any service or participates in any activity provided specifically for persons who fall within subsection (9),
(i) payments are made to him (or to another on his behalf) in pursuance of arrangements under section 57 of the Health and Social Care Act 2001 (c. 15), or
(j) he requires assistance in the conduct of his own affairs.

(2) Residential accommodation is accommodation provided for a person –

(a) in connection with any care or nursing he requires, or
(b) who is or has been a pupil attending a residential special school.

(3) A residential special school is a school which provides residential accommodation for its pupils and which is –

(a) a special school within the meaning of section 337 of the Education Act 1996 (c. 56);
(b) an independent school (within the meaning of section 463 of that Act) which is approved by the Secretary of State in accordance with section 347 of that Act;
(c) an independent school (within the meaning of section 463 of that Act) not falling within paragraph (a) or (b) which, with the consent of the Secretary of State given under section 347(5)(b) of that Act, provides places for children with special educational needs (within the meaning of section 312 of that Act);
(d) an institution within the further education sector (within the meaning of section 91 of the Further and Higher Education Act 1992) which provides accommodation for children.

(4) Domiciliary care is care of any description or assistance falling within subsection (5) whether provided continuously or not which a person receives in a place where he is, for the time being, living.

(5) Assistance falls within this subsection if it is (to any extent) provided to a person by reason of –

    (a)   his age;
    (b)   his health;
    (c)   any disability he has.

(6) Health care includes treatment, therapy or palliative care of any description.

(7) A person is in lawful custody if he is –

    (a)   detained in a prison (within the meaning of the Prison Act 1952 (c. 52));
    (b)   detained in a remand centre, young offender institution or secure training centre (as mentioned in section 43 of that Act);
    (c)   detained in an attendance centre (within the meaning of section 53(1) of that Act);
    (d)   a detained person (within the meaning of Part 8 of the Immigration and Asylum Act 1999 (c. 33)) who is detained in a removal centre or short-term holding facility (within the meaning of that Part) or in pursuance of escort arrangements made under section 156 of that Act.

(8) The reference to a welfare service must be construed in accordance with section 16(5).

(9) A person falls within this subsection if –

    (a)   he has particular needs because of his age;
    (b)   he has any form of disability;
    (c)   he has a physical or mental problem of such description as is prescribed;
    (d)   she is an expectant or nursing mother in receipt of residential accommodation pursuant to arrangements made under section 21(1)(aa) of the National Assistance Act 1948 or care pursuant to paragraph 1 of Schedule 8 to the National Health Service Act 1977 (c. 49);
    (e)   he is a person of a prescribed description not falling within paragraphs (a) to (d).

(10) A person requires assistance in the conduct of his own affairs if –

    (a)   a lasting power of attorney is created in respect of him in accordance with section 9 of the Mental Capacity Act 2005 (c. 9) or an application is made under paragraph 4 of Schedule 1 to that Act for the registration of an instrument intended to create a lasting power of attorney in respect of him;
    (b)   an enduring power of attorney (within the meaning of Schedule 4 to that Act) in respect of him is registered in accordance with that Schedule or an application is made under that Schedule for the registration of an enduring power of attorney in respect of him;
    (c)   an order under section 16 of that Act has been made by the Court of Protection in relation to the making of decisions on his behalf, or such an order has been applied for;
    (d)   an independent mental capacity advocate is or is to be appointed in respect of him in pursuance of arrangements under section 35 of that Act;

(e)   independent advocacy services (within the meaning of section 248 of the National Health Service Act 2006 (c. 41) or section 187 of the National Health Service (Wales) Act 2006 (c. 42)) are or are to be provided in respect of him;

(f)   a representative is or is to be appointed to receive payments on his behalf in pursuance of regulations made under the Social Security Administration Act 1992 (c. 5).

(11) The Secretary of State may by order provide that a person specified in the order or of a description so specified who falls within subsection (1) is not to be treated as a vulnerable adult.

Chapter 5

PROVISIONS FOR OLDER CHILDREN (LEAVING CARE) AND DISABLED CHILDREN

GENERAL

5.1 This Chapter covers the following areas. The first relates to leaving care provisions (which in turn concerns children aged over 16, and can in some circumstances extend local authority obligations to 25). The second relates to disabled children (which in part may be linked to leaving care provisions) and the support and resources that a local authority may be obliged to provide to them, and to their carers.

CHILDREN LEAVING CARE

5.2 The statute which governs leaving care provisions is the Children (Leaving Care) Act 2000. It is incorporated into the Children Act 1989 at ss 23A–24D. It is in turn subject to the Care Leavers (England) Regulations 2010, SI 2010/2571) and (in part) the Care Planning, Placement and Case Review (England) Regulations 2010, SI 2010/959). Both sets of Regulations came into force on 1 April 2011. Finally, the Department of Education has published Guidance, which is in itself issued under s 7 of the Local Authority Social Services Act 1970. Local authorities are reminded in the foreword that this means that the Guidance *must* be followed by local authorities. It replaces the previous Guidance (published by the Department of Health, on 8 October 2001). The new guidance is called 'The Children Act 1989 – Guidance and Regulations, Volume 3:Planning Transition to Adulthood for Care Leavers'. It was published in October 2010, and was implemented on 1 April 2011. It runs to 115 pages, and can be downloaded from the Department of Education website. The purpose behind the new guidance and regulations is in part intended to correct many of the problems that have arisen as a result of what is described as 'great local authority variability in the quality of "leaving care services" and the trend to premature discharge from care' (Explanatory Memorandum to the Care Leavers (England) Regulations 2010, para 7.3). Similar concerns are set out in the Explanatory Memorandum to the Care Planning, Placement and Case Review (England) Regulations 2010 to the effect that 'Many of the concerns about the failings in the care system are largely attributable to weak or absent care planning ...' (para 7.8).

5.3   It is unfortunate that the amendment of the Act has imported into what was otherwise an exceptionally lucid statute an almost impenetrable maze of definitions, exceptions and cross-references. The purpose of this section of Chapter 5 is to help to provide a route through the maze. To this end, there is some initial reference to the thinking that was behind its introduction in the first instance. It is hoped that this may also assist in interpreting any anomalies that arise in practice. A very thorough history of the legislation in its entirety together with an analysis of its purpose and progress is contained in *Beyond Care Matters: Future of the Care Population – Working Group Report* (DFER, Martin Narey).

CONSULTATION PAPER AND ORIGINS OF THE ACT

5.4   An initial consultation paper was issued by the Department of Health entitled *Me, Survive, Out There? New Arrangements for Young People Living in and Leaving Care* (July 1999). It primarily related to 16 and 17 year olds who were either voluntarily or compulsorily looked after by local authorities. Care leavers were those between the ages of 16 and 18 who leave care, and who qualified for advice and assistance under s 24 of the Children Act 1989.

5.5   The foreword to the paper (by the then Secretary of State for Health, Frank Dobson) stated:

> '... our determination [is] to end the practice of forcing some children as young as 16 to leave care and fend for themselves ... Local Authorities should look after young people of 16 and 17 and help them to develop the skills they need to look after themselves in the outside world.'

The purpose of the Act was therefore to enhance the prospects of those who had been in care into adulthood.

5.6   The practical implications of this were:

> '1.5 ... young people being looked after until they are willing and ready to leave care, which will mean more young people remaining in care until 18; improved arrangements for those young people leaving care; increased involvement of care leavers in education, training and employment; local authorities maintaining greater contact with formerly looked after children; ensuring that young people live in accommodation suited to their needs, thereby reducing the risk of homelessness and rough sleeping.'

It continued to state that this means:

> '1.7 ... local authorities to have a **duty to assess and meet the needs** of all eligible 16 and 17 year olds who are in care or care leavers. Wherever the young person lives the duty will rest with the local authority that looked after them; every young person in care on their sixteenth birthday to have a comprehensive **pathway** plan mapping out a clear pathway to independence; **new resources** for social services support and assistance for 16 and 17 year olds who are in care or who have left

care; local authorities to provide all eligible 16 and 17 year olds who are in care or care leavers with **personal and financial support** to meet their needs as identified in their pathway plans. Health and educational needs to be met by the relevant services; young people who are 16 and 17 and have been looked after for more than 3 months (continuously or in aggregate) to be eligible; young people not to be able to opt out of the new arrangements and claim social security benefits. Emergency assistance to be available to prevent those who go missing becoming destitute; each young person to have a **Young Persons Adviser** who will co-ordinate provision of support and assistance to meet the needs of the young person as identified in their pathway plan. Particular emphasis will be placed on helping the young person into education, training or employment; separate but linked arrangements of support and assistance to 18–21 year olds.'

As can be seen, the range of ages for a 'young person' had extended from 16 to 21.

5.7   It summarised the duties and powers of local authorities prior to the changes in legislation to the following: 16–18 years of ages – duty to advise and befriend; power to assist; 18–21 years of age – duty to advise and befriend; power to assist; 21 years of age and over – power to assist with education and training if commenced before 21st birthday. The intention was to make it a duty to assess and meet the needs of care leavers up to the age of 18 and give the local authority *power* to assist with training and education up to the age of 24 (regardless of when the training commenced) (paras 3.3 and 3.4). It also proposed that *all* young people in care should have a pathway plan by the age of 16. It would cover the period from 16 to beyond 18. It should contain coverage of the following areas: personal support; accommodation; education and training; employment; healthcare; life skills; financial management (para 3.9). It also suggested that there should be an Independent Review Panel in the case of disagreement, and regular reviews of the plans at intervals of no less than 6 months (paras 3.12 and 3.13). The tendency for young people to leave care early was attributed to a wish by local authorities to save money (para 3.14). It also proposed the creation of a 'Young Persons Adviser' (paras 3.39 et seq). It proposed that the new arrangements would apply *exclusively* to those between their 16th and 18th birthdays and who are in or leave care after their 16th birthday. Different arrangements were envisaged for those who had reached their 18th birthday (para 3.55). The minimum qualifying period in care was 3 months (either continuously or as an aggregate) (para 3.57). For 18–21 year olds a different regime was envisaged. This group would be eligible for state benefits. Accommodation for this group was seen as a priority (para 3.66). The majority of these proposals were enacted.

5.8   The Children (Leaving Care) Act 2000 came into force in October 2001. It was accompanied not just by the Guidance, but also by a Department of Health publication entitled 'Care Leaving Strategies – a good practice handbook'. This was not produced pursuant to s 7 of the Local Authority Social Services Act 1970, and therefore its status is as it describes itself – a handbook for good practice. It recommends eight areas upon which local authorities will need to concentrate:

(1) creating a strategy (eg an audit of requirements);

(2) improving preparation for leaving care (eg having a framework for an assessment);

(3) providing an appropriate range of accommodation (eg liaison between social services and housing departments);

(4) tailoring individual support for care leavers;

(5) accessing education, training and employment;

(6) improving participation of care leavers (eg involving young people in decision making);

(7) providing clear information for care leavers;

(8) monitoring, evaluating and future planning.

The handbook itself runs to some 81 pages. It has not been replaced, but it should be noted that the definitive guidance (and that which is binding on local authorities) is as set out and referred to at **5.2** above together with the relevant Regulations (which are set out within this Chapter).

5.9   Some of the most salient features of the Act are:

(1) the local authority retains responsibility wherever the young person lives;

(2) the local authority has a duty to keep in touch with young people up to the age of 21 (and in some cases, up to 25);

(3) local authorities may retain some responsibility for financially supporting vulnerable young people until they reach adulthood.

CHILDREN (LEAVING CARE) ACT 2000 – GUIDANCE

5.10 The following is a summary of the definitions and entitlements for different groups of young people. The precise details are to be found in the statute itself.

Definitions

Eligible children

Defined in paragraph 19B of Schedule 2 to the 1989 Act, and regulation 40 of the Care Planning Regulations as a child who is:
(a) looked after,
(b) aged 16 or 17, and
(c) has been looked after by a local authority for a period of 13 weeks, or periods amounting in total to 13 weeks, which began after he reached 14 and ended after he reached 16.

Main Statutory Obligations

The local authority has the same statutory obligations in relation to eligible children as they do towards other children looked after by them, including a duty to maintain their care plan, carry out regular reviews of their case and appoint an independent reviewing officer for the child. In addition they must:

- prepare an **assessment** of the eligible child's needs with a view to determining what advice, assistance and support it would be appropriate for them to provide him (both while he is still looked after and after he stops being looked after) [paragraph 19B(4) of Schedule 2 to the 1989 Act; the requirements for carrying out the assessment are set out in regulation 42 of the Care Planning Regulations]

- as soon as possible after the assessment of needs is completed, prepare a **pathway plan** (which includes the child's care plan) [paragraph 19B(4) of Schedule 2 to the 1989 Act; the requirements for preparing the pathway plan are set out in regulation 43 of the Care Planning Regulations]

- keep the pathway plan under **regular review** [paragraph 19B(5) of Schedule 2 to the 1989 Act]

- appoint a **personal adviser** for the child [paragraph 19C of Schedule 2 to the 1989 Act; the functions of the personal adviser are set out in regulation 44 of the Care Planning Regulations].

Relevant children

Defined in section 23A(2) of the 1989 Act as a child who is:

(a) not looked after,
(b) aged 16 or 17, and
(c) was, before he last ceased to be looked after, an eligible child.
Regulation 3 of the Care Leavers Regulations prescribes a further category of relevant child who is:
(a) not looked after,
(b) aged 16 or 17, and
(c) at the time he attained the age of 16 was detained (ie detained in a remand centre, a young offenders institution or a

The local authority that last looked after the relevant child must:

- take reasonable steps to **keep in touch** with the relevant child [section 23B(1) of the 1989 Act]

- prepare an **assessment** of the relevant child's needs with a view to determining what advice assistance and support it would be appropriate for them to provide him (unless they already did so when he was an eligible child) [section 23B(3)(a) of the 1989 Act; the requirements for carrying out the assessment are set out in regulations 4 and 5 of the Care Leavers Regulations] secure training centre, or any other centre pursuant to a Court order), or in a hospital, and immediately before he was detained or in hospital he had been looked after by a local authority for a period or periods amounting in all to at least 13 weeks which began after he reached the age of 14.

Regulation 3 of the Care Leavers Regulations also provides that a child who has lived for a continuous period of six months or more with:
(a) his parent,
(b) someone who is not his parent but who has parental responsibility for him or,
(c) where he is in care and there was a residence order in force immediately before the care order was made, a person in whose favour the residence order was made then that child is not a relevant child despite falling within section 23A(2). Where those living arrangements break down and the child ceases to live with the person concerned, the child is to be treated as a relevant child.

Former relevant children

Defined in section 23C(1) of the 1989 Act as a young person who is:

(a) aged 18 or above, and either
(b) has been a relevant child and would be one if he were under 18, or
(c) immediately before he ceased to be looked after at age 18, was an eligible child.

- as soon as possible after any assessment of needs is completed, prepare a **pathway plan** [section 23B(3)(b) of the 1989 Act; the requirements for preparing the pathway plan are set out in regulation 6 of the Care Leavers Regulations]

- keep the pathway plan under **regular review** [section 23E(1D) of the 1989 Act; the requirements for carrying out reviews are set out in regulation 7 of the Care Leavers Regulations]

- appoint a **personal adviser** for the child (unless they already did so when he was an eligible child) [section 23B(2) of the 1989 Act; the functions of the personal adviser are set out in regulation 8 of the Care Leavers Regulations]

- safeguard and promote the relevant child's welfare by **maintaining** him, providing him with or maintaining him in **suitable accommodation** and providing **assistance in order to meet his needs in relation to education, training or employment** as provided for in his pathway plan [section 23B(8) of the 1989 Act and regulation 9 of the Care Leavers Regulations; regulation 9 also makes provision about the meaning of "suitable accommodation"].

The local authority that last looked after the former relevant child must:

- take reasonable steps to **keep in touch** with the former relevant child, and if they lose touch with him, to re-establish contact [section 23C(2) of the 1989 Act]

- continue to keep the **pathway plan** under **regular review** [section 23C(3)(b) of the 1989 Act; the requirements for carrying out reviews are set out in regulation 7 of the Care Leavers Regulations]

- continue the appointment of the **personal adviser** for the child [section 23C(3)(a) of the 1989 Act; the functions of the personal adviser are set out in regulation 8 of the Care Leavers Regulations]

- if his welfare requires it, provide **financial assistance** by contributing to the former relevant child's expenses in living near the place where he is, or will be, employed or seeking employment [sections 23C(4)(a) and 24B(1) of the 1989 Act]

- if his welfare and educational and training needs require it, provide **financial assistance** to enable him to pursue education or training [sections 23C(4)(b) and 24B(2) of the 1989 Act]

- if the former relevant child pursues higher education in accordance with his pathway plan, to pay him the higher education bursary [section 23C(5A) and the Children Act 1989 (Higher Education Bursary) (England) Regulations 2009].

The duties in section 23C(2), (3) and (4)(b) continue until the former relevant child reaches 21 or, where the child's pathway plan sets out a programme of education or training which extends beyond his 21st birthday, they continue for so long as he pursues that programme

Former relevant children pursuing further education or training

Defined in section 23CA(1) as a former relevant child who is:
(a) aged under 25,
(b) in relation to whom the duties in 23C(2), (3) and (4) no longer apply, and
(c) he has informed the local authority that he wants to pursue or is pursuing a programme of education or training.

The local authority which owed duties to that former relevant child under section 23C of the 1989 Act must:

- appoint a **personal adviser** for that person [section 23CA(2) of the 1989 Act]

- carry out an **assessment** of the needs of that person with a view to determining what assistance (if any) it would be appropriate for them to provide him [section 23CA(3)(a) of the 1989 Act; the requirements for carrying out the assessment are set out in regulations 4 and 5 of the Care Leavers Regulations]

- prepare a **pathway plan** for him [section 23CA(3)(b) of the 1989 Act; the requirements for preparing the pathway plan are set out in regulation 6 of the Care Leavers Regulations]

- to the extent the person's educational or training needs require it, provide **financial assistance** [section 23CA(4) and (5) of the 1989 Act].

Persons qualifying for advice and assistance

Defined in section 24 of the 1989 Act as a person who is:
(a) aged at least 16 but is under 21,
(b) with respect to whom a special guardianship order is in force (or was in force when they reached 18) and was looked after immediately before the making of that order, or
(c) at any time after reaching the age of 16 but while he was still a child was, but is no longer, looked after, accommodated or fostered.

The relevant local authority (as defined in section 24(5) of the 1989 Act) must consider whether the person needs help of a kind the local authority can give:

- under section 24A – to **advise and befriend** and give **assistance**,

- under section 24B – to give **financial assistance** – see above; or where the person is in full time further or higher education, is under the age of 25 and qualifies for advice and assistance, or would have done if he was under 21, assistance in relation to securing vacation accommodation [sections 24A(2) and (3), and 24B of the 1989 Act].

Summary of different categories

Eligible children

5.11   An eligible child is 16 or 17 and who *has been* looked after for at least 13 weeks which *began* when he was 14 and ended after he reached the age of 16. An eligible child is entitled to all the provisions of the 'looked after system'. He is also entitled to a personal adviser, a needs assessment and a pathway plan. The assessment must be completed not more than 3 months after their 16th birthday. The pathway plan will include what advice, assistance and support it would be appropriate to provide him with while the local authority is still looking after him, and after it ceases looking after him. The plan should be produced as soon as possible after the 3-month period has expired. He may be entitled to the provision of suitable accommodation unless the local authority is satisfied that his welfare does not require it (s 23B(8)(b)).

Relevant children

5.12   A relevant child is aged 16 or 17 and who has been looked after for at least 13 weeks since the age of 14, and *has been looked after* at some time when aged 16 or 17, and who has now *left* care. In effect, he may well be a former eligible child. He will be entitled to a personal adviser; a needs assessment; a pathway plan; accommodation and maintenance; assistance to achieve the goals set out in the pathway plan (which may include cash); the local authority must keep in touch with him. The time limits for the assessment of needs and production of a care plan are the same as for an eligible child. The local authority will be the prime source of income for this category. He will not be a relevant child if he has lived with his family for 6 months (unless it breaks down in which case his status remains that of a relevant child). Similarly, the 13-week period excludes any time when the child was in any pre-planned short-term placements (none of which exceeded 4 weeks) and at the end of each placement he returned to either the care of his parent, or someone who has parental responsibility for him.

Additional relevant children

5.13   An additional relevant child is one who would have been a 'relevant child' but for the fact that on his 16th birthday he was detained in the criminal justice system or in hospital, or had been returned home but that return has broken down. He would be entitled to the same things to which a relevant child would be entitled.

Former relevant children and former relevant children pursuing further education and training

5.14   A former relevant child is aged 18 or over, and who was previously either an *eligible child* or a *relevant child*, or both. If at the age of 21 he is still being helped with education or training by the local authority, he remains a former relevant child until the training or education ceases (even if this takes him beyond the age of 21). His entitlements are that the local authority must keep in touch; provide a personal adviser; a pathway plan; assistance with employment; assistance with education and training; assistance in general and vacation accommodation for higher education or residential further education if needed. If pursuing further education and training, the obligations are as set out in the table above.

Persons qualifying for advice and assistance

5.15 Into this category falls any person either under the age of 21 (or 24 if in education or training) who ceases to be looked after or accommodated or privately fostered after the age of 16. It includes those who leave care after October 2001, either at or over the age of 16, but who do not fall within the definition of an eligible child. It also includes those who left care before October 2001. He is entitled to all the benefits to which he would have been entitled under s 24 of the Children Act 1989 prior to its amendment. The local authority must keep in touch as they think is appropriate in order to discharge its obligations under ss 24A and 24B. He is entitled to assistance with education and training up to the age of 25. He is entitled to vacation accommodation for higher education courses or residential further education courses if necessary (including paying for accommodation).

Unaffected children

5.16 An eligible child will not be an eligible child where the local authority has arranged to place him in a pre-planned series of short-term placements, none of which individually exceeds 4 weeks (even though they may amount in all to the prescribed period, and that at the end of each placement, the child either returns to the care of his parent, or a person who has parental responsibility for him. Further a relevant child will not be a relevant child if he has been in a family placement for a continuous period of 6 months. However, even these children will have the benefit of ss 24A and 24B. If a return home (which had been successful) breaks down, and the young person turns to the local authority prior to reaching 18, then he will revert to the status he would have had if there had been no return home in the first place. A local authority is also under a duty to seek out young people whom they have looked after, but who are neither eligible, relevant or former relevant children.

'Looked after, accommodated or fostered'

5.17 Section 24(2) defines the extent of this expression. It is very wide.

Complaints by children

5.18 Section 24D provides that a complaints procedure shall exist for relevant children, a young person falling within s 23C, a person qualifying for advice and assistance, and any person falling within s 24B(2).

Local authority planning and policy

5.19 Each local authority must publish information about services to be provided by them under ss 23, 23B–23D, 24A and 24B.

Needs assessments and pathway plans

5.20 The details of what should be contained in a plan, and the details of the assessment process are set out in Part 2 of the Care Leavers (England) Regulations 2010, SI 2010/2571, together with Sch 1, and also in regs 41–43 and Sch 8 of the Care Planning, Placement and Case Review (England) Regulations 2010 (also reproduced below). In summary, it should include the following: identify the person responsible for the assessment; a timetable for who is to be consulted; arrangements for recording the outcome of the assessment; representations in the event of disagreement; the views of the child; participation of the child. The local authority shall provide the child with copies of the plan, the results of his assessment and all reviews of the plan. In the case of an eligible child an assessment shall be completed not more than 3 months after the date he reaches 16 or becomes an eligible child after that date. In the case of a relevant child who does not already have a pathway plan, the period is no more than 3 months after the date he becomes a relevant child. As a part of the assessment, account shall be taken of; the child's health and development; his need for education, training or employment; the support available from his family or other relationships; his financial needs; the extent to which he possesses the practical and other skills necessary for independent living and his needs for care, support and accommodation. The local authority shall also take into account the views of his parents; anyone with parental responsibility; any person who is caring for the child on a day-to-day basis; any school or college he attends; any independent visitor; any person providing healthcare or treatment; the personal adviser appointed for the child; any other person who might be relevant (in the view of the local authority, or the child). The model used for assessment is intended to be similar to the same seven developmental areas identified in the *Looking after Children* materials. The plan must be completed as soon as possible after the assessment of the needs of the child. It should look to the child's 21st birthday, unless there is an anticipation of education beyond that date. The content of the pathway plan is contained in the Schedule to the Regulations. These largely reflect the contents of the assessment set out above (personal support; accommodation; education and training; employment; family and social relationships; practical and other skills; financial support; health needs and contingency planning). The manner in which the Courts have approached these obligations is set out in at **5.33–5.36** below.

Personal advisers

5.21 Part 3 of SI 2010/2571 covers the involvement of these individuals. There is a range of suggestions contained in the consultation paper as to the type of professionals from which these might be recruited. Chapter 3 of the Guidance provides detail as to their function. An appointment is a statutory requirement. The specific status of the personal adviser is considered in greater detail at **5.35** below.

Accommodation

5.22   Regulation 9 (SI 2010/2571) requires the local authority to take account of the accommodation needs of an eligible or relevant young person. The *Ordinary Residence: Guidance on the identification of people in need of community care services, England* suggests that:

> '141 A local authority which is responsible for providing a young person with leaving care services is not under a general duty to provide accommodation. Therefore, when a young person with assessed social care needs who is entitled to leaving care support reaches the age of 18 and requires residential accommodation, their accommodation is usually provided under the 1948 Act, by their local authority of ordinary residence.'

However, it is not correct that a local authority has no power to provide accommodation for a former relevant child (*R (SO) v London Borough of Barking and Dagenham (Secretary of State for the Home Department and the Children's Society Intervening)* [2010] EWCA Civ 1101, [2011] 1 FLR 734). For more details on the provision of accommodation to adults, please refer to Chapter 4.

Financial arrangements

5.23   Section 8 of the Guidance provides detail on this aspect of the duties of a local authority (including the position to be adopted if the young persons has capital or income of his own via a legacy or compensation).

5.24   A local authority is not expected to be able to fully meet all the demands in respect of financing young people and to this end is expected to provide a schedule of the areas for which they would normally provide funding. Items considered to be a priority for funding would include travel costs; educational materials; other education costs; costs associated with special needs; costs of childcare; clothing; costs of contact with family or other significant relationships; cultural/religious needs; counselling/therapy; hobbies/holidays. Plainly, there may be other items not included in this list.

5.25   A local authority may have to handle finances on behalf of a young person (for example where there are problems in managing money). The continuation of the provision of financial support is not affected by their location in the country. Some local authorities may provide leaving care grants.

5.26   Those care leavers who do not become relevant children but who qualify for advice under s 24(2) will look to the Department of Work and Pensions for financial support. Local authorities may provide additional assistance in particular cases.

Part 1
General

1 Citation, commencement and application

(1) These Regulations may be cited as the Care Leavers (England) Regulations 2010 and come into force on 1st April 2011.

(2) These Regulations apply in relation to England only.

2 Interpretation

(1) In these Regulations–

> "the 1989 Act" means the Children Act 1989;
> "personal adviser" means the person appointed –
>> (i)   under paragraph 19C of Schedule 2 to the 1989 Act for an eligible child,
>> (ii)   under section 23B(2) for a relevant child, or
>> (iii) under section 23CA(2) for a former relevant child;
>
> "placement" has the meaning given in section 22C(6);
> "relevant child" has the meaning given in section 23A(2) and regulation 3; and
> "responsible authority" means the local authority that last looked after the child.

(2) In these Regulations, save as otherwise appears, any reference to a numbered section is a reference to that section in the 1989 Act.

3 Relevant children

(1) For the purposes of section 23A(3), children falling within paragraph (2) are an additional category of relevant children.

(2) Subject to paragraph (3), a child falls within this paragraph if –

> (a)   the child is aged 16 or 17,
> (b)   the child is not subject to a care order, and
> (c)   on attaining the age of 16 the child was detained, or in hospital, and immediately before being detained or admitted to hospital had been looked after by a local authority for a period or periods amounting in total to at least 13 weeks, which began after the child attained the age of 14.

(3) In calculating the period of 13 weeks referred to in paragraph (2)(b), no account is to be taken of any period in which the child was looked after by a local authority in the course of a pre-planned series of short-term placements, none of which individually exceeded four weeks, where at the end of each such placement the child returned to the care of their parent, or a person who is not a parent but who has parental responsibility for them.

(4) For the purposes of this regulation –

> (a)   "detained" means detained in a remand centre, a young offender institution or a secure training centre, or any other institution pursuant to an order of a court, and

(b)   "hospital" has the meaning given in section 275(1) of the National Health Service Act 2006.

(5) Subject to paragraph (6), a child who has lived for a continuous period of six months or more (whether that period commenced before or after they ceased to be looked after) with –

(a)   their parent,

(b)   someone who is not their parent but who has parental responsibility for them, or

(c)   where they were in care and there was a residence order in force immediately before the care order was made, a person in whose favour the residence order was made,

is not a relevant child despite falling within section 23A(2).

(6) Where living arrangements described in paragraph (5) break down and the child ceases to live with the person concerned, the child is a relevant child.

Part 2
Assessments of Need and Pathway Plans

4 Involvement of relevant child or former relevant child

(1) In carrying out an assessment of needs under regulation 5, and in preparing or reviewing a pathway plan under regulation 6 or 7, the responsible authority must, unless it is not reasonably practicable –

(a)   seek and have regard to the views of the relevant or former relevant child to whom the assessment or pathway plan relates, and

(b)   take all reasonable steps to enable the relevant or former relevant child to attend and participate in any meetings at which their case is to be considered.

(2) The responsible authority must as soon as practicable provide the relevant or former relevant child with copies of –

(a)   the results of the assessment,

(b)   the pathway plan,

(c)   each review of the pathway plan

and must ensure that the contents of each document are explained to the relevant or former relevant child having regard to their level of understanding, unless it is not reasonably practicable to do so.

(3) The responsible authority must ensure that a written record is kept of the views obtained under paragraph (1)(a).

5 Assessment of needs

(1) The responsible authority must assess the needs of each relevant child who does not already have a pathway plan, and each former relevant child falling within section 23CA (*further assistance to pursue education or training*), in accordance with this regulation.

(2) The assessment of needs must be completed –

(a)   in the case of a relevant child who does not already have a pathway plan, not more than three months after the date on which the child becomes a relevant child, and

(b)   in the case of a former relevant child falling within section 23CA, not more than three months after the date on which the responsible authority are informed, in accordance with section 23CA(1)(c), that the former relevant child is pursuing, or wishes to pursue, a programme of education or training.

(3) The responsible authority must ensure that a written record is kept of –

(a)   the identity of the persons whose views have been sought for the purpose of carrying out the assessment,

(b)   the information obtained in the course of the assessment,

(c)   the deliberations at any meeting held in connection with any aspect of the assessment, and

(d)   the results of the assessment.

(4) In carrying out an assessment of the needs of a relevant child who does not already have a pathway plan, the responsible authority must–

(a)   take into account–
   (i)   the child's health and development,
   (ii)   the child's needs for education, training or employment,
   (iii)   the support available to the child from members of the child's family and other persons,
   (iv)   the child's financial needs,
   (v)   the extent to which the child possesses the practical and other skills necessary for independent living, and
   (vi)   the child's needs for care, support and accommodation, and

(b)   unless it is not reasonably practicable or appropriate to do so, seek and take into account the views of–
   (i)   the child's parents,
   (ii)   any person who is not the child's parent but has parental responsibility for the child,
   (iii)   any person who on a day to day basis cares for, or provides accommodation for the child,
   (iv)   any school or institution within the further education sector attended by the child,
   (v)   the local authority for the area in which the child lives where that is different from the responsible authority,
   (vi)   the designated teacher at the school where the child is a registered pupil,
   (vii)   any person providing health care or treatment to the child,
   (viii)   any person by whom assistance by way of representation is provided to the child by virtue of arrangements made by the responsible authority under section 26A (*advocacy services*),
   (ix)   the personal adviser, and
   (x)   any other person whose views the responsible authority, or the child, consider may be relevant.

(5) In carrying out an assessment of the needs of a former relevant child falling within section 23CA, the responsible authority must –

(a)   take into account –

    (i)   the former relevant child's needs for education, training or employment, and

    (ii)   any other considerations the responsible authority consider relevant, and

(b)   unless it is not reasonably practicable to do so, seek and take into account the views of –

    (i)   the personal adviser, and

    (ii)   any other person whose views the responsible authority, or the former relevant child consider may be relevant.

(6) In this regulation –

(a)   "institution within the further education sector" has the meaning given in section 91(3) of the Further and Higher Education Act 1992,

(b)   "registered pupil" has the meaning given in section 434(5) of the Education Act 1996, and

(c)   "school" has the meaning given in section 4 of the Education Act 1996.

6 Pathway plans

(1) A pathway plan prepared under section 23B(3) (*relevant children*) or 23CA(3) must be prepared as soon as possible after the assessment of needs referred to in regulation 5 is completed.

(2) The pathway plan must include, in particular –

(a)   in the case of a plan prepared under section 23B(3), the matters referred to in Schedule 1, and

(b)   in the case of a plan prepared under section 23CA, the matters referred to in paragraphs 1 to 4 of Schedule 1.

(3) The pathway plan must, in relation to each of the matters included in it by virtue of paragraph (2), set out –

(a)   the manner in which the responsible authority propose to meet the needs of the relevant or former relevant child, and

(b)   the date by which, and by whom, any action required to implement any aspect of the pathway plan will be carried out.

(4) The pathway plan must be recorded in writing.

7 Review of pathway plans

(1) The responsible authority must review the pathway plan of each relevant and former relevant child in accordance with this regulation.

(2) The responsible authority must arrange a review –

(a)   if requested to do so by the relevant or former relevant child,

(b)   if the responsible authority, or the personal adviser, consider a review necessary, and

(c)   in any event, at intervals of not more that six months.

(3) If the responsible authority provide the relevant child or former relevant child with accommodation under section 23B or section 24B, the responsible authority must also –

(a)   arrange a review as soon as is practicable after the end of a period of 28 days beginning on the day on which the accommodation is first provided, and

(b)   on completing a review under sub-paragraph (a), determine at what intervals (not exceeding three months) subsequent reviews will be carried out.

(4) In carrying out a review the responsible authority must –

(a)   to the extent it considers it appropriate to do so, seek and take account of the views of the persons mentioned in regulation 5(4)(b) or, as the case may be, regulation 5(5)(b), and

(b)   consider whether, in relation to each of the matters set out in the pathway plan, any change is necessary.

(5) The results of the review and any change to the pathway plan must be recorded in writing.

Part 3
Personal Advisers

8 Functions of personal advisers

(1) A personal adviser has the following functions in relation to the relevant child or former relevant child for whom they are appointed –

(a)   to provide advice (including practical advice) and support,

(b)   where applicable, to participate in the assessment and the preparation of the pathway plan,

(c)   to participate in reviews of the pathway plan,

(d)   to liaise with the responsible authority in the implementation of the pathway plan,

(e)   to co-ordinate the provision of services, and to take reasonable steps to ensure that the child makes use of such services and that they are appropriate to the child's needs,

(f)   to remain informed about the relevant child's or former relevant child's progress and wellbeing, and

(g)   to keep a written record of contacts with, and of services provided to, the relevant or former relevant child.

(2) In addition, where accommodation is provided to a relevant child or former relevant child by the responsible authority under section 23B or section 24B, the personal adviser must visit the relevant child or former relevant child at that accommodation –

(a)   within 7 days of the accommodation first being provided,

(b)   subsequently, before the pathway plan is reviewed under regulation 7(3), and

(c)   at subsequent intervals of not more than two months.

Part 4
Miscellaneous

9 Support and accommodation

(1) For the purposes of section 23B(8)(c) (*other support for relevant children*), the responsible authority must provide assistance in order to meet the relevant child's needs in relation to education, training or employment as provided for in the pathway plan.

(2) For the purposes of section 23B(10), 'suitable accommodation' means accommodation –

    (a)   which so far as reasonably practicable is suitable for the relevant child in the light of their needs, including any health needs and any needs arising from any disability,

    (b)   in respect of which the responsible authority have satisfied themselves as to the character and suitability of the landlord or other provider, and

    (c)   in respect of which the responsible authority have, so far as reasonably practicable, taken into account the relevant child's –

        (i)   wishes and feelings, and

        (ii)   education, training or employment needs.

(3) In determining for the purposes of paragraph (2)(a) whether accommodation is suitable for a relevant child, the responsible authority must have regard to the matters set out in Schedule 2.

(4) For the purposes of section 24B(5) (*provision of vacation accommodation* –

    (a)   "higher education" means education provided by means of a course of a description referred to in regulations made under section 22 of the Teaching and Higher Education Act 1998, and

    (b)   "further education" has the same meaning as in section 2(3) and (5) of the Education Act 1996 save that for the purposes of this regulation it only includes further education which is provided on a full-time residential basis.

10 Records

(1) The responsible authority must establish and maintain a written case record for each relevant child and former relevant child ('the case record').

(2) The case record must include the written records required by virtue of regulation 4(3), and regulation 5(3)(a) to (c), and the following records ('relevant records') –

    (a)   any assessment of needs,

    (b)   any pathway plan,

    (c)   any review of a pathway plan.

(3) Relevant records must be retained by the responsible authority until the seventy-fifth anniversary of the date of birth of the relevant or former relevant child to whom they relate or, if the child dies before attaining the age of 18, for a period of fifteen years beginning with the date of death.

(4) The requirement in paragraph (1) may be complied with by retaining the original written records or copies of them, or by keeping all or part of the information contained in them in some other accessible form such as a computer record.

(5) Relevant records must be kept securely and may not be disclosed to any person except in accordance with –

　　(a)　any provision of, or made under or by virtue of, a statute under which access to such records is authorised, or

　　(b)　any court order authorising access to such records.

SCHEDULE 1

Matters to be Dealt with in the Pathway Plan and Review

1 The nature and level of contact and personal support to be provided, and by whom, to the child or young person.

2 A detailed plan for the education or training of the child or young person.

3 How the responsible authority will assist the child or young person in relation to employment or other purposeful activity or occupation.

4 Contingency plans for action to be taken by the responsible authority should the pathway plan for any reason cease to be effective.

5 Details of the accommodation the child or young person is to occupy (including an assessment of its suitability in the light of the child's or young person's needs, and details of the considerations taken into account in assessing that suitability).

6 The support to be provided to enable the child or young person to develop and sustain appropriate family and social relationships.

7 A programme to develop the practical and other skills necessary for the child or young person to live independently.

8 The financial support to be provided to the child or young person, in particular where it is to be provided to meet accommodation and maintenance needs.

9 The health needs, including any mental health needs, of the child or young person, and how they are to be met.

10 Details of the arrangements made by the authority to meet the child's needs in relation to identity with particular regard to their religious persuasion, racial origin and cultural and linguistic background.

SCHEDULE 2

Matters to be Considered in Determining the Suitability of Accommodation

1 In respect of the accommodation, the –

　　(a)　facilities and services provided,
　　(b)　state of repair,
　　(c)　safety,
　　(d)　location,
　　(e)　support,
　　(f)　tenancy status, and

(g)   the financial commitments involved for the relevant child and their affordability.

2 In respect of the relevant child, their –

(a)   views about the accommodation,

(b)   understanding of their rights and responsibilities in relation to the accommodation, and

(c)   understanding of funding arrangements.

****

Care Planning, Placement and Case Review (England) Regulations 2010

Eligible children

40 Meaning of eligible child

(1) For the purposes of paragraph 19B(2)(b) of Schedule 2 to the 1989 Act (*meaning of eligible child*), the prescribed period is 13 weeks and the prescribed age is 14.

(2) For the purposes of paragraph 19B(3)(b) of that Schedule, if C is a child to whom regulation 48 applies, C is not an eligible child despite falling within paragraph 19B(2) of that Schedule.

41 General duties

If C is an eligible child, the responsible authority must –

(a)   assess C's needs in accordance with regulation 42, and

(b)   prepare C's pathway plan, in accordance with regulation 43.

42 Assessment of needs

(1) The responsible authority must complete the assessment of C's needs in accordance with paragraph 19B(4) of Schedule 2 to the 1989 Act not more than three months after the date on which C reaches the age of 16 or becomes an eligible child after that age.

(2) In carrying out their assessment of C's likely needs when C ceases to be looked after, the responsible authority must take account of the following considerations –

(a)   C's state of health (including physical, emotional and mental health) and development,

(b)   C's continuing need for education, training or employment,

(c)   the support that will be available to C from C's parents and other connected persons,

(d)   C's actual and anticipated financial resources and capacity to manage personal finances independently,

(e)   the extent to which C possesses the practical and other skills necessary for independent living,

(f)   C's need for continuing care, support and accommodation,

(g)   the wishes and feelings of –

　　　(i)   C,

(ii)   any parent of C's and any person who is not C's parent but who has parental responsibility for C,

(iii)   the appropriate person,

(h)   the views of –

(i)   any person or educational institution that provides C with education or training and, if C has a statement of special educational needs, the local authority who maintain the statement (if different),

(ii)   the IRO,

(iii) any person providing health (whether physical, emotional or mental health) or dental care or treatment to C,

(iv)   the personal adviser appointed for C, and

(v)   any other person whose views the responsible authority, or C, consider may be relevant.

43 The pathway plan

(1) The pathway plan must be prepared as soon as possible after the assessment of C's needs and must include, in particular –

(a)   C's care plan, and

(b)   the information referred to in Schedule 8.

(2) The pathway plan must, in relation to each of the matters referred to in paragraphs 2 to 10 of Schedule 8, set out–

(a)   the manner in which the responsible authority propose to meet C's needs, and

(b)   the date by which, and by whom, any action required to implement any aspect of the plan will be carried out.

44 Functions of the personal adviser

The personal adviser's functions in relation to C are to –

(a)   provide advice (including practical advice) and support,

(b)   participate in reviews of C's case carried out under Part 6,

(c)   liaise with the responsible authority in the implementation of the pathway plan,

(d)   co-ordinate the provision of services and take reasonable steps to ensure C makes use of such services,

(e)   remain informed about C's progress and wellbeing, and

(f)   maintain a written record of their contacts with C.

45 Additional functions of independent reviewing officers

(1) The IRO must ensure that, having regard to C's age and understanding, C has been informed by the responsible authority of the steps C may take under the 1989 Act and in particular, where appropriate, of –

(a)   C's rights to apply, with leave, for a section 8 order (*residence, contact and other orders with respect to children*) and, where C is in the care of the responsible authority, to apply for the discharge of the care order, and

(b)   the availability of the procedure established by them under section 26(3) for considering any representations (including complaints) C may wish to make about the discharge by the responsible authority of their functions, including the availability of assistance to make such representations under section 26A (*advocacy services*).

(2) If C wishes to take legal proceedings under the 1989 Act, the IRO must –

(a)   establish whether an appropriate adult is able and willing to assist C to obtain legal advice or bring proceedings on C's behalf, and

(b)   if there is no such person, assist C to obtain such advice.

(3) In the following circumstances the IRO must consider whether it would be appropriate to refer C's case to an officer of the Children and Family Court Advisory and Support Service –

(a)   in the opinion of the IRO, the responsible authority have failed in any significant respect to –

(i)   prepare C's care plan in accordance with these Regulations,

(ii)   review C's case in accordance with these Regulations, or effectively implement any decision taken in consequence of a review,

or are otherwise in breach of their duties to C in any material respect, and

(b)   having drawn the failure or breach to the attention of persons at an appropriate level of seniority within the responsible authority, it has not been addressed to the satisfaction of the IRO within a reasonable period of time.

(4) When consulted by the responsible authority about any matter concerning C, or when informed of any matter relating to C in accordance with these Regulations, the IRO must–

(a)   ensure that the responsible authority have ascertained and, subject to C's age and understanding, given due consideration to, C's wishes and feelings concerning the matter in question, and

(b)   consider whether to request a review of C's case.

46 Qualifications and experience of independent reviewing officers

(1) The IRO must be registered as a social worker in a register maintained by the General Social Care Council or by the Care Council for Wales under section 56 of the Care Standards Act 2000, or in a corresponding register maintained under the law of Scotland or Northern Ireland.

(2) The IRO must have sufficient relevant social work experience with children and families to perform the functions of an independent reviewing officer set out in section 25B(1) and under these Regulations in an independent manner and having regard to C's best interests.

(3) The responsible authority must not appoint any of the following as the IRO –

(a)   a person involved in preparing C's care plan or the management of C's case,

(b)   R,

(c)   C's personal adviser,

(d)   a person with management responsibilities in relation to a person mentioned in sub-paragraphs (a) to (c), or

(e)   a person with control over the resources allocated to the case.

SCHEDULE 8

Matters to be Dealt with in the Pathway Plan

1 The name of C's personal adviser.

2 The nature and level of contact and personal support to be provided to C, and by whom.

3 Details of the accommodation C is to occupy when C ceases to be looked after.

4 The plan for C's continuing education or training when C ceases to be looked after.

5 How the responsible authority will assist C in obtaining employment or other purposeful activity or occupation.

6 The support to be provided to enable C to develop and sustain appropriate family and social relationships.

7 A programme to develop the practical and other skills C needs to live independently.

8 The financial support to be provided to enable C to meet accommodation and maintenance costs.

9 C's health care needs, including any physical, emotional or mental health needs and how they are to be met when C ceases to be looked after.

10 The responsible authority's contingency plans for action to be taken in the event that the pathway plan ceases to be effective for any reason.

CHILDREN ACT 1989

5.27   The text of the amendments to the Children Act 1989 are set out below.

23A The responsible authority and relevant children

(1) The responsible local authority shall have the functions set out in section 23B in respect of a relevant child.

(2) In subsection (1) "relevant child" means (subject to subsection (3)) a child who –

    (a)   is not being looked after by any local authority;

    (b)   was, before last ceasing to be looked after, an eligible child for the purposes of paragraph 19B of Schedule 2; and

    (c)   is aged sixteen or seventeen.

(3) The Secretary of State may prescribe –

    (a)   additional categories of relevant children; and

    (b)   categories of children who are not to be relevant children despite falling within subsection (2).

(4) In subsection (1) the "responsible local authority" is the one which last looked after the child.

(5) If under subsection (3)(a) the Secretary of State prescribes a category of relevant children which includes children who do not fall within subsection (2)(b) (for example, because they were being looked after by a local authority in Scotland), he may in the regulations also provide for which local authority is to be the responsible local authority for those children.

23B Additional functions of the responsible authority in respect of relevant children

(1) It is the duty of each local authority to take reasonable steps to keep in touch with a relevant child for whom they are the responsible authority, whether he is within their area or not.

(2) It is the duty of each local authority to appoint a personal adviser for each relevant child (if they have not already done so under paragraph 19C of Schedule 2).

(3) It is the duty of each local authority, in relation to any relevant child who does not already have a pathway plan prepared for the purposes of paragraph 19B of Schedule 2 –

>   (a)   to carry out an assessment of his needs with a view to determining what advice, assistance and support it would be appropriate for them to provide him under this Part; and
>   (b)   to prepare a pathway plan for him.

(4) The local authority may carry out such an assessment at the same time as any assessment of his needs is made under any enactment referred to in sub-paragraphs (a) to (c) of paragraph 3 of Schedule 2, or under any other enactment.

(5) The Secretary of State may by regulations make provision as to assessments for the purposes of subsection (3).

(6) The regulations may in particular make provision about –

>   (a)   who is to be consulted in relation to an assessment;
>   (b)   the way in which an assessment is to be carried out, by whom and when;
>   (c)   the recording of the results of an assessment;
>   (d)   the considerations to which the local authority are to have regard in carrying out an assessment.

(7) The authority shall keep the pathway plan under regular review.

(8) The responsible local authority shall safeguard and promote the child's welfare and, unless they are satisfied that his welfare does not require it, support him by –

>   (a)   maintaining him;
>   (b)   providing him with or maintaining him in suitable accommodation; and
>   (c)   providing support of such other descriptions as may be prescribed.

(9) Support under subsection (8) may be in cash.

(10) The Secretary of State may by regulations make provision about the meaning of "suitable accommodation" and in particular about the suitability of landlords or other providers of accommodation.

(11) If the local authority have lost touch with a relevant child, despite taking reasonable steps to keep in touch, they must without delay –

    (a)   consider how to re-establish contact; and

    (b)   take reasonable steps to do so,

and while the child is still a relevant child must continue to take such steps until they succeed.

(12) Subsections (7) to (9) of section 17 apply in relation to support given under this section as they apply in relation to assistance given under that section.

(13) Subsections (4) and (5) of section 22 apply in relation to any decision by a local authority for the purposes of this section as they apply in relation to the decisions referred to in that section.

23C Continuing functions in respect of former relevant children

(1) Each local authority shall have the duties provided for in this section towards –

    (a)   a person who has been a relevant child for the purposes of section 23A (and would be one if he were under eighteen), and in relation to whom they were the last responsible authority; and

    (b)   a person who was being looked after by them when he attained the age of eighteen, and immediately before ceasing to be looked after was an eligible child,

and in this section such a person is referred to as a "former relevant child".

(2) It is the duty of the local authority to take reasonable steps –

    (a)   to keep in touch with a former relevant child whether he is within their area or not; and

    (b)   if they lose touch with him, to re-establish contact.

(3) It is the duty of the local authority –

    (a)   to continue the appointment of a personal adviser for a former relevant child; and

    (b)   to continue to keep his pathway plan under regular review.

(4) It is the duty of the local authority to give a former relevant child –

    (a)   assistance of the kind referred to in section 24B(1), to the extent that his welfare requires it;

    (b)   assistance of the kind referred to in section 24B(2), to the extent that his welfare and his educational or training needs require it;

    (c)   other assistance, to the extent that his welfare requires it.

(5) The assistance given under subsection (4)(c) may be in kind or, in exceptional circumstances, in cash.

(6) Subject to subsection (7), the duties set out in subsections (2), (3) and (4) subsist until the former relevant child reaches the age of twenty-one.

(7) If the former relevant child's pathway plan sets out a programme of education or training which extends beyond his twenty-first birthday –

    (a)   the duty set out in subsection (4)(b) continues to subsist for so long as the former relevant child continues to pursue that programme; and

    (b)   the duties set out in subsections (2) and (3) continue to subsist concurrently with that duty.

(8) For the purposes of subsection (7)(a) there shall be disregarded any interruption in a former relevant child's pursuance of a programme of education or training if the local authority are satisfied that he will resume it as soon as is reasonably practicable.

(9) Section 24B(5) applies in relation to a person being given assistance under subsection (4)(b) as it applies in relation to a person to whom section 24B(3) applies.

(10) Subsections (7) to (9) of section 17 apply in relation to assistance given under this section as they apply in relation to assistance given under that section.

23D Personal advisers

(1) The Secretary of State may by regulations require local authorities to appoint a personal adviser for children or young persons of a prescribed description who have reached the age of sixteen but not the age of twenty-one who are not –

   (a)   children who are relevant children for the purposes of section 23A;
   (b)   the young persons referred to in section 23C; or
   (c)   the children referred to in paragraph 19C of Schedule 2.

(2) Personal advisers appointed under or by virtue of this Part shall (in addition to any other functions) have such functions as the Secretary of State prescribes.

23E Pathway plans

(1) In this Part, a reference to a "pathway plan" is to a plan setting out –

   (a)   in the case of a plan prepared under paragraph 19B of Schedule 2 –
         (i)   the advice, assistance and support which the local authority intend to provide a child under this Part, both while they are looking after him and later; and
         (ii)   when they might cease to look after him; and
   (b)   in the case of a plan prepared under section 23B, the advice, assistance and support which the local authority intend to provide under this Part,

and dealing with such other matters (if any) as may be prescribed.

(2) The Secretary of State may by regulations make provision about pathway plans and their review.

24 Persons qualifying for advice and assistance

(1) In this Part "a person qualifying for advice and assistance" means a person to whom subsection (1A) or (1B) applies.

(1A) This subsection applies to a person –

   (a)   who has reached the age of sixteen but not the age of twenty-one;
   (b)   with respect to whom a special guardianship order is in force (or, if he has reached the age of eighteen, was in force when he reached that age); and
   (c)   who was, immediately before the making of that order, looked after by a local authority.

(1B) This subsection applies to a person to whom subsection (1A) does not apply, and who –

(a)   is under twenty-one; and

(b)   at any time after reaching the age of sixteen but while still a child was, but is no longer, looked after, accommodated or fostered.

(2) In subsection (1B)(b), "looked after, accommodated or fostered" means –

(a)   looked after by a local authority;

(b)   accommodated by or on behalf of a voluntary organisation;

(c)   accommodated in a private children's home;

(d)   accommodated for a consecutive period of at least three months –

    (i)   by any Local Health Board, Special Health Authority, Primary Care Trust or local education authority, or

    (ii)   in any care home or independent hospital or in any accommodation provided by a National Health Service trust or an NHS foundation trust; or

(e)   privately fostered.

(3) Subsection (2)(d) applies even if the period of three months mentioned there began before the child reached the age of sixteen.

(4) In the case of a person qualifying for advice and assistance by virtue of subsection (2)(a), it is the duty of the local authority which last looked after him to take such steps as they think appropriate to contact him at such times as they think appropriate with a view to discharging their functions under sections 24A and 24B.

(5) In each of sections 24A and 24B, the local authority under the duty or having the power mentioned there ("the relevant authority") is –

(za)   in the case of a person to whom subsection (1A) applies, a local authority determined in accordance with regulations made by the Secretary of State;

(a)   in the case of a person qualifying for advice and assistance by virtue of subsection (2)(a), the local authority which last looked after him; or

(b)   in the case of any other person qualifying for advice and assistance, the local authority within whose area the person is (if he has asked for help of a kind which can be given under section 24A or 24B).

24A Advice and assistance

(1) The relevant authority shall consider whether the conditions in subsection (2) are satisfied in relation to a person qualifying for advice and assistance.

(2) The conditions are that –

(a)   he needs help of a kind which they can give under this section or section 24B; and

(b)   in the case of a person to whom section 24(1A) applies, or to whom section 24(1B) applies and who was not being looked after by any local authority, they are satisfied that the person by whom he was being looked after does not have the necessary facilities for advising or befriending him.

(3) If the conditions are satisfied –

(a)   they shall advise and befriend him if he is a person to whom section 24(1A) applies, or he is a person to whom section 24(1B) applies and he was being looked after by a local authority or was accommodated by or on behalf of a voluntary organisation; and

(b)   in any other case they may do so.

(4) Where as a result of this section a local authority are under a duty, or are empowered, to advise and befriend a person, they may also give him assistance.

(5) The assistance may be in kind and, in exceptional circumstances, assistance may be given –

(a)   by providing accommodation, if in the circumstances assistance may not be given in respect of the accommodation under section 24B, or

(b)   in cash.

(6) Subsections (7) to (9) of section 17 apply in relation to assistance given under this section or section 24B as they apply in relation to assistance given under that section.

24B Employment, education and training

(1) The relevant local authority may give assistance to any person who qualifies for advice and assistance by virtue of section 24(1A) or section 24(2)(a) by contributing to expenses incurred by him in living near the place where he is, or will be, employed or seeking employment.

(2) The relevant local authority may give assistance to a person to whom subsection (3) applies by –

(a)   contributing to expenses incurred by the person in question in living near the place where he is, or will be, receiving education or training; or

(b)   making a grant to enable him to meet expenses connected with his education or training.

(3) This subsection applies to any person who –

(a)   is under twenty-four; and

(b)   qualifies for advice and assistance by virtue of section 24(1A) or section 24(2)(a), or would have done so if he were under twenty-one.

(4) Where a local authority are assisting a person under subsection (2) they may disregard any interruption in his attendance on the course if he resumes it as soon as is reasonably practicable.

(5) Where the local authority are satisfied that a person to whom subsection (3) applies who is in full-time further or higher education needs accommodation during a vacation because his term-time accommodation is not available to him then, they shall give him assistance by –

(a)   providing him with suitable accommodation during the vacation; or

(b)   paying him enough to enable him to secure such accommodation himself.

(6) The Secretary of State may prescribe the meaning of "full-time", "further education", "higher education" and "vacation" for the purposes of subsection (5).

24C Information

(1) Where it appears to a local authority that a person –

(a)   with whom they are under a duty to keep in touch under section 23B, 23C or 24; or

(b)   whom they have been advising and befriending under section 24A; or

(c)   to whom they have been giving assistance under section 24B,

proposes to live, or is living, in the area of another local authority, they must inform that other authority.

(2) Where a child who is accommodated –

(a)   by a voluntary organisation or in a private children's home;

(b)   by any Local Health Board, Special Health Authority, Primary Care Trust or local education authority; or

(c)   in any care home or independent hospital or any accommodation provided by a National Health Service trust or an NHS foundation trust,

ceases to be so accommodated, after reaching the age of sixteen, the organisation, authority or (as the case may be) person carrying on the home shall inform the local authority within whose area the child proposes to live.

(3) Subsection (2) only applies, by virtue of paragraph (b) or (c), if the accommodation has been provided for a consecutive period of at least three months.

24D Representations: sections 23A to 24B

(1) Every local authority shall establish a procedure for considering representations (including complaints) made to them by –

(a)   a relevant child for the purposes of section 23A or a young person falling within section 23C;

(b)   a person qualifying for advice and assistance; or

(c)   a person falling within section 24B(2),

about the discharge of their functions under this Part in relation to him.

(1A) Regulations may be made by the Secretary of State imposing time limits on the making of representations under subsection (1).

(2) In considering representations under subsection (1), a local authority shall comply with regulations (if any) made by the Secretary of State for the purposes of this subsection.

Schedule 2, Part II

Preparation for ceasing to be looked after

19A It is the duty of the local authority looking after a child to advise, assist and befriend him with a view to promoting his welfare when they have ceased to look after him.

19B (1) A local authority shall have the following additional functions in relation to an eligible child whom they are looking after.

(2) In sub-paragraph (1) "eligible child" means, subject to sub-paragraph (3), a child who –

(a)   is aged sixteen or seventeen; and

(b)   has been looked after by a local authority for a prescribed period, or periods amounting in all to a prescribed period, which began after he reached a prescribed age and ended after he reached the age of sixteen.

(3) The Secretary of State may prescribe –

(a)   additional categories of eligible children; and
(b)   categories of children who are not to be eligible children despite falling within sub-paragraph (2).

(4) For each eligible child, the local authority shall carry out an assessment of his needs with a view to determining what advice, assistance and support it would be appropriate for them to provide him under this Act –

(a)   while they are still looking after him; and
(b)   after they cease to look after him,

and shall then prepare a pathway plan for him.

(5) The local authority shall keep the pathway plan under regular review.

(6) Any such review may be carried out at the same time as a review of the child's case carried out by virtue of section 26.

(7) The Secretary of State may by regulations make provision as to assessments for the purposes of sub-paragraph (4).

(8) The regulations may in particular provide for the matters set out in section 23B(6).

Personal advisers

19C A local authority shall arrange for each child whom they are looking after who is an eligible child for the purposes of paragraph 19B to have a personal adviser.

Ordinary residence and responsible local authority

5.28   As set out above, the duties of the local authority now continue wherever the child lives. Arguments which were sustainable prior to the Act therefore no longer apply (cf *R v Kent CC ex p Salisbury and Pierre* [2000] 3 CCLR 38 and to a lesser extent *R (on the application of Stewart) v Wandsworth LBC, Hammersmith and Fulham LBC and Lambeth LBC* [2001] EWHC 709 (Admin), [2001] 4 CCLR 466 and *R (on the Application of M) v Barking & Dagenham LBC and Westminster CC (Interested Party)* [2002] EWHC 2663 (Admin), [2003] 6 CCLR 87).

5.29   However, whilst the issue of ordinary residence is very clear in respect of which local authority has responsibility under the Children (Leaving Care) Act 2000, the matter is not as straightforward when it comes to other community care services (including the provision of accommodation). The *Ordinary Residence: Guidance on the identification of the ordinary residence of people in need of community care services, England* sets out in some detail the provisions in these circumstances. These are set out below. The Guidance also contains a number of illustrative examples, but these are not included for reasons of space.

Determining ordinary residence

145. When a young person reaches 18 and is eligible for residential accommodation and/or services under the 1948 Act, their ordinary residence should be assessed to determine which local authority is responsible for the provision of such services under that Act. The local authority that had responsibility for the young person under the 1989 Act is not necessarily the young person's local authority of ordinary residence once they become eligible for services under the 1948 Act. However, where a child has been looked after, the local authority responsible for leaving care services will always be the local authority that had responsibility for their care under the 1989 Act.

146. Neither the 1989 Act nor the 1948 Act makes provision for how to determine ordinary residence when a young person moves from being eligible for services under the 1989 Act to being eligible for services under the 1948 Act. Therefore, when making decisions about the ordinary residence of young people in transition to adult services, local authorities should have regard to both Acts. **It is important to note that there is no set procedure for determining ordinary residence in this situation: every case must be decided on an individual basis, taking into account the circumstances of the young person and all the facts of their case.**

147. Although the provisions of the 1989 Act no longer apply once a young person reaches 18 (other than the leaving care provisions, if the young person is eligible for such services), local authorities could reasonably have regard to the 1989 Act and start from a presumption that the young person remains ordinarily resident in the local authority that had responsibility for them under the 1989 Act. Section 105(6) of the 1989 Act provides that, in determining the ordinary residence of a child for any purposes of that Act, any period in which a child lives in the following places should be disregarded:

- a school or other institution;
- in accordance with the requirements of a supervision order under the 1989 Act;
- in accordance with the requirements of a youth rehabilitation order under Part 1 of the Criminal Justice and Immigration Act 2008; or
- while he is being provided with accommodation by or on behalf of a local authority.

148. Therefore, where a local authority has placed a child in accommodation out of area under the 1989 Act, that local authority remains the child's place of ordinary residence for the purposes of the 1989 Act. In such a case, there would be a starting presumption that the young person's place of ordinary residence remains the same for the purposes of the 1948 Act when they turn 18.

149. However, this starting presumption may be rebutted by the circumstances of the individual's case and the application of the *Shah* or *Vale* tests (see Part 1 of this guidance). Under these tests, a number of factors should be taken into account when considering a person's ordinary residence for the purposes of the

1948 Act. These include: the remaining ties the young person has with the authority that was responsible for their care as a child, ties with the authority in which they are currently living, the length and nature of residence in this area and the young person's views in respect of where he/she wants to live (if he/she has the mental capacity to make this decision). If the young person is being provided with residential accommodation under Part 3 of the 1948 Act at the time ordinary residence falls to be assessed, the deeming provision in section 24(5) applies and it would be necessary to assess their place of ordinary residence immediately before such accommodation was provided.

150. In many cases, establishing a young person's local authority of ordinary residence will be a straightforward matter. However, difficulties may arise where a young person has been placed in residential accommodation out of area as a child under the 1989 Act. In this situation, the young person may be found to be ordinarily resident in the local authority that had responsibility for them under the 1989 Act, or they may be found to have acquired a new ordinary residence in the area in which they are living, depending on the facts of their case.

151. For example, where a young person (who has been placed out of area) moves out of their residential accommodation under the 1989 Act and into independent living arrangements in their 'host area' on or around their 18th birthday, the starting presumption would be that they are ordinarily resident in the area which had responsibility for them under the 1989 Act. However, in this situation, the starting presumption is more likely to be rebutted than in other situations. By the time the young person reaches the age of 18, they may have been accommodated in another local authority area for several years under the 1989 Act. Shortly before their 18th birthday, they may have a well established support network outside of their responsible authority under the 1989 Act which they wish to continue into adulthood. More importantly, they may have made a decision to stay in their host area for settled purposes. In such a case, a consideration of all the facts may lead to the conclusion that, for the purposes of the 1948 Act, the young person is ordinarily resident in the area in which they are living at the time of their 18th birthday. Scenarios 1, 2 and 3 below provide some examples of how ordinary residence is determined when a young person moves from accommodation provided under the 1989 to accommodation or services provided under the 1948 Act.

152. Similarly, where a young person is intending to move out of the area which had responsibility for him under the 1989 Act to go to university, the starting presumption would be that they are ordinarily resident in the area that had responsibility for them under the 1989 Act. Again, this presumption may be rebutted. If the young person moves to the area in which the university is located for settled purposes and has no intention to return to his responsible authority under the 1989 Act, then the facts of his case may lead to the conclusion that he has acquired an ordinary residence in that area.

153. Alternatively, if the young person has a base with his parents (or those with parental responsibility for him) in the local authority which had responsibility for him under the 1989 Act and he intends to return to this base during the university holidays (including the long summer holiday) then the facts of his case may lead to the conclusion that he remains ordinarily resident in the local authority which had responsibility for him under the 1989 Act.

154. It is not possible for a person to be ordinarily resident in two different local authorities under the 1948 Act (see paragraph 26 *(More than one place of residence)*). Therefore, where a young person goes away to university or college, it is necessary to establish, from all the facts of their case, to which local authority they have the stronger link. If it is the local authority which had responsibility for them under the 1989 Act, this local authority would be responsible for the provision of services under section 29 of the 1948 Act during term time at university. The young person's absence from their local authority of ordinary residence would not result in their ordinary residence being lost: it would be considered a temporary absence in line with the judgement in *Levene* (see paragraphs 23–24 *(Temporary absences)*). Scenarios 4 and 5 below provide further guidance on how ordinary residence is determined when a young person attends university in a different local authority area.

155. As detailed in paragraphs 139–140 above, a young person aged 18 or over may be entitled to leaving care services, provided by the responsible authority under the 1989 Act. As leaving care services do not include accommodation (with the exception of vacation accommodation and accommodation that is provided in exceptional circumstances, see paragraphs 142–144 above), any residential accommodation should be provided under Part 3 of the 1948 Act. If a former relevant child has been placed out of area as a looked after child, and wishes to remain in this area on reaching the age of 18, they may be found to be ordinarily resident there for the purposes of the 1948 Act. In this situation, their accommodation would be provided by the local authority in which they are living but the provision of their leaving care would remain the responsibility of the local authority that had responsibility for them under the 1989 Act.

156. Where this is the case, the 1989 Act and the 1948 Act would operate in parallel. This means the responsible authority under the 1989 Act and the authority of ordinary residence under the 1948 Act would need to work together to ensure the young person eligible for leaving care services was provided with joined up care and support.

157. It should be noted that where a child has been placed out of area under the 1989 Act and becomes eligible for leaving care services upon reaching the age of 18, this does not automatically mean they are ordinarily resident in the area that had responsibility for them under the 1989 Act. Whilst the young person remains entitled to leaving care support from their responsible authority, all the circumstances of their case must be considered. Scenarios 3 and 5 below provide examples of how the 1989 Act and the 1948 Act operate in parallel when a young person is eligible to leaving care services under the 1989 Act and accommodation and/or services under the 1948 Act.

DISPUTES OVER WHETHER A CHILD COMES WITHIN THE PROVISIONS OF THE ACT

Unaccompanied asylum-seeking children

5.30 In *R (on the Application of Berhe, Kidane, Munir and Ncube) v Hillingdon LBC and Secretary of State for Education and Skills (interested party)* [2003] EWHC 2075 (Admin), [2003] 6 CCLR 471, the general obligations of the local authority (under s 20 of the Children Act 1989) as against the specific provisions of the Children (Leaving Care) Act 2000 were considered. The claimants were all supported (with accommodation) by the local authority, and had gone on into higher education (as adults). It was held that the local authority had been providing them with accommodation (the local authority having argued that support with accommodation was not equivalent to providing support for that purpose), and that the claimants were not excluded from the Children (Leaving Care) Act 2000 whether housing was provided under ss 17 or 20 of the Children Act 1989. Advice on Unaccompanied Asylum-Seeking Children (UASC) is contained in Chapter 6(b) of the Guidance.

Detention

5.31 The claimant had been accommodated by the council for about 4 years prior to his 16th birthday, but shortly after that was sentenced to 10 months detention in a young offender's institution. It was asserted that he was an 'eligible child' and entitled to a personal adviser and a pathway plan. The council refuted this suggestion, and that it would treat him as a 'child in need' (s 17 of the Children Act 1989), and provided him with bed and breakfast accommodation, and £30 per week by way of financial assistance. It also made this decision upon the basis that the claimant had said that he did not wished to be categorised as having been 'in care'. It is perhaps unsurprising that the claim for judicial review succeeded (*R (W) v North Lincolnshire Council* [2008] EWHC 2299 (Admin), [2008] 2 FLR 2150. It should be noted that since April 2010 it is not permissible for local authorities to provide children with bed and breakfast accommodation (*Provision of Accommodation for 16 and 17 year old young people who may be homeless and/or require accommodation: Guidance to children's social services authorities and local housing authorities about their duties under Part 3 of the Children Act 1989 and Part 7 of the Housing Act 1996 to secure or provide accommodation for homeless 16 and 17 year old young people* para 3.1. This Guidance was issued pursuant to s 7 of the Local Authority Social Services Act 1970).

Housing

5.32 In *R (M) v Hammersmith and Fulham LBC* [2008] UKHL 14, [2008] 1 FLR 1384, an issue arose as to whether a child fell within the obligations of the local authority pursuant to the Housing Act 1996 or the Children Act 1989 and/or the Children (Leaving Care) Act 2000. Principally the case looks at the different statutory obligations as between the housing department of the local authority, and the children's social services department. However, it also considered whether on the facts of the case, M could ever have been considered to have been a 'relevant' and/or 'eligible' child. She had never been in care. She had never been 'looked after' but instead had been accommodated under s 188 of the Housing Act 1996. Children's Social Services had no connection with this accommodation. There had been no referral to Children's Social Services. There had been no services offered to M by Children's Social Services (although on the facts of the case it is very odd that she was not referred to that Department by the Housing Department). Consequently, she was not eligible for any of the support available via the Children (Leaving Care) Act 2000. The issue has been further considered in *R (on the application of G (FC)) v Southwark LBC* [2009] UKHL 26, [2009] 12 CCLR 437 (at **5.63** below).

Assessment of needs and pathway plans

5.33 A formal complaint had been made by the grandmother of a severely disabled boy regarding a failure to assess the needs of the child, and to prepare a pathway plan. The boy had been placed by the local authority at a children's centre, and was approaching his 18th birthday. The outcome of the complaint was not satisfactory, and proceedings were commenced by way of judicial review. It was held that the local authority had not complied with Sch 2, para 19B(4) of the Children Act 1989 or the Children (Leaving Care) (England) Regulations 2001. Orders were therefore made that there should be a statutory assessment and pathway plan prepared (*R (on the Application of P) v Newham LBC* [2004] EWHC 2210 (Admin), [2004] 7 CCLR 553).

5.34 In *R (on the application of J) (by his litigation friend MW) v Caerphilly CBC* [2005] EWHC 586 (Admin), [2005] 8 CCLR 255, [2005] 2 FLR 860, the issues of: (a) the function of the personal adviser; (b) the contents of a pathway plan; (c) a child who did not engage with the local authority; and (d) delay in complying with statutory obligations were all considered. It was held that whilst it was not unlawful or necessarily undesirable to appoint an employee of the local authority as a personal adviser, it was important that the appointee realised that he or she was acting in that role only. The personal adviser should not be responsible for undertaking the statutory assessment or the preparation of the pathway plan. In effect, in this case, the local authority had failed to provide a personal adviser. The manner in which the assessment and pathway plan had been produced was in breach of reg 7(2)(a) and reg 3(1) and Sch 2, para 19(c) of the Children Act 1989. Further, the attempts to involve the child were inadequate (reg 6(1)(a) and (b), (2)). The contents of the pathway plan were too vague, and did not state who would do what, and by when. If a child is likely to be uncooperative in the planning and assessment process, then this should be clearly documented, and a contingency plan devised.

5.35 Munby J, as he then was, re-visited the same points as he had made above in *R (G) v Nottingham City Council and Nottingham University Hospital* [2008] EWHC 400 (Admin), [2008] 1 FLR 1668. Two draft pathway plans had been prepared for the claimant, both of which were deficient in accordance with the Guidance and Regulations. A plan was required that set out in precise detail how the needs which arose from the assessment were to be met. The personal adviser had been involved in preparing the pathway plan. Given Munby's judgment as set out above, the local authority had been found to have acted unlawfully in that respect, as well as in almost all other respects.

5.36   In *R (on the application of A) v London Borough of Lambeth* [2010] EWHC 1652 (Admin) a personal adviser had also been involved in preparing the pathway plan. Applying and adopting *R (on the application of J) (by his litigation friend MW) v Caerphilly CBC* this was found to be unlawful. The process by which the claimant came within the Children (Leaving Care) Act 2000 is carefully dissected in the judgment, together with the deficiencies in that pathway plan (in similar terms to the criticism made in all of the cases referred to above).

Extent of obligation

5.37   In *Binomugisha v London Borough of Southwark* [2006] EWHC 2254 (Admin), [2007] 1 FLR 916, consideration was given to the interrelationship of the leaving care legislation, and the immigration status of the claimant. There were also alternative claims made in respect of the National Assistance Act 1948, and reliance was placed upon Art 8 of the European Convention on Human Rights. However, in terms of the subject matter of this chapter, the following principles emerged based upon the particular facts. The principal issue in the case was:

> '[918 [1]] ... whether the [local authority] has erred in law in their decision to cease providing support under sections 23C or 24A of the Children Act 1989 ... There are also issues as to whether [the local authority] is obliged to continue to provide the claimant with a personal adviser and a "pathway plan" also pursuant to the 1989 Act.'

It was common ground that:

> '[927 [33]] Before he was 18, [the local authority] provided support to the Claimant as a child in need as defined by section 17(10) of the 1989 Act. The support included accommodation under section 20. Once he reached 18 the claimant was no longer 'a child', but the local authority's duties towards him did not come to an abrupt end. It is not disputed that he was then within the statutory concept of a 'former relevant child' (see section 23C(1)). In such a case , the local authority must continue the appointment of a personal adviser and keep his pathway plan under regular review (see section 23(C)(3)).'

The claimant argued that by virtue of s 23C(4), the local authority had a duty to provide him with accommodation and to support him. At para [928 [36]] the relief which might have flowed from s 24 is set out thus:

> 'The claimant was under 21 and had, after reaching 16 years old, but while still a child, been looked after by the local authority. He was, therefore, a person who qualified for advice and assistance (section 24(1) and (1B)). The local authority then needed to consider if the claimant was in need of the kind of help which they could provide under section 24A, namely advising and befriending the claimant and giving him assistance. In exceptional circumstances, the assistance could take the form of providing accommodation and cash.'

A secondary issue arose as to whether the local authority was prevented from so doing as a result of the immigration status of the claimant and the interpretation of the wording of para 1(1)(g) of Sch 3 to the Nationality, Immigration and Asylum Act 2002. It was held that:

> '[943–944 [71]–[73]] … there is a continuing duty to provide a personal adviser and review a pathway plan even if the local authority is precluded from giving support and assistance, although the functions in each case will be very much truncated because of that restriction on the local authority's powers … pathway plans have some functions which are not dependent on the provision of "support and assistance". These functions are not, therefore, caught by paragraph 1 of Schedule 3 to the 2002 Act … there is a [sic] still a value in the personal adviser continuing in his role although the scope of the plan will be much reduced … I regard the continued provision of a personal adviser and reviews of pathway plans as a form of "advice" rather than "support or assistance" and a local authority's duties (modified as I have said) as continuing even though material support and assistance is prohibited by paragraph 1 of Schedule 3 … the obligations to continue reviews of the pathway plan and provide a personal adviser will continue in full … there would be a residual duty to advise the claimant in any ways which did not involve the provision of material support and assistance.'

Disabled children, leaving care and education

5.38   There is an overlap in respect of the education of disabled children, and disabled children who are leaving care. The Guidance adopts the definition provided by s 17(11) of the Children Act 1989 (see below). It adds (at Section 4, para 16):

> 'Disabled young people may well face more barriers than other young people who are being cared for or leaving care, and may also have needs specifically related to impairment. It is essential to ensure that these needs are met when preparing these young people for leaving care and subsequently, providing aftercare.'

In particular, it draws attention to the obligations that a local authority may have pursuant to other statutes:

> '23 Section 2(1) of the Chronically Sick and Disabled Persons Act 1970 lays on each Local Authority a duty to provide various welfare services to any person living within its area if this is necessary in order to meet the needs of that person. This includes meeting assessed needs for "practical assistance in the home".'

In addition, there are the provisions of the Children Act 2004 (s 9) which is set out at **5.71** and **5.72** below (and which refers to those who are leaving care and have learning disabilities).

DISABLED PERSONS (SERVICES, CONSULTATION AND REPRESENTATION) ACT 1986

5.39 Specifically in relation to education the Guidance stresses 'a smooth transition' from full-time education to adult life for a young person who is subject to a 'statement of special educational needs'. Their effect (that of ss 5 and 6 of the Disabled Persons (Services, Consultation and Representation) Act 1986) is to require the relevant education department to obtain the view of the (SSD) as to whether such a young person is disabled. This is done at the first annual review of the statement of special educational needs, or the first re-assessment of the young person's educational needs, following the young person's 14th birthday. If the SSD does consider that the young person is disabled, it must assess his needs, before he leaves full-time education, for the welfare services covered under s 2 of the 1986 Act' (Section 4 para 24).

Disabled Persons (Services, Consultation and Representation) Act 1986

5 Disabled persons leaving special education

(1) Where –

    (a)   a local education authority have made a statement under section 7 of the Education Act 1981 section 168 of the Education Act 1993 or section 324 of the Education Act 1996 (statement of child's educational needs) in respect of a child . . ., and

    (b)   the statement is still maintained by the authority at whichever is the earlier of the following times, namely –

        (i)   the time when they institute a review of the statement prescribed for the purposes of this paragraph, and

        (ii)   any time falling after they have carried out the review prescribed for the purposes of sub-paragraph (i) when they institute a re-assessment of his educational needs,

the authority shall at that time require the appropriate officer to give to the authority his opinion as to whether the child is or is not a disabled person.

(2) Where –

    (a)   a local education authority make any such statement in respect of a child after he has attained the age of 14, or

    (b)   a local education authority maintain any such statement in respect of a child in whose case the appropriate officer has, in pursuance of subsection (1), given his opinion that the child is not a disabled person, but the authority have become aware of a significant change in the mental or physical condition of the child giving them reason to believe that he may now be a disabled person,

the authority shall, at the time of making the statement or (as the case may be) of becoming aware of that change, require the appropriate officer to give to the authority his opinion as to whether the child is or is not a disabled person.

(3) In the following provisions of this section and in section 6 a person in respect of whom the appropriate officer has given his opinion that he is a disabled person is referred to as a "disabled student".

(3A) The responsible authority shall give to the appropriate officer written notification for the purposes of subsection (5) of the date on which any disabled student will cease to be of compulsory school age, and the notification shall state –

    (a)   his name and address; and

    (b)   whether or not he intends to remain in full-time education and, if he does, the name of the school or other institution at which the education will be received;

and shall be given not earlier than twelve months, nor later than eight months, before that date.

(3B) Where, in the case of a disabled student over compulsory school age who is receiving relevant full-time education, that is –

    (a)   full-time education at a school; or

    (b)   full-time further or higher education at an institution other than a school;

it appears to the responsible authority that the student will cease to receive relevant full-time education on a date ("the leaving date") on which he will be under the age of nineteen years and eight months, the responsible authority shall give written notification for the purposes of subsection (5) to the appropriate officer.

(3C) That notification shall state –

    (a)   his name and address; and

    (b)   the leaving date;

and shall be given not earlier than twelve months, nor later than eight months, before the leaving date.

(4) If at any time it appears to the responsible authority –

    (a)   that a disabled student has ceased to receive relevant full-time education or will cease to do so on a date less than 8 months after that time, and

    (b)   that no notification has been given under subsection (3B), but

    (c)   that, had the responsible authority for the time being been aware of his intentions 8 months or more before that date, they would have been required to give notification under that subsection with respect to him,

that authority shall, as soon as is reasonably practicable, give written notification for the purposes of subsection (5) to the appropriate officer of his name and address and of the date on which he ceased to receive, or will cease to receive, that education.

(5) When the appropriate officer receives a notification given with respect to a student under subsection (3A) that he does not intend to remain in full-time education or under subsection (3B) or (4), he shall (subject to subsections (6) and (7)) make arrangements for the local authority of which he is an officer to carry out an assessment of the needs of that person with respect to the provision by that authority of any statutory services for that person in accordance with any of the welfare enactments, and any such assessment shall be carried out –

(a)   in the case of a notification under subsection (3A) or (3B), not later than the end of the period of 5 months beginning with the date of receipt of the notification, or

(b)   in the case of a notification under subsection (4), before the date specified in the notification, if reasonably practicable, and in any event not later than the end of the period referred to in paragraph (a) above.

(6) If –

(a)   a notification has been given to the appropriate officer with respect to any person under subsection (3A) that he does not intend to remain in full-time education or under subsection (3B) or (4), but

(b)   it subsequently appears to the responsible authority that the person will be receiving relevant full-time education at a time later than the date specified in the notification,

the authority shall give written notification of the relevant facts to that officer as soon as is reasonably practicable; and on receiving any such notification that officer shall cease to be required under subsection (5) to make arrangements for the assessment of the needs of the person in question (but without prejudice to the operation of that subsection in relation to any further notification given with respect to that person under subsection (3A) that he does not intend to remain in full-time education or under subsection (3B) or (4)).

(7) Nothing in subsection (5) shall require the appropriate officer to make arrangements for the assessment of the needs of a person –

(a)   if, having attained the age of 16, he has requested that such arrangements should not be made under that subsection, or

(b)   if, being under that age, his parent or other person who is not a parent of his but who has parental responsibility for him has made such a request.

(8) Regulations under paragraph 7 of Schedule 27 to the Education Act 1996 (assessments and statements of special educational needs) may, in relation to the transfer of statements maintained under section 324 of that Act, make such provision as appears to the Secretary of State to be necessary or expedient in connection with the preceding provisions of this section.

(9) In this section –

"the appropriate officer", in relation to the child or person referred to in the provision of this section in question, means such officer as may be appointed for the purposes of this section by the local authority for the area in which that child or person is for the time being ordinarily resident;

"child" means a person of compulsory school age or a person who has attained that age but not the age of 19 and is registered as a pupil at a school or as a student at an establishment of higher or further education; and

"establishment of higher or further education" means an institution which provides higher education or further education (or both);

"prescribed" means prescribed in regulations made –

(a)   in relation to England, by the Secretary of State; and

(b)   in relation to Wales, by the National Assembly for Wales;

"the responsible authority" –

(a)   in relation to a child at school, means the local education authority who are responsible for the child for the purposes of Part IV of the Education Act 1996;

(b)   in relation to a person receiving full-time further education or higher education at an institution within the further education sector or the higher education sector, means the governing body of the institution; and

(c)   in relation to a person for whom the Learning and Skills Council for England or the National Assembly for Wales has secured full-time further education at an institution (other than a school) outside the further education sector or the higher education sector, the council or the National Assembly as the case may be

in each case whether any such opinion as is mentioned in subsection (3) was given to that authority or not;

and other expressions used in this section and in the Education Act 1996 or the Further and Higher Education Act 1992 (and not defined in this Act) have the same meaning in this section as in those Acts.

(10) This section applies to England and Wales only.

6 Review of expected leaving dates from full-time education of disabled persons

(1) The responsible authority shall for the purposes of section 5 above keep under review the date when any disabled student is expected to cease to receive relevant full-time education.

(2) Subsection (9) of section 5 shall have effect for the purposes of this section as it has effect for the purposes of that section.

Implementation of ss 5 and 6 of the Disabled Persons (Services, Consultation and Representation) Act 1986

5.40   Circular No LAC (88) 2 was issued in January 1988, and is intended to give guidance to local authorities in respect of the above provisions. The complete text is set out below.

DISABLED PERSON (SERVICES, CONSULTATION AND REPRESENTATION) ACT 1986 – Implementation of section 5 and 6

I. SUMMARY

This circular draws the attention of local authorities, Chief Education Officers and Directors of Social Services to the implementation of sections 5 and 6 of the Disabled Persons (Services, Consultation and Representation) Act 1986 and gives guidance on the effect pf those provisions.

II. SUMMARY

1. The Secretary of State for Social Services has made an order bringing sections 5 and 6 of the Disabled Persons (Services, Consultation and Representation) Act 1986 into effect on 1 February 1988.

2. The purpose of sections 5 and 6 is to ensure a smooth transition for a disabled child between full-time education and adult life. They aim to achieve this by providing for closer co-operation between the local education authority (LEA) and the Social Services Department (SSD) at two points, first as the child approaches the end of compulsory education, and second in the final year of full-time education.

3. LEAs and SSDs will need to review their procedures to achieve speedy and reliable transfers of information within and between their two departments, and to identify appropriate contact points.

4. ...

III. MAIN PROVISIONS OF SECTIONS

5. Section 5: This section refers to children with statements of special educational needs under the Education Act 1981.

a.   Under this section, the responsible local education authority (LEA) is required to seek an opinion from the SSD on whether a child who is the subject of a statement of special educational needs under section 7 of the Education Act 1981 is a disabled person.

b.   The SSD is required to provide an opinion to the LEA as to whether the child is or is not a disabled person.

c.   The LEA is required, having been notified that a child is a disabled person, to notify the SSD in writing of the date that that child will cease to receive full-time education.

d.   The SSD must then make arrangements to carry out an assessment of the needs of that disabled person with respect to the provision of any statutory services for that person in accordance with any of the 'welfare enactments'.

6. Section 6: This section requires LEAs to keep under review the leaving dates from full-time education at school or a further establishment of children who have been identified as disabled.

IV DUTIES OF EDUCATION AUTHORITIES

7. The LEA must obtain an opinion as to whether a child is or is not a disabled person as part of the first annual review or assessment or reassessment after the child's 14th birthday. In practice this will take place:

i.   as part of the mandatory reassessment of the child's special educational needs carried out when the child is between the ages of 13 and a half and 14 and a half, if that fails after the 14th birthday; or

ii.   a part of the annual review of the child's statement of special educational needs in his 15th year; or

iii.   at a later stage in the case of a child over 14 either being assessed for the first time, or those whose mental or physical condition has, in the view of the LEA, changed significantly since an opinion was last sought.

LEAs and SSDs will need to act quickly in the case of those children who fall into category 7.iii above, where only a short time remains before the child leaves full-time education.

8. Where an LEA seeks an opinion as to whether a child is disabled, they may wish to inform the family (parent or guardian or the child if he or she is aged 16 or over) that this is being done, and to explain the reasons for it.

V DUTY OF APPROPRIATE OFFICER TO IDENTIFY A CHILD WHO IS DISABLED

9. It will be necessary for the SSD to appoint an 'appropriate officer' to give an opinion as to whether any child referred to them by the LEA is or is not a disabled person and to notify the LEA accordingly.

10. When the appropriate officer is asked by the education authority to give an opinion as to whether or not a statemented child is a disabled person, it is important that this is done reasonably promptly. Where personal contact with the child is considered appropriate but the parent or guardian or child (as the case may be) does not cooperate, the appropriate officer will have to base his opinion as to whether or not the child is a disabled person on the information available. Delay in identifying a child as disabled could in turn prevent the LEA notifying the SSD of the expected date that the child will leave school and thereby restrict the time available for an assessment of welfare needs to be undertaken.

VI ARRANGEMENTS FOR NOTIFYING DATE OF LEAVING FULL-TIME EDUCATION

11. The LEA will have to notify the appropriate officer of the SSD not later than 8 months in advance (the 'relevant date' in the Act) of the date on which children who have been identified as disabled are expected to leave full-time education, whether school or further education. This must not be done, however, more than 12 months before the expected leaving date. For children transferring to a part-time place in a college of further education, notification must be given not later than 8 months before the child leaves school.

12. LEAs may not be able to state the precise date on which a child is expected to leave full-time education. The Act recognises this difficulty and allows for the procedures set out in paragraph 11 above to be varied in the following circumstances:

a.   If a notification has been given to the appropriate officer and the LEA finds out that the leaving date will be postponed or advanced the appropriate officer of the SSD must be notified of this fact as soon as is reasonably practicable.

b.   Where the LEA finds itself with less than 8 months in which to notify the appropriate officer of the SSD that the child is leaving school, it must take action to notify the appropriate officer of the social services department in writing of the leaving date as soon as possible.

VII YOUNG PEOPLE IN FULL-TIME EDUCATION AFTER THEIR NINETEENTH BIRTHDAY

13. Some young people who have been identified as disabled stay on beyond their 19th birthday in order to complete a course of full-time education in a school or college of further education. An LEA is not statutorily required to notify the SSD of the date when a disabled young person is expected to leave full-time education if, on the relevant date (ie 8 months before the expected leaving date), the young person is 19 or over. However, where disabled young people have continued in full-time education since the age of 16, it is hoped that authorities will exercise their discretion and accord them the same provision under sections 5 and 6 that they would have enjoyed had they elected to leave full-time education before the age of 19.

Any disabled young person will of course have the right, if he or she so requests, to have his or her needs assessed by virtue of section 4 of this Act, in accordance with section 2(1) of the Chronically Sick and Disabled Persons Act 1970 (See Circular LAC (87)6).

VIII ARRANGEMENTS TO BE UNDERTAKEN BY THE SSD ONCE THE LEAVING DATE HAS BEEN NOTIFIED

14. On receipt of the written notification from the LEA that a child who has been identified as a disabled person will leave full-time education, the appropriate officer is required to make arrangements for the local authority to carry out an assessment of the needs of the disabled person for the provision of statutory services under any of the welfare enactments. SSDs will need to have regard to the ability of the carer to provide care on a regular basis, where the disabled person is living at home (section 8(1) of this Act). Apart from assessing the need of the services specifically mentioned in the welfare enactments; and arranging for their provision, local authorities will wish to give such advice as they can about other matters affecting the welfare of the disabled person and his family or carers, and to refer them to other agencies as appropriate. Such advice might cover employment, higher and further education, health care and possible entitlement to social security benefits. The giving of such advice comes within the terms of section 1(2) of the CSDP Act as amended by section 9 of the Act. (See Circular LAC (87)6.)

...

IX TIMETABLE FOR ASSESSMENT

15. The assessment of the needs of the disabled person is required to be carried out according to the following timetable:

a.   Where the notification of leaving full-time education has been provided by the relevant date, within 5 months of that date, ie 3 months before leaving full-time education.

b.   Where the notification is received by the appropriate officer after the relevant date, (ie less than 8 months before leaving full-time education) before the school leaving date, if reasonably practicable, and in any event not later than 5 months after receiving the notification.

c.   Where notification is given to the appropriate officer that a person's leaving date will be postponed or advanced it is not necessarily to make arrangements for an assessment to be carried out until further notification under section 5(3) or 5(4) of the Act is received.

16. The appropriate officer should not make any arrangements for an assessment of the disabled person's needs to be undertaken where the parent or guardian (if the child is under 16) or the young person (if he is aged 16 or over) requests that this is not carried out.

GENERAL STATUTORY FRAMEWORK

5.41 Inevitably the legal framework for disabled children overlaps with the provision for the general population catered for in the Children Act 1989, together with the specific references to disabled children by virtue of s 28A of the Chronically Sick and Disabled Persons Act 1970. It also overlaps with the provision for the assessment of carers of disabled children and of those children themselves, and also impacts (in respect of older children) on the provisions of the Mental Capacity Act 2005.

5.42 The Office of the Deputy Prime Minister (Strategy Unit) published a final report (January 2005) which 'sets out an ambitious vision for improving the life chances of disabled people' (*Improving the Life Chances of Disabled People*). It stressed the need for early intervention in the life of disabled children in order to 'avoid long-term institutionalisation' (Part 5 'Early years and family support' p 115). It also expressed an aspiration to avoid long-term residential placements for disabled children, and that one way of achieving this was to provide 'adequate and early preventative support' (ibid). In Part 6 (p 138) it stated:

> '... by 2015, everyone with parental responsibility for a disabled young person will have access to the right support to enable them to cope, to enjoy being a parent, and to participate in the labour market if they choose ... families with disabled children often lose support as their child becomes an adult ... Families with a disabled young person have high levels of unmet need ... a survey of parents of disabled children found the highest levels of unmet needs among those whose children were older. The impact of unsuitable housing, for example, increases with age.'

It has been estimated that between 3 per cent and 5 per cent of all children in the UK are disabled (Jennifer Cousins, *Every Child is Special – Placing Disabled Children for Permanence Good Practice Guide* (BAAF, 2006)) which amounts to 327,000 children, 91 per cent of whom live at home, and 2.5 per cent are in foster care. It also cites evidence that 17,000 families in the community are caring for more than one disabled child. A disproportionately large percentage of disabled children are 'looked after'. Of those, 18 per cent were accommodated under s 20 of the Children Act 1989, and 70 per cent were subject to care orders or interim care orders; 11 per cent were freed for adoption.

DISABLED CHILDREN AND THE CHRONICALLY SICK AND DISABLED PERSONS ACT 1970 AND CHILDREN ACT 1989

5.43   Section 28A is reproduced in Chapter 3 but is repeated here for the sake of convenience.

Chronically Sick and Disabled Persons Act 1970

28A Application of Act to authorities having functions under the Children Act 1989

This Act applies with respect to disabled children in relation to whom a local authority have functions under Part III of the Children Act 1989 as it applies in relation to persons to whom section 29 of the National Assistance Act 1948 applies.

5.44   In effect, this imports into the Children Act 1989 a requirement upon a local authority to comply with its powers and duties under the Chronically Sick and Disabled Persons Act 1970 and the National Assistance Act 1948. Consequently, the case-law on those powers and duties as set out elsewhere apply (in general) and the specific case-law on the interaction between these statutes and the Children Act 1989 are set out below. Of particular significance in this context is s 17 of the Children Act 1989. The obligations of the local authority were considered in *R (on the application of Spink) v Wandsworth London Borough Council* [2005] EWCA Civ 302. This authority is also considered in Chapter 6, since it has a bearing on the ability of the local authority to charge for services. In this part of the book, however, its significance in terms of the obligations to provide services is considered. The historical aspect of the statutory provisions was traced by Lord Philips MR and started with ss 21(1) and 29 of the National Assistance Act 1948 (provision of accommodation and welfare services). He observed that when first enacted the provisions applied to both adults and children. He then moved on to s 2 of the Chronically Sick and Disabled Persons Act 1970 (which refers to s 29 of the National Assistance Act 1948, and then (for the purposes of this analysis) to s 17 of the Children Act 1989 (provision of services for children in need, their families and others) and Sch 2 (assessment of children's needs). The Court held:

'[33] The scheme of the Children Act involved removing children from, inter alia, the ambit of section 29 of the 1948 Act and this was achieved by the express amendment of Section 29 which restricted its application to persons over 18. It would be perverse to read section 2 of the 1970 Act, as amended by section 28A, as requiring local authorities to behave as if section 29 still applied to children.

[34] ... sections 21 and 29 of the 1948 Act were, when introduced, sections which conferred powers on local authorities to provide services and imposed general duties to exercise those powers. In this they resembled section 17 of the Children Act, as interpreted by the majority in the House of Lords in *R(G) v Barnet LBC*. It may be true that duties to individuals might be created under Section 29 of the Act once a scheme was approved by the Secretary of State. There is no warrant, however, for Mr Gordon's submission that local authorities could only discharge the duties imposed by section 2 of the 1970 Act by the exercise of their functions under section 29 of the 1948 Act because the latter was capable of giving rise to duties to individuals upon the directions of the Secretary of State. On the contrary, section 2 of the 1970 Act expressly provided that local authorities were to comply with their obligations under that section in the exercise of their functions under section 29 of the 1948 Act "notwithstanding anything in the scheme made by the authority under section 29". Just as the Secretary of State might be able to impose a duty on local authorities, enforceable by individuals, to exercise their functions under section 29, so section 2 of the 1970 Act could impose a similar duty.

[35] Once this is appreciated, there is no difficulty in interpreting sections 2 and 28A of the 1970 Act as requiring local authorities to comply with the requirements of section 2, in so far as these apply to children, by the exercise of their functions under Part III of the Children Act 1989, of which section 17 is particularly relevant ...'

He concluded:

'[45] The issue in this case is, essentially, whether Section 2 of the 1970 Act imposes on the Council the obligation to fund the considerable cost of making alterations to the ... family home. We question whether, when the 1970 Act came into force, it was capable of imposing such an obligation. The language describing the various matters itemised in section 2(1) differs significantly ... however the functions of a local authority under Section 17 of and Part 1 of Schedule 1 to the Children Act are in much wider terms than section 29 of the 1948 Act and the Council accepts that they can extend to providing the alterations that the boys are alleged to need.

[46] ... As a general proposition a local authority can reasonably expect that parents, who can afford the expense, will make any alterations to their home that are necessary for the care of their disabled children, if there is no alternative source of providing these ... having regard to these considerations, we agree with Richards J that a local authority can, in the circumstances such as those with which we are concerned, properly decline to be satisfied that it is necessary to provide services to meet the needs of disabled children until it has been demonstrated that, having regard to their means, it is not reasonable to expect their parents to provide these.'

Children Act 1989

Part III
Local Authority Support for Children and Families

Provision of services for children and their families

17 Provision of services for children in need, their families and others

(1) It shall be the general duty of every local authority (in addition to the other duties imposed on them by this Part) –

  (a)   to safeguard and promote the welfare of children within their area who are in need; and

  (b)   so far as is consistent with that duty, to promote the upbringing of such children by their families,

by providing a range and level of services appropriate to those children's needs.

(2) For the purpose principally of facilitating the discharge of their general duty under this section, every local authority shall have the specific duties and powers set out in Part I of Schedule 2.

(3) Any service provided by an authority in the exercise of functions conferred on them by this section may be provided for the family of a particular child in need or for any member of his family, if it is provided with a view to safeguarding or promoting the child's welfare.

(4) The Secretary of State may by order amend any provision of Part I of Schedule 2 or add any further duty or power to those for the time being mentioned there.

(4A) Before determining what (if any) services to provide for a particular child in need in the exercise of functions conferred on them by this section, a local authority shall, so far as is reasonably practicable and consistent with the child's welfare –

  (a)   ascertain the child's wishes and feelings regarding the provision of those services; and

  (b)   give due consideration (having regard to his age and understanding) to such wishes and feelings of the child as they have been able to ascertain.

(5) Every local authority –

  (a)   shall facilitate the provision by others(including in particular voluntary organisations) of services which the authority have power to provide by virtue of this section, or section 18, 20, 23, 23B to 23D, 24A or 24B; and

  (b)   may make such arrangements as they see fit for any person to act on their behalf in the provision of any such service.

(6) The services provided by a local authority in the exercise of functions conferred on them by this section may include providing accommodation and giving assistance in kind or, in exceptional circumstances, in cash.

(7) Assistance may be unconditional or subject to conditions as to the repayment of the assistance or of its value (in whole or in part).

(8) Before giving any assistance or imposing any conditions, a local authority shall have regard to the means of the child concerned and of each of his parents.

(9) No person shall be liable to make any repayment of assistance or of its value at any time when he is in receipt of income support under Part VII of the Social Security Contributions and Benefits Act 1992, of any element of child tax credit other than the family element, of working tax credit or of an income-based jobseeker's allowance.

(10) For the purposes of this Part a child shall be taken to be in need if –

    (a)   he is unlikely to achieve or maintain, or to have the opportunity of achieving or maintaining, a reasonable standard of health or development without the provision for him of services by a local authority under this Part;

    (b)   his health or development is likely to be significantly impaired, or further impaired, without the provision for him of such services; or

    (c)   he is disabled,

and "family", in relation to such a child, includes any person who has parental responsibility for the child and any other person with whom he has been living.

(11) For the purposes of this Part, a child is disabled if he is blind, deaf or dumb or suffers from mental disorder of any kind or is substantially and permanently handicapped by illness, injury or congenital deformity or such other disability as may be prescribed; and in this Part –

"development" means physical, intellectual, emotional, social or behavioural development; and

"health" means physical or mental health.

(12) The Treasury may by regulations prescribe circumstances in which a person is to be treated for the purposes of this Part (or for such of those purposes as are prescribed) as in receipt of any element of child tax credit other than the family element or of working tax credit.

5.45 One of the most useful parts of this section is s 17(10) and in particular 17(11) (which provides a statutory definition of a disabled child). Schedule 2(6) also sets out the provision of services that a local authority shall provide to minimise the effect upon disabled children within the area of their disabilities, and to give them the opportunity to lead lives which are as normal as possible. It should be noted that the case-law set out below does not provide an account of all the authorities in respect of s 17, but instead concentrates on disabled children. However, the principles established as to the overall function of s 17 will (of course) remain unaltered. Schedule 2, Part 1, para 2 of the Act requires a local authority to maintain a register of disabled children:

20 Provision of accommodation for children: general

(1) Every local authority shall provide accommodation for any child in need within their area who appears to them to require accommodation as a result of –

    (a)   there being no person who has parental responsibility for him;

    (b)   his being lost or having been abandoned; or

(c)   the person who has been caring for him being prevented (whether or not permanently, and for whatever reason) from providing him with suitable accommodation or care.

(2) Where a local authority provide accommodation under subsection (1) for a child who is ordinarily resident in the area of another local authority, that other local authority may take over the provision of accommodation for the child within –

(a)   three months of being notified in writing that the child is being provided with accommodation; or

(b)   such other longer period as may be prescribed.

(3) Every local authority shall provide accommodation for any child in need within their area who has reached the age of sixteen and whose welfare the authority consider is likely to be seriously prejudiced if they do not provide him with accommodation.

(4) A local authority may provide accommodation for any child within their area (even though a person who has parental responsibility for him is able to provide him with accommodation) if they consider that to do so would safeguard or promote the child's welfare.

(5) A local authority may provide accommodation for any person who has reached the age of sixteen but is under twenty-one in any community home which takes children who have reached the age of sixteen if they consider that to do so would safeguard or promote his welfare.

(6) Before providing accommodation under this section, a local authority shall, so far as is reasonably practicable and consistent with the child's welfare –

(a)   ascertain the child's wishes and feelings regarding the provision of accommodation; and

(b)   give due consideration (having regard to his age and understanding) to such wishes and feelings of the child as they have been able to ascertain.

(7) A local authority may not provide accommodation under this section for any child if any person who –

(a)   has parental responsibility for him; and

(b)   is willing and able to –
        (i)   provide accommodation for him; or
        (ii)   arrange for accommodation to be provided for him,
        objects.

(8) Any person who has parental responsibility for a child may at any time remove the child from accommodation provided by or on behalf of the local authority under this section.

(9) Subsections (7) and (8) do not apply while any person –

(a)   in whose favour a residence order is in force with respect to the child; . . .

(aa)   who is a special guardian of the child; or

(b)   who has care of the child by virtue of an order made in the exercise of the High Court's inherent jurisdiction with respect to children,

agrees to the child being looked after in accommodation provided by or on behalf of the local authority.

(10) Where there is more than one such person as is mentioned in subsection (9), all of them must agree.

(11) Subsections (7) and (8) do not apply where a child who has reached the age of sixteen agrees to being provided with accommodation under this section.

22 General duty of local authority in relation to children looked after by them

(1) In this Act, any reference to a child who is looked after by a local authority is a reference to a child who is –

    (a)   in their care; or

    (b)   provided with accommodation by the authority in the exercise of any functions (in particular those under this Act) which are social services functions within the meaning of the Local Authority Social Services Act 1970, apart from functions under sections 17, 23B and 24B.

(2) In subsection (1) "accommodation" means accommodation which is provided for a continuous period of more than 24 hours.

(3) It shall be the duty of a local authority looking after any child –

    (a)   to safeguard and promote his welfare; and

    (b)   to make such use of services available for children cared for by their own parents as appears to the authority reasonable in his case.

(3A) The duty of a local authority under subsection (3)(a) to safeguard and promote the welfare of a child looked after by them includes in particular a duty to promote the child's educational achievement.

(4) Before making any decision with respect to a child whom they are looking after, or proposing to look after, a local authority shall, so far as is reasonably practicable, ascertain the wishes and feelings of –

    (a)   the child;

    (b)   his parents;

    (c)   any person who is not a parent of his but who has parental responsibility for him; and

    (d)   any other person whose wishes and feelings the authority consider to be relevant,

regarding the matter to be decided.

(5) In making any such decision a local authority shall give due consideration –

    (a)   having regard to his age and understanding, to such wishes and feelings of the child as they have been able to ascertain;

    (b)   to such wishes and feelings of any person mentioned in subsection (4)(b) to (d) as they have been able to ascertain; and

    (c)   to the child's religious persuasion, racial origin and cultural and linguistic background.

(6) If it appears to a local authority that it is necessary, for the purpose of protecting members of the public from serious injury, to exercise their powers with respect to a child whom they are looking after in a manner which may not be consistent with their duties under this section, they may do so.

(7) If the Secretary of State considers it necessary, for the purpose of protecting members of the public from serious injury, to give directions to a local authority

with respect to the exercise of their powers with respect to a child whom they are looking after, he may give such directions to the authority.

(8) Where any such directions are given to an authority they shall comply with them even though doing so is inconsistent with their duties under this section.

23 Provision of accommodation and maintenance by local authority for children whom they are looking after

(1) It shall be the duty of any local authority looking after a child –

  (a)   when he is in their care, to provide accommodation for him; and
  (b)   to maintain him in other respects apart from providing accommodation for him.

(2) A local authority shall provide accommodation and maintenance for any child whom they are looking after by –

  (a)   placing him (subject to subsection (5) and any regulations made by the Secretary of State) with –
        (i)   a family;
        (ii)   a relative of his; or
        (iii) any other suitable person,

on such terms as to payment by the authority and otherwise as the authority may determine (subject to section 49 of the Children Act 2004);

  (aa) maintaining him in an appropriate children's home; or
  (f)   making such other arrangements as –
        (i)   seem appropriate to them; and
        (ii)   comply with any regulations made by the Secretary of State.

(2A) Where under subsection (2)(aa) a local authority maintains a child in a home provided, equipped and maintained by the Secretary of State under section 82(5), it shall do so on such terms as the Secretary of State may from time to time determine.

(3) Any person with whom a child has been placed under subsection (2)(a) is referred to in this Act as a local authority foster parent unless he falls within subsection (4).

(4) A person falls within this subsection if he is –

  (a)   a parent of the child;
  (b)   a person who is not a parent of the child but who has parental responsibility for him; or
  (c)   where the child is in care and there was a residence order in force with respect to him immediately before the care order was made, a person in whose favour the residence order was made.

(5) Where a child is in the care of a local authority, the authority may only allow him to live with a person who falls within subsection (4) in accordance with regulations made by the Secretary of State.

(5A) For the purposes of subsection (5) a child shall be regarded as living with a person if he stays with that person for a continuous period of more than 24 hours.

(6) Subject to any regulations made by the Secretary of State for the purposes of this subsection, any local authority looking after a child shall make arrangements to enable him to live with –

(a)   a person falling within subsection (4); or

(b)   a relative, friend or other person connected with him,

unless that would not be reasonably practicable or consistent with his welfare.

(7) Where a local authority provide accommodation for a child whom they are looking after, they shall, subject to the provisions of this Part and so far as is reasonably practicable and consistent with his welfare, secure that –

(a)   the accommodation is near his home; and

(b)   where the authority are also providing accommodation for a sibling of his, they are accommodated together.

(8) Where a local authority provide accommodation for a child whom they are looking after and who is disabled, they shall, so far as is reasonably practicable, secure that the accommodation is not unsuitable to his particular needs.

(9) Part II of Schedule 2 shall have effect for the purposes of making further provision as to children looked after by local authorities and in particular as to the regulations that may be made under subsections (2)(a) and (f) and (5).

(10) In this Act –

"appropriate children's home" means a children's home in respect of which a person is registered under Part II of the Care Standards Act 2000; and

"children's home" has the same meaning as in that Act.

Schedule 2

6 Every local authority shall provide services designed –

(a)   to minimise the effect on disabled children within their area of their disabilities; and

(b)   to give such children the opportunity to lead lives which are as normal as possible.

Extent of general obligations of local authorities

5.46   The main focus of this book is community care law as it applies to older and disabled children, although there is clearly an overlap with more mainstream legislation (eg under the Children Act 1989). For a full analysis of the latter, access to a specialist text will be required (eg Hershman & McFarlane, *Jordans*). The paragraphs below concentrate on a small portion of this mainstream legislation only as it impacts upon community care law. This is particularly the case when looking at accommodation needs.

5.47   In *R v Bexley LBC ex p B* [2000] 3 CCLR 15, a dispute arose as to whether it was lawful for a local authority to argue that only its general duties under s 17 applied, when it also had duties under the Chronically Sick and Disabled Persons Act 1970. On the facts in the case, all the service provision made for the child had been pursuant to that Act. The local authority withdrew the majority of the support that it had been providing. It was held that it was not open to a local authority to argue that the general target duty of a local authority pursuant to s 17 meant that it had no specific duties to a particular individual pursuant to s 2 of the Chronically Sick and Disabled Persons Act 1970.

5.48   In *R v Lambeth LBC ex p K* [2000] 3 CCLR 141 the assessment process itself was considered within the specific context of s 17, and a disabled child. It was held that there may be an enforceable duty to make provision for accommodation (cf *R v Wigan MBC ex p Tammadge*), and that the assessment itself should: (a) assess the needs of the disabled child (and the carers, if appropriate); (b) produce a care plan; and (c) provide the identified services.

5.49   In *R (JL) v Islington London Borough Council* [2009] EWHC 458 (Admin), [2009] 2 FLR 515, the local authority introduced eligibility criteria for disabled children. The concept of eligibility criteria for **adults** with community care needs is well established (although not without its difficulties, and legal challenges, as is set out in Chapters 3 and 4). The consequence for the child in this case of the introduction of a points system (which corresponded to three levels; low; medium; high) was a 50 per cent reduction in the services that were being provided. The local authority had adopted the position that the duty that they had towards the child was framed only by way of s 20(1) of the Children Act 1989 (which imposes an absolute duty upon it, as opposed to ss 17 and 20(4) which give rise to powers, and not absolute duties). Mrs Justice Black held that 'eligibility criteria cannot be used by a local authority in determining whether it has a duty to act under that section [20(1)]' [71].

5.50   In essence, what the local authority had done was to adopt the procedure for determining the eligibility for access to community care services for adults and transplanted it wholesale into eligibility for children's services (and a severely disabled child, in this case). In so doing, they had failed to consider the implications for so doing that have been so widely and exhaustively traversed in the this field of law as it applies to adults (for example, resources vs needs). In attempting to unravel the competing statutory obligations towards the child, the Court was faced with providing an audit of each separate statute, whether the obligation that flowed from that statute was a power or a duty, and finally, considering the development of the common law as to what extent the duty or power could be attenuated by reference to needs, resources, and eligibility criteria. It is not surprising that the penultimate paragraph in the judgment puts the problem thus:

> '[125] Without question, the use of eligibility criteria in determining provision for children is a very complex area. It is not possible in a judgment of this type to provide comprehensive guidance for local authorities generally as to when, precisely, it is acceptable to use eligibility criteria and as to the form they should take. The FACS Guidance seeks to fulfil that role in relation to adult services and there is no doubt that there is a pressing need for guidance in relation to children's services. Having read FACS carefully, I am not sure that if I were attempting, on

hehalf of a local authority, to determine how to use eligibility criteria and to draw up those criteria, I would find in it all the clarity and assistance I would need.'

5.51   There is no guidance on this point, and the replacement for FACS (see Chapters 3 and 4) would provide no more assistance now than it did in this case. In the judgment, the Court re-trod the road that has been travelled within adult community care law, and tried to square this with children. It identified four statutory obligations (ss 17(1), 20(1), 20(4) Children Act 1989; s 2 Chronically Sick and Disabled Persons Act 1970). Each of these are also considered in this Chapter. Section 17 is a target duty. Section 2 of the Chronically Sick and Disabled Persons Act 1970 (and specifically s 28A as it applies to children) imposes a specific duty to meet the needs of the child (if they are found within the limited range as adumbrated in the Act). When considering s 2/28A, then the decision of *Barry* in respect of resources and needs applies (see Chapters 3 and 4 at **3.37–3.48** and **4.7–4.8**). As Black J held 'if eligibility criteria are to be used in conjunction with s 2 their role must be properly confined so that resources considerations are not allowed to stray beyond the territory dictated by *Barry*' [103]. Section 20(1) is mandatory (*shall*) and s 20(4) is discretionary (*may*). The Court rejected the idea that *Barry* could apply to a mandatory obligation, but accepted that it could apply to any area of discretion in deploying resources to meet needs. The problem was that in this case the local authority seemed to have failed to import into its decision making process the significance of the established law as it applies to adult community care needs:

> '[110] Although I have determined that there is no reason in principle why eligibility criteria should not be used in conjunction with ss 17 and 20(4), it seems to me that the local authority in this case employed the wrong procedure in using their eligibility criteria to assess JL's case. FACS makes it clear ... that eligibility must be determined **following assessment.** The information collected in the assessment is used to identify risks – in the case of adults, risk to independence. Those risks are then compared to the eligibility criteria and, through identifying those that fall within the criteria, professionals should identify eligible needs. The same procedure must surely be followed in relation to children.'

The Court also considered the implications of s 49A of the Disability Discrimination Act (see **3.25, 3.48** and **3.64, 3.65** in Chapter 3), and found that the local authority had fallen foul of its provisions.

5.52   If nothing else, this case illustrates the confusion on the part of many children's social services departments of the overlapping duties that exist between community care law (as developed in respect of adults) and how those principles apply to children. That confusion is entirely understandable. Its consequences for JL were that the claim for judicial review succeeded, and the decision to reduce the services quashed upon the basis that there had been no lawful assessment of the needs of the child.

ACCOMMODATION NEEDS

5.53 In *R v Tower Hamlets LBC ex parte Bradford (Anita, Raymond and Simon)* [1998] 1 CCLR 294; (1997) 29 HLR 756, an 11-year-old child with special educational needs had been the subject of an assessment under s 17. However, the assessment had focussed on his educational needs, to the exclusion of his housing needs (which were considerable). The local authority had not conceded that housing needs formed a part of any analysis of the needs of a child pursuant to s 17. It was held that re-housing a child did come within s 17, and that there should have been an assessment including that aspect of the problem to discover whether there was: (a) a need for re-housing; and then (b) a decision made as to the appropriate service provision.

5.54 A similar issue arose in *R v Ealing LBC ex p C* [2000] 3 CCLR 122 in the Court of Appeal. It was held that where housing needs (for a severely disabled boy) were central, then it was a part of the duty of the local authority to consider providing him with accommodation (s 17(6)). In addition, the assessment had not contained any adequate analysis of the problem of accommodation.

5.55 In *R (on the Application of AB and SB) v Nottingham CC* [2001] 4 CCLR 295, a similar issue arose as those referred to above. Housing needs formed the main requirement for a (non-disabled) child. The local authority had not carried out any appropriate assessment of his needs, at all. It had simply referred the matter to its Housing Department. The claim for judicial review was allowed. It is should be noted that the guidance for assessment of children in need can be found in *Framework for the Assessment of Children in Need and their Families.* This is supplemented in *Assessing Children in Need and their Families: Practice Guidance.* Richards J considered the details of this assessment process closely in this judgment and held that:

> '[306G–306I] There should be a systematic assessment of needs which takes account of the three domains (child's developmental needs, parenting capacity, family and environmental factors) and involves collaboration between all relevant agencies ... It is important to be clear about the three stage process: identification of needs, production of care plan, and provision of identified needs. It seems to me that where a local authority follows a path that does not involve the preparation of a core assessment as such, it must nevertheless adopt a similar systematic approach with a view to achievement of the same objectives. Failure to do so without good cause will constitute an impermissible departure from the guidance.'

5.56 The following authority is definitive and significant in respect of s 17. In a conjoined appeal (*R (on the Application of G) v Barnet LBC; R (on the Application of W) v Lambeth LBC; R (on the Application of A) v Lambeth LBC* [2003] UKHL 57, [2003] 6 CCLR 500) the following main principle emerged. It re-emphasised that s 17 on its own produced a target duty only in respect of children in need, and did not create a specific duty. Neither did it impose upon a local authority a duty to meet all assessed needs, irrespective of resources. In respect of *A v Lambeth LBC* (which involved on the facts a degree of disability on the part of two out of three children in the family), Lord Nicholls and Lord Steyn dissenting, they held that there was an enforceable duty arising out of s 17, but it was not absolute. To what extent it had to be fulfilled would depend upon varying factors in each case. In respect of the obligation of a local authority to consider housing, s 17(6) (as amended by s 116 of the Adoption and Children Act 2002) now includes a specific reference to accommodation.

5.57   As a result of the decisions above having reached the Court of Appeal, and also as a result of the amendments to ss 17 and 22 of the Children Act 1989, introduced by the Adoption and Children Act 2002 (which received Royal Assent on 7 November 2002), the Department of Health issued Circular No LAC (2003) 13 (2 June 2003). It states:

> 'Those amendments have the effect of confirming the position ... that Section 17 ... includes the power for local authorities to provide accommodation for families and children; and that the provision of accommodation does not make a child looked after.'

5.58   In *The Queen (on the Application of J) v Enfield London Borough Council (Secretary of State for Health as Intervener)* [2002] EWHC 432 (Admin), [2002] 2 FLR 1, a number of issues arose as to the consequences of the legal status of the mother of a (non-disabled) child. She had argued that due to her own health problems she was entitled to housing (pursuant to s 21 of the National Assistance Act 1948 as a person in need of community care services). She also argued that she was entitled to financial assistance (pursuant to s 17) because her family included a child in need. It was held (*inter alia*) that the general duty of the local authority to promote the welfare of a child in need did not include the provision of financial assistance for accommodation.

5.59   The case of *R (on the Application of CD) (a child by her litigation friend VD) v Isle of Anglesey CC* [2004] EWHC 1635 (Admin), [2004] 7 CCLR 589, [2005] 1 FLR 59, considered the obligations and powers of the local authority within the context of ss 17, 20, 22, 23 of the Children Act 1989 and ss 2 and 28A of the Chronically Sick and Disabled Persons Act 1970. The facts of the case are particularly complex. A 15-year-old disabled child had lived in two homes. The first was with her mother (who was unable to look after her full-time) and the second with foster carers, where she spent the majority of her time. The home of the foster carers was unsuitable for the needs of the child, and the foster carers wished to move house. It was proposed that the local authority should assist in making funds available for the purchase of a new home. The care plan of the local authority was that the child should stay at her school (which had residential facilities) for about half of the time, with the balance of care to be provided by the mother, with assistance from support workers and respite care at the school. There would be visiting contact only to the foster carers. At the same time, the local authority de-registered the foster carers. It was held that the care plan was unlawful in that: (a) it ran counter to the wishes of the child; (b) it imposed responsibilities upon the mother that she plainly could not discharge; and (c) it did not acknowledge the significance of the foster carers in the life of the child. The local authority had also failed in its duty to promote the welfare of the child (pursuant to s 17(1)) by not providing a range and level of services appropriate to her needs, or to provide her with services designed to minimise the effect on her disabilities (s 17(2) and Sch 2, para 6), and that the accommodation with which it was proposing to supply her was unsuitable (and therefore not in accordance with s 23(8)). The local authority attempted to rely upon *Barry* but this was not determined by the Court other than by way of the comment:

> '[608C–608D] [The Local Authority] has House of Lords authority on her side for the proposition, perhaps surprising at first sight, that the 'needs' of a person to whom a local authority owe duties embrace consideration of the cost of providing them.'

This case was cited in *R (on the application of O) v London Borough of Hammersmith & Fulham* [2011] EWCA Civ 925. On the facts of the case, it was common ground that a child required accommodation (via s 20 of the CA 1989) for 52 weeks per year. The dispute was what type and location of accommodation met his needs. The assertion was to the effect that the only lawful conclusion would be the accommodation preferred by O's parents, and that the contrary conclusion by the council was unreasonable. Added to this argument was the proposition that the Administrative Court was bound to apply s 1(1) of the Children Act 1989 in reaching its decision (as it was determining a question with respect to the upbringing of a child) and that thus the child's welfare was the paramount consideration of the Court. The appeal failed, in all respects. Firstly, a difference of opinion between a council and a parent did not amount to an unreasonable decision. On the facts, the council had merely attached greater weight to some factors than had the parents. That in itself is not a foundation for a judicial review, and nor would such a decision amount to a breach of the Art 8 rights of the child. Secondly, although the fact that the hearing was not in the Family Division did not prevent an argument being advanced via s 1 of the CA 1989, it did have to be established that the Court was considering and determining a question in relation to the upbringing of the child (s 1(1)(a)). Lady Justice Black held that:

> '[50] the court is charged not with determining a question with respect to O's upbringing but rather a question with respect to the activities of the local authority, albeit that it was necessary to consider O's best interests as part of the judicial review process.'

In other words, the Court was not exercising a welfare, or best interests decision (citing *R (on the application of P) v Essex County Council and Basildon Council* [2004] EWHC 2027 (Admin) with approval on this point).

5.60   In *R (on the Application of BG) v Medway Council* [2005] EWHC 1932 (Admin), [2005] 8 CCLR 448, a local authority made proposals for funding alterations to the home occupied by a severely disabled boy and his family. Its proposals were that the finance would come from: (a) a disabled facilities grant; (b) an additional discretional non-repayable grant; and (c) a loan. The loan would be secured on the family home (for a term of 20 years) to be re-paid upon a move, the death of the child, repossession or bankruptcy. The terms of the loan were a subject of challenge. It was held that the conditions were proportionate and justified (since the loan itself was to enable the child to remain in his own home, and the conditions were designed to oblige re-payment if its original purpose was frustrated).

5.61   In *R (on the application of Mooney) v Southwark LBC* [2006] EWHC 1912, [2006] 9 CCLR 670, Mr Justice Jackson considered the historical development of the legislation in this area, and its interrelationship with the National Health Service and Community Care Act 1990. It also contains an exposition of the relevance of authorities considered elsewhere (*R v Islington London Borough Council ex parte Batantu; R (on the application of Wahid) v Tower Hamlets LBC; R v Wigan MBC ex parte Tammadge; R (on the application of G) v Barnet LBC*). As well as being authority for the points set out below, it is also therefore an excellent primer for the law in this context. The facts of the case concerned a disabled adult with sole care of two children (both of whom had behavioural problems). The accommodation provided by the local authority was unsuitable. The first part of the case was based upon s 21 of the National Assistance Act 1948 (provision of accommodation), together with Circular No LAC (93) 10 Appendix 1 (see **4.11** for the text). The second part of the case was based upon s 17 of the Children Act 1989. The third part of the case was based upon s 47 of the National Health Service and Community Care Act 1990. As Mr Justice Jackson observes in respect of the above:

> '[677 [29]] The community care services referred to in s 47(1) include, but certainly are not limited to, services provided under section 21 of the 1948 Act; see section 46(3) of the 1990 Act.'

In terms of the relief requested he held as follows:

> '[683 [51–52]] (i) there is a substantial gap between establishing a need for housing and triggering a duty under section 21(1) of the 1948 Act. The one does not automatically follow from the other: see the analysis of Section 21(1) by Hale LJ in *Wahid*. This analysis has additional authority because of the subsequent approval expressed by the House of Lords in [*R (on the Application of Westminster CC) v National Asylum and Support Service* [2002] UKHL 38] and by the Court of Appeal in *R (on the application of O) v Haringey LBC* [2004] 2 FLR 476] (ii) The needs of the children in this case, as revealed by various assessments, are real and obvious. Nevertheless, the needs of children cannot trigger any duty under Section 21 of the 1948 Act: see the judgment of Carnwath LJ in *O*.'

He continued:

> '[683 [58]] … was the Council being reasonable and rational in deciding that the claimant did not have a need triggering section 21? As Pill LJ and Hale LJ pointed out in *Wahid*, this is a decision for the local authority and not the court.'

In terms of the application pursuant to the National Assistance Act 1948, therefore, the claim failed. In respect of s 17 of the Children Act 1989, Mr Justice Jackson referred to *R (on the application of G) v Barnet LBC* (see above), and consequently this claim failed as well.

5.62 A number of associated issues were considered in *H, Barhanu, B v Wandsworth LBC, Hackney LBC, Islington LBC* [2007] EWHC 1082 (Admin), [2007] 10 CCLR 439, [2007] 2 FLR 822. In large part the case turned upon whether a local authority could opt to choose between s 17 or s 20 of the Children Act 1989 in terms of the provision of accommodation. Holman J defined the main issue thus:

'[453 [53]] ... whether the local authority can determine or specify that they did so [provide accommodation to the claimant] in exercise of the power under section 17 when, on the facts of the case, they were also under a duty to do so under section 20(1). In my view ... they cannot.'

There was also extensive argument as to whether the guidance provided by Circular No LAC (2003) 13 was lawful or not. It was held to be correct guidance, and the application in that respect was dismissed. Mr Justice Holman traced the respective obligations of the local authority through ss 17 (general duty), 20 (provision of accommodation for children), 23 (provision of accommodation for looked after children), and also 23A–23D (leaving care provisions). He held:

'[455 [60]] In my view, the approach which Wandsworth adopted in this case was not at all in accordance with either the Act or even the guidance and was accordingly unlawful. If the claimant has made plain that he did not wish to be provided with accommodation at all, then that might have been the end of the matter. But Wandsworth were wrong in law to present him with the three "options" ... and to require him to indicate a choice between section 17 and section 20.

[455 [61]]... Further, on the facts of this particular case, I regard confronting a child in the circumstances of this claimant with the need to make a choice between two statutory provisions on the basis of the document that was given to him as little short of bizarre.'

In effect, a local authority is obliged to determine what a child needs, irrespective of the implications which might follow from either s 17 or s 20.

5.63 The distinction between obligations owed as between s 20(1) Children Act 1989, and the Housing Act 1996 has been conclusively considered and determined in *R (on the application of G (FC)) v Southwark LBC* [2009] UKHL 26, [2009] 12 CCLR 437. There was also a consideration of the Children (Leaving Care) Act 2000. Baroness Hale commented:

'[5] It comes as something of a surprise that the issue had had to reach this House, in the light of the observations in *R v Hammersmith and Fulham LBC* ... as to what ought to have happened in the reverse situation.'

The latter case is considered at **5.32** above. On the facts in this case, the child had presented himself to the children's services department (as opposed to the housing department as had happened in *R v Hammersmith and Fulham LBC*) and requested assessment under s 17, and also for accommodation under s 20(1). There could have been no doubts on the facts of the case that the criteria for s 20(1) were made out [28]. It followed that the duty under s 20(1) was made out, and it was not open to the local authority to side step this by arguing that the child came within the homelessness provisions of the Housing Act 1996. A similar issue arose in *R (on the application of TG) v London Borough of Lambeth and Shelter (Intervener)* [2011] EWCA Civ 526, [2011] 14 CCLR 366. The claimant himself had the status of a 'former relevant child', and had informed his social worker that he intended to approach the housing department of the council for help. The social worker wrote a report, to assist him in that endeavour. It provided him with accommodation under s 188 of the Housing Act 1996, but did not refer him to the children's services department. Applying *R (M) v Hammersmith and Fulham LBC* it was held that by virtue of the involvement of the social worker, there was a connection between the child and the council as a result of which he was provided with accommodation. The decision at first instance refusing him relief was overturned, and he was granted a declaration as to his status in law (which in turn provided him with the continuing services of the council until the age of 21). A claim for damages was refused.

Ordinary residence

5.64　In *R v Kent County Council ex parte S* [2000] 1 FLR 155 an issue arose as to which local authority would be responsible for young adults who were approaching majority and whose capacity as to the intention to establish ordinary residence was compromised. On the facts in the case, this problem would not now arise as a result of the Children (Leaving Care) Act 2000, since for the relevant period they had been in care. However, the authority is still of use since some children may not have been looked after, and the local authority also has obligations arising out of s 28A of the Chronically Sick and Disabled Persons Act 1970. It was held that determining ordinary residence under this statute was a matter for the Court (unlike the National Assistance Act 1948 where disputes could be determined by the Secretary of State). It was also held that (in the facts) the young person had formed the necessary intention to stay (in Kent), and that if that was incorrect (and that she lacked capacity) she would be treated a small child and her ordinary residence would be that of her parents (in this case, her foster parents). Consequently, for the purposes of the 1970 Act, it was the local authority within which she was resident that had responsibility. The issue of ordinary residence is also considered at **5.28** and **5.29**.

Disabled children and the Carers and Disabled Children Act 2000

5.65　There remain some areas where the Children (Leaving Care) Act 2000 and the Carers and Disabled Children Act 2000 overlap (and these are set out below), but the main statute alongside which it falls to be considered is the Carers (Recognition and Services) Act 1995. It is the most recent in a series of statutes (referred to in Chapter 3) which impose greater obligations upon local authorities to assess not only disabled children (and adults) but also those who care for the disabled themselves. To that extent, it fits with the general strategy of the Government referred to above.

Summary

5.66 The main purpose of the Act can be summarised as follows. First, if an adult (or young person over the age of 16) is a carer for an individual (and that individual is over 18), and asks a local authority to assess his *own* ability to care for that person, then the local authority *must* carry out an assessment if it is satisfied that the person being cared for is someone for whom it may provide or arrange community care services. The case-law set out in Chapter 3 applies (in particular the low threshold for this test). Secondly, once the assessment has been carried out, the local authority must consider the assessment and decide whether the *carer* has needs in relation to the care that he provides, and if so whether those needs might be satisfied by services which could be provided by the local authority, and whether it will provide those services. Guidance in respect of children who have disabilities has been available for many years, and can be found in *The Children Act 1989: Guidance and Regulations Volume 6*. Again, the case-law in respect of needs and provision of services to satisfy those needs is applicable, as set out in Chapter 3. Thirdly, the Act cross-refers to s 1 of the Carers (Recognition and Services) Act 1995 in that if an assessment takes place under that Act, it may take into account an assessment under the Carers and Disabled Children Act 2000. Fourthly, if a person with parental responsibility for a disabled child requests an assessment of *his own* ability to care for that child, then the local authority must carry out such an assessment if it is satisfied that it comes within the ambit of s 17. The case-law set out within this Chapter is relevant for that purpose. Fifthly, it imposes upon the local authority has an obligation to notify a carer (both of an adult or a child) that he may be entitled to an assessment, if it appears to it that this would be the case. There are some exceptions to the latter (which are listed in s 6A(3)(a)–(c)). Practitioners should also note that local authorities should make specific allowances for young carers, and may indeed have separate obligations towards this group pursuant to s 17(3) of the Children Act 1989.

5.67 The Act is accompanied by *Carers and people with parental responsibility for disabled children Practice Guidance* (Deparment of Health, 2001) which sets out how the Policy Guidance on the Carers and Disabled Persons Act 2000 should be implemented. It covers all matters in respect of the Act, but perhaps the most significant within the context of this book is the emphasis upon transparency and clarity for the eligibility criteria for carers's assessments; the impact of the caring role; children and young people affected by caring situations (paras 74, 75); charging for services; direct payments and young carers; separation of financial contribution from any assessment under s 47 of the NHS and Community Care Act 1990.

Carers And Disabled Children Act 2000

1 Right of carers to assessment

(1) If an individual aged 16 or over ("the carer") –

(a)   provides or intends to provide a substantial amount of care on a regular basis for another individual aged 18 or over ("the person cared for"); and

(b)   asks a local authority to carry out an assessment of his ability to provide and to continue to provide care for the person cared for,

the local authority must carry out such an assessment if it is satisfied that the person cared for is someone for whom it may provide or arrange for the provision of community care services.

(2) For the purposes of such an assessment, the local authority may take into account, so far as it considers it to be material, an assessment under section 1(1) of the Carers (Recognition and Services) Act 1995.

(3) Subsection (1) does not apply if the individual provides or will provide the care in question –

(a)   by virtue of a contract of employment or other contract with any person; or

(b)   as a volunteer for a voluntary organisation.

(3A) An assessment under subsection (1) must include consideration of whether the carer –

(a)   works or wishes to work,

(b)   is undertaking, or wishes to undertake, education, training or any leisure activity.

(4) The Secretary of State (or, in relation to Wales, the National Assembly for Wales) may give directions as to the manner in which an assessment under subsection (1) is to be carried out or the form it is to take.

(5) Subject to any such directions, it is to be carried out in such manner, and is to take such form, as the local authority considers appropriate.

(6) In this section, "voluntary organisation" has the same meaning as in the National Assistance Act 1948.

2 Services for carers

(1) The local authority must consider the assessment and decide –

(a)   whether the carer has needs in relation to the care which he provides or intends to provide;

(b)   if so, whether they could be satisfied (wholly or partly) by services which the local authority may provide; and

(c)   if they could be so satisfied, whether or not to provide services to the carer.

(2) The services referred to are any services which –

(a)   the local authority sees fit to provide; and

(b)   will in the local authority's view help the carer care for the person cared
for,

and may take the form of physical help or other forms of support.

(3) A service, although provided to the carer –

(a)   may take the form of a service delivered to the person cared for if it is
one which, if provided to him instead of to the carer, could fall within
community care services and they both agree it is to be so delivered; but

(b)   if a service is delivered to the person cared for it may not, except in
prescribed circumstances, include anything of an intimate nature.

(4) Regulations may make provision about what is, or is not, of an intimate nature
for the purposes of subsection (3).

4 Assessments and services for both carer and person cared for

(1) In section 1 of the Carers (Recognition and Services) Act 1995 (which provides
for carers to be assessed as to their ability to care in connection with an
assessment of the needs of the individual cared for), after subsection (2) insert –

"(2A) For the purposes of an assessment under subsection (1) or (2), the local
authority may take into account, so far as it considers it to be material,
an assessment under section 1 or 6 of the Carers and Disabled Children
Act 2000."

(2) Subsection (4) applies if the local authority –

(a)   is either providing services under this Act to the carer, or is providing
community care services to or in respect of the person cared for (but not
both); and

(b)   proposes to provide another service to (or in respect of) the one who is
not receiving any such service,

and the new service, or any service already being provided, is one which could be
provided either under this Act, or by way of community care services.

(3) Subsection (4) also applies if –

(a)   the local authority is not providing services to the carer (under this Act)
or to the person cared for (by way of community care services), but
proposes to provide services to each of them following an assessment
under section 1 and under section 47 of the National Health Service and
Community Care Act 1990; or

(b)   the local authority is providing services both to the carer (under this
Act) and to the person cared for (by way of community care services),
and proposes to provide to either of them a new service,

and (in a paragraph (a) case) any of the services, or (in a paragraph (b) case) the
new service, is one which could be provided either under this Act, or by way of
community care services.

(4) In the case of each such service, the local authority must decide whether the
service is, or is in future, to be provided under this Act, or by way of community
care services (and hence whether it is, or is in future, to be provided to the carer, or
to the person cared for).

(5) The local authority's decision under subsection (4) is to be made without regard to the means of the carer or of the person cared for.

6 Assessments: persons with parental responsibility for disabled children

(1) If a person with parental responsibility for a disabled child –

    (a)   provides or intends to provide a substantial amount of care on a regular basis for the child; and

    (b)   asks a local authority to carry out an assessment of his ability to provide and to continue to provide care for the child,

the local authority must carry out such an assessment if it is satisfied that the child and his family are persons for whom it may provide or arrange for the provision of services under section 17 of the Children Act 1989 ("the 1989 Act").

(2) For the purposes of such an assessment, the local authority may take into account, so far as it considers it to be material, an assessment under section 1(2) of the Carers (Recognition and Services) Act 1995.

(2A) An assessment under subsection (1) must include consideration of whether the person with parental responsibility for the child –

    (a)   works or wishes to work,

    (b)   is undertaking, or wishes to undertake, education, training or any leisure activity.

(3) The Secretary of State (or, in relation to Wales, the National Assembly for Wales) may give directions as to the manner in which an assessment under subsection (1) is to be carried out or the form it is to take.

(4) Subject to any such directions, it is to be carried out in such manner, and is to take such form, as the local authority considers appropriate.

(5) The local authority must take the assessment into account when deciding what, if any, services to provide under section 17 of the 1989 Act.

(6) Terms used in this section have the same meaning as in Part III of the 1989 Act.

6A Duty to inform carers of right to assessment

(1) Subsection (2) applies if it appears to a local authority that it would be required to carry out a carer's assessment on being asked to do so by –

    (a)   the carer, or

    (b)   a person with parental responsibility for a disabled child ("the responsible person").

(2) The local authority must inform the carer or, as appropriate, the responsible person that he may be entitled to a carer's assessment (but this is subject to subsections (3) and (4)).

(3) Subsection (2) does not apply in relation to the carer if the local authority has previously –

    (a)   carried out a carer's assessment for him in relation to the person cared for,

(b)   informed him that he may be entitled to a carer's assessment in relation to the person cared for, or

(c)   carried out an assessment of him under section 4(3) of the Community Care (Delayed Discharges etc) Act 2003 in relation to the person cared for.

(4) Subsection (2) does not apply in relation to the responsible person if the local authority has previously carried out a carer's assessment for him in relation to the disabled child or informed him that he may be entitled to a carer's assessment in relation to the disabled child.

(5) In this section "carer's assessment" means –

(a)   in the case of the carer, an assessment under section 1 of his ability to provide and to continue to provide care for the person cared for,

(b)   in the case of the responsible person, an assessment under section 6 of his ability to provide and to continue to provide care for the disabled child.

The Community Care Assessment Directions 2004

5.67   These came into force on 1 September 2004. They amend the National Health Service and Community Care Act 1990. Circular No LAC (2004) 24 refers in part to the Carers and Disabled Children Act 2000 in that:

'Full involvement of individuals and their carers in both assessment and care planning has long been recognised as good practice and the importance of doing so has been highlighted in previous guidance. Carers are entitled, under the Carers and Disabled Children Act 2000, to request an assessment of their needs in supporting the person they care for.'

Reference has been made to the significance of these Directions in the context of adult social care provision in Chapters 3 and 4.

Delayed and deficient assessments

5.69   In *R (on the application of J) v Newham LBC* [2001] EWHC 992 (Admin), [2002] 5 CCLR 302, the local authority had failed to carry out any assessments at all (and had deferred such assessments on the basis of an anticipated change of circumstances). Further, it had provided no help to the mother of a disabled child, and the family were living in temporary accommodation. It was held that the local authority must carry out an assessment, both pursuant to s 17 of the Children Act 1989, and s 6 of the Carers and Disabled Children Act 2000 within the ordinary 35-working day period.

5.70   In *R (on the application of LH and MH) v Lambeth LBC* [2006] EWHC 1190 (Admin), [2006] 9 CCLR 622, the issue of proper assessment was considered. The factual context was that a mentally and physically disabled child was considered by his mother to require a residential placement. The local authority carried out assessments, but it was argued that they were incomplete and materially deficient. It was held that there had been a lack of concentration upon the needs of the child, or a clear identification of those needs, or upon the needs of the mother as a carer. Whilst the Court would not determine whether a residential placement was suitable or not, it was irrational to decide that a mere 'package of support' was appropriate in the absence of any proper analysis of the substantive needs. A declaration was made that the local authority was in breach of all its assessment obligations pursuant to Part III of the Children Act 1989 (as supplemented by the Children Act 2004), the Carers (Recognition and Services) Act 1995, and the Carers and Disabled Children Act 2000.

CHILDREN ACT 2004

5.71   The stated intention of the Act is (*inter alia*) to 'make provision for the establishment of a Children's Commissioner; to make provision about services provided to and for young people by local authorities …'. The relevant sections are reproduced below. The Act received Royal Assent on 15 November 2004.

Children Act 2004

9 Care leavers and young persons with learning disabilities

(1) This section applies for the purposes of this Part, other than section 2(11) and (12).

(2) Any reference to a child includes, in addition to a person under the age of 18, a person aged 18, 19 or 20 who –

    (a)   has been looked after by a local authority at any time after attaining the age of 16; or

    (b)   has a learning disability.

(3) For the purposes of subsection (2) –

    a person is "looked after by a local authority" if –

        (a)   for the purposes of the Children Act 1989 (c 41), he is looked after by a local authority in England and Wales;

        (b)   for the purposes of the Children (Scotland) Act 1995 (c 36), he is looked after by a local authority in Scotland;

        (c)   for the purposes of the Children (Northern Ireland) Order 1995 (SI 1995/755 (NI 2)), he is looked after by an authority in Northern Ireland;

    "learning disability" means a state of arrested or incomplete development of mind which induces significant impairment of intelligence and social functioning.

5.72   This corresponds in spirit to the provision of the Children (Leaving Care) Act 2000 in that its scope ranges in age from a child, to someone of the age of 20, and also inserts a definition of the term 'learning disability'. This term has some similarities in phraseology with s 17(10)(b) and (11) of the Children Act 1989, and s 1 of the Mental Health Act 1983.

10 Co-operation to improve well-being

(1) Each children's services authority in England must make arrangements to promote co-operation between –

  (a)   the authority;
  (b)   each of the authority's relevant partners; and
  (c)   such other persons or bodies as the authority consider appropriate, being persons or bodies of any nature who exercise functions or are engaged in activities in relation to children in the authority's area.

(2) The arrangements are to be made with a view to improving the well-being of children in the authority's area so far as relating to –

  (a)   physical and mental health and emotional well-being;
  (b)   protection from harm and neglect;
  (c)   education, training and recreation;
  (d)   the contribution made by them to society;
  (e)   social and economic well-being.

(3) In making arrangements under this section a children's services authority in England must have regard to the importance of parents and other persons caring for children in improving the well-being of children.

(4) For the purposes of this section each of the following is a relevant partner of a children's services authority in England –

  (a)   where the authority is a county council for an area for which there is also a district council, the district council;
  (b)   the police authority and the chief officer of police for a police area any part of which falls within the area of the children's services authority;
  (c)   a local probation board for an area any part of which falls within the area of the authority;
  (d)   a youth offending team for an area any part of which falls within the area of the authority;
  (e)   a Strategic Health Authority and Primary Care Trust for an area any part of which falls within the area of the authority;
  (f)   a person providing services under section 114 of the Learning and Skills Act 2000 (c. 21) in any part of the area of the authority;
  (g)   the Learning and Skills Council for England.

(5) The relevant partners of a children's services authority in England must co-operate with the authority in the making of arrangements under this section.

(6) A children's services authority in England and any of their relevant partners may for the purposes of arrangements under this section –

  (a)   provide staff, goods, services, accommodation or other resources;
  (b)   establish and maintain a pooled fund.

(7) For the purposes of subsection (6) a pooled fund is a fund –

  (a)   which is made up of contributions by the authority and the relevant partner or partners concerned; and
  (b)   out of which payments may be made towards expenditure incurred in the discharge of functions of the authority and functions of the relevant partner or partners.

(8) A children's services authority in England and each of their relevant partners must in exercising their functions under this section have regard to any guidance given to them for the purpose by the Secretary of State.

(9) Arrangements under this section may include arrangements relating to –

(a)   persons aged 18 and 19;

(b)   persons over the age of 19 who are receiving services under sections 23C to 24D of the Children Act 1989 (c. 41);

(c)   persons over the age of 19 but under the age of 25 who have a learning difficulty, within the meaning of section 13 of the Learning and Skills Act 2000, and are receiving services under that Act.

17 Children and young people's plans

(1) The Secretary of State may by regulations require a children's services authority in England from time to time to prepare and publish a plan setting out the authority's strategy for discharging their functions in relation to children and relevant young persons.

(2) Regulations under this section may in particular make provision as to –

(a)   the matters to be dealt with in a plan under this section;

(b)   the period to which a plan under this section is to relate;

(c)   when and how a plan under this section must be published;

(d)   keeping a plan under this section under review;

(e)   consultation to be carried out during preparation of a plan under this section.

(3) The matters for which provision may be made under subsection (2)(a) include in particular –

(a)   the arrangements made or to be made under section 10 by a children's services authority in England;

(b)   the strategy or proposals in relation to children and relevant young persons of any person or body with whom a children's services authority in England makes or proposes to make such arrangements.

(4) The power to make regulations conferred by this section shall, for the purposes of subsection (1) of section 100 of the Local Government Act 2003 (c 26), be regarded as included among the powers mentioned in subsection (2) of that section.

(5) In this section "relevant young persons" means persons, other than children, in relation to whom arrangements under section 10 may be made.

5.73 The provisions set out above require a local authority to publish information about (in effect) the coordination of children's services. The coordination is intended to ensure that not only do local authorities liaise with the appropriate departments within its own organisation (eg adult services and housing departments) but also with other bodies exercising functions relating to children within its area. The overall intention is to break down divisions between health, social care and education services, and the Act itself creates a positive duty on various agencies to work together to produce this outcome. The philosophy of the much overused expression 'joined up thinking' is also set out in the framework for children's trusts for use in planning and commissioning children's services (www.everychildmatters.gov.uk).

Transitional services

5.74 There is a considerable problem with the situation that arises when an older child (with community care needs) is approaching adulthood. The problem is created by an absence of liaison between children's services and adult services. It is compounded by the confusion within the respective departments as to what there legal obligations might be. Some attempts have been made to remedy this within the area of Mental Health Tribunals (eg Section E of *'Reports for Mental Health Tribunals'* (Tribunals Service) which deals with patients under the age of 18. However, as Mrs Justice Black has pointed out (para 5.49) albeit in a slightly different context, there is no definitive practice direction or government guidance with covers this area. As can be seen from **5.1** above, some attention has been paid to transition plans for care leavers, in the form of Regulations and Guidance which apply to that specific group.

5.75 The risks associated with this transition period have been recognised for some time (*Independence, choice and risk: a guide to best practice in supported decision making* Department of Health, May 2007). Paragraphs 2.59–2.61 cover this area and suggest that:

> 'Good practice in transition planning begins at least by the age of 14 and in some cases there may be very good reasons for adult services to start working with the young person and their family well before the age of 18 to ensure that there is consistency and trust built into their relationships ... in some cases it will be vital that the children's worker is also involved after the person reaches the age of 18. It may also be necessary for the court of protection to be involved from 16, to ensure that protection extends beyond the age of 18.'

The same document refers to *Transition: getting it right for young people* (Department of Health 2006). However, this concentrates exclusively upon health related matters (although some consideration is given to Children and Adolescent Mental Health Services). Further information is contained in *A Transition guide for all Services* (Department of Health 2007) and *Transition: moving on well* (Department of Health 2008). The guidance for the assessment of the eligibility for adult social care (*Prioritising need in the context of **Putting People First**: Guidance on Eligibility Criteria for Adult Social Care, 2010*) sets out what the problem is, and generally what should be done about it (early planning; co-ordinated multi-agency approach paras 135–138) but goes no further than this in stating how the solution actually might be achieved. The *Ordinary Residence Guidance* provides a trenchant summary of the legislative quagmire that exists in respect of young people in transition from children's services to adult services, and this is set out below.

The statutory framework on the provision of accommodation and services

138. Children who are in need of social care support, including children who are "looked after", are provided with accommodation and/or services under the Children Act 1989 (the "1989 Act"). They may also be provided with services under the Chronically Sick and Disabled Persons Act 1970 (the "1970 Act") (though they receive universal services such as access to schools and primary health care in the same way as all other children). When a young person with social care needs reaches the age of 18, the duty on local authorities to provide accommodation and services under the 1989 Act usually ceases. From their 18th birthday, residential accommodation is generally provided under section 21 of the 1948 Act, and other services are provided under section 29 of the 1948 Act, in conjunction with section 2 of the 1970 Act. These services are provided by the local authority in which the young person is ordinarily resident, which may or may not be the same local authority that was responsible for them under the 1989 Act (see paragraphs 145–158 below).

5.76 The case of *C (by his litigation friend the Official Solicitor) v A Local Authority* [2011] EWHC 1539 (Admin), [2011] 14 CCLR 471 (referred to in Chapter 2 at **2.111**) is an extreme but valuable example of the lack of planning in this area of practice. It can only be hoped that formal guidance on the best practice in this area is to be forthcoming, and in a format that makes it readily comprehensible to adult and children's social services. The Law Commission has turned its mind to this problem and had made specific recommendations to deal with it (paras 11.39–11.60 *Law Com No 326 May 2011*) but of course it is not known if the Government will adopt these recommendations (which in summary are to create a parity between the law in relation to children and adults, so that the legal complexities of the transition process are removed), or indeed when they might be implemented.

MENTAL CAPACITY ACT 2005

Children

5.77 The jurisdiction created by this Act in respect of children has been considered in Chapter 2 (at **2.107–2.111**). The Code of Practice defines children as 'people aged below 16' and young people as 'people aged 16–17'. It does not apply to those under the age of 16, except where decisions are to be made about a child's property of finances (if he lacks capacity on those matters) and is still likely to lack capacity to make financial decisions upon reaching the age of 18 (s 18(3)). The latter simply states:

'The powers under section 16 as respects any other matter relating to P's property and affairs may be exercised even though P has not reached 16, if the Court considers it likely that P will still lack capacity to make decisions in respect of that matter when he reaches 18.'

Young people

5.78   The Act applies to those over the age of 16, with three exceptions. The first is that only those over the age of 18 can make a Lasting Power of Attorney. The second is that only those over the age of 18 can make an advance decision to refuse medical treatment. The third is that the Court of Protection can only make a statutory will for a person aged 18 or over.

Chapter 6

FINANCE AND CHARGING

GENERAL

6.1 This Chapter considers those aspects of community care services for which charges may be made, or how those charges might be recovered. It also considers the regime by which payments may be made by local authorities to service users (direct payments) and includes matters arising out of the development of Individual Budgets.

ORIGINS OF THE NATIONAL ASSISTANCE ACT 1948

6.2 As is well known, the origins of the National Assistance Act 1948 lie in the *Beveridge Report* (*Beveridge Report on Social Insurance and Allied Services* (1943) Cmd 6404), and in the intention of Parliament in the immediate period after World War II to create a society in which the depredations of poverty and illness might be ameliorated by either national or local government. The spirit of this legislation can be seen in a small extract from one of the debates in the House of Lords as follows:

> 'Mine is an agreeable task this afternoon. I have to explain the main principles and provisions of a Bill which I know will receive a wholehearted welcome from noble Lords in all parts of the House. This is a Bill which makes a strong appeal to the sense of social justice which animates your Lordship's House, and it provides another opportunity for us to assist in mitigating undeserved distress and human misfortune ... The first thing which this Bill will achieve is the complete and final abolition of the Poor Law ... The point has been reached where the only way to deal with the Poor Law is to abolish it, so that the social services of the future, in every branch, may be services to which any member of the community will readily have recourse, without loss of self-respect and without fear of stigma, whenever his need may arise ... These new services fall naturally into two parts. On the one hand, it is necessary to meet the needs of those who for the most part live a normal home life, but find themselves in need of financial help. On the other hand, account must be taken of the person who, whether or not his financial resources are sufficient for his requirements, has a primary need of a different kind – namely, a need for care and attention that he cannot secure in ordinary home life. Any comprehensive scheme of assistance must necessarily make this twofold provision. The Government have decided completely to separate the duty of providing financial assistance from that of providing care and attention ... the latter will remain within the sphere of local government ...'
> (per Lord Henderson *Hansard* HL Deb, col 1095–1098 (6 April 1948)).

The role of local government (as can be seen from the previous chapters) has expanded considerably since 1948, but the issue of financing and charging for those services remains problematic.

PROVISION OF ACCOMMODATION

6.3   The circumstances in which a local authority may remain liable for providing accommodation are considered in Chapter 4, and s 21 of the National Assistance Act 1948 (NAA 1948) is set out within that chapter in its entirety. For the purposes of convenience, those parts of it that are relevant for this Chapter are repeated below.

National Assistance Act 1948

21 Duty of local authorities to provide accommodation

(2A) In determining for the purposes of paragraph (a) or (aa) of subsection (1) of this section whether care and attention are otherwise available to a person, a local authority shall disregard so much of the person's resources as may be specified in, or determined in accordance with, regulations made by the Secretary of State for the purposes of this subsection.

(2B) In subsection (2A) of this section the reference to a person's resources is a reference to his resources within the meaning of regulations made for the purposes of that subsection.

(3) ...

(4) Subject to the provisions of section 26 of this Act accommodation provided by a local authority in the exercise of their functions under this section shall be provided in premises managed by the authority or, to such extent as may be determined in accordance with the arrangements under this section, in such premises managed by another local authority as may be agreed between the two authorities and on such terms, including terms as to the reimbursement of expenditure incurred by the said other authority, as may be so agreed.

(8) ... nothing in this section shall authorise or require a local authority to make any provision authorised or required to be made (whether by that or by any other authority) by or under any enactment not contained in this Part of this Act or authorised or required to be provided under the National Health Service Act 2006 or the National Health Service (Wales) Act 2006.

6.4   Section 21(1) does not empower a local authority to make cash payments to enable an individual to acquire accommodation (or other commodity) (*R v Secretary of State for Health ex p M and K* [1998] 1 CCLR 495). Section 21(8) is considered within the context of the division of responsibilities between social services and health authorities below.

22 Charges to be made for accommodation

(1) Subject to section 26 of this Act, where a person is provided with accommodation under this Part of this Act the local authority providing the

accommodation shall recover from him the amount of the payment which he is liable to make in accordance with the following provisions of this section.

(2) Subject to the following provisions of this section, the payment which a person is liable to make for any such accommodation shall be in accordance with a standard rate fixed for that accommodation by the authority managing the premises in which it is provided and that standard rate shall represent the full cost to the authority of providing that accommodation.

(3) Where a person for whom accommodation in premises managed by any local authority is provided, or proposed to be provided, under this Part of this Act satisfies the local authority that he is unable to pay therefore at the standard rate, the authority shall assess his ability to pay ... , and accordingly determine at what lower rate he shall be liable to pay for the accommodation.

...

(4) In assessing for the purposes of the last foregoing subsection a person's ability to pay, a local authority shall assume that he will need for his personal requirements such sum per week as may be prescribed by the Minister, or such other sum as in special circumstances the authority may consider appropriate.

(4A) Regulations made for the purposes of subsection (4) of this section may prescribe different sums for different circumstances.

(5) In assessing as aforesaid a person's ability to pay, a local authority shall give effect to regulations made by the Secretary of State for the purposes of this subsection except that, until the first such regulations come into force, a local authority shall give effect to Part III of Schedule 1 to the Supplementary Benefits Act 1976, as it had effect immediately before the amendments made by Schedule 2 to the Social Security Act 1980.

(5A) If they think fit, an authority managing premises in which accommodation is provided for a person shall have power on each occasion when they provide accommodation for him, irrespective of his means, to limit to such amount as appears to them reasonable for him to pay the payments required from him for his accommodation during a period commencing when they begin to provide the accommodation for him and ending not more than eight weeks after that.

(6), (7) ...

(8) Where accommodation is provided by a local authority in premises managed by another local authority, the payment therefore under this section shall be made to the authority managing the premises and not to the authority providing accommodation, but the authority managing the premises shall account for the payment to the authority providing the accommodation.

(8A) This section shall have effect subject to any regulations under section 15 of the Community Care (Delayed Discharges etc) Act 2003 (power to require certain community care services and services for carers to be provided free of charge).

(9) ...

COMMUNITY CARE (DELAYED DISCHARGES ETC) ACT 2003

6.5   This statute and its purpose and effect is considered later in this Chapter. The significance of s 22(8A) above is as follows. The regulations referred to make specific provision for circumstances in which a qualifying service is to be provided free of charge. Qualifying services are defined as the provision of accommodation under Part 3 of NAA 1948, or any service referred to in s 17(2)(a)–(c) and (f) of the Health and Social Services and Social Security Adjudications Act 1983. The regulations may not require either provision of accommodation, or provision of personal care to a person at a place where that person is living (unless it is Part 3 accommodation), or a service provided under s 2 of the Carers and Disabled Children Act 2000 which consists of the provision of personal care to be provided free of charge for more than a maximum of 6 weeks (s 51(1)–(4)). The relevant regulations are the Community Care (Delayed Discharges etc) Act (Qualifying Services) (England) Regulations 2003, SI 2003/1196. These are set out below.

Community Care (Delayed Discharges Etc) Act (Qualifying Services) (England) Regulations 2003, SI 2003/1196

1 Citation, commencement and application

(1) These Regulations may be cited as the Community Care (Delayed Discharges etc) Act (Qualifying Services) (England) Regulations 2003 and shall come into force on 9th June 2003.

(2) These Regulations apply to England only.

2 Interpretation

In these Regulations –

(a)   "community equipment (aids and minor adaptations) service" means a qualifying service which consists of the provision of an aid, or a minor adaptation to property, for the purposes of assisting with nursing at home or aiding daily living; and, for the purposes of this paragraph, an adaptation is "minor" if the cost of making the adaptation is £1000 or less; and

(b)   "intermediate care" means a qualifying service which consists of a structured programme of care provided for a limited period of time to assist a person to maintain or regain the ability to live in his home.

3 Qualifying services

The qualifying services prescribed for the purposes of section 15(1) of the Community Care (Delayed Discharges etc) Act 2003 are intermediate care and community equipment (aids and minor adaptations) services.

4 Qualifying services to be provided free of charge

(1) A community equipment (aids and minor adaptations) service is required to be provided free of charge to any person to whom it is provided where the provision of that service begins on or after the date on which these regulations come into force.

(2) A period of intermediate care which begins on or after these regulations come into force is required to be provided free of charge to any person to whom it is provided for any period up to and including six weeks.

Charges for residential accommodation

6.6   The circumstances in which charges can be made, and the amount that can be charged, are hedged about by case-law, separate statutes, and subsidiary regulations. Those circumstances are set out below. In particular, the local authority can take into account resources (subject to the relevant regulations being taken into account in deciding whether those resources can be disregarded). Circular No LAC (92) 19 'Charges for Residential Accommodation' was issued by the Department of Health in December 1992. The rules have effect for all new residents from 1 April 1993 onwards. It was issued under s 7(1) of the Local Authority Social Services act 1970. It places upon the resident a responsibility to satisfy the local authority that he is unable to pay the whole charge. A resident may not withhold information that enables a local authority to make such a decision. There is an allowance (in terms of income) for personal expenses which is exempt. This figure is reviewed annually. There is a discretion (s 22(4) of NAA 1948) for the local authority itself to vary this figure. There is also an option for local authorities to use more expensive accommodation, provided that there is a third party able and willing to meet the difference in fees. The contribution of the third party is treated as part of the income of the resident.

Charges for Residential Accommodation Guide

6.7   The specific details of how the income and capital resources of a resident are to be assessed are contained in the *Charging For Residential Accommodation Guide* (usually referred to as CRAG). It is revised on an annual basis. It is issued in support of the National Assistance (Assessment of Resources) Regulations 1992, SI 1992/2977 (which in many respects mirror exactly the Income Support (General) Regulations 1987, SI 1987/1967). Practitioners looking for guidance as to what constitutes (for example) capital and income, or attempts to dispose of capital assets, will find that both the case-law (in the Courts) and decisions made by the Social Security Commissioner in respect of social security legislation is of considerable assistance. A survey of the subject is outside the scope of this book. The CRAG is available from the Department of Health Website (www.dh.gov.uk). It currently (April 2011) runs to just over 121 pages. It covers:

(1)   assessment of how much to charge and the ability to pay;

(2)   residents unable to manage their own affairs (eg who lack capacity);

(3)   charges for day services;

(4)   less dependent relatives;

(5)   temporary residents;

(6)   couples;

(7)   personal expenses allowance;

(8)   capital (and what constitutes capital);

(9)   income treated as capital;

(10) trust funds;

(11) real property;

(12) income other than earnings;

(13) earnings;

(14) Third Party Payment's and Top Up's;

(15) students.

Disputes in this area can be highly technical, and require interpretation of a labyrinthine interconnection of different areas of law, some of which remain unresolved even as a result of extensive litigation. Many difficulties can arise because of a lack of basic paperwork at the time that the resident is placed in accommodation. It is easy to see how this may happen, since (for example) the placement may have been in an emergency situation in the first instance, and the resident himself may have fluctuating capacity. The entire area itself is fraught with the possibility of disagreement as to what was agreed, and what was not agreed. It is often the case that a good deal of money is involved (whether the dispute be between the relatives of the resident and the local authority, or the resident and the local authority, or the owner of the residential home and the local authority) together with heightened emotions which may have coloured either decisions made or the perspective of the relevant parties to the dispute.

Capital

6.8   Where the resident is one of a couple, the resident must have in excess of £23,250 capital in his own right, or his share of jointly owned capital must be in excess of £23,250 before he is excluded from support on the grounds of capital

(CRAG 4.003). Examples of capital are buildings, land, National Savings Certificates, Premium Bonds, Stocks and Shares, Capital held by the Court of Protection or a deputy appointed by that Court, savings, cash, or trust funds (CRAG 6.002). A resident with capital of more than £23,250 is liable to pay the standard charge for the accommodation (CRAG 6.006) and capital of £14,250 or less is fully disregarded (CRAG 6.007). However, capital over £14,250 and up to and including £23,250 is taken into account in full for the purposes of calculating what is termed a 'tariff income' (CRAG 6.008 et seq). Tariff income is meant to represent 'an amount that a resident with capital over a certain limit should be able to contribute towards his accommodation costs, not the interest earning capacity of that capital'.

Capital to be disregarded indefinitely

6.9   The following are the main examples of capital that can be disregarded:

(1)   the value of a dwelling when the resident is placed temporarily;

(2)   where the dwelling is occupied by the partner of the resident, former partner, or civil partner (unless estranged or divorced, or unless the divorced or estranged partner is a lone parent), and where a relative is aged 60 or over, or is a child of the resident under 18, or where the relative is incapacitated (CRAG 7.003). The definition of the term 'relative' is at CRAG 7.004;

(3)   surrender value of life insurance policy or annuity;

(4)   payments from a charity;

(5)   personal possessions unless purchased in order to reduce capital for the purposes of reducing the local authority charge;

(6)   payments from a variety of third parties (for example the Independent Living Fund);

(7)   the value of funds held in trust or administered by a court which derive from a payment of damages for personal injury to the resident.

The complete list is at CRAG 6.030. It is extremely detailed. There are also extensive provisions for disregarding capital for various periods (6.031–6.039)

Deprivation of capital

6.10   It is not uncommon for a resident to deprive himself of capital in order to thwart the ability of the local authority to charge for accommodation. CRAG 6.066 gives a number of examples of this type of activity. It is the resident who is obliged to prove that he no longer has the resource. Examples of deprivation of capital are having given a lump sum away, substantial expenditure, transfer of ownership of real property, transfer of money into a trust which cannot be revoked, capital which has been converted into a form that can be disregarded (eg chattels) or capital which has been reduced by extravagant living. The difficulty that a local authority may face is in establishing that the deprivation of capital was for the sole purpose of avoiding being charged. Matters which will have a bearing on this will vary according to the specific facts of each case, but (for example) the timing of the alleged disposal will be relevant, as will be the pattern of the expenditure of the resident prior to being accommodated. If the local authority decides that deprivation has occurred then it will have to make a decision as to whether to treat the resident as having notional capital (that is to say that he still has the capital), and charge accordingly *or* to make use of the Health and Social Services and Social Security Adjudication Act 1983.

Income

6.11   Income is referred to as 'made in respect of a period and ... forms part of a series of payments' (CRAG 8.001). Income will be either fully taken into account, partially taken into account, or disregarded. A list of income that is taken fully into account is set out at CRAG 8.005–8.019. The main example is social security benefits and third party payments made to meet higher fees. A list of income that is partly disregarded is set out at CRAG 8.021–8.041. These include war disablement pensions, pensions, annuity income and mortgage protection insurance policies. A list of income that is fully disregarded is set out at CRAG 8.042 onwards. Earnings themselves are defined as 'any remuneration or profit derived from employment' (CRAG 9.001). Specific examples are given in CRAG Section 9, together with disregards. CRAG 8.074–8.075 deals with deprivation of income for the purposes of avoiding a charge.

Trust funds

6.12   CRAG Section 10 deals with trusts, which are defined as 'an arrangement for one person or a group of people ... to hold and administer capital in the form of money or property for the benefit of another person or group of people ...'. The creation of a trust is a common way in which a putative resident may deprive himself of income. Some trusts are entirely legitimate, and examples of this are those which have been set up as a result of compensation for a personal injury. In the latter case, a trustee may be the Court of Protection (or a deputy appointed for the purposes of administering the money held on behalf of P). The way in which a local authority may treat a trust is set out at CRAG 10.006, but will include establishing whether the resident is a beneficiary absolutely entitled to money from the trust, whether the trustees have a discretion to make payments, or whether the trust is as a result of a personal injury. If the value of the capital (including the value of the trust capital) is either less than £14,250 or more than £23,250, it will not be necessary to obtain a precise valuation of the trust.

6.13 There has been a good deal of debate and legal argument as to whether a local authority may have a claim as against a third party where a trust which has arisen from litigation is connected with personal injuries. For example, where the resident is in receipt of funds derived from a trust created as the result of a personal injury claim (and the tortfeasor has paid compensation as a result), it may seem anomalous from the perspective of the local authority that it is unable to seek recompense (either directly or indirectly) from the same tortfeasor even though it is the local authority who will be responsible for defraying the expense of such accommodation, through no fault of its own, but purely due to the negligence of the original wrongdoer. In *Islington LBC v University College Hospital Trust* [2005] EWCA Civ 596, [2005] 8 CCLR 337, an example of such a situation (of which there are many variations of fact involving local authorities across the UK) arose. The invidious position in which the local authority found itself was expressed thus:

> '[348D–348F] Viewing the matter as between the present parties, it indeed seems all of fair, just and reasonable that UCH rather than Islington should bear the cost of Mrs J's care. UCH has been negligent, Islington has not. It is not only unreasonable but also unfair that a tortfeasor should escape liability for part of the results of his negligence simply through the double accident of his victim being cared for by a public body rather than privately, and the victim not being able to pay for that care. And, in contrast to many claims for pure economic loss, the tortfeasor is not faced with liability for an uncertain and possibly infinite amount. All that Islington seeks from UCH is the very amount ... that UCH would have had to pay to Mrs J if Mrs J when injured had been sufficiently wealthy to be able to buy care for herself.'

The local authority accommodated a woman who had suffered a stroke as a result of the negligence of the health trust. As a result of that, she was provided with funds to purchase a house, and all the damages that were paid were under a structured settlement and held in trust. As can be seen from CRAG, this is an example of a trust which cannot be taken into account when considering resources. The local authority attempted to establish that it was a reasonably foreseeable consequence of the negligence of the Health Trust that she would need accommodation, and that the same Health Trust owed the local authority a duty of care. It was held that:

> 'It was reasonably foreseeable that Mrs J would suffer a need for care and accommodation and there was sufficient proximity for the trust to owe the local authority a duty of care. However, there were strong public policy reasons against imposing a duty of care ... the fact that the duty on the local authority to provide services was entirely separate from any issue in common law negligence and was essentially a matter for Parliament ....'

None of the claims involving the same or similar arguments made by local authorities have yet succeeded in fixing the tortfeasor with the responsibility of paying for any costs arising from the statutory obligations arising from s 21. In a slight variant on the above arguments the following issue was considered in *Peters v (1) East Midlands Strategic Health Authority (2) Halstead and (3) Nottingham City Council* [2009] EWCA Civ 145, [2009] 12 CCLR 299:

'[35] The question raised by this appeal is whether the principle also applies where the claimant has both a right of action against the wrongdoer to recover damages in respect of a head of loss and a statutory right to have the loss made good in kind by the provision of services by a local authority. In such a case, is the claimant entitled to recover damages from the wrongdoer as a matter of right, or can he do so only if, in all the circumstances of the case, it is reasonable for him not to enforce his statutory right against the public authority?'

The claimant (who lacked capacity to litigate) wanted damages to meet her wish to pay for her care needs, rather than to have those provided for as a statutory right, by the local authority. The Court held that she was entitled so to do, but in order to prevent any risk of 'double recovery' an undertaking was given to the Court by her Deputy (that is to say, the Deputy appointed within the Court of Protection to manage her property and affairs) not to seek any funding of her care via the Local Authority [64] and this was to be in addition to seeking from the Senior Judge of the Court of Protection a limit upon the authority conferred by the deputyship to the effect that he would be prohibited from seeking public funding of the claimant's care under s 21 of the National Assistance Act 1948. Finally, in *R (on the Application of Alyson Booker) v NHS Oldham and Direct Line Insurance PLC* [2010] EWHC 2593 (Admin), [2011] 14 CCLR 315 the level of damages in compensation for her personal injury included a provision for private treatment for some of her injuries. The PCT subsequently threatened to decline to provide her with treatment for those injuries upon the basis that she had elected to receive private treatment paid for by the tortfeasor. It should be noted that the settlement was also subject to similar undertakings to those given in *Peters v (1) East Midlands Strategic Health Authority (2) Halstead and (3) Nottingham City Council* (albeit the claimant had full capacity) and the purpose of the undertakings was to prevent 'double recovery'. The Court held that it was unlawful for the PCT to withhold services, it being the statutory obligation of the NHS to provide treatment free of charge, combined with the effect of s 2(4) of the Law Reform (Personal Injuries) Act 1948. This settlement was accompanied by an undertaking from her that she would use her best endeavours to secure such treatment from the NHS.

6.14 In *Crofton v National Health Service Litigation Authority* [2007] EWCA Civ 71, [2007] 10 CCLR 123, a reverse argument was raised, which was in effect that the level of damages should be *reduced* because the local authority would be obliged to shoulder the financial burden of providing care to the victim of the tort (by way of direct payments, in this instance). The appeal was allowed, and the matter remitted to the judge for further consideration. Perhaps unsurprisingly it was also held that it would be desirable if the local authority were to be joined as a party to the proceedings. Equally unsurprisingly the headnote reads:

'The court expressed dismay at the complexity and labrynthine nature of the relevant legislation and guidance, as well as (in some respects) its obscurity. Social Security law should be clear and accessible, but in this case it was neither.'

Other reported cases which consider this area are *Bell and Todd and Ryan v Liverpool Health Authority* [2001] All ER (D) 348 (Jun) and *Sowden v Lodge; Crookdale v Drury* [2004] EWCA Civ 1370, [2005] 1 WLR 2129. It should be emphasised that none of the above authorities have a direct bearing on either charging or on recovery of sums owed to a local authority.

Liability of relatives

6.15 The liability of relatives pursuant to ss 42 and 43 of NAA 1948 were repealed by the Health and Social Care Act 2008.

Students

6.16 A very small number of cases may arise in respect of students, and the detailed guidance in respect of this category of residents is set out at Section 12 of CRAG.

National Assistance (Assessment of Resources) Regulations 1992

6.17 These are made pursuant to s 22(5) of NAA 1948. They were introduced on 30 November 1992. They should be read alongside CRAG, and the relevant case-law.

Liability for charges and recovery of charges

6.18

National Assistance Act 1948

45 Recovery in cases of misrepresentation or non-disclosure

(1) If, whether fraudulently or otherwise, any person misrepresents or fails to disclose any material fact, and in consequence of the misrepresentation or failure –

   (a)   ... a local authority incur any expenditure under ... Part III of this Act, or
   (b)   any sum recoverable under this Act by ... a local authority is not recovered,

the ... authority shall be entitled to recover the amount thereof from the said person.

(2)–(4) ...

56 Legal proceedings

(1) Without prejudice to any other method of recovery, any sum due under this Act ... to a local authority (other than a sum due under an order made under section 43 of this Act) shall be recoverable summarily as a civil debt.

(2) Notwithstanding anything in any Act, proceedings for the recovery of any sum in the manner provided by the last foregoing subsection may be brought at any time within three years after the sum became due.

(3) Offences under this Act, other than offences under section 47(11) of this Act, may be prosecuted by any council which is a local authority for the purposes of the Local Authority Social Services Act 1970 and offences under section 47(11) of this Act may be prosecuted by the councils referred to in section 47(12) of this Act.

(4) ...

(5) This section shall apply to Scotland with the omission in subsection (1) thereof of the word "summarily", with the substitution for subsection (2) thereof of the following subsection –

"(2) Proceedings for the recovery of any such sum as aforesaid shall not be competent after the expiry of three years after the date when the sum became due."

and with the omission of subsection (3) thereof.

6.19 On the assumption that a local authority retains the power to recover money (for any purpose arising from sums owing under *any* part of the Act) then this may be a useful (and possibly underused) method of recovering funds. It is a simple remedy, and subject only to a 3-year limitation period.

Health and Social Services and Social Security Adjudications Act 1983

6.20 The section set out below explicitly provides that a local authority may recover charges, at its own discretion, for services provided pursuant to a list of specific statutes.

Health and Social Services and Social Security Adjudications Act 1983

17 Charges for local authority services in England and Wales

(1) Subject to subsection (3) below, an authority providing a service to which this section applies may recover such charge (if any) for it as they consider reasonable.

(2) This section applies to services provided under the following enactments –

    (a)   section 29 of the National Assistance Act 1948 (welfare arrangements for blind, deaf, dumb and crippled persons etc);

    (b)   section 45(1) of the Health Services and Public Health Act 1968 (welfare of old people);

    (c)   Schedule 20 to the National Health Service Act 2006 or Schedule 15 to the National Health Service (Wales) Act 2006 (care of mothers and young children, prevention of illness and care and after-care and home help and laundry facilities);

    (d)   section 8 of the Residential Homes Act 1980 (meals and recreation for old people); and

(e) paragraph 1 of Part II of Schedule 9 to this Act other than the provision of services for which payment may be required under section 22 or 26 of the National Assistance Act 1948;

(f) section 2 of the Carers and Disabled Children Act 2000.

(3) If a person –

(a) avails himself of a service to which this section applies, and

(b) satisfies the authority providing the service that his means are insufficient for it to be reasonably practicable for him to pay for the service the amount which he would otherwise be obliged to pay for it,

the authority shall not require him to pay more for it than it appears to them that it is reasonably practicable for him to pay.

(4) Any charge under this section may, without prejudice to any other method of recovery, be recovered summarily as a civil debt.

(5) This section has effect subject to any regulations under section 15 of the Community Care (Delayed Discharges etc) Act 2003 (power to require certain community care services and services for carers to be free of charge).

Section 29 of the National Assistance Act 1948

6.21 Thus, charges may be recovered for:

(1) giving persons instruction in their own homes or elsewhere;

(2) providing workshops;

(3) helping the same persons disposing of the produce of their work;

(4) providing them with recreational facilities; and

(5) accommodating them in a hostel.

It may also recover charges for services provided pursuant to s 2 of the Chronically Sick and Disabled Persons Act 1970. In *R v Powys CC ex pa Hambidge* [1998] 1 CCLR 458, (1998) *Times* 20 July the local authority had provided the applicant with services pursuant to s 2. It levied charges for those services. It was held that prior to the Chronically Sick and Disabled Persons Act 1970 coming into force the services referred to above were furnished by the local authority by way of s 29 of NAA 1948. The Chronically Sick and Disabled Persons Act 1970 had the effect of extending the circumstances in which there was an obligation to provide such services and that therefore a charge could be made.

6.22 In *R (on the application of Spink) v Wandsworth London Borough Council* [2005] EWCA Civ 302, [2005] 8 CCLR 272, a similar issue arose concerning whether or not it was permissible to recover charges for services provided from the parents of two disabled children. The Court considered the historical context in which the legislation had developed. It firstly considered s 21 of NAA 1948 and observed that when the Act first came into force, it applied to adults and children. The second statute that was considered was the Chronically Sick and Disabled Persons Act 1970 which in turn became subject to the charging provisions considered above under s 17. The third statute that the Court had to consider was the Children Act 1989 (s 17 – provision of services to children in need, their families and others). This in turn is subject to s 29, which permits a local authority to recoup the costs of some services provided pursuant to s 17 or 18. The persons against whom recoupment is possible are: (a) if the services are provided to a child under 16, his parents; (b) if the child has reached 16, the child himself; and (c) where it is provided to a member of the child's family, that member. The sums can be recovered by way of a civil debt. Schedule 2 of the Children Act 1989 provides that a local authority may simultaneously carry out an assessment pursuant to the Chronically Sick and Disabled Persons Act 1970. Further, the Chronically Sick and Disabled Persons Act 1970 was amended to include s 28A. Lord Phillips held as follows:

> 'This Act applies with respect to disabled children in relation to whom a local authority have functions under Part III of the Children Act 1989 as it applies in relation to persons to whom Section 29 of the National Assistance Act 1948 applies.'

It was held that (a) the scheme of the Children Act involved removing children from ... the ambit of s 29 of the 1948 Act and this was achieved by the express amendment of s 29 which restricted its application to persons over 18. It would be perverse to read s 2 of the 1970 Act, as amended by s 28A, as requiring local authorities to behave as if s 29 applied to children.

He continued:

> '... there is no difficulty in interpreting sections 2 and 28A of the 1970 Act as requiring local authorities to comply with the requirements of section 2, insofar as these apply to children, by the exercise of their functions under Part III of the Children Act, of which section 17 is particularly relevant. If follows that, where a local authority provides services in accordance with obligations imposed by section 2 of the 1970 Act by exercising functions under Section 17 of the Children Act, the provision of those services is subject to such rights to charge as are conferred by section 29 of the Children Act.'

The actual provision of services in this case related to alterations to the fabric of the family home. It was accepted by the local authority that these alterations did come within the ambit of s 17 of the Children Act 1989. It was held that:

> 'As a general proposition a local authority can reasonably expect that parents, who can afford the expense, will make any alterations to their home that are necessary for the care of their disabled children, if there is no alternative source of providing these. It is also reasonable to anticipate that some parents with means will not do so if they believe that this will result in the local authority making the alterations for them ... we agree ... that a local authority can, in circumstances such as those with which we are concerned, properly decline to be satisfied that it is necessary to

provide services to meet the needs of disabled children until it has been demonstrated that, having regard to their means, it is not reasonable to expect their parents to provide these.'

Both this case, and the statute considered below, are of significance in relation to children, and are should be cross-referred to Chapter 5, where relevant.

Section 2 of the Carers and Disabled Children Act 2000

6.23 This applies to services provided to the carers of a disabled child. Those services are not defined but may include any which the local authority see fit to provide (including physical help) and including community care services.

Charging and reasonableness

6.24 In any event, the power to charge for all of the above is predicated by significant caveats. The first is that the individual has satisfied the local authority that his means are insufficient for it to be reasonably practicable for him to pay for the services, the second is that the local authority shall not require him to pay more for it than appears reasonably practicable for him to pay.

6.25 The case-law which informs all of the above can be traced from *Avon CC v Hooper (A Minor) and Bristol and District Health Authority* [1998] 1 CCLR 366, [1997] 1 WLR 1605. The facts of the case are relatively complex, and need to be understood in order for the implications for local authorities to be clear. It also includes a judgment as to limitation periods in respect of such claims. The first defendant was a minor, who was severely handicapped as a result of the negligence of the second defendant. The child was cared for at the expense of the Claimant for a period of time. It was for this period of time that the Claimant sought to recover payment. The action in negligence between the child and the Health Authority was compromised upon the basis that the Health Authority would cover the cost of caring for the child for the rest of his life, and indemnify him and his estate against any claim that Avon CC might bring to recover the cost of care referred to above. In due course, Avon CC brought proceedings against the estate of the child for that purpose (that is to say, to recover the cost of services provided pursuant to s 29 via s 17 of the Health and Social Services and Social Security Adjudications Act 1983). It was held that:

(1) section 17 provides a power but not the obligation to charge, and that power must be exercised reasonably. If a local authority seeks to recover payment after a service has been provided, then it must be prepared to justify that decision. The reasonableness would be assessed at the time the charge was levied. There is no requirement to charge at the time the service is provided;

(2) it is for the service user to satisfy the local authority that his means are insufficient for it to be reasonably practicable for him to pay;

(3) 'means' includes all the financial resources of the individual, including an enforceable right to be indemnified as against another;

(4) the claim itself was partially statute barred because claims pursuant to s 17 are subject to s 9 of the Limitation Act 1980 (6 years).

6.26 In *R (on the Application of Stephenson) v Stockton-on-Tees BC* [2004] EWHC 2228 (Admin), [2004] 7 CCLR 459, the facts of the case involved an elderly woman who had been assessed as requiring significant home care. The daughter was already providing a large amount of this care, and the Claimant in the case had been paying her to offset the loss of earnings to her daughter. The local authority charged the Claimant for the home care services provided, and assessed them upon her income. That income was in itself assessed by calculating the amount that she was spending on her disabilities, but it refused to take into account as such an item of expenditure the money paid to her daughter. The Court considered s 17(1) and (3) and applied *Avon CC v Hooper* [1997] 1 WLR 1605 in that:

> '... there is an overriding criterion of reasonableness which governs the local authority's exercise of the power which is given by sub-section (1).'

It also referred to the guidance provided by the Secretary of State for Health *Fairer Charging Policies for Home Care and Other Non-residential Social Services*.

6.27 There was no dispute about the reasonableness of the decision to charge the Claimant, and therefore it was an issue as to whether the policy of the local authority of not taking into account the cost of care provided by a family member was rational. It was held that care provided by family members is normally voluntary, and if the Claimant chose to pay her daughter where she was prepared to provide it without payment, then the local authority were entitled to refuse to take that sum into account. The decision was appealed (*R (on the Application of Stephenson) v Stockton-on-Tees BC* [2005] EWCA Civ 960, [2005] 8 CCLR 517). The appeal was allowed, but only on the basis that the local authority had failed to exercise its discretion as to whether or not the sum could be taken into account, and had instead just relied upon its policy. The policy itself was not irrational.

6.28 A corollary to the above is *R (on the Application of Carton and Larrad) v Coventry CC; R (on the application of Morgan and Pickering) v Coventry CC* [2001] 4 CCLR 41. The Claimants were all disabled adults in receipt of day-care services. They were also all in receipt of disability living allowances. The local authority changed its policy in respect of assessing the means of the Claimants, which included assessing the amounts received by way of disability living allowance as income available for the purposes of charging for day care.

It was held that this change was irrational, unlawful and unfair. In *R v Powys CC ex p Hambidge (No 2)* [2000] 3 CCLR 231, the Claimant was also in receipt of disability living allowance. She received services from the local authority for which she paid. The local authority then changed its basis for charging (which resulted in an increase in the amount which the Claimant had to pay). An application was brought by way of judicial review, which failed at first instance (and had been based upon a failure to consult, and that the increase itself was perverse in a Wednesbury sense). An appeal was permitted upon the basis of the Disability Discrimination Act 1995. This too failed as there was no causal link between the different rates charged for different bands and the disability of the Claimant.

Section 21 of the Health and Social Services and Social Security Adjudications Act 1983

6.29 This Section has the potential to be the most useful to local authorities, although in practice its use is often hampered by poor practice and delay. The case-law which has constellated around the provision of various services under this and other statutes (and the extent to which charges can be made and/or recovered) is set out below. The law is by no means straightforward.

Health and Social Services and Social Security Adjudications Act 1983

21 Recovery of sums due to local authority where persons in residential accommodation have disposed of assets

(1) Subject to the following provisions of this section, where –

  (a) a person avails himself of Part III accommodation; and

  (b) that person knowingly and with the intention of avoiding charges for the accommodation –

    (i) has transferred any asset to which this section applies to some other person or persons not more than six months before the date on which he begins to reside in such accommodation; or

    (ii) transfers any such asset to some other person or persons while residing in the accommodation; and

  (c) either –

    (i) the consideration for the transfer is less than the value of the asset; or

    (ii) there is no consideration for the transfer,

the person or persons to whom the asset is transferred by the person availing himself of the accommodation shall be liable to pay the local authority providing the accommodation or arranging for its provision the difference between the amount assessed as due to be paid for the accommodation by the person availing himself of it and the amount which the local authority receive from him for it.

(2) This section applies to cash and any other asset which falls to be taken into account for the purpose of assessing under section 22 of the National Assistance Act 1948 the ability to pay for the accommodation of the person availing himself of it.

(3) Subsection (1) above shall have effect in relation to a transfer by a person who leaves Part III accommodation and subsequently resumes residence in such accommodation as if the period mentioned in paragraph (b)(i) were a period of six months before the date on which he resumed residence in such accommodation.

(3A) If the Secretary of State so directs, subsection (1) above shall not apply in such cases as may be specified in the direction.

(4) Where a person has transferred an asset to which this section applies to more than one person, the liability of each of the persons to whom it was transferred shall be in proportion to the benefit accruing to him from the transfer.

(5) A person's liability under this section shall not exceed the benefit accruing to him from the trade.

(6) Subject to subsection (7) below, the value of any asset to which this section applies, other than cash, which has been transferred shall be taken to be the amount of the consideration which would have been realised for it if it had been sold on the open market by a willing seller at the time of the transfer.

(7) For the purpose of calculating the value of an asset under subsection (6) above there shall be deducted from the amount of the consideration –

    (a)   the amount of any incumbrance on the asset; and
    (b)   a reasonable amount in respect of the expenses of the sale.

(8) In this Part of this Act "Part III accommodation" means accommodation provided under sections 21 to 26 of the National Assistance Act 1948, and, in the application of this Part of this Act to Scotland, means accommodation provided under the Social Work (Scotland) Act 1968 or section 25 (care and support services etc) of the Mental Health (Care and Treatment) (Scotland) Act 2003.

Deprivation of assets

6.30 An exposition of the principles behind ss 21, 22 and 24 is set out in Annex D of CRAG which also includes some illustrative case scenarios. In respect of s 21, the local authority would have to decide that there was sufficient evidence that the resident had transferred an asset *with the intention* of avoiding charges for accommodation. It may be difficult for a local authority to establish that such intention for that specific purpose existed. The transfer must have taken place no more than 6 months before admission (or 6 months before resuming admission to residential accommodation in the case of a resident who has been absent from such accommodation). Finally, there must have been either no consideration for the transfer, or the consideration must have been less than the value of the asset. There may be difficulties over the evidential basis for the latter. The 6 months before residing in Part 3 accommodation can only be applied from the date a local authority has assessed a person as needing residential care under Part 3 *and* has arranged a placement. The rule does not apply where a resident is self-funding in an independent sector home, has not been assessed, nor has had their placement arranged by a local authority. A local authority can only consider using this power if the asset disposed of is one which could have been taken into account for the purposes of assessing the charge. These assets are summarised above.

6.31   The section also permits the local authority to pursue the person to whom the asset has been transferred. The amount must be limited to the benefit accruing to him from the transfer. If the asset has been transferred to more than one person, each person can be held liable, but only up to the value of his share. The amount of liability of a third party should be the difference between the charge assessed including notional income or capital derived from the transferred asset and the amount actually being paid by the resident.

6.32   It is a moot point as to the manner in which a local authority might go about recovering any sums due (other than by way of using s 22). However, s 56 of NAA 1948 (see above) is the most direct route, or possibly via s 423 of the Insolvency Act 1986 (see *Derbyshire CC and another v Akrill and others*).

Subjective test for deprivation of assets

6.33   It is without any doubt that the test for treating a person as possessing assets of which they are alleged to deprive themselves is a subjective one (cf reg 25 of the National Assistance (Assessment of Resources) Regulations 1992, SI 1992/2977). In *R on the personal representatives of Beeson v Dorset CC and the Secretary of State for Health* [2001] EWHC Admin 986, [2002] 5 CCLR 5, the extent of this test was considered. The local authority had decided that the resident had deprived himself of capital (his house) for the purposes of decreasing the amount he might have been liable to pay for his accommodation. It then decided to use s 22 (placing a charge upon property) as a means of recovering the sums owed. The son of the resident made use of the Complaints Procedure Directions 1990 (pursuant to s 7B(3) of the Local Authority Social Services Act 1970). He gave evidence to the panel as to the circumstances in which the transfer took place (in effect that it was not related to an intention to deprive himself of assets for the purpose alleged by the local authority). The son judicially reviewed the decision of the panel (which had ruled against him). The Court considered (*inter alia*) *Yule v South Lanarkshire Council* as to the proper approach in terms of intention. The Court also relied to a certain extent upon the gloss provided on reg 25 by CRAG. The application succeeded upon the basis that:

(1)   the panel had not applied the correct test (which was a subjective one) and had not provided any comment upon the evidence of the son, or the reasons for rejecting it;

(2)   that Art 6(1) of the European Convention on Human Rights applied to the original decision to use s 22;

(3)   the panel itself was not independent (Art 6(1)) since it was comprised of councillors and chaired by the Director of Social Services and that therefore an independent complaints panel was required;

(4)   there was no breach of Art 14.

6.34 On a connected issue (the decision as to whether or not to provide long-term nursing care) the case of *Robertson v Fife* [2002] UKHL 35, [2002] 5 CCLR 543 is of significance. The facts of the case are indistinguishable from many others in that there had been a transfer by the resident of real property to family members for no consideration. When she was assessed, it was determined that she had insufficient capital to be able to pay for her accommodation. Subsequent to that first assessment, the local authority wished to move her into a nursing home (from long-term residential care). A second assessment of her means took place. This assessment resulted in a decision that the transfer had been with the intention of depriving herself of assets, and that it would not provide her with nursing care until her assets had fallen below the relevant sum. The case is in large part connected with the process of assessment itself. It was held that there was a requirement for the local authority to distinguish between a need for community care (placement in a nursing home) and the ability of the service user to pay for that care. Consequently, the local authority could not be denied such assistance simply because she could not afford to pay the local authority for those purposes. The assessment of need came first, and the local authority had erred in taking into account her resources when deciding on the question of need. The assessment of means (and the point at which notional capital can be taken into account) comes second.

6.35 In *Yule v South Lanarkshire Council* (Court of Session (Inner House) Extra Division) [2001] 4 CCLR 383, the issue was also in respect of an alleged deliberate intention to deprive by a service user. The Claimant had entered a nursing home. Prior to that she had transferred her house to a family member with no consideration. The local authority determined that she should have to pay for the costs of the nursing home, since there had been an intention to deprive (in accordance with the National Assistance (Assessment of Resources) Regulations 1992. On the appeal from an earlier decision the issue of the burden of proof was raised. It was held that s 22(3) of NAA 1948 provided that it was for the person to whom accommodation was provided to satisfy the local authority of an inability to pay. This then triggered an assessment process (including of capital) to see if the service user could pay. Analysis of the burden of proof was not appropriate. The local authority had to consider all the information made available to it, or found as a result of its assessment, in deciding whether there had been a deliberate intention to deprive. It was not a part of this that the service-user had to have been aware of the capital limit. On the facts of the case, it was reasonable for the local authority to have concluded that the service-user had indeed deprived herself of capital for the purpose of avoiding liability to pay.

6.36 In *Derbyshire CC and another v Akrill and others* [2005] EWCA Civ 308, [2005] 8 CCLR 173, the service-user had been living in a nursing home prior to his death (for which the local authority had paid most of the charges). He had arranged for a gift and leaseback of his house to some of his family members. The local authority asserted that this amounted to a deprivation of capital within the meaning of reg 25. On the facts of the case, there was an intention to deprive and the local authority were entitled to rely on s 423 of the Insolvency Act 1986 (which states that if a gift is made for the purposes of putting assets beyond the reach of someone who either is making a claim against those assets, or may do so, then the Court has the power to restore the position to that which existed prior to the transaction, or to protect the interests of the victims of the transaction). The case itself was remitted to the County Court for resolution by the County Court Judge.

22 Arrears of contributions charged on interest in land in England and Wales

(1) Subject to subsection (2) below, where a person who avails himself of Part III accommodation provided by a local authority in England, Wales or Scotland –

(a)   fails to pay any sum assessed as due to be paid by him for the accommodation; and

(b)   has a beneficial interest in land in England or Wales,

the local authority may create a charge in their favour on his interest in the land.

(2) In the case of a person who has interests in more than one parcel of land the charge under this section shall be upon his interest in such one of the parcels as the local authority may determine.

(2A) In determining whether to exercise their power under subsection (1) above and in making any determination under subsection (2) above, the local authority shall comply with any directions given to them by the Secretary of State as to the exercise of those functions.

(3) ...

(4) Subject to subsection (5) below, a charge under this section shall be in respect of any amount assessed as due to be paid which is outstanding from time to time.

(5) The charge on the interest of an equitable joint tenant in land shall be in respect of an amount not exceeding the value of the interest that he would enjoy in the land if the joint tenancy were severed but the creation of such a charge shall not sever the joint tenancy.

(6) On the death of an equitable joint tenant in land whose interest in the land is subject to a charge under this section –

(a)   if there are surviving joint tenants, their interests in the land; and

(b)   if the land vests in one person, or one person is entitled to have it vested in him, his interest in it,

shall become subject to a charge for an amount not exceeding the amount of the charge to which the interest of the deceased joint tenant was subject by virtue of subsection (5) above.

(7) A charge under this section shall be created by a declaration in writing made by the local authority.

(8) Any such charge, other than a charge on the interest of an equitable joint tenant in land, shall in the case of unregistered land be a land charge of Class B within the meaning of section 2 of the Land Charges Act 1972 and in the case of registered land be a registerable charge taking effect as a charge by way of legal mortgage.

The use of charges and cautions on land

6.37   Annex D of CRAG provides an exposition on this aspect of the Act. In particular, the Department of Health expresses the view that:

> '... because a specific power to create a charge is contained in the [1983 Act] the general powers contained in Section 111 of the Local Government Act 1972 cannot be used. Interest cannot be charged during the resident's lifetime on a debt which is covered by the creation of a charge on property under Section 22 of [the 1983 Act which] requires interest to be charged from the day after the resident's death.'

The remainder of the statute requires little explanation, simply that where there has been a failure to pay, a charge can be created on any land in which the resident has a beneficial interest, or on the proceeds of the sale of land held upon trust for sale. The local authority can select the land it prefers, if more than one is available. A charge is created by the local authority declaring in writing that the charge is being created. There may be difficulties when more than one person owns the land. If this is so then s 22(8) has the effect of preventing the registration of an interest in the proceeds of the sale of land. CRAG suggests:

> 'It would seem that registering a caution (which affords less protection than a registered charge) is the best step an authority can take in such circumstances.'

This aspect was considered in *R (on the Application of Kelly) v Hammersmith and Fulham LBC* [2004] EWHC 435 (Admin), [2004] 7 CCLR 542. The local authority had a duty to charge (under s 22 of NAA 1948) for accommodation provided to the service-user. After her death, the local authority registered a caution against dealing with her legal joint tenancy of a property. The Claimant alleged that no beneficial interest existed on the part of the deceased. She made an application by way of judicial review of the decision of the local authority not to vacate the caution. The headnote reads:

> 'The Claimant could not establish that the evidence that it was not mutually intended that the Claimant's mother should have any equitable interest was so overwhelmingly clear that the local authority's registration of a caution and refusal to vacate it was capricious, irrational and unlawful.'

Further, the Court suggested that disputes of this kind were better resolved under the provisions of s 56 of the Land Registration Act 1925.

Health and Social Care Act 2001

55 Power for local authorities to take charges on land instead of contributions

(1) Where a person ("the resident") –

   (a)   is availing himself of Part 3 accommodation provided by a local authority, or is proposing to do so, and

(b)   is liable, or would be liable, to pay for the accommodation (whether at the full standard rate determined in accordance with section 22(2) or 26(2) of the 1948 Act or at any lower rate),

the local authority may enter into a deferred payment agreement with the resident.

(2) The relevant authority may by directions require local authorities, where –

(a)   they provide or are to provide Part 3 accommodation for a person falling within subsection (1) ("the resident"), and
(b)   any conditions specified in the directions are satisfied,

to enter into a deferred payment agreement with the resident.

(3) A "deferred payment agreement" is an agreement whereby –

(a)   during the exempt period the resident will not be required to make payment to the authority of any relevant contributions in respect of periods (or parts of periods) falling within the exempt period, but
(b)   the total amount of the relevant contributions shall become payable to the authority on the day after the date on which the exempt period ends, and
(c)   the resident will grant the authority a charge in their favour in respect of any land specified in the agreement in which he has a beneficial interest (whether legal or equitable) for the purpose of securing the payment to the authority of the total amount payable to them as mentioned in paragraph (b).

(4) "The exempt period", in relation to a deferred payment agreement, is the period beginning with the time when the agreement takes effect and ending –

(a)   56 days after the date of the resident's death, or
(b)   with any earlier date which, in accordance with the agreement, the resident has specified in a notice given by him to the authority for the purposes of subsection (5)(b).

(5) The provisions of any deferred payment agreement and any such charge as is mentioned in subsection (3)(c) –

(a)   shall be determined by the authority in accordance with any directions given by the relevant authority; but
(b)   shall secure that the agreement and any such charge may be terminated by notice given to the authority by the resident on payment of the full amount which he is liable to pay as mentioned in subsection (3)(a) down to the date of the payment.

(6) Where a deferred payment agreement is in force in respect of the resident –

(a)   no interest shall accrue at any time on or before the date on which the exempt period ends in respect of any sum which he is liable to pay as mentioned in subsection (3)(a); but
(b)   as from the day after that date, any such sum shall bear interest at such reasonable rate as the relevant authority may direct or, if no such directions are given, as the authority may determine;

and accordingly any charge granted in pursuance of subsection (3)(c) shall secure payment to the authority of any interest falling due by virtue of paragraph (b) above.

(7) Any reference in this section to relevant contributions is a reference to so much of the payments which the resident is liable to pay to an authority for Part 3 accommodation (including any payments which are additional payments for the purpose of section 54) as may be specified, or determined in accordance with, regulations made for the purposes of this subsection.

(8) Any directions given by the relevant authority under this section shall be given to local authorities generally.

Deferred payments and charges

6.38   The information on the use of charges generally is set out above. The purpose and operation of this part of the Act is best understood by reference to Circular No LAC (2002) 11, the relevant parts of which are set out below. In essence, it permits an arrangement whereby instead of contributions being made, those payments may be deferred by way of a charge upon real property owned by the resident. The Circular states:

'... [it] allows councils to agree and operate deferred payments whereby they take legal charges on a persons main or only home in which they have a beneficial interest instead of contributions towards the cost of a person's residential accommodation. The aim is to allow people with property, but without income and other assets sufficient to meet their full assessed contribution, to have a legal charge placed on their property to meet any shortfall. Hence people will be able to keep their homes on admission to residential care and for the duration of the deferred payments agreement. The operation of deferred payments was fully described in LAC (2001) 25. Councils should promote the option of deferred payments when they become aware of residents whose property is taken into account by the financial assessment ... Councils should be prepared to put residents in contact with persons who can offer independent advice when it comes to completing the necessary paperwork for requesting and agreeing to deferred payments agreements. A lack of capacity does not debar residents from deferred payments. Where residents lack capacity, deferred payments can still be signed by those who hold a registered enduring power of attorney or where the resident's affairs are administered by the Court of Protection.'

The latter part will now be qualified by the operation of the Mental Capacity Act 2005 (see Chapter 2). The most relevant parts of LAC (2001) 25 are paras 4 and 8–17 inclusive. It also deals with resident and third party top-ups. Yet further information on related topics can be found in Circular No LAC (2001) 29.

Choice of accommodation and third party top-ups

6.39   Circular No LAC (2004) 20 is reproduced in part in Chapter 4. The remaining relevant sections are reproduced below for the sake of completeness, and provide a valuable and lucid commentary upon the financial implications of implementing the National Assistance 1948 (Choice of Accommodation) Directions 1992.

CIRCULAR NO LAC (2004) (20) – NATIONAL ASSISTANCE ACT 1948 (CHOICE OF ACCOMMODATION) DIRECTIONS 1992

3. More expensive accommodation

3.1 The guidance set out in paragraphs 3.2 to 3.5.11, applies only where a resident explicitly chooses to enter accommodation other than that which the council offers them, and where that preferred accommodation is more expensive than the council would usually expect to pay.

3.2 In certain circumstances, councils can make placements in more expensive accommodation than they would usually expect to pay for, provided a resident or a third party is able and willing to make up the difference (to 'top up'). Residents that are subject to the 12 week property disregard or have agreed a deferred payments agreement with the council may make top-ups from specified resources on their own behalf. These are the only situations where the resident may top up. The most common arrangement is that a third party is providing the top-up. A third party in this case might be a relative, a friend, or any other source. For liable relatives see paragraph 3.5.10.

3.3 When setting its usual cost(s) a council should be able to demonstrate that this cost is sufficient to allow it to meet assessed care needs and to provide residents with the level of care services that they could reasonably expect to receive if the possibility of resident and third party contributions did not exist.

3.4 Councils should not seek resident or third party contributions in cases where the council itself decides to offer someone a place in more expensive accommodation in order to meet assessed needs, or for other reasons. Where there are no placements at the council's usual rate, councils should not leave individuals to make their own arrangements having determined that they need to enter residential accommodation and do not have care and attention otherwise available to them. In these instances, councils should make suitable alternative arrangements and seek no contribution from the individual other than their contribution as assessed under the National Assistance (Assessment of Resources) Regulations 1992. Councils must never encourage or otherwise imply that care home providers can or should seek further contributions from individuals in order to meet assessed needs.

3.5 This paragraph deals with considerations that apply where either residents or third parties are making further contributions to costs over and above the resident's assessed contribution under the National Assistance (Assessment of Resources) Regulations 1992.

(a) Responsibility for costs of accommodation

3.5.1 When making arrangements for residential care for an individual under the National Assistance Act 1948, a council is responsible for the full cost of that accommodation. Therefore, where a council places someone in more expensive accommodation, it must contract to pay the accommodation's fees in full. The resident's or the third party's contribution will be treated as part of the resident's income for charging purposes and the council will be able to recover it in that way. However, under a deferred payments agreement, where the resident is topping up against the value of their home, their top-up contribution is added to their deferred contribution.

3.5.2 Councils will be aware that under section 26(3A) of the National Assistance Act 1948 (as inserted by the NHS and Community Care Act 1990), it is open to them to agree with both the resident and the person in charge of their accommodation that, instead of paying a contribution to the council, the resident may pay the same amount direct to the accommodation, with the council paying the difference. In such a case, the third party would also pay the accommodation direct on behalf of the resident. However, it should be noted that even where there is such an agreement for the resident to make payments direct to the accommodation, the council continues to be liable to pay the full costs of the accommodation should either the resident or relative fail to pay the required amount.

3.5.3 Where top-ups are required from a resident or third party, the resident will therefore need to demonstrate that either they or the third party is able and willing to pay the difference between the council's usual rate and the accommodation's actual fees.

3.5.4 In order to safeguard both residents and councils from entering into top-up arrangements that are likely to fail, the resident or the third party must reasonably be expected to be able to continue to make top-up payments for the duration of the arrangements. Councils should, therefore, assure themselves that residents or third parties will have the resources to continue to make the required top-up payments. Councils should seek similar assurances when residents top-up against the value of their home when the home is subject to a deferred payments agreement. When the home is eventually sold, it should be possible for the resident or their estate to pay back the deferred contribution including the resident top-ups.

(b) The amount of the resident or third party top-up

3.5.5 The amount of resident or third party top-up payments should be the difference between the actual fee for the accommodation and the amount that otherwise the council would usually have expected to pay for someone with the individual's assessed needs. In determining the precise amounts in individual cases, the council will take account of the guidance give in paragraphs 2.5.4 to 2.5.8 above.

3.5.6 The amount of the resident or third party top-up should be calculated on gross costs; that is, the difference between the preferred accommodation's fees and the fees that a council would usually expect to pay. The fact that a resident might not have been able to meet the full cost of the accommodation that the council would otherwise have arranged does not affect their ability to benefit from the additional top-up payments.

(c) Price increases

3.5.7 Arrangements between the council, resident and third party will need to be reviewed from time to time to take account of changes to accommodation fees. There will also be changes to the council's usual cost, which should be reasonable and set in accordance with paragraphs 2.5.4 to 2.5.8. However, fees and usual costs may not change at the same rate, and residents and third parties should be told that there cannot be a guarantee that any increases in the accommodation's fees will automatically be shared evenly between the council and/or the resident or third party, should the particular accommodation's fees rise more quickly than the costs the council would usually expect to pay for similar individuals. A council may find it useful to agree with the resident (or third party) that the resident's (or third party's) contribution will be reviewed on a regular basis on the understanding that clear explanations for proposed increases are given. It is also important that individuals know when, and in what circumstances, the fees for their accommodation will be reviewed.

(d) Responsibilities of residents and third parties

3.5.8 Councils should make clear to residents and third parties, in writing, the basis on which arrangements are to be made when they seek to exercise their right to more expensive preferred accommodation. It should be clear from the outset to the resident, third party and person providing the accommodation that:

- failure to keep up top-up payments may result in the resident having to move to other accommodation unless, after an assessment of need, it is shown that assessed needs can only be met in the current accommodation. In these circumstances, councils should make up the cost difference between the resident's assessed contribution and the accommodation's fees. Where a resident's top-ups are being made against the value of property subject to a deferred payments agreement, a council will have assured itself from the outset that top-up payments are viable and recoverable when the home is sold;
- an increase in the resident's income will not necessarily lessen the need for a top-up contribution, since the resident's own income will be subject to means testing by the council in the normal way;
- a rise in the accommodation's fees will not automatically be shared equally between council, resident (if making a top-up), and third party.

(e) Suitability and Conditions

3.5.9 With reference to paragraphs 2.5.1 to 2.5.3 and 2.5.16 to 2.5.17 above, the criteria of suitability and willingness to provide on the basis of normal conditions should be applied in the same way as for other preferred accommodation. An exception to this is that it would be reasonable to expect providers entering this kind of arrangement to agree to do so on the basis that the council has the right, subject to notice, to terminate the contract should the resident's or third party's top-up payments cease to be adequate.

Direct payments

6.40   The original act was the Community Care (Direct Payments) Act 1996 which has been replaced by the statute set out below, together with s 17A of the Children Act 1989. Generally speaking the aim of the original legislation was to confer greater autonomy on those who were in need of the relevant services, and also to permit a local authority to devolve and reduce its own involvement in the provision of such services. Further insight into its purpose and problems in its implementation can be found in *Modernising Adult Social Care – What's Working* (Department of Health, June 2007). For example, one area of difficulty was with those who may have mental health difficulties 'because of the episodic nature of their needs and the difficulty of using direct payments at times of crisis (the tendency was for one-off payments rather than continuing access to DP)' (para 70). The other problematic area identified was a lack of flexibility and imagination in terms of enabling access to appropriate services:

> '71 There are other significant barriers to change. These include attitudes to risk in the assessment process, and the use of "block contracts" that limit options for flexibility in service design, management and delivery ...
>
> 73 Individual budgets bring together the multiple funding streams that (can) support a person. They involve a shift towards self-assessment, and bring freedoms to use funding in any (legal) way that meets personal objectives. They have the potential to deliver much greater elements of service user control and choice, and open the possibility of greater social inclusion and well-being. The foreword to the Guidance states:
>
>> "The purpose of direct payments is to give recipients control over their own life by providing an alternative to social care services provided by a local council. A financial payment gives the person flexibility to look beyond 'off the peg' service solutions ... to meet their assessed needs".'

6.41   The primary legislation is supported by the Community Care, Services for Carers and Children's Services (Direct Payments) (England) Regulations 2009, SI 2009/1887 as amended by SI 2010/2246 (the Regulations). There are separate regulations for Wales (the Community Care, Services for Carers and Children's Services (Direct Payments) (Wales) Regulations 2011, SI 2011/831 (W 125)). The Department of Health has also published *Guidance on direct payments for community care, services for carers and children's services England 2009* (the Guidance). This has been issued pursuant to s 7 of the Local Authority Social Services Act 1970. The Chartered Institute of Public Finance and Accounting (CIPFA) has also provided guidance of what direct payments might reasonably be used to purchase (*Direct Payments and Individual Budgets: Managing the Finances* (2007)). The same guidance should be followed by local authorities in order that 'public funds are spent to produce the intended outcome' (para 230).

6.42   The foreword to the Guidance makes some reference to 'personal budgets' (see **6.66–6.70** below):

'The transformation of adult social services initiated by **Putting People First** builds on and reinforces these principles of choice and control. Central to the transformation programme is the concept of personal budgets ... direct payments and personal budgets should not be seen as separate mechanisms for delivering social care services ....'

There have been substantial amendments to the statute and Regulations (via amendments incorporated through the Health and Social Care Act 2008) the most significant of which effect direct payments to those who lack capacity to consent to the receipt of direct payments.

Recipients of direct payments

6.43 All of the following paragraphs are a summary of some of the Guidance. The relevant source paragraph is set in brackets after the summary or quotation. Direct payments must be made to all individuals who are eligible to receive them and who want them. There are a very limited number of individuals to whom payments must not be made. If the recipient agrees, there can be a mixed package of services provided by or arranged by the local authority and services paid for via direct payments. There is no obligation upon someone to receive direct payments.

6.44 In terms of managing the direct payments a local authority should consider what support can be offered to those who are in receipt of direct payments. This may include the provision of advocacy support. Direct payments may be made to a nominee, as long as the person who is eligible to receive the payments agrees to this.

Lack of capacity

6.45 For those who lack capacity, then subject to certain conditions, 'direct payments may now be made to another person on behalf of the person needing support' (para 20). This is termed 'suitable person' who is described as:

'25 ... a person appointed to receive and manage direct payments on behalf of someone who lacks capacity to consent to the making of direct payments. The suitable person will often, but not always, have been given a lasting power of attorney or have been appointed by the Court of Protection as a deputy under the Mental Capacity Act 2005. Usually the suitable person will be a family member or friend who may previously have been involved in the care of the person eligible for services.'

If payments are to be made for someone who lacks capacity, then the consent must be obtained from the 'suitable person' (para 186) and in addition if there is a surrogate of the person lacking capacity, then the consent of that surrogate must be obtained. A surrogate of a person is a donee of a lasting power of attorney created by that person or a deputy appointed by the Court of Protection 'who has been given powers relating to decisions about securing community care services to meet that person's needs' (paras 186 and 190). The process of selecting a suitable person must follow that set out in the Regulations and the Guidance suggests the most suitable candidates (paras 189–192) which effectively confines itself to either family or friends and/or those with a lasting power of attorney or a deputy appointed by the Court of Protection. The entire procedure is described in paras 189–198. The procedure for discontinuing payments in the case of those who lack capacity is contained in paras 257 and 258. An assessment of capacity would have to be in accordance with the Mental Capacity Act 2005, and in particular, be an assessment of capacity in respect of the specific issue of managing direct payments (paras 55–62 and see Chapter 2). The Guidance correctly stresses that:

> '66 Councils should not confuse whether somebody has the capability to manage direct payments with whether they have the mental capacity..to consent to such payments. It does not necessarily follow that because a person has capacity to consent they are also capable of managing direct payments.'

Termination of payments to those who lack capacity is dealt with at **6.59** below.

6.46 If someone consents, the local authority are under a positive duty to make direct payments, if it is satisfied that the person's needs for services can be met using a direct payment. A local authority is not under a duty to make a payment if it does not appear to it that the person is capable of managing the payment. Conditions can be attached to the payments, but these must be reasonable, since the overall aim of direct payments is to increase choice and control on the part of the recipient. Some of the excluded categories under the previousn system have been removed, for example, those who were detained under parts of the Mental Health Act 1983 and now 'local authorities will … be able to make direct payments to people who are subject to such mental health legislation, thereby enabling people previously excluded to benefit from greater choice and control over their support' [207]. In *R (on the application of H) v A City Council* [2011] EWCA Civ 403, [2011] 14 CCLR 381 an attempt by a council to impose conditions upon a recipient of direct payments (so that they would have to be made through a third party and a managed account) was held to be unlawful.

Use of direct payments

6.47 Direct payments cannot be used to buy anything for which the local authority would not be responsible (eg NHS provision), and they are not a substitute for disabled facilities grants (para 108). They cannot be used to pay for long term residential accommodation (para 101), but they can be used to buy non-residential care services for those who live in residential accommodation (para 106). However, where a person is entering residential accommodation temporarily then:

> '119b the council can determine this payment irrespective of the … means so an assessment of ability to pay a charge is not required. In such cases, where councils nonetheless decided to undertake a financial assessment, it should be in

accordance with the National Assistance (Assessment of Resources) Regulations 1992 which is supported by CRAG.'

They can be used to buy equipment or make adaptations that otherwise would have been provided by the council (para 107). Further prohibitions on the making of direct payments are set out at **6.71**.

Amount of direct payments

6.48 In calculating the amount of direct payments, the local authority will have to follow the Guidance as set out in paras 111–121 (which includes assessment of what financial contribution may have to be made to the services which are to be purchased). However, the basic premise is that:

'111 it must be equivalent to the council's reasonable cost of securing the provision of the service concerned, subject to any contribution from the recipient. This means that the direct payments should be sufficient to enable the recipient lawfully to secure a service of a standard that the council considers is reasonable to fulfil the needs for the service to which the payments relate. There is no limit on the maximum or minimum amount of direct payment either in the amount of care it is intended to purchase or on the value of the direct payment.'

6.49 There is no obligation upon the local authority to pay for the service users preferred option, if the cost exceeds the local authority's estimate of the reasonable cost of securing it *and* the service can be secured in a more cost effective manner, but still to the required standard (para 115). This is no more than a re-statement of the law on the deployment of local authority resources in the face of competing demands. It should also be noted that the local authority would also have to take into account the user's own assessed contribution to the cost of such provision in considering whether or not the cost is reasonable.

Charging/contribution to cost of service

6.50 Regulations 9 and 10 provides that the local authority shall determine, having regard to the recipients means, what amount, if any, it is reasonably practicable to pay towards the cost. The guidance as to charging those who have been assessed as needing community care services is contained in *Fairer Charging Policies for Home Care and Other Non-residential Social Services Guidance for Councils with Social Services Responsibilities* (Department of Health, September 2003). This is also issued pursuant to s 7 of the Local Authority Social Services Act 1970. In many ways this is the equivalent to CRAG for non-residential services and includes the following; services for which charges may or may not be made; disability related benefits; savings and capital; income from partners; setting the level of charges; issues in designing charging policies; carers; direct payments; Health Act 1999 partnerships.

6.51 The manner in which a recipient might make a contribution to the cost of care is summarised thus:

'[120] In considering whether to ask recipients of direct payments to make a financial contribution to the cost of their care package, the Regulations provide that the Council shall determine, having regard to the beneficiary's means, what amount or amounts (if any) it is reasonably practicable for the beneficiary to contribute towards their social care support. For people assessed as needing community care services or carer services that councils provide themselves, the relevant guidance is *Fairer Charging Policies for Home Care and other non-residential service.*'
[see **6.50** above].

It then states:

'[120] There are two ways in which an individual may make a financial contribution to the cost of their care. The council may make direct payments that are equivalent to its estimate of the reasonable costs of the service and subsequently seek reimbursement of the reasonable cost of the service (gross payment). Alternatively, the council may deduct from its estimate the assessed contribution before the payments are made and make direct payments net of the amount that the individual is expected to make (net payment). Councils should take into account the views of users when producing their policy on charging, allowing sufficient flexibility to respond to individual circumstances.'

Employment of close relatives

6.52 Unless the council is satisfied that it is necessary to meet a person's needs, a 'council may not allow people to use direct payments to secure services from: a spouse (husband or wife); a civil partner; the other member of the unmarried or same-sex couple of which they are a part; or a close relative with whom they live, or the spouse or partner of that close relative' [135]. The avowed purpose of this qualified prohibition is not stated in the Guidance, but it states that 'the restriction applies where the relationship between the two people is primarily personal rather than contractual, for example if the people living together would be living together in any event' [136]. If a payment is made to a member of the family, then it is counted as earnings (*Casewell v Secretary of State for the Home Department* [2008] EWCA Civ 524, [2008] 11 CCLR 684).

Disabled parents with parental responsibility for a child

6.53 The Guidance is worth citing in full here:

'160 Disabled people who are parents could be assessed as needing services under both community care legislation and/or the 1989 Act to assist them in their parenting role. This means that direct payments can be used to meet the social care needs of them, their children or their family that arise from their disability. It is important that the needs of the disabled person are looked at holistically, bearing in mind that specific duties may arise under particular legislation. In the interest of the family and to avoid duplication, councils should ensure that the assessment process is streamlined and co-ordinated between adult and children's services and other relevant departments.'

As has been observed elsewhere in this book, the need for liaison between adult social services and children's social services is honoured more often in its breach rather than its observance.

Seeking repayment of direct payments

6.54 If a local authority is satisfied that the money has not been used to secure the provision of the service to which it relates, it may require re-payment of all or some of it (para 244). If it decides to require repayment from someone who is also in receipt of payments from the Independent Living Funds (ILF), it should inform the ILF. Requirements for repayments should not be used for punishment of honest mistakes, or where the recipient has been the victim of fraud (para 245).

Stopping direct payments

6.55 The recipient may decide that he no longer wishes to receive direct payments (para 248). The local authority may decide that the use of the payments no longer provides for the needs of the user (para 249). The local authority may decide that the conditions attached to payments are not being met (para 252). It should be noted that the cessation of direct payments does not mean that the need for a service ceases – the local authority will still be under an obligation to provide for these to be provided (unless there has been a re-assessment of needs) (para 260).

Community Care, Services For Carers And Children's Services (Direct Payments) (England) Regulations 2009, SI 2009/1887

1 Citation, commencement, interpretation and application

(1) These Regulations may be cited as the Community Care, Services for Carers and Children's Services (Direct Payments) (England) Regulations 2009 and shall come into force on 9th November 2009.

(2) In these Regulations –

"the 1983 Act" means the Mental Health Act 1983;
"the 1989 Act" means the Children Act 1989;
"the 1990 Act" means the National Health Service and Community Care Act 1990;
"the 2001 Act" means the Health and Social Care Act 2001;
"direct payment" has the meaning given in regulation 7 or 8;
"prescribed person' means a person falling within the description prescribed by regulation 2 or 4 who falls within section 57(2) of the 2001 Act or section 17A(2) of the 1989 Act;
"P" means a person falling within the description prescribed by regulation 3 who falls within subsection (2)(a) of section 57 of the 2001 Act and subsection (5A) of that section or is reasonably believed by the responsible authority to fall within that subsection;
"relevant service" means –

(a)   in the case of direct payments under section 57(1) of the 2001 Act or section 17A(1) of the 1989 Act –

    (i)   a community care service within the meaning of section 46 of the 1990 Act,

    (ii)   a service under section 2 of the Carers and Disabled Children Act 2000 (services for carers), or

    (iii) a service which the responsible authority may provide in exercise of functions under section 17 of the 1989 Act (provision of services for children in need, their families and others); or

(b)   in the case of direct payments under section 57(1A) of the 2001 Act, a community care service within the meaning of section 46 of the 1990 Act;

"S" is the suitable person referred to in regulation 8(1).

(3) These Regulations apply in relation to England.

2 Prescribed descriptions of persons under section 57(1) of the 2001 Act – community care services and services for carers

For the purposes of section 57(1) of the 2001 Act a person is of a prescribed description if they are –

(a)   a person who appears to the responsible authority to be capable of managing a direct payment by themselves or with such assistance as may be available to them;

(b)   not a person who falls, or is reasonably believed by the responsible authority to fall, within section 57(5A) of the 2001 Act; and

(c)   not a person to whom Schedule 1 applies.

3 Prescribed descriptions of persons under section 57(1A) of the 2001 Act–community care services

For the purposes of section 57(1A) of the 2001 Act a person is of a prescribed description if they are not a person to whom Schedule 1 applies.

4 Prescribed descriptions of persons under section 17A(1) of the 1989 Act–children's services

For the purposes of section 17A(1) of the 1989 Act a person is of a prescribed description if they are –

(a)   a person who appears to the responsible authority to be capable of managing a direct payment by themselves or with such assistance as may be available to them; and

(b)   not a person to whom Schedule 1 applies.

5 Persons prescribed as representatives

For the purposes of section 57(5B) of the 2001 Act, a person is prescribed as a representative in relation to another person if they are –

(a)   a deputy appointed for that other person by the Court of Protection under section 16(2)(b) of the Mental Capacity Act 2005; or

(b)   a donee of a lasting power of attorney within the meaning of section 9 of the Mental Capacity Act 2005 created by that other person.

6 Prescribed powers for surrogates

For the purposes of section 57(5C) of the 2001 Act (which provides that a "surrogate", in relation to a person, means a person listed in that provision whose powers consist of or include such powers as may be prescribed), the prescribed powers are powers relating to decisions about securing the provision of a community care service within the meaning of section 46 of the 1990 Act.

7 Direct payments under section 57(1) of the 2001 Act or section 17A(1) of the 1989 Act

(1) If the conditions in paragraph (2) are satisfied, a responsible authority –

(a)   may, with that person's consent, make in respect of a prescribed person such payments under section 57(1) of the 2001 Act or section 17A(1) of the 1989 Act as are determined in accordance with regulation 9 ("direct payments") in respect of the prescribed person securing the provision of a relevant service which the person is obliged to receive as a result of an obligation imposed under an enactment mentioned in Schedule 2;

(b)   may, with that person's consent, make in respect of a prescribed person in respect of whom there is in force a condition imposed in accordance with section 42(2) or 73(4) (including such a condition which has been varied in accordance with section 73(5) or 75(3)) of the 1983 Act or who is a patient who has been conditionally discharged under section 193(7) of the Mental Health (Care and Treatment) (Scotland) Act 2003, direct payments in respect of the prescribed person securing the provision of a relevant service; and

(c)   in all other cases must, with that person's consent, make in respect of a prescribed person direct payments in respect of the prescribed person securing the provision of a relevant service.

(2) The conditions referred to in paragraph (1) are that the responsible authority are satisfied –

(a)   that the person's need for the relevant service can be met by securing the provision of it by means of a direct payment; and

(b)   in the case of a relevant service as defined in paragraph (a)(iii) of the definition of that term in regulation 1(2), that the welfare of the child in respect of whom the service is needed will be safeguarded and promoted by securing the provision of it by means of a direct payment.

8 Direct payments under section 57(1A) of the 2001 Act

(1) The responsible authority must take the steps in paragraph (2) before they may be satisfied that it is appropriate for a payment under section 57(1A) of the 2001 Act to be made to a suitable person ("S") in respect of S securing the provision of a relevant service for a person falling within the description prescribed by regulation 3 ("P").

(2) The steps referred to in paragraph (1) are that the responsible authority must –

(a)   so far as is reasonably practicable and appropriate, consult and take into account the views of –

> (i)   anyone named by P as someone to be consulted on the matter of whether a payment should be made to S for the purpose of securing provision for P of a relevant service or on matters of that kind,
>
> (ii)   anyone engaged in caring for P or interested in P's welfare, and
>
> (iii)   any representative or surrogate of P;

(b)   so far as is reasonably ascertainable, consider –

> (i)   P's past and present wishes and feelings (and, in particular, any relevant written statement made by P when P had capacity, within the meaning of the Mental Capacity Act 2005, to consent to the making of direct payments),
>
> (ii)   the beliefs and values that would be likely to influence P's decision if P had such capacity, and
>
> (iii)   the other factors that P would be likely to consider if P were able to do so;

(c)   obtain a criminal record certificate issued under section 113B of the Police Act 1997 –

> (i)   in respect of S where S is an individual and neither a person mentioned in paragraph (3) nor a friend of P who is involved in the provision of care for P, and
>
> (ii)   where S is a body corporate or an unincorporated body of persons, in respect of the individual who will, on behalf of that body, have overall responsibility for the day-to-day management of P's direct payments.

(3) The persons referred to in paragraph (2)(c)(i) are –

(a)   the spouse or civil partner of P;

(b)   a person who lives with P as if their spouse or civil partner;

(c)   a person who is P's –

> (i)   parent or parent-in-law,
>
> (ii)   son or daughter,
>
> (iii)   son-in-law or daughter-in-law,
>
> (iv)   stepson or stepdaughter,
>
> (v)   brother or sister,
>
> (vi)   aunt or uncle, or
>
> (vii)   grandparent;

(d)   the spouse or civil partner of any person specified in sub-paragraph (c); and

(e)   a person who lives with any person specified in sub-paragraph (c) as if that person's spouse or civil partner.

(4) Where, having taken the steps in paragraph (2), the responsible authority are satisfied of the matters listed in paragraph (5), the responsible authority –

(a)   may, with the requisite consent, make such payments under section 57(1A) of the 2001 Act as are determined in accordance with regulation 10 ("direct payments") to S in respect of S securing the provision of a relevant service for P which P is obliged to receive as a result of an obligation imposed under an enactment mentioned in Schedule 2;

(b)   in a case where there is in force, in respect of P, a condition imposed in accordance with section 42(2) or 73(4) (including such a condition which has been varied in accordance with section 73(5) or 75(3)) of the 1983

Act or in a case where P is a patient who has been conditionally discharged under section 193(7) of the Mental Health (Care and Treatment) (Scotland) Act 2003, may, with the requisite consent, make direct payments to S in respect of S securing the provision of a relevant service for P; and

(c)   in all other cases must, with the requisite consent, make direct payments to S in respect of S securing the provision of a relevant service for P.

(5) The matters referred to in paragraph (4) are that –

(a)   P's need for the relevant service can be met by securing the provision of it by means of a direct payment;

(b)   S –

    (i)   will act in the best interests, within the meaning of the Mental Capacity Act 2005, of P when securing the provision of services in respect of which the direct payment is made, and

    (ii)   appears to be capable of managing a direct payment by themselves or with such assistance as may be available to them, and

(c)   in all the circumstances it is appropriate for a direct payment to be made to S.

9 Amount and payment of direct payments under section 57(1) of the 2001 Act or section 17A(1) of the 1989 Act

(1) Subject to paragraphs (3) and (4), a direct payment under section 57(1) of the 2001 Act or section 17A(1) of the 1989 Act shall be made as a gross payment unless the responsible authority decide it shall be made as a net payment.

(2) Subject to paragraph (6), for the purpose of making the payment referred to in paragraph (1), the responsible authority shall determine, having regard to the prescribed person's means, what amount or amounts (if any) it is reasonably practicable for the prescribed person to pay towards securing the provision of the relevant service (whether by way of reimbursement as mentioned in section 57(4) of the 2001 Act or by way of a contribution as mentioned in section 57(5) of that Act).

(3) Where the relevant service is one which, apart from these Regulations, would be provided under section 117 of the 1983 Act (after-care) –

(a)   the payment shall be made at the rate mentioned in subsection (4)(a) of section 57 of the 2001 Act; and

(b)   subsection (4)(b) of that section shall not apply.

(4) Where a direct payment is made to a person falling within section 17A(5) of the 1989 Act –

(a)   the payment shall be made at the rate mentioned in subsection (4)(a) of section 57 of the 2001 Act; and

(b)   subsection (4)(b) of that section shall not apply.

(5) The payment referred to in paragraph (1) may be made to –

(a)   the prescribed person; or

(b)   a person nominated by the prescribed person to receive the payment on their behalf.

(6) For the purpose of making a direct payment under section 57(1) of the 2001 Act in respect of the prescribed person securing the provision of residential accommodation, the responsible authority may make the determination referred to in paragraph (2) irrespective of the prescribed person's means.

10 Amount and payment of direct payments under section 57(1A) of the 2001 Act

(1) A direct payment under section 57(1A) of the 2001 Act shall be made to S as a gross payment unless the responsible authority decide it shall be made as a net payment.

(2) Subject to paragraph (4), for the purpose of making the payment referred to in paragraph (1), the responsible authority shall determine, having regard to P's means, what amount or amounts (if any) it is reasonably practicable for P to pay towards securing the provision of the relevant service (whether by way of reimbursement as mentioned in section 57(4) of the 2001 Act or by way of a contribution as mentioned in section 57(5) of that Act).

(3) Where the relevant service is one which, apart from these Regulations, would be provided under section 117 of the 1983 Act (after-care) –

   (a)   the payment shall be made at the rate mentioned in subsection (4)(a) of section 57 of the 2001 Act; and
   (b)   subsection (4)(b) of that section shall not apply.

(4) For the purpose of making the payment referred to in paragraph (1) in respect of the prescribed person securing the provision of residential accommodation, the responsible authority, in making the determination referred to in paragraph (2), may do so irrespective of P's means.

11 Conditions in respect of direct payments under section 57(1) of the 2001 Act or section 17A(1) of the 1989 Act

(1) A direct payment under section 57(1) of the 2001 Act or section 17A(1) of the 1989 Act shall be subject to the condition that the service in respect of which it is made shall not be secured from a person mentioned in paragraph (2) unless the responsible authority are satisfied that securing the service from such a person is necessary –

   (a)   in the case of a relevant service as defined in paragraph (a)(i) or (ii) of the definition of that term in regulation 1(2), to meet satisfactorily the prescribed person's need for that service; or
   (b)   in the case of a relevant service as defined in paragraph (a)(iii) of the definition of that term in regulation 1(2), for promoting the welfare of the child in respect of whom the service is needed.

(2) The persons referred to in paragraph (1) are –

   (a)   the spouse or civil partner of the prescribed person;
   (b)   a person who lives with the prescribed person as if their spouse or civil partner;
   (c)   a person living in the same household as the prescribed person who is the prescribed person's –
         (i)   parent or parent-in-law,
         (ii)   son or daughter,
         (iii) son-in-law or daughter-in-law,

  (iv)   stepson or stepdaughter,
  (v)   brother or sister,
  (vi)   aunt or uncle, or
  (vii) grandparent;
(d)   the spouse or civil partner of any person specified in sub-paragraph (c) who lives in the same household as the prescribed person; and
(e)   a person who lives with any person specified in sub-paragraph (c) as if that person's spouse or civil partner.

(3) Paragraphs (2)(c)(ii) and (iii) do not apply in the case of a person mentioned in section 17A(2)(c) of the 1989 Act.

(4) A responsible authority may make a direct payment under section 57(1) of the 2001 Act or section 17A(1) of the 1989 Act subject to such other conditions (if any) as they think fit.

(5) The conditions referred to in paragraph (4) may, in particular, require that the payee –

(a)   shall not secure the relevant service from a particular person; and
(b)   shall provide such information to the responsible authority as the authority consider necessary in connection with the direct payment.

12 Conditions in respect of direct payments under section 57(1A) of the 2001 Act

(1) A direct payment under section 57(1A) of the 2001 Act shall be subject to the conditions in paragraph (2).

(2) The conditions referred to in paragraph (1) are that –

(a)   the service in respect of which the direct payment is made shall not be secured from a person mentioned in paragraph (3) unless the responsible authority are satisfied that securing the service from such a person is necessary to meet satisfactorily P's need for that service; and
(b)   S shall –
  (i)   act in the best interests, within the meaning of the Mental Capacity Act 2005, of P when securing the provision of services in respect of which the direct payment is made,
  (ii)   provide such information to the responsible authority as that authority consider necessary in connection with the direct payment,
  (iii) if S is an individual mentioned in regulation 8(2)(c)(i) or a body corporate or an unincorporated body of persons, obtain a criminal record certificate issued under section 113B of the Police Act 1997, or obtain verification that a satisfactory certificate under that Act has been obtained, in respect of any person from whom a service in respect of which a direct payment is made is secured,
  (iv)   notify the responsible authority if S reasonably believes that P no longer falls within section 57(5A) of the 2001 Act, and
  (v)   use the direct payment for securing the provision for P of the services for which the payment was made.

(3) The persons referred to in paragraph (2) are –

(a)   the spouse or civil partner of P;
(b)   a person who lives with P as if their spouse or civil partner;

    (c)   a person living in the same household as P who is P's –
        (i)   parent or parent-in-law,
        (ii)   son or daughter,
        (iii)   son-in-law or daughter-in-law,
        (iv)   stepson or stepdaughter,
        (v)   brother or sister,
        (vi)   aunt or uncle, or
        (vii) grandparent;
    (d)   the spouse or civil partner of any person specified in sub-paragraph (c) who lives in the same household as P; and
    (e)   a person who lives with any person specified in sub-paragraph (c) as if that person's spouse or civil partner.

(4) A responsible authority may make a direct payment under section 57(1A) of the 2001 Act subject to such other conditions (if any) as they think fit.

13 Maximum periods of residential accommodation which may be secured by means of a direct payment

(1) Subject to paragraph (2), a direct payment may not be made in respect of a person who falls within regulation 2 or 3 for the provision to that person of residential accommodation for a period in excess of 4 consecutive weeks in any period of 12 months.

(2) In calculating the period of 4 weeks mentioned in paragraph (1) a period in residential accommodation of less than 4 weeks shall be added to any succeeding period in residential accommodation where the two periods are separated by a period of less than 4 weeks but not otherwise.

(3) A direct payment may not be made in respect of a person who falls within regulation 4 for the provision of residential accommodation –

    (a) for any single period in excess of 4 weeks; and
    (b) for any period in excess of 120 days in any period of 12 months.

14 Displaced functions and obligations of the responsible authority

(1) Except as provided by paragraph (2), the fact that a responsible authority make a direct payment shall not affect their functions with respect to the provision under the relevant enactment of the service to which the payment relates.

(2) Where a responsible authority make a direct payment, they shall not be under any obligation with respect to the provision under the relevant enactment of the service to which the payment relates as long as they are satisfied that the need which calls for the provision of the service will be secured by –

    (a)   in the case of direct payments under section 57(1) of the 2001 Act or section 17A(1) of the 1989 Act, the payee's own arrangements; or
    (b)   in the case of direct payments under section 57(1A) of the 2001 Act, the arrangements made by S.

(3) In paragraphs (1) and (2), references to the relevant enactment, in relation to the provision of a service, are to the enactment under which the service would fall to be provided apart from these Regulations.

15 Repayment of direct payments

(1) A responsible authority which have made a direct payment may require the payment or part of the payment to be repaid where they are satisfied that –

    (a)   the direct payment or part of the payment has not been used to secure the provision of the service to which it relates; or

    (b)   a condition imposed under regulation 11 or 12 has not been complied with.

(2) Any sum falling to be repaid by virtue of paragraph (1) shall be recoverable as a debt due to the responsible authority.

16 Review

(1) A responsible authority must review the making of direct payments under section 57(1A) of the 2001 Act –

    (a)   at least once within the first year of the direct payments being made;

    (b)   at appropriate intervals, not exceeding twelve months, thereafter;

    (c)   where the responsible authority reasonably consider, on the basis of information given by S or by any other person, that P no longer falls within section 57(5A) of the 2001 Act; and

    (d)   whenever notified by any person of concerns that –

        (i)   the direct payment may not have been used to secure the provision for P of the services for which the payment was made, or

        (ii)   may mean that the responsible authority would no longer be satisfied of the matters listed in regulation 8(5)(b) or (c).

(2) A responsible authority must review the making of direct payments under section 57(1) of the 2001 Act where the responsible authority reasonably consider, on the basis of information given by any person, that P falls within section 57(5A) of that Act.

17 Termination of direct payments under section 57(1) of the 2001 Act or section 17A(1) of the 1989 Act

(1) Subject to paragraph (3), a responsible authority must terminate the making of direct payments under section 57(1) of the 2001 Act or section 17A(1) of the 1989 Act to a person if –

    (a)   the person ceases to be a prescribed person; or

    (b)   a condition mentioned in regulation 7(2) ceases to be met.

(2) A responsible authority may terminate the making of the whole or part of direct payments under section 57(1) of the 2001 Act or section 17A(1) of the 1989 Act to a prescribed person if –

    (a)   any condition imposed under regulation 11 or referred to in section 57(4)(b) of the 2001 Act is not complied with; or

    (b)   in all the circumstances the responsible authority consider it appropriate to terminate the making of direct payments.

(3) A responsible authority may continue to make direct payments to a person who ceases to satisfy regulation 2(b) who would otherwise be a prescribed person if –

(a)   the authority are reasonably satisfied that that person's lack of capacity to consent will be temporary;

(b)   another person who appears to the responsible authority to be capable of managing a direct payment is prepared to accept and manage such payments on behalf of that person during the period of their incapacity; and

(c)   the person with whom the arrangement for the provision of the relevant service has been made agrees to accept payment for the service from the person mentioned in sub-paragraph (b).

18 Termination of direct payments under section 57(1A) of the 2001 Act

(1) A responsible authority must terminate the making of direct payments under section 57(1A) of the 2001 Act to S if –

(a)   the person in respect of whom the payments are made ("the beneficiary") ceases to –
   (i)   fall within the description of persons prescribed by regulation 3, or
   (ii)   fall within section 57(2)(a) of the 2001 Act; or
(b)   the responsible authority are no longer satisfied of any of the matters listed in regulation 8(5).

(2) Subject to paragraphs (4) and (5), a responsible authority must terminate the making of direct payments under section 57(1A) of the 2001 Act to S if the beneficiary no longer falls within section 57(5A) of the 2001 Act or is reasonably believed by the responsible authority no longer to fall within that section.

(3) A responsible authority may terminate the making of the whole or part of the direct payments to S if any condition imposed under regulation 12 or referred to in section 57(4)(b) of the 2001 Act is not complied with.

(4) A responsible authority may continue to make direct payments under section 57(1A) of the 2001 Act to S notwithstanding that the beneficiary ceases to fall within section 57(5A) of the 2001 Act, if –

(a)   the authority are reasonably satisfied that the beneficiary's capacity to consent to the making of direct payments will be temporary; and

(b)   the direct payments are made subject to the additional condition that S shall allow the beneficiary to manage the direct payments themselves for any period in respect of which the responsible authority are satisfied that the beneficiary has capacity to consent to the making of direct payments and is capable of managing such payments.

(5) Where paragraph (2) applies and a responsible authority reasonably believe that the beneficiary's capacity to consent is not temporary, before terminating payments under section 57(1A), the authority shall consult the beneficiary with regard to whether the beneficiary consents to the making of direct payments under section 57(1) of the 2001 Act.

(6) Subject to paragraph (7), direct payments under section 57(1A) shall not be terminated under paragraph (2) until direct payments under section 57(1) of the 2001 Act are made where, in accordance with paragraph (5), the beneficiary consents to direct payments under section 57(1) of the 2001 Act, if the beneficiary –

(a)   is a prescribed person;

(b) falls within section 57(2)(a) of the 2001 Act; and

(c) the condition in regulation 7(2)(a) is met.

(7) Nothing in paragraph (6) affects the responsible authority's discretion not to make direct payments under section 57(1) of the 2001 Act under regulation 7(1)(a) or (b).

19 Consequential amendments

In regulation 19(b) of the Community Legal Service (Financial) Regulations 2000 and regulation 2(1) of the Criminal Defence Service (Financial Eligibility) Regulations 2006 for the words from "the Community Care, Services for Carers and Children's Services (Direct Payments) (England) Regulations 2003" to the end substitute "regulations made under section 57 of the Health and Social Care Act 2001 (direct payments) or section 17A of the Children Act 1989 (direct payments)".

The recipient

6.56 The person who is defined as being suitable for receiving direct payments is 'a person who appears to the responsible authority to be capable of managing a direct payment by themselves or with such assistance as may be available to them' (reg 2(a)). This is subject to a small number of exceptions set out at reg 2(b) and (c). In respect of children and direct payments, this is contained in reg 4(a) and (b).

Duty to make payments

6.57 If the responsible authority are satisfied that the person's needs for the relevant service can be met by securing the provision of it by means of a direct payment (in the case of an adult) and are satisfied that the welfare of the child will be safeguarded and promoted by securing the provision (in the case of a child), then it *must* make such payments (reg 7(1)(c), (2)(a), (b)). A relevant service means: (a) a community care service within s 46 of the National Health Service and Community Care Act 1990; (b) s 2 of the Carers and Disabled Children Act 2000; and (c) a service under s 17 of the Children Act 1989 ; (d) under s 57(1A) of the 2001 Act, a community care service within the meaning of s 46 of the 1990 Act (reg 1(2)(a)(i), (ii), (iii) and (b) The provisions for the *discretion* to make payments are set out in para 50 of the Guidance.

Conditions

6.58 There are only two conditions specified in the regulations. These are set out in regs 11 and 12.

Termination of payments to those who lack capacity

6.59 The Guidance provides information on this aspect at paragraphs 257–258. In essence, payments will cease if: (a) the suitable person to whom the payments are being made is no longer acting in the best interests of P; or (b) the person who lacks capacity has regained capacity (although there is a discretion to continue if that regaining of capacity is temporary).

Summary of changes to Direct Payment Regulations

6.60 The main changes are in respect of those who lack capacity (regs 5–8). However, the Health and Social Care Act 2001 (which is set out below) and which is the primary legislation from which direct payments flow, has also been amended, in order to make these alterations possible. There has also been a removal of the prohibition on direct payments to those detained under the Mental Health Act 1983 (although local authorities are still obliged to provide services under s 117 of the Act free – see Chapter 1).

6.61 The main amendments to the Act are at s 57(1A)–(1C) and (5A)–(5C) and (7A).

Health and Social Care Act 2001

57 Direct payments

(1) Regulations may make provision for and in connection with requiring or authorising the responsible authority in the case of a person of a prescribed description who falls within subsection (2) to make, with that person's consent, such payments to him as they may determine in accordance with the regulations in respect of his securing the provision of the service mentioned in paragraph (a) or (b) of that subsection.

(1A) Regulations may make provision for and in connection with requiring or authorising the responsible authority in the case of a person ("P") of a prescribed description—

    (a)   who falls within subsection (2)(a), and
    (b)   who falls within subsection (5A) or is reasonably believed by the authority to fall within that subsection,

to make, with the requisite consent, such payments as the authority may determine in accordance with the regulations to a suitable person other than P in respect of the other person's securing the provision for P of the service mentioned in subsection (2)(a).

(1B) In subsection (1A) "the requisite consent" means—

    (a)   the consent of the other person; and
    (b)   where the other person is not a surrogate of P but there is at least one person who is a surrogate of P, the consent also of a surrogate of P.

(1C) For the purposes of subsection (1A), a person (whether or not an individual) is "suitable" if—

    (a)   that person is a representative of P;
    (b)   that person is not a representative of P (or there is no-one who is a representative of P), but—
        (i)   a surrogate of P, and
        (ii)   the responsible authority,

consider that person to be a suitable person to receive the payments for the purpose of securing provision for P of the service concerned; or

(c) that person is not a representative of P (or there is no-one who is a representative of P), and there is no-one who is a surrogate of P, but the responsible authority considers that person to be a suitable person to receive the payments for that purpose.

(2) A person falls within this subsection if a local authority ("the responsible authority") have decided—

(a) under section 47 of the 1990 Act (assessment by local authorities of needs for community care services) that his needs call for the provision by them of a particular community care service (within the meaning of section 46 of that Act), or

(b) under section 2(1) of the Carers and Disabled Children Act 2000 (c 16) (services for carers) to provide him with a particular service under that Act.

(3) Regulations under this section may, in particular, make provision—

(a) specifying circumstances in which the responsible authority are not required or authorised to make any payments under the regulations to a person or in respect of a person, whether those circumstances relate to the person in question or to the particular service mentioned in paragraph (a) or (b) of subsection (2);

(b) for any payments required or authorised by the regulations to be made to a person by the responsible authority ("direct payments") to be made to that person ("the payee") as gross payments or alternatively as net payments;

(c) for the responsible authority to make for the purposes of subsection (4) or (5) such determination as to—
   (i) the payee's means in the case of direct payments under subsection (1) or, in the case of direct payments under subsection (1A), the means of the person ("the beneficiary") in respect of whom the payments are required or authorised to be made, and
   (ii) the amount (if any) which it would be reasonably practicable for him to pay to the authority by way of reimbursement or contribution,

as may be prescribed;

(d) as to the conditions falling to be complied with by the payee in the case of direct payments under subsection (1), or by the payee or by the beneficiary in the case of direct payments under subsection (1A), which must or may be imposed by the responsible authority in relation to the direct payments (and any conditions which may not be so imposed);

(e) specifying circumstances in which the responsible authority—
   (i) may or must terminate the making of direct payments,
   (ii) may require repayment (whether by the payee in the case of direct payments under subsection (1), or by the payee or by the beneficiary in the case of direct payments under subsection (1A), or otherwise) of the whole or part of the direct payments;

(f) for any sum falling to be paid or repaid to the responsible authority by virtue of any condition or other requirement imposed in pursuance of the regulations to be recoverable as a debt due to the authority;

(g)   displacing functions or obligations of the responsible authority with respect to the provision of the service mentioned in subsection (2)(a) or (b) only to such extent, and subject to such conditions, as may be prescribed;

(h)   authorising direct payments to be made to any prescribed person on behalf of the payee;

(j)   as to matters to which the responsible authority must, or may, have regard when making a decision for the purposes of a provision of the regulations;

(k)   as to steps which the responsible authority must, or may, take before, or after, the authority makes a decision for the purposes of a provision of the regulations;

(l)   specifying circumstances in which a person who has fallen within subsection (5A) but no longer does so (whether because of fluctuating capacity, or regaining or gaining of capacity) is to be treated, or may be treated, as falling within subsection (5A) for purposes of this section or for purposes of regulations under this section.

(4) For the purposes of subsection (3)(b) "gross payments" means payments—

(a)   which are made at such a rate as the authority estimate to be equivalent to the reasonable cost of securing the provision of the service concerned; but

(b)   which may be made subject to the condition that the payee in the case of direct payments under subsection (1), or the beneficiary in the case of direct payments under subsection (1A), pays to the responsible authority, by way of reimbursement, an amount or amounts determined under the regulations.

(5) For the purposes of subsection (3)(b) "net payments" means payments—

(a)   which are made on the basis that the payee will himself in the case of direct payments under subsection (1), or the beneficiary will in the case of direct payments under subsection (1A), pay an amount or amounts determined under the regulations by way of contribution towards the cost of securing the provision of the service concerned; and

(b)   which are accordingly made at such a rate below that mentioned in subsection (4)(a) as reflects any such contribution by the payee or (as the case may be) the beneficiary.

(5A) A person falls within this subsection if the person lacks capacity, within the meaning of the Mental Capacity Act 2005, to consent to the making of direct payments.

(5B) In this section "representative", in relation to a person, means such other person (whether or not an individual) as may be prescribed.

(5C) In this section "surrogate", in relation to a person, means—

(a)   a deputy appointed for the person by the Court of Protection under section 16(2)(b) of the Mental Capacity Act 2005, or

(b)   a donee of a lasting power of attorney created by the person,

whose powers, as deputy or donee, consist of or include such powers as may be prescribed.

(6) Regulations under this section shall provide that, where direct payments are made in respect of a service which, apart from the regulations, would be provided under section 117 of the Mental Health Act 1983 (c 20) (after-care)—

    (a)   the payments shall be made at the rate mentioned in subsection (4)(a); and

    (b)   subsection (4)(b) shall not apply.

(7) Regulations made for the purposes of subsection (3)(a) may provide that direct payments shall not be made in respect of the provision of residential accommodation for any person for a period in excess of a prescribed period.

(7A) For the purposes of subsection (3)(d), the conditions that are to be taken to be conditions in relation to direct payments include, in particular, conditions in relation to—

    (a)   the securing of the provision of the service concerned,
    (b)   the provider of the service,
    (c)   the person to whom payments are made in respect of the provision of the service, or
    (d)   the provision of the service.

(7B) Section 12 of the Social Care Charges (Wales) Measure 2010 makes further provision for and in connection with the determination of amounts by way of reimbursement as mentioned in subsection (4)(b) or contribution as mentioned in subsection (5)(a) in respect of chargeable services within the meaning of that Measure.

(8) In this section "prescribed" means specified in or determined in accordance with regulations under this section.

6.62 Having set out the summary of the Guidance and Regulations, the statute itself should need little by way of further explanation. However, there are certain discrete areas which require some further comment.

Use of direct payments to support education/care of disabled child

6.63 In *R (on the application of M) v Suffolk CC* [2006] EWHC 2366 (Admin), [2006] 9 CCLR 704, an issue arose as to the interpretation of the Regulations. This authority also illustrates the overlap between payments to parents of disabled children and the statutory framework which relates to them. The child herself was 17, and severely disabled. She lived with her father. The local authority carried out an assessment under s 17 of the Children Act 1989. This resulted in her placement at a local school and assistance at home. The father received direct payments for the care at home. He argued that he was unable to work and care for his daughter based upon the amount of direct payments made available to him, and arranged for his daughter to attend a residential school (partially funded by himself). He had asked the local authority to pay (with direct payments) for that part of the proportion of costs of the school that could be attributed to social care and practical assistance. The local authority contended that this was not permitted by the Regulations (reg 7(3)). It is perhaps unsurprising given the purpose of the statute that the Court held that the interpretation adopted by the local authority was wrong. The headnote reads (in part):

> 'There is no need to categorise formally the totality of fees as being for residence. In this way the parents are given a choice as to how an identified need should be met.'

Mr Justice Charles referred at length to the Guidance in his judgment, and in particular 'that it was also designed to give people choice. The backdrop of that, it seems to me, is choice in the way in which identified and assessed needs were to be met' [713B–713C]. There is no reason to suppose that the changes in the legislation would cause this case to be decided any differently.

6.64   The rationale behind the availability of direct payments to people with parental responsibility for a disabled child is summarised thus:

> '[5] The power to make direct payments to people with parental responsibility for disabled children and to disabled 16 and 17 year olds was created by the Carers and Disabled Children Act 2000. Section 17A of the 1989 Act, inserted by the 2001 Act, gave councils a duty to offer direct payments for children's services. In making payments under section 17A of the 1989 Act, councils are subject to the general duty provided by Part 3 of that Act to safeguard and promote the welfare of children in need, and to promote their upbringing by families when making these payments, in exactly the same way as when providing direct services. Before seeking any decision about providing direct payments, the council must ascertain and give due consideration to the child's wishes and feelings (section 17(4A) of the 1989 Act).'

Direct payments and s 17A of the Children Act 1989

6.65   The Guidance provides a helpful narrative to the intentions of the law in this area, both for children who are disabled, and (as above) those who have parental responsibility for disabled children, and in respect of older children who are making the transition between children's services and adult services. In respect of disabled young people (by which is meant principally those who are 16–17) it is suggested that 'Young people who receive direct payments may also find it helpful to have access to advocacy support. This should be separate from any support or advocacy provided to their parents (para 45). For parents who have parental responsibility for disabled children, paras 162–168 set out in considerable detail how a local authority should behave. In particular, it states:

> '167 Parents should be encouraged and supported to use direct payments with a view to enabling their disabled children to access the same kinds of opportunities and activities as their non-disabled peers. Direct payments to people with parental responsibility for a disabled child are provided within the framework of Part 3 of the 1989 Act, which requires councils to provide a range of services to safeguard and promote the welfare of children in need.'

Although not directly within the compass of s 17A, paras 175–183 cover the transition between childhood and adulthood (including what should happen if a child lacks capacity). Effectively, it emphasises the need to consult (with the child and those who have parental responsibility for him), to liaise between the relevant local authority departments, and also to consider the effect that the change in status between a child and an adult will have in terms of the primary legislation described throughout this text.

17A Direct payments

(1) The Secretary of State may by regulations make provision for and in connection with requiring or authorising the responsible authority in the case of a person of a prescribed description who falls within subsection (2) to make, with that person's consent, such payments to him as they may determine in accordance with the regulations in respect of his securing the provision of the service mentioned in that subsection.

(2) A person falls within this subsection if he is –

    (a)   a person with parental responsibility for a disabled child,
    (b)   a disabled person with parental responsibility for a child, or
    (c)   a disabled child aged 16 or 17,

and a local authority ("the responsible authority") have decided for the purposes of section 17 that the child's needs (or, if he is such a disabled child, his needs) call for the provision by them of a service in exercise of functions conferred on them under that section.

(3) Subsections (3) to (5) and (7) of section 57 of the 2001 Act shall apply, with any necessary modifications, in relation to regulations under this section as they apply in relation to regulations under that section.

(4) Regulations under this section shall provide that, where payments are made under the regulations to a person falling within subsection (5) –

    (a)   the payments shall be made at the rate mentioned in subsection (4)(a) of section 57 of the 2001 Act (as applied by subsection (3)); and
    (b)   subsection (4)(b) of that section shall not apply.

(5) A person falls within this subsection if he is –

    (a)   a person falling within subsection (2)(a) or (b) and the child in question is aged 16 or 17, or
    (b)   a person who is in receipt of income support ... under Part 7 of the Social Security Contributions and Benefits Act 1992 (c 4), of any element of child tax credit other than the family element, of working tax credit or of an income-based jobseeker's allowance.

(6) In this section –

"the 2001 Act" means the Health and Social Care Act 2001;
"disabled" in relation to an adult has the same meaning as that given by section 17(11) in relation to a child;
"prescribed" means specified in or determined in accordance with regulations under this section (and has the same meaning in the provisions of the 2001 Act mentioned in subsection (3) as they apply by virtue of that subsection).

Individual budgets, personal budgets, direct payments and resource allocation schemes

6.66   An informative and critically acute analysis of the recent development in the law and policy in this area can be found in *Individual budgets and irrational exuberance* (Luke Clements, [2008] 11 CCLR 413). The first observation that Clements makes is that:

> '[413/414] analysis of IBs is hampered by the absence of an agreed definition as to exactly what one is ... for the purpose of this article, a number of concepts associated with IBs are analysed and these include: (a) self-assessment: the idea that an individual controls the assessment of their needs for social care support ... (b) Resource allocation: a computation mechanism ... converts the self-assessment into a sum of money. The individual is informed of the value and of their entitlement to this sum – their 'IB'; (c) Service flexibility: the individual has considerable freedom to use their IB to purchase services that they consider best meets their social care needs ... (d) mixed funding streams: the resources to be allocated include, not just the funds that the individual is entitled to under the community care legislation but also funding relating to community equipment, Access to Work, Independent Living Funds, disability facilities grants and the Supporting People programme ...'

The second observation he makes (in the context of this book) is that:

> '[417] IBs are at best a policy initiative ... what little is clear about IB's however is that whatever they are, they must operate within the law, and this means that, in so far as they engage a local authority's community care obligations, it must ensure that: the person is assessed under s 47 of the NHS and Community Care Act 1990; the assessment complies with binding policy guidance and directions; qualifying carers are offered a carers assessment; the identified needs are compared to the relevant eligibility criteria; all "eligible needs" are met by service provision or by direct payments; 'financial resources' are not used as a reason for not meeting an eligible need; that the financial contribution the individual may need to make is assessed according to the relevant charging regimes, and that the assessment for this must follow on the individual's support needs; services/support must meet minimum human rights standards – most importantly the 'dignity' standard.'

Apart from the consequences of the decision in *McDonald* on the concept of 'dignity' (see Chapter 3) he adds:

> '[417] It follows that local authorities cannot, for example, operate costs ceilings on care packages; cannot offer cash payments that conflict with the Direct Payments regulations and cannot insist on a person having a Direct Payment. The IB pilot sites do not operate in a kind of free trade area or other zone immune from domestic law.'

6.67   Unfortunately, the concerns expressed by Clements in respect of the 'zone immune from domestic law' together with the ambiguity and confusion surrounding the definition of what an IB is, and the status of the idea being founded in policy documents and not actual law (either 'soft' or 'hard') has caused exactly the problems that he predicted (see **6.68–6.70**) although the Courts have thus far failed to find favour with the challenges made to the RAS system itself. His observation that:

> '[417] A particularly troubling dimension to this question concerns the extent to which a RAS-determined resource entitlement can trump an individual's community care entitlement. The simple answer, of course, is that it cannot – policy (speculative or otherwise) cannot negate a legal right.'

The concept of the RAS is described thus:

> '[425] A core element of the IB programme is a computation mechanism ... (RAS) ... that converts the individual's self assessment into a fixed sum ... the law however is framed in terms of an entitlement to have care needs met – not in terms of an entitlement to a financial payment (that may or may not meet "need"). The direct payment legislation too is framed in terms of a right to a payment that secures the provision of the assessed service needs.'

The difficulty is if the creation of an RAS system has been used to impose a maximum payment ceiling (which is not permissible within the direct payments scheme, for example) and is thus unlawful, and therefore has led to operating within a 'zone immune from domestic law'.

6.68 The documents produced by the relevant government departments are understandably rather more enthusiastic about the policies, albeit riddled with jargon. The greatest clarity is contained in the Guidance itself in which it is stated that:

> '[8] In this context, person centred planning and self-directed support should become mainstream mechanisms for delivery of social care support. Building on the success of direct payments, every person eligible for statutory services should be able to access a personal budget – a clear and upfront allocation of resources allowing them to decide how best to meet their needs ... it is helpful to think of "self-directed support" as an overarching term describing a variety of tools to give older and disabled people greater levels of control over how their support needs are met. A personal budget is the amount of money that a council decides is necessary to spend in order to meet an individual's needs and direct payments are one way in which the person can choose to use that money in order to meet those needs. As well as being made as a direct cash payment to the service user, a personal budget may also be held in trust by a third party, who will arrange services as directed by the person requiring support (an arrangement often described as a "notional budget".'

It will be recalled that this Guidance has been issued pursuant to s 7 of the Local Authority Social Services Act 1970 and thus has a far more enhanced status that a policy document. The concern is, of course, that in implementing this policy the focus will be rather more on saving money for the local authority, than actually either meeting the needs of the individual, or providing him with greater autonomy (which was the purpose of the direct payments scheme, and which has, indeed, proved successful in achieving that aim). The Guidance further comments that:

> '[30] Establishing systems based on choice, control and self-directed support will require councils to develop robust commissioning strategies to ensure the supply of high-quality, personalised services that people need and want to buy. This may required significant change to existing commissioning arrangements to meet changing patterns of demand as the uptake of personal budgets and direct payments increase.'

Whether or not local authorities have responded to that need for change is a moot point. The Guidance conflates personal budgets, an resource allocation systems (or 'schemes') at paras 111–118.

6.69   The first judgment to consider this area of law has been considered in *R (on the application of Savva) v Royal Borough of Kensington & Chelsea* [2010] EWCA Civ 1209, [2011] 14 CCLR 75. The judgment starts by citing the provisions of s 2 of the Chronically Sick and Disabled Persons Act 1970 and which observes that:

> '[1] Initially, local authorities carried out the duty by providing or procuring the provision of the relevant services. The disabled person was simply the recipient of the services. However, in recent years central government, through the Department of Health, has encouraged local authorities to discharge the duty by providing a disabled person with money in the form of a personal budget, thereby enabling the person to purchase the services required to meet his or her eligible needs. This is thought to enhance personal autonomy.'

In the case of the Claimant, this duty was discharged by virtue of reg 14(5). Lord Justice Kay then refers to the recurrent features of the Guidance referred to above as:

> '[6] an emphasis on "transparency" in the decision making process "clear, upfront allocation of funding", providing recipients with clarity on how decisions are made. Secondly, there is encouragement of the use of resource allocation systems (RAS's). No single RAS is prescribed. Several are described. It is clear that they are not seen as being in themselves precise methods of producing a definitive personal budget in an individual case. They produce a provisional or indicative figure.'

The contents of para 112 of the Guidance as follows:

> 'A resource allocation system should be applied as a means of giving an approximate indication of what it may reasonably cost to meet a person's particular needs according to their individual circumstances. It is important for councils to ensure that their resource allocation process is sufficiently flexible to allow someone's individual circumstances to be taken into account when determining the amount of resources they are allocated in a personal budget.'

This concept is then contrasted with the established law in respect of needs versus resources (see Chapters 3 and 4). The attack upon the decision of the local authority in this case was predicated by the assertion that the use of the RAS model selected, as it was argued that it imposed an unlawful cap on the budget. This was rejected upon the basis that:

'[18] It is very clear that the figure generated by the RAS was not used as anything other than a starting point or indicative allocation ... I do not think that it can be said that the Council ever lost sight of the fact that once Mrs Savva's eligible needs had been assessed, it was under an absolute duty to provide her with the services that would meet those needs or a personal budget with which to purchase them. The Council was entitled to use methodology recommended by the Department of Health which, in my judgment, did not have the effect suggested on behalf of Mrs Savva. It has never been suggested that the Department of Health's guidance is unlawful.'

Thus, if a local authority is to avoid operating in a 'zone immune from domestic law' it will be obliged to continue to steer by the existing common law in this area, and adhere to the Guidance provided by the Department of Health as cited above.

6.70 The second case is that of *R (on the Application of KM) v Cambridgeshire County Council* [2010] EWHC 3065 (Admin), [2011] 14 CCLR 83 (and subsequently on appeal *R (on the application of KM (by his mother and litigation friend JM)) v Cambridgeshire County Council* [2011] EWCA Civ 682, [2011] 14 CCLR 402). The arguments in this case were almost identical to those in *Savva*, and it is therefore not surprising that the claim failed. It was argued that (i) the defendant had failed to assess the claimant's needs; (ii) that the defendant had failed to provide reasons for its service provision decisions; (iii) that the defendant's methodology used to calculate care packages lacked transparency; (iv) that the defendant was in breach of its duty to adapt the claimant's home [1]. However, the central argument appeared to be 'that the defendant was in breach of what is contended to be an absolute obligation to provide him with a care package to meet his assessed needs [2]. Some criticism was made, however, of 'the shifts in the claimant's position' [4]. Mr Justice Bidder held that:

'[53] Kay LJ considered that the suggestion in *Savva* that an explanation of the RAS should be given went too far. Thus the absence of a detailed explanation as to the workings of the RAS at this stage would not, in my judgment, have been fatal had this been the end decision.'

He continued:

'[54] Mr Wise criticises the defendant for failing to provide an explanation setting out the **services** required to meet the claimant's needs. That appears to me to be a complete misunderstanding of the system of self-directed support. Both the RAS and the upper banding calculator ... were assessment of needs and not services but the RAS was a tool for translating needs into a sum which was adequate to provide the services for those needs by reference to the average costs of the provision by the authority of meeting those needs for other disabled people.

[55] ... the self-directed support system, however, was designed to provide a sufficient sum to meet the claimant's needs but it was up to the claimant and his advisers to determine how to spend that sum.

[56] Criticism of the council for failing to provide an explanation setting out the cost of the services required to meet the claimant's needs wholly fails to recognise how the self-directed support system works. The failure to recognise that characterises almost all of the correspondence from the claimant's advisers. They were assiduous and persistent but they were consistently at cross-purposes with the defendant because of their failure to appreciate how the scheme worked. *Savva* indicates that the use of such a scheme, **assuming that it is checked properly against an assessment of the claimant's needs, cannot be criticised** and the claimant's representatives have, as a result of *Savva* been driven eventually in these proceedings to accept that it cannot' [emphasis added].

So, for a local authority to avoid the kind of pitfalls outlined by Clements above, the approach taken by both local authorities in this case and *Savva* itself would render it unassailable by way of judicial review. It was held that:

'[72] The RAS, as far as an initial assessment is concerned, is an appropriate way of estimating the reasonable cost of meeting assessed needs. It is absolutely essential that at some stage in the process of care provision, resources must be taken into account. That is recognised both in *Savva* and *R v Gloucestershire County Council and another ex p Barry* [1997] AC 584.'

It is to be noted that in this case, the use of the RAS was purely as an indicator as to the needs of the claimant (not the services), and was used to calculate how much meeting those needs would cost. That is its function, and no more than that. The final decision as to how much the actual direct payment would be was not to be made until **after** a support plan was created which satisfied all the claimants assessed needs (pursuant to the relevant community care legislation and guidance). Neither of these cases have provided an effective challenge to the use of an RAS, as long as it is purely for the function for which it was designed. It remains to be seen whether all local authorities have been as astute as those who were involved in these two cases. The appeal against the decision at first instance failed, the Court of Appeal endorsing the logic of Bidder J.

Prohibition on purchase of NHS services

6.71 In *R (on the application of Harrison) v SoS for Health, Wakefield District Primary Care Trust, Wakefield Metropolitan District Council (interested parties); R (on the application of Garnham) v SoS for Health and Islington PCT, Islington LBC (interested party)* [2009] EWHC 574 (Admin), [2009] 12 CCLR 355 the approach to direct payments and the use of direct payments to purchase health care was re-considered (the subject matter having previously come before the Courts in the case of *R (on the application of Gunter) v South Western Staffordshire Primary Care Trust* [2005] EWHC 1894

(Admin), [2006] 9 CCLR 121). The scenario in the case is not uncommon. The claimants had been in receipt of direct payments (via the council) which had been used to provide them with funds to buy the care which they wanted (thus fulfilling the aim of direct payments). However, due to the particular nature of those needs, and a re-assessment, it was decided that these were health care related needs, and not social services needs. There was no dispute about this determination, but it prevented the local authority from providing direct payments (as these cannot be used to by NHS services). The consequence of this, however, is that because there is no equivalent of the direct payments system within the NHS, then the NHS will provide its services in the way that it sees as appropriate (which will almost certainly lead to a loss of choice and autonomy) particularly if the service user has built up a professional and personal relationship with the individuals who had been providing the care hitherto. Mr Justice Silber held that the decision of the PCT's was lawful, in that it was prohibited for cash payments to be made to purchase medical services. The ratio of the case is explored in more detail in Chapter 7. It should also be noted that s 11 of the Health Act 2009 has amended the NHS Act 2006 to allow the SoS to make monetary payments in lieu of providing them with health care services, but so far this has only been permissible within specified pilot schemes.

Chapter 7

HEALTH CARE AND SOCIAL CARE

DISTINCTION BETWEEN HEALTH CARE AND SOCIAL SERVICES

7.1 There has been a continuing debate over many years as to which services a local authority social services department should be funding, and which come within the ambit of health care. This section attempts to set that debate in its historical context (which is required in order to understand the problem) and to explain the most recent legislation (the National Health Service Act 2006 (and National Health Service (Wales) Act 2006)). A good deal of the argument involves responsibilities placed upon Strategic Health Authorities (SHAs) and Primary Care Trusts (PCTs), and therefore strictly speaking is outside the scope of this book. However, in order to try and determine what may fall to a local authority to provide, it obviously follows that it will be necessary to see what the Health Service may have to provide.

NURSING SERVICES

7.2 Equally obviously, perhaps, the significance for a local authority will be the amount it has to spend on community care services if what might be regarded as a healthcare provision falls within its responsibilities. For a service user, the implications largely follow from the preceding chapters on the obligation of local authorities to provide services under the relevant statutes, and the powers available to the courts to enforce local authorities to make provision. No such corollary exists as against a health service provider (as yet) since the National Health Service Act 2006 continues the previous statutory regime of a target duty only. As ever with this area of practice, there is a complex interrelationship between many of the statutes hitherto considered, and various regulations, guidance and circulars.

7.3 In *R v North and East Devon Health Authority, ex p Coughlan and Secretary of State for Health and Royal College of Nursing* [1999] 2 CCLR 285, [2000] 2 WLR 622, some guidance was given to the distinction between the two areas of provision. The judgment itself deals with the interrelation of the statutes in force at that time, but the principles remain illustrative of the salient issues in general terms. In particular, extensive reference is made to the National Health Service Act 1977, which has been repealed and replaced with the National Health Service 2006. The facts of the case are only relevant insofar as there was a dispute (in part) as to who should fund the nursing care for a disabled adult who had been placed in residential accommodation, and who required nursing care within that placement. It was held where a local authority was providing residential accommodation (pursuant to s 21(5) of the National Assistance Act 1948 that this together with s 21(8) (as it existed prior to amendment by the National Health Service Act 2006) enabled a local authority to provide nursing services.

7.4   The relevant issue was whether the nursing services were incidental or ancillary to the accommodation, and of a nature so that it can be expected that their provision should fall to be provided for by social services, or whether the primary need is a health need, in which case provision should be made by the NHS (irrespective of the fact that the individual had been placed in residential accommodation as a result of an assessment by the local authority).

7.5   The dilemma was summarised thus:

> '[289D–289E] The critical issue ... is whether nursing care for a chronically ill patient may lawfully be provided by a local authority as a social service (in which case the patient pays according to means) or whether it is required by law to be provided free of charge as part of the National Health Service.'

The Court of Appeal proceeded to consider a guideline document (HSG (92) (50)) which arose out of the National Health Service and Community Care Act 1990. The guidance referred to 'specialist nursing services' and 'general nursing care'. The latter (it suggested) should be paid for by the local authority. whereas the former was for the NHS to provide. The specific examples given for health authorities were 'physiotherapy, chiropody and speech and language therapy, with the appropriate equipment, and the provision of specialist nursing advice, e g continence advice and stoma care, for those people placed in nursing homes by local authorities with the consent of a DHA'. The Court also considered 1995 guidance in HSG (95) 8; LAC (95) 5 (subsequently cancelled on 28 June 2001) and commented:

> '[292D] It made clear that access to specialist medical and nursing services should be made available and provided at the expense of the NHS for those persons who were no longer eligible for in-patient care.'

It held that:

> '[298–299] The fact that some nursing services can be properly regarded as part of social services care, to be provided by the local authority, does not mean that all nursing services provided to those in the care of the local authority can be treated in this way. The scale and type of nursing required in an individual case may mean that it would not be appropriate to regard all or part of the nursing as being part of the "package of care" which can be provided by a local authority. There can be no precise legal line drawn between those nursing services which are and those which are not capable of being treated as included in such a package of care services ... as a very general indication as to where the line is to be drawn, it can be said that if the nursing services are (i) merely incidental or ancillary to the provision of accommodation which a local authority is under a duty to provide to

the category of persons to whom section 21 refers and (ii) of a nature which it can be expected that an authority whose primary responsibility is to provide social services can be expected to provide, then they can be provided under Section 21. It will be appreciated that the first part of the test is focusing on the overall quality of the services provided.'

7.6   A further gloss on this judgment has been provided by the Department of Health at Annex B (see below) of the National Framework for NHS Continuing Healthcare and NHS Funded Nursing Care (the National Framework). The latter document was first published in June 2007 (and is merely guidance) and was revised in July 2009 but directions (pursuant to both the National Health Service Act 2006 and the Local Authority Social Services Act 1970) have been subsequently implemented with effect from 1 October 2009. The latter are the NHS Continuing Healthcare (Responsibilities) Directions 2009 (the CHC Directions). To make matters even more complex, there are also 'The National Health Service (Nursing Care in Residential Accommodation) (England) Directions 2007' (referred to in this book as 'the nursing directions'. These documents are considered at greater length below.

The National Framework for NHS Continuing Healthcare and NHS funded Nursing Care – Annex B

R v North and East Devon Health Authority, ex parte Pamela Coughlan

Pamela Coughlan was seriously injured in a road traffic accident in 1971. Until 1993 she received NHS care in Newcourt Hospital. When the Exeter Health Authority wished to close that hospital and to move Miss Coughlan and other individuals to a new NHS facility at Mardon House the individuals were promised that Mardon House would be their home for life. In October 1998, the successor Health Authority (North and East Devon Health Authority) decided to withdraw services from Mardon House, to close that facility, and to transfer the care of Miss Coughlan and other disabled individuals to LA Social Services. Miss Coughlan and the other residents did not wish to move out of Mardon House and argued that the decision to close it was a breach of the promise that it would be their home for life and was therefore unlawful.

The arguments on the closure of Mardon House raised other legal points about the respective responsibilities of the Health Service and of Social Services for nursing care. The Court of Appeal's judgement on this aspect has heavily influenced the development of continuing care policies and the National Framework. The key points in this regard are as follows:

The NHS does not have sole responsibility for all nursing care. LAs can provide nursing services under section 21 of the National Assistance Act as long as the nursing care services are capable of being properly classified as part of the social services' responsibilities.

No precise legal line can be drawn between those nursing services which are and those which are not capable of being provided by a LA: the distinction between those services which can and cannot be provided by a LA is one of degree which will depend on a careful appraisal of the facts of an individual case.

As a very general indication as to the limit of LA provision, if the nursing services are:

(a)   merely incidental or ancillary to the provision of the accommodation which a LA is under a duty to provide pursuant to section 21; and

(b)   of a nature which it can be expected that an authority whose primary responsibility is to provide social services can be expected to provide, then such nursing services can be provided under section 21 of the National Assistance Act 1948.

By virtue of section 21(8) of the National Assistance Act a LA is also excluded from providing services where the NHS has in fact decided to provide those services.

The services that can appropriately be treated as responsibilities of a LA under section 21 may evolve with the changing standards of society.

Where a person's primary need is a health need, the responsibility is that of the NHS, even when the individual has been placed in a home by a LA.

An assessment of whether a person has a primary health need should involve consideration not only the nature and quality of the services required but also the quantity or continuity of such services.

The Secretary of State's duty under section 3 of (what is now) the National Health Service Act 2006 is limited to providing the services identified to the extent that she considers necessary to meet all reasonable requirements: in exercising his or her judgement the Secretary of State is entitled to take into account the resources available to her and the demands on those resources.

In respect of Ms Coughlan, her needs were clearly of a scale beyond the scope of LA services.

7.7   It is noteworthy that the annex emphasises the following. First, as long as nursing care falls within part of the function of social services, then the local authority can provide them. If the local authority provides them, then they become subject to the relevant charging regime *and* the element of compulsion (depending upon a variety of circumstances) whereas if they are provided by the relevant health service provider, they are free, *and* subject to s 3 of the National Health Service Act 2006 (summarised in Annex B as being predicated by resources within the overall context of a target duty only). Finally, it is beyond doubt that that where the NHS has decided to provide services, the local authority is prohibited from so doing.

SECTION 117 OF THE MENTAL HEALTH ACT 1983 AND HEALTH CARE

7.8   It is worth noting that the arguments in respect of provision of nursing care apply equally to the distinction between health care and social services responsibility for after-care under s 117 of the Mental Health Act 1983 (Chapter 1). However, as the National Framework states:

'[115] There are no powers to charge for services provided under Section 117, regardless of whether they are provided by the NHS or LA's. Accordingly, the question of whether services should be "free" NHS services rather than potentially charged-for social services does not arise. It is not therefore necessary to assess eligibility for NHS continuing healthcare if all the services in question are to be provided as aftercare under Section 117.

[116] However, a person in receipt of after-care services under section 117 may also have needs for continuing care which are not related to their mental disorder and which may therefore not fall within the scope of section 117. An obvious example would be a person who was already receiving continuing care in relation to physical health problems before being detained under the 1983 Act and whose physical health problems remain on discharge. Where such needs exist, it may be necessary to carry out a consideration for NHS Continuing Healthcare that looks at whether the individual has a primary health need on t the basis of the needs arising from their physical problems. Any mental health after-care needs that fall within section 117 responsibilities would not be taken into account in considering NHS continuing healthcare eligibility in such circumstances.'

7.9 Similar issues were the subject of a complaint to the Health Services Ombudsman, the results of which are contained in *Special Report – NHS funding for long term care – investigations into Complaints Nos E208/99-00 Dorset Health Authority and Dorset Health Care Trust; E420/00-01 Wigan and Bolton Health Authority and Bolton Hospitals NHS Trust; E814/00-01 Berkshire Health Authority; E 1626/01-02 Birmingham Health Authority* (Health Services Ombudsman, February 2003) [2003] 6 CCLR 397). This refers to guidance (HSC 2001/015) which states:

'... where all the nursing service is the NHS's responsibility because someone's primary health need is for health care rather than accommodation; where responsibility can be shared between the NHS and the council because nursing needs in general can be the responsibility of the council but the NHS is responsible for meeting other healthcare requirement; where the totality of the nursing service can be the responsibility of the local council.'

HSC 2001/015 was superseded by the first version of the National Framework upon its publication on 26 June 2007, and now by the revised version published in July 2009.

HEALTH AND SOCIAL CARE ACT 2001

7.10 The case of *Coughlan* was decided prior to the enactment of s 49 of the Health and Social Care Act 2001 (which came into force on 1 October 2001). It is an attempt to address the problems of nursing care by (in effect) prohibiting a local authority from providing a 'registered nurse' as a part of its obligations to provide community care services. The consequence of this should be that nursing care of this specific type will be provided by the NHS. For the avoidance of doubt, a registered nurse is a person registered by the UK Central Council for Nursing, Midwifery and Health Visitors. Community care services are those as set out in s 46(3) of the National Health Service and Community Care Act 1990.

Health and Social Care Act 2001

49 Exclusion of nursing care from community care services

(1) Nothing in the enactments relating to the provision of community care services shall authorise or require a local authority, in or in connection with the provision of any such services, to –

    (a)   provide for any person, or
    (b)   arrange for any person to be provided with,

nursing care by a registered nurse.

(2) In this section "nursing care by a registered nurse" means any services provided by a registered nurse and involving –

    (a)   the provision of care, or
    (b)   the planning, supervision or delegation of the provision of care,

other than any services which, having regard to their nature and the circumstances in which they are provided, do not need to be provided by a registered nurse.

7.11   The special report referred to above continued:

'From April 2003 NHS funding will be provided for such care for all care home residents. (In April 2002 the previous distinction between nursing and residential homes ended, and are all now known as care homes, with or without nursing care.)'

It also comments:

'408 As the *Coughlan* judgment points out, basing eligibility on the need for specialist care does not cater for the situation where the demands for nursing care are continuous and intense. It can also be unclear what constitutes specialist care: for instance, does that include input from mental health nurses.'

It recommends that the Department of Health should review the national guidance on eligibility for continuing NHS health care. This was duly carried out, and the first National Framework represented the new position as of June and October 2007 respectively, and now in the revised version (July 2009).

7.12   However, prior to that the matter was revisited in *R (on the application of Grogan) v Bexley NHS Care Trust and South East London Strategic Health Authority (First Interested Party) and Secretary of State for Health (Second Interested Party)* [2006] EWHC 44 (Admin), [2006] 9 CCLR 188. This considered (in part) the effects of s 49 of the Health and Social Care Act 2001. It also considered the criteria which were used by the Health Authorities in making decisions in respect of nursing care. These in themselves were in part based upon the 'registered nursing care contribution' (RNCC). The effect of s 49 was to transfer to the NHS the responsibility for funding registered nursing services. This in turn involved an assessment of the patient for such services (using the RNCC). A part of the issue was the manner in which such assessments took place. In terms of the distinction between nursing care and community care, the authority provides an extensive commentary upon this history of the legislation and guidance. It was held that the first stage of an assessment is to decide whether a patient is eligible for continuing NHS health care. Health care is not just nursing care. All aspects need to be considered. If a decision is made that the patient is not eligible for continuing NHS health care, then the second stage is to determine whether care is required from a registered nurse and to what extent. The second stage should not influence the decision made at the first stage. The Secretary of State was encouraged to re-visit guidance in this area.

7.13 This was provided ([2006] 9 CCLR 221) by the Department of Health following the *Grogan* judgment. It summarises the substance of the judgment in terms of the procedure for assessment. At para 13, it states:

> 'A primary health need signifies that the individual's overall care needs are such that, leaving aside the effect of section 49 of the 2001 Act, the responsibility for those needs cannot be met by the local authority and so must be the responsibility of the NHS, if anyone. In other words, there will be a primary health need if the nursing or other health services required by the individual are more than incidental or ancillary to the provision of accommodation which a local authority is under a duty to provide, and are of a nature beyond that which an authority whose primary responsibility is for social services could be expected to provide, but for section 49 of the 2001 Act, as part of a social services package. This issue can only be addressed by assessing the totality of the relevant needs and answering the question as to whether the nature and degree of the nursing care alone or together with other factors means that the local authority cannot lawfully provide it in its totality, and therefore, if it is to be provided its provision falls to the NHS.'

7.14 As will be considered below, the culmination of all of this can now be found in the National Framework. The gloss upon the *Grogan* judgment is contained in Annex C. It concludes:

> 'In assessing whether Mrs Grogan was entitled to NHS continuing Healthcare, the Care Trust did not have in place – and did not apply – criteria which properly identified the test or approach to be followed in deciding whether her primary need was a health need.
>
> The court identified the fact that there can be an overlap, or a gap, between social care and NHS provision, depending on the test, or tests, applied. The court accepted, as had been submitted by the Secretary of State, that the extent of her duties was governed by NHS legislation, not the upper limits of local authority lawful provision, and that therefore there was a potential in law for a gap between what the Secretary of State provided and those "health services" that the local authority could "lawfully" supply.

If the policy of the Secretary of State was that there should be no gap, then, when applying the primary health need approach, this should be considered against the limits of social services lawful provision, not just by reference to a "primary health need".

The Trust's decision that Mrs Grogan did not qualify for NHS Continuing Healthcare was set aside and the question of her entitlement to NHS Continuing Healthcare was remitted to the Trust for further consideration.

There was no finding, or other indication, that Mrs Grogan in fact met the criteria for NHS Continuing Healthcare.'

7.15 A claim for judicial review arose out of a dispute as to who should pay the care costs (as between a PCT and a local authority) was considered in *R (on the application of St Helens Borough Council) v Manchester Primary Care Trust* [2008] EWCA Civ 931, [2008] 11 CCLR 774. Essentially, the PCT had determined that the needs of an individual were not primarily health care needs, but that nevertheless it would contribute to the costs of the care of that individual. A subsequent decision was then to reverse the provision of the costs of the care. The local authority judicially reviewed the latter decision (but did not challenge the basis of the decision that the needs of the individual were not primarily healthcare needs). The Court drew attention to the existing division of responsibility of the local authority versus the PCT (as set out in all the paragraphs above) to the effect that the PCT is governed by the National Health Service Act 2006, and the local authority (in this instance) by the National Assistance Act 1948, the National Health Service and Community Care Act 1990, and the Chronically Sick and Disabled Persons Act 1970. There should be no gap in the provision to the individual. The PCT was the primary decision maker in respect of its responsibilities. The Court was not the appropriate forum to determine two conflicting decisions, both of which had been reached on a rational basis (ie in accordance with agreed procedures and unchallenged eligibility criteria). The application was dismissed, with the Court determining that expensive litigation as to which public body should pay was unsatisfactory. Thus, since the Court will be reluctant to consider it appropriate to adjudicate on this type of dispute, procedures for resolving the matter will be as between the relevant public bodies. The formalities for avoiding such disputes are considered below, although a seamless procedure does not exist. Consideration (on this point) is given to the NHS Continuing Healthcare (Responsibilities) Directions 2009 (see **7.35**) which, together with the National Framework, should lead to a resolution of disputes.

7.16 A slightly different perspective upon the law in this area was provided in *R (on the application of T and others) v Haringey LBC and another* [2005] EWHC 2235 (Admin), [2006] 9 CCLR 58. It involved one child directly, who had been discharged from hospital following a tracheostomy, and required nursing care. A dispute arose as to: (a) how much nursing care was required; and (b) what type of nursing care was required; and (c) who should provide it. The child was duly assessed under the Children Act 1989. The nursing care was (as a matter of fact) provided by registered nurses, and although this was not a prerequisite it was common ground that it would have been almost impossible to obtain nursing care that was not provided by a registered nurse. The local authority argued that is was prohibited from supplying the care by s 49 of the Health and Social Care Act 2001, and that this prohibition applied equally to the Chronically Sick and Disabled Persons Act 1970. On the particular facts of the case, it was held that the provision of the care fell outside the scope of s 17(1) of the Children Act 1989. The same conclusion followed in respect of the Chronically Sick and Disabled Persons Act 1970 and it was observed that:

> '[88] 77 ... one explanation for section 49 of the HSCA not including either Children Act or CSDPA functions is that it was not thought that the language in which their functions was couched would permit the potential for nursing care by registered nurses for medical conditions to arise as social services functions. It would be the reverse for NAA functions exercised by social services authorities.'

In other words, s 49 does not apply to the 1970 Act in respect of children (cf *Spink*). The PCT could not be under any compulsion, as its duty was merely a target duty (under the NHS Act 1977).

Community care (delayed discharges)

7.17 The implications for the issues set out above are re-visited below, under discussion of the National Framework and the National Health Service Act 2006. Before reaching that point, it is appropriate to consider the Community Care (Delayed Discharges) Act 2003. The effect of the Act is to penalise a local authority which fails to make arrangements in sufficient time in order for a patient to be discharged from hospital (by obliging it to pay the hospital). It also enables the Secretary of State to make regulations which remove the power of a local authority to charge for certain services. These have already been considered in part above. Part 2 of the Act considers those provisions that should be made available free of charge. The statute is supplemented by the Delayed Discharges (Continuing Care) Direction 2009 which came into force on 1 October 2009.

Community Care (Delayed Discharges Etc) Act 2003

1 Meaning of "NHS body" and "qualifying hospital patient"

(1) In this Part –

"NHS body" means –

  (a)   a National Health Service trust;
  (ab) an NHS foundation trust; or
  (b)   a Primary Care Trust (in England) or a Local Health Board (in Wales); and

"qualifying hospital patient" means, subject to subsection (2), a person being accommodated at –

  (a)   a health service hospital; or

(b)　an independent hospital in pursuance of arrangements made by an NHS body,

who is receiving (or who has received or is expected to receive) care of a description prescribed in regulations.

(2) The term "qualifying hospital patient" does not include any person who is ordinarily resident outside England and Wales.

(3) An NHS body may make arrangements with any person connected with the management of an independent hospital in the United Kingdom for that person (or any employee of his) to do, on behalf of the NHS body and in accordance with the arrangements, anything which is required or authorised to be done by the NHS body by or under this Part in relation to qualifying hospital patients accommodated in that hospital.

(4) Anything done or omitted to be done by or in relation to the authorised person (or any employee of his) in pursuance of such arrangements is to be treated as done or omitted to be done by or in relation to the NHS body.

(5) Nothing in subsection (3) or (4) prevents anything being done by or in relation to the NHS body.

2 Notice of patient's likely need for community care services

(1) This section applies where –

(a)　a person ("the patient") is or is expected to become a qualifying hospital patient at a particular hospital, and

(b)　the responsible NHS body considers that it is unlikely to be safe to discharge the patient from hospital unless one or more community care services are made available for him.

(2) It is the duty of the responsible NHS body to give notice of the patient's case for the purposes of this Part –

(a)　to the social services authority appearing to the NHS body to be the authority in whose area the patient is ordinarily resident when the notice is given, or

(b)　if it appears to them that the patient has no settled residence, to the social services authority in whose area the hospital is situated.

(3) That notice –

(a)　must state that it is given under this section; and

(b)　if given before the day on which the patient is admitted to the hospital, must not be given earlier than the beginning of the period of eight days ending with the day on which he is expected to be admitted.

(4) Before giving a notice under this section the responsible NHS body must consult –

(a)　the patient; and

(b)　if the responsible NHS body is aware of the identity of a person who is a carer in respect of the patient and it is reasonably practicable to consult him, that carer.

(5) In this Part "the responsible NHS body", in relation to a person who is or is expected to become a qualifying hospital patient, means –

(a) if the hospital concerned is a health service hospital, the NHS body managing the hospital; or

(b) if the hospital concerned is an independent hospital, the NHS body making the arrangements for the patient to be accommodated.

(6) In this Part "the responsible authority", in relation to a person whose case has been notified under this section, means (subject to any regulations under section 10) the social services authority to which the notice is given.

3 Notices under section 2: supplementary

(1) A notice under section 2 remains in force until the patient to which it relates is discharged, unless it has previously ceased to have effect by virtue of subsection (2) or (3).

(2) The responsible NHS body may withdraw the notice by giving notice of withdrawal to the responsible authority.

(3) Regulations may prescribe other circumstances in which the notice ceases to have effect.

(4) If the notice ceases to have effect before the patient is discharged –

(a) no further steps under section 4, 5 or 6 resulting from the notice shall be taken and no liability (or further liability) to make a payment under section 6(2) shall accrue; and

(b) the responsible NHS body may (subject to section 2(1)) give a fresh notice under section 2 in relation to the patient;

but paragraph (a) does not affect any liability which accrues before the notice ceases to have effect.

(5) Regulations may provide for –

(a) the form and content of –
(i) notices under section 2; and
(ii) notices of withdrawal under subsection (2),

and the manner in which such notices are to be given;

(b) circumstances in which notices under section 2 must be withdrawn; and

(c) determining the day on which a notice under section 2 or a notice of withdrawal under subsection (2) is given (including provision prescribing circumstances in which a notice under section 2 is to be treated for any specified purpose as having been given on a day other than that on which it was in fact given).

Notice of needs

7.18 These two sections provide for formal notification to the relevant local authority that a discharge will take place, and that community care services will be required. Those services will be under any of the following: s 29 of NAA 1948; s 45 of the Health Services and Public Health Act 1968; s 117 of the Mental Health Act 1983; s 2 of the Chronically Sick and Disabled Persons Act 1970; s 47 of the National Health Service and Community Care Act 1990.

4 Duties of responsible authority following notice under section 2

(1) The duties in this section apply where notice of a patient's case under section 2 has been given.

(2) The responsible authority must –

    (a)   carry out an assessment of the patient's needs with a view to identifying any community care services that need to be made available in order for it to be safe to discharge him; and

    (b)   after consulting the responsible NHS body, decide which of those services (if any) the authority will make available for the patient.

(3) The responsible authority must, in the circumstances mentioned in subsection (4), also –

    (a)   carry out an assessment of the needs of any person who is a carer in respect of the patient ("the carer") with a view to identifying any services which –

        (i)   the authority may provide under section 2 of the Carers and Disabled Children Act 2000 (c 16); and

        (ii)   need to be made available to the carer in order for it to be safe to discharge the patient; and

    (b)   after consulting the responsible NHS body, decide which of those services (if any) the authority will make available to the carer.

(4) The duties in subsection (3) apply only where the carer –

    (a)   asks the responsible authority to carry out an assessment under subsection (3); or

    (b)   has, within the period of twelve months ending with the day on which the notice under section 2 was given (or at any time after that day), asked the responsible authority to carry out an assessment under section 1 of the Carers and Disabled Children Act 2000.

(5) The duties in subsection (2) or (3) apply whether or not the patient's needs for community care services or the carer's needs for services (as the case may be) have previously been assessed.

(6) The responsible authority must keep under review –

    (a)   the needs of the patient; and

    (b)   the needs of any carer whose needs it has assessed under subsection (3)(a),

so far as affecting the services that need to be made available in order for it to be safe to discharge the patient.

(7) The responsible authority may, after consulting the responsible NHS body, alter –

    (a)   its decision under subsection (2)(b); or

    (b)   any decision taken by it under subsection (3)(b),

to take account of any change in circumstances since the assessment carried out under subsection (2)(a) or (3)(a) (as the case may be).

(8) The responsible authority must inform the responsible NHS body of the decision under subsection (2)(b), of any decision under subsection (3)(b) and of any alteration made under subsection (7).

(9) Anything done under subsection (2) above is to be treated as done under section 47(1) of the National Health Service and Community Care Act 1990 (c 19) (but without prejudice to anything to be done under that section in relation to any other community care services).

(10) Anything done under subsection (3) above is to be treated as done under section 1 or 2 of the Carers and Disabled Children Act 2000 (but without prejudice to anything to be done under that section in relation to other services which may be provided to the carer).

Duties of local authority

7.19 There is a mandatory duty to assess (in accordance with s 47(1) of the National Health Service and Community Care Act 1990). It also triggers the assessment for services under ss 1 and 2 of the Carers and Disabled Children Act 2000. It does not necessarily mean that a full s 47 assessment will be completed. A failure to assess will lead to an obligation upon the local authority to start making payments to the hospital.

5 Duties of responsible NHS body following notice under section 2

(1) The duties under this section apply where notice of a patient's case under section 2 has been given.

(2) The responsible NHS body, and any other NHS body which is considering whether to provide services to the patient after discharge, must consult the responsible authority before deciding what services (if any) it will make available to him in order for it to be safe to discharge the patient.

(3) The responsible NHS body must give the responsible authority notice of the day on which it proposes to discharge the patient.

(4) The notice under subsection (3) remains in force until the end of the relevant day, unless it has previously been withdrawn.

(5) The responsible NHS body may withdraw the notice under subsection (3) at any time before the end of the relevant day by giving notice of withdrawal to the responsible authority.

(6) For the purposes of this Part "the relevant day", in relation to a qualifying hospital patient, is the later of –

    (a)   the day specified in the notice under subsection (3); and

    (b)   the last day of the prescribed minimum interval after the notice under section 2 is given.

(7) Regulations may prescribe a period as the minimum interval after a notice under section 2 is given; but that period must –

    (a)   begin with the day after that on which the notice under section 2 is given; and

    (b)   be a period of at least two days.

(8) Until 31st March 2005 the period of two days referred to in subsection (7) is exclusive of Sundays and public holidays in England and Wales.

(9) If the notice under subsection (3) is withdrawn before the end of the relevant day –

(a)   the duty under subsection (3) applies again; and

(b)   when a fresh notice under subsection (3) is given, subsection (6) applies again for the purpose of identifying a new "relevant day".

(10) Regulations may provide for –

(a)   the time at which notices under subsection (3) are to be given;

(b)   the form and content of –

(i)   notices under subsection (3); and

(ii)   withdrawal notices under subsection (5);

and the manner in which such notices are to be given;

(c)   circumstances in which notices under subsection (3) must be withdrawn; and

(d)   determining the day on which a notice under subsection (3) or a notice of withdrawal under subsection (5) is given (including provision prescribing circumstances in which a notice under subsection (3) is to be treated for any specified purpose as having been given on a day other than that on which it was in fact given).

Duties of hospital

7.20   It is at this point that the hospital will be obliged to decide what services it will provide after discharge. It is also the point at which any disputes (pursuant to the sorts of situations set out above) should require resolution.

6 Liability to make delayed discharge payments

(1) This section applies where notice of a patient's case under section 2 and notice of the proposed discharge day under section 5(3) have both been given (and are in force).

(2) If by the end of the relevant day –

(a)   the patient has not been discharged and the responsible authority has not complied with its duties under section 4(2); or

(b)   it has not been possible to discharge the patient because, and only because, either of the conditions in subsection (3) is satisfied (or both are satisfied),

the responsible authority must make a payment of the amount prescribed in regulations for each day of the delayed discharge period.

(3) The conditions referred to in subsection (2) are that –

(a)   the responsible authority has not made available for the patient a community care service which it decided under section 4(2)(b) to make available for him;

(b)　the responsible authority has not made available for the patient's carer a service which it decided under section 4(3)(b) to make available to the carer.

(4) For this purpose "the delayed discharge period" is, subject to subsections (5) and (7), the period –

(a)　beginning with the day after the relevant day, and
(b)　ending with the day on which the patient is discharged.

(5) If on any day before that on which the patient is discharged the responsible authority gives notice to the responsible NHS body that –

(a)　it has complied with its duties under section 4(2),
(b)　every community care service that it decided under section 4(2)(b) to make available has been made available for the patient, and
(c)　every service that it decided under section 4(3)(b) to make available to a carer has been made available,

the delayed discharge period ends with that day.

(6) The references in subsections (3) and (5) to services "decided under" section 4(2)(b) or (3)(b) are, in a case where the decision in question has been altered under section 4(7), to any services specified in the altered decision.

(7) Regulations may –

(a)　require days after the relevant day not to be treated as days of the delayed discharge period;
(b)　prescribe circumstances (other than those mentioned in subsections (4) and (5)) in which the delayed discharge period ends;
(c)　make provision for determining the day on which a patient is discharged (including provision prescribing circumstances in which a patient is to be treated for the purposes of this section as having been discharged on a day other than that on which he was in fact discharged).

7 Delayed discharge payments: supplementary

(1) In prescribing an amount under section 6(2) the appropriate Minister must have regard (among other things) to either or both of the following matters –

(a)　costs to NHS bodies of providing accommodation and personal care to patients who are ready to be discharged; and
(b)　costs to social services authorities of providing community care services to, and services to carers in relation to, persons who have been discharged.

(2) Any payment which the responsible authority is required to make under section 6 in relation to qualifying hospital patient shall, subject to subsection (3), be made to the responsible NHS body.

(3) In cases of any description prescribed in regulations the payment shall be made to the person prescribed in relation to cases of that description.

8 Ordinary residence

(1) Any question arising under this Part as to the ordinary residence of a person who is or is expected to become a qualifying hospital patient shall be determined by the Secretary of State or by the Assembly.

(2) The Secretary of State and the Assembly must make and publish arrangements for determining which cases are to be dealt with by the Secretary of State and which are to be dealt with by the Assembly.

(3) Those arrangements may include provision for the Secretary of State and the Assembly to agree, in relation to any question that has arisen, which of them is to deal with the case.

9 Dispute resolution

(1) Regulations may make provision for panels appointed by Strategic Health Authorities in England and by Local Health Boards in Wales to assist in the resolution of disputes between two or more public authorities about matters arising under or in relation to this Part.

(2) The persons forming a panel for the purpose of a particular dispute must be appointed by a Strategic Health Authority or Local Health Board from lists of persons required by the regulations to be kept by the Authority or Board.

(3) The regulations must contain such provision as the appropriate Minister considers appropriate for ensuring that each social services authority situated (or any part of whose area is situated) in the area of a Strategic Health Authority or a Local Health Board is consulted about the persons whose names appear on any list kept by the Authority or Board for the purposes of subsection (2).

(4) The regulations may make provision about the panels, including in particular –

    (a)   provision for determining who is to appoint a panel in the case of a dispute between public authorities which are not all situated in the area of a single Strategic Health Authority or Local Health Board;

    (b)   provision specifying the descriptions of disputes which may be referred to a panel;

    (c)   provision about the recommendations (including recommendations relating to the payment of any amount by one party to another) which may be made by a panel in relation to any dispute referred to it.

(5) Regulations may prohibit a public authority from bringing legal proceedings against another public authority in relation to a dispute before such steps have been taken in relation to a panel appointed by virtue of this section as may be prescribed in the regulations.

(6) For the purposes of this section "public authority" means an NHS body or a social services authority.

Dispute resolution

7.21   If a dispute arises as to ordinary residence, then this must be referred to the Secretary of State. However, it also creates a mechanism for attempting to resolve a dispute arising out of the Act, which includes who should be providing after-care services, and whether they form part of social services responsibility or health care responsibility. Any dispute which is referred to the Secretary of State must conform to the Ordinary Residence Disputes (Community Care (Delayed Discharges etc) Act 2003) Directions 2010. These came into force on 19 April 2010. In effect, it provides a formal and mandatory requirement for 'constructive dialogue' and that a resolution of the problem should be reached within four months of the date upon which the dispute arose. Only after that, can the matter be referred to the Secretary of State. There is a lengthy list of documents that are required to be sent to the Department of Health for such a determination.

10 Adjustments between social services authorities

(1) Regulations may make provision as to the application of this Part in cases where, in relation to a qualifying hospital patient, it appears to the responsible authority for the time being that the patient is ordinarily resident in the area of another social services authority.

(2) The regulations may, among other things, authorise or require a social services authority –

    (a)   to accept a notice given to it under section 2 notwithstanding that it may wish to dispute that it was the right authority to be notified;

    (b)   to become the responsible authority for a patient's case in place of the social services authority previously responsible;

    (c)   to recover expenditure incurred –

        (i)   in the performance of functions under this Part in relation to a qualifying patient;

        (ii)   in the provision of community care services which are the subject of a decision under section 4(2)(b); or

        (iii)   in the provision of services to a carer which are the subject of a decision under section 4(3)(b),

from another social services authority.

(3) The regulations may modify the effect of any provision of this Part as it applies in any cases falling within subsection (1).

Adjustments

7.22 This simply provides for problems where there may also be disputes between local authorities over ordinary residence. Any of these types of dispute will involve the use of the Ordinary Residence Guidance (referred to in more detail at **7.53–7.54** in the context of this Chapter).

12 Interpretation

In this Part –

    "carer", in relation to a qualifying hospital patient, means a person who –

        (a)   provides or intends to provide a substantial amount of care on a regular basis for the patient; and

        (b)   is entitled to ask for an assessment under section 1 of the Carers and Disabled Children Act 2000 (c 16);

"community care service" has the meaning given by section 46(3) of the National Health Service and Community Care Act 1990;

"health service hospital" means a health service hospital within the meaning given by the National Health Service Act 2006 or the National Health Service (Wales) Act 2006;

"independent hospital" has the same meaning as in the Care Standards Act 2000;

"mental health care" means any health services relating to mental health which are of a description prescribed by order;

"NHS body" has the meaning given by section 1;

"qualifying hospital patient" has the meaning given by section 1;

"the relevant day" has the meaning given in section 5(6);

"the responsible authority" has the meaning given by section 2(6);

"the responsible NHS body" has the meaning given by section 2(5);

"social services authority" means a local authority for the purposes of the Local Authority Social Services Act 1970.

14 Power to apply Part 1 to NHS patients in care homes

(1) The appropriate Minister may by order provide for this Part to apply in relation to qualifying care home patients as it applies to qualifying hospital patients.

(2) An order under this section may –

    (a)   specify such modifications of this Part as appear to the appropriate Minister to be necessary for it to apply satisfactorily in relation to qualifying care home patients; and

    (b)   make supplementary, consequential, incidental, transitional or saving provision.

(3) In this section –

"care home" has the same meaning as in the Care Standards Act 2000 (c 14); and

"qualifying care home patient" means a person being accommodated at a care home, in pursuance of arrangements made by an NHS body, who is receiving (or who has received or is expecting to receive) care of a description prescribed in regulations.

(4) The care prescribed under subsection (3) must be care which is prescribed under section 1 for the purposes of the definition of "qualifying hospital patient" (or which as nearly as possible corresponds to care that is so prescribed).

Free provision of services

7.23   The part of the statute set out below and its interaction with NAA 1948, the Health and Social Services and Adjudication Act 1983 and the Carers and Disabled Children Act 2000 has already been considered above.

Part 2
Local Authority Community Care Services and Services for Carers

15 Free provision of services in England

(1) The Secretary of State may by regulations require that the provision of any qualifying service of a description prescribed in the regulations is to be free of charge to the person to whom it is provided.

(2) The regulations may (without prejudice to the generality of subsection (1)) –

(a)   prescribe circumstances in which a qualifying service is to be provided free of charge; and

(b)   limit the period for which a qualifying service is to be so provided.

(3) In this section "qualifying service" means –

(a)   the provision of accommodation under Part 3 of the National Assistance Act 1948 (c 29) in pursuance of arrangements made by a local authority in England; or

(b)   any service which is provided to a person by, or in pursuance of arrangements made by, a local authority in England under any enactment mentioned in section 17(2)(a) to (c) and (f) of the Health and Social Services and Social Security Adjudications Act 1983 (c 41) (charges for local authority services).

(4) The regulations may not require any of the following services to be provided free of charge for a period of more than six weeks –

(a)   the provision of accommodation under Part 3 of the National Assistance Act 1948;

(b)   the provision of personal care to a person in any place where that person is living, other than accommodation provided under that Part of that Act;

(c)   a service provided to a carer under section 2 of the Carers and Disabled Children Act 2000 which consists of the provision of personal care delivered to the person cared for (in accordance with subsection (3) of that section).

(5) The regulations may –

(a)   make different provision for different descriptions of qualifying service; and

(b)   make supplementary, consequential, incidental, transitional or saving provision.

(6) The power of the Secretary of State to make regulations under this section is exercisable by statutory instrument subject to annulment in pursuance of a resolution of either House of Parliament.

THE DELAYED DISCHARGES (ENGLAND) REGULATIONS 2003, SI 2003/2277

Acute care

7.24 The Regulations provide for a classification of the type of care that a patient must be receiving in order to become a 'qualifying hospital patient'. These are 'acute care' and 'not care in respect of which the patient has given an undertaking to pay'. Acute care is intensive medical treatment under the supervision of a consultant which is for a limited time after which the patient no longer benefits. Types of care that are *not* acute are maternity care; mental health care; palliative care; intermediate care; care provided for the purposes of recuperation or rehabilitation (reg 3).

Dispute resolution

7.25 Regulation 14 provides for the procedure to be adopted where there is a dispute about any matter arising out of Part 1 of the Act between two or more public authorities. Regulations 14, 15 and 16 deal with the Panel which will assist in resolving the dispute, and reg 17 places an embargo on legal proceedings until such dispute resolution has been concluded. Regulation 18 deals with procedures when there is a dispute as to ordinary residence.

THE NATIONAL HEALTH SERVICE ACT 2006

The National Framework for Continuing Healthcare and NHS Funded Nursing Care

7.26 As indicated above, the current National Framework is supplemented by directions and guidance. It is a concise and well-written document that provides a summary of the problems that have been in existence for some considerable time. It supersedes HSC (2001) 15 and LAC (2001) 18: *NHS Continuing Care: action following the Grogan judgment* (2006). From 1 October 2007 the previous guidance and circulars contained in LAC (2001) 26 and LAC (2003) 7 were cancelled. The first version stated:

> '1 It concentrates mainly on the process of establishing eligibility for NHS Continuing Healthcare and principles of care planning and dispute resolution relevant to that process, rather than specifying every aspect of planning NHS Continuing Healthcare.'

The revised version emerged as a result of reviews in 2008.

Definitions

7.27 The concept of continuing care is 'care provided over an extended period of time to a person aged 18 or over to meet physical or mental health needs which have arisen as the result of disability, accident or illness. NHS

Continuing Healthcare means a package of continuing healthcare arranged and funded solely by the NHS' (para 8).

Liaison between local authorities and NHS bodies

7.28 It continues:

> '9 An individual who needs "continuing care" may require services from NHS bodies and/or LAs. Both NHS bodies and LAs therefore have responsibilities to ensure that the assessment of eligibility for, and provision of, continuing care takes place in a timely and consistent fashion. If a person does not qualify for NHS continuing healthcare, the NHS may still have a responsibility to effectively contribute to that person's health needs – either by directly providing services or by part-funding the package of support. Where a package of support is provided or funded by both an LA and an NHS body, this is sometimes known as a "joint package" of continuing care ...'

It can be seen that the specific responsibility for liaison between the two public bodies is presaged by the Community Care (Delayed Discharges etc) Act 2003, and there are other aspects of the National Health Service Act 2006 which follow in a similar manner. The question of joint funding is considered at greater length below.

Changes arising from the National Health Service Act 2006

7.29 The changes brought about under the new regime are that there should firstly be 'one national approach on eligibility, with a common process and national tools to support decision making, for the NHS in England' (10a). Prior to this each of the 28 strategic health authorities had their own approach. Secondly, 'there should be one single band for NHS funded Nursing Care in a nursing home' (10b). The *Grogan* judgment (it will be recalled) in part was obliged to consider the different banding for eligibility for nursing care. A single band has been in operation since 1 October 2007. The specific directions on this are the National Health Service (Nursing Care in Residential Accommodation) (England) Directions 2007. These have been in force since 1 October 2007. It formalises the requirement on a PCT to carry out an assessment (reg 2) and makes arrangements for transitional provisions in respect of high, medium and low band payments (regs 4 and 5). Regulation 2 is set out below.

> **National Health Service (Nursing Care in Residential Accommodation) (England) Directions 2007**
>
> **2 Persons who enter relevant premises or who develop a need for nursing care on or after the relevant date**
>
> (1) Subject to paragraphs (2) and (3), where it appears to a Primary Care Trust that a person for whom it has responsibility –

(a)   is, on or after the relevant date, resident in relevant premises or may need to become resident in such premises; and

(b)   may be in need of nursing care,

that body shall carry out an assessment of his need for nursing care.

(2) Before carrying out an assessment under paragraph (1), the Primary Care Trust shall consider whether its duty under direction 2(2) of the Responsibilities Directions (duties of Primary Care Trusts – determining eligibility for NHS Continuing Healthcare) is engaged and if so, it shall comply with the requirements of those Directions prior to carrying out any assessment under this direction.

(3) Paragraph (1) shall not apply if the Primary Care Trust is providing the person with NHS Continuing Healthcare.

(4) Where –

(a)   the Primary Care Trust has carried out an assessment pursuant to direction 2(2) or (3) of the Responsibilities Directions, but

(b)   paragraph (3) does not apply because a decision has been made that the person is not eligible for NHS Continuing Healthcare,

that Trust shall nevertheless use that assessment, wherever reasonably practicable, to determine whether the person has a need for nursing care in making its assessment under paragraph (1).

(5) Where –

(a)   the Primary Care Trust determines that a person has a need for nursing care pursuant to this direction; and

(b)   the person has agreed with the Primary Care Trust with responsibility for him that he does want to be provided with such nursing care,

the Primary Care Trust shall pay to the person registered under Part 2 of the Care Standards Act 2000 in respect of the relevant premises the flat rate in respect of that person's nursing care.

National Health Service Act 2006 and other community care legislation

7.30   The guidance states:

'15 Primary legislation governing the health service does not use the expressions "continuing care", "NHS continuing healthcare" or "primary health need". However section 1 of the National Health Service Act 2006 requires the secretary of state to continue the promotion in England of a comprehensive health service, designed to secure improvement in (a) the physical and mental health of the people of England and (b) the prevention, diagnosis and treatment of illness ... a duty to provide services for the "care of persons suffering from illness" throughout England to whatever extent he or she considers it necessary to meet all reasonable requirements.'

This is the target duty referred to above, and is subject to resource restrictions.

Local authority assessment

7.31 If a local authority identifies someone who appears to need community care it is under a duty to assess those needs (s 47 of the National Health Service and Community Care Act 1990), which may include accommodation, as well as domiciliary care. The Local Authority must notify the PCT if:

> '16 ... it becomes apparent to the authority that the person has needs which may fall under the National Health Service Act 2006, and invite the PCT to assist in the making of the assessment (see section 47(3)(a) of the National Health Service and Community Care Act 1990).'

It will be recalled that there is a similar obligation upon the NHS body, in that it has to give notice to a local authority in certain circumstances, but prior to so doing it must carry out its own assessment (s 2(2) of the Community Care (Delayed Discharges etc) Act 2003).

Prohibition on provision

7.32 A local authority is prohibited from providing services which are required to be provided under the National Health Service Act 2006 (s 29(6)(b) of NAA 1948). As has been discussed above, similar considerations apply as a result of s 49 of the Health and Social Care Act 2001 (paras 18–20 of the National Framework).

The test for NHS versus local authority responsibility

7.33 The National Framework builds on previous authority and discussion on this controversial point. It states that:

> '[25] The Secretary of State has developed the concept of a "primary health need". Where a person's primary need is a health need, they are eligible for NHS continuing healthcare. Deciding whether this is the case involves looking at the totality of the relevant needs. Where an individual has a primary health need and is therefore eligible for NHS continuing healthcare, the NHS is responsible for providing all of that individual's assessed needs – including accommodation, if that is part of the overall need.
>
> [27] There should be no gap in the provision of care. People should not find themselves in a situation where neither the NHS nor the relevant LA (subject to the person meeting the relevant means test and having needs that fall within the appropriate local Fair Access to Care bandings) will fund care, either separately or together. Therefore, the 'primary health need' test should be applied, so that a decision of ineligibility for NHS continuing healthcare is only possible where, taken as a whole, the nursing or other health services required by the individual:
>
> (a) are no more than incidental or ancillary to the provision of accommodation which the LA Social Services are, or would be but for a person's means, under a duty to provide; and

(b)   are not of a nature beyond which a LA whose primary responsibility is to provide Social Services could be expected to provide [26] There are certain limitations to this test ... neither the PCT nor the LA can dictate what the other agency should provide, and the *Coughlan* judgment itself focused only on general and registered nursing needs.'

Specific criteria

7.34   The National Framework proposes the following:

'28 Certain characteristics of need – and their impact on the care required to manage them – may help to determine whether the "quality" or "quantity" of care required is more than the limits of LA's responsibilities as outlined in *Coughlan*:

1   Nature: ... the type of those needs ... the overall effect of those needs on the individual, including the type ("quality") of interventions required to manage them;
2   Intensity: ... both to the extent ("quantity") and severity ("degree") of the needs ... including the need for sustained/ongoing care ("continuity");
3   Complexity: ... how the needs present and interact to increase the skill needed to monitor and manage the care ...;
4   Unpredictability: ... the degree to which needs fluctuate ... the level of risk to the person's health if adequate and timely care is not provided ....'

The Guidance also refers to 'Decision Support Tools' which are intended to assist decision makers, and stresses that in order to make a decision, there needs to be evidence available from all assessments that are appropriate. These 'Decision Support Tools' are not reproduced at all in this text, but are on the Department of Health website. Further information about continuing healthcare can be found in companion guidance (*NHS Continuing Healthcare Practice Guidance* March 2010). This is a slightly more discursive text (and is only guidance) but it has this to say about the distinction between a social care need and a health need. Both descriptions are carefully hedged with the caveat that they are **not** legal definitions;

'4.11 a health care need ... in general terms ... is one related to the treatment, control or prevention of a disease, illness, injury or disability, and the care or aftercare of a person with these needs (whether or not the tasks involved have to be carried out by a health professional). In general terms ... a social care need is one that is focused on providing assistance with activities of daily living, maintaining independence, social interaction, enabling the individual to play a fuller part in society, protecting them in vulnerable situations and (in some circumstances) accessing a care home or other supported accommodation. Social care needs are directly related to the type of welfare services that LA's have a duty or power to provide ....'

An attempt to challenge (by way of judicial review) a decision that excluded a person from continuing care when the eligibility criteria devised by a PCT was in accordance with the relevant guidance failed (*R (on the application of Green (by her litigation friend Kempson)) v South West Strategic Health Authority and (1) North Somerset PCT (2) SoS Department of Health* [2008] EWHC 2576 (Admin), [2009] 12 CCLR 93).

Core values

7.35 These are summarised at paras 33–53 of the National Framework. A number of specific points emerge that may be of use to practitioners. The first is that the assessment and decision-making process should be 'person centred' (para 33). If there is any issue of mental capacity, then the use of the Mental Capacity Act 2005 should be considered, and also the necessity or otherwise of appointing an IMCA (see Chapter 2). Both PCTs and local authorities are reminded that a carer may have a right to a separate assessment of their needs as a carer (Carers and Disabled Children Act 2000). The setting of the care provided is irrelevant (para 47). Financial issues:

'48 ... should not be considered as a part of the decision about an individual's eligibility for NHS Continuing Healthcare.'

Finally the reasons given for a decision on eligibility should *not* be based on the person's diagnosis or:

'49 the setting of care; the ability of the care provider to manage care; the use (or not) of NHS employed staff to provide care ; the need for/presence of "specialist staff" in care delivery ; the fact that a need is well managed; the existence of other NHS funded care or any other input-related (rather than needs-related) rationale.'

The duty of the PCT to determine eligibility is set out in reg 2 of the NHS Continuing Healthcare (Responsibilities) Directions 2009. These have been made pursuant to both the National Health Service Act 2006 and the Local Authority Social Services Act 1970. The CHC Regulations came into force on 1 October 2009.

NHS Continuing Healthcare (Responsibilities) Directions 2009

Duties of Primary Care Trusts – determining eligibility for NHS Continuing Healthcare

2. (1) In exercising their functions under sections 2 and 3 of the 2006 Act, insofar as they relate to NHS Continuing Healthcare, Primary Care Trusts must comply with paragraphs (2) to (11).

(2) Subject to paragraph (12), a Primary Care Trust must take reasonable steps to ensure that an assessment of eligibility for NHS Continuing Healthcare is carried out in all cases where it appears to the Trust that –

  (a)   there may be a need for such care; or
  (b)   an individual who is receiving NHS Continuing Healthcare may no longer be eligible for such care.

(3) If an assessment for NHS Continuing Healthcare is required under paragraph (2)(a), the Primary Care Trust must ensure that it is carried out before any

assessment pursuant to direction 2(1) of the National Health Service (Nursing Care in Residential Accommodation) (England) Directions 2007.

(4) If a Primary Care Trust wishes to use an initial screening process to decide whether to undertake an assessment of a person's eligibility for NHS Continuing Healthcare it must –

(a)   complete and use the NHS Continuing Healthcare Checklist issued by the Secretary of State (as amended from time to time) to inform that decision;

(b)   inform that person (or someone acting on that person's behalf) in writing of the decision as to whether to carry out an assessment of that person's eligibility for NHS Continuing Healthcare; and

(c)   make a record of the decision.

(5) When carrying out an assessment of eligibility for NHS Continuing Healthcare a Primary Care Trust must ensure that –

(a)   a multi-disciplinary team –
    (i)   undertakes an assessment of needs, or has undertaken an assessment of needs that is an accurate reflection of that person's needs at the date of the assessment of eligibility for NHS Continuing Healthcare, and
    (ii)   uses that assessment of needs to complete the Decision Support Tool for NHS Continuing Healthcare issued by the Secretary of State (as amended from time to time); and

(b)   it makes a decision as to whether that person has a primary health need, using the completed Decision Support Tool to inform that decision.

(6) If the Primary Care Trust decides that the person has a primary health need, it must also decide that that person is eligible for NHS Continuing Healthcare.

(7) In deciding whether a person has a primary health need in accordance with paragraph (5)(b), a Primary Care Trust must consider whether the nursing or other health services required by that person are –

(a)   where that person is, or is to be, accommodated in a care home (within the meaning of section 3 of the Care Standards Act 2000), more than incidental or ancillary to the provision of accommodation which a social services authority is, or would be but for a person's means, under a duty to provide; or

(b)   of a nature beyond which a social services authority whose primary responsibility is to provide social services could be expected to provide,

and if it decides that the nursing or other health services required do, when considered in their totality, fall within sub-paragraph (a) or (b), it must decide that the person has a primary health need.

(8) Paragraphs (2) to (6) do not apply where an appropriate clinician decides that –

(a)   an individual has a primary health need arising from a rapidly deteriorating condition; and

(b)   the condition may be entering a terminal phase,

and has completed a Fast Track Pathway Tool stating reasons for the decision.

(9) Subject to paragraph (12), a Primary Care Trust must, upon receipt of a Fast Track Pathway Tool completed in accordance with paragraph (8), decide that a person is eligible for NHS Continuing Healthcare.

(10) Where an assessment of eligibility for NHS Continuing Healthcare has been carried out, or a Primary Care Trust has received a Fast Track Pathway Tool completed in accordance with paragraph (8), the Primary Care Trust shall –

- (a) notify the person assessed (or someone acting on that person's behalf), in writing, of the decision made about their eligibility for NHS Continuing Healthcare, the reasons for that decision and, where applicable, the matters referred to in paragraph (11), and
- (b) make a record of the decision.

(11) Where a Primary Care Trust has decided that a person is not eligible for NHS Continuing Healthcare, it must inform the person (or someone acting on that person's behalf) of the circumstances and manner in which that person may apply for a review of the decision if they are dissatisfied with the –

- (a) procedure followed by the Primary Care Trust in reaching that decision; or
- (b) primary health need decision made in accordance with paragraph (5)(b) of this direction.

(12) This direction does not apply in a case in which a Primary Care Trust or an English NHS Trust is obliged to comply with direction 2(2) to (11) of the Delayed Discharges Directions.

(13) In this direction –

- (a) "appropriate clinician" means a person who is –
  (i) responsible for the diagnosis, treatment or care of the person in respect of whom a Fast Track Pathway Tool is being completed,
  (ii) diagnosing, or providing treatment or care to, that person under the 2006 Act, and
  (iii) a registered nurse or is included in the register maintained under section 2 of the Medical Act 1983;
- (b) "healthcare profession" means a profession which is concerned (wholly or partly) with the physical or mental health of individuals (whether or not that person is regulated by, or by virtue of, any enactment); and
- (c) "multi-disciplinary team" means a team consisting of at least –
  (i) two professionals who are from different healthcare professions, or
  (ii) one professional who is from a healthcare profession and one person who is responsible for assessing individuals for community care services under section 47 of the National Health Service and Community Care Act 1990.

Involvement of local authority in NHS assessment

7.36 There is currently no mandatory requirement for social services and NHS bodies to work together in this respect. The National Framework states:

'55 PCTs should ensure that local protocols are developed between themselves, other NHS bodies, Las and other relevant partners. These should set out each organisation's role and how its responsibilities are to be exercised ....'

The extent to which it has been made mandatory is contained in direction 3 of the NHS Continuing Healthcare (Responsibilities) Directions 2009 which is set out below

3 Duties of Primary Care Trusts and social services authorities: joint working

(1) A Primary Care Trust shall, so far as is reasonably practicable, consult with the relevant social services authority before making a decision about a person's eligibility for NHS Continuing Healthcare.

(2) The relevant social services authority shall, so far as is reasonably practicable, provide advice and assistance to the Primary Care Trust who has consulted it pursuant to paragraph (1).

(3) Nothing in this direction affects a social services authority's duty to carry out an assessment of a person's needs for community care services pursuant to section 47 of the National Health Service and Community Care Act 1990, and if it has carried out such an assessment, it shall, so far as reasonably practicable, use the information obtained as a result of that assessment to comply with its duty under paragraph (2).

(4) Any dispute between a Primary Care Trust and the relevant social services authority about –

    (a)   a decision as to eligibility for NHS Continuing Healthcare; or

    (b)   where a person is not eligible for NHS Continuing Healthcare, the contribution of a Primary Care Trust or social services authority to a joint package of care for that person,

shall be resolved in accordance with a dispute resolution procedure agreed between the two bodies concerned.

Direct payments

7.37   The basic position in respect of direct payments and NHS services is still that cannot be purchased using direct payments. As the previous Guidance observed this may mean 'a loss of control over their care that they had previously exercised' (para 77). However, there are moves away from this basic proposition that may in the fairly near future import into the NHS a scheme which is almost identical to that which has so far developed and worked within the sphere of local authority activity. This area is only explored insofar as it may intersect with local authority obligations.

7.38   The issue is considered from a slightly different perspective at **6.71** (*R (on the application of Harrison) v SoS for Health, Wakefield District Primary Care Trust, Wakefield Metropolitan District Council (interested parties); R (on the application of Garnham) v SoS for Health and Islington PCT, Islington LBC (interested party)* [2009] EWHC 574 (Admin), [2009] 12 CCLR 355). However, the authority makes it clear that there is no power under the NHS Act 2006 to provide healthcare services by way of direct payments. However, it would still be permissible for a PCT to enter into an arrangement to directly employ carers (in a situation where these have previously been employed by way of direct payments from a council). Logically, there can be no good reason why the same regime should not apply when the need has either changed from a community care service to a continuing health care need – the same principles of enhanced autonomy apply. The problem is the quagmire of statute and regulation which prohibits such a course of action happening, as described above (albeit principally but not exclusively directed to nursing care of a particular type).

7.39 To that end s 11 of the Health Act 2009 amended the National Health Service Act 2006 to allow direct payments to be made. The National Health Service (Direct Payments) Regulations 2010 were also created for the same purpose. However, these have only taken effect in certain pilot scheme areas. The period of the pilot scheme is nearing its end, and there is already in existence an order that (once implemented) will make the system available to all PCT's. In *Primary Care & Community Services:Personal Health Budgets: first steps* (DoH 2009), health care direct payments are described as:

> '46 ... similar to the existing direct payment model in social care:individuals would be given cash payments to purchase and arrange the services they need.

> 47 At present , PCTs do not have the power to issue direct payments for healthcare to patients. It is not possible to make a direct payment for healthcare via a local authority under an arrangement under s 75 of the NHS Act 2007. Also, PCTs can only reimburse a local authority under section 256 of the NHS Act for expenditure incurred for the local authority's social services. Section 256 does not provide power to make a direct payment for healthcare.'

The most extensive commentary upon direct payments thus far is contained in *Direct Payments for Health Care – information for pilot sites* (DoH July 2010).

Personal health budgets and personalisation

7.40 A similar philosophy to 'personalisation' as set out in Chapter 6 in the context of community care services has been developing in respect of health care. Direct payments are one example of this. However, there are also the idea of a 'notional personal budget', and a 'real personal budget held by a third party'. These are described (respectively) as a situation where a patient is made aware of the treatment options 'within a budget constraint and ... the financial implications of their choices. The NHS underwrites overall costs and retains all contracting and service coordination functions' and allocation of a 'real budget, held by an intermediary (eg GP, care co-ordinator, advocate) on their behalf' (para 133(a) and (b), National Framework). A more thorough commentary upon personal health budgets is contained in *Primary Care & Community Services: Personal Health Budgets: first steps*. The programme was described as being 'at a very early stage of development' (*Executive Summary Direct Payments for Health Care* July 2010) and reviews will continue until a final report being due in October 2012 (in respect of personal budgets *The cost of implementing personal health budgets* PSSRU discussion paper DoH July 2011).

Specific NHS provision

7.41   The provision for NHS Funded nursing care is set out in Annex D of the National Framework and is reproduced below.

ANNEX D DETERMINING THE NEED FOR NHS-FUNDED NURSING CARE

1. In all cases, individuals should be considered for eligibility for NHS continuing healthcare before a decision is reached about the need for NHS-funded nursing care (NHS-funded nursing care provided by registered nurses) in residential accommodation. In most cases, therefore, the individual will already have been considered for NHS continuing healthcare and will have had an associated assessment, which should provide sufficient information to gauge the need for nursing care in residential accommodation. In certain circumstances, an individual who has been found not to be eligible for NHS continuing healthcare at the Checklist stage may still need an assessment of needs for NHS-funded nursing care. In such cases, an appropriate assessment should be completed. It may, therefore, be appropriate to use the Single Assessment Process (or similar), to ensure that all needs are identified and that the decisions reached are proportionate, reasoned and recorded.

2. Where the local authority (LA) also carries out an assessment of the individual's needs, it may be appropriate for the primary care trust (PCT) to carry out an assessment for NHS-funded nursing care jointly with this process. Where an individual is funding his or her own care needs (apart from NHS-funded nursing care), PCTs should take particular care to ensure that there is clarity on the part of themselves, the relevant LA and the individual as to who is taking responsibility for the assessment, case management and review of the individual's needs on an ongoing basis.

3. The outcome of the above process should provide the PCT with sufficient information to establish a contract with a care home for NHS-funded nursing services, and will trigger the PCT's responsibility to fund the care from a registered nurse through a single rate of payment.

4. Individuals who were in receipt of the high band of NHS-funded nursing care under the three-band system that was in force until 30 September 2007 are entitled to continue on the high band until:

a)   on review, it is determined that they no longer have any need for nursing care;

b)   on review, it is determined that their needs have changed, so that under the previous three-band system, they would have moved onto the medium or low bands. In this situation, the individual should be moved onto the single rate;

c)   they are no longer resident in a care home that provides nursing care;

d)   they become eligible for NHS continuing healthcare; or

e) they die.

Dispute resolution

7.41 There is no formal method of resolving disputes between a local authority and a PCT (although there is such a procedure for an aggrieved service user). The Community Care (Delayed Discharges etc) Act 2003 does contain a procedure for such resolutions, and it is perhaps unfortunate that it has not been adopted by the National Health Service Act 2006. The Framework explicitly refers to this and states as follows:

> '[161] Directions state that PCT's and LA's in each local area should agree a local disputes resolution process to resolve cases where there is a dispute between NHS bodies, or between and LA and a PCT, about eligibility for NHS continuing healthcare and/or about the apportionment of funding in joint funded care/support packages. Disputes should not delay the provision of the packet of the care package, and the protocol should make clear how funding will be provided pending resolution of the dispute. Where disputes relate to LA's and PCTs in different geographical areas, the relevant LA and PCT should agree a dispute resolution in a robust and timely manner. This should include agreement on how funding will be provided during the dispute, and arrangements for reimbursement to the agencies involved once the dispute is resolved. The above disputes process could operate in a similar way to the panels established under the Community Care (Delayed Discharges etc) Act 2003. *Resource Pack 2 – Understanding the tools and processes* offers advice on developing an NHS continuing healthcare disputes procedure.
>
> [162] *Who Pays?* sets out expectations for when there is a dispute between PCTs as to responsibility ....'

Further comment on '*Who Pays?*' is at **7.59** et seq below, and information about refunds at **7.51**.

The statute

7.42 The Act repealed the National Health Act 1977 in its entirety, and also most of the Health and Social Care Act 2001 and Health Act 1999. The significance of the partial repeal of the latter two statutes is that they respectively provided for the creation of joint social services and health bodies and for the pooling of budgets. This is all now provided for in the National Health Service Act 2006, and the relevant extracts are set out below, with commentary where appropriate.

National Health Service Act 2006

1 Secretary of State's duty to promote health service

(1) The Secretary of State must continue the promotion in England of a comprehensive health service designed to secure improvement –

  (a) in the physical and mental health of the people of England, and

(b)   in the prevention, diagnosis and treatment of illness.

(2) The Secretary of State must for that purpose provide or secure the provision of services in accordance with this Act.

(3) The services so provided must be free of charge except in so far as the making and recovery of charges is expressly provided for by or under any enactment, whenever passed.

2 Secretary of State's general power

(1) The Secretary of State may –

(a)   provide such services as he considers appropriate for the purpose of discharging any duty imposed on him by this Act, and
(b)   do anything else which is calculated to facilitate, or is conducive or incidental to, the discharge of such a duty.

(2) Subsection (1) does not affect –

(a)   the Secretary of State's powers apart from this section,
(b)   Chapter 1 of Part 7 (pharmaceutical services).

3 Secretary of State's duty as to provision of certain services

(1) The Secretary of State must provide throughout England, to such extent as he considers necessary to meet all reasonable requirements –

(a)   hospital accommodation,
(b)   other accommodation for the purpose of any service provided under this Act,
(c)   medical, dental, ophthalmic, nursing and ambulance services,
(d)   such other services or facilities for the care of pregnant women, women who are breastfeeding and young children as he considers are appropriate as part of the health service,
(e)   such other services or facilities for the prevention of illness, the care of persons suffering from illness and the after-care of persons who have suffered from illness as he considers are appropriate as part of the health service,
(f)   such other services or facilities as are required for the diagnosis and treatment of illness.

(2) For the purposes of the duty in subsection (1), services provided under –

(a)   section 83(2) (primary medical services), section 99(2) (primary dental services) or section 115(4) (primary ophthalmic services), or
(b)   a general medical services contract, a general dental services contract or a general ophthalmic services contract,

must be regarded as provided by the Secretary of State.

(3) This section does not affect Chapter 1 of Part 7 (pharmaceutical services).

Target duties

7.43   These are the so-called 'target duties' referred to in the text. It may well be the case that the execution of these duties could lead to a lower level of provision than that which is obliged from a local authority, and/or that which a local authority may be obliged to provide. No such equivalent compulsion exists in respect of an NHS body.

12 Secretary of State's arrangements with other bodies

(1) The Secretary of State may arrange with any person or body to provide, or assist in providing, any service under this Act.

(2) Arrangements may be made under subsection (1) with voluntary organisations.

(3) The Secretary of State may make available any facilities provided by him for any service under this Act –

    (a)   to any person or body carrying out any arrangements under subsection (1), or

    (b)   to any voluntary organisation eligible for assistance under section 64 or section 65 of the Health Services and Public Health Act 1968 (c 46).

(4) Where facilities are made available under subsection (3), the Secretary of State may make available the services of any person employed in connection with the facilities by –

    (a)   the Secretary of State,
    (b)   a Strategic Health Authority,
    (c)   a Primary Care Trust,
    (d)   a Special Health Authority, or
    (e)   a Local Health Board.

(5) Powers under this section may be exercised on such terms as may be agreed, including terms as to the making of payments by or to the Secretary of State.

(6) Goods or materials may be made available either temporarily or permanently.

(7) Any power to supply goods or materials under this section includes –

    (a)   a power to purchase and store them, and
    (b)   a power to arrange with third parties for the supply of goods or materials by those third parties.

7.44 Combined with Sch 3, para 15, this section confers an extremely wide discretion on a PCT to do whatever it would seem to require (including a local authority, although this is provided for explicitly below).

74 Supply of goods and services by local authorities

(1) In the Local Authorities (Goods and Services) Act 1970 (c 39) the expression "public body" includes –

    (a)   any Strategic Health Authority, Special Health Authority or Primary Care Trust, and

    (b)   so far as relates to his functions under this Act, the Secretary of State.

(2) Subsection (1) has effect as if made by an order under section 1(5) of the Local Authorities (Goods and Services) Act 1970 and may be varied or revoked by such an order.

(3) Each local authority must make services available to each NHS body acting in its area, so far as is reasonably necessary and practicable to enable the NHS body to discharge its functions under this Act.

(4) "Services" means the services of persons employed by the local authority for the purposes of its functions under the Local Authority Social Services Act 1970 (c 42).

7.45 See **7.44** above and also s 1 of the Local Authorities (Goods and Services) Act 1970 which states:

'... a local authority and a public body ... may enter into an agreement for all or any of the following purposes ... (a) the supply by the authority of any goods or materials (b) the provision by the local authority for the body of any administrative, professional or technical services.'

Pooling of resources

7.46 The repeal of the Health Act 1999 (and in particular s 31) has not affected the ability of NHS bodies and local authorities in terms of this area of practice and finance. Sections 29–31 encouraged this procedure and it is anticipated that the combination of PCTs (or the replacement bodies if they are abolished) and LA's for joint commissioning of services will increase in the foreseeable future. Sections 75–76 and 256–257 replicate the effect of the repealed Act. The equivalent regulations in Wales are the National Health Service Bodies and Local Authorities Partnership Arrangements (Wales) Regulations 2000, SI 2000/2993 (W193).

75 Arrangements between NHS bodies and local authorities

(1) The Secretary of State may by regulations make provision for or in connection with enabling prescribed NHS bodies (on the one hand) and prescribed local authorities (on the other) to enter into prescribed arrangements in relation to the exercise of –

  (a)   prescribed functions of the NHS bodies, and
  (b)   prescribed health-related functions of the local authorities,

if the arrangements are likely to lead to an improvement in the way in which those functions are exercised.

(2) The arrangements which may be prescribed include arrangements –

  (a)   for or in connection with the establishment and maintenance of a fund –
     (i)   which is made up of contributions by one or more NHS bodies and one or more local authorities, and
     (ii)   out of which payments may be made towards expenditure incurred in the exercise of both prescribed functions of the NHS body or bodies and prescribed health-related functions of the authority or authorities,
  (b)   for or in connection with the exercise by an NHS body on behalf of a local authority of prescribed health-related functions of the authority in conjunction with the exercise by the NHS body of prescribed functions of the NHS body,

(c) for or in connection with the exercise by a local authority on behalf of an NHS body of prescribed functions of the NHS body in conjunction with the exercise by the local authority of prescribed health-related functions of the local authority,

(d) as to the provision of staff, goods or services in connection with any arrangements mentioned in paragraph (a), (b) or (c),

(e) as to the making of payments by a local authority to an NHS body in connection with any arrangements mentioned in paragraph (b),

(f) as to the making of payments by an NHS body to a local authority in connection with any arrangements mentioned in paragraph (c).

(3) Regulations under this section may make provision –

(a) as to the cases in which NHS bodies and local authorities may enter into prescribed arrangements,

(b) as to the conditions which must be satisfied in relation to prescribed arrangements (including conditions in relation to consultation),

(c) for or in connection with requiring the consent of the Secretary of State to the operation of prescribed arrangements (including provision in relation to applications for consent, the approval or refusal of such applications and the variation or withdrawal of approval),

(d) in relation to the duration of prescribed arrangements,

(e) for or in connection with the variation or termination of prescribed arrangements,

(f) as to the responsibility for, and the operation and management of, prescribed arrangements,

(g) as to the sharing of information between NHS bodies and local authorities.

(4) The provision which may be made by virtue of subsection (3)(f) includes provision in relation to –

(a) the formation and operation of joint committees of NHS bodies and local authorities,

(b) the exercise of functions which are the subject of prescribed arrangements (including provision in relation to the exercise of such functions by joint committees or employees of NHS bodies and local authorities),

(c) the drawing up and implementation of plans in respect of prescribed arrangements,

(d) the monitoring of prescribed arrangements,

(e) the provision of reports on, and information about, prescribed arrangements,

(f) complaints and disputes about prescribed arrangements,

(g) accounts and audit in respect of prescribed arrangements.

(5) Arrangements made by virtue of this section do not affect –

(a) the liability of NHS bodies for the exercise of any of their functions,

(b) the liability of local authorities for the exercise of any of their functions, or

(c) any power or duty to recover charges in respect of services provided in the exercise of any local authority functions.

(6) The Secretary of State may issue guidance to NHS bodies and local authorities in relation to consultation or applications for consent in respect of prescribed arrangements.

(7) The reference in subsection (1) to an improvement in the way in which functions are exercised includes an improvement in the provision to any individuals of any services to which those functions relate.

(8) In this section –

"health-related functions", in relation to a local authority, means functions of the authority which, in the opinion of the Secretary of State–

    (a)   have an effect on the health of any individuals,

    (b)   have an effect on, or are affected by, any functions of NHS bodies, or

    (c)   are connected with any functions of NHS bodies,

"NHS body" does not include a Special Health Authority.

(9) Schedule 18 makes provision with respect to the transfer of staff in connection with arrangements made by virtue of this section.

76 Power of local authorities to make payments

(1) A local authority may make payments to a Strategic Health Authority, a Primary Care Trust or a Local Health Board towards expenditure incurred or to be incurred by the body in connection with the performance by it of prescribed functions.

(2) A payment under this section may be made in respect of expenditure of a capital or of a revenue nature or in respect of both kinds of expenditure.

(3) The Secretary of State may by directions prescribe conditions relating to payments under this section.

(4) The power under subsection (3) may in particular be exercised so as to require, in such circumstances as may be specified –

    (a)   repayment of the whole or part of a payment under this section, or

    (b)   in respect of property acquired with payments under this section, payment of an amount representing the whole or part of an increase in the value of the property which has occurred since its acquisition.

(5) No payment may be made under this section in respect of any expenditure unless the conditions relating to it conform with the conditions prescribed for payments of that description under subsection (3).

7.47   There is therefore the possibility of a complete fusion of funds, or of delegation of functions or resources to each other, or simply having one managed provider for both areas.

The relevant regulations are the NHS Bodies and Local Authorities Partnership Arrangements Regulations 2000, SI 2000/617.

77 Care Trusts

(1) Where –

(a)   a Primary Care Trust or an NHS trust is, or will be, a party to any existing or proposed LA delegation arrangements, and

(b)   the Secretary of State considers that designation of the body as a Care Trust would be likely to promote the effective exercise by the body of prescribed health-related functions of a local authority (in accordance with the arrangements) in conjunction with prescribed NHS functions of the body,

the Secretary of State may designate the body as a Care Trust.

(2) A Primary Care Trust or NHS trust may, however, be designated only in pursuance of an application made to the Secretary of State jointly by each prescribed body.

(3) If the application under subsection (2) requests the Secretary of State to do so, he may when designating a body as a Care Trust make a direction under subsection (4).

(4) The direction is that while the body is designated it may (in addition to exercising health-related functions of the local authority as mentioned in subsection (1)(b)) exercise such prescribed health-related functions of the local authority as are specified in the direction in relation to persons in any area so specified, even though it does not exercise any NHS functions in relation to persons in that area.

(5) Where a body is designated as a Care Trust under this section –

(a)   its designation may be revoked by the Secretary of State at any time –
(i)   of the Secretary of State's own motion, and
(ii)   after such consultation as he considers appropriate,

(b)   if an application for the revocation of its designation is made to the Secretary of State by one or more of the parties to the LA delegation arrangements, its designation must be revoked by the Secretary of State at the earliest time at which he considers it practicable to do so, having regard, in particular, to any steps that need to be taken in relation to those arrangements in connection with the revocation.

(6) The designation of a body as a Care Trust under this section must be effected by an order under section 18 or 25 which –

(a)   (in the case of an existing body) amends the order establishing the body so as to change its name to one that includes the words "Care Trust", or

(b)   (in the case of a new body) establishes the body with a name that includes those words,

and any revocation of its designation must be effected by a further order under section 18 or 25 which makes such provision for changing the name of the body as the Secretary of State considers expedient.

(7) The power of the Secretary of State to dissolve a Primary Care Trust or an NHS trust includes power to dissolve such a Primary Care Trust or NHS trust where he considers that it is appropriate to do so in connection with the designation of any other such body (whether existing or otherwise) as a Care Trust.

(8) Regulations may make such incidental, supplementary or consequential provision (including provision amending, repealing or revoking enactments) as the Secretary of State considers expedient in connection with the preceding provisions of this section.

(9) Regulations under subsection (8) may, in particular, make provision –

    (a)   prescribing –
        (i)   the manner and circumstances in which, and
        (ii)   any conditions which must be satisfied before,

    an application may be made for a body to be designated as a Care Trust under this section, or to cease to be so designated, and the information to be supplied with such an application,

    (b)   enabling the Secretary of State to terminate appointments of persons as members of a Primary Care Trust or of the board of directors of an NHS trust (or of a committee of such a Primary Care Trust or NHS trust) where he considers that it is appropriate to do so in connection with the designation of the Primary Care Trust or NHS trust as a Care Trust,
    (c)   requiring the consent of the Secretary of State to be obtained before any prescribed change is made with respect to the governance of a body so designated,
    (d)   for supplementing or modifying, in connection with the operation of subsection (3), any provision made by regulations under section 75.

(10) The designation of a body as a Care Trust under this section does not affect any of the functions, rights or liabilities of that body in its capacity as a Primary Care Trust or NHS trust.

(11) In connection with the exercise by a body so designated of any relevant social services functions under LA delegation arrangements –

    (a)   section 7 of the Local Authority Social Services Act 1970 (c 42) (authorities to exercise social services functions under guidance), and
    (b)   section 7A of that Act (directions as to exercise of such functions),

apply to the body as if it were a local authority within the meaning of that Act.

(12) In this section –

    "health-related functions" has the meaning given by section 75(8),
    "LA delegation arrangements" means arrangements falling within section 75(2)(b), whether or not made in conjunction with any pooled fund arrangements,
    "NHS functions" means functions exercisable by a Primary Care Trust or NHS trust in its capacity as such,
    "pooled fund arrangements" means arrangements falling within section 75(2)(a),
    "relevant social services functions" means health-related functions which are social services functions within the meaning of the Local Authority Social Services Act 1970.

7.48 This section provides for the creation of a separate entity which combines the functions of both an NHS body and a local authority. This is not the same as a partnership arrangement.

78 Directed partnership arrangements

(1) If the Secretary of State is of the opinion –

(a)   that a body to which this section applies ("the failing body") is not exercising any of its functions adequately, and

(b)   that it would be likely to lead to an improvement in the way in which that function is exercised if it were to be exercised –

(i)   by another body to which this section applies under delegation arrangements, or

(ii)   in accordance with pooled fund arrangements made with another such body,

the Secretary of State may direct those bodies to enter into such delegation arrangements or pooled fund arrangements in relation to the exercise of the appropriate function or functions as are specified in the direction.

(2) In subsection (1) "the appropriate function or functions" means –

(a)   the function of the failing body mentioned in that subsection, and

(b)   such other function of that body (if any) as the Secretary of State considers would, if exercised under or in accordance with the arrangements in question, be likely to contribute to an improvement in the exercise of the function referred to in paragraph (a).

(3) The bodies to which this section applies are –

(a)   Strategic Health Authorities,

(b)   Primary Care Trusts,

(c)   NHS trusts,

(d)   Local Health Boards, and

(e)   local authorities,

but in subsections (1) and (2) any reference to functions is, in relation to a local authority, a reference only to relevant social services functions of the authority.

(4) In this section any reference to an improvement in the way in which any function is exercised includes an improvement in the provision to any individuals of any services to which that function relates.

(5) In this section –

"delegation arrangements" means arrangements falling within section 75(2)(b) or (c), whether or not made in conjunction with any pooled fund arrangements,
"health-related functions" has the meaning given by section 75(8),
"pooled fund arrangements" means arrangements falling within section 75(2)(a),
"relevant social services functions" means health-related functions which are social services functions within the meaning of the Local Authority Social Services Act 1970 (c 42).

7.49   An element of compulsion is available to the Secretary of State in respect of 'the failing body'.

79 Further provision about directions and directed partnership arrangements

(1) A direction under section 78(1) (a "principal direction") may make provision with respect to –

- (a)   any of the matters with respect to which provision is required to be made by the specified arrangements by virtue of regulations under section 75, and
- (b)   such other matters as the Secretary of State considers appropriate.

(2) The Secretary of State may in particular (either in a principal direction or in any subsequent direction) make provision –

- (a)   for the determination, whether –
    - (i)   by agreement, or
    - (ii)   (in default of agreement) by the Secretary of State or an arbitrator appointed by him,

    of the amount of any payments which need to be made by one body to another for the purposes of the effective operation of the specified arrangements, and for the variation of any such determination,
- (b)   specifying the manner in which the amount of any such payments must be so determined (or varied),
- (c)   requiring a body specified in the direction to supply to the Secretary of State or an arbitrator, for the purpose of enabling any such amount to be so determined (or varied), such information or documents as may be so specified,
- (d)   requiring any amount so determined (or varied) to be paid by and to such bodies as are specified in the direction,
- (e)   requiring capital assets specified in the direction to be made available by and to such bodies as are so specified.

(3) The Secretary of State may, when giving a principal direction to any bodies to which section 78 applies, give such directions to any other such body as he considers appropriate for or in connection with securing that full effect is given to the principal direction.

(4) Before giving a principal direction to any bodies to which section 78 applies, the Secretary of State may –

- (a)   direct either or both of the bodies in question to take such steps specified in the direction, or
- (b)   give such other directions,

as he considers appropriate with a view to enabling him to determine whether the principal direction should be given.

(5) The revocation of a principal direction does not affect the continued operation of the specified arrangements.

(6) "The specified arrangements", in relation to a principal direction, means the arrangements specified in the direction in pursuance of section 78(1).

82 Co-operation between NHS bodies and local authorities

In exercising their respective functions NHS bodies (on the one hand) and local authorities (on the other) must co-operate with one another in order to secure and advance the health and welfare of the people of England and Wales.

7.50 There is therefore a positive duty imposed upon local authorities to cooperate for the purpose defined above.

191 Recovery of charges

(1) All charges recoverable under this Act by –

    (a)   the Secretary of State,

    (b)   a local social services authority, or

    (c)   any body established under this Act,

may be recovered summarily as a civil debt (but this does not affect any other method of recovery).

(2) If any person, for the purpose of evading the payment of any charge under this Act, or of reducing the amount of any such charge –

    (a)   knowingly makes any false statement or false representation, or

    (b)   produces or furnishes, or causes or knowingly allows to be produced or furnished, any document or information which he knows to be false in a material particular,

the charge or the balance of the charge, may be recovered from him by the person by whom the cost of the service in question was defrayed.

7.51 There are obvious similarities between this section and the Health and Social Security Adjudications Act 1983. It is unclear whether it could be used if a dispute arose between a local authority and a PCT as to money alleged to be owed by one to the other. However, the *NHS Continuing Healthcare Refunds Guidance – March 2010* (Department of Health, effective from 1 April 2010) specifically refers to s 256 in this context (para 11 of this Guidance, and para 7.52 below in this text). It also provides a complete answer to what to do if there has been unreasonable delay by a PCT and it is the LA that has funded the costs of the services in the meantime

7.52 The following sections (256–257) provide for payments to local authorities by PCTs in respect of any health related function, and vice versa in respect of prescribed functions. These functions have not been defined precisely. The equivalent regulations in Wales are the National Health Service (Payments by Local Authorities to NHS Bodies) (Prescribed Functions) (Wales) Regulations 2001, SI 2001/1543 (W108).

256 Power of Primary Care Trusts to make payments towards expenditure on community services

(1) A Primary Care Trust may make payments to –

    (a)   a local social services authority towards expenditure incurred or to be incurred by it in connection with any social services functions (within the meaning of the Local Authority Social Services Act 1970 (c 42)), other than functions under section 3 of the Disabled Persons (Employment) Act 1958 (c 33),

(b)   a district council, or a Welsh county council or county borough council, towards expenditure incurred or to be incurred by it in connection with its functions under Part 2 of Schedule 9 to the Health and Social Services and Social Security Adjudications Act 1983 (c 41) (meals and recreation for old people),

(c)   a local authority (as defined in section 579(1) of the Education Act 1996) (c 56), towards expenditure incurred or to be incurred by it in connection with its functions under the Education Acts (within the meaning of that Act), in so far as it performs those functions for the benefit of disabled persons,

(d)   a local housing authority within the meaning of the Housing Act 1985 (c 68), towards expenditure incurred or to be incurred by it in connection with its functions under Part 2 of that Act (provision of housing), or

(e)   any of the bodies mentioned in subsection (2), in respect of expenditure incurred or to be incurred by it in connection with the provision of housing accommodation.

(2) The bodies are –

(za)   a private registered provider of social housing,

(a)   a registered social landlord within the meaning of the Housing Act 1985 (see section 5(4) and (5) of that Act),

(b)   the Homes and Communities Agency,

(ba)   the Welsh new towns residuary body,

(c)   a new town development corporation,

(d)   an urban development corporation established under the Local Government, Planning and Land Act 1980 (c 65),

(e)   the Regulator of Social Housing.

(3) A Primary Care Trust may make payments to a local authority towards expenditure incurred or to be incurred by the authority in connection with the performance of any of the authority's functions which, in the opinion of the Primary Care Trust –

(a)   have an effect on the health of any individuals,

(b)   have an effect on, or are affected by, any NHS functions, or

(c)   are connected with any NHS functions.

(4) "NHS functions" means functions exercised by an NHS body.

(5) A payment under this section may be made in respect of expenditure of a capital or of a revenue nature or in respect of both kinds of expenditure.

(6) The Secretary of State may by directions prescribe conditions relating to payments under this section or section 257.

(7) The conditions include, in particular, conditions requiring, in such circumstances as may be specified –

(a)   repayment of the whole or part of a payment under this section, or

(b)   in respect of property acquired with a payment under this section, payment of an amount representing the whole or part of an increase in the value of the property which has occurred since its acquisition.

(8) No payment may be made under this section in respect of any expenditure unless the conditions relating to it conform with the conditions prescribed under subsection (6) for payments of that description.

(9) "A disabled person" is a person who has a physical or mental impairment which has a substantial and long-term adverse effect on his ability to carry out normal day-to-day activities or who has such other disability as may be prescribed.

Community services

257 Payments in respect of voluntary organisations under section 256

(1) This section applies where the expenditure in respect of which a payment under section 256 is proposed to be made is expenditure in connection with services to be provided by a voluntary organisation.

(2) Where this section applies, the Primary Care Trust may make payments to the voluntary organisation towards the expenditure incurred or to be incurred by the organisation in connection with the provision of those services, instead of or in addition to making payments under section 256(1) or (3).

(3) Where this section applies –

(a)   a body falling within any of paragraphs (a) to (d) of section 256(1) which has received payments under the paragraph, and

(b)   a local authority which has received payments under section 256(3),

may make out of the sums paid to it payments to the voluntary organisation towards expenditure incurred or to be incurred by the organisation in connection with the provision of those services.

(4) No payment may be made under subsection (2) or (3) except subject to conditions which conform with the conditions prescribed for payments of that description under section 256(6).

SCHEDULE 20
Further Provision about Local Social Services Authorities Section 254

1 Care of mothers and young children

A local social services authority may, with the Secretary of State's approval, and to such extent as he may direct must, make arrangements for the care of pregnant women and women who are breast feeding (other than for the provision of residential accommodation for them).

2 Prevention, care and after-care

(1) A local social services authority may, with the Secretary of State's approval, and to such extent as he may direct must, make the arrangements mentioned in sub-paragraph (2).

(2) The arrangements are for the purpose of the prevention of illness, for the care of persons suffering from illness and for the after-care of persons who have been suffering from illness and in particular for –

(a)   the provision, for persons whose care is undertaken with a view to preventing them from becoming ill, persons suffering from illness and persons who have been suffering from illness, of centres or other facilities for training them or keeping them suitably occupied and the equipment and maintenance of such centres,

(b)   the provision, for the benefit of such persons as are mentioned in paragraph (a), of ancillary or supplemental services, and

(c)   the exercise of the functions of the local social services authority in respect of persons suffering from mental disorder who are received into guardianship under Part 2 or 3 of the Mental Health Act 1983 (c 20) (whether the guardianship of the authority or of other persons).

(3) A local social services authority may not, and is not under a duty to, make under this paragraph arrangements to provide facilities for any of the purposes mentioned in section 15(1) of the Disabled Persons (Employment) Act 1944 (c 10).

(4) No arrangements under this paragraph may provide for the payment of money to persons for whose benefit they are made, except in so far as they fall within sub-paragraph (5).

(5) Arrangements fall within this sub-paragraph if –

(a)   they provide for the remuneration of such persons engaged in suitable work in accordance with the arrangements of such amounts as the local social services authority considers appropriate in respect of their occasional personal expenses, and

(b)   it appears to the authority that no such payment would otherwise be made.

(6) No arrangements under this paragraph may be given effect to in relation to a person to whom section 115 of the Immigration and Asylum Act 1999 (c 33) (exclusion from benefits) applies solely –

(a)   because he is destitute, or

(b)   because of the physical effects, or anticipated physical effects, of his being destitute.

(7) Section 95(2) to (7) of that Act apply for the purposes of sub-paragraph (6); and for that purpose a reference to the Secretary of State in section 95(4) or (5) is a reference to a local social services authority.

(8) The Secretary of State may make regulations as to the conduct of premises in which facilities are provided in pursuance of arrangements made under this paragraph for persons –

(a)   who are or have been suffering from mental disorder within the meaning of the Mental Health Act 1983, or

(b)   whose care is undertaken with a view to preventing them from becoming sufferers from mental disorder.

(9) "Facilities" means facilities for training such persons or keeping them suitably occupied.

(10) This paragraph does not apply in relation to persons under the age of 18.

(11) No authority is authorised or may be required under this paragraph to provide residential accommodation for any person.

3 Home help and laundry facilities

(1) Each local social services authority –

   (a)   must provide or arrange for the provision of, on such a scale as is adequate for the needs of its area, of home help for households where such help is required owing to the presence of a person to whom sub-paragraph (2) applies, and

   (b)   may provide or arrange for the provision of laundry facilities for households for which home help is being, or can be, provided under paragraph (a).

(2) This sub-paragraph applies to any person who –

   (a)   is suffering from illness,

   (b)   is pregnant or has recently given birth,

   (c)   is aged, or

   (d)   handicapped as a result of having suffered from illness or by congenital deformity.

4 Research

(1) A local social services authority may conduct or assist other persons in conducting research into matters relating to the functions of local social services authorities under this Schedule.

(2) Sub-paragraph (1) does not affect any powers conferred by any other Act.

ORDINARY RESIDENCE

7.53 Disputes may arise between local authorities and NHS bodies in respect of the same issue. It should be a relatively easy matter (in theory) to resolve the public body who has prime responsibility in respect of the service user. For example, s 24(5) of NAA 1948 (considered in *R (on the application of Greenwich LBC) v Secretary of State for Health and Bexley LBC* [2006] EWHC 2576 (Admin), [2007] 10 CCLR 60) makes it plain that where a local authority provides residential accommodation, then the service user will be deemed to be resident in the area in which he was ordinarily resident prior to accommodation. The dispute becomes more complex if the issue of health care needs versus social care needs then arises (that is to say, which NHS body will be responsible for defraying the costs of such care).

7.54 More up-to-date guidance has been provided in the form of Department of Health Guidance (*Who Pays? Establishing the Responsible Commissioner September 2007*). The latter is discussed at greater length below, and has been touched upon at **1.16** in respect of s 117 of the Mental Health Act 1983. In addition, the *Ordinary Residence Guidance* (referred to almost throughout this book in respect of the relevant context of the subject matter of each Chapter) provides specific help on determining ordinary residence where there is an issue on this point as between an LA and a Continuing Healthcare provision. A lot of difficulties are caused by a lack of liaison prior to such placements being made. Adhering to the principles set out below should ensure a lack of disputes. In addition to the extracts from the Ordinary Residence Guidance set out below, there is a very detailed account of what is to be done in respect of 'Shared Lives Schemes' or 'Adult Placement Schemes' (paras 120–128).

ORDINARY RESIDENCE:
Guidance on the identification of the ordinary residence of people in need of community care services, England

NHS Continuing Healthcare

...

113. Where a person is in receipt of NHS CHC, local authorities do not have a duty to provide social care services that are being provided by the NHS, although they do continue to have a wider role, for example in relation to safeguarding responsibilities. However, if a care review subsequently determines that a person's needs no longer meet the eligibility criteria for NHS CHC – perhaps because they needed intensive health and social care following an operation and they have now recovered – the NHS ceases to be responsible for the provision of the person's social care. Instead, the duty for the provision of social care falls to the local authority in which the person is ordinarily resident under Part 3 of the 1948 Act.

114. The deeming provision in section 24(6) of the 1948 Act, which sets out that prior ordinary residence is retained where a person is provided with NHS accommodation (see paragraphs 60–65), applies to people in receipt of accommodation as part of a package of NHS CHC. Therefore, where a person is placed in a care home (or other accommodation funded by the NHS) in another local authority area for the purpose of receiving NHS CHC, they continue to be ordinarily resident in the local authority area in which they were ordinarily resident before entering the NHS accommodation. Where a PCT places a person in such accommodation, it is good practice for it to inform the person's local authority of ordinary residence and, if the person is placed "out of area", it is also good practice for the PCT to inform the local authority in which the care home is located.

115. Where a person is accommodated in a care home as part of their package of NHS CHC, it is possible that they may cease to be eligible for NHS CHC, but still need to remain in their care home, or to be provided with Part 3 accommodation elsewhere. In such a case, the effect of the deeming provision in section 24(6) of the 1948 Act would be that the local authority in whose area the person was ordinarily resident immediately before being provided with NHS accommodation would be the authority responsible for funding the person's accommodation under Part 3 of the 1948 Act, as the following scenarios shows.

Scenario: a person is discharged from NHS Continuing Healthcare

Maureen is 72 years old. Three years ago, she suffered a stroke which left her severely disabled with complex care needs. She was assessed by her local PCT as needing NHS CHC and was moved from hospital to a rehabilitation unit within an independent sector care home in local authority B. This placement was fully funded by Maureen's local PCT. Before her stroke, Maureen had lived with her husband in local authority A.

Local authority B agrees to fund the placement on a 'without prejudice' basis but immediately falls into dispute with local authority A over Maureen's place of ordinary residence. Local authority B contends that Maureen remains ordinarily resident in local authority A, where she had been living with her husband before her placement at the care home began. Local authority A argues that Maureen has acquired an ordinary residence in local authority B due to the length of time she has spent at the care home.

In this situation, when Maureen first enters the care home she is receiving NHS CHC, therefore the deeming provision in section 24(6) of the 1948 Act applies. This section provides that any person for whom NHS accommodation is provided is deemed to be ordinarily resident in the area in which they were ordinarily resident immediately before being admitted to hospital or other NHS accommodation. Therefore, whilst Maureen is receiving NHS CHC at the care home she remains ordinarily resident in local authority A, where she was living before her stroke.

Once Maureen's NHS CHC ceases and she is instead provided with Part 3 accommodation under the 1948 Act, the deeming provision in section 24(5) of the Act applies. This section sets out that any person provided with Part 3 accommodation shall be deemed to be ordinarily resident in the area in which he or she was ordinarily resident immediately before the Part 3 accommodation was provided. Immediately before Maureen was provided with Part 3 accommodation she was living in the care home but was still ordinarily resident in local authority A due to the deeming provision in section 24(6). Therefore, Maureen remains ordinarily resident in local authority A, as that was where she was ordinarily resident **immediately before** she began receiving Part 3 accommodation.

A recent reassessment of Maureen's needs concludes that she is no longer eligible for NHS CHC and requires accommodation under Part 3 of the 1948 Act instead. The care home in which Maureen has been living offers her a place on a long-term basis and all those involved in her care agree that this arrangement best meets Maureen's needs.

115b. The deeming provision in section 24(6) of the 1948 Act does not apply to anyone who was receiving NHS CHC immediately before 19 April 2010 and this remains the case for as long as they continue to be provided with that NHS CHC accommodation. Therefore, in determining the ordinary residence of someone who went into NHS CHC accommodation on or before 18 April 2010 and continued to be there after that date, the ordinary residence rules that applied on the day they went into care should be applied – ie the dispute must be resolved in the light of the specific circumstances and not the deeming provisions.

Scenario: anyone receiving NHS CHC immediately before 19 April 2010

Lydia goes into NHS CHC accommodation on 10 April 2010 and stays there until 1 June, when it is decided that she is no longer eligible for NHS CHC and needs to be transferred into residential accommodation under the 1948

Act. In determining Lydia's ordinary residence, do not apply the deeming provision in section 24(6), as her case falls under the old rules, but look at Lydia's individual circumstances to determine where she was ordinarily resident at the date that her entitlement to NHS CHC ceased.

Joint packages of health and community care services

116. When a person has health needs as well as social care needs but does not qualify for NHS Continuing Healthcare (see paragraphs 112–115 above), they may be eligible for a joint package of care that contains both health and community care services.

117. Under section 47(1) of the NHS and Community Care Act 1990, local authorities have a duty to assess the needs of any person for whom they may provide or arrange the provision of community care services and who may be in need of such services (see paragraphs 6–8 (Community care assessments)). If it becomes apparent during the course of the assessment that the person has health needs, the local authority should notify the person's primary care trust (PCT) and invite them to assist in the assessment48.

118. It is the responsibility of the local authority in which the person is ordinarily resident to provide any community care services identified as necessary in the light of the assessment, as outlined in Part 1 of this guidance. Any health services identified by the assessment should be met by the person's PCT (see paragraphs 179–181 (Establishing the responsible commissioner) for guidance on how to establish the responsible PCT). PCTs and local authorities should work in partnership to agree their respective responsibilities in relation to the provision of the joint package of care.

119. Where a person is placed in Part 3 accommodation out of area, they remain ordinarily resident in the area of the placing local authority (see paragraphs 55–59 on the section 24(5) deeming provision) and the placing authority remains responsible for the provision of any community care services. However, the person's GP may be based in the area in which they are living and it is this PCT that is responsible for the provision of any health services. This may mean that a local authority and a PCT located several miles apart need to work together to provide a joint package of health and social care. In the case of a person in receipt of NHS Continuing Healthcare, the placing PCT remains responsible for the provision of care, even where the person changes their GP practice (see paragraphs 112–115 and paragraph 181).

Ordinary/usual residence and the PCT

7.55   There is an anomaly between the test set out in the NAA 1948 at s 24(5), and that which may be being used by an NHS body. In order to determine which PCT is responsible for providing free NHS care to a patient, it is necessary to look at the National Health Service (Functions of Strategic Health Authorities and Primary Care Trusts and Administration Arrangements) (England) Regulations 2002, SI 2002/2375. These have been amended many times, but first came into force on 1 October 2002. There are different regulations in Wales (Local Health Board (Functions) (Wales) Regulations 2003, SI 2003/150 (W20)).

7.56 In effect, the general rule is that the patient is taken to be the resident in the area of the PCT where he is registered with a GP. If there is doubt as to where he is 'usually' resident, then this is governed by reg 8, so that he will be treated as usually resident at the address he gives to the body providing him with services, or if there is still doubt, he will be usually resident in the area in which he is present. This is almost the reverse of the test under NAA 1948.

7.57 However, the matter does not end there. If a patient is receiving continuing NHS health care in a care home, it is the placing PCT which has arranged the care which remains responsible for the NHS payments for the care in that placement (but not, for example in-patient treatment in the area to which he has moved) (the above Regulations as amended by SI 2006/359). However, none of this applies if social services have made the arrangements, or if there has been an independent move by the individual concerned.

7.58 If there is a dispute as between PCTs then they should consult the Strategic Health Authority (which in effect means the Secretary of State). This method is analogous to s 32(3) of NAA 1948.

Who Pays? Establishing the Responsible Commissioner

7.59 The guiding principles are set out as:

'no treatment should be refused or delayed due to uncertainty or ambiguity as to which PCT is responsible for funding an individual's healthcare provision ... In general, the responsible commissioner will be determined on the basis of registration with a G.P practice or, where a patient is not registered, their place of residence' [Guiding Principles]. There is an explicit cross reference to "*Who Pays?*" at paragraphs 179–181 of the *Ordinary Residence Guidance.*'

No fixed abode

7.60 'Where a patient has no fixed abode, and they are not registered with a GP practice, the responsible PCT should be determined by the "usually resident" test' (para 17). This test is contained in Annex A (the principles of which are summarised below).

Usually resident

7.61 The guidance suggests that the principle is dependent upon 'the patient's perception of where they are resident (either currently, or failing that, most recently)'. This at least has the advantage of simplicity, except perhaps where the patient lacks capacity. There is no obligation for a patient to provide a precise address. Holiday or second homes are not acceptable as usual residences. A hostel address is acceptable. If a patient cannot give a current address, then the last address at which he considered himself usually resident will suffice. If a patient either refuses to give information, or is unable to do so, and there is no way of establishing usual residence by any other means, then it will be determined as being in the district where the treatment is being received. There should be no undue pressure placed on a patient in order to provide a usual residence in order to divert the funding implications to another district.

Patients who move

7.62   If a patient moves during the course of treatment then 'PCTs may wish to consider and agree flexible solutions, such as whether patient care should be provided by the originating PCT exercising functions on behalf of the receiving PCT for a specific length of time' (para 19).

Children and local authorities

7.63   This is an area which is fogged by lack of co-ordination and record keeping. The guidance suggests:

> '28 When a child is first placed by a Local Authority they have a shared responsibility with the relevant PCT or NHS Trust to ensure a full health assessment takes place and that a health plan is drawn up. The relevant PCT should be informed in writing by the responsible local authority of its intention to place a child in its area and should be advised whether the placement is intended to be long or short term. Some placements need to be arranged urgently and prior notification will not always be possible. In these cases the relevant PCT should be notified within two weeks or as soon as reasonably practicable.'

7.64   The guidance also adds:

> '30 ... the changes mean that where a PCT or a local authority, or a PCT and a local authority acting jointly, arrange such accommodation, the "originating PCT" remains the responsible PCT for secondary healthcare type services, even where the child changes their GP practice. The "originating PCT" is the PCT that make such an arrangement in the exercise of its functions, or the responsible PCT immediately before a local authority makes such an arrangement. As a matter of good practice, the originating PCT should notify the PCT in whose area the child is being place.'

7.65   Where the placement was effected prior to 1 April 2007, and a move took place after that date by the local authority then:

> '32 ... the responsible PCT will be the PCT in whose area the local authority is situated. This promotes consistency with the principle of the responsible commissioner being the PCT coterminous with the placing local authority. If there is more than one PCT, the PCT responsible is the PCT that was responsible for providing services to the child immediately before the local authority placed the child.'

The guidance identifies four groups of children to whom this will apply:

> '34–38 (1) Looked after children and Children Leaving Care; (2) pupils with statements of special educational needs attending residential special schools; (3) children with continuing healthcare needs requiring residential care who are not looked after children; (4) young adults with continuing healthcare needs.'

The *'Ordinary Residence Guidance'* in respect of this area is referred to at **5.74** in Chapter 5 as well as the specific obligations of a local authority to young people in transition between children's services to adult services.

Adults and long-term care placements

7.66 From 1 April 2006 where a PCT arranges such a placement (whether alone or with a local authority) it is the placing PCT which remains liable for the NHS aspect of that care (para 89). This also applies to NHS Continuing Healthcare Placements (para 90). The guidance stresses that:

> '92 For joint packages of care, where local authorities are placing residents who have health needs, they should work closely with the placing PCT responsible for commissioning the healthcare to ensure that a full assessment of health needs is made so that an appropriate joint package is put in place.'

Chapter 8

SOCIAL HOUSING

Adam Fullwood

INTRODUCTION

8.1 A secure and suitable home is a precondition for the success of any community care services. Whilst accommodation may be available under the community care legislation (for adults) and the Children Act (for children) the primary route into social housing is under the Housing Act 1996.

8.2 The purpose of this chapter is to provide an outline to the functions and responsibilities falling upon local housing authorities under Part VII (homelessness) and Part VI (allocation) of the Housing Act 1996. Emphasis has been placed on those features that overlap with community care and the other areas of law featured elsewhere in this book.

8.3 Statutory guidance has been produced in relation to both the homelessness and allocation provisions and extracts from the same will be reproduced where relevant below. For a more detailed analysis reference should be made to the excellent *Housing Allocation and Homelessness – Law and Practice* (Jordans, 2010) by Jan Luba QC and Liz Davies.

8.4 The Localism Act 2011, which received Royal Assent on 15 November 2011, will affect both social housing allocation and homelessness provisions. Details of some of the main changes are highlighted below, but at the time of writing these provisions were not in force.

ALLOCATION

The allocation scheme

8.5 When allocating accommodation to a new applicant for social housing or to an existing tenant seeking a transfer, the housing authority must comply with Part VI of the Housing Act 1996 (s 159) and to its own allocation scheme (s 167(8)).

159 Allocation of housing accommodation

(1) A local housing authority shall comply with the provisions of this Part in allocating housing accommodation.

(2) For the purposes of this Part a local housing authority allocate housing accommodation when they –

> (a)   select a person to be a secure or introductory tenant of housing accommodation held by them,
>
> (b)   nominate a person to be a secure or introductory tenant of housing accommodation held by another person, or
>
> (c)   nominate a person to be an assured tenant of housing accommodation held by a registered social landlord.

(3) The reference in subsection (2)(a) to selecting a person to be a secure tenant includes deciding to exercise any power to notify an existing tenant or licensee that his tenancy or licence is to be a secure tenancy.

(4) The references in subsection (2)(b) and (c) to nominating a person include nominating a person in pursuance of any arrangements (whether legally enforceable or not) to require that housing accommodation, or a specified amount of housing accommodation, is made available to a person or one of a number of persons nominated by the authority.

(5) The provisions of this Part do not apply to an allocation of housing accommodation to a person who is already a secure or introductory tenant unless the allocation involves a transfer of housing accommodation for that person and is made on his application.

(6) ...

(7) Subject to the provisions of this Part, a local housing authority may allocate housing accommodation in such manner as they consider appropriate.

Exceptions

8.6   Most housing authorities use a 'housing register' as a means of determining both eligibility and priority and to otherwise comply with the requirements of Part VI. However, there are a number of express exceptions to the normal allocation arrangements (s 160).

160 Cases where provisions about allocation do not apply

(1) The provisions of this Part about the allocation of housing accommodation do not apply in the following cases.

(2) They do not apply where a secure tenancy –

> (a)   vests under section 89 of the Housing Act 1985 (succession to periodic secure tenancy on death of tenant),
>
> (b)   remains a secure tenancy by virtue of section 90 of that Act (devolution of term certain of secure tenancy on death of tenant),
>
> (c)   is assigned under section 92 of that Act (assignment of secure tenancy by way of exchange),
>
> (d)   is assigned to a person who would be qualified to succeed the secure tenant if the secure tenant died immediately before the assignment, or
>
> (e)   vests or is otherwise disposed of in pursuance of an order made under –
>
> > (i)   section 24 of the Matrimonial Causes Act 1973 (property adjustment orders in connection with matrimonial proceedings),

    (ii)   section 17(1) of the Matrimonial and Family Proceedings Act 1984 (property adjustment orders after overseas divorce, &c),
    ...

    (iii)   paragraph 1 of Schedule 1 to the Children Act 1989 (orders for financial relief against parents)[, or

    (iv)   Part 2 of Schedule 5, or paragraph 9(2) or (3) of Schedule 7, to the Civil Partnership Act 2004 (property adjustment orders in connection with civil partnership proceedings or after overseas dissolution of civil partnership, etc).

(3) They do not apply where an introductory tenancy –

    (a)   becomes a secure tenancy on ceasing to be an introductory tenancy,

    (b)   vests under section 133(2) (succession to introductory tenancy on death of tenant),

    (c)   is assigned to a person who would be qualified to succeed the introductory tenant if the introductory tenant died immediately before the assignment, or

    (d)   vests or is otherwise disposed of in pursuance of an order made under –

        (i)   section 24 of the Matrimonial Causes Act 1973 (property adjustment orders in connection with matrimonial proceedings),

        (ii)   section 17(1) of the Matrimonial and Family Proceedings Act 1984 (property adjustment orders after overseas divorce, &c),
        ...

        (iii)   paragraph 1 of Schedule 1 to the Children Act 1989 (orders for financial relief against parents)[, or

        (iv)   Part 2 of Schedule 5, or paragraph 9(2) or (3) of Schedule 7, to the Civil Partnership Act 2004 (property adjustment orders in connection with civil partnership proceedings or after overseas dissolution of civil partnership, etc)].

(4) They do not apply in such other cases as the Secretary of State may prescribe by regulations.

(5) The regulations may be framed so as to make the exclusion of the provisions of this Part about the allocation of housing accommodation subject to such restrictions or conditions as may be specified.

In particular, those provisions may be excluded –

    (a)   in relation to specified descriptions of persons, or

    (b)   in relation to housing accommodation of a specified description or a specified proportion of housing accommodation of any specified description.

8.7   The *Allocation of Accommodation Code of Guidance for local housing authorities in England* (2002) sets out the following common situations that fall outside of the statutory provisions at Annex 1:

(a)   where a secure tenant dies, the tenancy is a periodic one, and there is a person qualified to succeed the tenant under the Housing Act 1985, s 89;

(b)   where a secure tenant with a fixed term tenancy dies and the tenancy remains secure by virtue the Housing Act 1985, s 90;

(c)   where a secure tenancy is assigned by way of exchange under the Housing Act 1985, s 92;

(d)   where a secure tenancy is assigned to someone who would be qualified to succeed to the tenancy if the secure tenant died immediately before the assignment; or

(e)   where a secure tenancy vests or is otherwise disposed of in pursuance of an order made under:

   (i)   the Matrimonial Causes Act 1973, s 24 (property adjustment orders in connection with matrimonial proceedings);
   (ii)   the Matrimonial and Family Proceedings Act 1984, s 17(1) (property adjustment orders after overseas divorce); or
   (iii) the Children Act 1989, Sch 1, para 1 (orders for financial relief against parents), or

(f)   where an introductory tenancy:

   (i)   becomes a secure tenancy on ceasing to be an introductory tenancy;
   (ii)   vests under the 1996 Act, s 133(2) (succession to an introductory tenancy on death of tenant); or
   (iii) is assigned to someone who would be qualified to succeed the introductory tenancy if the introductory tenant died immediately before the assignment; or
   (iv)   meets the criteria in para 3(e) above.

Eligibility

8.8   Accommodation can only be allocated to an 'eligible' person. The three main categories of ineligible person are those subject to immigration control (as defined by the Asylum and Immigration Act 1996) and other persons from abroad, those excluded from entitlement to housing benefit and those deemed unsuitable to be tenants due to unacceptable behaviour.

160A Allocation only to eligible persons

(1) A local housing authority shall not allocate housing accommodation –

   (a)   to a person from abroad who is ineligible for an allocation of housing accommodation by virtue of subsection (3) or (5);
   (b)   to a person who the authority have decided is to be treated as ineligible for such an allocation by virtue of subsection (7); or
   (c)   to two or more persons jointly if any of them is a person mentioned in paragraph (a) or (b).

(2) Except as provided by subsection (1), any person may be allocated housing accommodation by a local housing authority (whether on his application or otherwise).

(3) A person subject to immigration control within the meaning of the Asylum and Immigration Act 1996 (c 49) is (subject to subsection (6)) ineligible for an allocation of housing accommodation by a local housing authority unless he is of a class prescribed by regulations made by the Secretary of State.

(4) No person who is excluded from entitlement to housing benefit by section 115 of the Immigration and Asylum Act 1999 (c 33) (exclusion from benefits) shall be included in any class prescribed under subsection (3).

(5) The Secretary of State may by regulations prescribe other classes of persons from abroad who are (subject to subsection (6)) ineligible for an allocation of housing accommodation, either in relation to local housing authorities generally or any particular local housing authority.

(6) Nothing in subsection (3) or (5) affects the eligibility of a person who is already –

    (a)   a secure or introductory tenant;

    (b)   an assured tenant of housing accommodation allocated to him by a local housing authority.

(7) A local housing authority may decide that an applicant is to be treated as ineligible for an allocation of housing accommodation by them if they are satisfied that –

    (a)   he, or a member of his household, has been guilty of unacceptable behaviour serious enough to make him unsuitable to be a tenant of the authority; and

    (b)   in the circumstances at the time his application is considered, he is unsuitable to be a tenant of the authority by reason of that behaviour.

(8) The only behaviour which may be regarded by the authority as unacceptable for the purposes of subsection (7)(a) is –

    (a)   behaviour of the person concerned which would (if he were a secure tenant of the authority) entitle the authority to a possession order under section 84 of the Housing Act 1985 (c 68) on any ground mentioned in Part 1 of Schedule 2 to that Act (other than ground 8); or

    (b)   behaviour of a member of his household which would (if he were a person residing with a secure tenant of the authority) entitle the authority to such a possession order.

(9) If a local housing authority decide that an applicant for housing accommodation –

    (a)   is ineligible for an allocation by them by virtue of subsection (3) or (5); or

    (b)   is to be treated as ineligible for such an allocation by virtue of subsection (7),

they shall notify the applicant of their decision and the grounds for it.

(10) That notice shall be given in writing and, if not received by the applicant, shall be treated as having been given if it is made available at the authority's office for a reasonable period for collection by him or on his behalf.

(11) A person who is being treated by a local housing authority as ineligible by virtue of subsection (7) may (if he considers that he should no longer be treated as ineligible by the authority) make a fresh application to the authority for an allocation of housing accommodation by them.

8.9   The Code of Guidance contains a useful table to assist in determining eligibility at Annex 4:

Class of applicant	Conditions of eligibility	How to identify/verify
Existing social tenant (allocated accommodation by LA)	None	
British citizen	Must be habitually resident in the CTA[1]	Passport
EEA citizen[2]	Must be habitually resident in CTA, unless: – applicant is a 'worker'[3], or – applicant has a right to reside in the UK[4]	Passport or national identity card
Person subject to immigration control granted refugee status	None	Stamp in passport or Home Office letter
Person subject to immigration control granted exceptional leave to remain	ELR must not be subject to a condition requiring him/her to maintain him/herself and dependants	Stamp in passport or Home Office letter
Person subject to immigration control granted indefinite leave to remain	Must be habitually resident in CTA And, if ILR was granted on undertaking that a sponsor(s) would be responsible for maintenance & accommodation and 5 years has not elapsed since date of entry to UK or the undertaking – no sponsor remains alive	Stamp in passport or Home Office letter

Person subject to immigration control who is a citizen of a country that has ratified ECSMA[5] or ESC[6] (see Annex 9)	Must be lawfully present[7] in UK Must be habitually resident in CTA	Passport

[1] CTA: The Common Travel Area includes the UK, the Channel Islands, the Isle of Man and the Republic of Ireland.
[2] EEA countries are: Austria, Belgium, Denmark, Finland, France, Germany, Greece, Iceland, Ireland, Italy, Liechtenstein, Luxembourg, the Netherlands, Norway, Portugal, Spain, Sweden and the UK.
[3] A 'worker' for the purpose of Council Regulation (EEC) No. 1612/68 or (EEC) No.1251/70.
[4] A right to reside pursuant to Council Directive No.68/360/EEC or No.73/148/EEC.
[5] ECSMA is the European Convention on Social and Medical Assistance. Non EEA ratifying countries are: Malta and Turkey (See annex 9).
[6] ESC is the European Social Charter. Non EEA ratifying countries are: Cyprus, Czech Republic, Hungary, Latvia, Poland and Slovakia.
[7] Persons subject to immigration control are not lawfully present in the UK unless they have leave to enter or remain in the UK. Asylum seekers are generally granted 'temporary admission' and do not have leave to enter or remain.

8.10 Where housing authorities are uncertain about an applicant's immigration status, they are recommended to contact the Home Office. If such inquiries are considered necessary this should be conveyed to the applicant in the event that no further action is necessary if he prefers to withdraw his application (Code of Guidance, para 4.17).

8.11 An authority is entitled to refuse to offer a larger property to an eligible applicant on the basis that some members of her family were ineligible due to their immigration status (*R (Ariemuguvbe) v Islington LBC* [2009] EWCA Civ 1308).

8.12 Before an authority can lawfully conclude that an applicant is not eligible on the grounds of unacceptable behaviour it must be satisfied that a notional county court judge would make an outright order for possession in the circumstances of the case (*R (Dixon) v Wandsworth LBC* [2007] EWHC 3075 (Admin) at [17]).

8.13 The Code of Guidance provides examples of what constitutes unacceptable behavior serious enough to make an applicant unsuitable to be a tenant and the steps which housing authorities should take to satisfy themselves in this regard at paras 4.21 and 4.22:

> 4.21 Section 160A(8) provides that the only behaviour which can be regarded as unacceptable for these purposes is behaviour by the applicant or by a member of his household that would – if the applicant had been a secure tenant of the housing authority at the time – have entitled the housing authority to a possession order under section 84 of the Housing Act 1985 in relation to any of the grounds in Part I of Schedule 2, other than Ground 8. Theseare fault grounds and include behaviour such as conduct likely to cause nuisance or annoyance, and use of the

property for immoral or illegal purposes. Housing authorities should note that it is not necessary for the applicant to have actually been a tenant of the housing authority when the unacceptable behaviour occurred. The test is whether the behaviour would have entitled the housing authority to a possession order if, whether actually or notionally, the applicant had been a secure tenant.

4.22 Where a housing authority has reason to believe that section 160A(7) may apply; there are a number of steps that will need to be followed.

i)   They will need to satisfy themselves that there has been unacceptable behaviour which falls within the definition in s160A(8). In considering whether a possession order would be granted in the circumstances of a particular case, the housing authority would have to consider whether, having established the grounds, the court would decide that it was reasonable to grant a possession order. It has been established in case law that, when the court is deliberating, "reasonable" means having regard to the interests of the parties and also having regard to the interests of the public. So, in deciding whether it would be entitled to an order the housing authority would need to consider these interests, and this will include all the circumstances of the applicant and his or her household. In practice, courts are unlikely to grant possession orders in cases which have not been properly considered and are not supported by thorough and convincing evidence. It is acknowledged that in cases involving noise problems, domestic violence, racial harassment, intimidation and drug dealing, courts are likely to grant a possession order. Rent arrears would probably lead to a possession order, although in many cases it will be suspended giving the tenant the opportunity to pay the arrears. In taking a view on whether it would be entitled to a possession order, the housing authority will need to consider fully all the factors that a court would take into account in determining whether it was reasonable for an order to be granted. In the Secretary of State's view, a decision reached on the basis of established case law would be reasonable.

ii)   Having concluded that there would be entitlement to an order, the housing authority will need to satisfy itself that the behaviour is serious enough to make the person unsuitable to be a tenant of the housing authority. For example, the housing authority would need to be satisfied that, if a possession order were granted, it would not be suspended by the court. Behaviour such as the accrual of rent arrears which have resulted from factors outside the applicant's control – for example, delays in housing benefit payments; or liability for a partner's debts, where the applicant was not in control of the household's finances or was unaware that arrears were accruing – should not be considered serious enough to make the person unsuitable to be a tenant.

iii)   The housing authority will need to satisfy itself that the applicant is unsuitable to be a tenant by reason of the behaviour in question – in the circumstances at the time the application is considered. Previous unacceptable behaviour may not justify a decision to consider the applicant as unsuitable to be a tenant where that behaviour can be shown to have improved.

Advice and assistance

8.14 A local housing authority must secure that advice and information is available free of charge to persons in its district about the right to make an application for accommodation along with any necessary assistance in making such an application for those who are likely to need it (s 166(1) and Code of Guidance, paras 6.7–6.12).

8.15 A local housing authority must make its full scheme available for purchase on demand (s 168(2) and *R (Onuegbu) v Hackney LBC* [2005] EWHC 1277 (Admin)).

8.16 An application for accommodation cannot be divulged to any other member of the public without his consent (s 166(4)).

166 Applications for housing accommodation

(1) A local housing authority shall secure that –

(a) advice and information is available free of charge to persons in their district about the right to make an application for an allocation of housing accommodation; and

(b) any necessary assistance in making such an application is available free of charge to persons in their district who are likely to have difficulty in doing so without assistance.

(2) A local housing authority shall secure that an applicant for an allocation of housing accommodation is informed that he has the rights mentioned in section 167(4A).

(3) Every application made to a local housing authority for an allocation of housing accommodation shall (if made in accordance with the procedural requirements of the authority's allocation scheme) be considered by the authority.

(4) The fact that a person is an applicant for an allocation of housing accommodation shall not be divulged (without his consent) to any other member of the public.

(5) In this Part "district" in relation to a local housing authority has the same meaning as in the Housing Act 1985 (c 68).

Determining priorities

8.17 A local housing authority's allocation scheme must be framed so as to determine priorities between applicants and the procedure to be followed in allocating accommodation. The scheme must give 'reasonable preference' to persons falling within specific categories. A scheme *may* also give 'additional preference' to those with urgent housing needs.

8.18 Applicants may be entitled to priority on medical and/or welfare grounds. In such cases, the Code of Guidance provides helpful assistance at paras 5.13–5.15 as follows:

5.13 Where it is necessary to take account of medical advice, housing authorities should contact the most appropriate health or social care professional who has direct knowledge of the applicant's condition, as well as the impact his condition has on his housing needs.

5.14 "Welfare grounds" is intended to encompass not only care or support needs, but also other social needs which do not require ongoing care and support, such as the need to provide a secure base from which a care leaver or other vulnerable person can build a stable life. It would include vulnerable people (with or without care and support needs) who could not be expected to find their own accommodation.

5.15 Where accommodation is allocated to a person who needs to move on medical or welfare grounds, it is essential to assess any support and care needs, and housing authorities will need to liaise with social services, the Supporting People team and other relevant agencies, as necessary, to ensure the allocation of appropriate accommodation. Housing authorities should also consider, together with the applicant, whether his needs would be better served by staying put in his current accommodation if appropriate aids and adaptations were put in place.

8.19   In determining priorities the scheme may also allow three specific factors to be taken into account: (a) financial resources available to the applicant; (b) any behaviour of the applicant or a member of his household affecting his suitability to be a tenant; and (c) any local connection the applicant has with the authority's district (Code of Guidance, para 5.23).

8.20   In making accommodation offers to applicants who are supported by carers who do not reside with them, the authority should 'wherever possible' take account of any need for a spare bedroom (Code of Guidance, para 5.37).

8.21   Government policy has consistently expressed a need to support lone teenage parents under the age of 18 who are often moving into their first home. The Code of Guidance emphasises the need for multi-agency cooperation at para 5.41:

'Where an application for housing is received from a lone parent aged 16 or 17, the Secretary of State recommends that housing authorities have arrangements in place to ensure that they can undertake a joint assessment of the applicant's housing, care and support needs with social services. Housing authorities should obtain the consent of the young parent before involving social services, unless child protection concerns are present and to seek such consent might endanger the welfare of the child of the young parent.'

8.22   Where a minor is offered a tenancy the Code of Guidance suggests that social services consider underwriting the same until he reaches the age of 18. Whilst legal complications may arise in such circumstances the Code of Guidance offers some assistance assistance at para 5.49:

'In some circumstances, social services authorities may consider it appropriate to underwrite a tenancy agreement for an applicant who is under 18. There are legal complications associated with the grant of a tenancy to a minor because a minor cannot hold a legal estate in land. However, if a tenancy is granted, it probably takes effect as a contract for a lease and would be fully enforceable as a contract for necessaries (ie the basic necessities of life) under common law. Any guarantee given in those circumstances would remain valid in respect of any liability incurred by the minor notwithstanding that he or she may repudiate the agreement on or shortly after reaching 18.'

8.23 Once a lawful allocation scheme is adopted, the way in which choice and preference options are developed is largely a matter for the local housing authority. The Code of Guidance makes this clear at para 5.5:

'It is for housing authorities and their partner RSLs to decide in the light of local circumstances, and drawing on the experience of the choice based lettings pilot scheme, the ways in which they can amend or develop their existing arrangements so as to offer more choice to applicants.'

The principal features of the allocation scheme

8.24 Housing authorities must devise and apply its allocation scheme to reflect the requirements of Part VI.

167 Allocation in accordance with allocation scheme

(1) Every local housing authority shall have a scheme (their "allocation scheme") for determining priorities, and as to the procedure to be followed, in allocating housing accommodation.

For this purpose "procedure" includes all aspects of the allocation process, including the persons or descriptions of persons by whom decisions are to be taken.

(1A) The scheme shall include a statement of the authority's policy on offering people who are to be allocated housing accommodation –

(a)   a choice of housing accommodation; or
(b)   the opportunity to express preferences about the housing accommodation to be allocated to them.

(2) As regards priorities, the scheme shall, subject to subsection (2ZA), be framed so as to secure that reasonable preference is given to –

(a)   people who are homeless (within the meaning of Part 7);
(b)   people who are owed a duty by any local housing authority under section 190(2), 193(2) or 195(2) (or under section 65(2) or 68(2) of the Housing Act 1985) or who are occupying accommodation secured by any such authority under section 192(3);
(c)   people occupying insanitary or overcrowded housing or otherwise living in unsatisfactory housing conditions;
(d)   people who need to move on medical or welfare grounds (including grounds relating to a disability); and
(e)   people who need to move to a particular locality in the district of the authority, where failure to meet that need would cause hardship (to themselves or to others).

The scheme may also be framed so as to give additional preference to particular descriptions of people within this subsection (being descriptions of people with urgent housing needs).

(2ZA) People are to be disregarded for the purposes of subsection (2) if they would not have fallen within paragraph (a) or (b) of that subsection without the local housing authority having had regard to a restricted person (within the meaning of Part 7).

(2A) The scheme may contain provision for determining priorities in allocating housing accommodation to people within subsection (2); and the factors which the scheme may allow to be taken into account include –

   (a)   the financial resources available to a person to meet his housing costs;
   (b)   any behaviour of a person (or of a member of his household) which affects his suitability to be a tenant;
   (c)   any local connection (within the meaning of section 199) which exists between a person and the authority's district.

(2B) Nothing in subsection (2) requires the scheme to provide for any preference to be given to people the authority have decided are people to whom subsection (2C) applies.

(2C) This subsection applies to a person if the authority are satisfied that –

   (a)   he, or a member of his household, has been guilty of unacceptable behaviour serious enough to make him unsuitable to be a tenant of the authority; and
   (b)   in the circumstances at the time his case is considered, he deserves by reason of that behaviour not to be treated as a member of a group of people who are to be given preference by virtue of subsection (2).

(2D) Subsection (8) of section 160A applies for the purposes of subsection (2C)(a) above as it applies for the purposes of subsection (7)(a) of that section.

(2E) Subject to subsection (2), the scheme may contain provision about the allocation of particular housing accommodation –

   (a)   to a person who makes a specific application for that accommodation;
   (b)   to persons of a particular description (whether or not they are within subsection (2)).

(3) The Secretary of State may by regulations –

   (a)   specify further descriptions of people to whom preference is to be given as mentioned in subsection (2), or
   (b)   amend or repeal any part of subsection (2).

(4) The Secretary of State may by regulations specify factors which a local housing authority shall not take into account in allocating housing accommodation.

(4A) The scheme shall be framed so as to secure that an applicant for an allocation of housing accommodation –

   (a)   has the right to request such general information as will enable him to assess –

    (i)   how his application is likely to be treated under the scheme (including in particular whether he is likely to be regarded as a member of a group of people who are to be given preference by virtue of subsection (2)); and

    (ii)   whether housing accommodation appropriate to his needs is likely to be made available to him and, if so, how long it is likely to be before such accommodation becomes available for allocation to him;

(b)   is notified in writing of any decision that he is a person to whom subsection (2C) applies and the grounds for it;

(c)   has the right to request the authority to inform him of any decision about the facts of his case which is likely to be, or has been, taken into account in considering whether to allocate housing accommodation to him; and

(d)   has the right to request a review of a decision mentioned in paragraph (b) or (c), or in section 160A(9), and to be informed of the decision on the review and the grounds for it.

(5) As regards the procedure to be followed, the scheme shall be framed in accordance with such principles as the Secretary of State may prescribe by regulations.

(6) Subject to the above provisions, and to any regulations made under them, the authority may decide on what principles the scheme is to be framed.

(7) Before adopting an allocation scheme, or making an alteration to their scheme reflecting a major change of policy, a local housing authority shall –

(a)   send a copy of the draft scheme, or proposed alteration, to every registered social landlord with which they have nomination arrangements (see section 159(4)), and

(b)   afford those persons a reasonable opportunity to comment on the proposals.

(8) A local housing authority shall not allocate housing accommodation except in accordance with their allocation scheme.

8.25 The housing scheme must entitle an applicant to request general information relation to his application, is notified of a decision in writing, has a right to reasons for any such decision and a right of review (s 167(4A) and the Code of Guidance, paras 5.56–5.58). Once the internal right of review has been exhausted the decision may be challenged by way of judicial review.

8.26 Before adopting an allocation scheme or making any alternation to it reflecting a major change of policy, the authority shall send a copy of the draft scheme to all registered social landlords with which it has nomination arrangements along with a reasonable opportunity to comment on the same (s 167A(7) and the Code of Guidance, paras 6.4–6.6).

8.27 The courts have generally refused challenges brought against the adequacy of allocation schemes so long as the main features are explained. In *R (Ahmad) v Newham LBC* [2009] UKHL 14 Lord Neuberger said at [46]:

'... as a general proposition, it is undesirable for the courts to get involved in questions of how priorities are accorded in housing allocation policies. Of course, there will be cases where the court has a duty to interfere, for instance if a policy does not comply with statutory requirements, or if it is plainly irrational. However, it seems unlikely that thelegislature can have intended that Judges should embark on the exercise of telling authorities how to decide on priorities as between applicants in need of rehousing, save in relatively rare and extreme circumstances. Housing allocation policy is a difficult exercise which requires not only social and political sensitivity and judgment, but also local expertise and knowledge.'

8.28 In individual cases, an applicant would have to demonstrate that the decision breaches a requirement of either Part VI or the allocation scheme itself or is otherwise unlawful on public law grounds.

8.29 A reasons-based decision will normally be difficult to sustain so long as the reasons are stated in sufficient detail to enable the applicant to know what conclusion was reached on the 'principal important controversial issues' (*R (Dixon) v Wandsworth LBC* [2007] EWHC (Admin) at [26]).

8.30 Particular care is needed in cases involving medical needs assessment. Where medical advice has been commissioned by the authority caution must be applied to any non-medical opinions expressed (*R (Bauer-Czarnomski v Ealing LBC* [2010] EWHC 130 (Admin).

8.31 In exercising its functions under Part VI the authority shall have regard to guidance issued by the Secretary of State (Allocation of Accommodation: Code of Guidance for local housing authorities for England (2002)).

8.32 The Localism Act will give authorities more power to limit who can apply for social housing within their area. The objective behind this is to prevent people who have no need of social housing from joining the waiting list. The reforms will also make it easier for those in social housing to seek a transfer or otherwise move to different parts of the country.

Contracting out

8.33 Many local authorities have transferred ownership of their housing stock and 'contracted out' the operation and management of the housing allocation scheme pursuant to s 70 of the Deregulation and Contracting Out Act 1994 and the Local Authorities (Contracting Out of Allocation of Housing and Homelessness Functions) Order 1996, SI 1996/3205.

8.34 Other than: (i) adopting or altering the allocation scheme, including the principles on which the scheme is framed, and consulting registered social landlords; and (ii) making the allocation scheme available at the authority's principal office the majority of functions under Part VI may be contracted out.

8.35 It is important to note that where functions have been contracted out, the local authority retains responsibility for the scheme and for any acts /

omissions and decisions of its contractor save where the contractor fails to fulfill its contract or where criminal proceedings are brought against the contractor (s 72 of the 1994 Act and Code of Guidance, para 7.5).

HOMELESSNESS

8.36 It should be remembered that the homelessness provisions in Part VII of the Housing Act 1996 are primarily aimed at securing temporary accommodation pending the allocation of long-term housing.

8.37 Statutory guidance has been issued to local housing authorities that specifically deal with their functions and responsibilities. The principal guidance is currently the *Homelessness Code of Guidance for Local Authorities* (2006). This must be read subject to the *Supplementary Guidance on Intentional Homelessness* (2009). In terms of homelessness prevention, the Government has issued *Prevention of Homelessness – the role of health and social care* (2007) and *Joint Working between Housing and Childrren's Services, preventing homelessness and tackling its effects on children and young people* ((2008). Joint guidance has also been issued under Part III of the Children Act 1989 and Part VII of the Housing Act 1996 – *Provision of Accommodation for 16 and 17 year old young people ho may be homeless and/or require accommodation* (2010).[1]

8.38 Successive Governments have worked hard towards reducing the prevalence of homelessness and this continues to be a priority. However, despite the introduction of both national and local strategies homelessness continues to affect many parts of the country and is likely to continue in light of the current economic conditions.

Duty to cooperate

8.39 Local social services authorities must give the local housing authority such assistance as may be reasonably required in both carrying out local reviews and formulating homelessness strategies (Homelessness Act 2002, s 1(2) and Code of Guidance, para 1.6).

8.40 Perhaps more relevant to this book, social services authorities are also under a duty to take into account the relevant homeless strategy when carrying out its social services functions (Homelessness Act 2002, s 1(6)). This means that when community care assessments are being prepared under s 47 of the NHS and Community Care Act 1990, care should be taken to consider whether the homelessness strategy is relevant at the very least.

8.41 In light of the fact that many local housing authorities have transferred their housing stock to registered social landlords (RSLs) it is important to note

---

[1] Separate statutory guidance has been issued by the Welsh Assembly for Wales.

that RSLs are under a duty to cooperate with housing authorities to assist them in performing their functions under both Part VI and Part VII of the Housing Act 1996 so far as reasonable (ss 170, 213(1) and 213A).

Applications

8.42   Anyone who wants to make an application for homelessness assistance must be permitted to do so. Local housing authorities must have arrangements in place to enable a person to make an application at any time of the day or night (Code of Gudiance, para 6.8 and *R v Camden LBC ex p Gillan* (1988) 21 HLR 114).

8.43   A person cannot be prevented from making an application for assistance by being required to go through a 'home options interview' or similar process. This is considered to be unlawful 'gatekeeping' (*R (Aweys) v Birmingham CC* [2007] EWHC 52 (Admin)).

8.44   There is no residence requirement that needs to be fulfilled and so a person may apply to any local housing authority in the country (*R v Slough BC ex p Ealing LBC* [1981] QB 801, CA).

8.45   There is no requirement to make an application for assistance in a particular form or in writing at all (Code of Guidance, para 6.6 and *Aweys,* above at [8]) but a person who lacks mental capacity cannot make an application (*R v Oldham MBC ex p Garlick & another* [1993] AC 509, HL). In such circumstances, or where there is a dispute concerning a persons capacity to make an application himself, an application to the Court of Protection may be appropriate (see Chapter 2 above).

8.46   The threshold for making inquiries is low. It arises where the authority have reason to believe that an applicant may be homeless or threatened with homelessness (s 184(1)). The statute then sets out how that application should be determined.

184   Inquiry into cases of homelessness or threatened homelessness

(1) If the local housing authority have reason to believe that an applicant may be homeless or threatened with homelessness, they shall make such inquiries as are necessary to satisfy themselves –

    (a)   whether he is eligible for assistance, and

    (b)   if so, whether any duty, and if so what duty, is owed to him under the following provisions of this Part.

(2) They may also make inquiries whether he has a local connection with the district of another local housing authority in England, Wales or Scotland.

(3) On completing their inquiries the authority shall notify the applicant of their decision and, so far as any issue is decided against his interests, inform him of the reasons for their decision.

(3A) If the authority decide that a duty is owed to the applicant under section 193(2) or 195(2) but would not have done so without having had regard to a restricted person, the notice under subsection (3) must also –

(a)   inform the applicant that their decision was reached on that basis,
(b)   include the name of the restricted person,
(c)   explain why the person is a restricted person, and
(d)   explain the effect of section 193(7AD) or (as the case may be) section 195(4A).

(4) If the authority have notified or intend to notify another local housing authority under section 198 (referral of cases), they shall at the same time notify the applicant of that decision and inform him of the reasons for it.

(5) A notice under subsection (3) or (4) shall also inform the applicant of his right to request a review of the decision and of the time within which such a request must be made (see section 202).

(6) Notice required to be given to a person under this section shall be given in writing and, if not received by him, shall be treated as having been given to him if it is made available at the authority's office for a reasonable period for collection by him or on his behalf.

(7) In this Part "a restricted person" means a person –

(a)   who is not eligible for assistance under this Part,
(b)   who is subject to immigration control within the meaning of the Asylum and Immigration Act 1996, and
(c)   either –
         (i)   who does not have leave to enter or remain in the United Kingdom, or
         (ii)   whose leave to enter or remain in the United Kingdom is subject to a condition to maintain and accommodate himself, and any dependants, without recourse to public funds.

8.47   In making its inquiries, the authority must satisfy itself whether the applicant is eligible for assistance and, if so, whether any duty is owed under Part VII. In order to determine this, the authority will need to establish whether the application is homeless or threatened with homelessness, whether he became homeless or threatened with homelessness intentionally and whether he has a priority need for accommodation.

8.48   The duty to make inquiries and reach a decision rests with the authority and it is not for the applicant to 'prove their case'. At the same time applicants should always be given a fair opportunity to explain their circumstances particularly where material is received by the authority which is adverse to the applicant's interests (Code of Guidance, para 6.15).

8.49   There is no time limit imposed by statute. The Code of Guidance at para 6.16 provides:

Housing authorities should deal with inquiries as quickly as possible, whilst ensuring that they are thorough and, in any particular case, sufficient to enable the housing authority to satisfy itself what duty, if any, is owed or what other assistance can be offered. Housing authorities are obliged to begin inquiries as soon as they have reason to believe that an applicant may be homeless or threatened with homelessness and should aim to carry out an initial interview and preliminary assessment on the day an application is received. An early assessment will be vital to determine whether the housing authority has an immediate duty to secure accommodation under ssection 188 (see Chapter 7 for guidance on the interim duty to accommodate). Wherever possible, it is recommended that housing authorities aim to complete their inquiries and notify the applicant of their decision within 33 working days of accepting a duty to make inquiries under section 184. In many cases it should be possible for authorities to complete the inquiries significantly earlier.

8.50 When a decision is reached, the authority must notify the applicant in writing. Such notification must include its reasons where the decision is adverse to the applicant and reference to the right of review (s 184(3) and Code of Guidance, para 6.21).

Interim duty to accommodate pending decision

8.51 If the authority has reason to believe that an applicant 'may' be eligible for assistance, homeless and have a priority need, the authority comes under an 'immediate' duty to ensure that suitable accommodation is available for the applicant (and his household) pending the completion of inquiries (s 188(1) and Code of Guidance, para 6.5).

188 Interim duty to accommodate in case of apparent priority need

(1) If the local housing authority have reason to believe that an applicant may be homeless, eligible for assistance and have a priority need, they shall secure that accommodation is available for his occupation pending a decision as to the duty (if any) owed to him under the following provisions of this Part.

(2) The duty under this section arises irrespective of any possibility of the referral of the applicant's case to another local housing authority (see sections 198 to 200).

(3) The duty ceases when the authority's decision is notified to the applicant, even if the applicant requests a review of the decision (see section 202).

The authority may secure that accommodation is available for the applicant's occupation pending a decision on a review.

8.52 The use of the word 'may' has led the courts to determine that the duty to secure interim accommodation has a very low threshold (*R (Kelly & Mehari) v Birmingham CC* [2009] EWHC 3240 (Admin)).

8.53 A decision not to accommodate pending inquiries or a failure to make a decision at all is only challengeable by way of judicial review. Such challenges may, and often are, brought at very short notice to the duty judge of the Administrative Court. Care should be taken when making such applications to ensure that all relevant information is before the judge as they are by necessity ex parte applications (*R (Lawer) v Restormel BC* [2007] EWHC 2299 (Admin)).

Eligibility

8.54 Similar eligibility rules apply in relation to homelessness as they apply to the allocation provisions. A person who is subject to immigration control within the meaning of the Asylum and Immigration Act 1996 is not eligible along with those excluded from entitlement to housing benefit. In addition, certain classes of persons deemed eligible and ineligible are contained in regulations (Allocation of Housing and Homelessness (Eligibility) (England) Regulations 2006, SI 2006/1294).

8.55 As a general rule a person subject to immigration rule is a person who requires leave to enter or remain (whether or not such leave has been given).

8.56 The Code of Guidance provides a useful summary of those persons who do not require leave to enter or remain in the UK at para 9.7:

Only the following categories of person do not require leave to enter or remain in the UK:

(i)   British citizens;
(ii) certain Commonwealth citizens with a right of abode in the UK;
(iii) citizens of an EEA country, ("EEA nationals") and their family members, who have a right to reside in the UK that derives from EC law. The question of whether an EEA national (or family member) has a particular right to reside in the UK (or in another Member State e.g. the Republic of Ireland) will depend on the circumstances, particularly the economic status of the EEA national (e.g. whether he or she is a worker, self-employed, a student, or economically inactive etc.). See Annex 12 for further guidance on rights to reside;
(iv) persons who are exempt from immigration control under the Immigration Acts, including diplomats and their family members based in the United Kingdom, and some military personnel.

For the purposes of this guidance, "EEA nationals" means nationals of any of the EU member states (excluding the UK), and nationals of Iceland, Norway, Liechtenstein and Switzerland.

8.57 Anyone not falling into the four categories set out above may be ineligible unless they are rendered eligible by the regulations.

8.58 As already indicated in relation to eligibility for the allocation of accommodation under Part VI, any uncertainty about an applicant's immigration status should be resolved by the authority contacting the Home Office. Any intention to contact the Home Office should normally be notified to the applicant in the event that he does not wish to proceed.

Priority need

8.59   The main duties under Part VII will only be owed to a person who has a priority need for accommodation. Without priority need an authority will only owe a duty to assess his housing needs and then provide him with advice and assistance (s 190(3)).

8.60   A community care assessment prepared under section 47 of the NHS and Community Care Act 1990 may well be of real relevance to the question of priority need – especially when considering the issue of 'vulnerability' (see further below).

8.61   The categories of those applicants with a priority need are set out in s 189(1) and the Homelessness (Priority Need for Accommodation) (England) Order 2002, SI 2002/2051.

8.62   The Code of Guidance summaries the categories of applicant that have a priority need for accommodation at para 10.2:

(i)   a pregnant woman or a person with whom she resides or might reasonably be expected to reside (see paragraph 10.5);

(ii)   a person with whom dependent children reside or might reasonably be expected to reside (see paragraphs 10.6–10.11);

(iii)   a person who is vulnerable as a result of old age, mental illness or handicap or physical disability or other special reason, or with whom such a person resides or might reasonably be expected to reside (see paragraphs 10.12–10. 18);

(iv)   a person aged 16 or 17 who is not a 'relevant child' or a child in need to whom a local authority owes a duty under section 20 of the Children Act 1989 (see paragraphs 10.36–10.39);

(v)   a person under 21 who was (but is no longer) looked after, accommodated or fostered between the ages of 16 and 18 (except a person who is a 'relevant student') (see paragraphs 10.40–10.41);

(vi)   a person aged 21 or more who is vulnerable as a result of having been looked after, accommodated or fostered (except a person who is a 'relevant student') (see paragraphs 10.19–10.20);

(vii)   a person who is vulnerable as a result of having been a member of Her Majesty's regular naval, military or air forces (see paragraphs 10.21–10.23);

(viii) a person who is vulnerable as a result of:
   (a)   having served a custodial sentence,
   (b)   having been committed for contempt of court or any other kindred offence, or
   (c)   having been remanded in custody; (see paragraphs 10.24–10.27)

(ix)   a person who is vulnerable as a result of ceasing to occupy accommodation because of violence from another person or threats of violence from another person which are likely to be carried out (see paragraphs 10.28–10.29);

(x)   a person who is vulnerable for any other special reason, or with whom such a person resides or might reasonably be expected to reside (see paragraphs 10.30–10.35);

(xi)   a person who is homeless, or threatened with homelessness, as a result of an emergency such as flood, fire or other disaster (see paragraph 10.42).

8.63 A person's 'vulnerability' may give rise to a priority need for accommodation. The Code of Guidance provides some assistance in defining vulnerability at para 10.12:

> A person has a priority need for accommodation if he or she is vulnerable as a result of:
>
> (i)   old age;
> (ii)   mental illness or learning disability (mental handicap) or physical disability;
> (iii) having been looked after, accommodated or fostered and is aged 21 or more;
> (iv)   having been a member of Her Majesty's regular naval, military or air forces;
> (v)   having been in custody or detention;
> (vi)   ceasing to occupy accommodation because of violence from another person or threats of violence from another person which are likely to be carried out; or
> (vii) any other special reason.
>
> In the case of (i), (ii) and (vii) only, a person with whom a vulnerable person lives or might reasonably be expected to live also has a priority need for accommodation and can therefore make an application on behalf of themselves and that vulnerable person.

8.64 In assessing vulnerability the authority must consider whether, when homeless, the applicant would be less able to fend for him/herself than an ordinary homeless person so that he or she would suffer injury or detriment, in circumstances where a less vulnerable person would be able to cope without harmful effects (Code of Guidance, para 10.13). In *Osmani v Camden LBC* [2005] HLR 22 Lord Justice Auld at [38.6] expressed the meaning of, and approach to, the concept of vulnerability as follows:

> 'the test is a single one of a homeless person's less than normal ability to fend for himself such that he will suffer more harm than would an ordinary homeless person – a "composite assessment".'

Intentionality

8.65 An applicant will not be owed the main homelessness duties unless he is homeless or threatened with homelessness, eligible, has a priority need and is not homeless intentionally.

8.66 If an applicant satisfies all the requirements save for intentionality, the authority has a duty to secure accommodation is available for him but only for such period as they consider will give him a reasonable opportunity of securing accommodation. It must also provide him or secure that he is provided with advice and assistance in any attempts he may make in securing his own accommodation (s 190(2)).

8.67 Even if a person does not have a priority need, if he satisfies the other requirements the authority still has a power to accommodate (s 192(3)). The authority must therefore determine the issue of intentionality even if it has decided he does not have a priority need for accommodation.

191 Becoming homeless intentionally

(1) A person becomes homeless intentionally if he deliberately does or fails to do anything in consequence of which he ceases to occupy accommodation which is available for his occupation and which it would have been reasonable for him to continue to occupy.

(2) For the purposes of subsection (1) an act or omission in good faith on the part of a person who was unaware of any relevant fact shall not be treated as deliberate.

(3) A person shall be treated as becoming homeless intentionally if –

    (a)   he enters into an arrangement under which he is required to cease to occupy accommodation which it would have been reasonable for him to continue to occupy, and

    (b)   the purpose of the arrangement is to enable him to become entitled to assistance under this Part,

and there is no other good reason why he is homeless.

(4) (*repealed*)

8.68 Separate provision is made for determining whether a person becomes threatened with homelessness intentionally.

196 Becoming threatened with homelessness intentionally

(1) A person becomes threatened with homelessness intentionally if he deliberately does or fails to do anything the likely result of which is that he will be forced to leave accommodation which is available for his occupation and which it would have been reasonable for him to continue to occupy.

(2) For the purposes of subsection (1) an act or omission in good faith on the part of a person who was unaware of any relevant fact shall not be treated as deliberate.

(3) A person shall be treated as becoming threatened with homelessness intentionally if –

    (a)   he enters into an arrangement under which he is required to cease to occupy accommodation which it would have been reasonable for him to continue to occupy, and

    (b)   the purpose of the arrangement is to enable him to become entitled to assistance under this Part,

and there is no other good reason why he is threatened with homelessness.

(4) (*repealed*)

8.69 A common issue arising is identifying the person who has deliberately done or failed to do something which resulted in homelessness or threatened homelessness. The Code of Guidance states at para 11.9:

Every applicant is entitled to individual consideration of his or her application. This includes applicants where another member of their family or household has made, or is making, a separate application. It is the applicant who must deliberately have done or failed to do something which resulted in homelessness or threatened homelessness. Where a housing authority has found an applicant to be homeless intentionally, nothing in the 1996 Act prevents another member of his or her household from making a separate application. Situations may arise where one or more members of a household found to be intentionally homeless were not responsible for the actions or omissions that led to the homelessness. For example, a person may have deliberately failed to pay the rent or defaulted on the mortgage payments, which resulted in homelessness or threatened homelessness, against the wishes or without the knowledge of his or her partner. However, where applicants were not directly responsible for the act or omission which led to their family or household becoming homeless, but they acquiesced in that behaviour, then they may be treated as having become homeless intentionally themselves. In considering whether an applicant has acquiesced in certain behaviour, the Secretary of State recommends that the housing authority take into account whether the applicant could reasonably be expected to have taken that position through a fear of actual or probable violence.

8.70 It should be highlighted that an act or omission should not generally be treated as deliberate, even where deliberately carried out, if it was forced upon the applicant through no fault of his own (Code of Guidance, para 11.16).

8.71 Importantly in the context of this publication, where the local housing authority has reason to believe that an applicant was incapable of managing his or her affairs, for example by reason of age, illness or disability, his acts or omissions should not be considered 'deliberate' for the purposes of s 191(1) (Code of Guidance, para 11.17(i)).

8.72 An authority's decisions concerning eligibility, homeless or threatened with homelessness, priority need and intentionality are all decisions about which the applicant has a right of review by the authority (s 202(1)).

Interim accommodation pending review

8.73 Once a decision has been made, the authority has a power to accommodate. In *R v Camden LBC ex p Mohammed* (1998) 30 HLR 315 the court held that the following factors must be taken into account:

(a)   the strength of the applicant's case on review;

(b)   whether any new material, information or argument has been raised since the initial decision was made;

(c)   the personal circumstances of the applicant;

(d)   the consequences for the applicant if accommodation is not secured; and

(e)   any other relevant considerations.

8.74 To add to these factors, the authority may consider and rely upon the scarcity of its own resources (*R (Cole) v Enfield LBC* [2003] EWHC 1454 (Admin).

8.75 More than mere 'lip-service' should be paid to these factors (*R v Paul-Coker v Southwark LBC* [2006] EWHC 497 (Admin)) and general public law requirements should otherwise be applied.

Interim accommodation pending appeal

8.76 If the authority uphold the original decision on review, the applicant may appeal to the county court on a 'point of law' (s 204(1)).

8.77 Pending the outcome of the appeal the authority has a power to secure accommodation for the applicant where it was under a duty to secure accommodation pursuant to s 188, 190 or 200 (s 204(4)). Any challenge to the exercise of this power is to the county court as opposed to the Administrative Court by way of judicial review.

Main duty

8.78 An applicant who is eligible, homeless or threatened with homelessness, has a priority need and is not homeless intentionally will be owed a duty to secure suitable accommodation is made available for them (s 193(2)).

8.79 The authority will cease to be subject to the main duty in the circumstances prescribed by the Act (s 193(3)). At present the duty cannot be discharged by the offer of private rented accommodation unless the applicant consents to such an offer (s 193(7B), (7C)).

8.80 One of the main changes introduced by the Localism Act will be to allow local authorities to discharge their duties to homeless people by using private rented accommodation. A refusal of a reasonable offer of suitable accommodation in the private sector may lead to the end of the authority's duty.

EQUALITY AND DIVERSITY

8.81 Local housing authorities must consider its duties and responsibilities under the Equality Act 2010 when performing its housing related functions.

8.82 The homelessness Code of Guidance at para 7 states:

> 'When exercising their functions relating to homelessness and the prevention of homelessness, local authorities are under a statutory duty to ensure that their polices and procedures do not discriminate, directly or indirectly, on grounds of race, sex or gender, or disability. Authorities should also ensure that their policies and procedures do not discriminate on the basis of any other ground which is not

material to a person's housing application, including grounds of sexual orientation or religion or belief. Authorities should observe relevant codes of practice and adopt a formal equality and diversity policy relating to all aspects of their homelessness service, to ensure equality of access and treatment for all applicants. Appropriate provision will need to be made to ensure accessibility for people with particular needs, including those with mobility difficulties, sight or hearing loss and learning difficulties, as well as those for whom English is not their first language.'

8.83 In *Pieretti v Enfield LBC* [2010] EWCA Civ 1104 the Court of Appeal dismissed a local authority's argument that it did not have to consider the disability equality duty under s 49A of the Disability Discrimination Act 1995 (repealed and replaced with the public sector equality duty found at s 149 of the Equality Act 2010). Lord Justice Wilson at [31] said:

'I therefore have no hesitation in concluding that the duty in s 49A(1) of the Act of 1995 applies to local authorities in carrying out their functions – all of their functions – under Part VII of the Act of 1996...'

8.84 The equality duties are continuing duties which are capable of remedy following initial breach (*Barnsley MBC v Norton* [2011] EWCA Civ 834 at [26]). It is also of note that the duty to have regard to the need to take steps to take account of a person's disability pursuant to s 49A of the 1995 Act or s 149 of the 2010 Act means such regard as is appropriate in all the circumstances (*R (McDonald) v RB of Kensington and Chelsea* [2011] UKSC 33 at [33]).

Chapter 9

ASYLUM SUPPORT

Adam Fullwood

INTRODUCTION

9.1   Asylum seekers and former asylum seekers who are in need of community care services represent some of the most vulnerable people in society. This Chapter is aimed at providing an outline of the principal duties and responsibilities falling on the Secretary of State and those falling on local authorities for adults and children with community care needs under the National Assistance Act 1948 (NAA 1948) and Children Act 1989 (CA 1989).

9.2   The decision as to what duty (if any) is owed will often be determined by reference to that person's immigration status. Whilst an overview of immigration and asylum law will be provided where relevant, the reader is referred to McDonald's *Immigration Law and Practice* (8th edition, LexisNexis Butterworths), for a more in-depth analysis.

ASYLUM SUPPORT

Asylum seekers

9.3   Primary responsibility for supporting asylum seekers falls on central government under the provisions of the Immigration and Asylum Act 1999 (IAA 1999). From 3 April 2000 a destitute asylum-seeker would normally be entitled to initial accommodation pursuant to s 98 of IAA 1999 followed by interim support and accommodation pursuant to s 95.

9.4   Immigration and Asylum Act 1999, s 95(1) provides:

> The Secretary of State may provide, or arrange for the provision of support for –
>
> (a)   asylum-seekers, or
> (b)   dependents of asylum-seekers,
>
> who appear to the Secretary of State to be destitute or likely to become destitute within such period as may be prescribed.

The power to provide support has been interpreted as giving rise to a duty where all the criteria are met: *Husain v Asylum Support Adjudicator & Sec of State for the Home Department* [2001] EWHC 832 (Admin).

9.5   Asylum support under s 95 of IAA 1999 will normally be provided to an 'asylum seeker' and his or her 'dependant' who appears to be destitute or likely to become destitute within 14 days, or 56 days, if already in receipt of such support (s 95(1)). It is relevant to the subject matter of this book to highlight that an adult (over the age of 18) child or close member of the family who has resided with them for the preceding six of the last 12 months before the application and who is in need of care and attention from the applicant or a member of his household on account of his disability will qualify as a 'dependant'.

9.6   IAA 1999, s 95(3) defines 'destitute' as follows:

> For the purposes of this section, a person is destitute if –
>
> (a)   he does not have adequate accommodation or any means of obtaining it (whether or not his other essential living needs are met); or
>
> (b)   he has adequate accommodation or the means of obtaining it, but cannot meet his other essential living needs.

In deciding whether an asylum seeker is destitute or likely to become destitute the Secretary of State is entitled to consider whether he has any other income, support or assets that he or any dependent has or might be reasonably available pursuant to reg 6 of the Asylum Support Regulations 2000.

9.7   An 'asylum seeker' is a person aged 18 or over who has made a claim for asylum under the Refugee Convention or a claim under the European Convention on Human Rights that has been recorded but has not been determined (s 94(1)). Visitors and students falling outside of this definition are not eligible for asylum support even if destitute.

9.8   IAA 1999, s 94(1) provides:

> In this Part –
>
>> "asylum-seeker" means a person who is not under 18 and has made a claim for asylum which has been recorded by the Secretary of State but which has not been determined;
>> "claim for asylum" means a claim that it would be contrary to the United Kingdom's obligations under the Refugee Convention, or under Article 3 of the Human Rights Convention, for the Claimant to be removed from, or required to leave, the United Kingdom; ...

9.9   Care is needed to check whether an asylum seeker was required to make his claim at a 'designated place'. After 10 February 2003, a claim for leave to remain on the basis that return would breach his rights under the Refugee Convention and/or European Convention on Human Rights must be made in person at a place designated by the Secretary of State (Nationality, Immigration and Asylum Act 2002, s 113(1)).

9.10   If an asylum claim is refused and a second or 'fresh' claim is made or a claim under ECHR Art 3 is made, asylum support should be provided so long as the claim is 'recorded' by UKBA (s 94(1)). It will not be 'recorded' if the decision-maker does not consider that it amounts to a fresh claim. The test for a fresh claim is defined by para 353 of the Immigration Rules (available on the UKBA website). The leading case on 'fresh claims' remains *WM (Democratic Republic of Congo) v Sec of State for the Home Department* [2006] EWCA Civ 1495. If such a claim is recorded the claim will be determined along with the question of whether the person is destitute. There exists an in-country right of appeal against that decision.

9.11 A precondition for the provision of asylum support is that the asylum claim was made as soon as reasonably practicable after the person's entry into the United Kingdom unless such support is necessary to avoid a breach of their rights under the European Convention on Human Rights. This condition does not apply if the household includes a dependent child under the age of 18.

Failed asylum seekers

9.12 Once an asylum seeker without a dependent child has had his claim refused and has not appealed or has otherwise exhausted all his appeal rights he is not entitled to asylum support under s 95. In such circumstances, his entitlement will be limited to support under s 4 of IAA 1999 (otherwise known as 'hard cases' support).

9.13 A failed asylum seeker will only be entitled to hard cases support if he is destitute pursuant to reg 2 of the Immigration and Asylum (Provision of Accommodation to Failed Asylum-seekers) Regulations 2005. It should be noted that where such a person has a child under the age of 18 who was born before the final determination he will continue to be treated as an asylum seeker, and therefore eligible for asylum support under s 95, for as long as adult and child are in the United Kingdom (s 94(5)).

9.14 IAA 1999, s 4(2) provides:

> The Secretary of State may provide, or arrange for the provision of, facilities for the accommodation of a person if –
>
> (a)   he was (but no longer is) an asylum-seeker, and
> (b)   his claim for asylum was rejected.

9.15 IAA section 4(3) provides:

> The Secretary of State may provide, or arrange for the provision of, facilities for the accommodation of a dependant of a person for whom facilities may be provided under subsection (2).

9.16 The Immigration and Asylum (Provision of Accommodation to Failed Asylum Seekers) Regulations 2005 provides the criteria to be applied for determining whether to provide support. Regulation 3 provides:

> (1) Subject to regulations 4 and 6, the criteria to be used in determining the matters referred to in paragraphs (a) and (b) of section 4(5) of the 1999 Act in respect of a person falling within section 4(2) or (3) of that Act are –

(a)   that he appears to the Secretary of State to be destitute, and

(b)   that one or more of the conditions set out in paragraph (2) are satisfied in relation to him.

(2) Those conditions are that –

(a)   he is taking all reasonable steps to leave the United Kingdom ...;

(b)   he is unable to leave the United Kingdom by reason of a physical impediment to travel or for some other medical reason;

(c)   he is unable leave the United Kingdom because in the opinion of the Secretary of State there is currently no viable route of return available;

(d)   he has made an application for judicial review of a decision in relation to his asylum claim – (i) in England and Wales, and has been granted permission to proceed pursuant to Part 54 of the Civil Procedure Rules 1998 ...;

(e)   the provision of accommodation is necessary for the purpose of avoiding a breach of a person's Convention Rights ...

9.17   In *R (VC & ors) and R (K) v Newcastle City Council* [2011] EWHC 2673 (Admin) it was held that a local authority cannot automatically withdraw, or decline to offer, support under s 17 of the Children Act 1989 to a child whom it had assessed to be 'in need' simply on the basis that support was available under s 4 of IAA 1999. It could only do so in the very unlikely event that it could be shown that the secretary of state was able and willing, or could be compelled, to provide s 4 support and that the that that support would suffice to meet the child's assessed needs.

COMMUNITY CARE SERVICES

Introduction

9.18   An adult asylum seeker who may have a need for community care services might be entitled to receive the same from the relevant social services authority subject to: (a) an assessment of his needs; and (b) specific statutory provisions which may exclude him from accessing the same contained in the IAA 1999 and s 54 of and Sch 3 to the Nationality, Immigration and Asylum Act 2002 (NIAA 2002).

9.19   In relation to (a) it might be argued by local authorities that no duty arises because it does not have a power to provide community care services due to the effect of the exclusion provisions. However, in many cases an argument will be raised to the effect that a decision not to provide support may unlawfully interfere with Convention rights. In such circumstances, it would be prudent, to say the least, to carry out an assessment of need.

9.20   It is important to highlight at the outset that services provided under s 117 of the Mental Health Act 1983 are not excluded as a consequence of the person's immigration status.

Immigration and Asylum Act 1999

9.21 Services excluded by IAA 1999 are those covered by ss 116 and 117. Section 116 of IAA 1999 amended s 21 of the NAA 1948 to provide as follows:

(1A) A person to whom section 115 of the Immigration and Asylum Act 1999 (exclusion from benefits) applies may not be provided with residential accommodation under subsection (1)(a) if his need for care and attention has arisen solely –

(a) because he is destitute; or
(b) because of the physical effects, or anticipated physical effects, of his being destitute.

(1B) Subsections (3) and (5) to (8) of section 95 of the Immigration and Asylum Act 1999, and paragraph 2 of Schedule 8 to that Act, apply for the purposes of subsection (1A) as they apply for the purposes of that section, but for the references in subsections (5) and (7) of that section and in that paragraph to the Secretary of State substitute references to a local authority.

9.22 Section 115 applies to exclude from benefits that that are 'subject to immigration control' defined by s 115(9) as follows:

A person subject to immigration control" means a person who is not a national of an EEA State and who –

(a) requires leave to enter or remain in the United Kingdom but does not have it;
(b) has leave to enter or remain in the United Kingdom which is subject to a condition that he does not have recourse to public funds;
(c) has leave to enter or remain in the United Kingdom given as a result of a maintenance undertaking; or
(d) has leave to enter or remain in the United Kingdom only as a result of paragraph 17 of Schedule 4.

9.23 Section 117 of IAA 1999 creates additional restrictions in relation to the provision of services by health authorities by amending s 45 of the Health Services and Public Health Act 1968 (certain services for older people) by inserting the following:

(4A) No arrangements under this section may be given effect to in relation to a person to whom section 115 of the Immigration and Asylum Act 1999 (exclusion from benefits) applies solely –

(a) because he is destitute; or
(b) because of the physical effects, or anticipated physical effects, of his being destitute.

(4B) Subsections (3) and (5) to (8) of section 95 of the Immigration and Asylum Act 1999, and paragraph 2 of Schedule 8 to that Act, apply for the purposes of subsection (4A) as they apply for the purposes of that section, but for the references in subsections (5) and (7) of that section and in that paragraph to the Secretary of State substitute references to a local authority.

9.24 Section 117 also amends Sch 20 of the National Health Service Act 2006 by inserting the following:

(2A) No arrangements under this paragraph may be given effect to in relation to a person to whom section 115 of the Immigration and Asylum Act 1999 (exclusion from benefits) applies solely –

(a)   because he is destitute; or
(b)   because of the physical effects, or anticipated physical effects, of his being destitute.

(2B) Subsections (3) and (5) to (8) of section 95 of the Immigration and Asylum Act 1999, and paragraph 2 of Schedule 8 to that Act, apply for the purposes of subsection (2A) as they apply for the purposes of that section, but for the references in subsections (5) and (7) of that section and in that paragraph to the Secretary of State substitute references to a local social services authority.

9.25 Section 122(5) of IAA 1999 is of particular importance to s 17 CA 1989 cases. It provides:

No local authority may provide assistance under any of the child welfare provisions in respect of a dependant under the age of 18, or any member of his family, at any time when –

(a)   the Secretary of State is complying with this section in relation to him; or
(b)   there are reasonable grounds for believing that-
       (i)   the person concerned is a person for whom support may be provided under section 95; and
       (ii)   the Secretary of State would be required to comply with this section if that person had made an application under section 95.

9.26 A large number of asylum seekers and failed asylum seekers are excluded by NIAA 2002. Section 54 provides:

Withholding and withdrawal of support

Schedule 3 (which makes provision for support to be withheld or withdrawn in certain circumstances) shall have effect.

Schedule 3 provides:

SCHEDULE 3
Withholding and Withdrawal of Support

Ineligibility for support

1 (1) A person to whom this paragraph applies shall not be eligible for support or assistance under –

(a)   section 21 or 29 of the National Assistance Act 1948 (c. 29) (local authority: accommodation and welfare),
(b)   section 45 of the Health Services and Public Health Act 1968 (c. 46) (local authority: welfare of elderly),
(c)   section 12 or 13A of the Social Work (Scotland) Act 1968 (c. 49) (social welfare services),

(d) Article 7 or 15 of the Health and Personal Social Services (Northern Ireland) Order 1972 (S.I. 1972/1265 (N.I. 14)) (prevention of illness, social welfare, &c.),

(e) section 254 of, and Schedule 20 to, the National Health Service Act 2006, or section 192 of, and Schedule 15 to, the National Health Service (Wales) Act 2006 (social services),

(f) section 29(1)(b) of the Housing (Scotland) Act 1987 (c. 26) (interim duty to accommodate in case of apparent priority need where review of a local authority decision has been requested),

(g) section 17, 23C, 24A or 24B of the Children Act 1989 (c. 41) (welfare and other powers which can be exercised in relation to adults),

(h) Article 18, 35 or 36 of the Children (Northern Ireland) Order 1995 (S.I. 1995/755 (N.I. 2)) (welfare and other powers which can be exercised in relation to adults),

(i) sections 22, 29 and 30 of the Children (Scotland) Act 1995 (c. 36) (provisions analogous to those mentioned in paragraph (g)),

(j) section 188(3) or 204(4) of the Housing Act 1996 (c. 52) (accommodation pending review or appeal),

(k) section 2 of the Local Government Act 2000 (c. 22) (promotion of well-being),

(l) a provision of the Immigration and Asylum Act 1999 (c. 33), or

(m) a provision of this Act.

(2) A power or duty under a provision referred to in sub-paragraph (1) may not be exercised or performed in respect of a person to whom this paragraph applies (whether or not the person has previously been in receipt of support or assistance under the provision).

(3) An approval or directions given under or in relation to a provision referred to in sub-paragraph (1) shall be taken to be subject to sub-paragraph (2).

Exceptions

2 (1) Paragraph 1 does not prevent the provision of support or assistance –

(a) to a British citizen, or

(b) to a child, or

(c) under or by virtue of regulations made under paragraph 8, 9 or 10 below, or

(d) in a case in respect of which, and to the extent to which, regulations made by the Secretary of State disapply paragraph 1, or

(e) in circumstances in respect of which, and to the extent to which, regulations made by the Secretary of State disapply paragraph 1.

(2) Regulations under sub-paragraph (1)(d) may confer a discretion on the Secretary of State.

(3) Regulations under sub-paragraph (1)(e) may, in particular, disapply paragraph 1 to the provision of support or assistance by a local authority to a person where the authority –

(a) has taken steps in accordance with guidance issued by the Secretary of State to determine whether paragraph 1 would (but for the regulations) apply to the person, and

(b) has concluded on the basis of those steps that there is no reason to believe that paragraph 1 would apply.

(4) Regulations under sub-paragraph (1)(d) or (e) may confer a discretion on an authority.

(5) A local authority which is considering whether to give support or assistance to a person under a provision listed in paragraph 1(1) shall act in accordance with any relevant guidance issued by the Secretary of State under sub-paragraph (3)(a).

(6) A reference in this Schedule to a person to whom paragraph 1 applies includes a reference to a person in respect of whom that paragraph is disapplied to a limited extent by regulations under sub-paragraph (1)(d) or (e), except in a case for which the regulations provide otherwise.

3 Paragraph 1 does not prevent the exercise of a power or the performance of a duty if, and to the extent that, its exercise or performance is necessary for the purpose of avoiding a breach of –

    (a)   a person's Convention rights, or
    (b)   a person's rights under the Community Treaties.

First class of ineligible person: refugee status abroad

4 (1) Paragraph 1 applies to a person if he –

    (a)   has refugee status abroad, or
    (b)   is the dependant of a person who is in the United Kingdom and who has refugee status abroad.

(2) For the purposes of this paragraph a person has refugee status abroad if –

    (a)   he does not have the nationality of an EEA State, and
    (b)   the government of an EEA State other than the United Kingdom has determined that he is entitled to protection as a refugee under the Refugee Convention.

Second class of ineligible person: citizen of other EEA State

5 Paragraph 1 applies to a person if he –

    (a)   has the nationality of an EEA State other than the United Kingdom, or
    (b)   is the dependant of a person who has the nationality of an EEA State other than the United Kingdom.

Third class of ineligible person: failed asylum-seeker

6 (1) Paragraph 1 applies to a person if –

    (a)   he was (but is no longer) an asylum-seeker, and
    (b)   he fails to cooperate with removal directions issued in respect of him.

(2) Paragraph 1 also applies to a dependant of a person to whom that paragraph applies by virtue of sub-paragraph (1).

Fourth class of ineligible person: person unlawfully in United Kingdom

7 Paragraph 1 applies to a person if –

    (a)   he is in the United Kingdom in breach of the immigration laws within the meaning of section 11, and
    (b)   he is not an asylum-seeker.

Fifth class of ineligible person: failed asylum-seeker with family

7A (1) Paragraph 1 applies to a person if –

    (a)   he—
        (i)   is treated as an asylum-seeker for the purposes of Part VI of the Immigration and Asylum Act 1999 (c. 33) (support) by virtue only of section 94(3A) (failed asylum-seeker with dependant child), or
        (ii)   is treated as an asylum seeker for the purposes of Part 2 of this Act by virtue only of section 18(2),
    (b)   the Secretary of State has certified that in his opinion the person has failed without reasonable excuse to take reasonable steps –
        (i)   to leave the United Kingdom voluntarily, or
        (ii)   to place himself in a position in which he is able to leave the United Kingdom voluntarily,
    (c)   the person has received a copy of the Secretary of State's certificate, and
    (d)   the period of 14 days, beginning with the date on which the person receives the copy of the certificate, has elapsed.

(2) Paragraph 1 also applies to a dependant of a person to whom that paragraph applies by virtue of sub-paragraph (1).

(3) For the purpose of sub-paragraph (1)(d) if the Secretary of State sends a copy of a certificate by first class post to a person's last known address, the person shall be treated as receiving the copy on the second day after the day on which it was posted.

(4) The Secretary of State may by regulations vary the period specified in sub-paragraph (1)(d).

Travel assistance

8 The Secretary of State may make regulations providing for arrangements to be made enabling a person to whom paragraph 1 applies by virtue of paragraph 4 or 5 to leave the United Kingdom.

Temporary accommodation

9 (1) The Secretary of State may make regulations providing for arrangements to be made for the accommodation of a person to whom paragraph 1 applies pending the implementation of arrangements made by virtue of paragraph 8.

(2) Arrangements for a person by virtue of this paragraph –

    (a)   may be made only if the person has with him a dependent child, and
    (b)   may include arrangements for a dependent child.

10 (1) The Secretary of State may make regulations providing for arrangements to be made for the accommodation of a person if –

    (a)   paragraph 1 applies to him by virtue of paragraph 7, and
    (b)   he has not failed to cooperate with removal directions issued in respect of him.

(2) Arrangements for a person by virtue of this paragraph –

    (a)   may be made only if the person has with him a dependent child, and
    (b)   may include arrangements for a dependent child.

Assistance and accommodation: general

11 Regulations under paragraph 8, 9 or 10 may –

(a)   provide for the making of arrangements under a provision referred to in paragraph 1(1) or otherwise;

(b)   confer a function (which may include the exercise of a discretion) on the Secretary of State, a local authority or another person;

(c)   provide that arrangements must be made in a specified manner or in accordance with specified principles;

(d)   provide that arrangements may not be made in a specified manner;

(e)   require a local authority or another person to have regard to guidance issued by the Secretary of State in making arrangements;

(f)   require a local authority or another person to comply with a direction of the Secretary of State in making arrangements.

12 (1) Regulations may, in particular, provide that if a person refuses an offer of arrangements under paragraph 8 or fails to implement or cooperate with arrangements made for him under that paragraph –

(a)   new arrangements may be made for him under paragraph 8, but

(b)   new arrangements may not be made for him under paragraph 9.

(2) Regulations by virtue of this paragraph may include exceptions in the case of a person who –

(a)   has a reason of a kind specified in the regulations for failing to implement or cooperate with arrangements made under paragraph 8, and

(b)   satisfies any requirements of the regulations for proof of the reason.

Offences

13 (1) A person who leaves the United Kingdom in accordance with arrangements made under paragraph 8 commits an offence if he –

(a)   returns to the United Kingdom, and

(b)   requests that arrangements be made for him by virtue of paragraph 8, 9 or 10.

(2) A person commits an offence if he –

(a)   requests that arrangements be made for him by virtue of paragraph 8, 9 or 10, and

(b)   fails to mention a previous request by him for the making of arrangements under any of those paragraphs.

(3) A person who is guilty of an offence under this paragraph shall be liable on summary conviction to imprisonment for a term not exceeding six months.

Information

14 (1) If it appears to a local authority that paragraph 1 applies or may apply to a person in the authority's area by virtue of paragraph 6, 7 or 7A, the authority must inform the Secretary of State.

(2) A local authority shall act in accordance with any relevant guidance issued by the Secretary of State for the purpose of determining whether paragraph 1 applies or may apply to a person in the authority's area by virtue of paragraph 6, 7 or 7A.

Power to amend Schedule

15 The Secretary of State may by order amend this Schedule so as –

    (a)   to provide for paragraph 1 to apply or not to apply to a class of person;

    (b)   to add or remove a provision to or from the list in paragraph 1(1);

    (c)   to add, amend or remove a limitation of or exception to paragraph 1.

Orders and regulations

16 (1) An order or regulations under this Schedule must be made by statutory instrument.

(2) An order or regulations under this Schedule may –

    (a)   make provision which applies generally or only in specified cases or circumstances or only for specified purposes;

    (b)   make different provision for different cases, circumstances or purposes;

    (c)   make transitional provision;

    (d)   make consequential provision (which may include provision amending a provision made by or under this or another Act).

(3) An order under this Schedule, regulations under paragraph 2(1)(d) or (e) or other regulations which include consequential provision amending an enactment shall not be made unless a draft has been laid before and approved by resolution of each House of Parliament.

(4) Regulations under this Schedule to which sub-paragraph (3) does not apply shall be subject to annulment in pursuance of a resolution of either House of Parliament.

Interpretation

17 (1) In this Schedule –

    "asylum-seeker" means a person –
        (a)   who is at least 18 years old,
        (b)   who has made a claim for asylum (within the meaning of section 18(3)), and
        (c)   whose claim has been recorded by the Secretary of State but not determined,

    "Convention rights" has the same meaning as in the Human Rights Act 1998 (c. 42),
    "child" means a person under the age of eighteen,
    "dependant" and "dependent" shall have such meanings as may be prescribed by regulations made by the Secretary of State,
    "EEA State" means a State which is a contracting party to the Agreement on the European Economic Area signed at Oporto on 2nd May 1992 (as it has effect from time to time),
    "local authority" –
        (a)   in relation to England and Wales, has the same meaning as in section 129(3),

(b)   in relation to Scotland, has the same meaning as in section 129(4), and

(c)   in relation to Northern Ireland, means a health service body within the meaning of section 133(4)(d) and the Northern Ireland Housing Executive (for which purpose a reference to the authority's area shall be taken as a reference to Northern Ireland),

"the Refugee Convention" means the Convention relating to the status of Refugees done at Geneva on 28th July 1951 and its Protocol, and
"removal directions" means directions under Schedule 2 to the Immigration Act 1971 (c. 77) (control of entry, &c.), under Schedule 3 to that Act (deportation) or under section 10 of the Immigration and Asylum Act 1999 (c. 33) (removal of person unlawfully in United Kingdom).

(2) For the purpose of the definition of "asylum-seeker" in sub-paragraph (1) a claim is determined if –

(a) the Secretary of State has notified the claimant of his decision,
(b) no appeal against the decision can be brought (disregarding the possibility of an appeal out of time with permission), and
(c) any appeal which has already been brought has been disposed of.

(3) For the purpose of sub-paragraph (2)(c) an appeal is disposed of when it is no longer pending for the purpose of –

(a) Part 5 of this Act, or
(b) the Special Immigration Appeals Commission Act 1997 (c. 68).

(4) The giving of directions in respect of a person under a provision of the Immigration Acts is not the provision of assistance to him for the purposes of this Schedule.

9.27   The interplay between the rights and responsibilities arising under the community care and Children Act schemes and the exclusions arising under the immigration and asylum scheme has been the subject of significant analysis by the courts. A full account is not possible for the purposes of this Chapter but the following represent some of the important decisions.

9.28   In *R (Westminster City Council) v National Asylum Support Service* [2002] 1 WLR 2956 the House of Lords looked at the difference between the able-bodied and infirm destitute asylum seeker in the context of community care services under s 21 NAA 1948. Lord Hoffmann at [32] said:

> 'The use of the word "solely" makes it clear that only the able bodied destitute are excluded from the powers and duties of section 21(1)(a). The infirm destitute remain within. Their need for care and attention arises because they are infirm as well as because they are destitute. They would need care and attention even if they were wealthy. They would not of course need accommodation, but that is not where section 21(1A) draws the line.'

9.29   To determine whether a person's need for care and attention has arisen solely because he is destitute or because of the physical effects, or anticipated physical effects, of his being destitute under s 21(1A) of NAA 1948 regard should be had to the decision of the Court of Appeal in *R v Wandsworth LBC* *ex p O* [2000] 1 WLR 2539. In that case Lord Justice Brown (as he then was) concluded that the meaning of s 21(1A) was that if an applicant's need for care and attention is 'to any material extent made more acute by some circumstance other than the mere lack of accommodation and funds, then, despite being subject to immigration control, he qualifies for assistance.' The duty under CA 1989 to a child does not extend to the parent (see: Lord Justice Carnwath at paras [50] [52] and [64]).

9.30 In *R (On the application of M) v Slough BC* [2008] 1 WLR 1808 Baroness Hale applied the distinction between the healthy or 'able-bodied' asylum seeker and the 'infirm' asylum seeker by reference to the proper analysis of the words 'care and attention'. At [33] she said:

> 'But "care and attention" must mean something more than "accommodation". Section 21(1)(a) is not a general power to provide housing. That is dealt with by other legislation entirely, with its own criteria for eligibility. If a simple need for housing, with or without the means of subsistence, were within section 21(1)(a), there would have been no need for the original section 21(1)(b). Furthermore, every homeless person who did not qualify for housing under the Housing Act 1996 would be able to turn to the local social services authority instead. That was definitely not what Parliament intended in 1977. This view is consistent with *Ex parte M*, in which Lord Woolf emphasised, at p 20, that asylum seekers were not entitled merely because they lacked money or accommodation. I remain of the view which I expressed in *Wahid*, at para 32, that the natural and ordinary meaning of the words "care and attention" in this context is "looking after". Looking after means doing something for the person being cared for which he cannot or should not be expected to do for himself: it might be household tasks which an old person can no longer perform or can only perform with great difficulty; it might be protection from risks which a mentally disabled person cannot perceive; it might be personal care, such as feeding, washing or toileting. This is not an exhaustive list. The provision of medical care is expressly excluded. Viewed in this light, I think it likely that all three of Mrs Y-Ahmed, Mrs O and Mr Bhikha needed some care and attention (as did Mr Wahid but in his case it was available to him in his own home, over-crowded though it was). This definition draws a reasonable line between the "able bodied" and the "infirm".'

What this means is that responsibility for the 'able-bodied' destitute asylum-seeker falls on the Secretary of State but responsibility for the 'infirm' destitute asylum-seeker falls on the relevant social services authority. Lord Brown at [40] agreed with Baroness Hale.

9.31 The meaning of 'not otherwise available' was subject to further analysis by the Court of Appeal in *SL v Westminster City Council (1) Medical Foundation (2) MIND* [2011] EWCA Civ 954. This was a case concerned with s 21(1)(a) where SL had been granted leave to remain after the first instance decision and before the matter came before the Court of Appeal. Lord Justice Laws concluded at [38] and [39] that these words meant:

> '... care and attention is not "otherwise available" unless it would be reasonably practicable and efficacious to supply it without the provision of accommodation.'

In that case the Court concluded that a man with a history of mental health problems who required regular visits by a care coordinator to access appropriate services was in need of care and attention not otherwise available to him.

9.32 Local authorities have the power to fund travel arrangements for EEA refugees and EEA nationals to return to the relevant country pursuant to the Withholding and Withdrawal of Support (Travel Assistance and Temporary Accommodation) Regulations 2002. Further, where there is a dependent child, the authority has a power to accommodate them pending their return and for so long as they cooperate.

Age disputes

9.33 There has been much litigation arising from disputed assertions by those who claim to be under the age of 18. The outcome of such disputes is important to both local authorities and the individual concerned because children will generally be owed a wider range of services than adults including the 'looked-after' duties arising under the Children (Leaving Care) Act 2000. The determination of this issue is also important because if a claim is rejected when the child is under the age of seventeen and a half, the Home Secretary will not remove him for 3 years or until he reaches seventeen and a half, whichever is the earlier, unless there are adequate arrangements to look after him in his country of origin.

9.34 A local authority has a duty to assess a putative child under s 17(1) of the Children Act 1989. This might lead to a duty to provide accommodation to the child under s 20. The crucial question is whether s/he is a child? Whether an applicant is a child is ultimately a question of fact to be determined by the court where there is a dispute (see *R (A) v LB or Croydon & ors* [2009] UKSC 8 at [27]).

9.35 In that case reference was made to the approach adopted by Stanley Burnton J in *R (B) v Merton LBC* [2003] EWHC 1689 (Admin), [2003] 4 All ER 280. This decision and its guidance have led to the development of what is sometimes referred to as a 'Merton compliant' interview or process. The assessment does not require anything approaching a trial and judicialisation of the process is to be avoided. The matter can be determined informally provided that there are minimum standards of inquiry and fairness. Except in clear cases, age cannot be determined solely from appearance. The decision-maker should explain to the young person the purpose of the interview. Questions should elicit background, family and educational circumstances and history, and ethnic and cultural matters may be relevant. The decision-maker may have to assess the applicant's credibility. Questions of the burden of proof do not apply. The local authority should make its own decision and not simply adopt a decision made, for instance, by the Home Office, if there has been a referral. It is not necessary to obtain a medical report, although paediatric expert evidence is sometimes provided in these cases, and there is some difference of view as to its persuasiveness in borderline cases. If the decision-maker forms a view that the young person may be lying, he should be given the opportunity to address the matters that may lead to that view. Adverse provisional conclusions should be put to him, so that he may have the opportunity to deal with them and rectify misunderstandings. The local authority is obliged to give reasons for its decision, although these need not be long or elaborate.

9.36   In *R (FZ) v Croydon LBC* [2011] EWCA Civ 59 the Court of Appeal has given guidance as to how the courts should determine such cases. Upon an application for permission to move for judicial review the test was framed at [9] as follows:

> ' …We consider that at the permission stage in an age assessment case the court should ask whether the material before the court raises a factual case which, taken at its highest, could not properly succeed in a contested factual hearing. If so, permission should be refused. If not, permission should normally be granted, subject to other discretionary factors, such as delay ….'

The court also held that where permission is granted, the claim for judicial review will be transferred for determination by the Upper Tribunal pursuant to the Senior Courts Act 1981, s 31A(3).

9.37   Local authorities must analyse the methodology used to support a claimant's assertion concerning age. In *R (R) v Croydon LBC* [2011] EWHC 1473 the methodology employed by a commonly used paediatrician was discredited and the court relied instead on the opinion of the social worker.

9.38   In many cases the issue of a claimant's age will have been determined in immigration proceedings. In *R (PM) v Hertfordshire County Council* [2010] EWHC 2056 the Court held that a local authority assessing the age of a young asylum seeker was not bound by an age assessment that the First-tier Tribunal (Immigration and Asylum Chamber) had made while hearing the asylum seeker's asylum appeal. It is recommended local authorities carefully consider any such determinations and provide reasons to support any decision not to follow the same.

INDEX

References are to paragraph numbers.

Abduction

capacity, and   2.36, 2.37

Abuse

Health Select Committee's Inquiry
     into Elder Abuse   3.92

meaning   3.89

Accommodation

adult placements   4.69

after care obligations   1.3

charges for residential   6.6

     capital   6.8

     Charges for Residential
         Accommodation Guide   6.7

     deprivation of capital   6.10

     disregarded capital   6.9

     income   6.11

     liability of relatives   6.15

     students   6.16

     trust funds   6.12–6.14

children   5.56–5.58

children leaving care   5.22

choice of   4.44

     availability   4.45

     capacity, and   4.45, 4.68

     cost   4.45

     disputes between care home
         owners and local
         authority   4.49

     Guidance   4.44, 4.45

     suitability   4.45

     third party top-ups, and   6.39

     top up payments   4.45

closure of care homes   4.23

disabled children   5.53, 5.59–5.64

housing and care schemes   4.67

Independent Mental Capacity
     Advocates   1.24

promise of home for life   4.26

provision of   4.1

     analysis of legislation   4.2

     charges   6.4

     lack of re-assessment   4.17

     local authority duties and
         powers   4.1

     National Assistance Act 1948   4.4, 6.3,
         6.4

     needs and resources   4.7–4.10

     ordinary housing and needs   4.11–4.16

     payment   4.2

     psychological need   4.5

Accommodation—*continued*

     provision of—*continued*

         reasonableness of need   4.6

         relevant legislation   4.3

         unaccompanied asylum-seeking
             children   5.30

         regulation of   4.54

             Care Standards Act 2000   4.54–4.57

         sale of home   4.25

         social housing *see* Housing,
             provision of

Acute care

     definition   7.24

Adult contact

     capacity, and   2.14

Adults

     long term care placements   7.66

     placements scheme   4.69

After care   1.1

     care plans   1.3

     charges for services   1.19

         interest   1.23

         limitation periods   1.21

         maladministration   1.22

         proactive reimbursement   1.20

         prohibition on   1.19

         repayment of   1.20

         restitution   1.20

         state benefits, and   1.20

     Code   1.2

         guidelines under   1.2

     continuation of   1.12

     definition   1.3

     definition of services   1.17

         Code guidance on   1.17

         nursing care   1.18

         residential facilities   1.18

         scope   1.18

     end of need for   1.9

     geographic jurisdiction   1.13

     identifying appropriate   1.4

     judicial review, and   1.12

     local authority

         duties   1.8

         relevant   1.9

     Mental Capacity Act 2005, and   2.72

     MHA 1983, under   1.15

     objectives   1.2

     ordinary residence, and   1.13–1.15

         basic principle   1.15

After care—*continued*
  ordinary residence, and—*continued*
    dual residence | 1.15
    guidance | 1.14
    temporary absence | 1.15
  persons who cease to be detained | 1.6
  relevant bodies | 1.9
  Report of Inquiry into Care and
    Treatment of Christopher
    Clunis | 1.10
  responsible commissioner,
    establishing | 1.16
  retrospective assessments | 1.12
Allocation of housing *see* Housing,
  provision of
Approved mental health professional *see*
  also Independent Mental
  Capacity Advocates; Nearest
  relative; Responsible clinician
  definition | 1.33
  guardianship, and
    role | 1.51
Assessment
  Carers (Recognition and Services)
    Act 1995 | 3.78
  ability of carer | 3.79
  alterations to property | 3.83
  disabled child | 3.80
  entitlement to own assessment | 3.81
  exclusions | 3.82
  interaction with other
    legislation | 3.78
  children leaving care | 5.20, 5.33–5.36
  closure of care homes
    flawed assessment | 4.37
  community care | 7.31
  delay in | 3.76, 3.77
  disabled children | 3.54
  Carers and Disabled Children
    Act 2000 | 5.66, 5.67
  delayed and deficient
    assessments | 5.69
  disabled parents | 6.53
  flaws in | 3.50–3.52
  funding for health care | 7.12
  inadequate | 3.70–3.72
  legislation governing | 3.1
  maladministration | 3.76, 3.77
  non-assessment | 3.73–3.75
  older people | 3.27, 3.84
  ordinary residence, and | 3.66
  parents with learning disabilities | 3.34,
     | 3.59, 3.60
  promise of home for life, and | 4.27–4.29
  provision of accommodation | 4.11–4.16
  re-assessment | 4.17
  refusal to assess | 3.73–3.75
Assets
  deprivation of
    charges, and | 6.30

Asylum seekers
  claims for asylum | 9.7, 9.8
  'designated place' requirement | 9.9
  community care services,
    entitlement | 9.18–9.20
    case law | 9.27–9.32
    exclusions | 9.21–9.25
      NIAA 2002 | 9.26
  failed
    hard case support, for | 9.12–9.17
  meaning | 9.7, 9.8
  provision of accommodation | 4.6
  second/fresh claims | 9.10
  support, for | 9.1, 9.2
    conditions | 9.11
    'dependents' | 9.5
    destitute, requirement | 9.3, 9.4, 9.6
    hard cases | 9.12–9.17
    statutory provisions | 9.3, 9.4
  unaccompanied children
    age disputes | 9.33–9.38
    assessment, of | 9.34
    decision-making process | 9.35
    'looked after' duties | 9.33
    provision for | 5.30

Best interests principle *see also*
  Capacity | 2.3, 2.8, 2.9, 2.23–2.25, 2.64,
     | 2.65, 2.67, 2.73, 2.76, 2.80, 2.82,
     | 2.86, 2.87, 2.97
  adult contact/residence disputes | 2.16,
     | 2.17, 2.19
  checklist | 2.79
  children, and | 2.107
  choice of residence | 2.21, 2.22
  contraception | 2.30
  deprivation of liberty | 2.39–2.41, 2.43,
     | 2.44, 2.46, 2.47, 2.56, 2.58,
     | 2.60–2.62
  interim orders | 2.89
  marriage, and | 2.20
  medical treatment | 2.11–2.13
  removal from UK | 2.35
  statutory provision | 2.78
  tenancy agreements | 2.32
Bournewood Gap | 2.39–2.41
  MCA 2005 amendments, and | 2.41
  restriction on deprivation of liberty | 2.41

Capacity *see also* Best interests
  principle | 2.1
  abduction, and | 2.36, 2.37
  adult contact/residence disputes,
    and | 2.14, 2.15
    declaratory relief | 2.16
    disputed issues of fact | 2.17
    independent living, opportunity,
      for | 2.19
    parental relationship | 2.16
    right to family life | 2.16, 2.17
    spouse | 2.18
  assessment of | 2.1
  children | 5.77

Capacity —*continued*
choice of accommodation, and   4.45, 4.68
choice of residence, and   2.21, 2.22
community care assessment, and   3.13
contraception, and   2.26, 2.30, 2.31
contracts, entering into   2.81
deprivation of liberty   2.38–2.41
  The Bournewood Gap   2.39–2.41
diagnosis   2.77
general concepts   2.3
inability to make decisions   2.77
injunctive relief   2.3
judicial review of local authority
    decisions   2.23–2.25
law of   2.2
main principles   2.3
marriage, and   2.20
  best interests test   2.20
  protection of vulnerable adults   2.20
medical treatment, and   2.10, 2.11, 2.79
  demanding treatment   2.13
  doctor's duty of care   2.13
  GMC guidance   2.13
  inter partes hearings   2.12
  surgical or invasive treatment
      guidelines   2.11
Mental Capacity Act 2005   2.64
  Code of Practice   2.87
  Independent Mental Health Act
      Advocates   2.87
payment for goods and services   2.80
person lacking   2.75
  temporary   2.77
presumption of   2.76
removal from UK, and   2.35
reports   2.90
sexual relationships, and   2.26–2.29
standard of proof   2.77
statutory provisions   2.75–2.90
tenancy agreements, entering
    into   2.32–2.34
test for   2.4–2.9
  best interests   2.8
  burden of proof   2.7, 2.9
  capacity to consent   2.8
  Code of Practice guidance   2.9
  evidence   2.7
  fluctuating nature of capacity,
      and   2.5
  inherent jurisdiction   2.9
  judicial determination   2.7
  litigation capacity   2.8
  purpose and nature of act   2.8
  specificity   2.7
  standard of proof   2.9
  subject matter capacity   2.8
young people   5.78
Care homes
closure   4.23, 4.30–4.32
  alternatives to litigation   4.33
  draft guidance   4.33
  eligible needs and resources   4.40–4.42
  failure to renew contract   4.36
  flawed assessment   4.37

Care homes—*continued*
closure—*continued*
  home for life   4.34
  inadequate consultation   4.35
  mandatory and permissive
      functions   4.43
  movement of resident   4.37
  National Assistance Act 1948,
      s 29   4.38, 4.39
  ordinary residence   4.43
  private care/public body   4.23, 4.24
  procedure for   4.33
  re-assessment   4.34
  resources   4.34
definition   4.57
  what constitutes   4.58–4.62
disputes between local authorities,
    and   4.46
eligibility to register as   4.65
Health and Social Care Act 2008,
    effect of   4.61, 4.62
  regulation   3.85, 4.54
Care plans   1.3
accomodation   1.3
breach of duty, and   1.4
consultation with professionals   1.4
devising   1.4
inadequate   3.70–3.72
key elements   1.3
prior to discharge   1.4
undeveloped   1.4
Care Standards Act 2000   4.54–4.57
definition of care home   4.57
scope   4.56
Care trusts
nursing services, and   7.47
Carers
assessment of needs   3.14, 5.65–5.67
Cautions on land
use of charges, and   6.37
Charges
avoidance of   6.29
cautions on land, and   6.37
choice of accommodation   6.39
  third party top ups, and   6.39
Community Care (Delayed
    Discharges etc) Act 2003   6.5
charges for residential
    accommodation   6.6, 6.7
contribution to cost of service   6.50, 6.51
deferred payments, and   6.38
deprivation of assets   6.30
  liability of third parties   6.31
  manner of recovery   6.32
  subjective test for   6.33–6.36
  transfer to avoid charges   6.30
direct payments   6.40, 6.42, 6.43
  amount of   6.48, 6.49
  conditions   6.58
  Direct Payment Regulations   6.60–6.62
  duty to make payments   6.57
  education/care of disabled
      child, for   6.63, 6.64

Charges—*continued*
  direct payments—*continued*
    individual budgets   6.66–6.70
    legislation   6.41
    local authority duties   6.46
    managing   6.44
    personal budgets   6.66–6.70
    persons lacking capacity   6.45, 6.46
    purchase of health care,
        prohibition   6.71
    recipient   6.56
    recipients of   6.43
    resource allocation schemes 6.66–6.70
    s 17A Children Act 1989   6.65
    seeking repayment   6.54
    stopping   6.55
    termination   6.59
    use of   6.47
  employment of close relatives   6.52
  Health and Social Services and
    Social Security
    Adjudications Act 1983 6.20, 6.29
  introduction   6.1
  liability   6.18, 6.19
  National Assistance (Assessment of
    Resources) Regulations 1992 6.17
  National Assistance Act 1948   6.2
    origins   6.2
    s 29   6.21
  nursing services   7.7
  provision of accommodation   6.4
  reasonableness, and   6.24
    care provided by family
        member   6.26, 6.27
    case law   6.25
    disability living allowance, and 6.28
    limitation periods   6.25
    recovery   6.18, 6.19, 6.21
    National Health Service Act
        2006, under   7.50
    parents of disabled children 6.22
    scope   6.21
  s 2 Carers and Disabled Children
    Act 2000   6.23
  students   6.16
  use of   6.37
Charges for Residential
  Accommodation Guide   6.7
Children *see also* Disabled children;
  Older children
  accommodation needs   5.55–5.57
    legal status of parent   5.58
  disabled   3.53, 5.38
  exclusion of welfare provisions 9.25
  local authorities, and   7.63–7.65
  older   5.1
  ordinary residence, and   3.36
    test   3.36
  patients, of
    information provided to   1.59
  unaccompanied
    age disputes   9.33–9.38

Civil partners
  guardianship, and   1.44
Clunis, Christopher   1.10
Community care
  delayed discharges   7.17–7.20
  free provision of services   7.23
  local authority assessment   7.31
  National Health Service Act 2006
    changes under   7.29
    definitions   7.27
    liaison between local authorities
        and NHS   7.28
    other community care
        legislation, and   7.30
    prohibition on provision   7.32
    responsibility test   7.33
      capacity, and   7.35
      carer, assessment   7.35
      core values   7.35
      financial issues   7.35
      local authority involvement in
        NHS assessment   7.36
      person centred approach   7.35
      specific criteria   7.34
Community care services
  assessments
    flaws in   3.50–3.52
    assessment   3.1
    Fair Access to Care Services
        (FACS)   3.2, 3.3
      mental capacity   3.13
      needs of carers   3.14
      process   3.11, 3.12
  asylum seekers, for *see* Asylum
    seekers
  autonomy of user   3.7
  charges, for   3.9
  commissioning, of   3.17
  determining eligibility   3.6, 3.7
  Directions (2004)   3.12
  disabled children, for *see* Disabled
    children
  'eligible needs'   3.6
  historical development   3.4
  individual entitlement   3.5
  ineligible for support,
    determination   3.15
  local authority obligations   3.5
  personal budgets   3.23
  'presenting needs'   3.6
  resource allocation systems 3.24–3.26
  resources and assessment to pay 3.8–3.10
  support plan
    contents   3.18
      minimum   3.20
    FACS   3.20
    format   3.19
    Guidance   3.18, 3.22
    personal involvement   3.22
    review   3.21
  withdrawal of support   3.16

Community treatment order
applications to tribunals 1.57
Confidentiality
Code of Conduct 1.60
generally 1.60
guardianship, and 1.42
Consultation
closure of care homes 4.35
Contraception
capacity, and 2.26, 2.30, 2.31
Contribution to cost of service 6.50, 6.51
Controlled activity
vulnerable adults, and 4.73
Court of Protection
aims of 2.73
application forms 2.93
applications within proceedings 2.95
telephone and video hearings 2.95
urgent applications 2.95
without notice 2.95
best interests decision 1.26
children, and 2.107, 2.108
transfer to Family
Division 2.109–2.111
commencement of proceediings 2.94
Application Form 2.94
family members 2.94
regulation of 2.94
costs 2.100
damages, jurisdiction to award 2.102,
2.103
deputies, appointment of *see also*
Deputy 2.82
disclosure 2.98
expert evidence 2.97
guidance on tenancy agreements 2.32
hearings 2.69
privacy 2.96
inherent jurisdiction 2.9
interim orders 2.89
jurisdiction 2.91
litigation friend 2.99
ordinary residence issues 2.104–2.106
permission 2.93
persons without capacity 2.14
power to make declarations 2.81, 2.82
powers 2.74
Practice Directions 2.101
procedure 2.91
rules
notification of P 2.92
transfer of proceedings 2.109–2.111

Day care facilities
withdrawal 4.43
Deferred payments
charges, and 6.38
Deprivation of liberty
capacity, and 2.39
authorisation of 2.44–2.46
capacity, and 2.38, 2.40, 2.41
ECHR 2.49
meaning 2.51–2.54, 2.56–2.62

Deprivation of liberty—*continued*
no DOLS
role of local authority 2.47–2.50
safeguards 2.41, 2.86
Code of Practice 2.42–2.46
general principles, for 2.43
Deputy
appointment of 2.82, 2.84
family member, as 2.83
local authority, as 2.85
mismanagement, by 2.83
powers
personal welfare decisions 2.82, 2.83
property decisions 2.82–2.85
Detention *see also* Deprivation of
liberty 1.2
after care services, and 1.2
discharge
nearest relative, and 1.56
persons who cease to be detained 1.5
remedies 1.56
Direct payments
charges, and 6.40–6.43
persons lacking capacity 6.45, 6.46
nursing services 7.37–7.39
personal budgets 7.40
stopping 6.55
Directed partnership arrangements 7.48
Disability Discrimination Acts
vulnerable adult parents, and 3.64
Disabled children *see also* Children;
Older children 3.53
accommodation needs 5.53, 5.62, 5.63
alterations to accommodation 5.60
foster parents, and 5.59
local authority duties 5.54
ordinary residence 5.64
unsuitable accommodation 5.61
care, leaving 5.38
Carers and Disabled Children Act
2000 5.65
assessment under 5.66
guidance 5.66, 5.67
main purpose 5.66
Children Act 2004 5.71–5.73
Community Care Assessment
Directions 2004 5.67
community care services 3.56
assessment of 3.56
mandatory provision for
assessment 3.58
planning for 3.56
promotion and planning of 3.57
delayed and deficient assessments 5.69,
5.70
direct payments supporting 6.63, 6.64
legislation 3.54, 5.39, 5.43
general statutory framework 5.41
implementation 5.40
Office of Deputy Prime
Minister final report 5.42
local authority duties 3.54

Disabled children —*continued*
local authority obligations   5.38
  extent of   5.46–5.52
local authority powers and duties   5.44
  case law   5.44
  obligations to provide services   5.44
  scope   5.45
Mental Capacity Act 2005   5.77
  children   5.77
  young people   5.78
provision of welfare services   3.55
  enforcement   3.55
  response   3.55
  trigger   3.55
recovery of charges   6.22
transitional services   5.74–5.76
Disabled parents
needs assessments   6.53
Disclosure
Court of Protection   2.98
guardianship, and   1.42
hospital manager's duties   1.58
Dispute resolution   7.25
nursing services, and   7.41
ordinary residence   7.21
Doctors
duty of care
  capacity, and   2.13
Domiciliary care   4.66

Education
disabled children   5.38
**European Convention on Human Rights
and Fundamental Freedoms**
claims for aylum under   9.7, 9.8
  'designated place' requirement   9.9
disclosure, and   1.42
Expert evidence
change of mind   2.97
questions in writing   2.97
Rules   2.97
Extra care housing   4.67

Fair Access to Care Services (FACS)   3.2
eligibility criteria   3.2, 3.3
Guidance   3.3
legislation   3.2
local authority obligations   3.3
Fostering   5.17
accommodation needs, and   5.59

Guardianship   1.26
alteration   1.35
applications to tribunals   1.57
appropriateness   1.26
basis for   1.26
best interests decision   1.26
consent to treatment, and   1.40
discharge by nearest relative   1.37
  restrictions, on   1.37
format of application   1.28

Guardianship—*continued*
inappropriate/anomalous
  applications   1.30–1.32
local authority aims   1.26
Mental Capacity Act 2005   1.27
  Code of Guidance   1.27
  implications of   1.27
  interaction with MHA 1983   1.27
nearest relative   1.41
  AMHP, role of   1.51
  barring orders   1.56
  choice of   1.43
  civil partners   1.44
  Code of Practice   1.41
  concurrent detention, and   1.55
  consultation with   1.47–1.51
  determination of nature of   1.43
  disclosure, and   1.42
  displacement of   1.51
  displacement of unsuitable   1.45
  function   1.41
  grounds for displacement   1.52
  homosexual partner as   1.43
  hospital manager's obligations   1.56
  identification of   1.47–1.51
  information provided to,
    obligations   1.59
  interim orders   1.55
  meaning of consultation   1.50
  Mental Health Act 2007, and   1.44
  misuse of functions by   1.46
  objections to   1.43
  patients lacking capacity   1.56
  procedure for application to
    displace   1.52–1.54
  purpose of consultation with   1.50
  role   1.41
  scope of role   1.42
  Secretary of State's powers   1.56
nearest relative and   1.36
  conflicts of interest   1.36
necessity   1.28
orders of Court in respect of   1.38
powers conferred   1.34
purpose   1.26
responsibility for providing
  information   1.39
time period   1.29
  automatic renewal   1.29
  discharges   1.29
  ending   1.29
  RC examination   1.29
  renewal   1.29
transfer   1.34
typical scenario for   1.26

Health care
adults and long term placements   7.66
children   7.63–7.65
local authorities   7.63–7.65
no fixed abode   7.60
patients who move   7.62
responsible commissioner   7.59

Health care—*continued*
social services distinguished   7.1
usually resident   7.61
Homelessness
applications   8.42–8.50
   arrangements, for   8.42
   capacity requirement   8.45
   no form, for   8.45
   no residence requirement   8.44
   no time limit   8.49
   notification of decision   8.50
   right of review   8.50
becoming intentionally
   homeless   8.65–8.67, 8.69–8.71
   incapacity   8.71
becoming threatened with
   homelessness
   intentionally   8.68–8.71
   incapacity   8.71
Code of Guidance   8.37, 8.39, 8.42, 8.45,
   8.48, 8.49, 8.56, 8.62–8.64, 8.69,
   8.82
cooperation with housing
   authorities
   registered social landlords, by   8.41
   social service, by   8.39
decisions about
   right to review   8.72
economic climate, effect of   8.38
eligibility   8.54–8.58
   immigration control, persons
      subject to   8.54–8.58
equality issues   8.81–8.84
government strategy   8.38
homelessness strategies   8.39
   social services' duty to take
     account of   8.40
housing authority's duty   8.78–8.80
inquiries
   eligibility for assistance   8.47
   housing authority's duty   8.48
   threshold   8.46
interim accommodation pending
   appeal   8.76, 8.77
interim accommodation pending
   review   8.73–8.75
interim duty to accommodate   8.51–8.53
local reviews   8.39
priority need   8.59–8.64
   categories   8.61, 8.62
   vulnerability, meaning   8.63, 8.64
statutory provisions   8.36, 8.37
Hospital
community care duties   7.20
Hospital managers
disclosure requirements   1.58
Housing and care schemes   4.67
Housing associations
closure of care homes   4.23

Housing, provision of *see also* Local
   housing authorities
advice and assitance,
   availability   8.14–8.16, 8.25
   purchase on demand   8.15
allocation scheme *see also*
   Homelessness   8.5
   adoption, of   8.26
   alteration of   8.26
   challenges, to   8.27–8.31
     code of guidance   8.31
     medical reasons   8.30
   code of guidance   8.7, 8.9, 8.13, 8.14,
     8.35
   court's view   8.27
   exceptions   8.6, 8.7
   information to RSLs   8.26
   Localism Act 2010   8.32
   right of review   8.25
   statutory requirements   8.24–8.26
applications for
   privacy   8.16
contracting out   8.33–8.35
eligibility   8.6, 8.8–8.13
   categories of ineligible persons   8.8
   immigration control, persons
     subject to   8.8
   ineligible family members   8.11
   notification of reasons for
     ineligibility   8.8
   unacceptable behaviour   8.8, 8.12
equality issues   8.81–8.84
housing register   8.6
introductory tenancy   8.6, 8.7
priority need   8.6, 8.17–8.23
   'additional preference'   8.17
   applicants support by carers   8.20
   code of guidance   8.18–8.23, 8.25, 8.26
   determination
     housing authority, by   8.23
   determination, of   8.19
   lone teenage parents   8.21
   medical/welfare grounds   8.18
   minors   8.22
   'reasonable preference'   8.17
secure tenancy   8.6, 8.7
statutory provisions   8.1–8.4

Ill-treatment or neglect
local authority powers   2.88
statutory provisions   2.87
Immigration control
persons subject to *see also* Asylum
   seekers
   ineligibility for homelessness
     assistance   8.54–8.58
     uncertainty as to
       immigration status   8.58
   ineligibility for housing   8.8, 8.11
     uncertainty as to
       immigration status   8.10

Independent Barring Board
  provision of information to   4.74
Independent Mental Capacity
    Advocates *see also* Approved
    mental health professional;
    Nearest relative; Responsible
    clinician   1.24, 2.87
  accommodation, and   1.24
  discretion to appoint   2.87
  purpose   1.25
  role   1.25
  services of
    qualifying patients   1.25
Independent Mental Health Advocates
  (Mental Health Act 1983)   1.24
Informal patients   1.59
Inherent jurisdiction
  local authority duty of care   3.96–3.99
Interim orders   2.88, 2.89

Judicial review
  after care services   1.12

Learning disabilities
  parents with   3.34
Leaving care grants   5.25
Liberty and security, right to   2.49
Liberty, deprivation of *see* Deprivation
  of liberty
Life sustaining treatment *see* Medical
  treatment
Litigation capacity   2.8
Litigation friend   2.99
  suitability to act as   2.99
Local authority
  accommodation
    Independent Mental Capacity
      Advocates   1.24
  children leaving care
    duties and powers   5.7
    responsibility   5.28
  children, and   7.63–7.65
  community care assessment   7.31
  community care duties   7.19
  community care services,
    obligations   3.5
  direct payments duties   6.46
  disabled children
    accommodation needs   5.54
    duties and powers   5.44
    obligations   5.38
  disputes with care home owners   4.46, 4.50
    additional payments   4.53
    choice of accommodation   4.49
    choice of contractors   4.46
    Health and Social Care Act
      2001   4.52
    LASSA Guidance 1990   4.48
    legislation   4.46
    legislative background   4.47

Local authority—*continued*
  disputes with care home
    owners—*continued*
    levels of charges   4.51
    'mixed economy'   4.46
    third party payments   4.52
  duties
    after care services   1.8
    employment of close relatives   6.52
    FACS obligations   3.2, 3.3
    guardianship, and   1.26
    health care   7.63–7.65
    judicial review of decisions of
      capacity, and   2.23–2.25
    nursing care   4.26
    nursing services, provision   7.7
    persons without capacity, and   2.14
    prescribed information, disclosure   4.74
    duty to refer   4.74
    provision of accommodation   4.1
    liability for   4.17
    sale of home   4.25
    social services responsibilities   4.63
    adult placements   4.69
    care homes   4.65
    domiciliary care   4.66
    extra care housing   4.67
    Guidance   4.63
    personal care   4.64
    supply of goods and services by   7.44, 7.45
  vulnerable adults
    duty of care   3.93–3.99
    inherent jurisdiction   3.96–3.99
Local housing authority *see also*
  Housing, provision of
  Allocation of Accommodation
    Code of Guidance   8.7, 8.9, 8.13, 8.14, 8.18–8.23, 8.25, 8.26, 8.31, 8.35
  allocation scheme   8.5
    adoption, of   8.26
    alteration of   8.26
    challenges, to   8.27–8.31
      medical reasons   8.30
    contracting out   8.33–8.35
    court's view   8.27
    information to RSLs   8.26
    Localism Act 2010   8.32
    right of review   8.25
    statutory requirements   8.24–8.26
  housing register   8.6
  housing stock
    transfer of ownership   8.33
  priority of housing need
    determination, by   8.23
  provision for homelessness *see*
    Homelessness
  provision of advice and assitance,
    by   8.14–8.16, 8.25
    purchase on demand   8.15
  responsibilities, statutory provisions   8.2

Long term care placements
adults and 7.66

Marriage
capacity, and 2.20
Medical treatment
best interests principle 2.11–2.13
capacity, and 2.10–2.13, 2.79
religious beliefs 2.79
wishes of patient 2.79
Mental Capacity Act 2005
after-care 2.72
capacity, determination under 2.66–2.68
Court of Protection, and 2.63
effect of 2.63
interaction with MHA 1983 2.70, 2.71
principles of 2.65
provisions of 2.75–2.90
Mental Health Act 1983 1.1
after care 1.1
obligations under 1.1
Mental Health Act 2007
new terms under 1.33

National Assistance Act 1948
provision of accommodation, and 4.4
National Care Standards Commission 3.85
National Framework for Continuing
Healthcare and NHS Funded
Nursing Care 7.26
National Service Framework for Older
People (NSF) 3.28
categories of older people 3.29
mental health 3.31, 3.32
progress of 3.33
rationale behind 3.28
standards 3.30
Nearest relative *see also* Approved
mental health professional;
Independent Mental Capacity
Advocates; Responsible
clinician 1.41
AMHP, role of 1.51
applications for discharge of
patients 1.36
barring orders 1.56
choice of 1.43
Code of Practice 1.41
concurrent detention, and 1.55
conflicts of interest 1.36
consultation with 1.47–1.51
determination of nature of 1.43
discharge of guardianship 1.37
displacement of 1.51
displacement of unsuitable 1.45
function 1.41
grounds for displacement 1.52
homosexual partner as 1.43
hospital manager's obligations 1.56
identification of 1.47–1.51
information provided to,
obligations 1.59

Nearest relative *—continued*
interim orders 1.55
meaning of consultation 1.50
misuse of functions by 1.46
objections to 1.43
patients lacking capacity 1.56
procedure for application to
displace 1.52–1.54
purpose of consultation with 1.50
role 1.41
Secretary of State's powers 1.56
NHS provision 7.41
No fixed abode 7.60
Nursing care
after care service, as 1.18
provision 4.26
Nursing services 7.2
areas of provision 7.3
charging regime 7.7
community care 7.17
adjustments 7.22
dispute resolution 7.21
free provision of services 7.23
hospital duties 7.20
local authority duties 7.19
notice of needs 7.18
direct payments, and 7.37–7.39
dispute resolution 7.41
eligibility for funding 7.12
procedure for assessment 7.13–7.16
general 7.5
guideline document 7.5
Health and Social Care Act
2001 7.10–7.16
health service provider, provision
by 7.7
incidental or ancillary, whether 7.4
legislation governing 7.2
Mental Health Act 1983
s 117 7.8, 7.9
National Framework 7.6
National Health Service Act 2006 7.26,
7.42
care trusts 7.47
directed partnership
arrangements 7.48, 7.49
goods and services 7.44, 7.45
National Framework 7.26
pooling of resources 7.46
Primary Care Trusts payment
powers 7.52
recovery of charges 7.50, 7.51
target duties 7.43
NHS provision 7.41
ordinary residence, and 7.53, 7.54
provision by local authority 7.7
specialist 7.5

Older children *see also* Children;
Disabled children 5.1
capacity 5.78
care, leaving 5.2
accommodation 5.22

Older children —*continued*
  care, leaving—*continued*
    additional relevant children   5.13
    categories of   5.11
    child in detention   5.31
    Children Act 1989   5.27
    commencement of legislation   5.8
    complaints by children   5.18
    consultation paper   5.4–5.6
    definitions   5.10
    Dept of Work & Pensions
        financial support   5.26
    disabled children   5.38
    duty to advise and befriend   5.7
    eligible children   5.11
    extent of obligations   5.30–5.32, 5.37
    features of Act   5.9
    financial arrangements   5.23
    former relevant children   5.14
    good practice handbook   5.8
    Guidance   5.2
    handling finances   5.25
    history of legislation   5.3
    items considered priority for
        funding   5.24
    leaving care grants   5.25
    legislation   5.2
    local authority duties and
        powers   5.7
    local authority planning and
        policy   5.19
    'looked after, accommodated or
        fostered'   5.17
    needs assessments   5.20, 5.33–5.36
    ordinary residence   5.28
    origins of Act   5.4–5.6
    pathway plans   5.7, 5.20, 5.33–5.36
    personal advisers   5.21
    power to assist   5.7
    power to assist with training
        and education   5.7
    provision of housing   5.32
    qualifying children   5.15
    relevant children   5.12
    responsible local authority   5.28
    scope of entitlements   5.10
    unaccompanied asylum-seeking
        children   5.30
    unaffected children   5.16
    young people 16+   5.15
    Young Persons Adviser   5.7
Older people   3.27, 3.84–3.86
  assessment   3.27
  healthcare, role of   3.86
  local authority obligations   3.84
  mental health in   3.31, 3.32
  National Care Standards
    Commission   3.85
  National Service Framework for
    Older People (NSF)   3.28
  single assessment process   3.84
Ordinary housing
  needs, and   4.11–4.16

Ordinary residence   3.35, 7.53, 7.54
  assessment, and   3.66
  basic principle   1.15
  children leaving care, and   5.28
  children, and   3.36
  definition   3.66
  disabled children, and   5.64
  dispute resolution   7.21
  disputes between NHS and local
    authority   7.53, 7.54
  dual residence   1.15
  geographic jurisdiction   1.13
  guidance   1.14
  meaning   1.15
  no settled residence   3.67–3.69
  Primary Care Trust, and   7.55–7.58
  provision of accommodation,
    and   4.18–4.22
  'resident'   1.14
  temporary absence   1.15

Parents with learning disabilities   3.34
  assessment   3.59
  legislation   3.34
  needs   3.37
  ordinary residence   3.35
    children, and   3.36
  resources, relevance of   3.38–3.49
    criteria   3.39
    local authority duties   3.40
Pathway plans
  children leaving care   5.20, 5.33–5.36
Patients who move   7.62
Personal advisers
  children leaving care, and   5.21
Personal care
  local authority responsibilities   4.64
Persons who cease to be detained   1.5
  conditional discharge   1.6
  definition   1.5
  duty of service provision   1.7
    extent   1.7
    purpose   1.7
POVA list   4.70
Practice Directions
  Court of Protection   2.101
Primary Care Trusts
  ordinary residence, and   7.55–7.58
  power to make payments   7.52
Primary health need
  concept of   7.33
Promise of home for life   4.26–4.29
  closure of care homes, and   4.34
  legality   4.26
  transfer of patient to community   4.29
Protection of Vulnerable Adults Scheme   3.91

Qualifying hospital patient
  classification as   7.24

Reasonable adjustments
  vulnerable adult parents, and   3.64

Re-assessment
closure of care homes 4.34
provision of accommodation 4.17
sale of home 4.25
Refugee Convention
claims for aylum under 9.7, 9.8
'designated place' requirement 9.9
Registered Nursing Care Contribution 7.12
Registered social landlord
housing allocation schemes, and 8.26
Regulated activity
vulnerable adults, and 4.71
Relatives
employment of 6.52
liability for accommodation
charges 6.15
Report of Inquiry into Care and
Treatment of Christopher Clunis
recommendations 1.10, 1.11
Residence
capacity, and 2.14
choice of residence 2.21, 2.22
parents with learning disabilities 3.35
Residential accommodation
charges for 6.6, 6.7
Residential facilities
after care services, and 1.18
Responsible clinician *see also* Approved
mental health professional;
Independent Mental Capacity
Advocates; Nearest relative
definition 1.33
examinations, by 1.29
Responsible commissioner 7.59
establishing 1.16
guidance 1.16

Safeguarding Vulnerable Groups Act
2006 4.70
Sale of home 4.25
Sexual relationships
capacity, and 2.26–2.29
Social care
adults and long term placements 7.66
children 7.63–7.65
local authorities 7.63–7.65
no fixed abode 7.60
patients who move 7.62
responsible commissioner 7.59
usually resident 7.61
Social services
health care distinguished 7.1

State benefits
repayment of after care charges 1.20
Students
charges for accommodation 6.16
Subject matter capacity 2.8
Supervised Community Treatment 1.59

Telephone and video hearings
Court of Protection 2.95
Tenancy agreements
capacity to enter into 2.32–2.34
Third party top-ups
choice of accommodation, and 6.39
Tribunals
applications to 1.57
Trust funds
charges for accommodation,
and 6.12–6.14

Unaccompanied children *see* Asylum
seekers
Usual residence 7.54
Usually resident
meaning 7.61

Vulnerable adult parents 3.61
eligibility thresholds 3.62
Disability Discrimination Acts 3.64
no settled residence 3.67–3.69
ordinary residence 3.66
reasonable adjustments 3.64
statistics 3.63
promotion of well-being 3.65
Vulnerable adults 3.87
abuse 3.89
inter-agency framework and
policy 3.90
controlled activity 4.73
definition 4.75
guidance 3.88
inherent jurisdiction 3.96–3.99
legislation 3.87
local authority's duty of care 3.93–3.99
Protection of Vulnerable Adults
Scheme 3.91
regulated activity 4.71
definition 4.71
provider 4.72
Safeguarding Vulnerable Groups
Act 2006 4.70

Young people *see* Older children
Young Persons Adviser 5.7